SAP PRESS e-books

Print or e-book, Kindle or iPad, workplace or airplane: Choose where and how to read your SAP PRESS books! You can now get all our titles as e-books, too:

- By download and online access
- For all popular devices
- And, of course, DRM-free

Convinced? Then go to www.sap-press.com and get your e-book today.

Architecting EDI with SAP® IDocs

SAP PRESS is a joint initiative of SAP and Rheinwerk Publishing. The know-how offered by SAP specialists combined with the expertise of Rheinwerk Publishing offers the reader expert books in the field. SAP PRESS features first-hand information and expert advice, and provides useful skills for professional decision-making.

SAP PRESS offers a variety of books on technical and business-related topics for the SAP user. For further information, please visit our website: *www.sap-press.com*.

Aron, Gakhar, Vij
SAP Integration Suite
2021, 343 pages, hardcover and e-book
www.sap-press.com/5326

Bilay, Gutsche, Krimmel, Stiehl
SAP Cloud Platform Integration:
The Comprehensive Guide (3rd Edition)
2020, 906 pages, hardcover and e-book
www.sap-press.com/5077

Bönnen, Jegadeesan, Mary, Vij
SAP API Management
2019, 365 pages, hardcover and e-book
www.sap-press.com/4928

John Bilay, Roberto Viana Blanco
SAP Process Orchestration: The Comprehensive Guide (2nd Edition)
2017, 908 pages, hardcover and e-book
www.sap-press.com/4431

Emmanuel Hadzipetros

Architecting EDI with SAP® IDocs

The Comprehensive Guide

Editor Emily Nicholls
Acquisitions Editor Kelly Grace Weaver
Copyeditor Pamela Siska
Cover Design Graham Geary
Photo Credit iStockphoto.com/15949465/© sara_winter
Layout Design Vera Brauner
Production Kelly O'Callaghan
Typesetting Publishers' Design and Production Services, Inc.
Printed and bound in Canada, on paper from sustainable sources

ISBN 978-1-59229-871-6

© 2022 by Rheinwerk Publishing, Inc., Boston (MA)

2nd edition 2014, 2nd reprint 2022

Library of Congress Cataloging-in-Publication Data
Hadzipetros, Emmanuel.
Architecting EDI with SAP IDocs : the comprehensive guide / Emmanuel Hadzipetros. — 2nd edition.
pages cm
ISBN-13: 978-1-59229-871-6
ISBN-10: 1-59229-871-0
ISBN-13: 978-1-59229-872-3
ISBN-13: 978-1-59229-873-0
1. SAP ERP. 2. Electronic data interchange. 3. Enterprise application integration (Computer systems)
I. Title.
HF5548.33.H35 2013
650.0285'53—dc23
2013031002

Contents at a Glance

Dear Reader,

As readers, we value authors who offer creative, clear, and fresh approaches to technical topics—especially ones with innumerable moving parts and connected processes. Similarly, as editors, we enjoy working alongside those energetic authors to execute these visions, sharing in our readers' delight with unexpected examples and colorful characters.

So you can imagine my excitement about beginning work on the second edition of a project fondly known around the SAP PRESS office as "the Hollywood book" by Emmanuel Hadzipetros. It stands out as a technical resource with a delightfully reimagined premise—that of legendary B-movie studio founder Darryl Q. Fernhausen's beloved Acme Studios, which seeks to implement an Electronic Data Interchange system in an SAP environment.

Emmanuel's brilliant, inventive account of the implementation process is a unique answer to traditional technical style. As he made adjustments and updates and optimized illustrations for color e-book editions, Emmanuel was organized, reliable, and judicious as he fine-tuned both the technical content and the story itself. Perhaps he has a future in film-making.

So as you follow along through the project affectionately called "Plan Q from Outer Space" by implementation personnel, join our growing Acme team. Since your comments and suggestions are the most useful tools to help us improve our books, we encourage you to visit our website at *www.sap-press.com* and share your feedback about *Architecting EDI with SAP IDocs: The Comprehensive Guide*.

Emily Nicholls
Editor, SAP PRESS

Rheinwerk Publishing
Boston, MA

emilyn@rheinwerk-publishing.com
www.sap-press.com

Contents

ACT III   Realizing the Dream—Building Acme's SAP EDI System

11 Processing the Incoming Supplier Invoice 413

ACT IV   Finishing Touches

19   Extending the Interface: Custom IDoc Tools 739

Prologue

Let's return to Hollywood and once again take the studio tour of Acme Pictures and revisit its legendary founder, Darryl Q. Fernhausen.

Since the first edition of this book was published, we've had time to reconsider Acme's implementation of an Electronic Data Interchange (EDI) system in an SAP environment. While the first edition covered a lot of ground, it left out even more. And, frankly, we made some mistakes, not all of which were typos.

This second edition is our attempt to plug some of these gaps. While much of the original remains, we've tried to put more emphasis on the business context and have added new interfaces from the purchasing cycle.

We have consolidated and expanded our discussions of message control and added a number of new custom tools and utilities. We have changed our IDoc format from ASCII to XML and introduced some basic concepts of working with, and extending, XML schema.

All in all, we hope that the result is a tighter book that covers more subjects in a clearer manner. But this book is still about SAP and EDI. And the basics haven't changed.

EDI is still the most widely used form of electronic commerce in the world today. It is highly unlikely that this will change anytime soon. EDI has been around for decades. It is reliable, proven, stable, and supported by long-established standards developed and maintained by such global bodies as the United Nations, the International Organization for Standardization (ISO), GS1, and the American National Standards Institute (ANSI).

If money talks, EDI has the eloquence of a Shakespearean actor. It supports trillions of dollars in transactions every year in a wide variety of industries. Many companies will not buy goods or services from suppliers that cannot exchange standard business documents through EDI.

In the United States, Wal-Mart, the world's largest retailer, is at the heart of a gigantic global EDI ecosystem with thousands of suppliers that rivals most governments in its use of information and communications technology. If you want to sell to Wal-Mart, you can do it only through EDI.

The importance of EDI as an enterprise integration application for thousands of SAP customers is beyond dispute. EDI, and the large-volume batch processing of business transactions that it enables, is a key element of the SAP environment in thousands of locations around the world. Where EDI is present, most of the transactional data that flow between SAP and external trading partners are carried by EDI.

With more than 70 percent of the global business software market, SAP is the business system of record that a majority of EDI consultants, developers, and production support teams work with every day.

Together, SAP and EDI are the heart, bones, arteries, and brains of modern business and government organizations.

So why are we touring an imaginary Hollywood studio? Look beyond the glitz and the glitter and it is just another business. Acme Pictures is a good model for the challenges faced by many businesses when they implement SAP and EDI together.

Acme Pictures sells movies on DVD, a consumer product sold through retail, not all that different from other products that wind up on store shelves around the world. We could just as easily be talking about video games, pharmaceuticals, carpet, shoes, software, beverages, snack foods, or the book that I hope you are now enjoying.

For Acme Pictures, it's a simple equation: The volume of business it does with large retail chains across North America, and the huge number of documents that this business generates, can only be managed through EDI.

The other thing, of course, is that Hollywood is a lot of fun. But so is SAP and EDI, even if the details can get a little dry at times. I'll never forget the advice of a project manager during kick-off for an SAP implementation at a steel mill in Ohio: "Work hard and have lots of fun!"

The fun is in the creative process of designing and building a system that fits the client's business. It's discovering how far you can push the limits of your knowledge to provide your client with a useful system that will support its business for years to come.

The Book and Its Audience

Audiences are the lifeblood of Hollywood. Books, too. And while this book will never be made into a movie, it may provide some useful information to SAP and EDI consultants, developers, managers, and anyone else implementing, supporting, or considering EDI in an SAP environment.

This book is the culmination of my 20-year odyssey as an SAP consultant and developer with a perennial fascination for data flows and integration. It represents ideas about integration architecture considered throughout my SAP career, which includes project work in four countries, three continents, and such industries as beverages, electrical utilities, steel, electronics, textiles, pharmaceuticals, and entertainment.

We will take the studio tour of an SAP EDI implementation project, lovingly referred to as Plan Q from Outer Space, or just plain Plan Q—in honor of our imaginary studio's most famous film.

This project-based approach attempts to deal in a holistic manner with the entire SAP EDI ecosystem at Acme Pictures, beginning with an overview of the business it supports, just enough to discuss technical solutions. The real-world business of a Hollywood studio is far more complex and nuanced than we could describe in these pages.

This book is not an SAP or EDI programming guide. It does assume an ability to follow program logic and visualize end-to-end systems. We rely on standards and standard functionality wherever possible.

Where potential solutions to common problems are presented, we will step through the process flow and logic. But we will not write the code for you. Consider our logic as starting points for your own creative exploration. And forgive me in advance if some of our ideas don't add up for you.

Our real hope is that this book helps you formulate questions that you may not have considered. After all, every business, no matter how big or how small, is as unique as the people who run it.

Structure of the Book

The book loosely follows the phases of our imaginary SAP project with detours for background information about IDocs and EDI.

In deference to our Hollywood theme, the book is organized into four acts, which are meant to build your knowledge of Acme's business, its systems, and SAP IDoc and EDI development. A summary of each chapter follows.

Act I—Hollywood, DVDs, and the After Life of Movies

▶ **Chapter 1—Hollywood's B-Movie Queen Does SAP and EDI**
This chapter introduces Acme Pictures, its visionary founder, Darryl Q. Fernhausen, and its unique approach to the movie business. We also touch on SAP EDI development strategy.

▶ **Chapter 2—The Blueprint: Discovery and Documentation**
In this chapter we document Acme's DVD business and the legacy systems that support it. It also provides an overview of key customer and vendor processes, including purchasing and order-to-cash.

▶ **Chapter 3—Designing the New SAP EDI Architecture**
We present the vision for the new system. We'll introduce to-be systems and interfaces, and the Resource Integration Manager (RIM). We also examine the key business processing cycles enabled by EDI.

Act II—Taming Chaos with Standards: EDI in an SAP Environment

▶ **Chapter 4—EDI: The Ugly Stepsister of E-Commerce**
This chapter covers EDI for SAP professionals, including a brief tour of its fascinating history and introduce the major EDI standards, with special emphasis on EDIFACT and ANSI X12.

▶ **Chapter 5—Real-World Business Process Integration with EDI**
Relationships and integrating processes between trading partners are at the heart of EDI. In this chapter we look at the role of Acme's EDI RIM, with its adapters and services, and its connections to SAP.

▶ **Chapter 6—EDI Architecture in SAP: IDoc Basics**
In this chapter we discuss Intermediate Documents (IDocs)—the intelligent messages defined by the Data Dictionary and the underlying logic that determines how they are used.

▶ **Chapter 7—Configuring IDocs in SAP for EDI Exchange**
From partner profiles to message control and mapping tables, inbound and outbound IDoc configuration and processing flows in SAP are the focus of this chapter.

► **Chapter 8—Custom IDocs and IDoc Extensions**
An introduction to IDoc development in SAP. We go over development tools and process flows and build, code, and configure one custom and one extended IDoc.

Act III—Realizing the Dream: Building Acme's SAP EDI System

► **Chapter 9—Generating the PO for Replication Services**
This chapter defines the function and technical setup for the outbound purchase order for replication services to Acme's contract manufacturer, including configuration of message control to output an ORDERS IDoc.

► **Chapter 10—The Inbound Goods Receipt**
In this chapter we discuss the functionality and configuration of inbound inventory adjustments and goods receipt through an EDI X12 867 transaction.

► **Chapter 11—Processing the Inbound Supplier Invoice**
We review posting requirements for the inbound supplier invoice for contract manufacturing services, including invoice verification and configuration.

► **Chapter 12—The Inbound Customer Purchase Order**
This chapter examines the inbound X12 850 to ORDERS IDoc customer purchase order, including logic for SDQ processing and code to block posting of duplicate POs to SAP Sales Orders.

► **Chapter 13—Building the Outbound Order Confirmation**
Covers the generation of the outbound ORDRSP confirmation from an SAP sales order. We'll build an extended IDoc and look at logic for a custom program to bundle multiple sales orders from the same SDQ PO into a single X12 855 interchange.

► **Chapter 14—Sending a Shipping Order to the Supplier**
We discuss the outbound SHPORD to X12 830 shipping order to the supplier, including message control configuration enabling output of IDocs from the SAP delivery document.

► **Chapter 15—The Inbound Shipping Confirmation**
This chapter focuses on the X12 856 shipping confirmation from the vendor, which updates pick quantity and posts goods issue in the delivery document in Acme's SAP system after the order ships.

► **Chapter 16—The Advanced Shipping Notice to the Customer**
In this chapter we focus on the advanced ship notice (ASN), which tells the

customer what to expect in its shipment. We will emphasize the critical business requirement for accuracy and timeliness and discuss conditions for creating the DESADV IDoc.

▶ **Chapter 17 — Generating the Outbound Customer Invoice**
Here we cover the INVOIC to X12 810 customer invoice, generated from the SAP billing document. We detail output requirements for the IDoc and step through a custom ALV grid program for changing the PO number in the IDoc.

▶ **Chapter 18 — Processing the Inbound Payment Advice**
The focus of this chapter is the inbound payment advice, which records details of a customer payment on all invoices, including debits and credits. We also discuss common issues with very large X12 820 files.

Act IV — Finishing Touches

▶ **Chapter 19 — Extending the Interface: Custom IDoc Tools**
Fun with ABAP, ALE, and XML as we look at custom utilities that take advantage of standard SAP functionality.

▶ **Chapter 20 — Testing the EDI System in SAP**
Acme's testing strategy is the focus of this chapter. We examine the composition and role of the test team and outline the key test phases.

▶ **Chapter 21 — Troubleshooting and Recovery**
Defining success and failure in Acme's SAP EDI architecture. We'll look at standard monitoring tools and consider situations that appear successful but could lead to errors in later stages of the EDI cycle.

▶ **Epilogue**
With the project complete, the integration team relaxes at a famous Hollywood watering hole to toast the successful release of an Acme *film noir* classic and the success of the new SAP EDI system.

Acknowledgments

If no man is an island, as the English poet and preacher John Donne once observed, the same is especially true for authors, who often labor in solitude and obscurity. During the long, lonely hours spent writing a book, it is easy to forget the many people who enrich our lives and our work every day.

The quest to define, begin, complete, and rewrite this book was a labor of love that extended over many years. It would have been a mission impossible without the people—family, friends, and colleagues—who sometimes endured yawn-inducing dissertations of SAP integration issues.

First and foremost, this is dedicated to my son and two daughters and especially to the grandchildren that I've been blessed with since publication of the first edition. The future belongs to you.

To all my family and friends, wherever in or out of this crazy, beautiful world you may find yourselves: thank you for being you.

A good programmer never stops learning. A good consultant learns so that he can pass on his knowledge to benefit his client. A passion to learn and to acquire and pass on new skills is the key to success and to having fun in this business. Learning means working with other people—listening, studying, discussing, playing, and poking around systems.

I've been lucky in the colleagues that I've worked with over the years. I've learned so much from so many people that it's impossible to remember them all. So thanks to everybody. You know who you are. It's been a privilege working with you.

I also want to thank the folks at SAP PRESS for their support and continuing belief in this project.

Finally, I want to express a heartfelt thank you to the countless numbers of extraordinary working people in Hollywood who labor quietly every day in the offices and back lots of the studios beyond the glare of the klieg lights.

When the director shouts "Lights…cameras…action!" they turn on the lights, run the cameras, build the sets, feed the crews, park the star wagons, clean up, and run the IT systems that keep the business humming.

They are, always have been, and always will be the real stars of Hollywood.

ACT I
Hollywood, DVDs, and the After-Life of Movies

Hollywood studios use SAP and EDI to run their home entertainment business. Acme Pictures is no exception. We'll look at its history and unique business model and introduce Acme's new SAP EDI implementation. Hold on to your hats—we're in for an interesting ride.

1   Hollywood's B-Movie Queen Does SAP and EDI

Welcome to Hollywood, the world's most fabulous dream factory. If it's true that dreams are made in this town, these dreams can only be realized on a solid foundation of business.

Like all modern businesses, the dream factory depends on business systems to manage its processes, keep its documents flowing, and deliver timely and accurate information to support decision making across the enterprise.

It's no wonder then that Acme Pictures, our imaginary Hollywood dream factory, has decided to implement SAP to run its Home Entertainment division, which is responsible for selling the studio's movies on DVD to big box stores across the United States and Canada.

Buying and selling is what Acme Home Entertainment, abbreviated as AHE, is all about. AHE doesn't manufacture its own DVDs, nor does it maintain warehouses to store them. The studio outsources this work to a vendor: Disc Services International (DSI).

DSI is a replicator that has the facilities to burn millions of images of Acme's movies onto DVDs, and to package, store, and ship them to AHE's retail customers across North America. DSI also orders raw materials for AHE when required to complete a replication order or to replenish inventory in anticipation of future orders.

All this buying and selling would be impossible without electronic data interchange, more commonly referred to as EDI.

As in so many other SAP implementation projects around the world, Acme Pictures plans to build a new EDI system that will connect its trading partners to the new SAP system. The EDI system will feed SAP virtually all of its transactional data and route all outbound business documents from SAP to Acme's customers.

1.1   SAP and EDI: Getting to Know Each Other

The SAP and EDI teams should understand each other's requirements. On all too many projects, the two teams operate almost as if the other inhabited a separate universe.

On the surface, it appears that the structure, conversion, and delivery of IDocs are the key links between SAP and EDI: the Basis/technical architecture, configuration, and development.

▶ Basis/technical architecture relates to overall system design and connectivity, including the connections between SAP and EDI and the details of communications between EDI and the trading partners.

▶ Configuration and development in SAP is primarily about setting up the IDoc interface, customizing IDocs, and writing ABAP code.

▶ Configuration and development in EDI is primarily about trading partner management, adapters, mapping, and business process development.

Within SAP, IDocs are objects that encapsulate a business document or a data object such as a customer or material master record. Behind each IDoc is program intelligence that determines the business meaning, the semantics, of the object encapsulated by the IDoc as well as its place within the document flow that completes a full-cycle business process (BP).

In other words, the business stands behind each IDoc through the classic SAP modules of Sales and Distribution (SD), Materials Management (MM), and Financial Accounting (FI) in the case of Acme Pictures' current implementation.

The EDI side rarely ventures beyond an imperfect understanding of how you use IDoc structure in a map. EDI's focus is rightly on its own realm. At least during the implementation phase, it dwells on the technical details of trading partner management, communications and connectivity, mapping, and business process development.

But EDI has a mission-critical business function: It ties together the business processes enabled by the backend business systems of Acme Pictures and its trading partners.

EDI is not just about exchanging documents. Business documents don't exist in a vacuum; they exist as milestone participants in an end-to-end business processing cycle that results in the completion of a business activity, such as purchasing or sales, and that ends in an update to accounting and speaks directly to the company's bottom line.

It's in everybody's interests—the SAP and EDI teams, the implementation project as a whole, and, most importantly, the business—that both teams understand more about what each is doing and what each requires. This provides the rich context for each group to proceed with its own tasks within the overall implementation.

Acme Pictures understands how critical EDI is to the success of its business and its SAP implementation. The SAP and EDI teams will work closely together throughout the project to deliver a clean and efficient EDI architecture across both systems to support the business and its users.

Since we're in Hollywood, let's take the quick studio tour. Acme Pictures has a colorful history and a very interesting business model.

1.2   A Brief History of Fame: Our Imaginary Dream Factory

Let us introduce you to Acme Pictures, affectionately known in the industry as the *B-Movie Queen of Hollywood*.

Acme won this accolade the hard way, with a diligent devotion to producing high-quality works of transcendent mediocrity. Acme's pictures are stinkers by design. The studio specializes in low-grade science fiction, pulp horror, alien zombie invasions, and the occasional salacious romp across multiple historical eras; its movies are so vulgar and incompetently produced that they become objects of a cult-like devotion.

Acme stumbled on its successful formula more than 50 years ago with the release of its first smash hit, *I Married an Alien from Planet Q in Outer Space*. Its poorly written and ill-conceived plot, scratchy soundtrack, and cheap black-and-white cinematography stunned critics into silence but delighted moviegoers around the world.

The critics have since warmed to this cult classic, reading into it a metaphor for Senator Joe McCarthy's anti-communist witch hunts then sweeping the United States, particularly the fear they spread through Hollywood. But this was far from the intent of Acme's visionary founder, Darryl Q. Fernhausen, who only wanted to make a quick buck by taking advantage of the science fiction craze at the time.

Fernhausen, who was known around the studio as Darryl Q or The Great Mr. Q, knew a winning formula when he saw it. He proceeded to build a successful business around it. His films never won any Oscars. But they made Fernhausen rich and transformed Acme into an underappreciated and unloved Hollywood institution, except for the loyal fans who continue to flock to the theaters for each of the studio's much-hyped stink bombs.

Darryl Q was in Hollywood heaven: a movie mogul who could afford to indulge his taste for Cuban cigars, cocktails at the perpetually *film noir* Formosa Café, and platinum blondes with stars in their eyes. Acme Pictures made him more than enough money to indulge all his pleasures to his heart's content.

Acme's fortunes really took off with the birth of the Home Entertainment division and the release of the studio's movies to VHS and DVD. Acme's extensive catalog of B-movies became a rich source of ongoing revenue. Acme's new releases inspire tremendous excitement among legions of loyal fans, many of whom have been known to line up for days before the very popular DVD release of a particularly bad film.

Today, at about $500 million a year, Acme's DVD sales are still booming across North America, accounting for 60 percent of its revenues, even with the downturn in the DVD business for other studios. Acme's biggest customer is Gordy's Galaxy of Games & B Flix, affectionately known around Acme as Gordy or Gordy's Galaxy. Among other things, Gordy is renowned for geriatric greeters who dress as space aliens from Acme's most memorable films.

But most of all, Gordy is all about the business. With more than 2,000 retail outlets across North America, Gordy's Galaxy provides Acme Pictures with more than half of its DVD revenues.

The success of Acme's business depends on getting DVD movies on to the customers' shelves, particularly Gordy. Without EDI in Purchasing and Sales, this would be an impossible mission.

But this is almost irrelevant. Gordy's Galaxy mandated that it will do business with its vendors only through EDI using AS2 (applicability statement 2) communications across the Internet. It also mandated that ANSI ASC X12 version 5010 be the standard format for all EDI transactions in North America.

Acme Pictures will do anything to keep Gordy's Galaxy happy and fully stocked. If Gordy wants AS2 and X12 5010, that's what Gordy will get.

1.2.1 A Bird's-Eye View of the Business

Let's fly up to 100,000 feet and get a bird's-eye view of the Purchasing and Sales processes at Acme Pictures to introduce ourselves to the business context for our interfaces.

The purchasing process begins with planning and forecasting, as outlined in Figure 1.1. There are important differences between new releases and catalog, but the key to both is being able to predict demand for particular DVD products from key customers.

Forecasting is an arcane science and a delicate art that requires data from numerous sources, including open sales orders, inventory, and, for some key customers (including Gordy), point of sales (POS) data reporting daily and weekly sales and inventory from all stores.

Purchase orders (POs) for finished goods and raw materials are planned and approved based on requirements for new release or replenishment product calculated by the forecast.

For finished goods, a manufacturing PO is released and sent to the replicator, Disc Services International (DSI). DSI pulls the necessary raw materials from inventory and burns and packages the disks.

Acme Pictures owns the stock, but DSI keeps the inventory in its warehouse. When the inventory is consumed and transformed by manufacturing and packaging into DVDs, DSI sends Acme a goods receipt that updates the PO and posts the finished goods to inventory in Acme's system. Raw materials are then flushed from Acme's inventory.

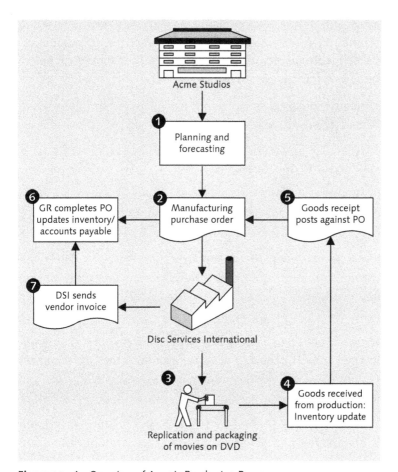

Figure 1.1 An Overview of Acme's Purchasing Process

The process is completed when DSI sends Acme an invoice that closes the PO and updates accounts payable (AP).

The sales process is outlined in Figure 1.2. At its most basic, a customer purchase order is sent to Acme for a set number of movie DVDs for each store in the customer's chain.

AHE receives the PO, verifies it, and then drops a shipping order (SO) to the warehouse run by DSI, which also manages distribution to the customer.

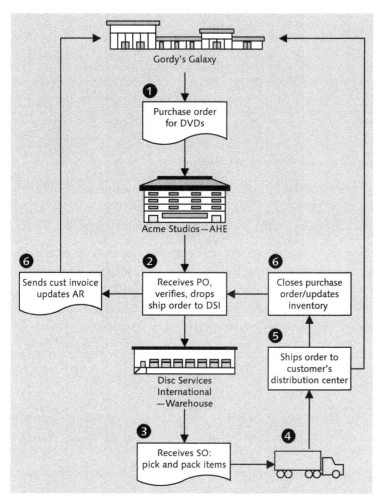

Figure 1.2 Sales Processing Begins with a Customer PO

DSI receives the SO and picks the product from inventory, if there is enough product in inventory to fill the order. DSI then packs the product, puts it onto trucks, and ships it to the customer.

As the truck leaves the loading dock, DSI sends Acme a shipping confirmation that updates inventory with picking and packing quantities, posts a goods issue, and closes the order in Acme's system.

The sales processing cycle ends when Acme sends the customer an invoice for the shipped DVD movie products. The invoice updates accounts receivable (AR) in Acme's finance system.

This is the heart of Acme's DVD business, at its most basic, stripped of all the messy complexities that reside in each leg of these processes. Now we need to consider the project.

1.2.2   Enter Plan Q: A New Project Is Born

Acme's Home Entertainment division already has an extensive network of highly customized legacy systems, including EDI, running mostly on AS400s. These legacy applications are linked through a complex web of point-to-point file-based interfaces.

We'll look at these legacy systems in more detail as we examine the as-is state in the blueprint phase of the project. For now, it is enough to know that Acme management decided that it was time to simplify and modernize its technical architecture, replace key business systems with SAP, upgrade its EDI system, and come up with a better way to manage the file-based interfaces that will remain after go-live.

They also had to consider the competition: Every major Hollywood studio had already implemented, was implementing, or planned to implement SAP along with a new or improved EDI system.

Acme couldn't afford to stand still. A steering committee of key management decision makers was formed, an SAP integrator was hired to provide project management and consultants, and business users were appointed to an implementation team. Luckily for Acme, the integrator had a small number of developers who were experienced with both SAP and EDI.

And so Plan Q from Outer Space, or more simply Plan Q, the name given to Acme's SAP project in honor of the studio's first smash hit, was born with great fanfare and a flurry of PowerPoint presentations.

Plan Q is a full-cycle SAP implementation for SD, MM, SAP Project Systems (PS), and FI-CO that includes building a modern EDI middleware system based on Java, Extensible Markup Language (XML), and business process modeling. There will also be interfaces between all SAP modules and a number of legacy systems.

It was a project worthy of the Great Mr. Q himself, who long ago joined the Hollywood immortals in that great sound stage in the sky, or wherever else it may be.

Acme management paid homage to Darryl Q at the kick-off meeting and expressed the belief that he would have approved and was even now smiling on their efforts from wherever he happened to be in Hollywood Heaven—or that other, much hotter, place that lies somewhere in the San Fernando Valley.

1.2.3 We Define Our Scope

Plan Q is a big project, but we're concerned with only one piece of it: a self-contained subproject focused on the SAP EDI build of the purchasing and order-to-cash cycle for Gordy's Galaxy. This includes the following interfaces (direction is in relation to Acme's new SAP system):

1. Outbound purchase order for replication services
2. Inbound goods receipt
3. Inbound supplier invoice
4. Inbound customer purchase order
5. Outbound customer purchase order acknowledgment
6. Outbound shipping order to supplier
7. Inbound shipping confirmation
8. Outbound advanced shipping notification (ASN) to customer
9. Outbound invoice to customer
10. Inbound payment advice

Functional and technical specifications for each EDI interface will be documented, including supporting configuration, mapping specifications, and all related development work in SAP and EDI.

Standard SAP IDoc processing is used as much as possible. However, in any SAP implementation, the ideal of using standard functionality always runs up against the reality of how business is actually done. There are always complications that can only be handled with custom configuration or code.

We'll consider custom solutions to a number of common problems that often crop up in a real-world SAP EDI implementation, such as ensuring that duplicate POs don't post to a sales order in SAP and an approach to handling SDQ—Destination Quantity—segments in X12 transactions, which group order quantities for up to 10 ship-to locations in one segment.

Before we begin the build, we need to lay the foundation. This means documenting Acme's key business processes as they exist now and as the project team determines that they should exist in the future, paying special attention to the order-to-cash cycle for Gordy's Galaxy. This will give us a better understanding of the business that Acme's new SAP EDI architecture will support.

We'll look at the special role that vendor-managed inventory (VMI) plays in Gordy's Galaxy order-to-cash cycle and how legacy systems currently support the business. At that point, we'll be ready to present the architecture of the new SAP EDI system, with its key systems and interfaces.

Laying the foundation also means providing our team members with detailed background information on EDI and the IDoc interface. It's important to understand our processes, tools, and development requirements before we begin building our interfaces.

1.3 Defining Some Basic Ground Rules

Before we begin, we need to lay down some basic ground rules about our technical environment and interface development strategy. So let's outline the major points of our common approach.

1.3.1 The Technical Environment

Our application servers and LAN will run on Windows Enterprise Server. It's not an optimal environment, but it's fairly easy to maintain and to describe. It can handle all of Acme's requirements for the foreseeable future.

We'll be implementing SAP ERP Central Component (ECC) version 6.05 with the 7.2 GUI. It's not state of the art, but Acme plans an upgrade about a year after go-live.

1.3.2 The EDI System

There are a lot of EDI systems on the market, and we won't favor any in our implementation. We will describe a generic no-name system that, like many others, is built on Java and XML, makes extensive use of business process modeling, uses XPath to evaluate and process interface data at runtime, and runs in a Java EE (J2EE) application server on its own Windows Enterprise Server box.

Interfaces are developed in the EDI system as business processing models (BPMs) or workflows using the Business Process Modeling Language (BPML), a dialect of XML used to construct end-to-end workflow models made up of services, adapters, and connectors implemented as Java objects in the runtime engine of the EDI system.

BPML and its successor BPEL (Business Process Execution Language), which is used in workflow modeling systems such as Aris Toolset and the SAP NetWeaver Process Integration (SAP NetWeaver PI) business process modeling tool, are similar to scripting languages such as KornShell in that they trigger execution of commands and program objects within a runtime execution environment.

In the case of SAP NetWeaver PI (formerly known as Exchange Infrastructure, or XI), this runtime business process engine is an integral part of the integration server. The integration engine within SAP NetWeaver PI provides services that enable the execution of program steps that are relevant to transformation and routing of an interface.

In our generic EDI system, the service and adapter objects each perform one function, such as the following:

▶ Identify whether a message is X12, EDIFACT, or any other standard

▶ Execute a map

▶ Envelope or de-envelope an EDI transaction

▶ Pull metadata from a document

▶ Do an SQL read of a table through a JDBC adapter

▶ Connect to SAP and send in an IDoc

The BPML code can be handcrafted or generated by a visual modeling tool as services or adapters are selected, connected, and configured, a little like assembling Lego blocks.

The BPML code sample in Listing 1.1 describes an SAP adapter that is called by the EDI runtime engine. Parameters are passed to the adapter by the `<assign>` tag from processing data available at runtime using XPath statements for the following:

▶ The SAP application and gateway servers

▶ The Gateway host

▶ Client number

- ▶ User name and password
- ▶ EDI port
- ▶ The SAP function module that will import and process the IDoc
- ▶ The full path and file name of the IDoc that is being passed

```
<operation name="SAPAdapter">
  <participant name="ACM_SAPAdapter_FILE_RFC"/>
  <output message="SAPAdapterInputMessage">
    <assign to="Ashost" from="string(Param/APPServer)">
    </assign>
    <assign to="Client" from="string(Param/Client)">
    </assign>
    <assign to="Gwhost" from="string(Param/GatewayHost)">
    </assign>
    <assign to="Gwserv" from="string(Param/GatewaySrvc)">
    </assign>
    <assign to="IDocPathName"
        from="string(Param/PATHNAME)"></assign>
    <assign to="Passwd" from="string(Param/Pword)"></assign>
    <assign to="Port" from="string(Param/SNDPOR)"></assign>
    <assign to="ProgramID" from="string(Param/PgmID)">
    </assign>
    <assign to="Function" from="string(Param/Function)">
    </assign>
    <assign to="User" from="string(Param/User)"></assign>
  </output>
</operation>
```

Listing 1.1 Example of an SAP Adapter Defined in BPML

The adapter object is embedded within a chain of connected objects comprising a business process workflow, which at runtime, would do the following:

1. Execute an SQL statement through a JDBC adapter to read parameters for the target SAP system from a database table.

2. Call a generic map to plug key values into the control segment of the IDoc being handed off to SAP.

3. Provide a name for the IDoc file.

4. Call a file system adapter to transfer the IDoc file to a folder on the SAP application server.

5. Call the SAP adapter to log in to the target SAP system and make a remote function call (RFC) to function module `EDI_DATA_INCOMING`.

The workflow works like a function in SAP. Other business process workflows
performing different runtime tasks, such as routing to or from a trading partner
or de-enveloping, call the SAP adapter workflow at some point during their processing cycles.

The SAP adapter manages connections through the SAP Java Connector (JCo). On
the inbound, the adapter makes the RFC to an SAP function through JCo. On the
outbound, the IDoc interface makes the call through an SAP RFC destination, which
calls a listener BP in the EDI system through JCo.

We'll look at these end-to-end processes in more detail as we cover the EDI system,
installing and using the JCo connector, and RFC communications between SAP and
the EDI system in Chapter 5, Section 5.4.1.

1.3.3   Nothing but IDocs

The IDoc is the warm and fuzzy blanket of SAP interface development strategies,
but skeptical audiences sometimes must be convinced because they may be more
comfortable writing ABAP code to import or export custom flat files.

After a lot of consultation and not a little arguing, Plan Q's ABAP team lead decided
that all interfaces, whether standard or custom, would be developed using IDocs.

If a standard IDoc and function exists for a particular interface, we'll use the standard. If we have to customize or extend it, we'll customize. If no IDoc exists that
meets the needs of a particular interface, we'll either extend a standard or build
a custom IDoc from scratch. The extended and custom IDocs will be processed
through a customer exit or a custom IDoc function.

Obviously, we're preaching to the choir here, or you wouldn't be reading a book
about architecting EDI using IDocs, but we wanted to repeat the arguments often
used in the past.

The IDoc interface is a wonderful plug-and-play development platform that gives
you most of what you need before you even begin coding, as you will see when
we go through the steps to build and configure custom IDocs in Chapter 8, Custom
IDocs and IDoc Extensions.

Consider the effort involved in developing an IDoc from scratch. You build a custom IDoc, beginning with its data elements and segments, and assemble the segments into a basic type. You then write a function module to process the data.

On the outbound, you populate the IDoc and export it by calling a standard function module. Inbound IDocs are imported by a standard function and handed off by the IDoc interface to your custom function where data are read from the IDoc and posted to a transaction or a table through a function, a batch or direct input program, or an SQL insert.

Once this is done, a few simple configuration steps plug your custom IDoc and function into the standard IDoc interface, transforming each into an SAP business object representing a complete transactional or master data record type with its own standard interface and self-contained and predictable logic. Your custom IDoc can then be monitored, processed, reprocessed, reported on, and audited by all the standard programs and tools available to SAP's delivered IDocs. It will behave like every other IDoc in the system.

This is an incredible benefit. The effort required to develop a new IDoc from scratch isn't that much greater than the effort to write an ABAP program to process and export or import a custom flat file.

It's a win-win situation. Not only do you plug your interfaces into the wide array of standard IDoc services, you gain tremendous strategic benefits. You can plan custom interfaces within an architectural framework that provides consistency, reliability, and a suite of standard tools that is faithful to SAP standards.

You can design and build integration architecture, rather than merely recreate point-to-point legacy interfaces that use custom programs to shuttle files between trading partners and internal systems. It future-proofs your client's investment in the new system.

1.3.4 Batch Processing of Large Files

It's impossible to escape a fundamental reality about EDI: it's mostly about batch processing of low- to high-volume transmissions that include a wide array of file sizes, from very small to extraordinarily large.

Acme's relationship with Gordy's Galaxy is a case in point. With more than 2,000 stores across North America, Gordy's Galaxy sends Acme massive quantities of transactional data.

This begins with daily feeds of store-level sales recorded at the cash register whenever an Acme DVD is sold. These daily sales are augmented by a weekly transmission of inventory remaining on the shelves of each store.

Thousands of sales orders and deliveries are processed for Gordy's Galaxy every day involving high-volume data processing and transmission, in both directions by Acme's systems.

The relationship also involves ordering large quantities of finished goods and raw materials from Disc Services International, updates to inventory in multiple systems and generation of complex customer invoicing with multiple pricing schemes for goods delivered to stores in all 50 US states and 10 Canadian provinces, a variety of discounts and special promotions often at the store level, returns processing, and on and on.

The icing on this cake is the monthly X12 820 Payment Advice sent by Gordy's Galaxy. Acme gets only one 820 a month, but each includes detailed payment information for all invoices and debit and credit memos for the preceding 30-day payment period. The largest 820 transmissions, recording $20 million in payments or more, can exceed 30MB at the peak of the holiday shopping season.

So we're not going to try to reinvent the wheel here. The relationship with Gordy's Galaxy is too important to experiment with. Our EDI architecture will be built on file-based remote function calls (RFCs) into SAP with IDocs collected in the IDoc database and schedules for batch processing of IDocs defined in the SAP job scheduler (Transaction SM36).

1.3.5 XML File Ports

File ports can send or receive IDocs in ASCII or XML format. We'll use XML for all of Acme's IDocs. XML IDocs are easier to read. It's also easier to build test XML IDoc files from scratch.

We'll define one XML file port for all of Acme's IDocs: XML_IDOC.

XML file ports are used in the partner profile to convert IDocs to XML format and route them to and from SAP as physical files on the application server. They define the IDoc file name and the path where it will be stored.

The file port also routes IDocs to and from an external EDI system through RFCs or scripts or batch files on the SAP application server.

1.3.6   Partner Profiles

Customer partner profiles will be created only for the sold-to partner, not the ship-to or any other customer type, regardless of how many ship-to locations exist for any customer.

This implies that the customer master record is set up with the partner function populated. Each sold-to partner references each one of its ship-to partners (store locations and distribution centers) in the partner function tab of the customer master record.

Each ship-to master record, in turn, references its sold-to partner. These data are stored in table KNVP.

The link between the external customer store location that is mapped to the IDoc by the EDI transaction and the internal SAP ship-to partner will be managed in table EDPAR, which is accessible through Transaction VOE4.

1.3.7   EDI Mapping Strategy

EDI mapping strategy can be a topic of debate, particularly if EDI is being implemented for the first time. The basic question is whether to develop one map per trading partner or a generic map per transaction and version for all trading partners that use that transaction.

A large number of trading partners means a lot of maps. Many of these maps will be very similar to maps developed for other partners using the same EDI transaction and version.

Designing a common map for a number of trading partners who use the same EDI transaction and version works as long as there aren't that many differences in the way each of these partners uses the various segments, data elements, and qualifiers within the standard. If you have to write a lot of conditional IF . . . THEN statements in your mapping logic to deal with partner-specific usage, you'll want one or more unique maps.

You also need to consider that different trading partners change their use of EDI standards over time at different rates. If you build a common map that includes a trading partner who changes his use of the standard—for example, includes new data elements or upgrades to a more recent version—you could use the common map to create a unique map for that partner. This protects you from needing to do regression testing on the common map when one partner changes his use of the standard.

The policy for the Acme SAP EDI team will be to thoroughly analyze all trading partners' EDI guidelines and production data and, where feasible, to build common maps for groups of partners using the same EDI transaction and version. Where this isn't possible, we'll build unique maps for one trading partner, transaction, and version.

Gordy's Galaxy is one of those special cases because of volume, importance to the business, command of the standards, and mandates to suppliers. It's a no-brainer: Acme will build customer-specific maps for all of Gordy's EDI transactions.

This illustrates an important point. EDI is more than just an exchange of electronic documents: It is a relationship with a business partner. And when it comes to a customer, the old adage holds true: The customer is always right, even when he's wrong. After all, the customer is paying the bills.

We also need to consider business logic. It may seem obvious, but SAP will be the business system of record, and all relevant master and transactional data will live there. The SAP EDI team will ensure that each map translates accurately. But all business logic, calculations, and lookups will be confined to SAP, even if this means writing custom ABAP code.

Our goal, then, is to build maps that simply translate IDocs to X12. We want to avoid data processing, database lookups, or calculations in the map itself. The customer deserves to receive his business documents directly from Acme's business system of record.

1.4   Summary

We've introduced Acme Pictures, its unique business, and its need for a new SAP EDI system. The project is approved, business users are identified, and the consultants are on board. Project scope has been determined.

A lot of interesting development work awaits us. The team is eager to push on. But first we need to understand the present state of the business and the legacy systems that support it. That's where the blueprint phase comes in, which we shall consider next.

"The past is what you see in your rear-view mirror," Darryl Q was fond of saying when he courted a new wife or reconciled with an old director. "It's a lot closer than it seems to be." And so it is for our project team: The past is the key to the future, as we uncover Acme's as-is business processes and legacy systems.

2 The Blueprint: Discovery and Documentation

The project kicks off with a blueprint aimed at getting a complete picture of Acme's as-is business processes and legacy systems. Visio, Word, and Excel will be our best friends through this process. Functional consultants will hold weeks of workshops with business users where they will hammer out Acme Home Entertainment's core business processes bit by bit.

The following questions are fundamental:

- What do you do?
- How do you do it?
- Why do you do it?
- With whom?
- What happens next?

Functional consultants step the business users through each task within each process. The goal of these workshops is to capture as much detail as possible about the business process flows and to identify the points of integration. The information is sketched out on whiteboards and notepads as business users discuss their jobs with each other and with the functional consultants, who poke and prod their memories with questions and comments.

This information feeds Visio process flows and Word narratives that give us a visual map of the home entertainment business. Describing the present is about planning for the future: doing business in the new SAP environment.

The SAP EDI team is deeply involved. Our focus is Acme's relationship with Gordy's Galaxy of Games & B Flix. We need to understand how the legacy systems and interfaces support the business. We won't participate in every workshop, but we need a basic understanding of the key process flows in Purchasing, Sales and Distribution, and Finance, particularly the data flows that support them, including internal interfaces and EDI.

2.1 A Business Process Overview

Acme Home Entertainment (AHE) sells movies on DVD to big box stores across North America. EDI is the critical component that enables the timely and efficient electronic transmission of the key business documents that support the buying and selling that's at the heart of this business. And so blueprinting begins with the as-is purchasing process flow.

2.1.1 The As-Is Purchasing Process Flow

AHE outsources the manufacturing, packaging, and distribution of DVDs to a vendor: Disc Services International (DSI). Purchasing is the process of ordering the goods and services required to manufacture and distribute AHE's DVDs, including the following:

▶ Raw materials such as blank disks, cases, cover and marketing artwork, stickers, and plastic wrapping

▶ Manufacturing services such as DVD replication, packaging, assembly, and stickering

▶ Inventory and distribution services such as storage of raw materials and finished goods, picking, packing, and shipping to customer locations

Two categories of DVD are promoted and sold by AHE: new release and catalog. Each has its own requirements in terms of purchasing.

▶ New release is a movie title that has completed its theatrical run and is about to be released to DVD. This process is driven by marketing and promotional timelines as well as sales planning and demand forecasting.

▸ Catalog is the library of DVD movie titles already in the sales pipeline. Catalog is primarily about replenishment and is dependent on planning around customer sales and inventory.

We'll look at each process flow in a little more detail to give us an overview of the business context in which EDI operates at AHE.

The Purchasing Process for New Release Titles

Purchasing for new releases is largely about planning around the street date. The street date is more than just a release date for the new DVD. It's a sales policy driven by marketing goals and communicated to all customers at least two weeks before the release date.

The aim is to control release of the title to the market, build marketing buzz, and ensure that no retail customer gets the jump on any other for a new DVD product, particularly one with good sales potential.

Marketing sets the goals for the new release. Sales comes up with a plan to sell it. This begins about four months before the street date and is focused on the title rather than on any specific DVD products.

Title is a key concept in the software, video games, publishing, and movie industries. Title is the highest level of abstraction for the product. It is the object of copyright and the legal name for the creative work. When copied to a DVD, the title is assigned attributes and a bill of materials (BOM), transforming it into a product for sale, or an SAP finished good.

The announce date is another milestone in the marketing and sales plan. It is the date the DVD release is announced to Acme's customers, which is about 10 weeks before the street date.

By the time the announce date rolls around, Sales has reached out to all customers and has a feel for the demand for the title. A forecast for an initial target quantity is calculated in Excel based on the emerging marketing goals and sales plan. This is where the as-is purchasing process flow for new releases begins, outlined in Figure 2.1.

The forecast is fed into the legacy VMI system and used to calculate components required to build the DVD product. Marketing and Sales review and update the initial requirements calculations and approve a final forecast. This happens about 10 weeks before the street date.

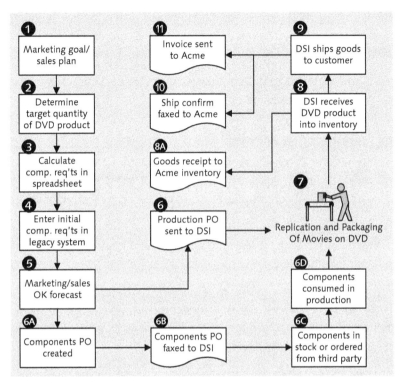

Figure 2.1 As-Is Purchasing Process Flow for New Release

When the final forecast is approved and released, production POs are sent to DSI for the replication and packaging of about a third of the projected volume for the title on DVD. These expectations for sales of the new release raised by planning are based largely on experience and faith.

At the same time, POs are released to DSI for the raw material components required to manufacture the DVD products. DSI maintains inventory for AHE and order raw materials from third-party suppliers.

DSI orders the necessary components and begins replicating and packaging product. The completed DVDs are put into inventory at DSI's warehouse for shipping, and its inventory system is updated. DSI also sends a goods receipt that updates Acme's inventory when production is completed.

About five weeks before the street date, Acme creates sales orders for each customer—and drops component and manufacturing POs to DSI—for the remaining two-thirds of projected shipments from the final forecast.

One week before the street date, customers begin to place their own orders based on their sales projections. AHE uses these orders to calculate replenishment demand for the first month after street date.

DSI ships the completed DVDs to all customers two days before the street date to ensure they have the product by 12:01 a.m. on the release date. After the DVDs have been put on the truck, and the truck pulls away from the loading dock, DSI faxes a shipping confirmation to AHE to complete the PO and update AHE's inventory systems.

DSI then sends invoices to AHE for all services rendered. Accounts payable (AP) is updated and the new release purchasing cycle is closed.

The Purchasing Process for Catalog Titles

Requirements calculations for the catalog forecast begin with daily feeds of point of sales (POS) data and weekly store level inventory counts.

These are fed into the vendor-managed inventory (VMI) system that's used to calculate replenishment requirements for Acme's seven biggest customers, which account for 75 percent of the business. We look at VMI a little more closely in Section 2.2.3.

In addition to VMI data, the catalog forecast needs master and transactional data from Acme's legacy systems, including products, BOMs, customer store locations, open and closed orders, inventory counts, shipments, and a variety of forecasts and sales plans.

An overview of the catalog processing flow is depicted in Figure 2.2.

The forecast looks at open customer orders, compares ordered products and quantities against available inventory, and estimates what finished goods and components AHE will order from DSI to fulfill its customer requirements. The forecast then calculates replenishment order proposals and AHE's manufacturing system generates planned orders that are sent to DSI for replication or fulfillment.

The forecast calculations also check on-hand inventory for the components in the BOMs for all ordered DVD products to determine whether additional component purchases are required. Calculated reorder quantities are entered into an Excel spreadsheet, and component POs are created in AHE's manufacturing system and sent to DSI for processing.

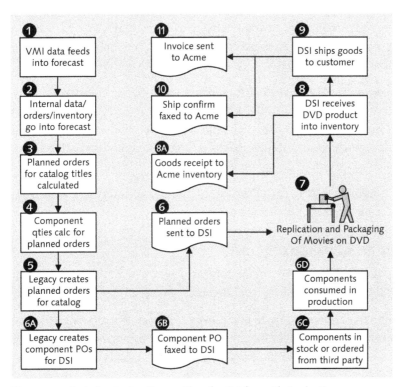

Figure 2.2 As-Is Purchasing Process Flow for Catalog with Production

DSI checks its own inventory and determines the quantity of finished goods for manufacture and of components it needs to order from external suppliers. It then begins to fulfill the orders with its on-hand inventory and schedules production for product that will consume ordered components.

As DSI completes replication and packaging of DVD products, the finished goods are received into inventory and a goods receipt is sent to Acme.

DSI picks and packs the DVDs and ships them to the customer's location. When the truck leaves the loading dock, a shipping confirmation is sent to Acme system and inventory is manually updated in legacy.

DSI then send its invoices for all goods and services performed for Acme and AP is updated. The catalog purchasing cycle is now complete.

2.1.2   The As-Is Sales and Distribution Processing Flow

We'll look at Acme's sales and distribution cycle with Gordy's Galaxy in this section, outlined in Figure 2.3.

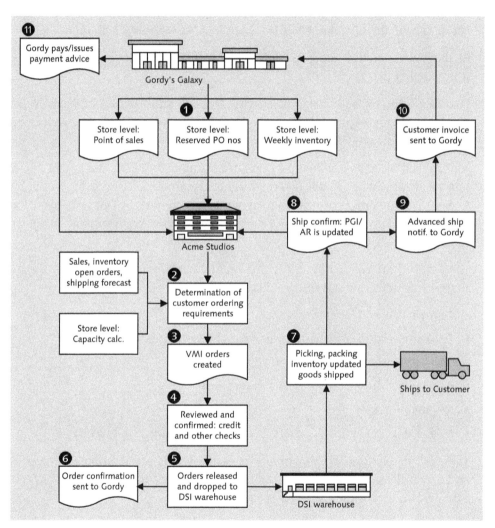

Figure 2.3   As-Is Sales and Distribution Process Flow with Inventory

Gordy's Galaxy is AHE's biggest customer and the focus of our EDI team's efforts. Gordy is also the main driver behind Acme's adoption of VMI ordering.

It all begins with data flows from Gordy's more than 2,000 store locations across North America to AHE's legacy systems. Each time an Acme DVD is bought at one of Gordy's stores, the purchase is scanned at the cash register and a record of the sale is captured to a companywide POS system. The data recorded includes the store number where the sale was made, Gordy's item number for the product, the number of units in the sale, the selling price per unit, and the total amount of the sale.

At the same time, the goods are subtracted from Gordy's inventory against the store number that made the sale.

Two data feeds are built from this activity. One bundles daily POS for each store and is sent every night to AHE. The other bundles weekly inventory counts by store and is sent to AHE once a week.

A third feed includes reserved purchase order numbers (RPOs) and is sent on an as-needed basis, when Gordy determines that all current RPOs have been used by Acme. These are ranges of customer PO numbers generated by Gordy's Galaxy for AHE. This is a key element of the VMI process that allows Acme to create customer POs to replenish all of Gordy's stores.

These orders are created by calculating requirements based on a variety of data sources, including but not restricted to the following:

▶ Gordy's POS and inventory feeds

▶ Minimum and maximum ordering levels by store number and SKU

▶ Shelf dimension data for each of Gordy's stores

▶ Acme's open and closed orders and inventory

▶ Shipping forecasts

▶ Master data, including products, BOMs, store locations, and so on

These calculations produce VMI orders for each of Gordy's stores using the reserved purchase order numbers. The orders determine how many of each of Acme's DVD titles will be sent to each of Gordy's stores.

After the VMI orders are created, AHE's Customer Operations department reviews them, does a credit check, checks stock, and determines purchasing requirements for raw materials. Customer Operations then releases the order, drops it to the DSI warehouse, and faxes a copy to Gordy's as an order acknowledgment that they can enter into their system as a PO.

DSI checks its inventory and begins to fill the order with on-hand finished goods. DSI picks and packs the goods from its warehouse, updates its inventory, and records the movements for transmission to Acme after the goods have been shipped.

If the finished goods are not in stock, DSI manufactures them, checking inventory for the raw materials to replicate the requested product.

After picking and packing, the DVDs are loaded onto trucks and shipped to one of Gordy's distribution centers. When the trucks leave DSI's loading dock, a shipping confirmation that includes the pick quantity is sent to Acme.

AHE receives the shipping confirmation and posts it against the shipped order, closing it and updating inventory. This also updates accounts receivable (AR). At the same time, Customer Operations generates a copy of the order and sends it to Gordy's Galaxy as an advanced ship notice (ASN) to let Gordy know that the shipment is en route to its distribution center. The ASN must arrive before the shipment gets to Gordy's receiving dock.

This ASN gives Gordy's distribution center a heads-up about what DVD products are in the shipment and how much of each product is destined for each store. Gordy won't accept an invoice until it receives the ASN followed by the product that is then matched perfectly against the ASN.

So now, AHE can issue an invoice to Gordy's Galaxy for the shipment. The invoice is created and sent, and AR is updated. Gordy normally pays after 30 days, with an electronic transfer to AHE's bank and the transmission of a payment advice to AHE's AR department where the invoice is closed and all relevant general ledger (GL) accounts are cleared.

The monthly payment is the net of all invoices, debits, credits, returns, promotions, and so on generated within the 30-day payment period.

2.1.3   Selling the Dream with Vendor Management Inventory

Acme initially jumped into vendor-managed inventory (VMI) because of a mandate from Gordy's Galaxy. Gordy wanted to partner with its key vendors to streamline ordering and manage supply chain costs.

VMI is a relationship between trading partners that is wholly dependent on computer systems and EDI data flows. It gives the vendor the freedom to make decisions about replenishment based on real-world data.

Trading partners share key ordering information such as new and changed store locations, sales and marketing plans, and actual sales and inventory levels at each customer store. The goal is to create a replenishment system focused on the buying habits of shoppers, which is captured by the POS data recorded for each sale and transmitted to Acme.

This real-world data capture creates unique opportunities to analyze the effectiveness of marketing and sales plans and to quickly adjust strategy and ordering requirements when initial assumptions don't quite pan out.

To achieve this symbiotic relationship, the trading partners loosely integrate their computer systems through EDI transmissions. For Acme Pictures, VMI is an unqualified success. The studio has expanded VMI relationships to its seven largest customers that account for 75 percent of its total revenues.

The VMI relationship with Gordy, as outlined in Figure 2.4, is driven by AHE's systems, particularly EDI data transmissions.

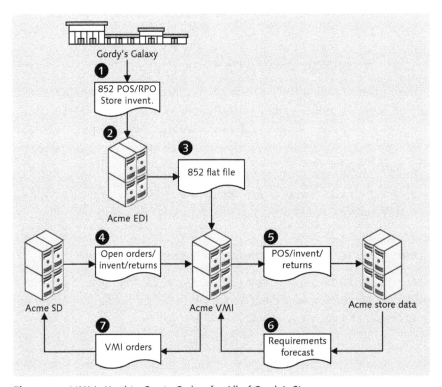

Figure 2.4 VMI Is Used to Create Orders for All of Gordy's Stores

We've already touched briefly on the store-level POS and inventory feeds, and the reserved purchase order numbers (RPOs) that Acme receives from Gordy's Galaxy. These data are sent in an EDI X12 852 transaction. This is characteristic of EDI, where one transaction can serve multiple purposes.

POS data are identified where the XQ segment has only one date, and there is no XPO segment, as in the 852 data fragment in Listing 2.1.

```
ST*852*0001~
XQ*H*20081218~
N9*AD*693887~
```
Listing 2.1 Identifying POS Data in an 852 Transaction

Weekly inventory is distinguished in the same way as POS but includes a second end date to the XQ segment to indicate a date range for the count (see Listing 2.2).

```
ST*852*0001~
XQ*H*20081214*20081220~
N9*AD*693887~
```
Listing 2.2 Weekly Inventory Identified by a Date Range

RPOs are identified by the presence of one or more XPO segments that contain PO number ranges assigned to the vendor, as illustrated in the 852 fragment in Listing 2.3.

```
ST*852*13730001
XQ*G*20081218
XPO*000011408145*000011408175*9*1033917530001
XPO*000020506131*000020506175*9*1033917530002
```
Listing 2.3 Populated XPO Segments Define RPO Transmissions

The RPO transaction can also include details of products that have already been ordered but not yet delivered. This is provided at the line-item level of the transaction and includes the following:

▶ The product code in the LIN segment, which, in the case of Gordy's Galaxy, is the UPC number

▶ The expected delivery date in the ZA segment

▶ Quantities of the item expected by each store

This is illustrated in the 852 fragment in Listing 2.4. LIN is the highest level of the item detail loop. The SDQ segment can hold quantity ordering information for up to 10 stores.

```
LIN**UP*035143019723*IN*113499
PO4*20
ZA*QP***007*20060307
SDQ*EA*92*00001*40*00002*80*00006*80*00008*100*00009*80
SDQ*EA*92*00022*60*00024*80*00025*96*00028*60*00029*72
```
Listing 2.4 The SDQ Segment in an 852

We delve more deeply into the structure of EDI transactions in Chapter 4, EDI: The Ugly Stepsister of E-Commerce. For now, it's enough to look at the data samples.

The RPOs provide the PO numbers required to post a customer order in Acme's system that will be recognized by Gordy's Galaxy when it receives the ASN announcing delivery of the ordered goods.

Gordy transmits its POS data every night and its inventory once a week. Acme's EDI system receives the data, recognizes the sending and receiving systems, identifies the transaction, determines and executes a translation map that transforms the EDI file into an internal flat file format, and then posts the flat file to the VMI system.

At the same time, Acme's legacy systems send VMI daily extracts of master and transactional data, including customers, store locations, finished goods, open orders, inventory, sales forecasts, and so on.

VMI sends this legacy, POS, and inventory data to StoreData, a custom system that maintains a variety of store-level data, including the following:

▶ Titles and product numbers

▶ Minimum and maximum order levels by title and product

▶ Shelf dimensions and positioning

These data drive a complex series of calculations that figure out how much of each DVD product to order for each of Gordy's stores. The results of these calculations are sent back to the VMI system. VMI then creates orders for the customer from these calculations and assigns the next free PO number from the RPO range that came in separate 852 transmissions.

Finally, the suggested PO is sent to Acme's SD system, where a customer order posts. At this point, the regular sales processing flows kick in.

The 852 is a key transaction in the sales and distribution processing flow between Gordy's Galaxy and AHE. The 852 provides critical POS data used to generate customer orders and to validate sales and marketing plans. The 852 will not directly post to SAP in the brave new world, except through the VMI orders calculated and created by VMI and its associated data feeds.

The VMI system remains untouched in the new SAP EDI architecture. SAP replaces many of the systems that feed VMI; it also replaces the Legacy SD system that receives the VMI order feed. VMI is a critical piece of the overall business data flows and system architecture. We'll treat the 852 feeds with the deference and respect they so richly deserve.

2.2   Legacy Systems, Data Flows, and Interfaces

The time has come to look a little more closely at Acme's legacy systems and interfaces and to reconsider business processes that we've superficially touched on from the perspective of the EDI data flows.

Some of Acme's core legacy business systems and interfaces that impact EDI are outlined in Figure 2.5.

There are far more legacy systems, and most will be replaced by SAP. There are, for example, multiple data warehouses, forecasting systems, databases, systems that track and manage advertising revenue and royalty payments, and many more. All ultimately feed into finance and the bottom line. Our focus, however, is on a snapshot of the legacy environment so that we can plan our SAP EDI implementation for Gordy's order-to-cash cycle.

Like most companies, Acme built its legacy systems in a piecemeal fashion over a long period of time. They reside on a variety of boxes and include packaged software and custom applications. The packaged software has been highly customized, usually by outside consultants, over 15 years. Interfaces between systems are handled by file transfers using FTP scripts run as batch scheduled jobs. This is not necessarily a bad thing, but a lot of redundant data are passed around.

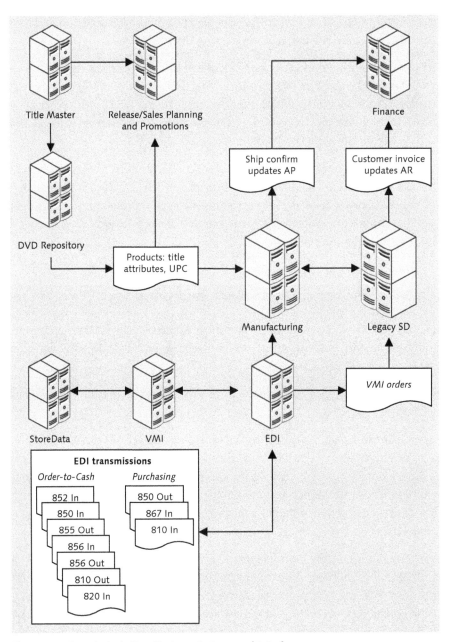

Figure 2.5 Acme's As-Is Core Business Systems and Interfaces

As is often the case with legacy systems that have grown organically from new requirements, none of these systems are well documented, although IT has produced a number of very messy Visio flow charts with high-level overviews of the key systems and data flows.

So though legacy systems might not be pretty, they work. AHE's business users have grown comfortable with their idiosyncratic inefficiencies. Users are not particularly interested in elegant architectures, consolidated data stores, or efficiently written code. All they care about is being able to do their jobs.

Acme IT wants a more streamlined systems environment. SAP will replace many of these legacy systems and reduce the number of interfaces. A key benefit for IT is the consolidation of master and transactional data currently stored across multiple systems into the SAP data model. In most cases, the users will have to deal with only one system to do their jobs: SAP.

But that's future state. Before we can get there, we need to understand how things work today.

The key systems and data flows refer to a few of the core systems and data feeds that impact the business of selling Acme's movies on DVD. This includes purchasing the goods and services needed to manufacture, store, and ship the finished product.

2.2.1 Title Master and DVD Repository

Title is the approved legal name of the creative work; it is the highest level of abstraction for a movie. It's not a product that can be sold to a consumer at a retail outlet. Title is a property, a legal entity, and the basis for products sold at retail. Title Master stores only one record for each creative work owned by AHE.

The DVD Repository transforms the title into a product. It assigns specific attributes such as format (wide screen or standard), ISBN and UPC numbers, language, packaging, sticker requirements, and so on. Each title is linked to many records in the DVD Repository.

The DVD Repository is the equivalent of the SAP material master for finished goods. It feeds the product master for both new release and catalog items to Manufacturing, Legacy SD, and the planning, forecasting, and promotions systems. Key data flows include the following:

▶ An on-demand feed of titles to the DVD Repository for the assignment of attributes and creation of products

65

▸ Nightly feeds of DVD Repository product master data to Manufacturing, Legacy SD, and other systems

The Title Master and DVD Repository are custom SQL Server databases with a Visual Basic frontend.

2.2.2 Release Planning and Promotions Systems

Release planning and promotions are handled by a number of custom systems built in MS Access, Excel, and MySQL with browser or Visual Basic frontends.

The release planning system plots key milestones in the new release cycle for DVDs, including such dates as theatrical, announce, release, replication, street, and others.

The promotions system is used to run promotional campaigns. It stores key marketing data such as campaign costs and funding; regional, national, and customer marketing goals; and customer contact information. Planning reports and sales forecasts used to predict new release ordering requirements are generated. Key data flows include the following:

▸ On-demand feeds of DVD Repository product attributes inbound

▸ Nightly feeds of customers, items, purchase requirements, sales, returns, open orders, and forecasts from Legacy SD, Manufacturing, and VMI

2.2.3 Legacy SD

Legacy SD is the sales and distribution system that is the entry point for EDI on the sales side. It is responsible for all types of customer orders, VMI, EDI, returns, and so on. Shipping orders, invoices, and other customer documents are also processed here.

Legacy SD holds the complete customer master, including bill-to, store locations, and contact information, as well as a copy of the finished goods master and current inventory from Manufacturing. Key data flows include the following:

▸ VMI orders from VMI

▸ Customer POs, shipping confirmations, and payments from EDI

▸ Customer PO acknowledgments, ASNs, and invoices to EDI

▸ Finished goods master data, customer item cross-reference, on-hand inventory, and open vendor POs from Manufacturing

► Open customer orders, returns, and deliveries to VMI and Manufacturing

► Updates to AR in Finance, including customer invoices, and payments

Legacy SD is built on a highly customized JDEdwards system on an AS400.

2.2.4 Manufacturing

Legacy Manufacturing is responsible for issuing POs to vendors for the replication of DVD movie products. It is also used to purchase raw material components for replication and packaging, and supplies for creative and marketing materials.

Manufacturing is the entry point for EDI in purchasing. It gets finished goods master data from the DVD Repository and finished goods and some raw material inventory through EDI transmissions from DSI.

Master data include vendors, materials, some BOMs, and a cross-reference between the customer and Acme item numbers.

Manufacturing receives vendor invoices and passes them to Finance for AP processing. It also handles basic material resource planning (MRP) using its own on-hand inventory and open shipping order data from Legacy SD. Key data flows include the following:

► Vendor POs and invoices to EDI

► Goods receipts and inventory adjustments from EDI

► Open and closed customer orders from Legacy SD

► BOMs and forecast requirements to Release and Sales Planning

► Updates to AP in Finance through goods receipts and vendor invoices

Manufacturing resides on its own highly customized JDEdwards instance on the AS400.

2.2.5 Finance

As the heart and soul of the existing architecture, all key systems feed into Finance. It handles all financial processing, balancing, and period closings. It contains AP, AR, cost accounting, fixed assets, and the GL. The Finance system is responsible for paying the bills, collecting and clearing payments, and providing a variety of fiscal reports that management loves to pore over.

Key data flows into Finance include the following:

- From manufacturing: open and closed vendor orders, forecasts, inventory adjustments, vendor invoices
- From SD: open and closed customer orders, sales forecasts, goods receipts, customer invoices, and payments for clearing

Finance is a standalone module of the customized JDEdwards system.

2.2.6   VMI and StoreData

VMI is a complex custom application built on an SQL Server database. To most of Acme's employees, it is a black box with a voracious appetite for data, including the following:

- Daily POS data from customer store locations
- Open and closed customer orders, daily shipments, and returns
- RPO numbers from Gordy
- Open and closed vendor orders for replication of DVD products and for the purchase of components and services
- Sales and purchasing forecasts
- On-hand inventory from customer store locations and DSI
- Material master data and BOMs

StoreData is a critical element of the VMI environment. It holds shelf-level dimensions for each of Gordy's stores. It knows how many DVDs can be displayed on any particular shelf in any of Gordy's stores in a variety of display options.

This is key to helping VMI calculate how much to deliver to each of Gordy's stores to keep shelves stocked and products moving. Key data flows include the following:

- POS, store level inventory, and new or changed locations from VMI
- Shelf location and dimension data from Gordy
- Product packaging dimensions and special display characteristics

StoreData is a custom application built on a MySQL database with a Visual Basic frontend.

2.2.7 EDI

The dedicated EDI system communicates directly with VMI, Manufacturing, and Legacy SD. It handles all the normal functions of an EDI system, including trading partner management, communications, mapping, and routing to Acme's internal systems.

EDI has been around for nearly 15 years and has been largely customized. Most of its functionality is undocumented, and there are no mapping specifications, although it can generate mapping reports with code listings for all custom logic. Its maps cannot be reused by any other EDI system.

Legacy EDI does not support AS2 communications over the Internet. EDI files are moved to a folder on the network and sent to the trading partner by an AS2 server rented from an EDI service bureau.

Gordy's Galaxy, Acme's most important customer, has mandated that it will exchange EDI files with vendors only through AS2, so Acme has no choice.

An advantage of AS2 is that it eliminates transmission charges imposed by value added networks (VANs), which was Acme's traditional means of EDI communications. The VAN charges Acme per byte of data transmitted, and these can add up. At the height of the busy Christmas holiday shopping season, Acme can pay $15,000 or more a month in VAN usage fees alone.

Though there are setup and maintenance fees with AS2, these monthly charges are eliminated once it's up.

2.3   Legacy EDI Data Flows

EDI is mission critical for AHE. Without EDI, it would be impossible to keep all of Gordy's more than 2,000 stores across North America stocked with DVDs. Besides, Gordy will do business with its vendors only through EDI. And what Gordy wants, Gordy gets.

So now we look a little more closely at the key EDI document transfers that enable the purchasing, sales, and distribution processes in the legacy systems that we've been touching on.

2.3.1 Replicating Success: Outsourcing Production

Hollywood studios make movies, not DVDs. They don't have the replication facilities to image and package them, the warehouses to store the raw material and finished product inventories, or the distribution facilities to ship DVDs to their customers' store locations.

So thank God for vendors such as Disc Services International. Manufacturing and shipping DVDs is DSI's business. DSI has been in that business for years: replicating, packaging, and shipping DVDs and CDs for movie studios and the music, software, and publishing industries.

EDI document flows are the backbone of this purchasing process, which is outlined in Figure 2.6.

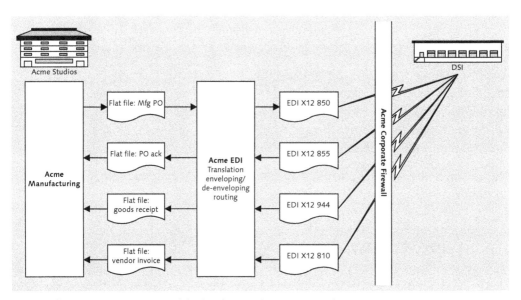

Figure 2.6 An Overview of the Purchasing EDI Document Flow

Acme's Legacy EDI Outbound Process Flow

The EDI document processing flow begins when Acme's Manufacturing system issues a vendor PO for replication and packaging of DVDs or for the purchase of raw materials for manufacturing.

We'll look at ordering titles in stock from DSI. The process is the same for all outbound interfaces in purchasing and sales and is outlined in Figure 2.7.

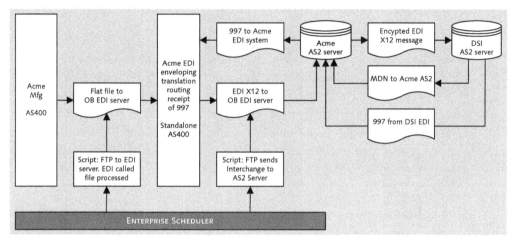

Figure 2.7 Legacy Outbound EDI Processing Depends on Scheduled Batch Jobs to Move Files from System to System

The PO is exported from the Manufacturing system as a flat file. It is picked up by an FTP script at the operating system level, which is triggered by a job scheduler. The job checks for the existence of a file in an outbound PO directory every hour.

The FTP process moves the file to an inbound PO directory on the EDI server, which is on a separate box from the Manufacturing system. It triggers a script on the EDI server that calls a job in the EDI system to pick up the PO file and check the header for transaction and receiver codes used to identify a conversion map and execute it.

The map translates the PO flat file to an outbound X12 850 and saves the individual transactions to another outbound directory for batching and enveloping of multiple 850s into a single transmission.

DSI expects three 850 transmissions a day from Acme: at 5:00 a.m., 3:00 p.m., and 11:00 p.m. The enveloping job is called an hour before each transmission. It picks up all 850 transactions in the batch directory and wraps each one in an ST-SE envelope. It then collects each ST transaction into a single file and wraps it in one GS-GE group envelope. The group is then wrapped in one ISA-IE envelope to create an X12 interchange file.

The ISA envelope includes Acme's EDI sender ID, DSI's EDI recipient ID, the date and time of transmission, and an interchange control number. This information is used in routing the transmission to the proper recipient and in providing a unique code to allow easy identification of the interchange in the event of an error or a failure in transmission.

When the enveloping job completes its run, it saves the consolidated EDI file to a DSI outbound interchange directory. Another job polls that directory every hour. When it finds an interchange file, the job picks up the file and runs an FTP process that transfers the interchange to an outbound directory on an AS2 server at the EDI service bureau that Acme uses for its AS2 transmissions. The service bureau then encrypts the interchange and sends by AS2 as a secure HTTP/S transmission across the Internet to DSI's AS2 server, which decrypts the message and passes it to DSI's EDI system for translation and routing to DSI's business systems.

We need to note two other exchanges before moving on. When the AS2 transmission is received by DSI's AS2 server, a technical acknowledgment known as a message disposition notification (MDN) is sent back to Acme's EDI service bureau.

The MDN informs the sending system that the encrypted EDI message has been received. It does not imply that the message has been decrypted, translated, and posted to the recipient's business system—only that it's been received.

When the 850 hits the recipient's EDI system, while it's being de-enveloped and just before translation, a 997 acknowledgment interchange is built and sent back to Acme's EDI system by AS2 with the following data:

▶ The group control number from the GS envelope of Acme's 850 EDI transmission

▶ A code identifying the transaction sent by Acme

▶ Status codes reporting on the success or failure of structural and syntax checks on the EDI file

The 997 tells the sender that the interchange was received and checked. It does not imply that the file was successfully translated and posted to the target system.

Acme's Legacy EDI Inbound Process Flow

This process is reversed for the inbound to Acme. The inbound processing flow is the same for all inbound EDI transmissions in Purchasing and Sales. The inbound EDI processing flow is outlined in Figure 2.8.

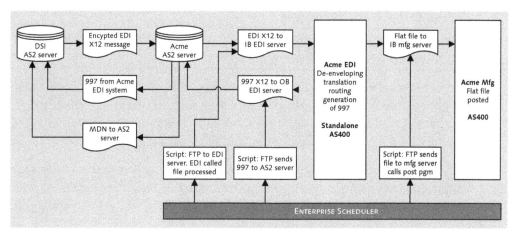

Figure 2.8 The Legacy Inbound Process Sends Both an MDN and a 997 to DSI as Acknowledgments

When DSI posts the 850 PO from AHE, it issues an acknowledgment in a flat file that its EDI system translates to an 855 order acknowledgment. The 855 is sent by AS2 through a secure HTTP/S transmission to the AS2 server at Acme's EDI service provider.

When the encrypted transmission is received by the AS2 server at Acme's EDI service bureau, an MDN is generated and sent back to DSI's AS2 server through an AS2 HTTP/S transmission. The MDN is always sent to confirm receipt of an AS2 message by an AS2 server.

The 855 is decrypted and sent by FTP to an 855 interchange directory on Acme's EDI application server. This directory is polled by a job every hour. If the job finds a file in the directory, it calls a program in the EDI system that strips the envelopes away from the transmission.

The de-enveloping job reads the ISA, GS, and ST envelopes to identify the send and receive partners, the X12 version, and transaction. This information is used to do the following:

▸ Generate a 997 group level acknowledgment to send back to DSI by AS2 to let them know that the interchange has been received and has passed or failed the structural and syntax checks

▸ Identify a translation map to transform the X12 855 transactions within the interchange to a custom flat file using an internal Acme format

- Execute the translation map
- Store the translated file to an outbound order acknowledgment directory on the EDI system application server

Another scheduled job polls this directory every hour, 15 minutes after the initial job imports the 855 interchange into the EDI system. If a translated file is found, a script kicks off an FTP process that moves the translated file into an inbound directory on the Manufacturing system's application server.

The FTP script includes a call to a job in the Manufacturing system that imports the flat file and calls an acknowledgment program that updates the original PO with the date of acknowledgment and the date the order will be ready for shipping, and any changes that DSI made to the quantities.

We look at enveloping, de-enveloping, acknowledgments, and other EDI processes in greater detail in Chapter 4. For now, it's enough to get a feel for how this all works in Acme's legacy EDI system.

Completing the Purchasing Cycle

DSI replicates and packages the DVD order. Any adjustments to inventory throughout production are sent to Acme's EDI system in an 867 inventory adjustment that updates Acme's inventory in the Manufacturing system.

When replication is complete, the DVDs are picked, packed, and put on a truck for shipment to Gordy's distribution centers. As the truck leaves the loading dock, DSI generates a warehouse receipt in a flat file from its delivery system that includes the shipped quantity of all items in the original vendor PO and a flag to indicate whether the entire order was shipped.

This file is translated by DSI's EDI system to a 944 warehouse receipt and transmitted to Acme's EDI system by AS2.

Acme's EDI system translates the 944 to an internal flat file format. It's picked up and sent by FTP to the Manufacturing server where it's imported and posted against the original vendor PO. It updates the quantities shipped against the open quantities on each item of the PO. After all items have been confirmed and if the completion flag is set, a goods receipt is posted against the PO, and the order is closed.

Acme's inventory is updated with the finished goods and the raw materials consumed in production are flushed. The flushed materials are determined by reading BOMs for the finished goods. AP is updated through an internal interface: it now expects to receive a vendor invoice.

After DSI issues the warehouse receipt, it generates and sends an invoice to its EDI system. The invoice is translated to an 810 invoice transaction and sent to Acme's EDI system by AS2. The 810 is translated to a flat file that is moved by FTP to the Manufacturing system's application server.

The invoice file is then uploaded and posted into Manufacturing and sent to AP in the Finance system through an internal interface.

2.3.2   Order-to-Cash and Legacy EDI

The main focus for our exploration of an EDI architecture in SAP is Gordy's Galaxy order-to-cash cycle. We'll look at how this works in Acme's legacy systems. The technical details of the inbound and outbound processing flows for EDI documents in Sales and Distribution are identical to those in Purchasing. MDNs and 997s are generated and sent for each inbound transmission and received for each outbound.

Figure 2.9 is an overview of the base sales and distribution EDI flows. For Gordy's Galaxy and all VMI customers, it begins with the transmission of an 852 POS transaction detailing daily sales for all of Acme's DVD products at each of Gordy's retail outlets.

The daily POS is supplemented by weekly transmissions of 852 store-level inventory and intermittent transmissions of reserve PO numbers.

The three 852 feeds are sent to Acme's EDI system and translated to flat files that are moved by a scheduled FTP process to the VMI system. The 852 posts to VMI and replenishment calculations are run, including data from StoreData and other systems.

Individual orders are generated for each of Gordy's stores that will receive replenishment product. The orders are collected, consolidated into a single file, and exported to an outbound directory on the VMI application server.

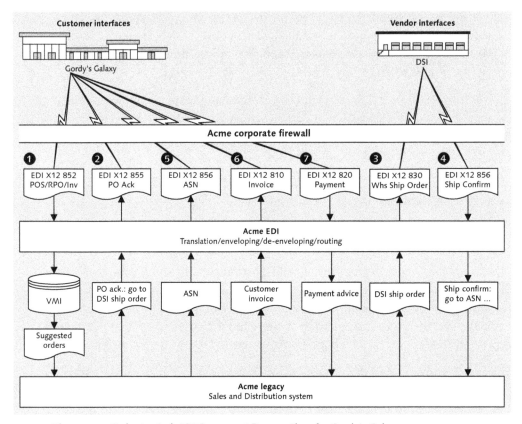

Figure 2.9 Order-to-Cash EDI Document Process Flow for Gordy's Galaxy

From there, a scheduled job kicks off that picks up the file and moves it by FTP to an inbound orders directory on the Legacy SD application server and triggers a program that imports the file and posts it to a customer order.

The order is not finalized until Acme's customer operations approves it. This involves a credit check and other confirmations. After the order is approved, a flat file is exported to an outbound acknowledgment directory on the legacy application server.

This acknowledgment is both a simple and a complex process. The acknowledgment is a copy of the order posted. But the order that posts is by individual store number. We need to collect all of the orders for each store against one PO number and bundle them into a single EDI transaction with store-level ordering details at the item level.

Legacy SD consolidates each order into a single file before exporting it to the application server. Once in the acknowledgment directory, the scheduler kicks off a KornShell script that loops through the flat file and reformats it so that product ordering details for each store are at the item level.

The acknowledgment file is then passed to the EDI system where it is identified, translated to an 855 transaction set, enveloped, and sent to Acme's AS2 service bureau. The AS2 server encrypts and transmits the interchange to Gordy's AS2 server, which passes it to the EDI system.

At this point, we need to tell DSI how much product to ship to each of Gordy's stores. We're assuming that they've already been fed enough POs to replicate all the DVD products we need to ship. A shipping order is generated in Legacy SD detailing the quantities of specific DVD product to ship to each of Gordy's stores.

The shipping order outputs a flat file to the application server. The flat file is picked up by an FTP process and sent to the EDI system, where it is translated to a 940 warehouse ship order transaction, enveloped, and sent to DSI by AS2. DSI receives the 940 and goes into its warehouse to pick and pack the DVD product and apply any stickers that Gordy's stores may be expecting. This is detailed in the shipping order.

The truck is loaded and sent off to Gordy's distribution centers. DSI's delivery system closes the shipping order and generates a flat file shipping confirmation. DSI's EDI system translates this file to an 856 shipping confirmation and sends it to Acme's EDI system.

The 856 is translated to a flat file and sent into Acme's legacy system, where it updates the pick quantity in the open shipping order. When all pick quantities have been confirmed, the order is closed and inventory released. AR in Finance is updated through an internal interface.

But the invoice cannot be issued yet. Gordy's Galaxy must be informed that the shipment is on its way. Closing the shipping order triggers output of a flat file copy of the order. This is passed to the EDI system, where it is translated to an 856 ASN, enveloped, and sent to Gordy's EDI system.

Gordy won't accept an invoice until it receives the DVD products and the 856 at its distribution center and confirms that the goods described in the 856 have all been received.

If the invoice arrives before the 856 ASN, Gordy issues an 864 error message listing the rejected invoices and the reasons for their rejection. We know that Gordy received the 856 because Gordy sends a 997 confirming receipt of the 856. This generally comes within an hour of sending the 856.

So now we can generate the invoice. Legacy SD spits it out as a flat file that is translated by EDI to an 810 customer invoice. The 810 is enveloped and transmitted to Gordy's EDI system by AS2.

By agreement, Gordy pays within 30 days of receiving the invoice. AR is anxious that invoices are received and posted, so the 997s and 864s for the 810s are closely monitored by the EDI support group. AR regularly checks Gordy's partner website. If the invoices don't show up within a couple of days, they call Gordy's AP department to track down the invoices.

Assuming everything goes well, Gordy sends an electronic payment to the bank and issues a payment document that is sent by EDI as an 820 payment advice. This contains details of all invoices, debits, credits, rebates, promotional pricing, returns, and so on, paid by the electronic funds transfer. These are all supported by documents that exist in Acme's Legacy SD and Finance systems: invoices, returns orders, and debit or credit memos sent by Gordy by fax or through an 812 EDI transmission.

The payments, credits, and debits on the 820 must match all invoices and other documents in Acme's systems to clear, or the payment won't be recorded and the accounts will be out of balance.

2.4   Summary

So ends our whirlwind tour of Acme's as-is business and legacy systems process flows. We spent some effort describing it because it is the basis for our brave new world of SAP and EDI. Our consultants have been very busy uncovering all this stuff, and we're only looking at a simple piece of it.

It's time now to turn our attention to describing how this will translate to our new SAP EDI environment.

"Never look back," Darryl Q, the visionary founder of Acme Pictures, would say whenever he fired a writer who couldn't get a scene straight—or crooked, depending on the film. The Great Mr. Q always looked ahead to the next picture, the next season, the next dollar. And so our project team looks ahead as we design the architecture for our new SAP EDI system.

3 Designing the New SAP EDI Architecture

For weeks, our functional consultants and their business partners have been busy as beavers defining Acme's as-is business processes as completely as the workshops and memories of business users have allowed.

Our SAP EDI specialist attended many of the workshops to learn what he could and to offer his views on how EDI could help improve business process flows. He interviewed key IT and EDI business owners and built a picture of Acme's legacy systems and their key interfaces, outlined in Chapter 2.

The technical team documented all internal file formats used to exchange EDI data with Acme's trading partners, obtained mapping reports for all legacy maps, and cataloged all the scripts, batch files, and scheduled jobs that keep the data flowing.

A key working document came out of this exercise: a spreadsheet listing all EDI transactions by trading partner. It includes columns for the following:

- EDI sender and receiver IDs, direction, and frequency
- EDI standards (X12, EDIFACT, TRADACOMS, etc.) and version
- Communications method (VAN, AS2, or FTP)
- IP addresses or URLs for VAN mailboxes or AS2 (applicability statement) servers

This is the starting point for our definition of Acme's new EDI interfaces. If we add columns to map IDoc messages and basic types to EDI transactions, we have a preliminary inventory of EDI interfaces in the new system.

It's been a lively and stimulating process of discovery. But everybody is anxious to put it behind them and begin building the new system. First we flesh out the SAP EDI architecture. And then we need to sell it to Acme Home Entertainment's business owners and management.

3.1 The To-Be Systems and Interfaces Emerge

This is the most creative phase of the project. We take what we know about the business, legacy systems, and interfaces, and then design solutions for our system build. We'll take it as a given that Acme has decided on its new EDI system and that a sandbox is up and running.

Our first task is to define an overall architecture that provides a high-level conceptual vision of how the various systems will work together in the brave new world. This includes SAP, the key legacy systems that will remain after go-live, and Acme's EDI trading partners.

3.1.1 The Resource Integration Manager

Figure 3.1 presents an overview of the team's vision of the new integration architecture, including EDI.

The integration system is the focal point of the new environment, the traffic cop managing and monitoring all data flows. The team responsible for EDI and internal interfaces christened it the Resource Integration Manager (RIM).

All internal and EDI data feeds flow to the RIM. The RIM identifies the source and target systems and converts the feed to a target format. It then routes the file to its target system for posting. Internal interfaces move through FTP while EDI uses a new AS2 perimeter server.

The new integration architecture emerging from the Plan Q's blueprint phase is much slimmer than the legacy environment we outlined in Chapter 2. While most legacy systems are being replaced, some key systems remain:

▶ Title Master will feed Project Systems (PS) in SAP

▶ Planning and promotions will receive sales data from SAP

▶ VMI and StoreData

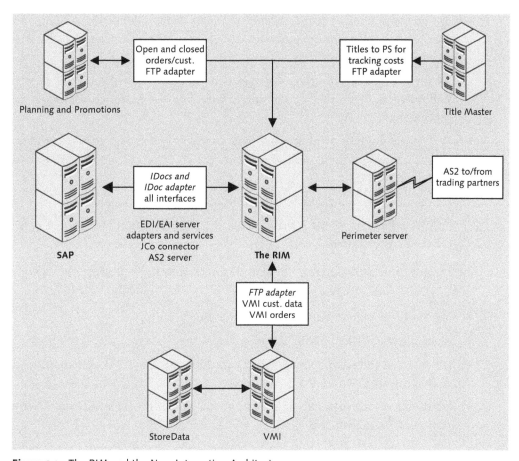

Figure 3.1 The RIM and the New Integration Architecture

Some of these systems will be replaced in a future Plan Q Phase 2, although not the Title Master. But that doesn't affect our current build of the order-to-cash cycle with Gordy's Galaxy of Games & B Flix.

Most legacy functionality is rolling into SAP, including the following:

▶ General ledger (GL), accounts payable (AP), accounts receivable (AR), payment clearing, period closings, costing, financial reporting, and all other financial functions from Finance and other systems to the Financial Accounting and Controlling (FI-CO) module

▶ Project planning and costing for titles to the PS module, supported by daily feeds from the Title Master through the RIM

- Customer master data management, customer orders, deliveries, billing, and other sales and distribution functions from Legacy SD to the Sales and Distribution (SD) module in SAP

- Vendor and finished goods master data management, finished goods inventory, vendor orders, and other purchasing functions to the Materials Management (MM) module in SAP

- DVD finished goods attributes and characteristics, such as genre, street date, theatrical release, ratings, and so on, from the DVD Repository to MM, in two ways:

  - Classifications and characteristics within the finished goods master

  - Custom fields in a MARA material master table extension or in one or more linked custom tables

At the same time, functionality that didn't exist in legacy is being introduced with SAP. Some of this new functionality that will impact EDI includes the following:

- Complete raw materials and component master data

- Bill of material (BOM) master data

- Raw material and component inventory tracking in Acme's SAP system through EDI feeds from DSI

- Purchasing of raw materials and components by EDI through DSI and directly from third-party suppliers

- Daily EDI feeds to DSI of new and changed customer sold-to and ship-to partners, finished goods, raw materials, and BOM master data

- Daily feeds of master and transactional data from SAP to VMI and other Acme backend systems and data warehouses, including the following:

  - Customer sold-to and ship-to parties

  - Finished goods and raw materials

  - BOMs

  - Open customer orders

  - Open POs

  - Open deliveries

3.1.2 Let's Get Technical: A More Intimate Look at the RIM

AHE opted for an integration system that features an automated workflow engine rooted in Business Process Modeling Language (BPML). It runs on a J2EE application server and uses services and adapters that are strung together with connectors to build workflows.

The workflows and the objects that they contain are described in BPML and executed by Java programs in the runtime workflow engine. The workflows process, transform, route, and move data from system to system. They encapsulate specific functionality, like SAP functions. Workflow processing data are stored in XML documents similar to the Web Services Description Language (WSDL) structured documents used by SAP NetWeaver PI.

The system is built on a two-tier environment with separate database and application servers and a browser GUI. The database is accessed through services that implement Java Database Connectivity (JDBC) connections.

The adapters—including an SAP IDoc adapter—introduced in Chapter 1, Section 1.3.2, The EDI System, support data transfer and remote application triggering in a variety of protocols and standards:

▶ SAP RFC through the Java Connector (JCo)

▶ AS2 through a built-in server that supports encrypted AS1 and AS2 by HTTP and HTTP/S

▶ SOAP transfers through HTTP and HTTP/S

▶ FTP and FTP/S

▶ DOS and Windows enterprise server file transfers

▶ Execution of operating system level programs, commands, and scripts

Mapping

The RIM has a graphical mapping tool and a library of EDI standards that can be used as interfaces in mapping. IDoc metadata—data that describe the structure, syntax, and attributes of IDoc basic types—can be imported in a number of ways:

▶ XML schema or document type definitions (DTDs), or traditional parser format in a text file, all generated from Transaction WE60

▶ EDIFECS gXML, a widely supported standard that stores detailed structural and attribute information in an XML document validated by an accompanying DTD

▶ An RFC through the SAP adapter and the JCo to two SAP function modules in function group `EDIMEXT`:

  ▶ `IDOC_RECORD_READ`

  ▶ `IDOCTYPE_READ_COMPLETE`

`EDIMEXT` is a standard API that allows external middleware systems, or any programmer, to extract IDoc metadata from SAP for use in mapping and other applications.

`IDOC_RECORD_READ` returns field level metadata—field name, lengths, position, data types, and so on—for each of the three record types, or segments, that form the underlying structure of all basic types: the control record (EDI_DC40), data record (EDI_DD40), and status record (EDI_DS40).

Function `IDOCTYPE_READ_COMPLETE` returns detailed information about every segment, data element, and qualifier used by an IDoc basic or extended type and all logical messages linked to it.

To see for yourself, run `IDOCTYPE_READ_COMPLETE` with the function module test tool in Transaction SE37 and enter the following values into the TEST FUNCTION MODULE: INITIAL SCREEN:

▶ `PI_IDOCTYP` = IDoc basic type name

▶ `PI_RELEASE` = IDoc release number

▶ `PI_CIMTYP` = IDoc extension name if IDoc has a custom segment

Figure 3.2 shows a slice of the metadata returned for the segments ORDERS05. Displayed is the segment number, which defines its order in the basic type, name, version, and segment length.

Both functions read a number of tables that contain the complete structure and syntax of an IDoc type or extension:

▶ IDOCSYN for the order and hierarchical relationships of the segments in an IDoc type, including the following:

  ▶ Segment name

  ▶ Sequential numbering of segment with the type

  ▶ Hierarchical level of a segment

- Name of the parent segment
- Sequential number of the parent segment
- Flag marking a parent segment as the beginning of a segment group
- Minimum and maximum number of segments in a sequence

- CIMSYN for the order and hierarchical relationships of the segments in an Extended IDoc type
- EDIMSG for the link between a basic type and extension and its associated logical messages
- EDISEGMENT for header attribute information for all segments in an IDoc basic or extended type
- DD04L and DD04T for information on all data elements within each segment in an IDoc basic or extended type
- DD03L and DD03T for all field names within each segment
- DD07L and DD07T for field values stored in domains behind data elements within each segment

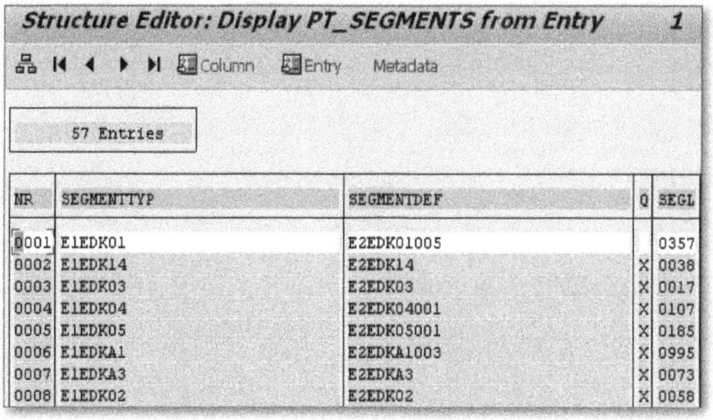
Structure Editor: Display PT_SEGMENTS from Entry 1

Column Entry Metadata

57 Entries

NR	SEGMENTTYP	SEGMENTDEF	Q	SEGL
0001	E1EDK01	E2EDK01005		0357
0002	E1EDK14	E2EDK14	X	0038
0003	E1EDK03	E2EDK03	X	0017
0004	E1EDK04	E2EDK04001	X	0107
0005	E1EDK05	E2EDK05001	X	0185
0006	E1EDKA1	E2EDKA1003	X	0995
0007	E1EDKA3	E2EDKA3	X	0073
0008	E1EDK02	E2EDK02	X	0058

Figure 3.2 A Portion of the Report Listing Segment Metadata

The functions and tables are great fun to play with in the ABAP debugger. They provide a comprehensive description of how all elements of an IDoc type tie together to create a coherent and intelligent structure.

In addition, because IDoc segments are structures defined in the SAP Data Dictionary, these functions expose you to the tables that store the metadata for all tables, data types, fields, data elements, domains, and other objects in the dictionary itself.

The DD* class of tables read extensively by both functions are the heart and soul of the SAP Data Dictionary.

We repeat this fact more than once as we work our way through this book: Regardless of what you do in SAP, the SAP Data Dictionary is your best friend. Learn the Data Dictionary, and you'll learn a lot about SAP.

EDI Trading Partner Management

Acme's new integration system includes functionality to create and manage EDI trading partner profiles. This is critical to supporting Acme's trading partner relationships and includes the following:

▶ Identification and location data such as trading partner ID, address, time zone, and country
▶ Communications information for each trading partner, including:
  ▶ Sending and receiving protocol such as AS2, HTTP, FTP, and so on
  ▶ Target URL for outbound transmissions for AS2
  ▶ Target IP address for outbound transmission via VAN
  ▶ User name, password, and other login information for trading partner AS2 servers, VANs, and other systems
  ▶ Mailbox address at source or target VAN
  ▶ Response timeout and retry values
  ▶ Security information such as encryption algorithms and certificates
  ▶ Synchronous or asynchronous delivery mode
  ▶ Acknowledgment receipt and signature types
▶ Envelope configuration for each trading partner to support enveloping and de-enveloping processes, including the following:
  ▶ Interchange, group, and transaction set envelopes by EDI standard (X12, EDIFACT, TRADACOMS, etc.)
  ▶ EDI sending and receiving trading partner IDs and qualifiers
  ▶ Direction of transmissions

▸ EDI transactions and versions

▸ Control number sequences for each envelope type

▸ Translation map required to convert each transaction

▸ Need for a 997 functional acknowledgment and timing of transmission

3.2 Laying the Foundations for EDI: Master Data

It goes without saying that both SAP and EDI depend on a solid foundation of master data. Before we can consider the processing flows in our system design, we'll outline key master data conversions that will impact EDI.

3.2.1 A Brief Word on Conversion Strategy

The conversion strategy at AHE is simple and straightforward. Legacy data are extracted into flat files and analyzed to see how closely they fit the SAP data model. Gaps are identified and plugged by business users in spreadsheets.

The data are then saved on the application server in linked flat files that match the views of the SAP master data object for loading mostly through projects created in the Legacy System Migration Workbench (LSMW).

While the technical team works out these conversion processes, the business defines master data creation and maintenance procedures for the production system.

The key master data objects, and their sequence of conversion, are illustrated in Figure 3.3.

There are a few main points to take away:

▸ Customers, vendors, and materials can be loaded in parallel.

▸ Ship-to parties are loaded after the sold-to parties.

▸ The sold-to partner function is updated with its ship-to parties after the ship-to parties are loaded.

▸ BOMs, pricing conditions, and customer material info records are loaded after the material master, either in parallel or sequentially.

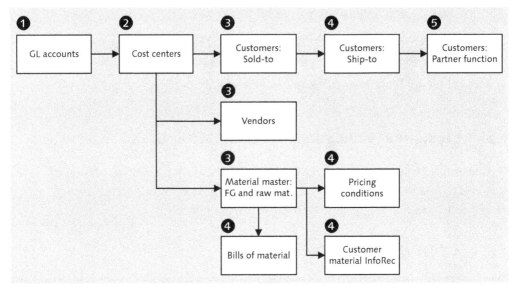

Figure 3.3 Key Master Data Conversion Objects That Impact EDI

But we digress. This is not the time or the place to get into the nitty-gritty details of conversion strategy. Instead, we'll briefly cycle through the key master data objects that will impact our new SAP EDI environment.

3.2.2 General Ledger Chart of Accounts and Cost Centers

The General Ledger chart of accounts and cost centers are the keys to the financial system. The chart of accounts is collected from the legacy finance systems into a spreadsheet where it is cleaned up and restructured for SAP. The chart of accounts is the first master data object loaded, followed by cost centers.

3.2.3 Customer Master Sold-To

The sold-to customer master record is created next, in this case for Gordy's Galaxy. There's only one sold-to partner for each customer in the North American business. Invoices are issued to, and payments received from, the sold-to partner.

The sold-to record is the key to building customer EDI partner profiles—partner type KU—in Transaction WE20. We'll set up only one partner profile per customer using the SAP sold-to number. Ship-to parties will not be used to create partner profiles.

The sold-to record posts against Transaction XD01 and is loaded through an LSMW project using standard conversion program `RFBIDE00`. Some of the key tables populated in the customer master load include the following:

▶ **KNA1**
General data; only one record per customer.

▶ **KNB1**
Company code data; one record for each company code to which the customer is assigned.

▶ **KNKA**
Credit management; customer credit limit.

▶ **KNVV**
Sales area data.

▶ **KNVP**
Customer master partner functions, which link the sold-to party to other customer records or partners such as bill-to, payer, and ship-to.

3.2.4 Customer Master Ship-To

The ship-to partner is the customer location—store or distribution center—that receives a shipment for the sold-to partner. Sales orders, representing goods ordered by location, are created by ship-to and sold-to partners.

Ship-to partners are loaded after the sold-to customer in a two-step process:

1. The ship-to customer master is created. Each store or distribution center in the customer's organization is set up as a ship-to party in SAP. More than 2,000 ship-to customer records will be created in Acme's SAP system, one for each of Gordy's stores and distribution centers.

2. The ship-to customer is linked to the sold-to party through the PARTNER FUNCTIONS tab of the ship-to master.

The ship-to party is created with Transaction XD01 through an LSMW project using standard conversion program `RFBIDE00`. It writes to the same tables as the sold-to master.

The next step is to create a link between the sold-to party and all of its ship-to partners, which is displayed in the PARTNER FUNCTIONS tab of the SALES AREA DATA level of the customer master record. This link validates the ship-to party against the sold-to partners during creation of sales orders.

This is a critical relationship throughout the order-to-cash processing cycle in SAP and for design of our EDI system. In Chapter 5, you'll see how the ship-to party is mapped to the sold-to party during standard processing of both inbound and outbound IDocs.

The update to the sold-to customer record is done against Transaction XD02 through an LSMW project using standard conversion program `RFBIDE00`. The update is to partner function table KNVP.

3.2.5 Vendor Master

Vendors, or suppliers, sell AHE goods and services that enable the sale of movies on DVD. They are critical to EDI processing and receive purchase and shipping orders and send inventory and invoices, among other documents.

Vendors also manage inventory and shipping for AHE. We'll focus on one vendor in our SAP EDI build for AHE: Disc Services International (DSI).

Vendor partner profiles are created in WE20 with partner type LI.

Vendors are loaded against Transaction XK01 through an LSMW project using standard conversion program `RFBIKR00`. Some of the key tables populated in the vendor master load include the following:

▶ **LFA1**
General data; only one record per vendor.

▶ **LFB1**
Company code data; one record for each company code the vendor has been assigned to.

▶ **LFM1**
Purchasing organization data; one record for each purchasing organization and company code the vendor is assigned to.

3.2.6 Material Master

The material master includes both finished goods and raw materials.

Finished goods are the DVD products sold to AHE's customers. They are fully defined with specific display formats, broadcast standards, languages, country and customer versions, packaging, stickers, and so on.

Raw materials include all of the components used to manufacture, promote, market, and sell movies on DVDs. This includes blank discs, packaging, artwork, cellophane wrapping, stickers, promotional displays, and artwork for promotional posters.

Raw materials are purchased from AHE's vendors. Finished goods are manufactured and packaged. AHE buys manufacturing, packaging, and shipping services from its vendors, who also manage inventory for both raw materials and finished goods. AHE owns the inventory. The finished goods are then sold to AHE's customers.

All of these activities are enabled by the flow of electronic business documents that the new EDI RIM will manage.

Materials are loaded with Transaction MM01 through an LSMW project using standard direct input conversion program RMDATIND.

An important link for EDI is created by populating field MARA-EAN11. This maps the internal SAP material number to either the Universal Product Code (UPC), the European Article Number (EAN), or GS1's Global Trade Item Number (GTIN), which supersedes both.

Some of the key tables populated in the material master load include the following:

- **MARA**
  General data for material master; one record per material.

- **MARM**
  Base and alternative units of measure for the material.

- **MVKE**
  Sales data for the material master; one material record per sales organization and distribution channel. Relevant for sales and delivery.

- **MARC**
  Plant data for material; one material record per vendor plant. Relevant for purchasing, production planning, inventory, and delivery.

- **MBEW**
  Valuation area data for material by vendor plant. Relevant for valuation and accounting.

▶ **MARD**
Storage location for material by vendor plant and storage location. Relevant for inventory.

3.2.7 Customer Material Info Records

The customer material info record (CMIR) links the SAP customer, sales organization, distribution channel, and material number to the item number used by that customer.

This is a key reference for EDI. CMIR is read during IDoc processing to convert a customer's item number to the internal SAP material number. We look at this conversion process in Chapter 7, Section 7.1.4, subsection KNMT: Customer Material Info Record.

For AHE, only active finished goods that are being sold to customers will be entered in CMIR.

CMIRs are loaded against Transaction VD51. There's no standard conversion object that can be used in the LSMW. You can run a batch input recording within the LSMW, but VD51 populates a table control, and each line needs to be populated with an index. You can't do this in a batch data communication (BDC) recording, although you can edit the ABAP code generated by the recording.

A much easier approach is to write a custom ABAP that calls function RV_CUSTOMER_MATERIAL_UPDATE. Pass a file to the function with the customer, sales organization, SAP material, and customer item number to table parameter XKNMT_TAB, and set the update indicator (field XKNMT-UPDKZ) to "I" (for Insert).

Existing records can be updated by setting XKNMT-UPDKZ to "U" or deleted by populating table parameter XKNMT_TAB instead and setting YKNMT-UPDKZ to "D" (Delete).

The structure of both table parameters is defined by data type VKNMT in the data dictionary.

Function RV_CUSTOMER_MATERIAL_UPDATE is used by VD51 to create the CMIR and VD52 to update it. Key tables populated include the following:

▶ **KNMTK**
CMIR header for customer and sales organization data.

▶ **KNMT**
CMIR data table.

3.2.8 Bill of Materials

Next is the bill of materials (BOM), the recipe for the manufactured product. Every finished good that is manufactured and sold has a BOM.

The BOM is the bedrock of production. It links the SAP finished good with each raw material component required to produce it.

We'll load BOMs by calling Transaction CS01 in an LSMW project using standard BDC conversion program RCSBI010. Key tables populated for the BOM include the following:

▶ **MAST**
Links the finished good master to the BOM by vendor plant.

▶ **STKO**
BOM header-level data, including BOM ID.

▶ **STAS**
Links BOM header to item level data.

▶ **STPO**
Item-level raw material component data for BOM.

3.2.9 Pricing Conditions

Pricing conditions assign prices for a finished good—by customer, sales organization, and distribution center—to a condition type for a specified validity period.

Condition types can hold amounts or calculated values based on specified variables, such as percentages, quantity, weight, volume, and so on, that are invoked by predefined procedures.

Incoming EDI orders include prices that post to the sales order against a condition type that stores the agreed price set for that partner in SAP. If the two match or are within an accepted tolerance limit, the EDI price is used by SAP. Otherwise, the buyer and seller work it out.

Pricing condition types include everything that can have a price assigned to it, in both unit prices and percentages, including the following:

▶ Standard unit price for a finished good
▶ Sales taxes

- Special and standard customer discounts, rewards, and rebates
- Promotional pricing
- Customer cash advances
- Freight and shipping surcharges
- Gross and net prices

Load pricing conditions through an LSMW project with conversion program RV14BTCI or IDoc basic type COND_A02 with message COND_A. We've generally used the IDoc.

There are two key pricing condition tables populated and read during IDoc processing:

- **KONH**
  Header and administrative data.

- **KONP**
  Item details.

3.3   The Typical Lifecycle of an Order from Gordy

And so we have a typically beautiful day in southern California. It's not too hot, and there are no fires, earthquakes, or mudslides. AHE has even brought a massage therapist to the back lot to help the team relieve some tension.

You couldn't ask for a better day for a presentation. You can almost feel the irascible Darryl Q smiling in anticipation from his director's chair in that great studio in the sky.

We'll go over our overall SAP EDI system design by following a typical day in the lifecycle of an order from Gordy's Galaxy. The purpose of this exercise is to inform Acme's business process owners and managers of our implementation plans and to get their sign-off.

Figure 3.4 outlines the processing cycles that we'll focus on. To keep things simple, our presentation is limited to catalog sales for Gordy's Galaxy.

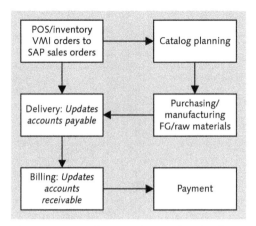

Figure 3.4 Key Elements of Our Lifecycle of an Order Tour

Our own slice of this day in the life links six discrete processing chains that close the circle for buying the goods and services required to sell Acme's movies on DVD to stores in Gordy's chain:

▶ VMI orders

▶ Catalog planning

▶ Purchasing of replication services and components

▶ Delivery to the customer

▶ Billing

▶ Payment

Our interest here is in how EDI supports Gordy's order-to-cash cycle. This will help us understand the EDI data flows within the context of the overall business processing cycle.

3.3.1 VMI Sales Orders

Our day begins with sales order processing, outlined in Figure 3.5.

Gordy's Galaxy sends an X12 852 to the AHE EDI RIM. The message holds daily point of sales (POS) or weekly inventory data captured from check-out scans at each of Gordy's stores in North America.

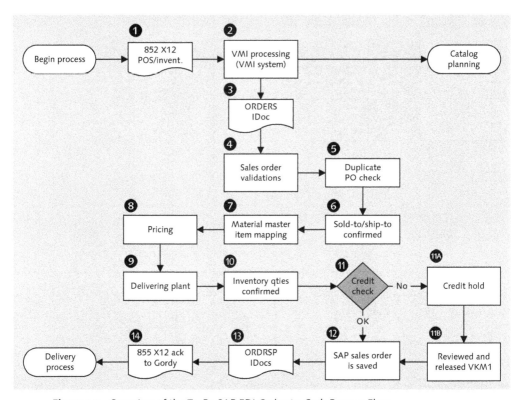

Figure 3.5 Overview of the To-Be SAP EDI Order-to-Cash Process Flow

The 852 also carries reserved purchase order (RPO) numbers. The RPOs provide a range of numbers that AHE uses to create POs for Gordy. These POs will post to SAP as sales orders, one for each store.

The 852 transmissions are translated by the EDI RIM to an internal flat file format and are posted to the VMI system. To support its calculations, VMI relies on an interface with DataStore and daily feeds of master and transactional data from SAP.

Daily Data Extracts

These nightly extracts are handled by standard and extended IDocs in SAP that map to flat files in the RIM for VMI. They include complete and delta extracts. The most important of these feeds are the following:

▶ Customer sold-to and ship-to parties using message type DEBMAS

▶ Finished goods and raw material masters using message type MATMAS, with a custom extended type for attributes and additional data stored as classifications, extensions to MARA, or custom tables linked to MARA

▶ BOMs using message type BOMMAT

▶ Finished goods inventory using message type MBGMCR

▶ Open customer orders using message type ORDERS

▶ Open deliveries using message type DESADV

The extracts are triggered by custom programs that populate the IDocs and send them to the RIM as if they were normal EDI transactions. The RIM recognizes them as internal interfaces from the IDoc control record fields:

▶ PARTYP—Partner Type: equals LS, for logical system

▶ SNDPFC—Sending Partner Function: equals ZI, internal interface

They can be further distinguished for programming purposes by populating the MESSAGE CODE field in the partner profile, which matches the MESCOD field in the IDoc control record.

But we're jumping ahead of ourselves. We discuss the IDoc control record and partner profile setup in more detail in Chapter 5, Real-World Business Process Integration with EDI.

Replenishment Calculations

VMI uses these data, along with the calculations from StoreData, to determine replenishment levels for catalog product for Gordy's stores. VMI uses these calculations to build a customer PO for Gordy in a flat file format that bundles the ordered quantity of each DVD product for each store at the line-item level.

This arrangement is similar to the SDQ segment of an X12 transaction that we saw illustrated in our brief discussion of the 852 in Chapter 2, Section 2.1.3, Selling the Dream with Vendor Management Inventory. The line-item level of the order flat file looks like Listing 3.1.

```
ITEM*025143
STORE*GRDY01001*40* GRDY01002*80* GRDY01003*15* GRDY01004*92
STORE*GRDY01005*40* GRDY01006*80* GRDY01007*15* GRDY01008*92
ITEM*026825
```

```
STORE*GRDY01001*40* GRDY01002*80* GRDY01003*15* GRDY01004*92
STORE*GRDY01005*40* GRDY01006*80* GRDY01007*15* GRDY01008*92
```

Listing 3.1 Line Item Segments with Multiple Store Ordering Data by Product, Just Like the SDQ Segment of an X12 Transaction

The VMI order file is mapped to an ORDERS IDoc message type for posting to SAP.

The challenge is to unravel the line item store order detail so that one SAP sales order—referencing the VMI order number—is created for each store. Each order will group all items by one store.

The map needs to create multiple ORDERS IDocs for one VMI order. For a customer as large as Gordy, this could result in thousands of sales orders posting to SAP against the same customer PO.

We'll have the same issue with non-VMI customers who use SDQ segments in their 850 PO transactions. We look at mapping strategies to handle this in our build of the inbound VMI orders interface in Chapter 9, Generating the PO for Replication Services.

One Order per Store

The newly translated ORDERS IDoc will flow into SAP, one IDoc for each store. A number of validations will be run during processing of the IDocs before they create SAP sales orders.

We first confirm that the incoming customer PO has not posted before. Duplicate orders can result in duplicate shipment of product, which in turn can lead to unnecessary shipping expenses and penalties from the customer.

This is a custom check that we will program in an IDoc enhancement. We look at how to code this in Chapter 9, Generating the PO for Replication Services.

Next, the system checks to ensure that the sold-to and ship-to partners exist against the sales organization defined for the order and that each product ordered exists in the material master.

Pricing is then calculated at the line-item level using the pricing condition types defined for the sold-to customer, sales organization, material, and validity date combination. This includes all unit, discount and promotional prices, and percentages, as well as all relevant taxes.

Then inventory is checked to ensure that there are sufficient open quantities of the ordered items in stock to fill the order. If this check fails, the items must be ordered from DSI, and the purchasing process kicks off.

If there is enough stock in inventory to cover the order, a credit check runs to ensure that there's no credit hold on the customer due to unpaid bills. If the credit check passes, the sales order is saved.

Under Acme's VMI arrangement with Gordy, we need to tell them what we've ordered when the sales orders post. Gordy will not accept delivery of product until this information is in its system. We do this with an order acknowledgment.

When sales orders are saved in SAP, an ORDRSP IDoc is generated for each order. It's a copy of the SAP order that will be mapped to an X12 855 order acknowledgment.

Bundling Acknowledgments

The wrinkle in all this is that Gordy wants one acknowledgment per PO, not one per store-level sales order. Our challenge is to bundle each sales order that posted against the one VMI suggested order into a single EDI transmission with ordering data for each DVD product at the line-item level by store and quantity in SDQ segments.

We can't do this in a map and there are no standard IDocs with SDQ segments. We need to write a program or a script in the EDI RIM or in SAP. One approach is to extend an ORDRSP IDoc with a custom SDQ segment as a child of item-level segment E1EDP01 and to process it with a custom ABAP program.

When multiple SAP sales orders are saved against one PO with SDQ segments, one standard ORDRSP IDoc is generated for each sales order and parked in the database at status 64 with message code BND (bundle) in control record field MESCOD.

The ABAP program then reads all IDocs with BND in the MESCOD field of the control record. The BND IDocs are bundled into a single custom IDoc by PO number and sold-to partner. Order quantities for each store are in the custom SDQ segment at the line-item level.

This leverages the powerful data processing capabilities of ABAP and the fact that all business data resides in SAP. It also simplifies mapping in the EDI RIM.

We look at the pieces of this process in more detail in our build of the outbound order acknowledgment in Chapter 13, Building the Outbound PO Acknowledgment.

When this processing completes, the 855 is sent to Gordy's EDI system and posted to its backend business system as an open PO. Gordy now knows what Acme ordered. We're ready to move on to delivery processing.

But first we need to do a little planning to accommodate ordering finished products that we don't have in stock.

3.3.2   Catalog Planning

Planning is about purchasing manufacturing services to produce finished goods in Acme's relationship with DSI, which includes figuring out what components need to be ordered to complete replication. A simplified view of the catalog planning process is outlined in Figure 3.6.

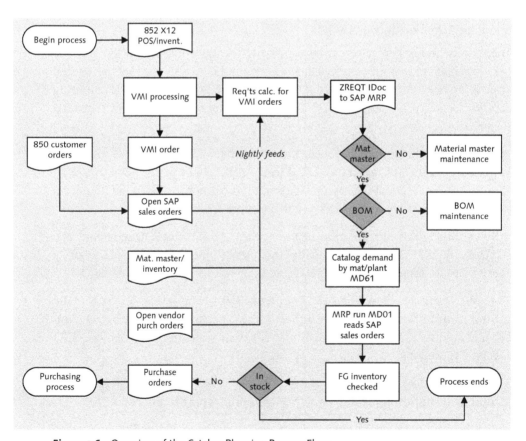

Figure 3.6 Overview of the Catalog Planning Process Flow

Purchasing is dependent on planning, which begins with EDI POS and store-level inventory feeds from Gordy's Galaxy in the 852. This flows into RIM, is transformed to an internal flat file format, and is sent to VMI, where it feeds a customer forecast.

The customer forecast is also fed by StoreData calculations and by the daily data extracts we discussed in Section 3.3.1, including open sales orders, material masters, inventory, and open vendor POs.

VMI then sends a flat file to the RIM with forecast data for finished goods that will be used by MRP in SAP to build an independent requirement for customer product. This provides an estimate of how much of a DVD product needs to be produced by a particular date. The VMI file includes the following:

- Finished goods material number
- Vendor plant
- Schedule date
- Quantity required

Generate IDoc from Business Object

This flat file is mapped to a custom IDoc that we'll call ZREQTS. This development is outside the scope of our order-to-cash cycle for Gordy, but we'll briefly touch on the process.

The IDoc is generated from business object BUS3027 for method CREATEFROMDATA with Transaction BDBG. This converts function BAPI_REQUIREMENTS_CREATE to an IDoc and generates a function module to process it.

The developer can then add an extension to the custom IDoc in the Segment Editor (Transaction WE31) to store data that will check the material number, plant, requirement type, and version to determine if the independent requirement already exists.

If the requirement doesn't exist, a new requirement for finished goods is created using the standard direct input processing in the generated function module. If a requirement does exist, custom code in the function triggers an update of the requirement by calling BAPI_REQUIREMENTS_CHANGE.

Before the requirement is either created or changed, the product is validated against the SAP material master and the BOM. If either check fails, the relevant master data record is created.

MRP takes all of these data, reads open sales orders and inventory, and produces a forecast for finished goods. The basic question is whether this projected demand can be fulfilled from existing inventory.

If the answer is yes, the process ends, and no further action is taken. If the answer is no, POs are created for replication and for ordering component materials from DSI or from a third-party supplier.

3.3.3 Purchasing/Manufacturing

The purchasing process continues our day by picking up where planning leaves off, as outlined in Figure 3.7.

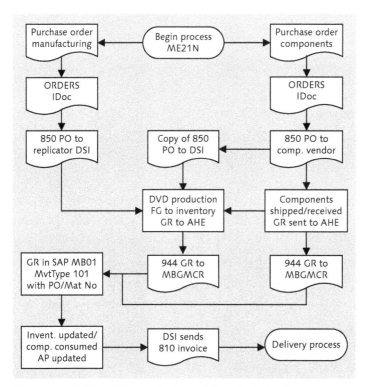

Figure 3.7 Outline of the Purchasing and Manufacturing Flow

Before DSI can manufacture DVDs for Acme, it needs to know what it's dealing with. Every night, Acme sends DSI a number of complete and delta data feeds from SAP, including the following:

► **Finished goods and components master data**
Extracted to extended message type MATMAS. RIM translates the IDoc to an X12 888 item maintenance message and sends it to DSI.

► **Bill of materials master data**
Extracted to an extended message type BOMMAT. The EDI RIM translates it to an X12 832 price and sales catalog and sends it to DSI.

Manufacturing Purchasing Order

The manufacturing or replication PO is created in Acme's SAP system to purchase manufacturing services from DSI for a DVD product.

When the PO is saved with Transaction ME21N, an ORDERS IDoc is generated and sent to the EDI RIM where it is transformed into an X12 850 PO. It is then routed to DSI's EDI system, which passes the PO to its backend business system for posting to an internal order.

DSI generates an acknowledgment to a flat file, which is transformed by its EDI system to an X12 855 PO acknowledgment. The 855 is sent to the Acme EDI RIM and transformed to an inbound ORDRSP IDoc. This updates the acknowledgment number field in the CONFIRMATIONS tab at the item level of the vendor PO.

Component PO

Acme needs to order raw materials to use in the manufacture of its finished goods. A component PO is created with Transaction ME21N, generating an ORDERS IDoc that's mapped to an 850 X12 in the EDI RIM and sent to the third party component supplier.

A copy of the order is also sent to DSI in a separate 850 X12 transmission.

The components are shipped to DSI and received into inventory. DSI then sends Acme a 944 stock transfer with a goods receipt against the third-party components order.

The 944 goods receipt is transformed by the RIM to an MBGMCR IDoc message type. The IDoc posts to SAP inventory against the PO number with Transaction MB01 and movement type 101.

As an interesting aside, seven transactions can be called by MBGMCR, which was converted from BAPI_GOODSMVT_CREATE business object BUS2017 method CREATE-FROMDATA. These transactions are recorded in table T158G and identified by the GM code in the IDoc's GM code segment.

Production Completed

Meanwhile, back at DSI, replication and packaging is done. Component materials have been consumed—blank discs, labels, clamshell cases, cardboard wraparounds, artwork, stickers, and so on—and the finished goods moved into the warehouse.

This triggers a goods receipts against the PO that is sent as an X12 944 transmission to the EDI RIM, where it is converted to an MBGMCR IDoc and routed into SAP.

The IDoc posts a goods receipts against the manufacturing PO item using Transaction MB01 with movement type 101. The goods receipt also relieves inventory of the components consumed during production. The PO is completed after a goods receipt posts against the full quantity of each item in the order. AP is then updated, and Acme is ready to receive the vendor invoice.

DSI creates an invoice in its AR system that is sent to their EDI system and transformed into an X12 810. Acme's RIM receives and translates the 810 to an INVOIC IDoc, which posts a vendor invoice in SAP against the manufacturing PO number.

3.3.4 Delivery

DSI is also the distributor for Acme's DVDs. It ships product to all of Gordy's customer distribution centers or directly to their stores. To support delivery processing, AHE sends several master data extracts from SAP to DSI every night.

The most important of these feeds is the ship-to customer master. It includes all relevant contact information for customer distribution centers and stores. It is extracted from SAP into IDoc message types DEBMAS (customer) and ADRMAS (addresses). These IDocs are converted in the EDI RIM to an X12 816 organizational relationships transaction and sent to DSI.

Acme collects these data from its customers. Each one handles it differently. Gordy's Galaxy regularly sends Acme an 816 with new store locations, address changes, and store closings, but some customers send an Excel spreadsheet, an ASCII file, a Word document, or even an email.

DSI needs to know what to ship from its warehouse to Gordy. This is handled by delivery documents from Acme's SAP system, generated by running the Delivery Due List with Transaction VL10 or SAP menu path LOGISTICS • SALES AND DISTRIBUTION • SHIPPING AND TRANSPORTATION • OUTBOUND DELIVERY • CREATE • COLLECTIVE PROCESSING OF DOCUMENTS DUE FOR DELIVERY • DELIVERY. This begins the delivery process outlined in Figure 3.8.

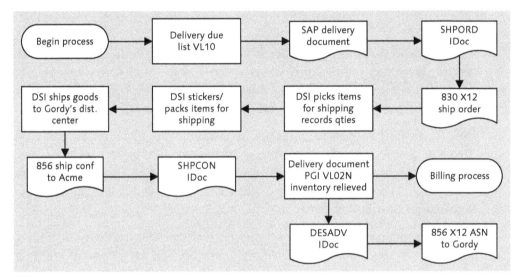

Figure 3.8 Outline of the Delivery Business Processing Flow

Before deliveries can be created, sales orders must meet certain conditions:

▶ There is no delivery block for a credit check or any other reason at the header or schedule line item levels.

▶ The schedule line is due for shipping on the selected date.

▶ Delivery quantity is confirmed by an availability check.

Each SAP delivery is generated from one sales order with one ship-to party. The delivery tells DSI how many units of what items to ship from which DSI warehouse to which one of Gordy's distribution centers or stores.

When the delivery is saved, a SHPORD IDoc is generated and sent to the EDI RIM, which transforms it to an X12 830 warehouse shipping order. The 830 is then sent to DSI's EDI system.

DSI picks, stickers, and packs the DVDs and loads them onto a truck. DSI updates its inventory at each stage through barcode scans.

When the truck pulls away from the loading dock, the pick quantities for each store and item in the shipment are bundled into a flat file and sent to DSI's EDI system. The file is transformed into an 856 shipping confirmation and sent to Acme's EDI RIM where it is converted to a SHPCON IDoc and sent into SAP to post against the delivery document, update the pick quantity, and trigger a post goods issue (PGI) with Transaction VL02N.

PGI completes the delivery, which relieves inventory and updates AR in preparation for invoicing. Before Gordy will accept an invoice from Acme, they need to know that a shipment is on its way, what ordered items it contains, and which distribution center or store it's bound for.

After Acme's delivery document is updated with the pick quantity and the PGI, a DESADV IDoc is generated as an advanced shipping notice (ASN) to the customer. The IDoc is sent to the RIM, transformed into an 856 ASN, and sent to Gordy's EDI system. The ASN must post to Gordy's business system before the shipment arrives at its distribution center.

When the shipment arrives, Gordy confirms the items against the ASN. If there are no errors, the goods are received into inventory and AP is updated. Gordy is now ready to receive AHE's invoice.

If the ASN is received after the shipment arrives, or there are discrepancies between the ASN and the shipment, an 824 application advice is sent to Acme detailing the errors. The errors must be fixed within 24 hours and the ASN resent; otherwise Acme will not be able to invoice.

If the invoice is sent before the ASN is confirmed, it is rejected, and an X12 864 text message is returned explaining why the invoice was rejected.

3.3.5 Billing

The billing process, outlined in Figure 3.9, kicks off after Gordy receives and confirms the ASN against the shipment.

Invoices are generated in SAP by running the Billing Due List for deliveries that have been PGI'd, with Transaction VF04 or menu path LOGISTICS • SALES AND DISTRIBUTION • BILLING • BILLING DOCUMENT • MAINTAIN BILLING DUE LIST.

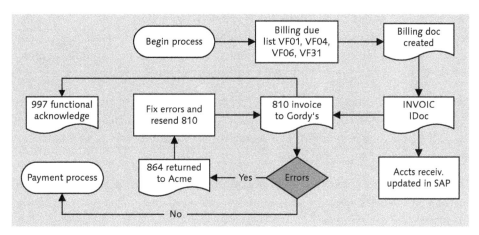

Figure 3.9 Billing Kicks Off After the Delivery Has Been PGI'd

Key selections are date range, billing type, and delivery-related flag. We'll capture all completed deliveries over a wide date range because they become available for invoicing on different dates.

As billing documents are created, AR is updated and the system is primed to accept payment according to the customer's payment terms—within 30 days in the case of Gordy's Galaxy.

Each billing document generates an INVOIC IDoc that is sent to the RIM, transformed into an X12 810 customer invoice, and sent to Gordy's EDI system, which posts the invoice to its AP system.

The billing process isn't quite done yet. We need to confirm that the invoice has been received. One milestone is receipt of the 997 functional acknowledgment from Gordy referencing the group control number of Acme's 810 customer invoice transmission.

We'll look at the 997 in more detail in Chapter 4, EDI: The Ugly Stepsister of E-Commerce. It is triggered during deconstruction of the envelope of the inbound 810 by Gordy's EDI translator and immediately sent to AHE.

Acme's EDI production support team watches for this transaction whenever invoices are sent. It is no guarantee that the invoices were posted in the customer's system—just proof that they were received.

The other EDI transaction to look for is the 864 text report, which is sent when errors occur during posting of the invoices to Gordy's business system. The error reports are sometimes a little cryptic, but if an 864 comes in for one or more invoices, the problem must be fixed quickly and the invoice resent.

Acme's AR department will anxiously check Gordy's partner website to ensure that the invoice posted. Even if everything works smoothly, it's not unusual for the EDI team to be asked by AR to resend invoices. Sometimes it's just anxiety, but sometimes it needs to be done.

The billing process ends when we can confirm that the invoice has posted in the customer's business system and is being processed in the normal manner by the customer's AP department.

3.3.6 Payment

There's nothing like a timely payment to cap off a perfect day of business, particularly from a customer as cooperative and generous as Gordy. Payment is one process that senior management cares about...a lot.

Just 30 days after the invoice posts to Gordy's business system, payment is transferred electronically to AHE's bank account, and the payment process, outlined in Figure 3.10, kicks off.

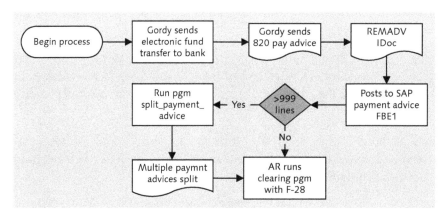

Figure 3.10 Overview of the 820 Payment Advice and Clearing Process

At the same time that the funds are transferred, Gordy's system generates a payment file that its EDI system maps to an X12 820 payment advice.

Gordy sends only a few 820s each month, but they can be extremely large, complex files. They reference every invoice and debit or credit memo issued for any purpose that impacted the net amount of the referenced payment.

The peak holiday shopping season between September and December can lead to monthly payments of $20 million or more. The 820 reporting of these payments can contain more than 100,000 segments referencing thousands of documents with thousands of adjustments for discounts, returns, promotions, rewards, penalties, and countless other pricing tweaks.

Because of its size, complexity, and high visibility to management, the 820 presents unique challenges. Did we say "challenges"? What we meant to say was "opportunities for growth."

The 820's size is its most daunting challenge. A $20 million payment can result in an 820 that exceeds 20MB, which can convert to a REMADV IDoc file greater than 200MB. We look at strategies for processing a very large payment in our build of the payment advice interface in Chapter 18.

Gordy's EDI system transmits its 820 to Acme's RIM, where it is converted to a REMADV IDoc and sent into SAP to post to a payment document for clearing by AR against Transaction FBE1.

The SAP payment advice is a holding tank, a temporary document that fronts for three tables: AVIK (payment header), AVIP (payment documents detail), and AVIR (subitems of line items). The only purpose for these tables is to feed the clearing process in AR.

Acme's AR department clears payments with Transaction F-28 after they have posted a payment document, which is purged after the payment is cleared.

There is one catch: Payment documents can post with an unlimited number of line items. The clearing process can handle only 999 lines or less. SAP provides an ABAP program that is hard-coded to split the payment into documents of 900 lines or less: `SPLIT_PAYMENT_ADVICE`.

The program calls function `REMADV_SPLIT_PAYMENT_ADVICE` in function group `FRAD` (Payment Advices).

If you want to control the maximum number of lines, copy the split program into a custom ABAP program that adds the maximum number of lines to a selection screen parameter.

For EDI, posting of the payment document ends the payment process.

3.4 Interfaces in the Order-to-Cash Cycle

Our overview of the to-be day-in-the-life processing cycle for an order from Gordy took us through purchasing and sales. We have a pretty good sense of our business by now and of where we're going with the EDI interfaces that will support it. Our focus is the order-to-cash cycle with Gordy's Galaxy.

The following are EDI interfaces:

▶ **Outbound purchase order for replication services**
DVDs ordered by Gordy's are produced by DSI. Acme creates a manufacturing PO for replication services with Transaction ME21N. The PO generates an ORDERS IDoc that is sent to the RIM, converted to an outbound X12 850 PO, and sent to DSI. Covered in Chapter 9.

▶ **Inbound goods receipt**
DSI produces the DVDs and receives the finished goods into inventory, which also prepares accounts payable for invoicing. The inventory posting sends a file to DSI's EDI system, which converts it to a 944 stock transfer with goods receipt. The 944 is transmitted to Acme's RIM, converted to an MBGMCR IDoc, and posted to finished goods stock with Transaction MB01, movement type 101. Covered in Chapter 10.

▶ **Inbound invoice from the supplier**
DSI generates an invoice for Acme's manufacturing PO and transmits an 810 to Acme's RIM. The RIM converts the 810 to an INVOIC IDoc and sends it into Acme's SAP system, where it posts to an MM invoice against the manufacturing PO. Covered in Chapter 11.

▶ **Inbound VMI customer purchase order**
Gordy sends an X12 852 to the RIM, where it is mapped to a flat file and sent to VMI to be used to calculate and generate POs for Gordy's stores. An order with a reserved PO number is sent from VMI to the RIM, where it maps to one or more ORDERS IDocs that post to sales orders in SAP, one for each store. Covered in Chapter 12.

▶ **Outbound customer order acknowledgment**
Each VMI PO can create multiple sales orders, one for each store. When each

sales orders is saved, one ORDRSP IDoc is generated as an acknowledgment. The IDocs are bundled into one IDoc per PO with all store item orders in a custom SDQ segment at the line-item level. The ORDRSP SDQ IDoc is sent to the RIM to be mapped to an 855 X12 order acknowledgment and transmitted to Gordy's Galaxy. Covered in Chapter 13.

▶ **Outbound shipping order to vendor**
When a delivery document is generated from a completed sales order, a SHPORD IDoc is output and sent to the RIM to be translated to an 830 ship order and transmitted to DSI with picking, packing, and shipping instructions. Covered in Chapter 14.

▶ **Inbound shipping confirmation**
DSI picks, packs, and loads the delivery, and the truck pulls away from the shipping dock. An 856 shipping confirmation is sent to Acme's EDI RIM and converted to a SHPCON IDoc, which updates the delivery document in SAP with the pick quantity and the post goods issue, relieving inventory. Covered in Chapter 15.

▶ **Outbound advance shipping notification**
When the PGI posts to Acme's delivery, a DESADV IDoc is generated, sent to the RIM, and converted to an X12 856. The ASN is then sent to Gordy's Galaxy, which uses it to confirm the delivered goods. Covered in Chapter 16.

▶ **Outbound customer invoice**
After Acme sends the ASN, the Billing Due List is run, and billing documents created. Each billing document generates an INVOIC IDoc that is sent to the RIM, converted to an X12 810 invoice, and routed to Gordy's Galaxy. Covered in Chapter 17.

▶ **Inbound payment advice**
Gordy pays the invoice with an electronic funds transfer to the bank. At the same time it sends an X12 820 payment advice to Acme's RIM with details of the payment. The 820 is converted to a REMADV IDoc and posted to a payment advice in Acme's SAP system for clearing by the AR department. Covered in Chapter 18.

3.5 Considering the Project Plan

We know from experience that any plan, even Plan Q from Outer Space, will be revised over the course of the project. But we need a baseline, so we build the first cut of our project plan and identify key deliverables, milestones, and tasks that must be completed before we can bring our baby home.

This important exercise allows our team to think in a detailed way about the tasks that need to be done to complete this project. A few of the key deliverables, milestones, and tasks include the following:

▶ System builds for the RIM and SAP

▶ Technical architecture and data flows for all systems

▶ Data migration and conversion strategies

▶ Identification and compilation of RICEF (reports, interfaces, enhancements, and forms) list for all SAP and EDI custom development

▶ Development tasks for each object on the RICEF list

▶ EDI configuration in SAP and the RIM for all trading partners

▶ Testing and training strategies and documentation for all phases of testing, cut-over, and go-live

▶ Development and implementation of archiving strategy in SAP and the EDI RIM

3.6   Summary

Our day-in-the life of the to-be SAP EDI system draws to a close. We went over the new systems and interfaces and touched on the Resource Integration Manager (the RIM), and its handling of EDI traffic in the new environment. We went over master data requirements and looked at the typical lifecycle of an order from Gordy's Galaxy, from VMI processing to catalog planning, purchasing, delivery, billing, and payment.

In true Hollywood tradition, the day-in-the-life was a smash hit and management signed off on our vision. The more superstitious among Acme's management poured a glass of bourbon onto the pavement before the main entrance to Soundstage 13, which is said to be haunted by the tuxedo-clad spirit of the Great Mr. Q.

Acme management asked the team to put together a few papers on EDI and the IDoc interface, so they could understand better what they were getting into. So before we begin to build our system, the SAP EDI team agreed to collect some background information on both. For those who are interested, we will proceed in Chapter 4 with an introduction to EDI.

ACT II
Taming Chaos with Standards—
EDI in an SAP Environment

"I may be drunk and I may be ugly," Darryl Q once quipped at a Hollywood party. "But I have lots of money. And that makes me very sexy." It's the same with EDI. There may be more elegant ways to exchange data, but EDI works and it supports trillions of dollars in business each year. And that makes EDI very sexy.

4   EDI: The Ugly Stepsister of E-Commerce

Saying "I don't get no respect" is how the late, great, bug-eyed American comedian Rodney Dangerfield punctuated his self-deprecating jokes. "I played hide-and-seek and they wouldn't even look for me."

EDI is the Rodney Dangerfield of enterprise systems, the ugly stepsister of e-commerce. Underappreciated, misunderstood, and unloved, EDI has been consigned by many to the graveyard to be replaced by a grab bag of technologies identified by an alphabet soup of acronyms.

But to paraphrase Mark Twain's famous quip about his own death, rumors of EDI's demise are greatly exaggerated. EDI's continued success is guaranteed by the long-term business relationships of the companies that use it.

If you have an important customer, like Gordy's Galaxy of Games & B Flix, who will do business only through EDI, you will continue to use EDI until your customer is ready to tear up his infrastructure and replace it with something new, at great cost and risk to himself and his partners.

Consider Acme Pictures. Before SAP, all e-commerce was EDI. Acme traded exclusively with key customers and suppliers through EDI for years. The SAP project provided an opportunity to streamline the data flows. But the plan was to improve EDI, not replace it.

In addition, since EDI will provide the new SAP system with more than 90 percent of its transactional data, it is in our interests to have more than a passing understanding of EDI.

4.1   A Brief History of e-Commerce

EDI is one of the most successful business technologies ever devised.

A significant proportion of global commerce depends on the more than 20 million daily worldwide EDI transactions, according to a report published by Ken Vollmer of the Forester Foundation in 2007 called *B2B Integration Trends: Message Formats, Alternatives Grow, But EDI Standards Remain The Leading Option For B2B Messaging*. In it, Vollmer asserts that EDI comprises up to 90 percent of all business-to-business (B2B) e-commerce volume and directly supports more than one-third of US Gross Domestic Product (GDP).

The US Census Bureau tries to measure this economic activity in its annual e-commerce survey available from their website E-STATS—MEASURING THE DIGITAL ECONOMY at *www.census.gov/eos/www/ebusiness614.htm*.

Based on the Bureau's most recent survey (May 2012), the dollar value of EDI shipments, sales, or revenues in the United States alone in 2010 was around $3 trillion...that's trillion with a capital T.

This figure is based on total e-commerce bookings of $4.129 trillion in four industry sectors: manufacturing, merchant wholesale, retail, and selected services. EDI statistics are tracked only for merchant wholesale, where 34.4 percent of total revenues are e-commerce, of which 73.1 percent is EDI.

But this is a conservative estimate. Manufacturing is the biggest B2B consumer in this group: 55.3 percent of its total revenues are through B2B transactions, but its EDI statistics are not tracked by the Bureau.

In addition, the survey does not track B2B activity for such heavy EDI sectors as government. Nor does it account for the value of efficiencies gained when an organization automates its business processes and relationships with EDI. It can't measure the value of an automated supply chain or of improved service and regulatory compliance through EDI.

No matter how you cut it, we're talking real money here, which would put a big smile on the face of the Great Darryl Q, who always knew which side his bread was buttered on. And even if statistics make you dizzy, it doesn't take a rocket scientist to see that EDI follows the money.

4.1.1 A Flowery Beginning for e-Commerce

A rose is but a rose and would be just as sweet by any other name, to loosely paraphrase Shakespeare. So what do these beautiful symbols of our love for each other have to do with EDI?

The earliest use of e-commerce can be traced back to a group of florists in the United States who in 1910 created a cooperative around the brilliant idea of using communications technology to allow their customers to send flowers to anybody anywhere in the country on the same day.

The new cooperative used the telegraph to electronically transmit a customer order to the partner store that was closest to the recipient's address. The success of the Florists' Telegraph Delivery (FTD) created a rich national market that is profitable to this day. FTD is still a giant in the floral industry.

4.1.2 The Berlin Airlift, the Supply Chain, and Transportation

Another watershed moment occurred amid the drama and saber rattling of the Berlin Airlift of 1948. West Berlin, with its 2.5 million people, was jointly administered by the US, Britain, and France, but was surrounded by East Germany, then controlled by the Soviet Union.

On June 28, 1948, Soviet dictator Josef Stalin ordered an embargo of all rail, road, and barge traffic to Berlin from West Germany. The West responded with a massive airlift that would supply the city with more than 4,500 tons of food and other necessities each day.

Logistics were identified as the critical issue on the first day when only 80 tons were flown into the besieged city. The response was to set up a logistics team under Major General William H. Tunner, who had honed his craft ferrying goods by air between India and China during World War II.

The supply chain was the easy part. Warehouses were clustered on one side of West Berlin so that goods could be quickly transported from the airfields for distribution. Flights were scheduled in groups of 20 and landed in Berlin at three-minute intervals around the clock.

The challenge was delivering paperwork, particularly requests for supplies and cargo manifests detailing what was onboard each plane. Because Berlin was cut off, manifests couldn't be sent in advance of any flight's arrival. In addition, the paperwork came from multiple military organizations with different formats, languages, and required numbers of copies.

The solution was to design standard forms that could be transmitted by the communications technologies of the day: telex, teletype, and telephone.

It was a huge success. Over 13 months, more than 2 million tons of goods were flown into West Berlin. The West won a strategic victory in the Cold War when the Soviets backed down and reopened the land corridor.

This victory made a lasting impression on the logistics experts who participated in it. The cooperative effort at standardization in support of the distribution of real-world goods through a well-organized supply chain spawned the birth of EDI and the ongoing organized development and spread of standards across industries and between nations.

Shipping and the Birth of Cross-Industry Standards

US Army Supply Sergeant, Edward A. Guilbert—who worked on the standard manifest during the Berlin Airlift—in the 1960s designed the first set of EDI-like electronic messages for sending cargo data between his employer, DuPont, and Chemical Leaman Tank Lines, one of their shippers.

The importance of Guilbert's achievement is recognized today by the Edward A. Guilbert E-Business Professional Award given by the Data Interchange Standards Association (DISA), the body that administers ASC X12 EDI standards, to recognize contributions in e-commerce message development.

Holland American Lines closed the EDI circle in 1965 by transmitting shipping manifests by telex that were converted to tape and fed to a computer.

The Transportation Data Coordinating Committee

Railroads, truckers, shippers, and airlines all began to use electronic manifests. But one critical element was missing: cross-industry standards. A cacophony of proprietary standards was emerging, making it difficult and expensive for two companies with different standards to trade through EDI.

In 1968 a group of logistics specialists who had served during the Berlin Airlift formed the Transportation Data Coordinating Committee (TDCC) to design standards for cross-industry EDI transaction sets that could be used by all firms in the transportation industry regardless of mode.

In 1975 the TDCC published the Electronic Data Interchange Standards that later became the basis for ASC X12 EDI. The first successful transmission of one of the new transactions soon followed in the railway industry. Within ten years, 90 percent of all railway waybills were transmitted electronically.

The TDCC also worked with computer and communications experts to develop business applications to process electronic transactions, which led to direct computer-to-computer data exchanges and the first electronic purchase order and invoice.

At the same time, large retailers, grocers, auto manufacturers, and others jumped into the fray, developing proprietary POs and invoices, and aggressively pushing EDI technologies throughout their web of suppliers. To paraphrase Mao Tse Tung, a thousand flowers bloomed in the multitude of proprietary message formats designed by the early adopters of EDI.

4.1.3   The Birth of ASC X12

Enter the American National Standards Institute (ANSI), the folks who gave us ASCII. In 1979 ANSI created the Accredited Standards Committee (ASC) X12 to drive the development of open, generic EDI message standards for all industries.

In 1979 ASC released its first EDI standard based on the pioneering work of the TDCC. Also that year, the grocery and food industry published its Uniform Communication Standard (UCS), based on TDCC EDI standards. Eventually UCS merged with X12 and is identified today by the suffix UCS in the version data element of the GS group control segment.

In 1987 the Data Interchange Standards Association (DISA) was founded as the administrative arm of ASC X12 and today plays a key role in developing and distributing e-business standards through national, international, and industry groups and associations.

TDCC moved its transportation, warehousing, and retail standards to X12 in 1989. These standards became the core of X12M, a dialect of X12 designed for the supply chain, one of seven, each managed by an industry subcommittee, including the following:

- X12C Communications/controls

- X12F Finance

- X12G Government

- X12I Transportation

- X12J Technical Assessment

- X12M Supply Chain

- X12N Insurance

ASC X12 is the most widely used EDI standard in the world, by more than 300,000 companies in all industries and public service sectors. EDI in North America is overwhelmingly X12. Our very own Acme Pictures is a busy X12 shop, except for its overseas customers, who use the UN global standard EDIFACT in continental Europe and TRADACOMS in the UK.

We look at ASC X12 in more detail in Section 4.3, The Anatomy of an X12 Interchange.

4.1.4 Global Trade and E-Commerce: UN/EDIFACT

International trade was the driving force behind the evolution of global EDI standards. In the beginning, this meant paper—lots of it.

The cost of paperwork to international trade was measured in a survey by the US Department of Transportation (DOT) in 1971. DOT found that 46 different documents, on average, were used for one unit of export/import business with more than 360 copies. DOT estimated that the US produced 6.5 billion copies of 828 million documents each year to support its international trade.

This mountain of paper generated huge costs. Documentation for an average unit of export/import business consumed 64 man hours at a cost of $351.04 for a total of one billion man hours and $6.5 billion a year in the US.

The United Nations was the only body that could address this issue on a global basis. In the 1960s the UN Economic Council for Europe (UN/ECE) began designing standard forms that could be used across countries and industries. This led to broad international adoption of UN global standards for document size and format, number of characters per line, number of lines per box, grouping of field headings by function, and so on.

With the expanding use of computers in business, the focus shifted in 1972 to developing standard data terminologies and a uniform system for automatic processing and transmission of trade data and streamlining business processes.

Requirements for electronic data exchange were published in May 1975 in a document with the euphonious title of TRADE/WP.4/GE.I/R.54, also known as the Stockholm Charter. While the technical title may lack poetic resonance, its conclusions are an EDI Magna Carta, defining the principles and ground rules for developing global EDI standards, including the following:

▶ Rules for structuring data should be independent of systems or media.

▶ Transmitted data should be legible to humans.

▶ The character "'" (Hex 27) should be used to identify segments, while "+" (Hex 2B) and ":" (Hex 3A) delimit data elements and sub-elements.

▶ Data element design should be based on existing paper documents.

▶ Groups, segments, and data elements should be independent of each other so that one could be changed without affecting any of the others.

Two teams were set up to begin building global EDI standards based on the Stockholm Charter: one focused on standard data elements and codes and the other on data exchange standards for electronic transmission and computer media such as magnetic tapes.

The Birth of UN/EDIFACT

The first set of EDI rules for international trade was published in 1981: The Guidelines for Trade Data Interchange (GTDI). A joint European North American group—UN-JEDI—was then charged with trying to reconcile GTDI with US X12 standards.

The UN-JEDI recommendations came out in September 1986 and were used to design the UN/EDIFACT (UN/Electronic Data Interchange for Administration, Commerce, and Transport) standard. EDIFACT syntax rules received ISO certification (ISO 9735) in 1988 followed by publication of the first message: an invoice INVOIC. By 2003, responsibility for development of EDIFACT and other global e-business standards was transferred to the UN Center for Trade Facilitation and Electronic Business (UN/CEFACT).

4.1.5 Other EDI Standards

A number of other EDI standards emerged, including some that grew out of vertical industry groups and the UN/GTDI guidelines. We'll touch briefly on a few of these standards.

ODETTE

The Organization for Data Exchange by Teletransmission in Europe (ODETTE) was born in London in 1984 to group national automotive organizations from the UK, Benelux, France, Germany, Italy, Spain, and Sweden.

OFTP (ODETTE File Transfer Protocol) was published in 1986. It supports direct transmission of electronic documents across the Internet or through ISDN or X.25 networks. It features encryption, digital signatures, and authentication. Unlike AS2, OFTP can transmit in both directions (push or pull).

The first three EDI messages, built on UN/GTDI syntax rules, were published the same year: delivery instruction (DELINS), despatch advice (AVIEXP), and invoice (INVOIC). By 1989, more than 30 ODETTE messages covered the full spectrum of the automotive supply chain.

ODETTE began migrating to UN/EDIFACT in 1990 as a subset of the global standard. Full compliance followed in 2000, when ODETTE agreed with the world's largest national auto industry groups to adopt UN/EDIFACT. Today, ODETTE has been largely replaced by UN/EDIFACT, although the old standards are still in use at many European auto industry EDI sites.

TRADACOMS

Used primarily in the UK retail sector, TRADACOMS is an early implementation of UN/GTDI syntax. It was introduced in 1982 and is maintained by GS1 UK, the British branch of the global GS1 standards body.

TRADACOMS features 26 transactions including orders, invoices, product information, delivery confirmation, and so on. It differs from EDIFACT in a number of important ways:

▸ STX/END segments define interchange envelopes instead of UNB/UNZ.

▸ MHD/MTR segments define message envelopes rather than UNH/UNT.

▸ The "=" (Hex 3D) character is used to identify the first data element in a segment rather than the standard data delimiter "+" (Hex 2B).

▸ It is UK-specific, so it does not support any currency other than the pound.

Development of TRADACOMS ended in 1995, but British retailers continue to use it with no sign of changing, even though GS1 UK actively discourages its use in favor of EDIFACT.

VDA

Germany's *Verband der Automobilindustrie* (Association of the Automotive Industry) began developing EDI standards in 1977 in the wake of an earlier effort to standardize paper forms, well before release of the UN/GTDI guidelines. Messages and implementation guidelines were developed for planning, distribution, and invoicing.

VDA messages are flat files with a header, payload, and trailer records, each of which is identified by a numeric code. The structure of VDA 4905/1 (delivery instruction), for example, is defined by four segment characteristics:

1. Record type code identifying the function of the segment—for example, 511 header record, 517 packaging data, or 519 trailer record

2. Version number for the record type

3. M/C that identifies field characteristics such as mandatory, conditional, alphanumeric (left-justified), or numeric (right-justified)

4. Repetition with a value of 1 or R (for repeat)

Some very large EDI operations, such as Volkswagen, continue to use VDA, along with ODETTE, ODETTE/EDIFACT, and EDIFACT. The goal, however, is to move entirely to EDIFACT over time.

4.1.6   Communications, VANs, and the Internet

Even with the emergence of message standards, EDI remained an expensive proposition. In the days before widespread adoption of SAP, business software was largely built over time as needed by in-house programmers or contractors, who rarely documented their work, resulting in a multitude of custom systems with different levels of functionality and a bewildering array of file formats.

Data communications proved particularly complex and expensive. In the early days of EDI point-to-point communication, often across a telephone line at very slow speeds, was the only option. This was difficult to maintain as the number of potential EDI partners for any company grew.

Value added networks (VANs) emerged in the 1970s to provide a single secure point of communications between EDI trading partners. Delivery was guaranteed across a secure network, and audit tools and reports helped manage data flows. Costs were high. Charges were by the number of kilo-characters—blocks of 1,024 bytes—transmitted per month, with a monthly minimum. But VANs promised peace of mind.

AS2

The dramatic growth of the Internet brought new communications standards that enabled secure transfer of encrypted EDI transactions across the web.

Applicability Statement 2 (AS2) was developed by the Internet Engineering Task Force (IETF) to enable secure data transmission through HTTP and Secure Multi-purpose Internet Mail Extensions (SMIME) standards.

EDI, or any other structured data format, files are sent as encrypted SMIME attachments in an AS2 message through an HTTP or HTTP/S post method with synchronous or asynchronous return of a message disposition notification (MDN) to confirm that the transmission was received. Security is provided by digital certificates and authentication.

The biggest advantage of AS2 is cost. Data transmission across the Internet is free, eliminating VAN costs. But "free" comes at a price, including an AS2 server; static IP, always-on Internet connection; maintenance of multiple point-to-point interfaces; management of certificates; and ongoing personnel costs for maintaining networks and connections.

In Acme's case, Gordy's Galaxy mandated that all its suppliers use AS2. After the initial investment, Acme had the infrastructure to handle AS2 exchanges with any trading partner who could support it. Within two years, more than 70 percent of Acme's EDI traffic was AS2 and VAN costs plummeted.

The great Darryl Q. wouldn't have studied EDI's history or analyzed its global economic impact. If his customers wanted EDI, he would have built it, and paid others well to learn everything he needed to know about it, beginning with an overview of the two major standards that will work with Acme's new SAP system. We'll begin with EDIFACT, but most of our focus will be ASC X12.

4.2   The Anatomy of an EDIFACT Interchange

The structure of all EDIFACT interchanges follows the same pattern, as illustrated by the ORDERS message in Figure 4.1.

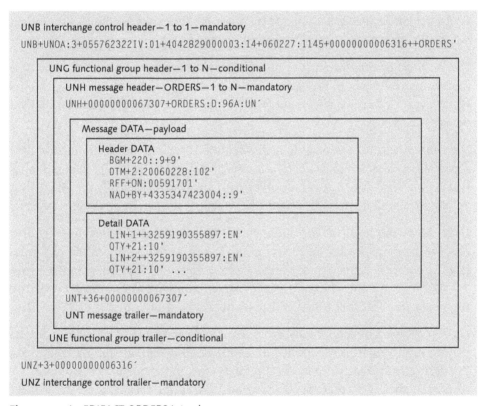

Figure 4.1   An EDIFACT ORDERS Interchange

EDIFACT is built from the bottom up in a thoughtful and consistent manner. Messages represent common business documents such as purchase orders and invoices and are assembled from a reusable library of common segments, data elements, and qualifier codes maintained in a data dictionary by a UN committee that includes experts from around the world.

From the inside, every EDIFACT transmission is composed of the following:

- One-to-many *messages*, each defined by one UNH message header and one UNT trailer. Each message corresponds to one business document such as a PO or invoice. The message is within the innermost envelope.

- An optional *functional group* within one UNG header and one UNE trailer, storing one or more messages of the same business document type. One or more functional groups can appear in each interchange, but the group is rarely used outside North America.

- A mandatory *interchange* defined by one UNB interchange control header and one UNZ trailer. This is the outermost envelope.

The message is constructed of relatively short segments that carry a specific type of data that can be used in many different business documents. Each segment is identified by a three-character tag followed by a "+" character and is terminated by a " ' " character.

Segments are made up of data elements identified by a four-character numeric code separated by the colon character (:). There are two basic types of data elements: ones that simply store data, in a variety of formats, and ones that qualify the segment or adjoining data elements with a particular function, format, or other characteristic.

DTM, for example, is the date/time/period segment used in every message. No other segment carries a date. The type of date or time period stored and its format in any instance is defined by a qualifier code. Take our DTM segment in the Figure 4.1 sample. The 2 after the tag is a code that identifies the date as the delivery date requested. The 102 following the date identifies the date format as CCYYMMDD.

Nearly 800 types of dates, times, or periods for documents and events and dozens of date/time formats are identified by an EDIFACT code. This approach supports use of the standard across borders and time zones and is characteristic of its international scope. Every other segment works in the same way.

EDIFACT and IDoc Messages

EDIFACT messages follow the same naming conventions as IDoc logical message types: a six-character capitalized name that identifies the business document it represents, although IDocs have strayed from this nomenclature in recent years. They share the same name for many messages: ORDERS (purchase order), DESADV (despatch advice), INVOIC (invoice), and REMADV (remittance advice), and so on.

Both IDoc and EDIFACT messages are designed for global use by as wide an array of industries as possible.

Conceptually, at a structural design level, EDIFACT and IDoc messages follow a similar approach. Both have a hierarchical structure composed of sequenced segments grouped in the following zones:

▶ Header control record (IDoc) or envelopes (EDIFACT) defining the parameters and contents of each message

▶ Header data area with document-wide records such as document numbers, dates, totals and summaries, and so on

▶ Detail data area with granular line-item level records

Each segment is assembled from standard data elements that store discrete fields from the business document they represent. Segments represent a particular type of data and can be qualified with codes for reuse. They can be collected in hierarchical groups of related segments that can be populated once or repeat as often as necessary to pass all relevant data. Groups of segments can themselves be grouped within other groups.

The similarity ends there, however. EDIFACT — and all EDI messages — are bridge documents between two or more systems. They are meant to accurately represent the output of the sending system. An EDI purchase order has the full legal force of a paper purchase order. It is a contract and must faithfully represent the data generated by the sending system.

It's up to the receiver to accurately convert the EDI bridge document to a format that can be posted it to the receiving business system. The EDIFACT document is a neutral container, and the specifics of its use are agreed to by the two partners in a relationship, usually driven by the buyer.

IDocs are intelligent messages unique to SAP with standard application processing logic behind them. They are key elements of a mature programming interface with impressive application processing right out of the box as well as unlimited customization.

IDocs are not neutral containers. They represent the business document, with its logic and rules, as it has been defined in SAP, the business system of record.

4.3 The Anatomy of an X12 Interchange

The inbound X12 850 purchase order is an iconic X12 transaction with its own unique challenges and a critical interface in Acme's implementation. Its hierarchical structure, as illustrated in Figure 4.2, is universal across all X12 transactions.

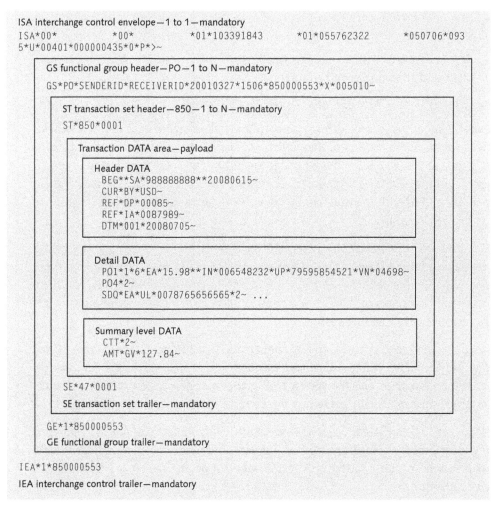

Figure 4.2 The Structure of an ASC X12 Interchange

From the inside out, every X12 interchange includes the following elements:

- One to many *transaction sets* defined by the innermost ST transaction set envelope and the SE trailer. The transaction set is a single instance of a business document such as a PO or invoice. Each transaction set is identified by a three-digit code such as 850 (PO), 810 (invoice), or 820 (payment advice).

- One to many *groups* defined by the GS functional group envelope and the GE trailer. The group collects one or more transactions of the same set such as POs or payment advices identified by a function code. In our example, the function code is PO for purchase order.

  The GS envelope identifies the version of its X12 transaction sets. Gordy's transactions to Acme are always version 5010. While multiple groups can be included in one interchange, in practice there's usually only one.

- The *interchange* is defined by the ISA interchange control envelope and the IEA trailer. The interchange contains one or more GS groups, each of which has one or more transaction sets.

The payload in the transaction set is one instance of a business document, a PO in our example. It is constructed from sequenced segments, each of which is identified by a two- or three-character code.

For example, BEG is the beginning segment of the X12 850 transaction set with identifying data for the document such as PO number and PO date. Unlike EDIFACT, which only presents dates in the DTM segment, X12 stores dates in many other segments besides DTM. But X12 also uses DTM in the same way as EDIFACT: to qualify many different types of dates, times, and periods in many different formats.

In both X12 and IDocs segments are constructed to store a specific type of data often qualified by codes for use in different documents and contexts. But common data elements are often shared across multiple segments, which is not consistent with the EDIFACT standard of a more abstracted architecture where the segment defines the data element contents.

For example, X12 data elements 0373 (date), 0380 (quantity), and 0234 (product ID) are used in many different segments besides DTM (Date/Time), QTY (Quantity), and LIN (Item Identification), including segments that do not deal with these objects as the central subject.

There's a much tighter relationship between the data element and segment in EDIFACT. Date (2380) appears only in DTM; quantity (6060) only in QTY; and product ID (7140) only in segments that directly deal with ordered product as the central subject; these are LIN (Item Number), PIA (Additional Product Info), BII (Bill Item Identification), and TCC (Transport Charge/Rate Calculations).

IDocs follow X12 in this less strict use of data elements and segments.

4.3.1 Syntax and Semantics: X12 as Language

Let's consider ASC X12 as a language for a moment. Like all languages, it has syntax and semantics, two wonderful Greek words that loosely translate as grammatical structure and meaning or content.

Syntax is defined by grammar, a set of rules about structuring transaction sets maintained by ASC X12 but harmonized, where relevant, with the syntax rules developed by UN/CEFACT for EDIFACT. Syntax rules are spelled out in EDI implementation guidelines available for a price from DISA.

The semantics—or vocabulary—that infuses the grammatical structure with meaning is applied through a data dictionary that includes the following:

► **Code sources**

  ► Devised by various industry groups to meet their needs

  ► Used as qualifiers for data elements

► **Data element dictionary**

  ► Defines all data elements available for use by all segments

  ► Links data elements that require qualifiers to all available codes

► **Segment dictionary**

  ► Identifies all segments that can be used

  ► Tags segments for use in the header, detail, and/or summary sections of the data area

  ► Defines the data elements used within each segment

  ► Defines the sequence of data elements used within each segment

► **Transaction set tables**

  ► Identifies all transaction sets by a three-digit code for all versions of ASC X12, such as 850

  ► Identifies all segments that can be used in each transaction set and version

▸ Defines the sequence of allowable segments for each transaction set and version

An overview of how the X12 language is realized is illustrated in Figure 4.3.

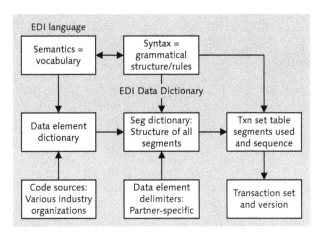

Figure 4.3 The EDI Language Is Realized through Semantics and Syntax

At the highest level, the data dictionary imparts meaning to the grammatical structure by linking the data elements and their qualifiers from the code list to the segments, and linking the segments to the transaction sets and version.

But the standards are flexible so that each partner can adapt them to meet the specific requirements of his own business and industry, creating something like a local X12 dialect, to push our language analogy one step further. There's no dramatic deviation from the standard. The differences are along the lines of:

▸ Selection of transaction sets and version to map to the documents used in the partner's business processes

▸ Choice of optional data elements and segments to use

▸ Selection of a small set of qualifiers from the code lists, which determine business usage of segments and data elements

▸ Delimiters to use between data elements within segments; X12 delimiters are selected by the partner, unlike EDIFACT, which provides a set of standard delimiter characters that all messages must use

The details of each partner's usage are spelled out in his EDI implementation guidelines, the starting point for our analysis of his data. It's important to understand the partner's usage so that we can map the X12 to the IDoc in SAP.

But first we need to get a handle on the structure of the X12. We'll stick with the 850 and begin with an overview of the envelopes.

4.3.2 The Envelope Segments

Envelopes provide the high-level organization and identity for the EDI interchange. Together, the three envelopes answer the basic questions of who is the sender, who is the receiver, and what is being sent. We'll start at the highest level and work our way down.

The ISA-IEA Interchange Control Envelope

The ISA interchange header and IEA trailer envelope segments define the interchange. Unlike all other X12 segments, the ISA header has a fixed length with a delimiter. Unpopulated data elements filled in with spaces. All other X12 segments are built of variable-length delimited data elements.

The ISA packages the interchange into a transmission from one sender to one receiver, allowing the EDI system to identify the source and destination for the transmission. The key data elements of the ISA segment include the following:

- A fixed interchange sender ID qualifier
- Interchange sender ID number
- A fixed interchange receiver ID qualifier
- Interchange receiver ID number
- Interchange creation date
- Interchange creation time
- Interchange control segment version number
- Unique interchange control ID number for the partner and transaction

The IEA trailer has two fields:

- Number of functional groups in interchange
- Interchange control ID number from the ISA header

The GS-GE Group Control Header

The GS group header envelope and GE trailer segments collect one or more ST transaction sets into a functional group for one transaction type defined by a function code.

The GS envelope assigns a sender, a receiver, and a version of the X12 standard to its transaction sets. The sender and receiver do not have to be the same as in the ISA and can be used to identify different departments for internal routing of the group and its transactions.

We won't get that fancy in Acme's implementation, however. Gordy's group sender and receiver will be the same as in the ISA. And Gordy Galaxy will never send more than one group per interchange.

The following are the key data elements of the GS envelope segment:

▶ Functional code that identifies the business function of the transaction sets within the group — PO for purchase order

▶ Sender's EDI ID number

▶ Receiver's EDI ID number

▶ Group control number identifying the current group within the interchange (often is the same as the Interchange Control ID and is sent back to the sending party by the receiving party in an X12 997 to acknowledge receipt of an EDI transmission)

▶ Version of the transaction sets in the group (Gordy uses 00510)

The GE trailer only has two fields:

▶ Number of transaction sets in group

▶ Group control number from GS segment

The ST-SE Transaction Set Header

The ST transaction set header and SE trailer segments identify transaction sets in a group. Each transaction is one instance of a business document in the sender's system and is identified by a three-digit code: 850 for a PO. X12 version 5010 has 318 transaction sets.

We will map the transaction set to and from the IDocs in Acme's SAP system. The key data elements of the ST segment include the following:

▸ Transaction set code: 850 for a PO

▸ Unique transaction set control ID number

The SE trailer has two fields:

▸ Number of transaction set segments including the ST and SE envelopes

▸ Unique transaction set control ID number from the ST segment

4.3.3 Dissecting Gordy's 850 to Acme

Listing 4.1 offers a sample 850 X12 transaction from Gordy.

```
ST*850*0001~
BEG*00*SA*0099969569**20081202~
CUR*BY*USD~
REF*DP*0099~
REF*IA*0099989~
ITD*05*15*****30~
DTM*001*20081222~
DTM*002*20081205~
DTM*010*20081205~
N9*L1*SPECIAL INSTRUCTIONS~
MTX**IF MULTIPLE DESTINATIONS HAVE SAME SHIP DATE PLEASE~
MTX**SHIP TO FURTHEST DESTINATION FIRST AND CLOSEST LAST~
N1*BT**UL*0999567891299~
N1*SU*ACME STUDIOS~
PO1*1*6*EA*15.98**IN*0065832*UP*999956535219*VN*04698~
PO4*2~
SDQ*EA*UL*0099965656565*2*0099965656566*2*0099965656567*2~
PO1*2*2*EA*15.98**IN*006548234*UP*99995854525*VN*04693~
PO4*2~
SDQ*EA*UL*0099965656568*2~
CTT*2~
AMT*GV*127.84~
SE*23*0001~
```

Listing 4.1 An 850 PO Transaction Sent by Gordy to Acme

Let's step through each segment to get a better handle on the transaction. Not all of these segments will be mapped to our SAP ORDERS IDoc.

The ST Segment

A transaction set always begins with an ST segment and ends with an SE segment. It identifies the document, assigns a sequential control number within its functional group, and counts the number of segments in the transaction set. The ST segment also begins the header zone of the data area.

The BEG First Segment

BEG is the first segment of the business document for the 850. Its sole purpose is to identify the beginning of the 850 and to transmit key document numbers and dates. It is mandatory and occurs only once in the transaction set.

The BEG segment that Gordy sends to Acme is defined in Table 4.1.

Ref	ID	Data Element Description	Usage	Value
BEG01	0353	Transaction set purpose code	M	00
BEG02	0092	PO type code	M	SA
BEG03	0324	PO number	M	02999
BEG04	0328	Release number	O	
BEG05	0373	PO date	M	20080615

Table 4.1 Structure of the BEG Segment Sent by Gordy to Acme

Each data element is identified by two IDs:

▸ A reference (i.e., BEG01) that links it to the segment and to its sequence within the segment

▸ A data element ID assigned by the X12 data element dictionary: 0373 in version 5010, for example, is an eight-digit date with format CCYYMMDD that can be used in any other segment where a date is required

There are 12 data elements in segment BEG in version 5010 of the X12 standard, but Gordy only sends Acme these five, and BEG04 is always null. Data elements left out are optional and can be used to refine the business process.

For example, BEG07 — data element 0587 — holds the acknowledgment type code that specifies the type of acknowledgment expected from the vendor for the PO. Data elements 0324 (PO number) and 0373 (PO date) are both mapped to the SAP IDoc.

Codes and Qualifiers

We should note the use of the qualifiers in data elements 0353 (BEG01) and 0092 (BEG02). These codes are defined by various industry groups and are linked to data elements by the version of the X12 standard through the data elements dictionary. Once assigned, however, codes are not removed.

Data element 0353 defines the purpose of the PO transmitted. It qualifies the entire transaction. Value 00 defines the transmitted document as an original PO and is a trigger for action: Create this customer PO in your system. The only other value that Gordy uses for this element is 22 (information copy) which is never transmitted to Acme.

The action implied by this code is further qualified by data element 0092, with the value SA for standalone order, identifying the type of PO being sent, which points to the business document and process that should follow. This is underlined by the other qualifiers that Gordy can send in 0092:

► BE: Blanket order with estimated quantities and no firm commitment

► RL: Release or delivery order against an existing contract or blanket order

These values point to very different types of business documents that may need to be created—or not—in the receiving SAP system.

This could lead to widely different follow-on business processes. A value of BE in data element 0092, for example, could trigger a report that is emailed to users rather than creation of a PO in SAP.

The way these codes are used is one of the key elements that define Gordy's dialect of the X12 EDI language. Usage is fully documented in Gordy's EDI implementation guidelines for the transaction and version.

We'll look at codes a little more closely when we discuss the DTM segment in Section Header Position 060: The DTM Segment below.

The CUR Segment

The CUR segment follows BEG in position 030 of the header. It identifies the transaction currency. Both data elements reference codes:

► CUR01: Data element 0098. Entity identifier code. Value: BY for buyer. Qualifies trading partner type whose currency is stored.

► CUR02: Data element 0100. ISO currency codes. Value: USD. This is mapped to the IDoc.

The REF Segment

The REF Reference Information segment provides identification data for a variety of objects, including the customer, vendor, order, and even associated documents and events.

It can occur multiple times and uses codes in data element 0128 (REF01) to identify the nature of the data transmitted in 0127 (REF02). Only two codes are sent by Gordy to Acme:

▶ DP: Department number. Identifies an order for Gordy (0099) or for its deep discount club chain Klub Kazoo (0100). The two are set up as different customer accounts in Acme's SAP system. Gordy expects separate delivery and invoices for both, although it issues only one payment.

▶ IA: Internal vendor number. The code Gordy uses in its business system to identify Acme Studios.

The ITD Segment

ITD stores terms of payment for the order. Terms of payment with Gordy are entered in Acme's SAP customer master for Gordy's sold-to partner record, in the billing document screen of the sales area data.

When a sales order is created from Gordy's purchase order in SAP, terms of payment are pulled from this record. They are not brought in through the IDoc, so we don't have to map them.

The segment can occur more than once, but Gordy only sends one instance with the following data elements:

▶ ITD01: Data element 0336. Terms of payment type code. 05 for discount not applicable.

▶ ITD02: Data element 0333. Terms of basis date code. 15 for receipt of goods.

▶ ITD07: Data element 0386. Terms of net days. 30 for payment 30 days after receiving ordered goods.

The DTM Segment

DTM is the date segment and can occur up to 10 times. Each instance holds a different type of date identified by the qualifier in data element 0374 (DTM01). All of these dates are mapped to the SAP IDoc. Gordy's use of the DTM header segment is described in Table 4.2.

Ref	ID	Data Element Description	Usage	Value
DTM01	0374	Date/time qualifier	M	001
DTM02	0373	Date	M	20080701

Table 4.2 Structure of the DTM Segment Sent by Gordy to Acme

Data element 0374 qualifies the segment and data element 0373. It tells us what action is expected by what date. It also points to where this date will be mapped in the IDoc. The following codes are used in data element 0374 in our sample:

▶ 001: Cancel after date. Order is to be canceled if goods haven't been delivered by this date.

▶ 002: Requested delivery date. Goods to be delivered to the ordering store location by this date.

▶ 010: Requested ship date. Latest date that goods can be shipped to Gordy's distribution center to make requested delivery date to the store.

In addition, the selection process for determining what codes to use point to the way that the business process is managed by the sending partner and to details of Gordy's implementation of X12. Of the more than 1,280 possible codes linked to data element 0374 in X12 version 5010, Gordy uses only seven.

The N9 Extended Reference Loop

We've looked at two types of segment so far: standalone single instance and standalone repeating segments.

Segments BEG and CUR each occur only once, whereas REF, ITD, and DTM can be repeated multiple times. All present a flat structure, following one after the other, and none has any children.

N9, on the other hand, is a proud parent. It is a loop, a repeating virtual group that includes more than one child. N9 is the parent and all instances of MTX that follow are its children.

Our sample transaction features a number of loops, including N9, N1, PO1, and CTT. We'll look at each of these in turn.

All loops are identified in the ASC X12 850 version 5010 standard by a loop ID and by beginning and end flags. The standard identifies five segments that can occur within the N9 loop. Each is tagged with the N9 loop ID. N9, the first segment and the parent, is also tagged with the begin flag. EFI, the last segment, is tagged with the end flag.

The loop is optional but can occur up to 1,000 times in the transaction. If the N9 loop occurs, the parent N9 segment must appear only once each time the loop is repeated. All other segments are optional.

Once again, the 850 that Acme receives from Gordy doesn't include all of the possible segments in the standard. The structure of Gordy's N9 loop virtual group is illustrated in Figure 4.4.

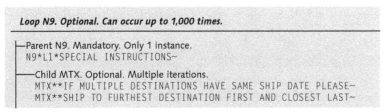

Figure 4.4 The N9 Loop Is a Virtual Group with a Parent-Child Relationship

N9 is the parent and appears only once in our sample. MTX is the child and occurs twice, although it can occur many more times. Like the loop itself, MTX is optional and does not have to occur when an N9 segment is present. However, Gordy uses this loop to send Acme text messages. N9 never appears more than once in the transactions that Acme receives from Gordy, and it's always accompanied by one or more MTX segments.

Codes qualify the loop and identify the nature of the information being transmitted. The code L1 in data element 0128 (N901) means letters or notes. The nature of these notes is specified by data element 0127 (N902), which is hard-coded to read "SPECIAL INSTRUCTIONS."

The instructions are detailed in the subsequent MTX segments in data element 1551 (MTX02), which holds text. The standard allows up to 4,096 characters in this data element, but Gordy never sends more than 80.

We don't have to pass this data element to SAP. If we did, it would be mapped to a text segment in the IDoc with a text element qualifier. It would then post to a text element at the header level of the SAP sales order and would pass to the delivery document when it's generated.

There are 1,731 possible codes for data element 0128, but Gordy only uses three of them and sends only L1 to Acme. In addition to L1, Gordy uses two others:

▶ L9: Customer part number

▶ LA: Shipping label serial number

The rules for this are documented in Gordy's 850 implementation guidelines.

The N1 Party ID Loop

When there's no SDQ segment present, we use the N1 party identification loop to map the ship-to party to the IDoc, a particularly important piece of data for posting the SAP sales order. In our 850 sample, N1 isn't relevant for mapping because the SDQ segment provides us with the ship-to party.

The mandatory N1 loop can occur up to 200 times. The X12 standard includes 15 segments within the N1 loop, but Gordy uses three (N1, N3, and N4) and generally only sends Acme one: N1. The other two are for address information and not relevant to posting sales orders in SAP.

N1 is the parent segment and occurs only once for each iteration of the loop. The N1 segment that Gordy sends Acme in the 850 is defined in Table 4.3.

Ref	ID	Data Element Description	Usage	Value
N101	0098	Entity identifier code	M	BY
N102	0093	Partner name	O	
N103	0066	Identification code qualifier	M	UL
N104	0067	Party ID number	M	0234567891299

Table 4.3   Gordy's N1 Party Identification Segment

Data element 0098 (N101) identifies the type of party stored in the segment: partner, organization, location, or individual. There are 1,500 codes in version 5010 of the ASC X12 standard but Gordy only sends four to Acme:

- ▶ BY: Buying party for the purchasing organization. Ordered goods will be shipped to a distribution center for later allocation to stores on an as-needed basis. BY is always accompanied by another ST N1 segment.

- ▶ ST: Ship-to party, either a store or distribution center. When ST is present there is no SDQ segment. Each SAP sales order is created for one sold-to and one ship-to party. When ST is present in the N1 segment, there is only one ship-to party for the PO. The ship-to party is the only value we'll map to the IDoc from Gordy's N1 segment.

- ▶ BT: Bill-to party.

- ▶ SU: Supplier/manufacturer for the vendor.

BY, ST, and BT are further qualified by the Global Location Number (GLN) in data element 0067 (N103). We know it's a GLN from the code UL in data element 0066.

GLN is a unique 13-digit universal code that identifies one department, location, legal entity, or trading partner. It's assigned and maintained by GS1, the global standards organization that replaced European Article Numbering (EAN) International and the US-based Uniform Code Council (UCC). More than 100 GS1 national member organizations share this global standard.

UCC is now GS1 US, which is responsible for the uniform product code (UPC) numbers embedded in bar codes. Gordy sends UPC numbers, along with other item number types, to identify product it wants to order from suppliers.

Another important GS1 standard related to UCC is the Global Trade Item Number (GTIN), a unique global product code. GTINs identify products, inner packs, cases, and pallets bearing products in a delivery environment. They show up on purchase orders, delivery, and payment documents.

GLNs, UPCs, and GTINs share the same basic structure: a company prefix, followed by a location or item number, and a check digit at the last position. UPCs are 12 digits and GTINs can be 8, 12, 13, or 14 digits in length.

GS1 standards simplify mapping because we only have to deal with one code for each partner or item—as long as the standards are being used, of course.

In this, Gordy's has followed the path of virtue. It uses GLNs for all its organizational units, including purchasing organizations, accounts payable, store locations, and distribution centers.

But Acme, like most companies, continues to use its internal SAP identifiers for customers and products, although it does get UPC numbers for all its finished goods that are sold.

The only value that we pass to the IDoc from Gordy's N1 segment is the GLN when data element 0098 equals ST. In our current example, the ship-to party is in the SDQ segment, so we map nothing from N1.

The PO1 Item Loop

The PO1 loop stores details of the goods ordered for each of Gordy's stores or distribution centers: item numbers, quantities, unit prices, and, when the SDQ is present, store locations.

The PO1 loop is mandatory and can occur up to 100,000 times in one order. Under the X12 standard, the PO1 loop can include as many as 36 segments, but Gordy only sends Acme the three illustrated in Figure 4.5.

```
Loop PO1. Mandatory. Can occur up to 100,000 times.

— Parent PO1. Mandatory. Only 1 instance.
  PO1*1*6*EA*15.98**IN*006548232*UP*795958545212*VN*04698~
—— Child PO4. Optional. Up to 999,999 iterations.
  PO4*2~
—— Child SDQ. Optional. Up to 999,999 iterations.
  SDQ*EA*UL*0078765656565*2*0078765656566*2*0078765656567*2~
```

Figure 4.5 Structure of the PO1 Loop in Our Sample of Gordy's 850 to Acme

The PO1 segment is the parent, and PO4 and SDQ are its children. PO1 can occur only once in each instance of the loop, whereas PO4 and SDQ can both occur up to 999,999 times...in other words, more than once.

Baseline item data is sent in PO1, including item number, total quantity ordered, and unit price. The structure of the PO1 segment that Gordy sends to Acme is detailed in Table 4.4.

Ref	ID	Data Element Description	Usage	Value
PO101	0350	Line item number	M	1
PO102	0380	Total quantity ordered for item	M	6

Table 4.4 Gordy's PO1 Item Details Segment

Ref	ID	Data Element Description	Usage	Value
PO103	0355	Unit of measure	O	EA
PO104	0212	Unit price	O	15.98
PO105	0639	Basis of unit price	O	
PO106	0235	Item qualifier: Buyer's item no.	M	IN
PO107	0234	Item	M	006548232
PO108	0235	Item qualifier: UPC	M	UP
PO109	0234	Item	M	795958545212
PO110	0235	Item qualifier: Vendor's item no.	M	VN
PO111	0234	Item	M	04698

Table 4.4 Gordy's PO1 Item Details Segment (Cont.)

When an SDQ segment is present, data element 0380 (PO102) contains the total quantity ordered for the item. Data element 0380 is only mapped to the IDoc when there is no SDQ present.

Data element 0235 qualifies 0234, which contains the item number. Neither can appear without the other. In Gordy's usage, the pair is repeated three times. The X12 standard allows the two to be repeated up to 10 times in the PO1 segment. Each pair qualifies a different type of item number.

We'll map all three to the IDoc. The IN item, the material number set up in Gordy's business system, isn't used in SAP. The VN item is Acme's SAP material master number. The UP item is the 12-digit UPC identifier for Acme's item number. It is stored in the material master record in SAP, in field EAN11 in table MARA. We'll see how these item numbers are evaluated during our discussion of inbound IDoc processing in SAP in Chapter 5, Real World Business Process Integration with EDI.

Pricing is applied when the sales order is created through pricing conditions associated with the material and customer. SAP treats the unit price from the X12 850 as a customer expected price. The customer's price is compared to the price set in pricing conditions during processing of the IDoc.

If the customer price is different but falls within an accepted tolerance range set for the pricing condition, say $15 up or down, SAP uses its own price in the sales order. If the customer price falls outside the tolerance limit, the sales order is put on incompletion hold, and pricing is manually corrected after contacting the customer and working out who had the correct price.

Segment PO4 is about the physical details of the item, including packaging, weights, and dimensions. The only value that Gordy ever sends is in data element 0356, which is the pack quantity. In the examples that we're looking at here, this value refers to the number of "eaches" within each pack.

We introduced the SDQ segment in our discussion of the 852 and VMI processing in Chapter 2, Section 2.1.3, Selling the Dream with Vendor Management Inventory. It has a simple structure and a single-minded purpose: to report the quantity of the item ordered by each store location. The base structure of the SDQ is detailed in Table 4.5.

Ref	ID	Data Element Description	Usage	Value
SDQ01	0355	Unit of measure	M	EA
SDQ02	0066	SDQ location qualifier: GLN	M	UL
SDQ03	0067	Store location	M	0099965656565
SDQ04	0380	Quantity ordered	M	2

Table 4.5 The SDQ Segment Tells How Much Each Store Is Ordering

Each SDQ segment always has the unit of measure, a qualifier to identify the type of location codes reported (GLN identified by qualifier UL), and at least one pair of data elements: 0067, which holds the GLN number, and 0380, which has the quantity ordered by that store.

Each SDQ segment that Gordy sends Acme can hold up to 10 pairs of data elements 0067 and 0380. Each PO1 loop can have up to 500 SDQ segments.

The SDQ isn't as complex as it may seem. The purchasing department orders Acme movies on DVD for all stores in Gordy's chain. One bill-to party (AP) gets the invoice for the order. The PO consolidates ordering requirements for all stores in the SDQ within each PO1 loop. This is an efficient way to transmit data for a large organization with a lot of locations.

The challenge is in the mapping. The IDoc build is driven by the way SAP sales orders are created. Each sales order is for one sold-to and one ship-to party. The item-level SDQ represents one SAP sales order for each item-location-quantity combination. The GLN store location in SDQ at the item level must be mapped to the E1EDKA1 partner segment at the header level of a new ORDERS message on the IDoc side.

If, for example, we have a PO from Gordy with SDQ segments that hold item-quantity ordering data for 2,000 stores, we need 2,000 ORDERS IDocs, one for each store. Each ORDERS IDoc creates one sales order for one ship-to party.

This SDQ unraveling is a common challenge in EDI implementations. We can do it through a script at the operating system level before the transaction is translated, we can do it in the map during translation, or we can do it in SAP by writing custom ABAP code, which is what we're going to do for Acme.

We'll look at this challenge more closely when we build our 850-ORDERS interface in Chapter 12, Inbound Customer Purchase Order.

The CTT Summary Group

Summary information for the transaction is stored in the CTT group. Its use is optional. Many of Acme's partners do not include it, but Gordy does. The CTT segment is the parent and AMT the child. Like the group, both segments can occur only once.

Gordy uses the CTT segment to report the number of PO1 segments included in the transaction. This value is in data element 0354 (CTT01).

The AMT segment reports the gross value of all items in the transaction, including all charges minus allowances. This value is in data element 0782 (AMT02) and is identified by the GV qualifier in data element 0522 (AMT01).

None of the data in the CTT loop will be mapped to the IDoc.

4.4   Enveloping and De-enveloping: The X12 in Action

EDI envelopes are critical to the processing of an interchange by the integration system, whether that system is in-house, at a service bureau, or in a cloud-based platform. The envelopes define and identify the interchange.

The integration system needs to know who the message came from, who it's going to, and what it contains. This is done through de-enveloping for inbound messages or enveloping for outbound messages. This is the critical step that routes the message to the receiver's business system, regardless of direction. It's a good place to start our exploration of message process flows.

4.4.1 Unwrapping an Inbound EDI Interchange

We'll use the inbound X12 850 PO that maps to an ORDERS IDoc and posts to an SAP sales order for this example. We'll assume that there is only one X12 PO in the batch as we walk through these steps.

1. Acme's EDI system receives the interchange from the customer. The first step is to verify that the first segment in the interchange is a valid ISA control envelope.

2. The EDI sender and receiver trading partner ID and qualifiers are identified and confirmed. The interchange control ID is then checked to confirm that it hasn't been sent before.

3. The ISA header and IEA trailer are then stripped from the interchange and the EDI system is queried for the GS envelope using the sender and receiver IDs, X12 version (5010), and the function code (PO).

4. The GS header and GE trailer segments are then stripped from the interchange, and the EDI system queries for the ST envelope linked to the GS envelope using the transaction set code from the incoming ST – 850.

5. At this point, the system identifies the translation map, which is linked to the ST envelope through key values from all three: sender, receiver, qualifiers, version, and transaction code.

6. The translation map is called and the 850 converted to an ORDERS IDoc file. The map populates the control segment with the sender, receiver, message and basic types, and other key values needed to pass checks before being written to the SAP IDoc database.

7. The IDoc file is sent into SAP by calling a standard RFC function module.

The envelopes are defined in the EDI subsystem and are specific to the trading partner and X12 version and transaction set.

At Acme Pictures, the inbound ISA points to only one external trading partner ID and qualifier. All GS functional group and ST transaction set envelopes for that trading partner link to the ISA through the trading partner ID.

The inbound GS group envelope is further distinguished from the ISA by its version and function code, read from the incoming interchange. These keys tie it to the transaction set envelope which is associated with the translation map and the IDoc message and basic type: ORDERS.ORDERS05 for the 850.

Gordy's uses a GLN as their EDI trading partner ID. Acme's SAP system expects its customer number in the SNDPRN field of the control segment before it will post a sales order from Gordy's incoming PO in the ORDERS IDoc.

We could always hard-code the SAP customer number in the translation map, assuming we build one map for each trading partner. A better way would be to look up the SAP number at runtime based on the trading partner IDs and such other variables as the transaction set, direction, and IDoc types.

We can build this table in the EDI system or in SAP and read it at runtime to identify the SAP partner number during inbound processing or the EDI trading partner ID during outbound processing. Not surprisingly, we're going to build it for Acme Pictures in SAP. We'll use a customer exit to do our conversions before the IDoc interface checks the partner ID.

We look at building and using this custom EDI conversion table in greater detail in later chapters. For now, it's enough to know that during inbound processing it will be read in SAP using key values from the control segment to provide the SAP customer number to field SNDPRN and the SAP logical system to field RCVPRN.

4.4.2 Building an Outbound EDI Interchange

We'll use the outbound INVOIC message to Gordy's Galaxy for this example and assume two IDocs.

1. The IDocs are batched and exported to a file from Acme's SAP system and sent to the EDI system through an RFC to a listening process.

2. The IDoc file is translated in a loop, one at a time, to an ASC X12 810 EDI invoice.

3. Each transaction is packaged into a transaction set by wrapping it with an ST header and SE trailer.

4. A sequential transaction set control number is assigned to each ST transaction in the batch.

5. The transaction sets are then packaged into one group by wrapping them in a GS functional header and GE trailer.

6. A group control number is assigned to the GS-GE group by reading and incrementing the last number used stored in a group control ID table in the EDI system database.

7. The group is packaged into one interchange by wrapping it in an ISA header and IEA trailer envelope.

8. An ISA interchange control ID is assigned to the envelope. The last ISA control number used for an outbound Gordy's interchange is read from a table in the EDI system and incremented.

9. The interchange is passed to a communications process for transmission to Gordy's by AS2.

4.5   Summary

We've completed our brief introduction to EDI and have seen that it has a long and interesting history. In spite of the numerous predictions of its imminent demise, it remains a critical part of the world's economic infrastructure, supporting more than 20 million transactions a day.

While the ASC X12 standard grew out of the Berlin Airlift and the push to standardize documents and communications in the transportation industry in the US, the global UN/EDIFACT standard developed out of the need to rationalize international trade.

We went over the structure of sample EDIFACT and X12 messages and saw that while there are differences between them, both are consistent standards for the electronic transmission of business documents based on a data dictionary maintained by committees of experts.

In all this, an understanding of the envelopes is critical. The envelopes are the starting point for both the packaging of an EDI interchange and its processing, regardless of direction or standard for that matter. The envelopes are also key to the relationship between EDI and the IDoc interface through their link to the control segment.

We'll see this in greater detail in the next chapter as we begin our exploration of how EDI will actually work with SAP through IDocs at Acme Pictures.

For Darryl Q, services and standards meant that his writers stayed sober long enough to finish a movie. But for the Cinderella studio he built, services and standards mean an integrated business system built around SAP and fed by EDI. So let's look at the nuts and bolts of how our project team will keep the data flowing seamlessly in and out of SAP.

5 Real-World Business Process Integration with EDI

The US Department of Commerce defines EDI on its website in a typically understated bureaucratic fashion as:

A computerized system that allows linked computers to conduct business transactions, such as invoicing and ordering, over a telecommunications network.

This bare-bones definition misses the boat on standards and on the independence of EDI from communications technology. We could throw the baby out with the bath water and demand a more precise definition for our tax dollars from the bureaucrats at Commerce. But their definition hits the mark in one crucial way: It focuses on the links between remote systems through business transactions created by EDI.

This link is critical. EDI is about relationships enabled by standards that bring together trading partners—and their business processes—into a cooperative exchange. The electronic business documents they exchange are only the tip of the iceberg.

Each PO, shipping order, invoice, or payment is the result of the business process that produced it: the sequence of actions, both automated and manual, taken by both trading partners that impact each other.

At the same time, each transacted document is part of a greater business processing cycle—order-to-cash—that involves both TPs. The processing cycle is only completed after the last document for each partner posts to his business system and completes whatever follow-up processing he requires, such as updates to inventory or AR or AP or to some GL account.

The EDI standard used by the partners doesn't care what computer system runs at either end, nor does it care what data format feeds each system or how the interchanges are transmitted from one to the other.

The key thing is that the partners agree on how the standard is going to be used. One is the buyer, and the other the seller; the buyer drives the relationship and usage of the standard. In EDI, as in life, he who pays the piper calls the tune.

This relationship can have a dramatic impact on the way both the buyer and seller end up doing business with each other, and within their own systems and organizations. We'll see how this can work in the VMI process. But first, let's look at what we need to make this EDI thing work.

5.1   The Basic EDI Interface

A base EDI interface process flow is illustrated in Figure 5.1. This document exchange is at the heart of all EDI processes.

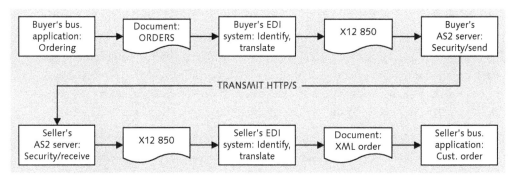

Figure 5.1   Base EDI Interface Process Flow

The business application in the buyer's system issues a purchase order. The PO is exported to a file in an internal format, such as an ORDERS IDoc. The IDoc is sent to the EDI system, which identifies the sender and receiver; business document type; EDI standard (X12 or EDIFACT), version, and transaction; the envelope and translation map; and what happens next.

The EDI system translates the ORDERS IDoc to an X12 850 EDI PO and passes it to the AS2 server, which encrypts the interchange, applies relevant security parameters, and sends it to the seller's AS2 server through an HTTP/S POST.

The seller's AS2 server authenticates the message, decrypts it, extracts the X12 850 and hands it off to the seller's EDI system, which runs the same identification steps that occurred in the buyer's system. The EDI PO is then translated to an internal customer order data file format and sent into the seller's business system where it posts to an internal customer order.

This is how the business systems at both ends are linked. The key is the X12 EDI standard that both parties use to transfer structured order data between them. The X12 standard mediates between the different file formats used by each business system.

This loosely coupled architecture preserves each partner's independence and binds them in a business relationship that provides the foundation to support extensive customization and rationalization.

5.2   Trading Partner Management

The exchange of documents seems simple enough, doesn't it? But before we can begin building our interfaces, the foundation for the relationship needs to be in place: knowledge of each partner's requirements.

The key points of this knowledge, from Acme's point of view for the VMI process with Gordy's Galaxy of Games & B Flix, are outlined in Figure 5.2.

Trading partner management is a central feature of any EDI system. It lays the ground rules and defines the parameters for the business relationship.

Trading partner management begins with a formal agreement. This usually involves a contract or other document that spells out the relationship and provides technical information about transactions, security requirements, and communications protocols.

This agreement feeds trading partner management in Acme's EDI system. The trading partner is set up with base contact information and an EDI ID number and qualifier that will be linked to Acme's EDI ID and qualifier. Acme can have different EDI IDs and qualifiers for different partners, but we're not going to go there. There are customers who maintain a separate trading partner ID for each transaction, but this only complicates what should be a very simple and straightforward relationship.

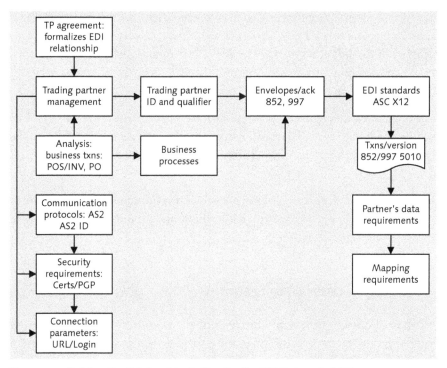

Figure 5.2 Building the Relationship: Setting Up the EDI Partner for VMI

The combination of trading partner ID, Acme EDI ID, and qualifier is the key that identifies the envelopes in Acme's EDI RIM for each transaction that will be exchanged. This key matches the sender and receiver in the ISA interchange and GS group control envelopes:

▶ Inbound: Sender is the trading partner; receiver is Acme's EDI ID.

▶ Outbound: Sender is Acme; receiver is the trading partner EDI ID.

Before we decide what envelopes to set up, we determine what transactions to exchange with the partner. This was analyzed during the blueprint phase. It resulted in a number of spreadsheets and other documents that achieved the following:

▶ Identified required EDI transactions from legacy and from the design work on the business process flows for the new SAP EDI environment

▶ Mapped the EDI transactions to corresponding IDocs and to the business documents that they will match up to in SAP

- Fit these EDI transactions within the process flows that describe the new business environment in the to-be SAP EDI system

For Gordy's Galaxy, we'll exchange EDI transactions within the order-to-cash processing cycle. For now, we're interested in only one VMI transmission—the 852, with its three types of data: daily POS, weekly inventory, and reserved purchase order (RPO) numbers. The to-be process flow for VMI is discussed in greater detail in Chapter 3, Section 3.3.1, VMI Sales Orders.

The VMI process includes the following internal interfaces:

- From EDI to the VMI system
- Between VMI and StoreData and StoreData and VMI
- Between VMI and SAP

We'll need envelopes for an X12 852 transaction. Because Gordy needs Acme to return a 997 functional acknowledgment (FA) for each inbound transaction we receive, we also need envelopes for an outbound 997. So the following envelopes are required for the inbound X12 852, with Gordy as the sender and Acme the receiver:

- Generic inbound ISA interchange
- Inbound GS group for function code PD (POS or INV or RPO) and ASC X12 version 5010
- Inbound ST transaction set for transaction code 852

For the outbound 997, Acme is the sender and Gordy the receiver. We need the following:

- Generic outbound ISA interchange
- Outbound GS group for function code FA (functional acknowledgment) and ASC X12 version 5010
- Outbound ST transaction set for transaction code 997

Our analysis expanded beyond the simple identification of EDI transactions and corresponding IDoc message types in SAP. We also analyzed data from production samples of 852 transactions sent by Gordy in the past few months. This meant weeks of studying Gordy's 852 guidelines and poring over EDI data to identify recurring and occasional patterns of data usage. The goal is to document Gordy's real-world usage so that we can build mapping specifications to support our development of translation maps.

In addition, trading partner setup includes the communications and security agreements with Gordy's Galaxy. This begins with Gordy's mandate that Acme use AS2 for EDI transmissions.

The AS2 setup includes defining an AS2 ID that can be different from the EDI ID number. Each partner has its own AS2 ID that it uses for all its AS2 partners. We could use GLNs or DUNs but whatever we decide to use, it must be documented in the trading partner agreement.

This ID is entered in the partner's AS2 profile and included in the header area of all AS2 transmissions between the two partners.

Connection parameters need to be set up, including the URL endpoint for the HTTP/S POST to the trading partner's AS2 server; user name, password, and any other login parameters required. At the same time, security requirements such as encryption logarithms—in this case, PGP (Pretty Good Privacy)—are entered, and AS2 certificates are exchanged between the partners to authenticate transmissions.

5.3   The Impact of VMI Collaboration through EDI

And so Acme's trading partner relationship with Gordy's Galaxy for the 852 processing cycle is defined and encoded in the RIM. The foundation for the business collaboration is in place.

So what does this give us? VMI, or vendor-managed inventory, is a particularly good example because it is a relationship of trust that grants Acme the power to take over ordering and replenishment for Gordy. Without the close integration between the systems of both partners enabled by EDI, VMI would be impossible to pull off.

As the vendor, Acme is responsible for ensuring that Gordy has the stock it needs in its stores to sell movies on DVD. To do this, Gordy needs to keep Acme informed of how much stock it's selling every day and how much it has left in inventory at the end of each week.

This is done through the 852 POS and inventory data that feed Acme's VMI system so that it can run complex calculations to determine ordering levels for Gordy. This results in VMI POs for Gordy that are sent into Acme's SAP system. These POs post as sales orders and trigger the order-to-cash cycle that stocks Gordy's store and ends with a payment for product to Acme.

The impact of this business processing cycle, which is only possible because of EDI, is profound and far-reaching. Above and beyond the efficiencies that automated data transfers bring to the back office, the cost savings in reduced paperwork, and the speed in which business processing cycles complete, EDI has wrought a significant cultural shift for Gordy's Galaxy.

Take the issue of store-level inventory. Before VMI and EDI, store managers were responsible for controlling inventory in their own stores. There was no such thing as just in time (JIT) delivery of stock. Store managers predicted their own needs as best they could, which meant they often ordered more than they could sell, resulting in higher inventory costs.

VMI enabled by EDI freed store managers of this responsibility. They were able to focus instead on running the store and hiring and firing staff. The enterprise was able to reduce the level of skills required for this role, which resulted in lowering the costs of hiring and maintaining store managers.

5.4   The Role of Acme's EDI RIM

Trading partner management defines the EDI relationship and provides the foundation for the exchange of business documents with Acme's partners. Acme's EDI system—the RIM—provides other services that are supported by trading partner management and are critical to the completion of the business processing cycle enabled by EDI. We look at some of them in the following sections.

5.4.1   Outbound Services

Services used to support outbound processing through the EDI RIM are illustrated in Figure 5.3. We're using an ORDRSP IDoc to X12 855 interface in our illustration of the outbound process.

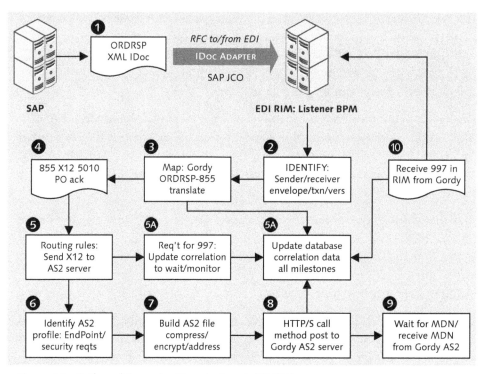

Figure 5.3 Outbound Processing Steps in Acme's EDI RIM

Connecting to SAP—The IDoc Adapter and JCo

An IDoc is exported in XML format to a file on the SAP application server. An RFC is then made to a business process workflow (BP) in the EDI RIM. The export is handled by standard functions in the IDoc interface, including MASTER_IDOC_DIS-TRIBUTE, which applies application link enabling (ALE) checks to the IDoc before calling function EDI_OUTPUT_NEW to export the IDoc through an XML file port and trigger the RFC.

The BP responds because it was identified as the listener process for outbound RFCs in the RIM's IDoc adapter. The workflow picks up the IDoc file from the SAP application server and passes it to the next processing stage in the EDI RIM, a process that identifies the sender and receiver, the message type, and map.

The connection between SAP and EDI is through the RIM's IDoc adapter, which works through methods in Java classes in the SAP Java Connector (JCo).

The IDoc adapter is a Java object and can exchange RFCs with SAP if JCo is installed on the RIM application server and a program name is registered as a service with Windows server. JCo, through the IDoc adapter, is the RFC server for SAP and the EDI RIM.

The RIM's IDoc adapter handles the registration in a configuration screen where we name a program, a tag that identifies the adapter as a service that can send or receive RFCs from SAP. The naming convention we use for this registered program tag is:

```
EDI_<SAP_SYSTEM>_<SAP_CLIENT>
```

In the three systems and clients in Acme's base SAP environment, this name becomes:

```
EDI_DEV_100
EDI_QAS_100
EDI_PRD_100
```

We also need to configure an RFC destination in SAP that identifies the program name we created in the RIM IDoc adapter as a registered server program using Transaction SM59.

JCo is the connecting tissue between the RFC destination and the IDoc adapter. It is a middleware toolkit that provides an application programming interface (API) for exchanging data by RFC communications between SAP and external third-party Java-based applications, such as Acme's EDI RIM.

Different EDI systems provide different tools for accessing JCo methods, but installation boils down to three files:

▶ **sapjco.jar**
Java classes for connecting to SAP in synchronous, asynchronous (tRFC for transactional RFC), and queued (qRFC) modes. We'll be using tRFC for the file-based transfer of EDI documents.

The jar file must be in the Java class path. Acme's EDI RIM stores it in a \sapjco\ directory in the directory it uses to store its .jar files.

▶ **librfc32.dll**
Stored with the EDI RIM's .dll library files in a \sapjco\ directory.

▶ **sapjcorfc.dll**
Stored in the same directory as librfc32.dll.

In addition, a number of Microsoft runtime libraries must be present in the *WINNT\\ system32* directory, if they aren't already there:

- mfc71.dll
- mfc71u.dll
- msvcp60.dll
- msvcp71.dll
- msvcr71.dll
- msvcrt.dll

Complete details for installation and use of JCo are on the CONNECTORS page on the SAP Service Marketplace (*http://service.sap.com/connectors*). You'll need login credentials to get in.

JCo Java classes can also be used to do the following:

- Create direct connections or connection pools to SAP
- Create a repository of BAPI and RFC function metadata to enable the population of function parameters and tables at runtime
- Directly call RFC functions in SAP through the IDoc adapter
- Process and manipulate table and field data
- Handle errors and messages

The EDI team is shielded from all of this because the IDoc adapter in the RIM takes care of it. All we need to do is configure the adapter to connect to SAP and call an inbound function to trigger IDoc processing. This adapter configuration includes the following:

- Setup of the transfer as file-based RFC rather than ALE
- SAP application server name or IP address
- SAP gateway host and service
- SAP system and client
- Login credentials: user name, password, and language
- SAP XML file port. Our naming convention is EDI_IDOC for all ports in all environments and clients.
- Registered server program ID: EDI_DEV_100

▸ Name of listener BP called by the SAP RFC server when it triggers the RIM during export of IDocs.

▸ Parameters such as maximum number of connections and timeout.

▸ RFC function module to call for inbound IDocs: `EDI_DATA_INCOMING`

Configuration options are fed as parameters to the JCo class methods called by the IDoc adapter at runtime. We don't have to do any coding to make this happen. The adapter and JCo work together to open up the pipe between SAP and the EDI RIM.

Identification and Application of Standards

Before the EDI system can translate our ORDRSP IDoc to an X12 version 5010 855 PO Acknowledgment for Gordy's Galaxy, it needs to know what it's dealing with. The RIM already knows that the file came from SAP and that it's an IDoc. It needs three crucial pieces of information:

▸ EDI sender (Acme) and receiver IDs (Gordy's Galaxy)

▸ EDI standard (X12), version (5010), and transaction (855)

▸ The X12 ST envelope, the first to be called in the enveloping process

Control data for the IDoc are held in the control segment EDI_DC40. Key fields for identifying the ST envelope are RCVPRN (SAP receiving partner), which can be mapped to the EDI receiver ID, and IDOCTYP (IDoc Basic Type), which can be linked to the EDI transaction code.

We also need to pass the EDI sender and receiver partner IDs to complete identification of the ST envelope. We'll pass these two values in the fields SNDLAD (EDI sender ID) and RCVLAD (EDI receiver ID) of the IDoc control segment EDI_DC40. We got these from a look-up table during IDoc processing in SAP, as we will see in Chapter 7, Section 7.2.4.

Identifying the ST envelope gives us the translation map and leads to the GS and ISA envelopes, each of which provides additional information that helps move the process along.

Translation

The IDoc is translated at the transaction level. While more than one IDoc per trading partner can be processed by the RIM, they are translated one at a time in a loop.

During the translation loop through each IDoc, the map writes key document data such as IDoc number and SAP document number—the PO and sales order number for an outbound ORDRSP-855 translation—to a correlation table in the EDI system database, one value per correlation record. If the translation fails, these values are not written to the correlation table, although an error record is. In fact, every key milestone in the IDoc's processing cycle through the RIM is recorded in the correlation table.

This correlation table is used by the EDI support team to find transactions and business documents that have been processed by the RIM for auditing, reporting, and troubleshooting in production.

The map is developed in a mapping tool included with the integration system and is specific to Gordy's Galaxy.

The mapping tool comes with a database of EDI standards that provide the metadata it needs to build maps. Once imported into the mapping tool, the EDI structures can be exported as XML Schema (XSD), DTDs, EDIFECS ECS, Sterling DDF, and other metadata formats for use in custom programs or other mapping and XML development tools.

The IDocs come out of SAP in a variety of ways, as we saw in Chapter 3, Section 3.1.2, Let's Get Technical: A More Intimate Look at the RIM, in our discussion of mapping and IDoc metadata.

Completed maps are checked into the RIM and are available for use in a translation object as a service in a BP. The translation service is a Java object that is described and consumed through BPML code and is connected to other Java services in a process flow. The relationships between each object, the data that pass between them, and logical conditions that may be applied to program flow through XPath evaluations are spelled out in the BPML code.

At runtime, the BPML triggers execution of the BPM one service at a time, in the sequence, and according to the conditions, defined in the BPML.

Enveloping

Translation is intertwined with enveloping and driven by logic in the map and in BPML and Java code.

The identification of the ST envelope leads to the identification of the map. This triggers translation of the IDoc file in a loop, one transaction at a time, and the application of the ST-SE envelope. As packaging of each transaction set is completed, the GS functional group and ISA interchange envelopes are identified and applied.

As enveloping proceeds and control numbers are applied to each envelope level, the correlation table is updated with control and status data about the transaction, group, and interchange, one value per correlation record, along with date and timestamps and other values, including the following:

- Sending EDI partner ID and qualifier
- Receiving EDI partner ID and qualifier
- ISA-IEA envelope control number
- GS-GE envelope control number, function code PR, and EDI version 00510
- ST-SE control number and transaction set code 855

The system updates correlation data at every event during the processing flow for each interface, regardless of direction. It stores complete end-to-end control and status data and pointers to every document generated or processed for every interface, from transmission to translation to receipt of the 997 acknowledgment. We will look at how we can use correlation data to provide status information for monitoring our EDI interfaces in SAP.

Functional Acknowledgment

Creation of the GS-GE group envelope during construction of our outbound 855 triggers insertion of a record in the correlation table telling the system that a 997 acknowledgment is expected within a set time limit—48 hours for Acme's X12 interfaces, which is more than enough time to indicate a problem with the interchange at the receiver's end.

Acme expects Gordy to send back the following details about its receipt of the EDI transmission:

- Group control ID and function code for Acme's outbound 855
- Date and time transmission received by Gordy
- Number of transaction sets in the group
- Transaction set ID for each business document in the interchange

- ▶ Status codes reporting whether or not the group and its transaction sets were accepted, partially accepted, or rejected

A 997 does not confirm successful translation or posting of the 855 PO Acknowledgment to Gordy's business system.

Routing, Communications, and Security

Routing rules are applied through a BP that passes the translated X12 855 to Acme's AS2 server for transmission to the trading partner. The AS2 server is a set of services in Acme's RIM accessed through workflow that are implemented in BPML, just like all other BPs in the system.

The AS2 server includes such services as the following:

- ▶ AS2 profile management
- ▶ Building AS2 messages from EDI and other documents
- ▶ HTTP client and server adapters
- ▶ Encrypting EDI messages and decrypting AS2 messages
- ▶ Building and parsing AS2 message header data
- ▶ Synchronous and asynchronous send of MDNs
- ▶ AS2 duplicate message checking and error handling
- ▶ File management and database lookups
- ▶ AS2 mailbox creation and support

The BP that passes EDI to the AS2 server reads the AS2 ID from a table in the EDI database that maps it to the EDI trading partner ID. The AS2 ID points to an AS2 profile that includes such information as:

- ▶ AS2 ID
- ▶ End point URL for the AS2 HTTP/s method post call
- ▶ EDI standards and data types being exchanged
- ▶ SSL settings and cipher strength
- ▶ Certificates used to enforce security provided by the trading partner
- ▶ Encryption and signing protocols and algorithms
- ▶ Delivery mode, which is synchronous for all of Acme's interfaces

- ▸ Requirement and delivery mode for an MDN

- ▸ Response timeout values

The AS2 server builds the AS2 message by encrypting the EDI interchange and prefixing it with a text header that includes transmission and disposition details. Listing 5.1 shows an example of an AS2 text header.

```
Host:99.999.9.999:5070
User-Agent:EDI AS2 server
Date:Thu, 2 Dec 2008 21:15:13 GMT
From:NimbyNnNM
AS2-Version:1.1
AS2-From:9998888999001
AS2-To:9999888888001
Subject:EDIINTDATA Batch [#444444]
Message-ID:<20081202161510CEB9999X@9999888888001>
Disposition-Notification-To:NimbyNnNM
Disposition-Notification-Options:signed-receipt-protocol=
optional,pkcs7-signature; signed-receipt-micalg=optional,
sha1
Content-Type:application/pkcs7-mime; smime-type=enveloped-
data; name="smime.p7m"
Content-Disposition:inline; filename="smime.p7m"
Content-Length:1707
URI:/b2bhttp/inbound/as2
```

Listing 5.1 AS2 Message Text Header

Most of this is self-explanatory. The host is the IP address of the sending AS2 system. The sender and receiver are both AS2 IDs linked to the EDI trading partner IDs in a lookup table. The URI identifies a directory in the target AS2 server where the transmitted file will be deposited.

The disposition lines tell the receiving system that a notification receipt—an MDN (message disposition notification)—is expected. They also provide send options for the receipt such as security requirements and file name for the MDN.

Acme's AS2 server sends the message through an HTTP/S Post call to Gordy's server. The post method transmits the encrypted message and triggers a service in Gordy's AS2 server that picks up the file and kicks off its own internal processing.

An MDN is immediately returned to Acme by AS2 to acknowledge receipt of the message in Gordy's system. When the AS2 message is decrypted and the GS envelope identified, and the 855 is verified, a 997 is generated and sent back to Acme's RIM where it updates correlation with a date and time stamp that completes the outbound process.

5.4.2 Inbound Services

We'll use an 850 customer PO to ORDERS IDoc interface to illustrate services that support inbound processing, outlined in Figure 5.4.

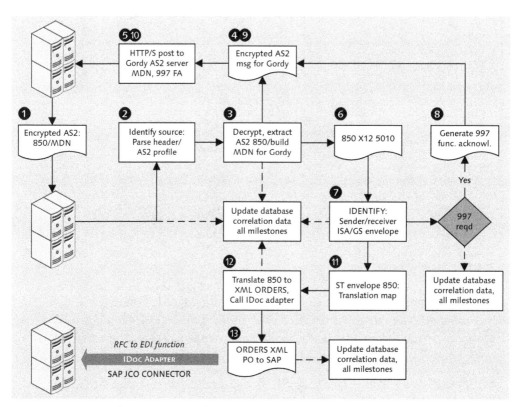

Figure 5.4 Inbound Services in the EDI RIM

Communications, Security, and Routing

Acme's AS2 server receives an encrypted message carrying an 850 purchase order from Gordy's AS2 server by HTTP/S Post. This triggers a BP in the RIM that applies AS2 server services that does the following:

- Parses the AS2 message header and identifies the sender and receiver and an AS2 profile
- Checks that the sender and message type match a valid certificate
- Identifies MDN requirements for the sender
- Confirms that the incoming AS2 message ID isn't a duplicate
- Generates and send an MDN to Gordy by AS2
- Updates correlation data with details of the transmission and the MDN

The MDN is sent to Gordy before the message is processed and the 850 PO extracted. It's an electronic handshake that tells the remote partner that its AS2 message has been received.

The EDI sender and receiver IDs are identified through a link to the AS2 IDs when the message is decrypted and the EDI transaction extracted. The server knows from the AS2 profile that it will hand off the decrypted EDI transaction to another BP that will de-envelope and translate it.

De-enveloping: Identification and Application of Standards

De-enveloping services are invoked to identify the EDI standard and transaction—ASC X12 850—and to strip away the envelopes for translation, as discussed in Chapter 4, Section 4.4.2, Unwrapping an Inbound EDI Interchange.

The interchange is first identified as an X12 message. From the standard, it knows that the first envelope is an ISA. It reads the sender and receiver IDs and qualifiers, strips away the ISA IEA interchange envelope, and identifies the GS-GE group envelope.

The service gets the function code and X12 version from the GS header—PO for purchase order—which leads to the ST transaction set envelope and the map. But before the transaction sets are translated, the interchange must be acknowledged.

As each envelope is identified and stripped away, the correlation table is updated with key EDI control and processing data:

- Sending and receiving EDI partner numbers and qualifiers, as well as the ISA control number
- GS-GE envelope control number, function code PO, and X12 version 005010

▶ ST-SE control number, envelope transaction code 850, and linked IDoc message and basic type ORDERS.ORDERS05

▶ Map to call for the 850 to ORDERS XML IDoc translation

Functional Acknowledgment

The inbound GS group envelope identifies the need to send a 997 functional acknowledgment when a transaction is received. Gordy expects a 997 within six hours of every 850 it sends and this requirement is identified when the GS envelope is unwrapped in Acme's EDI RIM.

The 997 is generated after all transaction sets in the inbound 850 interchange have been identified and tested for syntax. The number of transactions in the interchange is pulled from the GE group trailer and the ST control IDs are read as the transactions sets are unwrapped for translation. At the same time, this control and processing status data are inserted into the correlation table.

The 997 provides Gordy with the following details about the inbound 850: PO interchange:

▶ Group control number for the inbound 850

▶ Date and time that the 997 was generated

▶ Group function code (PO) for the inbound 850

▶ Number of transaction sets in the group

▶ Transaction code 850 for the transaction sets in the group

▶ Status codes reporting if the group and transaction sets were accepted, partially accepted, or rejected by the syntax checks in Acme's EDI RIM

The 997 FA does not imply that any transaction was successfully translated or that translated documents posted to Gordy's business system.

Application errors in the receiving business system are handled by other EDI transmissions that report application problems to the sender, by phone calls between the EDI teams or business users, by troubleshooting in the receiving EDI or business systems, or some combination of these.

The segments in the 997 that Acme returns to Gordy are listed in Table 5.1.

Seq	ID	Segment Description	Usage	Repeat
010	ST	Transaction set header	M	1
020	AK1	Functional group response header	M	1
AK2 Loop			O	999999
030	AK2	Transaction set response header	O	1
020	AK5	Transaction set response trailer	M	1
030	AK9	Functional group response trailer	M	1
040	SE	Transaction set trailer	M	1

Table 5.1 The X12 997 Version 5010 that Acme Sends to Gordy

The AK1 segment contains the following data elements:

▸ 0479: Data element AK101. Inbound transaction function code. PO for the 850 purchase order.

▸ 0028: Data element AK102. Group control number for incoming 850.

The AK2 loop stores transaction set response information. Not every partner sends these data. Acme and Gordy do, which simplifies tracking the response to individual EDI transactions.

AK2 is a loop and can occur multiple times. But each of its two segments occurs only once. The AK2 header contains the following data elements:

▸ 0143: Data element AK201. Transaction set identifier code: 850 for the incoming customer PO being acknowledged.

▸ 0329: Data element AK202. Transaction set control number identifies the specific 850 transaction set being acknowledged.

The AK5 trailer segment includes the following data elements:

▸ 0717: Data element AK501. Transaction set acknowledgment code. Reports on syntax check on 850 transaction in the EDI RIM. Values:

　▸ A = Accepted

　▸ E = Accepted but errors noted

　▸ R = Rejected

- 0718: Data element AK502. Transaction set syntax error code. Identifies syntax errors if 0717 = R or E in current transaction.

The AK9 segment carries status information about the interchange. Acme uses four data elements:

- 0715: Data element AK901. Function group acknowledgment code. Reports status of syntax check on group in the EDI RIM. Values:

  - A = Accepted
  - E = Accepted but errors noted
  - R = Rejected

- 0097: Data element AK902. Number of transaction sets in group.
- 0123: Data element AK903. Number of transaction sets received from count of transactions de-enveloped.
- 0002: Data element AK904. Number of accepted transactions from the syntax check of transaction sets during de-enveloping.

Translation

Translation is at the transaction level in a loop, one document at a time, in the same sequence that the transaction sets occur in the functional group.

The translation service calls the map, and each X12 850 is converted to an ORDERS IDoc one transaction set at a time. Each newly translated IDoc is appended to the bottom of the batch.

The correlation table is updated with the inbound customer PO number. The IDoc number is not inserted into correlation during inbound processing because the IDoc number has not been assigned by SAP yet. It's only assigned when SAP saves it to the IDoc database.

Inbound Connection to SAP—The IDoc Adapter and JCo

When all transactions have been translated by the map and the translation service, another BP is called to invoke the services required to move the IDoc file into SAP.

A file adapter service moves the IDoc file to an inbound directory on the SAP application server. The IDoc adapter then swings into action. It logs on to SAP through

JCo and calls function EDI_DATA_INCOMING, the starting point of the IDoc's journey through the IDoc interface.

The IDoc adapter manages the connection and logon to SAP and calls the inbound RFC-enabled function through a number of JCo classes:

▶ Connection: Works through client and server classes to connect to SAP. Uses parameter information from attributes and relies on a number of other classes to maintain the connection, set traces, manage throughput, return errors, and break the connection.

▶ Attributes: Provides parameters required to log in to SAP.

▶ Function template: Gets all metadata and import, export, and table parameters for RFC-enabled functions from SAP.

▶ Function: Represents an RFC function module in SAP with metadata, import, export, and table parameters provided by the function template.

These classes, their constructors and methods are fully documented in the */docs* directory of the archive containing the JCo .jar and .dll files.

5.4.3   Archiving EDI Data

In a perfect world, everything always works perfectly. But since we don't live in a perfect world, sometimes things go wrong no matter how well we plan.

That's why we archive. The RIM needs to be set up to archive EDI files. Because archiving is not implemented as a service, we must develop a generic archiving BP that can be called by outbound and inbound process flows at both the pre-translation and post-translation stages.

It's not just about the auditors, although they do demand it. IDocs and EDI messages are business documents with a lot of money riding on them.

Archiving is required for production support. The EDI support team can't do its job without it. There will always be situations when they need to dig up an EDI transmission or find a 997 to resolve a production problem or answer a customer or user question.

Good archiving means that it's easy to find stuff after it's been archived. We need simple naming conventions for the archive directories that make it easy for even the most technophobic AR clerk to find data when he needs to.

Forget about nodes and numbers and exotic extensions that don't allow you to search using a simple tool like Windows search. We want to make life as easy as we can for everybody else.

The naming convention for all archived EDI files at Acme will be:

<TradingPartnerID>_<EDITxn>_<Date_Time>_<WorkflowID>.txt

For example:

9999888888001_850_20081202_210233_498786.txt

The naming convention for all archived IDoc files will be:

<SAPPartner>_<MesType>_<Date_Time>_<WorkflowID>.txt

For example:

GRDY01_INVOIC_20081202_210233_498786.txt

Both sort archived files by partner ID and transaction or message. This naming convention assumes that our BPs will be tagged by Acme's EDI RIM with a workflow ID for monitoring and troubleshooting.

Archive folders include direction and date in their naming convention. The convention for naming archive folders will be:

\Archive\<DIR>\<TYPE>\<CCYY>\<MM>\<DD>

The archived files will be saved in the lowest folder level DD, as in these examples:

\Archive\IB\EDI\2013\12\02
\Archive\IB\IDOC\2013\12\02
\Archive\OB\IDOC\2013\12\02
\Archive\OB\EDI\2013\12\02

The archiving BP is invoked by both outbound and inbound translation processes. Data for construction of the file and directory names for the pre-translation and post-translation archives is passed from the calling BP, regardless of direction. The folder and file names are built on the fly using XPath statements.

XPath is also used to apply rules to determine the direction and interface of the message. The system date is pulled and concatenated by XPath into the directory and file name. XPath is also used to concatenate other data elements into path and file names such as constants, transactions, IDocs, and BP workflow IDs.

The archive folder path is built only once each day, the first time that a file hits the system and is archived. After the file name is built, a file system adapter is called to write the EDI or IDoc file to the DD directory for the date that the file is processed.

5.5 Reporting EDI Status to SAP

SAP provides a handy tool for reporting status information about processing milestones for outbound IDocs in an external EDI system back to SAP: the STATUS IDoc.

The STATUS IDoc—message type STATUS with basic type SYSTAT01—is used to update outbound IDocs in SAP with a new status record for key processing milestones in the EDI system.

Because STATUS is an IDoc, a status interface is processed with the same EDI RIM interface services used for all other IDocs.

Our first decision is the EDI milestones that we want to capture. We'll begin with the success or failure of the translation step. Later, we may want to add successful receipt of MDN or the 997. This last requires capturing data during outbound processing of an IDoc through the RIM that can be read during inbound 997 processing.

We will discuss requirements for a 997 STATUS interface here, but will stop short of a full-scale design.

5.5.1 SAP Status Codes

First some background about the status interface. SAP reserves a number of status codes for reporting the success or failure of outbound IDoc processing in a third-party EDI system. The codes reference EDI events—processing milestones—for the IDoc through the EDI system.

The status interface can capture the results of these processing milestones and bring them into SAP to update the outbound IDoc and make them part of its processing history as detailed in its control segment and status records.

Table 5.2 lists the SAP status codes reserved for the EDI system.

Status Code	Code Description
04	Error within control information of EDI subsystem
05	Error during translation
06	Translation OK
07	Error during syntax check
08	Syntax check OK
09	Error during interchange handling
10	Interchange handling OK
11	Error during dispatch
12	Dispatch OK
13	Retransmission OK
14	Interchange acknowledgment positive
15	Interchange acknowledgment negative
16	Functional acknowledgment positive
17	Functional acknowledgment negative
22	Dispatch OK, acknowledgment still due
23	Error during retransmission
24	Control information of EDI subsystem OK
36	Electronic signature not performed (timeout)
40	Application document not created in receiving system
41	Application document created in receiving system

Table 5.2 Status Codes for Outbound Processing of IDocs in the EDI RIM

The control segment holds the most recent status recorded against the IDoc, and the status record stores every status captured throughout the IDoc's lifecycle, representing each processing phase from creation to the endpoint.

For inbound IDocs, the endpoint is status 53—*Application document posted*. It means that the business document represented by the IDoc has been created successfully in SAP. An ORDERS IDoc, for example, successfully created an SAP sales order.

We can define our own endpoint for outbound IDocs using a status interface. The endpoint for Phase 1 of the Acme implementation will be the successful translation of an IDoc to an EDI message. The following status codes and messages will get us there:

- 05: Translation failed for ISA <ISAControlNumber> for TP <ReceiverTradingPartnerID>.
- 06: Translation OK for ISA <ISAControlNumber> for TP <ReceiverTradingPartnerID>.

We'll know if the translation was successful by looking at the IDoc status code in any of the IDoc monitoring tools such as BD87 or WE02.

If the control segment status equals 06, we only need to confirm that the X12 interchange was transmitted to the trading partner. If the status equals 05, we know that there's an error in the translation that needs to be investigated.

When we implement the 997-STATUS interface, the endpoint will be the successful receipt of the FA from the partner's EDI system. The following status codes and messages will get us there:

- 16: OK. 997 recv'd for Txn set <TransactionSetID> Group <GroupControlID> with status A (Accepted).
- 17: Error. 997 recv'd for Txn set <TransactionSetID> Group <GroupControlID> with status R (Rejected).

The status interface is a custom process driven by our map between the outbound and STATUS IDocs. We can send SAP any text message that we choose. To send the custom messages that we're proposing, we need to do three things:

- Create two custom messages in SAP with two parameters each. We use standard message class IDOC_ADAPTER, which is designed for IDoc messages. SAP reserves the number range 900 to 999 for customer messages, so we begin with 900.
- Map the message class and message number to the status IDoc.
- Map the ISA control number and trading partner ID to parameter fields in the STATUS IDoc.

5.5.2 Creating Custom Messages

You create the custom messages in the SAP Repository (Transaction SE80) by following these steps.

1. Select REPOSITORY INFORMATION SYSTEM and click EDIT OBJECT to open the OBJECT SELECTION dialog. Select the MORE tab.

2. Select MESSAGE CLASS and enter "IDOC_ADAPTER", as shown in Figure 5.5. Click EXECUTE.

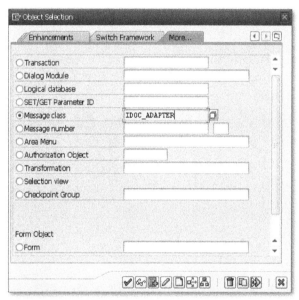

Figure 5.5 Custom Messages Are Created in Message Class

3. Click the MESSAGES tab, and select menu option MESSAGE CLASS • DISPLAY • CHANGE to turn on editing.

4. Press ⌈Ctrl⌉+⌈End⌉ to get to the end of the number range in the EDIT MESSAGES screen. This takes you to message 999. Scroll up to 900.

5. Enter the following text into message 900. The & (ampersand) character tells SAP to insert a parameter variable:

   TRANSLATION OK FOR ISA & FOR TP &

6. Enter the following into message 901:

   TRANSLATION FAILED!

7. Since you're here, also enter custom messages for a future 997 status interface into message numbers 902 and 903 (Figure 5.6):

OK: 997 RECV'D FOR TXN SET & GROUP & WITH STATUS A (ACCEPTED)

ERROR. 997 RECV'D FOR TXN SET & GROUP & WITH STATUS R (REJECTED)

Message class	IDOC_ADAPTER	Activ		

Attributes | Messages

Mess...	Message short text	Self-explan...	
900	Translation OK for ISA & for TP &	☑	
901	Translation Failed!	☑	
902	OK: 997 recv'd for Txn set & Group & with Status A (Accepted)	☑	
903	Error: 997 recv'd for Txn set & Group & with Status R (Rejected)	☑	

Figure 5.6 Our Custom Messages in Message Class IDOC_ADAPTER

8. Save the messages, and SAP prompts for a transportable workbench request for each new message in IDOC_ADAPTER. Assign the new messages to a transport request, and you're done.

5.5.3 Mapping the STATUS IDoc

For the translation status, we'll build a generic STATUS IDoc map that transfers data from the control segment of any outbound IDoc (EDI_DC40) to the control and data segments of the STATUS IDoc. This map won't translate any of the data segments of the outbound IDoc.

The structure of the STATUS IDoc includes a control segment (EDIDC) and one data segment (E1STATS) that can be repeated up to 6,500 times. Table 5.3 defines the IDoc structure.

Segment	Description	Usage	Repeat
EDIDC	Control segment for IDoc version 3	M	1
E1STATS	CA-EDI: Status record	M	6500

Table 5.3 Structure of the STATUS IDoc

All fields in the E1STATS segment hold reference information or message data and parameters. Table 5.4 details the segment's fields.

Pos	Field	Data Element	Description
01	TABNAM	EDI_TABNA3	IDoc table name
02	MANDT	MANDT	SAP client number
03	DOCNUM	EDI_DOCNUC	Outbound IDoc number
04	LOGDAT	EDI_LOGDAT	Date of status information
05	LOGTIM	EDI_LOGTIM	Time of status information
06	STATUS	EDI_STATUS	Status of outbound IDoc
07	UNAME	EDI_UNAME	User name
08	REPID	EDILREPID	ABAP program name
09	ROUTID	EDI_ROUTID	Name of called subroutine
10	STACOD	EDI_STACOD	Status code
11	STATXT	EDI_STATX_	Text message for status code
12	SEGNUM	IDOCSSGNUC	SAP segment number reported on
13	SEGFLD	EDILSEGFLD	Segment field reported on
14	STAPA1	EDILSTAPA1	Status message parameter 1
15	STAPA2	EDILSTAPA2	Status message parameter 2
16	STAPA3	EDILSTAPA3	Status message parameter 3
17	STAPA4	EDILSTAPA4	Status message parameter 4
18	REFINT	IDOCSRFINT	EDI control ID
19	REFGRP	IDOCSRFGRP	EDI group control ID
20	REFMES	IDOCSRFMES	EDI transaction/message control ID
21	ARCKEY	IDOCSARKEY	Archive link key to file in 3rd party archive
22	STATYP	EDI_SYMSTY	Message type (A, W, E, S, I)
23	STAMQU	EDI_STAMQU	Status message qualifier
24	STAMID	EDI_STAMID	Status message ID
25	STAMNO	EDI_STAMNC	Status message number

Table 5.4 Fields for Segment E1STATS

The STATUS map populates many of these fields with data from the outbound IDoc control segment.

First we populate the inbound STATUS control segment so that it will pass IDoc interface checks in SAP. Without the correct values in the control segment, the STATUS IDoc will fail when it hits SAP.

Table 5.5 details the mapping requirements for the STATUS control segment. All values are pulled from the control segment (EDI_DC40) of the outbound IDoc or are hard coded. In some cases, receiver fields in the outbound IDoc control segment are mapped to sender fields in the inbound STATUS IDoc control segment.

Source IDoc	STATUS	Comments
MANDT	MANDT	SAP target client
2	DIRECT	Direction 2 = Inbound. Hard-code.
SYSTAT01	IDOCTYP	IDoc basic type for STATUS. Hard-code.
STATUS	MESTYP	IDoc Logical message type STATUS. Hard-code.
RCVPOR	SNDPOR	OB receiver to IB sender port—EDI_IDOC in all clients and systems
RCVPRT	SNDPRT	OB receiver to IB sender partner type
RCVPFC	SNDPFC	OB receiver to IB sender partner function
RCVPRN	SNDPRN	OB receiver (SAP customer) to IB send partner
SNDPOR	RCVPOR	OB sender to IB receiver port
SNDPRT	RCVPRT	OB send to IB receiver partner type
SNDPFC	RCVPFC	OB sender to IB receiver partner function
SNDPRN	RCVPRN	OB sender (SAP Logical System) to IB receiver partner

Table 5.5 Mapping of OB EDI_DC40 to IB SYSTAT01 Control Segment

Table 5.6 details mapping requirements for the E1STATS segment. All values are pulled from the EDI_DC40 control segment of the outbound IDoc, the EDI envelopes, or are hard-coded.

Source/Data	STATUS	Comments
EDI_DS40	TABNAM	SAP IDoc status record table name. Hard-code.
MANDT	MANDT	SAP target client
DOCNUM	DOCNUM	IDoc number of outbound IDoc
06	STATUS	If translation OK, 06, else 05. From map.
EDISYS	REPID	Processing program identified as EDI system. Hard-code.
ISACtrlNo	STAPA1	ISA interchange control number, from enveloping data for outbound transaction
EDI Receiver ID	STAPA2	EDI partner ID for receiver, from enveloping data for outbound transaction
ISACtrlNo	REFINT	ISA interchange control number from enveloping data for outbound transaction
GSCtrlNo	REFGRP	GS group control number from enveloping data for outbound transaction
STCtrlNo	REFMES	ST transaction set control number from enveloping data for OB transaction
S	STATYP	If status = 06, S (Success), else E (Error). Map.
SAP	STAMQU	Origin of OB message: SAP. Hard-code.
IDOC_ADAPTER	STAMID	SAP message class for IDocs. Hard-code.
900	STAMNO	Custom SAP message number: if status = 06, 900, else 901. Map.

Table 5.6 Mapping the SYSTAT01 E1STATS Segment

These mapping parameters will build one populated STATUS IDoc type for each outbound IDoc that was translated, or not, to an X12 transaction during outbound processing.

The message class in STAMID and message number in STAMNO will pull our custom SAP messages into the status record of the outbound IDoc. The parameter values in STAPA1 and STAPA2 will replace the ampersand (&) character in the status record message in BD87 or any of the other SAP tools that display the IDoc.

The following updates also occur to the outbound IDoc in SAP:

▶ The status code in field E1STATS-STATUS updates the STATUS field in the control segment (table EDIDC) and the status record (table EDIDS) of the outbound IDoc.

▶ The ISA interchange control number in field E1STATS-REFINT populates the outbound IDoc control segment field EDIDC-REFINT.

▶ The GS group control number in E1STATS-REFGRP plugs into the outbound IDoc control segment field EDIDC-REFGRP.

▶ The ST transaction set control number in E1STATS-REFMES populates field EDIDC-REFMES in the outbound IDoc control segment.

These enveloping values create an explicit link between the outbound IDoc, the SAP business document it encapsulates, and the EDI transaction, group, and interchange sent to the trading partner. This is a valuable tool for monitoring, reporting, and troubleshooting in production.

5.5.4   So How Do We Get the Enveloping Data?

It seems simple enough, doesn't it? The issue is getting at these enveloping data so we can map them. Different EDI systems handle translation, enveloping, and de-enveloping differently. We're making some assumptions about how Acme's EDI RIM handles this critical functionality.

1. A correlation table is updated whenever an IDoc is enveloped, de-enveloped, or translated.

2. IDocs are translated in a loop, one at a time.

3. All data in the source structure are available at runtime when the map is executed. Source data can be processed programmatically before the translation begins to write data to the target structure.

4. The mapping tool supports writing rules or exits to identify translation errors for each outbound IDoc that fails to translate.

5. The mapping tool supports writing rules or exits to read envelope data from the correlation table during translation.

6. The mapping tool also supports writing rules or exits to insert records in the RIM database. We're also assuming that we can build custom tables in the database.

The outbound map will insert the IDoc number for each IDoc successfully translated into the correlation table with a key that identifies the number as an IDoc number. The STATUS map will insert EDI envelope control values from correlation into a custom table in the RIM database: tbl_STATAck. The structure of tbl_STATAck is detailed in Table 5.7.

Seq	Field	Description
010	IDocNum	Number of outbound IDoc that was successfully translated
020	TPID	EDI TP ID for receiving partner of outbound IDoc
030	ISACtrl	ISA interchange control number for EDI transaction built from outbound IDoc
040	GSCtrl	GS group control number for outbound IDoc
050	STCtrl	ST transaction set control number for EDI transaction translated from outbound IDoc
060	FuncCode	GS envelope function code for outbound IDoc
070	TxnCode	EDI transaction code for outbound IDoc
080	Date	Date stamp
090	Time	Timestamp
100	BP_ID	BP ID for translation BP that triggered table insertion

Table 5.7 Structure of Custom Table tbl_STATAck

The STATUS map reads the correlation table through an exit in a rule to identify each translated IDoc number as it loops through each outbound IDoc during creation of the STATUS IDoc. SQL access to correlation is through the IDoc number key:

```
SELECT IDocNum from tbl_correlation
   WHERE IDocKey = <idoc_key_value>
     and value   = <current_IDoc_no>;
```

The same SQL approach is used for every other value that needs to be pulled from correlation:

▶ EDI receiving partner, the trading partner that will receive the outbound transmission and return the inbound 997

- ISA interchange control number for the outbound EDI transmission
- GS group control number for the outbound transmission
- ST transaction set number for the EDI transaction translated from the outbound IDoc
- EDI transaction code
- BP ID for the process that translated the outbound IDoc

These correlation values go into both the STATUS IDoc and the custom table tbl_STATAck.

In the STATUS IDoc, the correlation values are sent back to SAP to update the original outbound IDoc with a *Translation OK* or *Failed* status.

Correlation values inserted into table tbl_STATAck link the inbound 997 to the outbound IDoc number it is acknowledging through the Group control ID of the outbound EDI interchange, which is in the 997. This gives us the connections then to build an inbound STATUS IDoc map that will update the original outbound IDoc in SAP with status information from the 997, closing the EDI circle. This kills two birds with one stone:

1. The STATUS map identifies translated and failed IDocs. Correlation is only updated with IDoc numbers if the translation succeeds.

   If an 810 customer invoice is generated from an INVOIC IDoc, correlation is updated with the invoice number and the IDoc number. If the translation fails, correlation is not updated.

2. The STATUS map creates a link between the invoice that Acme sends to Gordy in the IDoc and the 997 that Gordy sends back.

   The INVOIC IDoc in SAP is updated by Gordy's 997 through the STATUS IDoc as soon as it comes in. The EDI team know that Gordy received the invoice 810.

So what? Imagine a batch of customer invoices. The INVOIC IDocs are translated to 810 transactions, wrapped in a group and an interchange. That interchange is then sent to the customer and an MDN is received.

An hour later, an X12 997 FA is transmitted, translated by the 997-STATUS map, and sent into SAP where it updates the INVOIC IDoc with status 16—*997 received with no errors reported*.

The customer doesn't pay, and its AP department asserts that it did not receive the invoice. But we have an SAP report that checks our IDocs for status 16 (*997 OK*) or 17 (*997 Error*) that Acme's AR department can run for itself. The report tells the department that the invoice was sent, received, and acknowledged.

Before AR had this report, it would call EDI and complain loudly and demand that the invoices be resent. Now the people in AR know that the invoices have been received so they phone their contacts in the customer's AP department and tell them so. The customer's AP folks check with their EDI team and learn that the invoices were indeed received but generated a translation error in their EDI system that forced a minor change to their map.

The fix was tested and put into production, but when they reran the invoice file, it failed because the ISA control number had already been processed, and duplicate checking was turned on. At this point, it was a holiday weekend, everybody was busy, and the invoices fell through the cracks. Stuff happens.

It goes without saying that you'll need to know how your own EDI system and mapping tool works to translate this approach into an actual design.

5.5.5 The Status Interface Business Process Workflow

The status interface will be implemented in a BP workflow that will be called after translation and enveloping is completed in the outbound IDoc process. Every outbound IDoc will return a STATUS IDoc to SAP.

The basic processing steps for the status interface BP are illustrated in the example of an outbound INVOIC IDoc in Figure 5.7.

Two billing documents for Gordy's Galaxy are created in SAP generating two INVOIC IDocs with IDoc numbers 123456788 and 123456789. The IDocs are bundled into a file and exported to the EDI system where they hit the translation step of the outbound process.

IDoc 123456789 translates successfully but 123456788 fails. Gordy's INVOIC-810 map inserts IDoc number 123456789 into the EDI system's correlation table. There is no insert for IDoc 123456788.

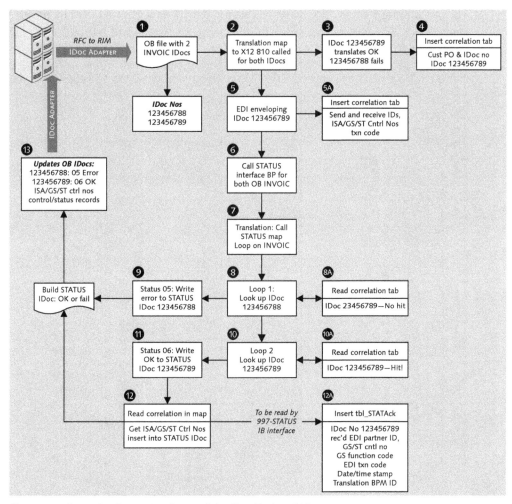

Figure 5.7 Reporting Processing Status of the IDoc Back to SAP

One X12 810 version 5010 EDI transaction comes out of the batch file for IDoc 123456789 and is enveloped. The enveloping process inserts a number of EDI control and status records into the correlation table, including sender and receiver partner ID and envelope control numbers, as described in the discussion of outbound enveloping in Section 5.4.1, subsection Enveloping.

The file containing both the failed and translated IDocs is handed off to a translation service in the status interface BP that maps the outbound INVOIC IDoc file to the STATUS IDoc.

The STATUS map loops through the IDocs one at a time. IDoc 123456788 is the first up. It failed to translate to an 810. Using a mapping rule, the status map reads the correlation table for IDoc 123456788, and there is no hit.

The status map then builds the EDI_DC control segment for the STATUS IDoc from the EDI_DC40 control segment of IDoc 123456788, as described in the mapping specifications in Table 5.5. The values that will be inserted into segment E1STATS are listed in Table 5.8.

Value	Field	Comments
123456788	DOCNUM	Identifies outbound INVOICE IDoc that will be updated by STATUS.
05	STACOD	Error status for translation failure.
EDISYS	REPID	Identifies the RIM as originating program or routine for the status.
E	STATYP	E = Error status.
SAP	STAMQU	Identifies SAP message.
IDOC_ADAPTER	STAMID	Identifies EDI message class.
901	STAMNO	Identifies custom error message number we created in message class IDOC_ADAPTER.
EDI_DS40	TABNAM	IDoc status record table.
100	MANDT	SAP target client number.

Table 5.8 STATUS Values in Segment E1STATS for Failed IDoc

The first STATUS IDoc in the inbound file is now ready to be sent into SAP after the file is completed.

IDoc 123456789 is mapped next. It successfully translated to an 810. The status map reads correlation in a mapping rule for IDoc 123456789 and gets a hit. EDI control data are pulled from the correlation table.

The status map builds the EDI_DC control record for the STATUS IDoc from the EDI_DC40 control segment of IDoc 123456789. The values that it will insert into data segment E1STATS are listed in Table 5.9.

Value	Field	Comments
123456789	DOCNUM	Identifies outbound INVOICE IDoc that will be updated by STATUS.
06	STACOD	Success status for translation OK.
EDISYS	REPID	Identifies the RIM as originating program or routine for the status.
S	STATYP	S = Success status.
SAP	STAMQU	Identifies SAP message.
IDOC_ADAPTER	STAMID	Identifies EDI message class.
900	STAMNO	Identifies custom error message number we created in message class IDOC_ADAPTER.
987456	STAPA1	ISA interchange control number for 810. Replaces first ampersand (&) in message 900.
9998888999001	STAPA2	EDI trading partner ID for Gordy. Replaces second ampersand (&) in message 900.
987456	REFINT	ISA control number for 810. Links IDoc to X12 interchange through control record.
987456	REFGRP	GS control number for 810. Links IDoc to function group through control record.
1	REFMES	ST transaction set control number for 810. Links IDoc to transaction through control record.
EDI_DS40	TABNAM	IDoc status record table.
100	MANDT	SAP target client number.

Table 5.9 STATUS Values in Segment E1STATS for Translated IDoc

At the end of the translation loop through IDoc 123456789, tbl_STATAck is populated with the IDoc and correlation values listed in Table 5.10.

Value	Field	Comments
123456789	IdocNum	Successfully translated IDoc.
9998888999001	TPID	EDI trading partner ID for Gordy.
987456	ISACtrl	ISA interchange control number for 810.
987456	GSCtrl	GS group control number for 810.
1	STCtrl	ST transaction set control number for 810.
IN	FuncCode	GS group function code for invoice.
810	TxnCode	EDI transaction code or message for 810.
20131202	Date	System date in RIM at processing time.
063029	Time	System time in RIM at processing time.
154879	BP_ID	Work flow ID for OB translation BP.

Table 5.10 IDoc and EDI Values in tbl_STATAck for Translated IDoc

The SQL insert is called in a mapping rule after the outbound IDoc has been successfully mapped to the STATUS IDoc:

```
INSERT into tbl_STATAck (IDocNum)
    VALUES (<current_idoc_no>,<recv_tp_id>,<isa_cntl_no>,
            <gs_cntl_no>,<st_txn_cntl_no>,<gs_func_code>,
            <edi_txn_code>,<date>,<time>,<bp_id>);
```

The second STATUS IDoc is appended to the inbound IDoc file, and the file is completed. The file with its two IDocs is then moved to an inbound directory on the SAP application server, and the SAP adapter calls function EDI_DATA_INCOMING. The file is picked up and processed by SAP and IDocs 123456788 and 123456789 are updated with their new status.

5.5.6   The 997 Functional Acknowledgment Interface

Now that custom table tbl_STATAck is populated, we can briefly consider the future inbound 997 FA interface.

We already have our custom table, and if outbound interfaces are set up as described, we'll have the data we need to match the outbound INVOIC IDoc with an inbound acknowledgment, whether that's an X12 997 or an EDIFACT CONTRL Syntax and Service Report message.

We'll need a map to translate 997 (or EDIFACT CONTRL) to a STATUS IDoc for each partner that acknowledges outbound EDI transactions.

For now we're only concerned with Gordy. It acknowledges Acme's outbound X12 transmissions at the transactional level. Its 997 includes the AK2 loop, which stores transaction code and transaction set control numbers for Acme's outbound X12 810.

This simplifies Gordy's 997-STATUS map. When the 997 is received and the map called, a rule or exit will loop through AK2 and read tbl_STATAck for the IDoc number. The SQL read will look something like this:

```
SELECT IDocNum ISACtrl from tbl_STATAck
    WHERE TPID = <997_ISA_send_tp_id>
      and GSCtrl = <997_AK102_gsctrl>
      and STCtrl = <997_AK202_stctrl>
      and FuncCode = <997_AK101_func_code>
      and TxnCode = <997_AK201_txncode>
```

The map then builds the STATUS IDoc, beginning with the EDI_DC control segment with the values listed in Table 5.11.

Value	Field	Comment
100	MANDT	SAP target client. Hard-code.
2	DIRECT	Direction 2 = Inbound. Hard-code.
SYSTAT01	IDOCTYP	IDoc basic type for STATUS. Hard-code.
STATUS	MESTYP	IDoc Logical message type STATUS. Hard-code.
EDI_IDOC	SNDPOR	Sender port. Hard-code.
KU	SNDPRT	Sender partner type. Hard-code.
BP	SNDPFC	Sender partner function. Hard-code.
9998888999001	SNDPRN	EDI send partner ID. The EDI partner ID will be converted to the SAP sold-to partner through a customer exit in the IDoc control segment.
SAPPRD	RCVPOR	SAP logical receiver port. Hard-code.
LS	RCVPRT	Logical system receive partner type. Hard-code.
SAPPRD100	RCVPRN	SAP logical system ID for receive partner. Hard-code.

Table 5.11 STATUS Values in Segment E1STATS for Translated IDoc

The map then plugs the values listed in Table 5.12 into the E1STATS data segment of the SYSTAT01 IDoc type.

Value	Field	Comments
123456789	DOCNUM	Read from tbl_STATAck-IdocNum.
16	STACOD	If 997-AK501 = A (Accepted), then write 16 to target, else write 17 for transaction syntax error.
EDISYS	REPID	Identifies the RIM as originating program or routine for the status.
S	STATYP	If 997-AK501 = A, then write S to target, else write E for error.
SAP	STAMQU	Identifies SAP message.
IDOC_ADAPTER	STAMID	Identifies EDI message class.
902	STAMNO	If 997-AK501 = A, then write 902 (OK) to message number, else write 903 (Error).
987456	STAPA1	ISA interchange control number for 810.
9998888999001	STAPA2	EDI trading partner ID for Gordy from 997.
987456	REFINT	ISA control IB for OB 810 from tbl_STATAck-ISACtrl.
987999	REFGRP	GS control ID for OB 810 from 997-AK102 validated against tbl_STATAck-GSCtrl.
1	REFMES	ST transaction set number for OB 810 from 997 AK202 validated against tbl_STATAck-STCtrl.
EDI_DS40	TABNAM	IDoc status record table.
100	MANDT	SAP target client number.

Table 5.12 STATUS Values in Segment E1STATS for Returned 997

This will update the control and status segments of outbound INVOIC IDoc 123456789 with the status reported for the 810 by Gordy's 997, closing the circle on the IDoc processing cycle, at least as far as transmission goes.

Most customers send acknowledgments at the group level, which means the transaction set control number for the outbound EDI is not available in the 997.

The key here is the group control number, which is unique for each partner, function code (transaction), and version. The SQL read of tbl_STATAck depends on this unique combination. It is enough to pull all the transaction set IDs and IDoc numbers from tbl_STATAck for the function group. The SQL read would look something like this:

```
SELECT IDocNum ISACtrl STCtrl from tbl_STATAck
   WHERE TPID = <997_ISA_send_tp_id>
     and GSCtrl = <997_AK102_gsctrl>
     and FuncCode = <997_AK101_func_code>
     and TxnCode = <If FuncCode = IN, 810, etc>
```

The other issue with group-level acknowledgments is that we don't have transactional level status. So we need to pass the group status to each IDoc as the transaction status, which we'll get from AK901 of the 997.

To do this, we'll write a mapping rule that calls the SQL read and pulls all of the IDocNum, ISACtrl, and STCtrl values from all records linked to the group control number in tbl_STATAck into an array in memory, an internal table in ABAP terms.

The code would then loop through that array to provide E1STATS with the transaction set status that would otherwise come from AK501 of the 997 to build one inbound STATUS IDoc for each outbound ISACtrl, IDocNum, and STCtrl combination.

The problem is that if AK901 returns a status code of E (accepted but errors noted), we have no way of identifying the transaction set that failed syntax test. We have the number of accepted transaction sets in AK904, but this doesn't identify the specific ones that failed.

The critical information that we're trying to collect from this interface is confirmation that the EDI transmission was received by the customer and whether it passed the syntax check. If there was an error, it will be dealt with by the EDI teams, probably over the phone. How to handle this situation will no doubt fuel future discussions about the interface.

The good news is that in a production environment, syntax errors are rare.

5.6   Putting All the Pieces Together

The beauty of a workflow-based system is that it allows us to design a core business processing architecture that leverages reusable, discrete processes to manage routings or transformations for all of Acme's data flows between SAP, the RIM, internal business systems, and external trading partners.

The point of this long and winding sentence is to define a design philosophy: Keep it simple, clean, and consistent. Our core processing model is built on discrete BPs—workflows—defined in BPML that link services together to do a specific job such as communications, routing, translation, archiving, reporting status, sending data to SAP, and so on.

The base architecture separates communications from data processing and translation. Whether inbound or outbound, the processing outline can be summarized in three simple points:

▶ Data transmission

▶ Message identification, routing, and translation

▶ Data transmission

The key to maintaining this simplicity is recognizing the data and their context as they flow through the system. If each of the base BPs that make up this architecture can recognize from the data and the environment the four Ws—who, what, where, and when—of the interface, we'll be able to drop new trading partners into the system by doing four things:

▶ Building a map

▶ Configuring envelopes and other trading partner information

▶ Setting up AS2 or other communications profiles or reference tables

▶ Writing the occasional XPath rule to provide custom processing for a special situation for a particular partner

We can't emphasize strongly enough the importance of maintaining this consistency. EDI is a lynchpin of the enterprise. The vast bulk of business data that will flow into or out of SAP—sales orders, deliveries, invoices, payments, and all of their underlying follow-on processing and postings—depend either directly or indirectly on EDI.

So let's see how it works. We'll put the pieces together and follow the end-to-end process flow between Acme's new SAP-EDI RIM and its most important customer, Gordy's Galaxy of Games & B Flix.

5.6.1   Inbound

The core processes that handle inbound message flow in Acme's RIM are outlined in Figure 5.8.

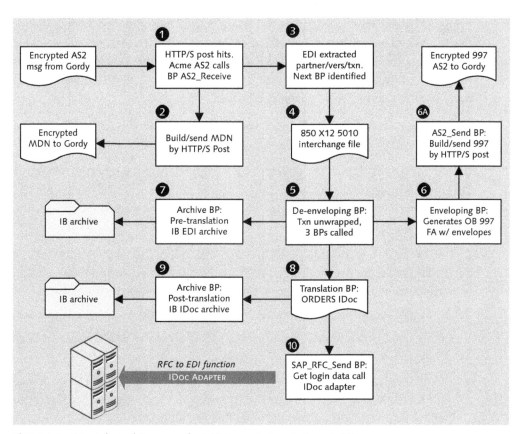

Figure 5.8   Core Inbound Processes for X12 Transmissions in Acme's RIM

The encrypted transmission is sent by Gordy's AS2 server to the AS2 server in Acme's EDI RIM by an HTTP/S Post that triggers BP AS2_Receive. It reads the header, identifies the partner's AS2 profile, and immediately sends an MDN to Gordy's AS2 server to acknowledge receipt of the message.

The AS2 message is decrypted and the de-enveloping BP called. The de-enveloper identifies the format as X12 and uses the EDI sender and receiver IDs and qualifier to get the ISA, GS, and ST envelopes; the X12 version, and the transaction set 850.

De-enveloping then calls three different BPs, not necessarily in sequence. One generates a 997 to Gordy; another calls a pre-translation archiving process; the third calls the translation BP, which in turn calls a post-translation archive before it sends the IDoc into SAP.

The outbound enveloping BP builds a 997 FA in response to the inbound 850, triggered by the acknowledgment flag in the 850's GS group envelope. It identifies the 997 envelopes from the EDI sender and receiver IDs and qualifiers, builds the transaction, and wraps it with ST, GS, and ISA envelopes. The 997 includes the group control number from Gordy's 850 in the AK1 segment and the status of each 850 transaction set de-enveloped in AK5.

Enveloping then calls the AS2_Send workflow to transmit the 997 to Gordy and wait for an MDN response.

Back to the de-enveloper. The envelopes are stripped from the inbound 850 interchange, the translation map is identified, and parameters are collected from the system. Runtime processing data in XML format are then passed along with the EDI file to the follow-up BPs:

1. The archive BP to store the 850 in a pre-translation X12 archive folder using XPath to build the path and file name from the direction, date and time, sending partner, transaction set, and work flow ID number.

2. The translation BP to convert the 850 to an ORDERS.ORDERS05 XML IDoc file.

3. The archive BP from translation to save the IDoc file to the post-translation IDoc archive folder.

4. SAP_RFC_Send to move the IDoc file to an inbound folder on the SAP application server, read login parameters from a custom table, login to SAP, and call the IDoc adapter. Login parameters include the following:

   ▸ Application server, gateway host, and gateway service

   ▸ File port

   ▸ System number and system ID

   ▸ SAP client

   ▸ EDI IDoc user name and password

The IDoc adapter invokes JCo connection classes to log in to SAP and call RFC function `EDI_DATA_INCOMING`, passing the full path and file name of the IDoc file and XML file port. The function confirms that all IDocs in the file are valid. If they are, the file is deleted from the application server. If not, an error is returned and processing stops.

5.6.2 Outbound

The core outbound EDI process flows are outlined in Figure 5.9. It shows a customer invoice, but all outbound transmissions follow the same path.

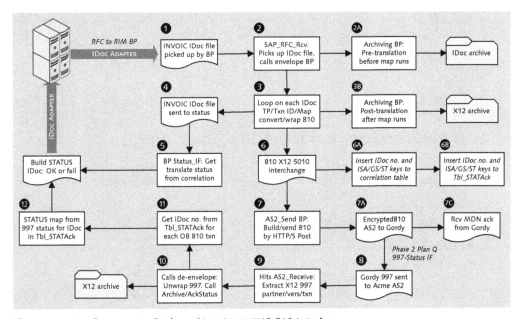

Figure 5.9 Key Processes in Outbound Invoice to X12 810 Interface

It begins when a billing document is created in SAP. An outbound IDoc is generated through message control and exported to an outbound directory on the application server.

BP SAP_RFC_Rcv in the RIM is called through the RFC destination in the XML file port. SAP_RFC_Rcv is the *registered server program* in the RFC destination set up with Transaction SM59, which matches the registered program name in the IDoc adapter in the RIM.

The RFC sends the path and file name of the IDoc file to SAP_RFC_Rcv, which invokes a file system adapter to pick up the IDoc file from the SAP application server.

SAP_RFC_Rcv passes the IDoc file to enveloping, which extracts the IDoc control record to read the following keys:

▶ **RCVPRN**
SAP receiving partner. For the invoice, this is Gordy's bill-to partner in SAP, which is the same as his sold-to number.

▶ **RCVPRT**
Receiving partner type. KU for customer.

▶ **RCVPFC**
Receiving partner function. BP for bill-to partner.

▶ **RCVLAD**
Gordy's receiving EDI partner number, read from a custom table in SAP into the control segment through customer exit code.

▶ **SNDLAD**
Acme's sender EDI partner number, read by the customer exit.

▶ **MESTYP**
Logical message type. INVOIC for the invoice.

▶ **IDOCTP**
IDoc Basic type. INVOIC02.

These values are used, along with direction, to identify and retrieve the envelopes. The ST envelope identifies and runs the map, converting the INVOIC IDoc to an X12 810 version 5010 customer invoice.

The enveloping BP loops through each IDoc, translates it, wraps it in an ST envelope, and assigns a sequential transaction set control number, beginning with 1. Successful translation inserts the IDoc, billing document, ST control numbers, enveloping BP instance ID, and other keys into the correlation table. Unsuccessful translation does not update correlation.

The GS envelope then wraps the translated transaction sets into a group and assigns a group control number, which is inserted along with the BP instance ID into correlation. This is followed by the ISA envelope, which updates correlation with the interchange control number and the BP instance ID.

Archiving is called twice. First the INVOIC file is saved to an outbound pre-translation IDoc archive folder and then the translated 810 interchange is saved to an outbound post-translation X12 archive file and folder.

Enveloping then passes the INVOIC IDoc file to BP Status_IF, which loops through the file and reads correlation for each IDoc number, before mapping the IDoc control segment to a STATUS IDoc.

If a correlation record is found for the IDoc, status code 06—*Translation Successful*—is inserted into a STATUS IDoc. If no correlation record is found, status code 05—*Translation Failed*—is inserted instead. This is the current endpoint for IDoc processing in Acme's new SAP system.

After all IDocs have been translated, BP Status_IF sends the STATUS IDocs into SAP through the IDoc adapter to update the control and status records of the original outbound INVOIC IDoc.

Meanwhile, enveloping calls AS2_Send and hands off the 810 interchange. BP AS2_Send identifies Gordy's AS2 profile (sender and receiver IDs, AS2 endpoint, and so on), encrypts the 810 interchange, and bundles it into an AS2 message with a text header.

It then sends the encrypted AS2 message through an HTTP adapter that hits the endpoint URL in Gordy's AS2 server with an HTTP/S Post method.

Assuming there are no hiccups, the AS2 message triggers a receiving process in Gordy's AS2 server. AS2_Send waits for the MDN, which should come immediately after the message has been received by Gordy's system.

The process is completed when Gordy returns an X12 997 FA referencing the GS and ST transaction set control numbers of the outbound 810 invoice interchange.

The 997 is returned through a normal AS2 inbound process that triggers AS2_Receive and is handed off to de-enveloping.

During a future phase of Acme's Plan Q from Outer Space project, a 997-STATUS interface will be added to feed acknowledgment data to SAP through the STATUS IDoc. Status 16—*Successful receipt of the 997 with no syntax errors*—will then be the endpoint for IDoc processing in SAP.

5.7   Archiving and Deleting IDocs in SAP

One thing we can be sure of in Acme's new SAP EDI system is that we are going to produce a lot of data, particularly if we build the STATUS interface.

The team estimated data volumes for Acme from previous implementations at several other comparable studios that included a STATUS interface for translation and 997 acknowledgment.

The team projected that in the first four weeks after go-live about 1.5 million IDocs would be created with more than 75 million records, including all segments, for a daily average of about 73,000 IDocs. Nearly 40 percent of these were STATUS IDocs, or just under 30,000 a day.

But it doesn't stop there. STATUS IDocs are processed by workflow tasks, each of which creates dozens of records across at least seven workflow tables, including a complete history of every action performed.

Workflow tasks also process a range of IDoc errors. Each time an ORDERS IDoc fails, for example, a task handles the error processing and updates the workflow tables. This means that even a relatively small implementation can quickly accumulate millions of work item records for IDocs, as well as for all the other business objects processed through work flow tasks.

All of this can impact performance of applications that read these tables, particularly SAP Business Workplace Inbox and Outbox, which are often configured to receive or send error messages for failed IDocs and other business processes.

Clearly, there is a need to define an archiving and deletion policy for IDocs and the workflow records that they spawn. We're not going to get into the weeds of policy here, but we are going to look at the tools that we would use to archive and delete IDocs in Acme's SAP system, bearing in mind that we've already decided to archive IDocs files in the EDI RIM.

5.7.1   Archive and Delete

Deleting IDocs from SAP is a two-step process: first you archive, then you delete. Figure 5.10 outlines the overall process in SAP.

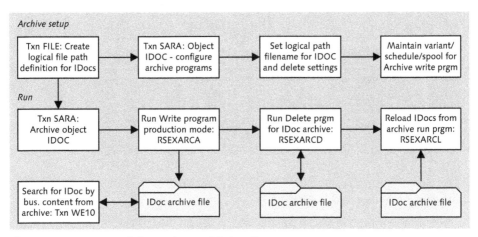

Archive setup

| Txn FILE: Create logical file path definition for IDocs | → | Txn SARA: Object IDOC - configure archive programs | → | Set logical path filename for IDOC and delete settings | → | Maintain variant/schedule/spool for Archive write prgm |

Run

| Txn SARA: Archive object IDOC | → | Run Write program production mode: RSEXARCA | → | Run Delete prgm for IDoc archive: RSEXARCD | → | Reload IDocs from archive run prgm: RSEXARCL |

| Search for IDoc by bus. content from archive: Txn WE10 | ← → | IDoc archive file | | IDoc archive file | | IDoc archive file |

Figure 5.10 Overview of IDoc Archive and Delete Process

The basic rule is that only completed IDocs can be archived. IDocs in an error status can still be reprocessed. This state is recorded in the STATUS field of the control segment and enforced by an archive flag in Transaction WE47, status maintenance. Only the status codes listed in Table 5.13 can be archived.

Status Code	Description
03	Data passed to port OK
12	Dispatch OK
13	Retransmission OK
18	Triggering EDI subsystem OK
31	Error—no further processing
33	Original of an IDoc that was edited
35	IDoc reloaded from archive
38	IDoc archived
40	Application document not created in target system
41	Application document created in target system
53	Application document posted

Table 5.13 IDoc Status Codes that are Valid for Archiving and Deletion

Status Code	Description
68	Error—no further processing
70	Original of an IDoc that was edited
71	IDoc reloaded from archive
73	IDoc archived

Table 5.13 IDoc Status Codes that are Valid for Archiving and Deletion (Cont.)

Configure Archiving and Delete

Archive configuration begins with a logical path and file name, created with client-independent Transaction FILE. First we create the logical path.

1. In the LOGICAL FILE PATH DEFINITION OVERVIEW screen, click NEW ENTRIES to open the OVERVIEW OF ADDED ENTRIES screen.

2. Enter the new logical path name as shown in Figure 5.11. The custom object name should begin with a Z or a Y. Save and the system prompts for a transport request.

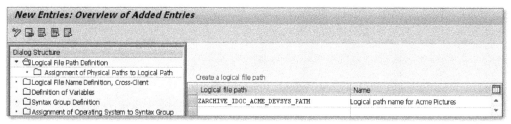

Figure 5.11 Creating a New Logical Path Name for the Archive

3. Next assign an operating system for the archive server and a physical file path to the logical path.

4. Select the logical path name and double-click the ASSIGNMENT OF PHYSICAL PATHS TO LOGICAL PATH folder.

5. Click NEW ENTRIES and select WINDOWS NT from the SYNTAX GROUP dialog. Enter a physical path on the SAP application server for the archive file. Don't forget the <FILENAME> token at the end of the path name. It should look like Figure 5.12.

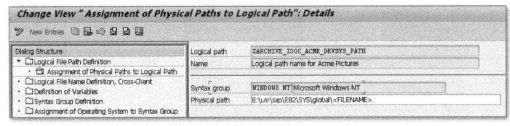

Figure 5.12 Assigning a Physical Path to the Logical Path

6. Next define a logical system file name and link it to the logical path.

7. Double-click the LOGICAL FILE NAME DEFINITION, CROSS-CLIENT folder and click NEW ENTRIES.

8. Enter the following values (as shown in Figure 5.13). Don't forget to save.

   ▶ LOGICAL FILE field: "ZACME_IDOC_DEV"

   ▶ NAME field: "Acme dev archive logical file"

   ▶ PHYSICAL FILE field: "AcmeIDocArchive" (We're hard-coding here but this can be built from system variables that can be replaced at runtime)

   ▶ DATA FORMAT field: "ASC" for ASCII

   ▶ APPLICATION AREA field: "BC" for SAP NetWeaver

   ▶ LOGICAL PATH field: "ZARCHIVE_IDOC_ACME_DEVSYS_PATH" for the link

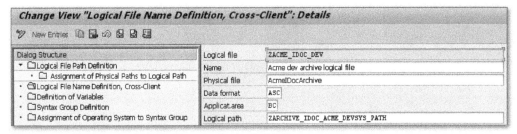

Figure 5.13 Linking a Logical File Name to the Logical Path

Now we link the archive object IDOC to our logical path and filename with Transaction SARA. SAP archives by business object, which for IDocs is, reasonably enough, IDOC. Note the four ACTIONS buttons in Figure 5.14. They correspond to the four programs that archive, delete archived IDocs, read, and manage the archive.

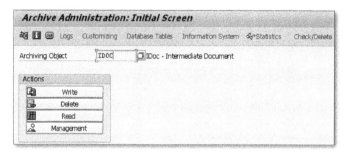

Figure 5.14 Initial Screen for Archiving Transaction SARA

We still need to do a little more configuration.

1. Click CUSTOMIZING and select TECHNICAL SETTINGS from ARCHIVING OBJECT-SPECIFIC CUSTOMIZING in the dialog box that pops up.

2. The CUSTOMIZING VIEW FOR ARCHIVING screen loads. Enter the new logical file name to link the archive object IDOC to the logical path and file name, as illustrated in Figure 5.15.

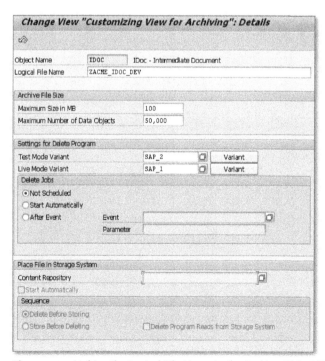

Figure 5.15 Linking the Logical File Name to the Archive Object IDOC

3. You can also set parameters for the archive and delete program in this screen, but leave the defaults as they are.

4. Save. The system prompts for a transport request.

Run Write

The WRITE button triggers ABAP report RSEXARCA. It runs with a variant that defines selection parameters for the archive, a scheduled job, and spool parameters for output of the report generated on completion of the job. The variant (as shown in Figure 5.16) can be used to select IDocs by a variety of parameters common to most IDoc selection programs in SAP.

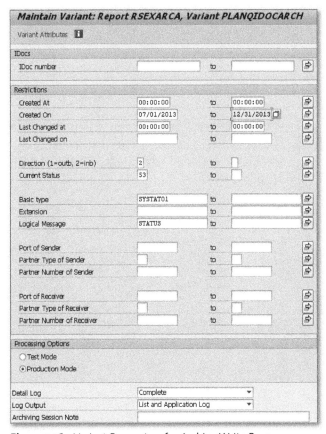

Figure 5.16 Variant Parameters for Archive Write Program

Please note the PROCESSING OPTIONS. TEST MODE will simulate an archive run but will not create any archive file. Only PRODUCTION MODE will create an archived file in the logical directory configured for the archive.

When the variant, schedule, and spool print parameters are configured, the write job is ready to run, as illustrated in Figure 5.17. Click EXECUTE (or press F8) and the archive job will run.

Figure 5.17 Write Is Locked and Loaded and Ready to Run

To check the status of the archive, click the green JOB OVERVIEW button next to ARCHIVE DIRECTORY. It will take you directly to the JOB OVERVIEW screen of the SAP job scheduler (Transaction SM37) where the job report in the print spool will list all IDocs, including the number of control, data, and status segments archived for each IDoc (see Figure 5.18).

Graphical display of spool request 775325 in system E82

```
02/17/2013                              Archiving IDocs

Production Mode: Statistics on Written Data Objects


Archive File Key                  000920-001IDOC
Number of Written Data Objects                  1
Size of Archive File in MB                  0.007
Proportion of Header Data in %               84.9
Occupied Database Space in MB             0.008
- Tables                                   0.003
- Indexes                                  0.001
- Structures                               0.004
```

Type	No.	Description
EDIDC	1	Control record (IDoc)
EDIDD	4	Data record (IDoc)
EDIDS	5	Status Record (IDoc)

Figure 5.18 Sample Spool Request Report for the IDoc Archive Job

Run Delete

The DELETE button in TRANSACTION SARA runs ABAP report RSEXARCD, which reads an archive file and deletes its IDocs from the SAP database.

1. To delete archived IDocs from SAP, click DELETE to load the EXECUTE DELETE PROGRAM run screen (as shown in Figure 5.19).

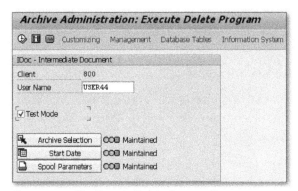

Figure 5.19 The Execute Delete Program Screen

2. An archive is selected to identify the IDocs in SAP to delete. Click the ARCHIVE SELECTION button to open the selection pop-up (as shown in Figure 5.20).

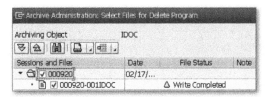

Figure 5.20 Select an Archive to Delete Its IDocs from SAP

3. The archive selection dialog will list all archives successfully saved with the write program. Select an archive or archive file and click CONTINUE to return to the EXECUTE DELETE PROGRAM screen.

4. As with the write program, create a job by clicking START DATE and configure the output device by clicking SPOOL PARAMETERS.

5. When all parameters have been maintained, click EXECUTE to kick off DELETE at its scheduled time. To delete IDocs, do not set the TEST flag.

   ▸ Check the spool report in the job scheduler for the deletions by clicking the green JOB button, just as with the write program.

The read program (ABAP RSEXARCR) returns control record keys and link information for archived IDocs. Management returns administrative data for the archive, including IDoc number, status, physical filename, size, date archived, current jobs, number of objects, and so on.

To reload an archive, use ABAP report RSEXARCL. To find an IDoc in the archive, use Transaction WE09 or Transaction WE10 (ABAP RSEIDOC9) to search by the contents of specific data elements and segments. We look at this in more detail in Chapter 21, Section 21.2, Monitoring and Recovery Tools.

5.7.2 Deleting IDoc Generated Work Items

SAP provides standard programs for mass deletion of work items and their history. Transaction SWWL (ABAP RSWWWIDE) deletes work items while Transaction SWWH (ABAP RSWWHIDE) cleans up their history.

But we need to exercise caution. Work items are not only about IDocs. They are also used for many other processes, including basis, security, and application objects. As shown in Figure 5.21, the selection screen for SWWL allows us to restrict the damage to IDocs by selecting tasks. The key is knowing what tasks to use for IDoc selection and not deleting immediately.

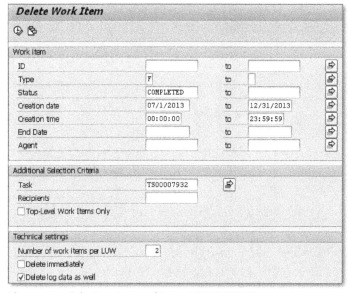

Figure 5.21 Selection Screen of Report RSWWWIDE

The easiest way to understand tasks is as an ABAP program used by SAP workflow to do one job within a process flow. They are triggered when a specified condition is met in the processing flow of an IDoc.

For example, task TS30000020 runs when an RFC is made into SAP with an empty IDoc file. The task sends an error message to the SAP Business Workplace Inbox (Transaction SBWP) from where it can be used to troubleshoot the problem.

The tasks listed in Table 5.14 are related to IDoc processing and can be used to select work items for deletion in Transaction SWWL.

Task	Description
TS00007989	Outbound, error handling with IDoc. Failed to save IDoc to file.
TS00008068	Inbound, error message with IDoc. Errors with control segment values.
TS00008070	Outbound, syntax (structural) error in IDoc.
TS00008074	Inbound, syntax (structural) error in IDoc.
TS30000020	Error message without IDoc. IDoc file empty.
TS60001307	Outbound, error message with IDoc packet. Batching error.
TS70008037	Display MC document (outbound w/o IDoc). Failed to generate an IDoc from message control.
TS70008125	IDoc status report with post-processing (after export).
TS00008068	Inbound, error message with IDoc (configuration).
TS00008070	Outbound, syntax (structural) error in IDoc.
TS00008074	Inbound, syntax error in IDoc (structural, segments).
TS30200090	Processing inbound IDoc by application failure.
TS20000051	IDoc application inbound error. Application posting and system errors (such as authorization).
TS30000206	IDOC_START_INBOUND. Runs each time a STATUS IDoc comes into SAP.

Table 5.14 IDoc Tasks for Selection of Work Items to Delete

There are many other relevant tasks, including one to handle errors for each major application IDoc. For example, task TS00008046 handles errors for inbound ORDERS, TS00007949 for REMADV, TS00008056 for INVOIC, and so on.

Tasks are maintained in Transaction PFTC and stored in infotype HRS1201, which can be viewed with Transaction SE16 if you have authorization. Search for IDoc tasks by entering *IDOC* into the SWOTP (object type) field in the SE16 selection screen for the infotype.

Execute Transaction SWWL to return a report that lists all relevant work items for the tasks and date range entered in the selection screen (as shown in Figure 5.22). Double-click any task to follow its trail all the way back to the IDoc.

Work Items to Be Deleted (68 Entries)

ID	Del	Type	Text	Status	Creation date	Creation time
1035802		W	Messages have been issued: number 0000000000932474 S-FG300	READY	03/12/2010	01:06:33
1068214		W	EDI: Partner profile not available	READY	06/22/2010	17:25:40
1087646		W	Get details from previous status records with status 26	READY	11/09/2010	16:39:52
1087647		W	Get details from previous status records with status 26	READY	11/10/2010	16:18:32
1087654		W	Get details from previous status records with status 26	READY	11/11/2010	09:03:17

Figure 5.22 Sample Task Delete Report from Transaction SWWL

Tasks can be deleted one at a time, in groups, or all at once from the report. Select the task or tasks and click DELETE (the trashcan icon).

Important Tip

Before deleting any tasks, download all the work item IDs for all the tasks you intend to delete. You'll need them to delete work item history with Transaction SWWH. The ALV List report has a download button at the top of the screen that will output the report to a text file or spreadsheet. Or select the ID column and press Ctrl + C to copy only the IDs.

Deleting Work Item History

Use Transaction SWWH to delete work item history, as shown in Figure 5.23.

Use the work item IDs from Transaction SWWH to select history for deletion.

Delete Work Item History

Work item				
ID	1109800	to		

Method				
Date		to		
Time	00:00:00	to	00:00:00	
Time Stamp	..,130,221,232,005	to	..,130,222,232,005	
Agent		to		
Return code		to		

Technical settings

Number of work items per LUW   10

☐ Delete immediately

Figure 5.23   Delete Work Item History with Work Item IDs

Execute but do not check DELETE IMMEDIATELY. A work item history report is returned displaying every action recorded against the work item ID, as illustrated in Figure 5.24.

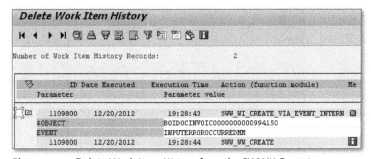

Delete Work Item History

Number of Work Item History Records: 2

	ID	Date Executed	Execution Time	Action (function module)	Me
Parameter			Parameter value		
	1109800	12/20/2012	19:28:43	SWW_WI_CREATE_VIA_EVENT_INTERN	
$OBJECT			BOIDOCINVOIC0000000000994150		
EVENT			INPUTERROROCCURREDMM		
	1109800	12/20/2012	19:28:44	SWW_WW_CREATE	

Figure 5.24   Delete Work Item History from the SWWH Report

As with the work item report in Transaction SWWL, history items can be deleted one at a time, in groups, or all at once.

5.8   Summary

In this chapter we took a deeper dive into the processing flows in Acme's new SAP EDI system. We looked at the services that will be used by all processes and outlined an archiving approach for EDI transactions and IDocs on the RIM.

We also looked at the STATUS interface that will report to SAP the status of processing milestones for IDocs as they pass through the RIM to the trading partner, including 997 functional acknowledgments.

All this means a lot of data. We won't archive IDocs in SAP at Acme Pictures, but we will need a strategy to delete them. So we went over SAP's standard tools for archiving and deleting IDocs.

Now it's time to look at IDocs themselves, and to get a better handle on their structure and basic configuration. So before we go any further, let's work on building the foundations of our knowledge of these intelligent messages.

Darryl Q didn't know IDocs or EDI from a hole in the head, but he knew a winning team when he saw one. IDocs are the building blocks of EDI in SAP, and EDI is critical to the success of the Great Mr. Q's DVD business. It's time, then, to begin lifting the veil and learning how IDocs work in SAP.

6   EDI Architecture in SAP: IDoc Basics

Things are getting interesting for the SAP EDI implementation team at Acme Pictures.

We've learned a little about EDI standards and technology and where it all fits in the grand scheme of Acme's new SAP system, particularly when it comes to its most important customer, Gordy's Galaxy of Games & B Flix.

We've designed our EDI architecture, the system is installed, and workflows are being built. The first maps are in the hands of map developers.

The JCo connector has been installed on the EDI application server and the IDoc Adapter configured for file-based RFC transfer between the RIM and Acme's SAP development client in logical system DEV100.

We'll step through EDI configuration in SAP shortly. But first, our SAP EDI team lead is a writing fiend who insists on documenting IDoc structure and processing for the team and for Acme's future folks.

"You can't build a house without a foundation," he's fond of saying. "And that foundation always starts with a document and at least one Visio."

Acme project management is delighted. Many consultants have built systems for Acme without writing a word about what they did (or thought they did) along the way. Their systems usually did the job, but Acme IT spent a lot of time, money, and energy trying to figure out how.

6.1   Intelligent Messages: The Anatomy of an IDoc

SAP defines "IDoc" as an intermediate document, pointing to its role in the transfer of data to or from an SAP business document or object, such as a PO, delivery document, invoice, or customer master record.

This is an accurate definition as far as it goes. Like EDI messages, IDocs are independent of the complex application objects — the database and program logic — that store and process the business documents and objects that are encapsulated by the IDoc. The IDoc is "intermediate" in that it is a phase, a bridge, in the transfer of a business document into, out of, or within SAP.

An IDoc is a structured vessel, like an EDI message, with defined hierarchical relationships. But unlike an EDI message, an IDoc is an intelligent document plugged into a standard interface with a full suite of message processing services enabled through database tables and structures, programs, functions, and ABAP classes for processing, monitoring, displaying, auditing, testing, editing, and building IDocs.

The beauty of this interface is that it's truly plug and play. A developer can use all these standard objects in his own custom IDocs, processing functions, and programs to extend the functionality of the standard interface to meet specific issues for particular clients.

The word "IDoc" is thrown around a lot on an SAP project. It can mean different things at different times to different people. We can use the term "IDoc" for any one of five distinct objects that we will consider here:

1. Logical message type

2. IDoc basic type

3. IDoc extended type

4. IDoc instance

5. IDoc file

Let's walk through each one.

6.1.1   Logical Message Type

An IDoc can be the name of a logical message type that represents the abstraction of a business document or record in SAP. It identifies the nature of the object that will be transferred and, to a certain extent, its function within a business process. It also links to the processing logic that will either populate or post the IDoc.

A logical message type can have multiple purposes. Message type ORDERS, for example, can serve as an outbound supplier purchase order, an inbound customer sales order, a returns order, and so on.

In addition, message type ORDERS posting to a sales order can be followed by logical message ORDRSP sent to a customer to confirm receipt of an order or an ORDCHG sent to request a change in an existing order.

The use of a logical message type within a particular interface or business process is defined by the following:

▶ The application logic it triggers, which provides its transactional context

▶ An IDoc basic type, which gives it a structure

▶ The data that populates its structure at runtime, which gives it meaning

Naming conventions for logical message types are largely the same as for EDIFACT EDI standards, but there are key differences between the two:

▶ An EDIFACT message has a structure defined by the standard and applied by a data dictionary.

▶ Logical message types have no structure. They derive structure through their link to a basic type.

▶ Logical message types are linked to application and routing logic, while EDIFACT messages are independent of any processing logic.

The logical message type is the brain of the operation. It bridges structure and logic through links applied in configuration. It is about the business document, the data that will inhabit the IDoc, and the ABAP code that will process it, whether that's a function module or a workflow task.

We'll use the following logical message types to build our EDI interfaces at Acme pictures:

▶ ORDERS: Outbound purchase orders and inbound sales orders

▶ ORDRSP: Outbound order acknowledgments

▶ SHPORD: Outbound deliveries

▶ MBGMCR: Inbound goods receipt

- SHPCON: Inbound ship confirmations
- DESADV: Outbound advanced shipping notices (ASNs)
- INVOIC: Inbound supplier and outbound customer invoices
- REMADV: Inbound payment advice

6.1.2 IDoc Record Types: External Representation

IDocs get their record structure, syntax, and hierarchical format from three record types defined in the SAP Data Dictionary in the following sequence:

- *One control record* that contains message-wide administrative data
- *One-to-many data records* with application data prefixed by control fields that link each record back to the control segment and:
  - Identify the segment name of each record
  - Define the sequence of each segment within the IDoc
  - Define the hierarchy level and hierarchical relationships of each segment within the IDoc.
- *One-to-many status records* with a complete audit trail from the moment the IDoc is written to the database to its final endpoint status

This is true for ASCII and XML IDocs. But the presentation of these record types for ASCII IDocs is different for an external EDI system than it is for internal use by SAP. XML IDocs have a simpler, more consistent structure driven by an XSD schema externally and the IDoc database internally.

SAP outputs the external structure of IDoc record types for use in mapping by EDI systems when the IDoc metadata is generated in parser format with Transaction WE60.

External Control Record

The external control record holds message-wide administrative data and is defined by structure EDI_DC40 (EDI_DC in IDoc Version 3) in the SAP Data Dictionary. It has a record length of 524 bytes. Table 6.1 is an example of a control record populated by an external EDI system for an inbound ORDERS message to Acme's DEV 100 system.

Field	Value	Description
TABNAM	EDI_DC40	Name of the Data Dictionary structure that defines the external control record type.
MANDT	100	SAP target client number.
DOCNUM		IDoc number. Generated by SAP when the IDoc is saved to the IDoc database. If the map writes a value to this field, it will be overwritten by SAP when the IDoc is written to the database.
DOCREL	702	SAP version.
STATUS		IDoc status. Generated by SAP.
DIRECT	2	Direction. 1 = Outbound, 2 = Inbound.
OUTMOD		Output processing mode.
EXPRSS		Inbound processing override flag.
TEST		Test flag. Only populated if set in the partner profile.
IDOCTYP	ORDERS05	IDoc basic type for inbound sales order. Partner profile key.
CIMTYP		IDoc extended type name names custom segment.
MESTYP	ORDERS	Logical message type. Partner profile key.
MESCOD		Message code. Only populated if used in partner profile in WE20. It then becomes part of the key to read partner profile table EDP21 (inbound).
MESFCT		Message function. See MESCOD.
STD	X	EDI standard. X = X12, E = EDIFACT.
STDVRS	5010	EDI version.
STDMES	850	EDI transaction code or message.
SNDPOR	XML_IDOC	SAP sender port. Defined as a file port in WE21.
SNDPRT	KU	Sender partner type. Partner profile key.
SNDPFC	SP	Sender partner function. Only if set in partner profile.
SNDPRN	GRDY01	Sender partner number. Partner profile key.

Table 6.1 IDoc Control Record Populated by an External EDI System

Field	Value	Description
SNDSAD		Sender address. Reserved for future use by SAP.
SNDLAD	01234567US0	EDI sender trading partner ID. To be read from custom SAP table by user exit on control segment.
RCVPOR	SAPDEV	SAP receiver port. Always <SAP>+<SysID>.
RCVPRT	LS	Receiver partner type always logical system.
RCVPFC		Receiver partner function.
RCVPRN	DEVCLNT100	Receiver partner number. Always SAP logical system for receiving (DEV) client.
RCVSAD		Receiver address. Reserved for future use by SAP.
RCVLAD	9999999USD	EDI receiver trading partner ID to be read from custom SAP table by user exit on control segment.
CREDAT		IDoc create date. Generated by SAP.
CRETIM		IDoc create time. Generated by SAP.
REFINT	00000133	EDI interchange control number.
REFGRP	133	EDI group control number.
REFMES	1	EDI transaction set control number.
ARCKEY		External archive system key for IDoc.
SERIAL		Serialization key. Used to process batched IDocs in a defined sequence.

Table 6.1 IDoc Control Record Populated by an External EDI System (Cont.)

All of these values, except for the EDI trading partner IDs, are provided by the EDI system. Assuming that the file port, partner profile, and other IDoc configuration options are in place, this control segment will get the message through the door and written to the IDoc database.

During outbound processing the interchange, group, and transaction control IDs are inserted into the control segment by the STATUS interface we discussed in Chapter 5, Section 5.5, Reporting EDI Status to SAP.

This simplifies the work of the EDI production support team after the system goes live. It allows us to write reports that link our business document to the IDoc and

EDI transaction, group, and interchange. This approach involves a little more planning and creativity, but the benefits are enormous.

Use Transaction SE11 to view the structure of the external control record. Enter "EDI_DC40" in the DATA TYPE selection field, and click DISPLAY.

External Data Record

The external data record type is defined by Data Dictionary structure EDI_DD40 (EDI_DD for IDoc Version 3). It has a 63-byte control area and a 1,000-byte SDATA field for unstructured application data, as illustrated in Figure 6.1.

IDoc record type EDI_DD40	
Control key fields—63 bytes	SDATA unparsed data field—1000 bytes

Figure 6.1 The External Base IDoc Data Record Type

The control fields include the external name of the IDoc segment and the keys that define the placement and hierarchical relationships of the record within the IDoc. The data record type structure is detailed in Table 6.2.

Field	Value	Description
SEGNAM	E2EDK01005	External segment name. The segment name can be used as a record tag in the EDI mapping tool.
MANDT	100	SAP client number.
DOCNUM		IDoc number. Generated by SAP. Links segment to IDoc number in control record.
SEGNUM	000001	Sequential segment number. Shows position of segment within the IDoc.
PSGNUM		Parent segment number. SEGNUM for parent in a parent-child relationship. Doesn't need to be mapped. SAP identifies this number from the syntax for the internal IDoc Basic type.
HLEVEL	1	Hierarchy level of segment.
SDATA		Unparsed 1,000-byte application data field.

Table 6.2 The Structure of the External IDoc Data Record Type

External Status Record Type

Defined by Data Dictionary structure EDI_DS40 (EDI_DS for IDoc Version 3), the external status record stores the complete lifecycle of an IDoc from creation to endpoint status. The length of the external status record type is 562 bytes.

The external status record type is not processed by the EDI system, nor is it exported with the IDoc from SAP.

6.1.3   IDoc Record Types: Internal Representation

Just as the ancient Romans believed that arms make the man, internal IDoc record types make the IDoc. They provide the structure and hierarchical organization for IDoc data in the IDoc database and for the schema that format XML IDocs, greatly simplifying their structure and readability.

Internal record types aren't seen by the EDI system if they're working with ASCII IDocs. But XML IDocs perfectly mirror the structure and naming conventions of internal record types, except for the control record, which still uses the EDI_DC40 external structure.

Internal record types are about the IDoc database. They are used by SAP to structure incoming or outgoing application data for insertion into the three tables of the IDoc database.

During inbound processing, external record types are converted to internal record types after the IDoc has been imported from the EDI system and before it is written to the IDoc database.

During outbound processing, the IDoc is generated from the business document, structured with the internal record types, assigned a unique IDoc ID number, and then written to the IDoc database.

After the IDoc has been created in the database, output functions are called and it is read into a communications IDoc that is structured by the external record types. It is sent out of SAP to the EDI system.

The three tables of the IDoc database provide the structure for the internal record types. These tables also store the IDoc records created in the IDoc interface:

- ▸ EDIDC: One control record per IDoc with a unique IDoc number
- ▸ EDID4: One to many data records linked to the control record through the unique IDoc number
- ▸ EDIDS: One or more status records linked to the control and data records through the unique IDoc number

Understanding these tables and the record types that they define is key to understanding IDocs in SAP. As far as SAP is concerned, an IDoc does not exist until it is written to the three tables of the IDoc database.

The organization and structure of an IDoc as defined by the internal record types of the IDoc database is illustrated in Figure 6.2.

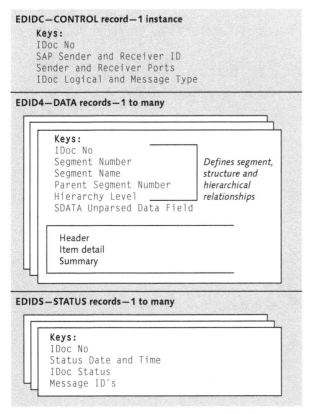

EDIDC—CONTROL record—1 instance
Keys:
IDoc No
SAP Sender and Receiver ID
Sender and Receiver Ports
IDoc Logical and Message Type

EDID4—DATA records—1 to many
Keys:
IDoc No
Segment Number
Segment Name   *Defines segment,*
Parent Segment Number   *structure and*
Hierarchy Level   *hierarchical*
SDATA Unparsed Data Field *relationships*

Header
Item detail
Summary

EDIDS—STATUS records—1 to many
Keys:
IDoc No
Status Date and Time
IDoc Status
Message ID´s

Figure 6.2 Internal Record Types Are Defined by the IDoc Database

The Internal Control Record Type

The internal control record is defined by the structure of table EDIDC. It identifies the IDoc message and basic type and holds the most up-to-date administrative and control information about the IDoc's current processing state in SAP. It has a record length of 542 bytes.

The key fields of a populated EDIDC control record for an inbound ORDERS IDoc are listed in Table 6.3. This message posted to Acme DEV 100 from the external IDoc in Table 6.2. An SAP sales order successfully posted from this IDoc.

Field	Value	Description
MANDT	100	SAP client number.
DOCNUM	675478	IDoc number. Generated after the IDoc was converted to the internal format, just before it was written to the IDoc database.
DOCREL	702	SAP version.
STATUS	53	IDoc status. 53: Application document posted.
DIRECT	2	Direction. 1 = Outbound; 2 = Inbound.
RCVPOR	SAPDEV	SAP receiver port. Always <SAP>+<SysID>.
RCVPRT	LS	Receiver partner type: Always logical system.
RCVPRN	DEVCLNT100	Receiver partner number. Always SAP logical system for receiving (DEV) client.
RCVLAD	9999999USD	EDI receiver trading partner ID for Acme.
STD	X	EDI standard. X = X12; E = EDIFACT.
STDVRS	5010	EDI version.
STDMES	850	EDI transaction code or message.
MESCOD		Message code. Populated only if used in partner profile in WE20.
SNDPOR	XML_IDOC	SAP sender port. File port in WE21.
SNDPRT	KU	Sender partner type. Partner profile key.
SNDPRN	GRDY01	Sender partner number. Partner profile key.

Table 6.3 Table EDIDC Structures the Internal Control Record

Field	Value	Description
SNDLAD	01234567US0	EDI sender trading partner ID for Gordy.
REFINT	00000133	EDI interchange control number.
REFGRP	133	EDI group control number.
REFMES	1	EDI transaction set control number.
CREDAT	200080915	Date created on IDoc database.
CRETIM	102454	Time created on IDoc database.
MESTYP	ORDERS	Logical message type.
IDOCTYP	ORDERS05	IDoc basic type for inbound sales order.
CIMTYP		IDoc extended type name.
RCVPFC		Receiver partner function.
SNDPFC	SP	Sender partner function.
UPDDAT	200080915	Date IDoc was last changed in the database. Reflects the most recent status change.
UPDTIM	102632	Time IDoc was last changed in the database.
MAXSEGNUM	100	Total number of data records in the IDoc.

Table 6.3 Table EDIDC Structures the Internal Control Record (Cont.)

The internal control record includes fields that match configuration set up before we begin exchanging IDocs and it tracks the most recent processing information about the IDoc, such as date and time of the last update to the control and status records and the total number of data segments.

It defines the beginning of the IDoc, which exists as a linked set of physical records in the database. The key is the unique IDoc number that links the control record in EDIDC to its associated data records in EDID4 and status records in EDIDS. These linked physical records are the IDoc.

The complete structure of EDIDC can be viewed with Transaction SE11.

Internal Data Record Type

The structure of the internal data record type is defined by transparent table EDID4, which also stores the IDoc's data records.

The internal data record includes a control area of 71 bytes and a 1,000-byte SDATA field. The control area stores the IDoc number, the internal segment name, its sequence, and hierarchical level and relationships within the IDoc. Table 6.4 shows the structure of the internal data record type.

Field	Value	Description
MANDT	100	SAP client number.
DOCNUM	675478	IDoc number.
COUNTER	000	Cluster table counter.
SEGNUM	000001	Sequential number of segment within the IDoc.
SEGNAM	E1EDK01	Internal segment name.
PSGNUM	000000	Parent segment. SEGNUM of its parent segment.
HLEVEL	01	Hierarchy level of segment.
DTINT2	1000	Length of unparsed SDATA field.
SDATA		Unparsed 1,000-byte application data field.

Table 6.4 Table EDID4 Provides the Structure for the Internal Data Record

The application data in SDATA is parsed into discrete fields at runtime by Data Dictionary structures that use the internal segment name.

Internal Status Record Type

The structure of the internal status record type is defined by transparent table EDIDS, which is also used to store the status records generated by the IDoc interface at key processing milestones in the IDoc's lifecycle. The length of the status record is 522 bytes.

Except for status information passed from the external EDI system by the STATUS interface, status records are created purely within SAP and are never seen by the EDI system.

Table 6.5 shows the fields and contents of the status record for our inbound ORDERS IDoc after it successfully posted a sales order.

Field	Value	Description
MANDT	100	SAP client number.
DOCNUM	675478	IDoc number.
LOGDAT	20131231	Date status record last updated.
LOGTIM	10:26:32	Time status record last updated.
COUNTR	00003	Sequential counter for status record beginning with 0.
CREDAT	20131231	Date status record created on IDoc database.
CRETIM	102454	Time status record created on IDoc database.
STATUS	53	IDoc status. 53 = Document successfully posted.
UNAME	SAP_EDI	User name for EDI system in SAP. Used to process IDocs and run background batch programs.
REPID	EDISYS	Program that created status record—EDI system.
STATXT	&1 &2 has been saved	Constant text and variables (&) for generation of text message in status record.
STAPA1	Standard Order	Message parameter 1. Variable for assembly of text message for status record. Replaces & character in STATXT. Standard text constant.
STAPA2	20000099	Message parameter 2. Sales order number created by IDoc.
STAPA3		Message parameter 3.
STAPA4		Message parameter 4.
STATYP	I	Type of system message: ▶ A: Abend ▶ W: Warning ▶ E: Error ▶ S: Success
STAMQU	SAP	System that created the message.
STAMID	V1	Message class invoked.
STAMNO	311	Standard status 53 information message number.

Table 6.5 Table EDIDS Structures and Stores the Status Record

One status record is created for each processing milestone in the IDoc's lifecycle. The status sequence provides the complete history of the IDoc as it moves through SAP and, at Acme Pictures, the EDI RIM.

For inbound IDocs, this sequence is displayed in Table 6.6 from oldest to final endpoint.

Status	Description
50	IDoc added to database.
64	IDoc ready to be transferred to application.
62	IDoc passed to application.
51	Error: Application document not posted.
53	Application document posted. Endpoint.

Table 6.6 The Basic Happy Path Inbound Lifecycle with One Error

For outbound IDocs, the basic IDoc lifecycle is outlined in Table 6.7.

Status	Description
01	IDoc created on database.
30	IDoc ready for dispatch to the EDI system.
03	Data passed to port OK.
18	Triggering EDI system OK.
05	Translation failed.
06	Translation OK. Returned by STATUS interface. Current endpoint.
16	Functional acknowledgment positive. Endpoint for future 997-STATUS interface.

Table 6.7 Outbound IDoc Lifecycle Processing Sequence

You can view table EDIDS with Transaction SE11. Check out the complete list of status codes with Transaction WE47.

6.1.4   IDoc Basic Type

The IDoc basic type is a data structure, not a data container. The basic type gives the logical message type, and its business document, a structure for the data that will be processed by the IDoc function.

IDoc data are stored in records that derive their structures from the control, data, and status record types.

The basic type is composed of one or more segments that exist as structures in the Data Dictionary. The segments provide the field structure to parse application data in the SDATA field of the data record for processing by the IDoc interface or for mapping in the EDI system. The layout of a populated instance of basic type ORDERS05 in the TEST TOOL FOR IDOC PROCESSING screen (Transaction WE19) in Figure 6.3 illustrates this organization.

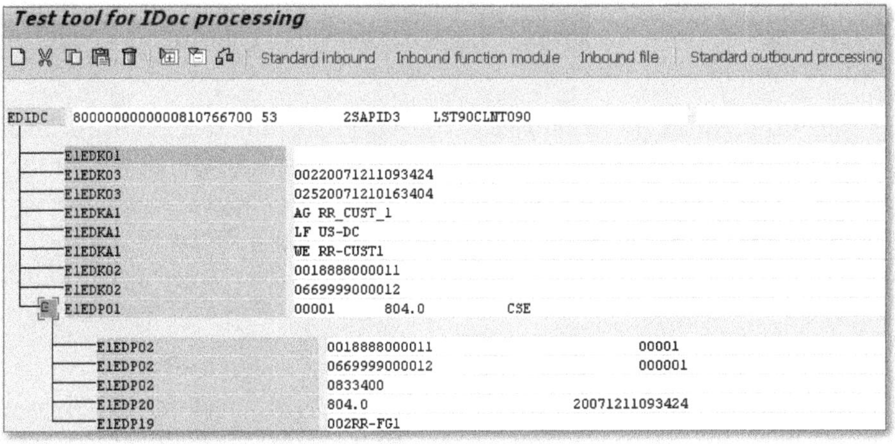

Figure 6.3   ORDERS05 IDoc Basic Type in WE19 Test Tool

It shows the hierarchy of segments beginning with the EDIDC control record at the top, the segment name of each data record to the left below EDIDC, and the unformatted SDATA field in white to right of each data record.

Double-click the segment name and a pop-up appears with the parsed fields from the segment structure in the Data Dictionary. Figure 6.4, for example, shows the parsed field structure for segment E1EDK02.

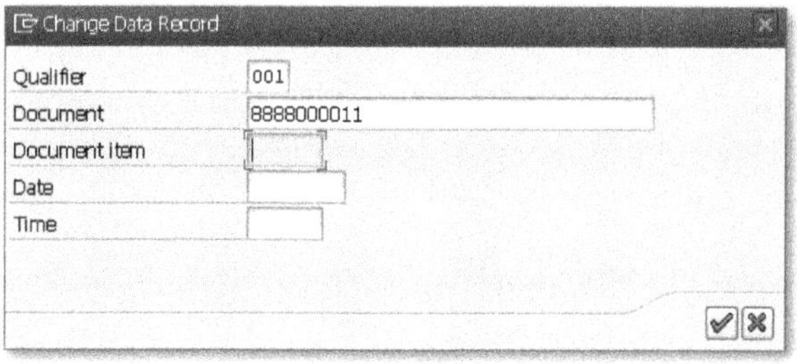

Figure 6.4 Parsed Data Dictionary Field Structure of Segment E1EDK02

A basic type can be shared with several logical message types. ORDERS05, for example, is linked to message types ORDERS (purchase or sales orders), ORDRSP (order response), ORDCHG (order change), REQOTE (request for quotation), QUOTES (quotation), and DELORD (delivery request). This allows a common data structure for a variety of business objects—POs, quotes, delivery orders, and so on—that can populate an instance of the basic type according to their own needs. The logical message type, through its link to the processing function, determines the data in the populated IDoc.

Basic types that are shared by multiple message types have comprehensive structures that can accommodate a variety of application uses. Only a small number of segments and fields in ORDERS05, for example, are used to create a sales order. The mapping documents that we produce for Acme's X12 to IDoc translation identify the segments and fields that we actually use, after the SD functional team determines what data they need to create a sales order and support all follow-on functionality.

The syntax for each IDoc basic type—the sequence in which each segment falls and its hierarchical relationships to other segments—is stored in table IDOCSYN and is read by function IDOCTYPE_READ_COMPLETE called during IDoc processing from function EDI_IDOC_SYNTAX_GET.

The link between the message and basic types is passed in the IDoc control record in fields MESTYP and IDOCTYP. If these fields are not populated by the EDI system for inbound processing, the IDoc will fail.

The system populates these fields during outbound processing. They match the message and basic types entered in the outbound partner profile. We look at this works in our discussions of configuration and output control.

6.1.5   IDoc Extended Type

An IDoc extended type is a basic type with one or more custom segments. As customer objects, they begin with a Z.

For Acme's Plan Q implementation, the naming convention for extended types is Z_<Basic_Type>. An extended type for ORDERS05 would be Z_ORDERS05. Extended segments require customization to process them, usually written in customer exits.

The extension must be identified in the outbound partner profile and in the CIMTYP field of the IDoc control record. It must be passed to SAP in the control segment for inbound processing as well.

6.1.6   IDoc Instance

An IDoc exists in SAP only after it has been written to the IDoc database.

This means one control record in table EDIDC, one or more data records in EDID4, and one or more status records in EDIDS, linked together through a common unique IDoc number. Application data are stored in the SDATA field of the EDID4 data records. The segment name and number, which represent its sequence in the IDoc, fall in the control key area of the record.

The hierarchical relationships between segments are defined in the parent segment (PSGNUM) and hierarchy level (HLEVEL) fields in the data record control area. The parent segment points to the segment number (SEGNUM) of the parent in a parent-child relationship.

The IDoc is the application object that drives follow-up processing in the interface after it has been created in the IDoc database. It's a permanent SAP data object that lives in the database until it's archived and purged. Like all data objects, it can be read, processed, edited, and otherwise manipulated by standard and custom ABAP programs.

On the inbound, the IDoc creates the SAP business document, such as a customer sales order (logical message type ORDERS). On the outbound, the IDoc pulls application data from the SAP business document and passes it to an externally formatted Communications IDoc that is converted to XML through the XML file port and transmitted to the EDI RIM.

6.1.7   IDoc File

We refer to a *file* here because we're using a file-based RFC connection between SAP and the RIM. It could just as easily be a batch of IDoc data sent into or out of SAP by ALE transfer through memory.

The IDoc file holds either an XML (which we'll use at Acme Pictures) or an ASCII IDoc with the external record format and segment names. The XML IDoc, on the other hand, is formatted with the internal segment names and the external control record with the field structure of EDI_DC40. We look at XML IDocs in the next section.

On the inbound, the IDoc file contains data that has been translated or generated by an external system. An ASCII IDoc is converted to the internal record types before it is written to the IDoc database using these functions:

▶ IDOC_CTRL_INBOUND_CONVERT for the control record
▶ IDOC_DATA_INBOUND_CONVERT for the data records

On the outbound, the externally formatted ASCII IDoc is generated by the system, after it has been built and written to the IDoc database, by functions:

▶ IDOC_CONTROL_OUTBOUND_CONVERT for the control record
▶ IDOC_DATA_OUTBOUND_CONVERT for the data records

Status records do not leave SAP and are not converted.

These functions convert IDoc versions 3 and 4 (control records EDI_DC and EDI_DC40). The system can convert an incoming version 3 to a version 4 IDoc. On the outbound, the version is determined by the file port, as you'll see when we consider file port configuration.

The IDoc file only exists at runtime, although a record of its passage is saved to the EDI file archive. As far as SAP is concerned, it's a temporary object with no status record and no existence until it has been written to the IDoc database.

6.1.8   XML IDocs

Listing 6.1 shows an example of basic purchase order IDoc from Gordy's to Acme in XML format.

```xml
<?xml version="1.0" encoding="UTF-8"?>
<ORDERS05>
  <IDOC BEGIN="1">
    <EDI_DC40 SEGMENT="1">
      <TABNAM>EDI_DC40</TABNAM>
      <MANDT>100</MANDT>
      <DOCNUM>0000000134206118</DOCNUM>
      <DOCREL>702</DOCREL>
      <STATUS>30</STATUS>
      <DIRECT>2</DIRECT>
      <IDOCTYP>ORDERS05</IDOCTYP>
      <MESTYP>ORDERS</MESTYP>
      <SNDPOR>XML_IDOC</SNDPOR>
      <SNDPRT>KU</SNDPRT>
      <SNDPRN>GRDY01</SNDPRN>
      <RCVPOR>SAPDEV</RCVPOR>
      <RCVPRT>LS</RCVPRT>
      <RCVPRN>DEVCLNT100</RCVPRN>
    </EDI_DC40>
    <E1EDK01 SEGMENT="1">
      <BELNR>8196733288</BELNR>
    </E1EDK01>
    <E1EDK03 SEGMENT="1">
      <IDDAT>012</IDDAT>
      <DATUM>20131231</DATUM>
    </E1EDK03>
    <E1EDKA1 SEGMENT="1">
      <PARVW>AG</PARVW>
      <PARTN>0001013694</PARTN>
    </E1EDKA1>
    <E1EDKA1 SEGMENT="1">
      <PARVW>LF</PARVW>
      <PARTN>0001014700</PARTN>
    </E1EDKA1>
    <E1EDKA1 SEGMENT="1">
      <PARVW>WE</PARVW>
      <LIFNR>0001013699</LIFNR>
      <NAME1>Pharma1 Pharma</NAME1>
      <STRAS>123 Victory Blvd</STRAS>
      <ORT01>Newark</ORT01>
      <PSTLZ>07103</PSTLZ>
      <LAND1>US</LAND1>
      <REGIO>NJ</REGIO>
```

```
    </E1EDKA1>
    <E1EDK02 SEGMENT="1">
      <QUALF>001</QUALF>
      <BELNR>8196733288</BELNR>
      <DATUM>20110117</DATUM>
    </E1EDK02>
    <E1EDP01 SEGMENT="1">
      <POSEX>000010</POSEX>
      <MENGE>25000.000</MENGE>
      <MENEE>PCE</MENEE>
      <WERKS>CH01</WERKS>
      <E1EDP19 SEGMENT="1">
        <QUALF>001</QUALF>
        <IDTNR>000000000000991182</IDTNR>
        <KTEXT>SORITOL SR FCT 20MG 3X10 IL</KTEXT>
      </E1EDP19>
      <E1EDP19 SEGMENT="1">
        <QUALF>002</QUALF>
        <IDTNR>8612791311828</IDTNR>
      </E1EDP19>
    </E1EDP01>
  </IDOC>
</ORDERS05>
```

Listing 6.1 XML IDoc ORDERS.ORDERS05 PO from Gordy's to Acme

The message is identified by the basic type, which gives the IDoc structure and is stored within `<ORDERS05></ORDERS05>` and `<IDOC></IDOC>`. `<IDOC>` defines the start of the data payload by setting the `BEGIN` attribute to "1". Each new segment is identified by a `SEGMENT` attribute set to "1". The control segment is structured by its external representation EDI_DC40, but every other segment uses the internal segment name in table EDID4.

The control area in ASCII IDocs that identifies each segment, its sequential order, and its hierarchical relationships, is absent from XML. Note also that the EDID4 field name for each data element clearly identifies the data in the XML IDoc. ASCII IDocs store data in fixed length format in SDATA. Field names are not sent. It's much easier to read and hand-roll an XML IDoc.

The structure and syntax of the XML IDoc is defined by a schema (XSD) that is generated by SAP with Transaction WE60 and used by the EDI RIM mapping tool to identify and convert the message. A small snippet of the XSD schema—up to definition of data element MANDT in EDI_DC40—in Transaction WE60 is illustrated in Figure 6.5.

```
<?xml version="1.0" encoding="utf-8" ?>
- <xsd:schema xmlns:xsd="http://www.w3.org/2001/XMLSchema" version="1.0">
  - <xsd:element name="ORDERS05">
    - <xsd:annotation>
        <xsd:documentation>Purchasing/Sales</xsd:documentation>
      </xsd:annotation>
    - <xsd:complexType>
      - <xsd:sequence>
        - <xsd:element name="IDOC">
          - <xsd:complexType>
            - <xsd:sequence>
              - <xsd:element name="EDI_DC40">
                - <xsd:annotation>
                    <xsd:documentation>IDoc Control Record for Interface to External System</xsd:documentation>
                  </xsd:annotation>
                - <xsd:complexType>
                  - <xsd:sequence>
                    - <xsd:element name="TABNAM" type="xsd:string" fixed="EDI_DC40">
                      - <xsd:annotation>
                          <xsd:documentation>Name of Table Structure</xsd:documentation>
                        </xsd:annotation>
                      </xsd:element>
                    - <xsd:element name="MANDT" minOccurs="0">
                      - <xsd:annotation>
                          <xsd:documentation>Client</xsd:documentation>
                        </xsd:annotation>
                      - <xsd:simpleType>
                        - <xsd:restriction base="xsd:string">
                            <xsd:maxLength value="3" />
                          </xsd:restriction>
                        </xsd:simpleType>
                      </xsd:element>
```

Figure 6.5 A Small Slice of the Schema for ORDERS05

The full schema is 7,182 lines of descriptive XML instructions. It's complex and verbose, but SAP takes care of all that. All you need to do is generate the schema in Transaction WE60, download it by selecting menu option XML • DOWNLOAD, import it into your mapping application, and build an XML map.

It's even easier to process an XML IDoc in SAP. All it takes is an XML file port. We look at how to do this in Section 6.3.4, XML File Port. For now, we look at how the IDoc interface processes XML IDocs.

Inbound Processing

The IDoc file is picked up from the application server by function module EDI_ DATA_INCOMING. The EDI RIM triggers the function and passes it the full path and filename, and the sender file port name.

The first thing `EDI_DATA_INCOMING` does is call a function that reads the port and identifies the incoming as either a file or XML port: `EDI_PORT_READ`. It then confirms that the file is a valid XML message and calls function `IDOC_XML_FROM_FILE` to convert the XML file to an internal format that SAP can process and save to the IDoc database.

Outbound Processing

The beauty of the IDoc interface is that it is consistent. Outbound processing of XML IDocs isn't all that different from inbound.

Function `MASTER_IDOC_DISTRIBUTE` is called by the interface after the communications IDoc has been built and before it is written to the IDoc database. After some preliminary house-keeping, it calls function `EDI_OUTPUT_NEW`, which reads the port from the control segment field RCVPOR and identifies its type with function `EDI_PORT_READ`.

If the port is XML, function `IDOCS_OUTPUT_IN_XML_FORMAT` is called to convert the communications IDoc to XML format and write the file to a directory on the application server based on the XML port settings so that the EDI RIM can pick it up.

6.2   IDoc Architecture and the Data Dictionary

Everything in SAP is defined by the Data Dictionary. The data that describe and process every object are stored in Data Dictionary tables, including the objects of the Data Dictionary itself and the ABAP code that runs the entire system.

Get comfortable with digging through the Data Dictionary and you'll get a really good handle on SAP. Here's a tip: All tables that define and describe Data Dictionary objects begin with "DD".

IDocs are no different. All objects that make up the structure and syntax of an IDoc are defined, stored, and linked to each other in the Data Dictionary. A high-level view of how these relationships work for IDocs is illustrated in Figure 6.6.

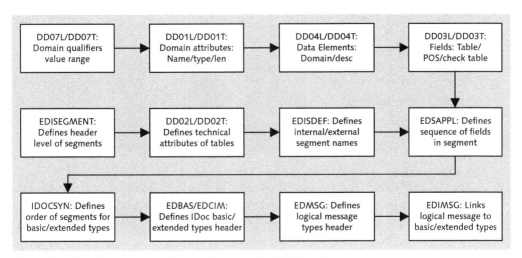

Figure 6.6 IDoc Structure Is Built from Objects in the SAP Data Dictionary

6.2.1 Domains

The domain is the atom of the Data Dictionary and the building block for data elements and fields.

Domain EDIF1225A is typical. It provides base formatting information and a range of qualifier values for the ACTION field in segment E1EDK01 in basic type ORDERS05.

Formatting characteristics defined in the domain include data type "CHAR" and length "3".

Domain EDIF1225A includes a value range that drives processing options for the IDoc at runtime. Qualifier options are listed in Table 6.8.

Value	Description
Null	This field is not used in the message.
000	No particular action required.
001	Reverse entire document.
002	Changes in document header.
003	Changes in one or more items.

Table 6.8 Qualifier Values for Domain EDIF1225A

Value	Description
004	Changes in header and items.
005	Credit memo display/ERS method.
006	Retroactive price change/clearing invoice.
007	Non-valuated goods receipt.

Table 6.8 Qualifier Values for Domain EDIF1225A (Cont.)

The default action for a null value or for a 000 in an inbound customer PO is to create a sales order. The value in the IDoc at runtime is provided by the translation in the EDI system, which is driven by the functional requirement for the document. In our case, we will only be using the inbound ORDERS to create a sales order.

Domains are defined in table DD01L with text descriptions in multiple languages in DD01T. Domain qualifiers—value ranges—are stored in tables DD07L and DD07T, which store text descriptions for each value in multiple languages.

You can view domains in the Data Dictionary with Transaction SE11. Enter "EDIF1225A" in the DOMAIN selection field, and click DISPLAY.

6.2.2 Data Elements

The data element is linked to a domain. It inherits the domain's field length, value range, and other attributes and adds a text description and field labels of varying lengths.

Data element EDIF1225_A, which is built on domain EDIF1225A, adds the text description "Action code for the whole EDI message."

Data elements are defined in table DD04L (links to the domain) and table DD04T (stores the text description in multiple languages).

Data elements can be viewed in the Data Dictionary with Transaction SE11. Enter data element name "EDIF1225_A" in the DATA TYPE selection field, and click DISPLAY.

6.2.3 Fields

The field is a local instance of a data element created in a table or structure. It inherits all the attributes of the domain and data element—formatting, field labels, text description, value ranges, and so on from the data element.

Fields provide a field structure to the segment through the order of their placement. The field ACTION, the first field in segment E1EDK01, is built on data element EDIF1225_A.

A field is created in a table or structure. ACTION was created in the IDoc Segment Editor (Transaction WE31) for segment E1EDK01. A data element was assigned to it when it was created, pulling all the properties of the data element and its underlying domain into the field.

Field definitions are stored in table DD03L through their link to the structure or table, in this case, E1EDK01, and the data element. Their position in the structure is one of the keys in DD03L. Field text is stored in table DD03T.

6.2.4 Segments

Segments are the building blocks of IDoc basic and extended types. They are created in the IDoc Segment Editor (Transaction WE31) and exist as structures in the SAP Data Dictionary. Their attributes and field structure are stored in a number of tables, including the following:

▶ EDISEGMENT: Header level data for segment.

▶ DD02L: Technical details at header level for tables and structures, including segments. Text descriptions in multiple languages are in table DD02T.

▶ EDISDEF: Internal and external segment names, versions, number of fields, and create dates and times.

▶ DD03L: Field names and attributes for tables and structures, including order of fields in segments.

▶ EDSAPPL: Application structure defining the sequential position of each field within the segment.

Segments are used in ABAP processing of IDocs to parse application data in the SDATA field of the data record into discrete fields. Segment names can also be used in standard and custom monitoring reports to search for IDocs by segment name and content or to otherwise process them.

The structure of any of these tables can be displayed in the Data Dictionary with Transaction SE11. The field structure of any segment can be displayed in the Segment Editor using Transaction WE31 or in the Data Dictionary with Transaction SE11.

6.2.5 IDoc Basic and Extended Types

As we have indicated, IDoc basic and extended types are defined through the sequence and hierarchical relationships of their segments, whether those segments are standard or custom. IDoc basic or extended types are created in the DEVELOP IDOC TYPES editor (Transaction WE30) by assembling released segments that have a field structure. Each segment is assigned a number of characteristics:

▶ Name

▶ Mandatory or not

▶ Minimum and maximum occurrence within basic type

▶ Parent segment number

▶ Hierarchy level

A number of tables are used to define basic and extended types and link them to one or more logical messages, including the following:

▶ EDBAS: Header level create and update information about IDoc basic types

▶ EDCIM: Header level create and update information about IDoc basic types with custom segments

▶ IDOCSYN: Syntax description for basic types. Defines the selection and sequence of segments in an IDoc basic or extended type, including the following attributes:

  ▶ Segment name

  ▶ Sequence number within the basic type

  ▶ Name and sequence number of parent segment

  ▶ Mandatory segment flag

  ▶ Minimum and maximum occurrences of segment

  ▶ Hierarchy level

▶ EDMSG: Stores logical message types created with Transaction WE81

▶ EDIMSG: Stores the link between logical message type and IDoc basic and extended types created with Transaction WE82

> **Tip: Tracing IDoc Construction**
>
> If you know how to read or debug ABAP code, go through function `IDOCTYPE_READ_ COMPLETE`. It reads all the key tables used in building the structure of an IDoc basic type, with all of its segments, data elements, and qualifiers, from the domain level right through to the link between the logical message and basic types.

6.3   One-Time EDI Configuration for IDocs in SAP

In the next chapter we look at details of inbound and outbound IDoc configuration for EDI in SAP. There are a number of one-time configuration tasks that set up SAP for exchanging IDocs with an external EDI system, regardless of the direction of any interface. More often than not these tasks are handled by the Basis team.

Some of this one-time setup can done through the ALE IMG (Transaction SALE). For Acme Pictures, these one-time EDI configuration settings include the following:

▶ Create an EDI background user to process IDocs in SAP

▶ Define a logical system for the SAP client and EDI system

▶ Create a connection to the Acme EDI RIM

▶ Create a file port for IDoc transfers

The beauty of the ALE IMG is that it presents all IDoc configuration options and scenarios for EDI or ALE in one screen in the order that they would be set. If you want more information about the configuration options in the ALE IMG, click on the page icon next to each heading. An HTML page will open with details about what that setting does.

6.3.1   EDI User Name

The IDoc adapter in the EDI system needs a user name and password to log in to SAP to trigger the IDoc interface. We'll copy WF-BATCH, a standard CPI/C communications user provided by SAP for workflow and background processing, into a new EDI_USER for Acme's IDoc processing.

The password for EDI_USER will be DARYLQF1, in honor of Daryl Q. Fernhausen, the indomitable founder of Acme Pictures.

Neither WF-BATCH nor EDI_USER can be used to log in to the SAP front-end GUI. But both can trigger background batch processing jobs in SAP. EDI_USER will have authorization to call RFC functions and run IDocs and other programs in background mode, including create and change of business documents in SAP.

The security will set up EDI_USER with Transaction SU01.

In addition to the EDI username and password, the EDI team will need the following information for all SAP systems they'll exchanging IDocs with:

- Client number
- Application server
- System number
- Gateway host and service
- Port or ports to be used for IDoc exchange

6.3.2 Logical System

The logical system represents an SAP system and client that participates in an exchange of IDocs with the EDI RIM. We'll also create a logical system for the EDI RIM to point to the destination for our EDI interfaces.

The SAP logical system name is used by the IDoc interface as the sending partner in outbound and the receiving partner in inbound exchanges.

The Basis team creates logical systems. To create the logical system for the EDI RIM, use Transaction BD54 or ALE IMG (Transaction SALE) path APPLICATION LINK ENABLING (ALE) • BASIC SETTINGS • LOGICAL SYSTEMS • DEFINE LOGICAL SYSTEMS.

You then enter the logical system name for the EDI RIM: EDIDEV100 (see Figure 6.7). This identifies the EDI DEV box that will exchange IDocs with Client 100 of Acme's SAP DEV system. Don't forget to save.

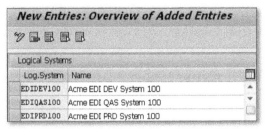

Figure 6.7 Three New Logical Systems in BD54

Logical systems are transportable, so we'll also create one for QAS and PRD:

▶ EDIQAS100

▶ EDIPRD100

Logical systems are stored in tables TBDLS and TBDLST. Logical systems can be transported between SAP environments.

The logical system will also be assigned to the client that will exchange the IDocs with the EDI RIM. This assignment cannot be transported between clients and must be entered manually every a new system client is created that will exchange IDocs.

The Basis team assigns the SAP logical system to a client through the IMG path APPLICATION LINK ENABLING (ALE) • BASIC SETTINGS • LOGICAL SYSTEMS • ASSIGN LOGICAL SYSTEM TO CLIENT. This assignment is stored in table T000.

6.3.3 Connecting Systems to SAP

The EDI RIM is connected to SAP through an RFC destination. There are different types of RFC connections, many of which are used to connect internal SAP systems. Connection type TCP/IP supports communications with an external system.

The TCP/IP RFC destination represents the target for an RFC through the JCo connector to a listener work flow on the EDI RIM that picks up outbound IDocs for processing within the EDI system.

The RFC destination is a logical system that points to another system that will be involved in an exchange of data. It allows an external system to call RFC functions in SAP and for SAP functions to call target programs in an external system. It's the key enabler for communications with the EDI RIM in SAP.

The Basis team normally creates the RFC destination with input from the SAP EDI team. The RFC destination cannot be transported and must be manually created in each new client.

RFC destinations are created with Transaction SM59 or the ALE IMG path APPLICATION LINK ENABLING (ALE) • COMMUNICATIONS • CREATE RFC CONNECTIONS.

1. Select TCP/IP connections and click CREATE.

2. Enter the name of the registered program ID in the RFC DESTINATION field: EDI_DEV_100. This is the registered program name we up in the RIM's IDoc adapter in Chapter 5, Section 5.4.1, Outbound Services.

3. Select connection type T for TCP/IP from the CONNECTION TYPE dropdown list.

4. Enter a description in the DESCRIPTION 1 field and any additional information that might be relevant in DESCRIPTION 2 and 3.

5. Make sure the TECHNICAL SETTINGS tab is selected.

6. Select the REGISTERED SERVER PROGRAM radio button.

7. Enter the name of the RFC Destination in PROGRAM ID. This is the registered program name that we used in the RFC destination's name field. This identifies the target work for the RFC in the EDI system.

8. Enter the local SAP Gateway name or IP address in the GATEWAY HOST FIELD.

9. Enter the SAP Gateway service name in the GATEWAY SERVICE FIELD.

10. Save the RFC destination.

To test the RFC destination, click the TEST CONNECTION button. If JCo is installed correctly on the EDI application server and the IDoc Adapter is set up on the RIM, SAP will find the external system and make the connection, at least if both systems are installed in a Windows environment.

Base RFC destination options are stored in table RFCDES.

During outbound IDoc processing, the RFC destination is identified from table EDI-POX (EDIPOD for ASCII IDoc file ports), through its link to the XML file port. It's called by a C function: RFC_REMOTE_EXEC from function IDOCS_OUTPUT_IN_XML_FORMAT (IDOCS_OUTPUT_TO_FILE for ASCII file-based transfer), after the IDoc has been converted to XML, written to the IDoc database, and written to a file in a directory on the SAP application server. This C function is the trigger that starts the listener work flow on Acme's EDI RIM.

6.3.4 XML File Port

As its name implies, the XML file port enables the transfer of a physical XML IDoc file from SAP. It points to where the file will be written, gives it a name, and triggers the EDI RIM through the RFC destination.

It is a critical piece of configuration for IDocs in SAP for both inbound and outbound IDocs, as we have already seen.

The SAP EDI team creates the XML file port, although this can also be done by Basis. The XML file port cannot be transported and must be created manually in each new client.

The XML file port is created with Transaction WE21 or through the SAP EASY ACCESS path SAP MENU • TOOLS • ALE • ALE ADMINISTRATION • RUNTIME SETTINGS • PORT MAINTENANCE.

1. Select port type XML FILE and click CREATE.

2. Enter a name into the PORT field: "XML_IDOC". We'll use the same XML file port name in all three Acme clients.

3. Enter a text description for the port in the DESCRIPTION field.

4. Select the UNICODE radio button. This will add an encoding attribute to the XML tag at the top of the XML IDoc file:

   ```
   <?xml version="1.0" encoding="utf-8" ?>
   ```

5. In the OUTBOUND FILE tab, do the following:

   ▶ Select PHYSICAL DIRECTORY, and enter a directory path name. Use a logical directory if you've defined one for your IDoc outbox.

   ▶ In the FUNCTION MODULE field, select a function to name the IDoc file. We'll use EDI_PATH_CREATE_MESTYP_DOCNUM. This uses the logical message type name and IDoc number of the first IDoc in the XML file as the file name (see Figure 6.8).

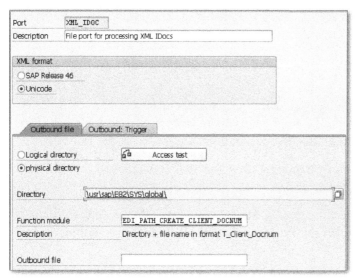

Figure 6.8 Outbound File Parameters for XML File Port XML_IDOC

6. Save the record, and click on the OUTBOUND: TRIGGER tab (see Figure 6.9).

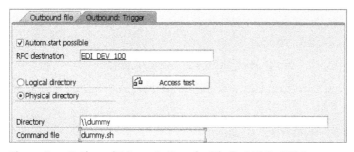

Figure 6.9 Outbound Trigger Options for File Port XML_IDOC

7. Click the AUTOM.START POSSIBLE checkbox. This is mandatory if you want to use the RFC destination to trigger processing of outbound IDocs in the EDI RIM.

8. Enter "EDI_DEV_100" in the RFC DESTINATION field.

9. Enter a dummy directory name in the DIRECTORY field and a dummy script name in the COMMAND FILE field (see Figure 6.9).

10. Save the file port.

Only outbound settings are defined in the file port, although the port is checked by the interface during inbound processing as well, as we have seen. The EDI RIM takes care of the file name and path and the RFC trigger for inbound interfaces. But the file port name must be in the control segment field SNDPRN of the incoming IDoc.

We'll only create one XML file port for all EDI transfers at Acme Pictures. Some sites create multiple file ports to distinguish IDoc flows in the IDoc database for different departments or organizations or for other reasons. This is a design decision. We only really need one port, so we're keeping things simple at Acme Pictures.

XML file port definitions are stored in table EDIPOX. ASCII IDoc file port definitions are stored in table EDIPOD.

An Undocumented Opportunity

The DIRECTORY and COMMAND FILE fields in the OUTBOUND: TRIGGER tab of the XML file port reflect the days when scripts were called in the operating system to move files between SAP and an external EDI system. Scripts are not required when an RFC destination is invoked because it triggers the external application, which pulls in the IDoc file.

The two fields are still mandatory. Their contents are passed to the external application when the RFC is made, along with the path and file name of the IDoc file. The contents of the command file fields are passed as export parameters through the C function call that triggers the EDI RIM through the RFC destination.

The contents of the command file fields are available to the EDI system and can be used to pass additional information from SAP for custom processing within the EDI system if this information can be read with XPath queries.

6.4 Summary

We've begun to explore IDocs and the IDoc interface in a little more detail. We've looked at IDoc terminology, architecture and its various objects, from domains and data elements to segments and basic types. The SAP Data Dictionary plays a critical role in the construction of IDocs. Its tables and structures make it a useful tool for understanding how IDocs are assembled and structured.

We looked at the differences between internal and external representations of ASCII IDocs and went over the structure of the all-important control segment that marks the beginning of every IDoc.

The SAP EDI team at Acme Pictures decided to use XML IDocs because they're easier to read and hand-build than the more traditional ASCII IDocs. So the team lead insisted that we introduce the anatomy of an XML IDoc to all of our stakeholders.

We also went over some one-time configuration to enable a communications link between SAP and an external EDI system that must be set up before we can begin exchanging IDocs with the EDI RIM.

It's time to dive deeper now and go over IDoc configuration to support the exchange of business documents with an external EDI system. In the next chapter we lay out how we configure Acme's SAP system to send and receive IDocs with Gordy's Galaxy of Games & B Flix through the new EDI RIM.

"Make it work!" was one of Darryl Q's signature lines whenever one of his directors struggled with the talents of a favorite would-be starlet. Darryl Q understood that his protégés needed an environment that supported their potential. Same thing with IDocs—they can do their job only in an environment that's been set up to support them. So enter, stage left... configuration!

7 Configuring IDocs in SAP for EDI Exchange

There's an old Hollywood saying: "The only thing worse than people talking about you is people not talking about you." Acme Pictures' legendary founder Darryl Q. Fernhausen understood the truth of this deep in his bones: it's all about recognition.

Hollywood lives and dies on recognition. From the stars to their agents and the studio executives, this is a business that can thrive only when it is readily recognized by millions of people around the world.

It's the same thing with IDocs. They can do their jobs only if the system recognizes them. After all, IDocs by themselves are only entries in tables linked to other records and to processing functions. Until SAP is told what they are going to do, with what business document, and for what customer or vendor, they remain passive, unrecognized records scattered across multiple tables with lots of potential but no ability to realize it.

Configuration, then, is about setting up the system to recognize when, how, and for whom to process an IDoc. This recognition, as we will see, is critical at runtime. So we'll begin by looking at inbound setup and processing.

7.1 Inbound Configuration is About Posting IDocs

The basic fact about inbound IDocs is that they create a business document in the receiving SAP system just as a data entry operator would if he or she were entering data manually from, for example, a paper purchase order.

Inbound configuration tells the system what function to run to post an IDoc to a business document for one or more trading partners or external systems. This means matching up control segment keys to system data that are used to recognize the IDoc, the sending partner or system, and the process to call to post the business document.

7.1.1 Key Values for Inbound IDoc Posting

SAP knows what to do with an incoming IDoc from fields in the control segment EDI_DC40 that must match the inbound partner profile and system keys in the receiving client. These fields are listed in Table 7.1 in the order in which they appear in the control record.

Field	Description	Value
RCVPOR	Receiving port. Always a concatenation of SAP+<SystemID>.	SAPDEV
RCVPRT	Receiving partner type. Always logical system.	LS
RCVPRN	Receiving partner. Always the logical system for the receiving SAP client.	DEVCLNT100
MESCOD	Message code. Identifies different use cases for the same partner/logical message. Value can be null or anything else.	
MESFCT	Message function. Same as MESCOD.	
SNDPOR	Sending port. The outbound XML port set up with Transaction WE21.	XML_IDOC
SNDPRT	Sending partner type (i.e., customer, vendor, etc.) as configured in Transaction WE44.	KU
SNDPRN	Sending partner. Must exist in receiving system master data. We'll be using the sold-to partner for Gordy, at least for orders.	GRDY01
MESTYP	Logical message type for IDoc.	ORDERS
IDOCTP	IDoc basic type.	ORDERS05
RCVPFC	Receiver partner function. Always null for inbound IDocs.	

Table 7.1 Control Segment Keys Match Inbound Partner Profile

Field	Description	Value
SNDPFC	Receiver partner function (i.e., sold-to partner). Value can be null or one of a defined list of functions per partner type.	SP

Table 7.1 Control Segment Keys Match Inbound Partner Profile (Cont.)

7.1.2 Partner Type

Partner type is a critical concept—and a mandatory key—in the creation of a partner profile, regardless of direction. It defines the type of partner that for the general header of the partner profile and is used to confirm that the partner exists in master data.

The confirmation is handled by a form routine in an ABAP program defined with Transaction WE44. The partner type identifies the master data table to read to confirm the partner number. The only partner type that is not checked is User. The seven standard partner types are listed in Table 7.2.

Partner Type	Description	Table Read
B	Bank	T012
BP	Benefits provider	BUT000
GP	Business partner	BUT000
KU	Customer	KNA1
LI	Vendor	LFA1
LS	Logical system	TBDLST
US	User—not checked	N/A

Table 7.2 Standard Partner Types for Partner Profiles

Custom partner types can be added with Transaction WE44, although it's not commonly done. You would first create or identify a table to store the partner master data. Next you would create a form in a custom ABAP program with a simple SQL statement to check the table each time a new partner number is entered into a partner profile with the custom partner type. Then you would add the custom partner type and check program to the table in Transaction WE44.

There are two basic ways to configure partner profiles for an external EDI system.

The first is to use partner type LS (logical system) for all trading partners and IDocs that would point at the EDI RIM. The advantage of this is that you maintain only one partner profile for all partners. But it adds a little more complexity to outbound configuration and makes it more difficult to identify IDocs for specific trading partners using standard SAP reporting tools.

Logical system is appropriate for system-to-system ALE exchange of IDocs. If you were working with SAP's process integration middleware (SAP NetWeaver Process Integration, for example), you would set up an LS type partner profile for PI and use other means to identify IDocs for specific trading partners.

The cleaner and more traditional approach to partner profile configuration for EDI is to use specific partner types such as customer (KU) and vendor (LI). This means one partner profile for each EDI customer or vendor, which simplifies production support, reporting, and auditing in SAP because it's easy to identify IDocs by partner number.

We'll take the old-school approach and work exclusively with customer and vendor partner types in our Acme Pictures SAP EDI project. For now, we'll look at inbound configuration, which is simpler than outbound configuration and includes the following tasks:

▶ Create an inbound partner profile for all inbound IDocs

▶ Enter inbound reference data to EDI configuration tables for inbound purchase orders that will post to sales orders

7.1.3 Inbound Partner Profile for an ORDERS PO

Partner profiles exist at a general and directional level, each corresponding to a table in the SAP Data Dictionary.

Partner profiles define IDoc traffic between the local SAP client and the outside world, whether that's another SAP system, SAP NetWeaver PI, or an external, third-party integration platform, regardless of where it lives.

This definition includes linking a sending (inbound) or receiving (outbound) trading partner to a logical message and process (function module or workflow) that triggers application services in the IDoc interface.

It also links to underlying system configuration that is not explicitly entered into the partner profile. This is especially true for inbound IDocs, illustrated in the base configuration trail for an inbound partner profile in Figure 7.1.

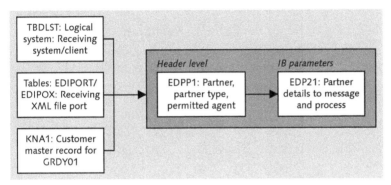

Figure 7.1 Underlying Relationships of the Inbound Partner Profile

This configuration trail includes background values in the master data used by the system to validate IDocs during inbound processing and explicit values entered into the partner profile at the header level (stored in table EDPP1) and inbound parameters level (stored in table EDP21).

Inbound partner profiles must be unique even if the same partner is sending the same logical message for different interfaces. This is enforced by the following key fields in table EDP21:

▸ MANDT: SAP client (mandatory; system-assigned)

▸ SNDPRN: Sending partner (mandatory)

▸ SNDPRT: Sending partner type (mandatory)

▸ SNDPFC: Partner function or role (optional)

▸ MESTYP: Logical message type (mandatory)

▸ MESCOD: Message code (optional)

▸ MESFCT: Message function (optional)

▸ TEST: Test flag indicating IDoc a test message (optional)

All of these fields must be populated in the IDoc control record and they must match the values in the inbound partner profile. In addition, the IDoc basic type is not identified in the inbound partner profile, but it is mandatory in the control record. The system needs this to identify the structure of the incoming IDoc.

Partner profiles are created with Transaction WE20 or through the SAP EASY ACCESS menu SAP MENU • TOOLS • ALE • ALE ADMINISTRATION • RUNTIME SETTINGS • PARTNER PROFILES.

We'll create an inbound partner profile to receive an ORDERS message type for a customer purchase order from Gordy's Galaxy in this section. The principles are the same for all partners and inbound IDocs.

Transporting Partner Profiles

Partner profiles cannot be transported from client to client. Typically, they are recreated manually each time you move to a different SAP system.

If you have a large number of partner profiles, you can build a custom load program using standard functions that SAP uses in the Transaction WE20 program to build its partner profiles. We look at a sample load program in Chapter 19, Section 19.2, Mass Upload of Partner Profiles to SAP.

An IDoc can also be generated to send partner profiles to a remote system. The logical message type is SYPART with basic type SYPART01.

Generate IDoc in Transaction WE20 by selecting menu option UTILITIES(M) • IDOC OUTPUT or [Ctrl]+[F8]. A pop-up dialog will prompt for a partner number and partner type. Click the OK checkmark and another dialog will ask for the following values:

- Partner number
- Partner type
- Partner role
- Message code
- Message function

All it needs is an outbound partner profile for message type SYPART and a logical system partner.

This functionality is not meant for mass transport of IDocs. To generate the IDoc, you need an outbound partner profile for SYPART and the receiving partner whose partner profile you want to send.

The SYPART partner profile needs to exactly match the key for the call to SYPART and for the partner profile you want to pull. While not really useful for transporting IDocs, this is a good way to play with the functionality and data behind partner profiles. It is recommended as a learning tool.

Create Header Level

The header level is common to inbound and outbound partner profiles. To create the partner profile header level for Gordy's Galaxy, follow these steps:

1. Click CREATE or press function key F5 in Transaction WE20.

2. Enter "GRDY01" (Gordy's SAP customer number) in the PARTNER NO. field and "KU" in PARTNER TYPE.

3. Enter the values shown in Figure 7.2 into the fields in the POST PROCESSING: PERMITTED AGENT tab.

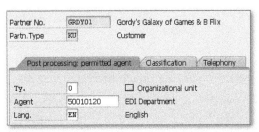

Figure 7.2 The Header Level of the Partner Profile for Gordy

Use your own post-processing permitted agent and don't forget to save. You can now add any number of unique inbound and outbound partner profiles for Gordy's Galaxy.

Post-Processing Permitted Agent

This is a mandatory entry and is used by the workflow system to route error messages to SAP Office mail inboxes if workflow error processing is turned on and configured.

The post-processing agent can be a work center, job, organization, person, position, or user. It's best to use an organization or position dedicated to IDoc monitoring and support.

Except for the user, which is created by the Basis team, permitted agent types are generally created by the HR team within an organizational structure in SAP that supports HR processing.

Inbound Parameters for Gordy's ORDERS

To create the inbound partner profile for message type ORDERS, follow these steps:

1. Click the CREATE INBOUND PARAMETER icon below the inbound parameters table control on the main PARTNER PROFILES screen, as illustrated in Figure 7.3.

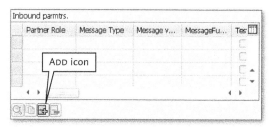

Figure 7.3 Add a New Inbound Partner Profile

2. Enter "AG" or "SP" (sold-to) into the PARTNER ROLE field. The partner number in control segment field SNDPRN must now be Gordy's sold-to number. If you enter "AG", it will be converted to "SP" for display. But it is saved as "AG" in the database.

   Partner role or partner function is an optional parameter that can be used to describe a particular type of partner so the values are linked to the partner type. For example, a customer partner type can be a sold-to, bill-to, ship-to, or many other partner types. Partner function can be used to create a unique entry for the same message and partner type.

   If the partner function is used, it becomes part of the unique partner function key in EDP21 and must be populated in the SNDPFC field in the control segment of an inbound IDoc.

3. Enter "ORDERS" in MESSAGE TYPE.

4. Enter ORDE in the PROCESS CODE field. This links the logical message type to IDoc function IDOC_INPUT_ORDERS, which posts the IDoc to a sales order. Double-click ORDE and you'll see the link to the function module (as shown in Figure 7.4).

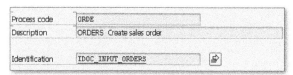

Figure 7.4 Link Between Process Code and Function

Double-click the function name and you'll land in the ABAP code, if you have authorization to view code.

Click the right-pointing arrow icon and you'll land in the DISPLAY VIEW "FUNC-TION MODULES FOR INBOUND ALE-EDI": DETAILS screen. This links the process code to the function, and objects for the IDoc, IDoc packet or batch of IDocs, and application (see Figure 7.5).

The two IDoc and IDoc packet objects link to workflow methods and events that control error processing for the linked message type. These generate the workflow tasks that we looked at deleting in Chapter 5, Section 5.7.2, Deleting IDoc Generated Work Items.

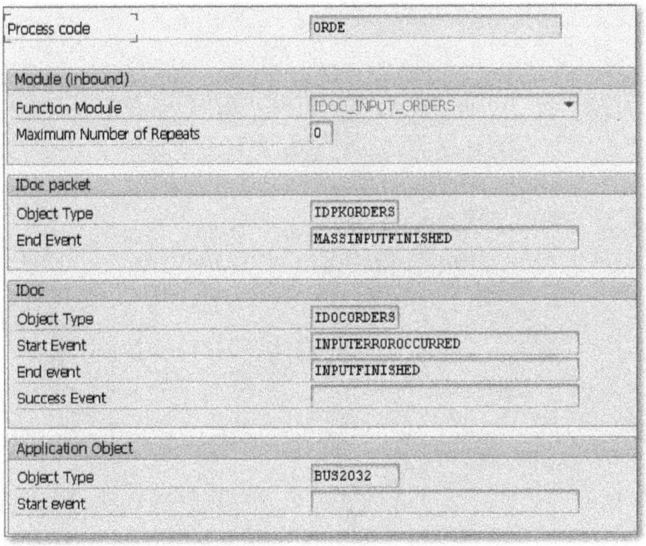

Process code	ORDE
Module (inbound)	
Function Module	IDOC_INPUT_ORDERS
Maximum Number of Repeats	0
IDoc packet	
Object Type	IDPKORDERS
End Event	MASSINPUTFINISHED
IDoc	
Object Type	IDOCORDERS
Start Event	INPUTERROROCCURRED
End event	INPUTFINISHED
Success Event	
Application Object	
Object Type	BUS2032
Start event	

Figure 7.5 Another View from the Inbound Partner Profile

The application object links the IDoc to a particular business document, such a sales or purchase order. It represents an object in the Business Object Repository. The link is configured with Transaction WE57. The application object can also be used to search for IDocs that are linked to particular types of business document.

5. Back in the PARTNER PROFILES: INBOUND PARAMETERS screen, select TRIGGER BY BACKGROUND PROGRAM under PROCESSING BY FUNCTION MODULE.

This batches IDocs at status 64—*IDoc ready to be transferred to application*—until program RBDAPP01 is run to kick off posting of the IDoc to a sales order. This is a design decision aimed at controlling the flow of IDoc data posting business documents in Acme's SAP system.

Selecting TRIGGER IMMEDIATELY will post the IDoc to a sales order as soon it has been saved to the IDoc database.

6. Save. The inbound partner profile will look like Figure 7.6.

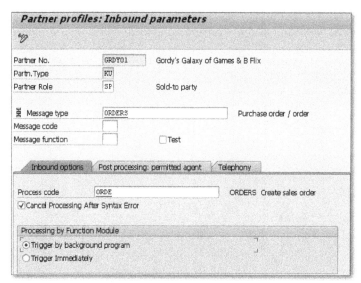

Figure 7.6 Inbound Options for Message Type ORDERS

MESSAGE CODE and MESSAGE FUNCTION are optional fields that correspond to the control segments fields MESCOD and MESFCT. Their purpose is to allow creation of additional inbound (or outbound) partner profiles for the same message type and partner.

They can be used, for example, to trigger custom processing on an ORDERS (or any other) message type to handle a requirement that is not covered by the standard IDoc.

7.1.4 Inbound EDI Reference Data

Three EDI conversion tables are relevant to the creation of a sales order from an incoming customer PO, including the following:

▸ EDPAR: Converts external to internal SAP partner numbers. Also used for outbound orders, order acknowledgments, and invoice IDocs. Another table—PUMA—converts between external and internal partner numbers for delivery documents.

▸ EDSDC: Identifies sales organization and document type by vendor.

▸ KNMT: Customer Material Info Record. Converts external customer material number to internal SAP material number.

In addition, we'll build a custom EDI mapping table—ZEDIXREF—in Acme's SAP system. It will map the EDI interchange partner ID to the SAP partner number in the SNDPRN field of the IDoc control segment. The IDoc control segment must match the partner profile set up for the customer or vendor, direction, and message type.

EDPAR External Partner Number Conversion

The structure of EDPAR is detailed in Table 7.3. The key fields are critical to partner number conversion.

Field	Key	Description
MANDT	X	SAP client.
KUNNR	X	Internal SAP customer or vendor number. This can come from SNDPRN, or from an application table depending on the IDoc and direction being processed.
PARVW	X	Partner type (such as sold-to, ship-to, vendor, supplier, and so on) checked against table TPAR.
EXPNR	X	External partner number in the remote system.
INPNR		Internal SAP partner number read linked to KUNNR, PARVW, and EXPNR. System does not check that this is a valid SAP partner number.

Table 7.3 Field Structure of the EDPAR Partner Conversion Table

Gordy's Galaxy has more than 2,000 store locations and distribution centers across the United States and Canada. Each one has a unique identification number in Gordy's internal business system.

Acme has its own unique partner ID for each of its customers, including Gordy's sold-to and ship-to partners, assigned by their new SAP system. EDPAR's job is to convert the sold-to and ship-to location numbers that Gordy sends in their 850 X12 PO to Acme's corresponding internal SAP partner number.

This is important. Each sales order is created against one sold-to and one ship-to partner using Acme's SAP numbers. Other partner relationships are pulled into the order from the customer master record of the sold-to partner, including bill-to and payer partners.

When Gordy sends an 850 PO, its bill-to number, which is an internal purchasing organization, is stored in the N1 segment with qualifier BT.

The store location is in a header level N1 segment with qualifier UL for Universal Locator, which is how X12 identifies the GLN. It can also be in one or more SDQ segments at the line item level, but we're not concerned with that for now.

Gordy's supplier ID (that is, the number its system uses to identify Acme Pictures) is also stored in the N1 segment, with qualifier SU. We'll see how this is used when we look at table EDSDC.

We'll map Gordy's bill-to, ship-to, and supplier numbers to the E1EDKA1 segment of the ORDERS IDoc. The bill-to and ship-to will be converted to Acme's internal SAP numbers through EDPAR. The supplier number will not be converted by EDPAR.

There's an interesting wrinkle here. Gordy has a chain of club stores—Klub Kazoo— with their own customer accounts in Acme's SAP system: sold-to, bill-to, and ship-to numbers used for ordering, shipping, and invoicing.

But Gordy pays the bills and is set up as Klub Kazoo's payer (partner type PY) in Acme's customer master. Furthermore, Gordy orders for all its retail and Klub Kazoo stores in the same 850 interchange using the same EDI sender ID in the ISA segment and the same sold-to partner in N1 with qualifier BT.

In the control segment, and the partner profile, Acme only uses the sold-to number for Gordy's retail for both organizations. But each sales order must post to Acme's SAP system with the correct sold-to number and ship-to in E1EDKA1, whether that's Gordy's retail or Klub Kazoo.

Thankfully, retail and club sold-to numbers can be distinguished in the 850 transaction by the department code in the REF segment. If the department code in REF02 is 0001, Acme's SAP sold-to number is for Gordy's retail. If REF02 is 0005, the SAP sold-to number is for Klub Kazoo.

In either case, we will map the department code to E1EDKA1-LIFNR, where PARVW equals AG.

The ship-to GLNs will also be mapped to E1EDKA1-LIFNR but PARVW will be set to WE. The supplier number won't be converted by EDPAR but it will be used to read EDSDC, as we shall soon see. It will map to E1EDKA1-PARTN and PARVW will be set to LF.

The control segment partner number in SNDPRN, which must match up with Gordy's partner profile, will be read from a custom EDI lookup table in SAP before the IDoc is written to the IDoc database and is assigned a number, as we'll see when we look at custom table ZEDIXREF.

External partner conversion for the inbound purchase order with EDPAR is called in function `IDOC_INPUT_ORDERS`, after the IDoc has been written to the database and is ready for application processing. It occurs in a loop on the data segments within the form routine `INTERPRET_IDOC_ORDERS`.

Segment E1EDKA1 can occur up to 99 times. Each time it loops, the code evaluates the qualifier in PARVW in the following order:

1. AG: Sold-to partner, read from the SNDPRN field of the IDoc control segment unless the partner type is LS (logical system) or the sold-to is in E1EDKA1-PARTN.

2. LF: Vendor.

3. WE: Ship-to location.

4. SP: Shipping carrier.

5. RE: Invoice recipient.

6. RG: Payer.

7. WK: Destination plant.

8. OTHERS: other partner types recorded in table TPAR.

The logic to convert external to internal SAP partner numbers in EDPAR is the same for all inbound partner types, and is outlined in Figure 7.7.

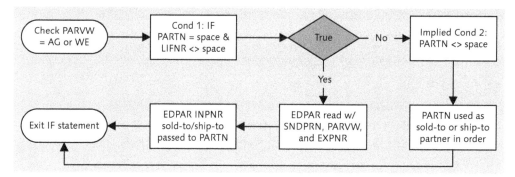

Figure 7.7 EDPAR Inbound Partner Number Conversion for Sold-To

1. Partner type is determined from E1EDKA1-PARVW. First up is AG, the sold-to partner.

2. Condition 1 is true: E1EDKA1-PARTN is null, and E1EDKA1-LIFNR is not null. The internal SAP partner number is read from EDPAR using the key:

```
KUNNR = IDOC_CONTROL-SNDPRN (GRDY01)
PARVW = E1EDKA1-PARVW (AG)
EXPNR = E1EDKA1-LIFNR (0001)
```

3. If EXPNR equals 0001, then INPRN returns Gordy's internal sold-to number, which will post to the sales order.

4. If EXPNR equals 0005, then INPRN returns Klub Kazoo's internal sold-to number.

5. If INPRN is not found, an error message is returned and the IDoc fails to post to a sales order.

6. If E1EDKA1-PARTN is not null, it posts to the sales order as the internal SAP sold-to partner number.

The basic principle is that if PARTN is populated, the system assumes that it is the internal SAP partner number and there is no conversion. If LIFNR is populated and PARTN is null, the partner number is external and EDPAR conversion is run. The ship-to partner is converted in the same way.

The key to making this work is the data we enter into EDPAR with Transaction VOE4. Figure 7.8 lists the entries we made for this example.

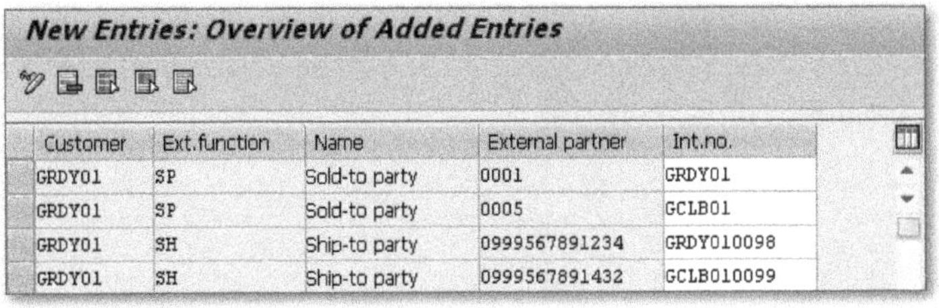
New Entries: Overview of Added Entries

Customer	Ext.function	Name	External partner	Int.no.
GRDY01	SP	Sold-to party	0001	GRDY01
GRDY01	SP	Sold-to party	0005	GCLB01
GRDY01	SH	Ship-to party	0999567891234	GRDY010098
GRDY01	SH	Ship-to party	0999567891432	GCLB010099

Figure 7.8 EDPAR Entries for Gordy and Klub Kazoo

The left-most column labeled CUSTOMER holds Gordy's sold-to number pulled from the control segment field SNDPRN. The external (partner) function SP in column two (labeled EXT.FUNCTION; converted from AG by the system) and the EXTERNAL PARTNER number in column four—the department ID from the REF segment of the X12 850 transaction—maps to the internal SAP sold-to partner in the fifth column (labeled INT.NO.).

Record one holds the internal sold-to partner for Gordy's retail. Record two has the internal sold-to partner for Klub Kazoo. Records three and four are ship-to locations, identified by partner function SH—one for Gordy's retail and the other for Klub Kazoo.

The newly converted SAP partner numbers now are ready to be used by the system to create the sales orders from Gordy's PO.

EDSDC: Sales Organization

EDSDC does a simple but important conversion critical to the creation of a sales order. It identifies the sales organization and order type by linking to the internal sold-to partner number and the vendor number sent by the customer in the 850 transaction.

These values are required to create the sales order with Transaction VA01, whether the order is being created manually (as in Figure 7.9) or automatically by an IDoc.

The sales organization and order type values can be passed in the IDoc in segment E1EDK14 (Organizational Data). But they are internal Acme values and Gordy has no need to keep them or transmit them. We can hard-code them in the map, but we may need to use different sales organizations or order types based on the contents of the X12 850 transaction.

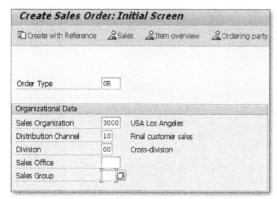

Figure 7.9 Creating a Sales Order Manually with EDSDC Values

The vendor can be used to drive different sales organizations or order types for a customer. It's not checked by EDSDC, so it can be anything we need it be. But we're going to keep this simple in our example.

The structure of EDSDC is detailed in Table 7.4.

Field	Key	Description
MANDT	X	SAP client
KUNNR	X	Customer number 1 (generally an SAP partner number)
LIFNR	X	Customer's internal vendor number
VKORG		Sales organization
VTWEG		Distribution channel
SPART		Division
AUART		Sales document type

Table 7.4 EDSDC Identifies the Sales Organization

As we have seen, Gordy sends its internal vendor number for Acme in the N1 segment of the 850 PO with the qualifier SU for supplier. This is mapped to E1EDKA1-PARTN in the IDoc with partner type LF in PARVW.

EDSDC is also read in function IDOC_INPUT_ORDERS. During the partner processing loop in form INTERPRET_IDOC_ORDERS through segment E1EDKA1, the vendor number in PARTN (PARVW equals LF) is passed to variable LIEFERANT.

This variable, with the sold-to number converted through EDPAR, is used to read the sales organization and order type in EDSDC in form `CHECK_IDOC_ORDERS` using two keys:

```
KUNNR = VBAK-KUNNR (Sold-to Partner GRDY01)
LIFNR = LIEFERANT (from E1EDKA1-PARTN with PARVW LF)
```

We need to create mapping records in EDSDC for Gordy's retail and Klub Kazoo sold-to numbers with Transaction VOE2, New Entries. Gordy's retail entry is shown in Figure 7.10.

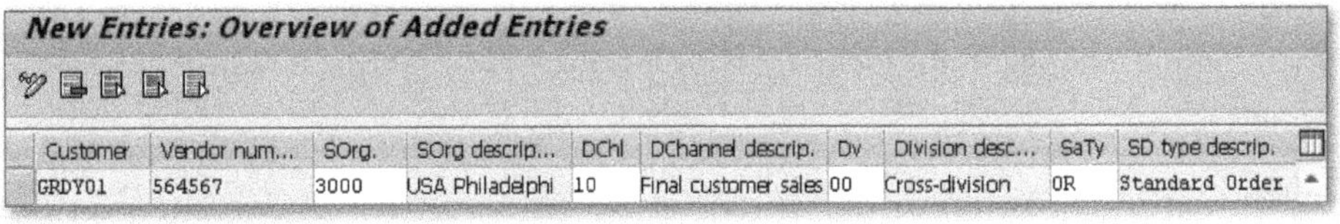
New Entries: Overview of Added Entries

Customer	Vendor num...	SOrg.	SOrg descrip...	DChl	DChannel descrip.	Dv	Division desc...	SaTy	SD type descrip.
GRDY01	564567	3000	USA Philadelphi	10	Final customer sales	00	Cross-division	OR	Standard Order

Figure 7.10 EDSDC Sales Organization and Order Type Mapping to Gordy

KNMT: Customer Material Info Record

The Customer Material Info Record (CMIR) in tables KNMTK (CMIR header) and KNMT (CMIR details) converts the customer's item number to the internal SAP material number in the supplier's system.

The customer's item number is sent in the PO1 segment at the item detail level of the 850 transaction. It can occur up to 10 times within PO1 in data element 0234 qualified by data element 0235.

Most of Acme's customers send between one and three instances of the item number in the 850. Gordy sends Acme two with the following qualifiers:

- IN: Buyer's item number
- UP: The 12-digit UPC number

The 850 item numbers are mapped to E1EDP19-IDNTR at the item level of the IDoc with the following qualifiers in field QUALF:

- 001: Customer material number
- 003: EAN (European Article Number), which stores either the UPC or GTIN number

The UPC or GTIN numbers are stored in the SAP material master record in the EAN/UPC field in the Basic data 1 screen (field MARA-EAN11). If sent in the IDoc, they're stored in the sales order at the item level in field VBAP-EAN11 and displayed in the EAN/UPC field in the Sales A screen.

The conversion process for the external material number is called from form DETERMINE_MATERIAL in form CHECK_IDOC_ORDERS in function IDOC_INPUT_ORDERS.

It runs after all data have been extracted from the IDoc segments, in a loop on internal table XVBAP, which stores the item level details of the sales order.

The first check determines whether the sales order is being created against a quote or contract. If yes, the material in the IDoc is ignored and the item number is pulled instead from the quote or contract.

If the internal SAP material is present (whether it was pulled from E1EDP19 with QUAL 002 or from a quote or contract item number), conversion logic is not run.

If, on the other hand, an external item number is sent in E1EDP19 with QUAL 001, CMIR is read to get the SAP material number with function RV_CUSTOMER_MATE-RIAL_READ. The following values are passed to the function:

```
CMR_KDMAT = XVBAP-KDMAT (Customer item from E1EDP19)
CMR_KUNNR = XVBAK-KUNNR (Internal SAP customer number)
CMR_VKORG = XVBAK-VKORG (Sales organization)
CMR_VTWEG = XVBAK-VTWEG (Distribution channel)
CMR_SPART = XVBAK-SPART (Division)
```

The function reads table KNMT and returns the complete record that matches the parameters fed to it. The key fields for the CMIR conversion in KNMT are listed in Table 7.5.

Field	Key	Description
MANDT	X	SAP client
VKORG	X	Sales organization
VTWEG	X	Distribution channel
KUNNR	X	SAP customer number
MATNR	X	SAP material number
KDMAT		Customer material number

Table 7.5 KNMT Keys Used in CMIR Item Number Conversion

If the function makes a hit, the SAP material number is returned in a KNMT string and plugged into the MATERIAL field at the item level of the sales order, through the internal table field XVBAP-MATNR. If there is no hit, an error is returned and the order does not post.

The customer material number is also posted to the sales order, to the table field VBAP-KDMAT and the CUSTOMER MATERIAL field in the item level ORDER DATA screen, which references customer purchase order data.

The customer material information record is master data. If it is to be used, it should be part of the standard master data creation process for EDI materials.

CMIR is populated by Transaction VD51 or from the SAP menu path LOGISTICS • SALES AND DISTRIBUTION • MASTER DATA • AGREEMENTS • CUSTOMER MATERIAL INFORMATION • CREATE. CMIR records are changed with Transaction VD52 and displayed with Transaction VD53.

To create a CMIR record linking Acme's internal SAP to Gordy's material numbers, go to Transaction VD51 and follow these steps:

1. Enter Gordy's sold-to partner number ("GRDY01") in the CUSTOMER field.

2. Enter the sales organization "3000".

3. Enter the distribution channel "10 and click EXECUTE.

4. Enter Acme's SAP item ("245", in our example) in the MATERIAL NO. field of the table control.

5. Enter the customer's item number ("89478522851") in the CUST. MATERIAL field.

6. Save the record. It should look like the example in Figure 7.11.

Figure 7.11 CMIR Maps Acme's SAP to Gordy's Item Number

This assumes, of course, that all the supporting master data have already been created: customers, plants, sales organizations, materials, and so on.

ZEDIXREF: Custom EDI SAP Trading Partner ID Conversion

We also need to convert the EDI trading partner ID that Gordy uses to send and receive EDI interchanges to the SAP partner numbers that Acme uses to set up its inbound partner profiles.

As we've seen, the IDoc control segment field SNDPRN must match the SAP partner number in the partner profile before SAP can recognize who the IDoc is from. The RIM is not an extension of SAP and does not natively map between the EDI trading partner ID's and the SAP partner numbers.

Besides, it's not always a one-to-one relationship. Each customer usually has only one EDI trading partner ID, but not always. There are companies that use multiple trading partner IDs for different internal organizations.

And SAP can have multiple partner profiles set up for the same customer, with different partner types and numbers. An inbound sales order, for example, might be set up for the sold-to partner. But an inbound or outbound delivery could be set up by the customer's ship-to location with a different customer number. An invoice or payment could be set up for a bill-to or payer or other partner type with a different number from the sold-to.

So we need a table somewhere in the RIM or in SAP that maps the incoming EDI trading partner ID to the internal SAP partner number, which matches the inbound partner profile.

For Acme Pictures we'll build this custom table—we'll call it ZEDIXREF—in SAP. Luckily, there is a customer exit called just before the IDoc is written to the IDoc database that allows us to make last minute changes to the control segment. The exit—in enhancement SIDOC001—is called during both inbound and outbound IDoc processing.

We'll write code in this user exit to read ZEDIXREF during inbound processing to pick up what we need to complete our control segment.

The structure of ZEDIXREF is listed in Table 7.6.

Field	Key	Description
MANDT	X	SAP client number
DIRECT	X	IDoc Direction
STDMES	X	EDI transaction or message
MESTYP	X	IDoc logical message type
IDOCTP	X	IDoc basic type
CIMTYP		IDoc extension
SNDPRN		SAP sender partner number
RCVPRN		SAP receiver partner number
SNDLAD		EDI sender trading partner number
RCVLAD		EDI receiver trading partner number

Table 7.6 Structure of Custom Table ZEDIXREF

During inbound processing, we'll read fields SNDPRN and RCVPRN into the same fields in the IDoc from ZEDIXREF using the following control segment keys:

▶ EDIDC-DIR: Direction

▶ EDIDC-STDMES: EDI transaction or message, mapped from the EDI transaction set

▶ EDIDC-MESTYP: IDoc logical message type

▶ EDIDC-IDOCTP: IDoc Basic type

▶ EDIDC-CIMTYP: IDoc extension

▶ EDIDC-SNDLAD: EDI sender trading partner number, mapped from the interchange sender ID

▶ EDIDC-RCVLAD: EDI receiver trading partner number, mapped from the interchange receiver ID

We get into the details of the development effort in Chapter 19, Section 19.1, Mapping the EDI Trading Partner to the Control Segment.

This table needs to be populated for each IDoc EDI interface we configure in SAP. For Gordy's inbound ORDERS purchase order message, we'll add the values listed in Table 7.7.

Field	Value	Description
DIRECT	2	Direction inbound
STDMES	850	EDI PO transaction
MESTYP	ORDERS	IDoc message type
IDOCTP	ORDERS05	IDoc basic type
CIMTYP		IDoc extension
SNDPRN	GRDY01	SAP send partner: Gordy's customer number in Acme's system
RCVPRN	DEVCLNT100	SAP receive partner: Acme SAP logical system
SNDLAD	01234567US0	EDI send trading partner ID
RCVLAD	9999999USD	EDI receive trading partner ID

Table 7.7 ZEDIXREF Entry for the Inbound 850 from Gordy

These entries will allow our code to find the correct SAP send and receive partner numbers and then pass them to the SNDPRN and RCVPRN fields of the IDoc control segment before it is written to the database. Without these values, the IDoc would fail.

7.1.5 Tying It All Together: The SAP EDI Inbound Processing Flow

The beauty of the IDoc interface is that all IDocs are processed in the same way. When you understand how one works, you pretty well understand how they all work.

This is especially true for inbound processing, which is all about posting a business document in SAP. In our example, this would be a sales order created from an inbound XML ORDERS.ORDERS05 IDoc converted from an 850 customer PO from Gordy.

To enable inbound processing for Gordy's ORDERS, we need the following:

▸ An XML file port: XML_IDOC
▸ A partner profile for Gordy with inbound parameters:
  ▸ Partner function SP (AG in database) for sold-to partner
  ▸ Message type ORDERS

- ▸ Process code ORDE, linked to function `IDOC_INPUT_ORDERS`
- ▸ Trigger by background program selected

▸ Inbound EDI reference data set up for Gordy in EDPAR, EDSDC, and our custom table ZEDIXREF

The inbound EDI IDoc process flow in SAP for this configuration is outlined in Figure 7.12.

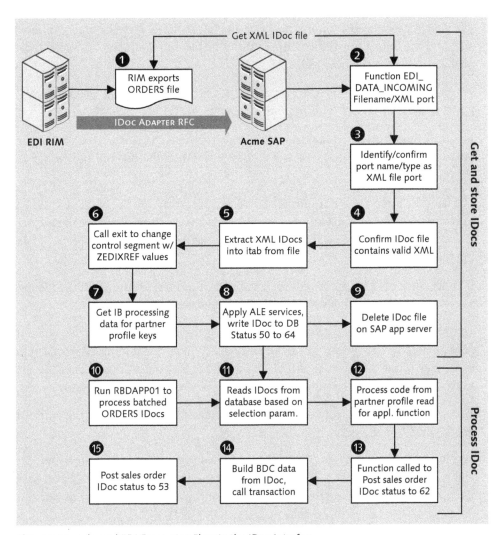

Figure 7.12 Inbound EDI Processing Flow in the IDoc Interface

These steps are implemented by a series of standard function modules that perform the real work of the IDoc interface. Functions that retrieve and kick off inbound processing of IDocs are in function group EDIN. Other function groups are called on to post the IDoc to a business document. We'll look at the key processing steps as we go through the flow for a typical inbound ORDERS.ORDERS05 IDoc. Here's how it works.

Getting and Storing the IDocs

The EDI RIM calls RFC function EDI_DATA_INCOMING in SAP through the IDoc adapter. The full path and file name to the IDoc file and the name of the XML file port are passed to the function.

The port type (in this case, XML) is identified and verified for XML file port XML_IDOC in table EDIPORT with function EDI_PORT_READ.

If it isn't found, an error message is returned. Otherwise, the system checks the port type and calls function IDOC_XML_FROM_FILE with the file and port name as parameters.

The IDoc file is read into an internal table through a string and the first line checked to confirm that it is valid XML. The system then checks to see whether the file has already been processed by reading table EDFI2 with function EDI_EDFI2_READ in function group EDFI2.

If an instance of the current record in the IDoc file is found in EDFI2, the file has already been processed, an error is returned, and the import fails.

This means that there was an interruption during an earlier run and the file was not fully processed. The system creates an entry in EDFI2 during inbound processing to keep track of the last processed IDoc in the file. This entry is deleted once the file is processed, unless there's an interruption for any reason, and processing ceases.

To reprocess the IDocs from the failed file, you need to either change the name of the file or delete the entry from EDFI2.

You'll probably want to get Basis involved if you decide to delete the entry. Or you can call function EDI_EDFI2_DELETE to delete the entry from EDFI2. Just pass the full path and file name to the function import parameter from the test tool in the FUNCTION BUILDER through Transaction SE37 or SE80.

If there is no record of the current IDoc in EDFI2, the system writes one.

A process of confirmation and conversion then begins. The second node of the XML file is read to confirm that the tag name for each IDoc is `<IDOC BEGIN="1">` and the control record is identified to confirm the beginning of each IDoc.

The control record is then converted from XML to a structured string. Next the external control segment structure EDI_DC40 is converted to the internal EDIDC with function `IDOC_CTRL_INBOUND_CONVERT`, and it is updated with direction, client number, receiver port, and release number, and the IDoc number field is cleared.

The IDoc data are then converted from XML into a string with the EDIDD structure and appended to the control segment.

Once these conversions are run and the IDocs are built into strings within the internal table, the IDocs are written to the IDoc database with function `IDOC_INBOUND_WRITE_TO_DB`.

But first the system offers a last chance to modify the control record by calling function `EDI_CONTROL_RECORD_MODIFY` that invokes `EXIT_SAPLEDI1_001` in enhancement SIDOC001 (Transaction SMOD). The entire control record is passed to the user exit and all of its fields can be changed before the IDoc is saved to the database.

This is where we'll read our custom EDI lookup table ZEDIXREF to get the internal SAP partner number linked to the EDI trading partner ID, direction, and transaction.

Function `IDOC_INBOUND_PROCESS_DATA_GET` is then called to confirm that the control record matches the partner profile key, defined in the key structure EDK21 using the following control segment values:

▶ SNDPRN: SAP send partner number (mandatory)

▶ SNDPRT: Partner type (mandatory)

▶ SNDPFC: Partner function (optional)

▶ MESTYP: Message type (mandatory)

▶ MESCOD: Message code (optional)

▶ MESFCT: Message function (optional)

▶ TEST: Test flag (optional)

The IDoc will fail if these control record fields do not exactly match the values in the partner profile key. All optional fields are mandatory if they have been set in the partner profile.

IDOC_INBOUND_PROCESS_DATA_GET reads the process code linked to the application function that posts the IDoc to the business document. It also retrieves the processing mode that determines if the IDoc is batched or posted immediately. In our example, the function returns 3, which means the IDoc posts through background batch processing.

The system is now ready to save the IDoc to the database. This is managed by a number of functions:

▶ EDI_DOCUMENT_OPEN_FOR_CREATE
  Builds a control record structure and the first status record: 50—*IDoc added to database*.

▶ EDI_SEGMENTS_ADD_BLOCK
  Builds data records.

▶ EDI_DOCUMENT_STATUS_SET
  Builds status records and sets the final create status: 64—*IDoc ready to be transferred to application*. Updates the control record structure with the final status.

▶ EDI_DOCUMENT_CLOSE_CREATE
  Checks IDoc syntax, assigns the next available IDoc number (function NUMBER_GET_NEXT), and inserts IDoc control, data, and status records to the IDoc database.

The IDoc has now been created on the IDoc database and is ready to post to a business document, assuming there have been no errors and the status has been set to 64.

The last piece of house-keeping run by EDI_DATA_INCOMING is to delete the XML IDoc file from its folder on the application server and to delete its record in EDFI2 using function EDI_EDFI2_DELETE.

Posting the Application Document

Because the partner profile was set for background processing, the IDoc is parked in the database at status 64 until ABAP report RBDAPP01 runs, either in the background by a scheduled job or directly online.

In a nutshell, RBDAPP01 reads IDocs stored at status 64 or 66 (waiting for predecessor IDoc in serialization) from parameters in its selection screen. It then identifies and calls the IDoc processing function that posts them to their business documents (in this example, a vendor's sales order) from a customer purchase order.

The selection screen for RBDAPP01 offers several options that correspond to fields in the IDoc control segment (as shown in Figure 7.13), including the following:

- IDoc number or numbers.
- Creation date and time.
- IDoc status.

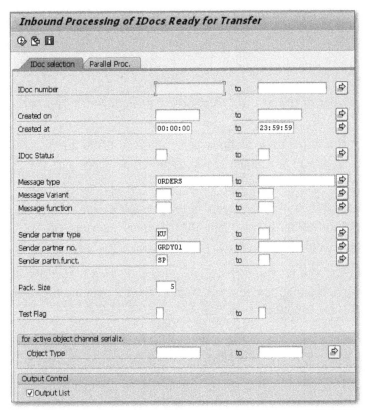

Figure 7.13 Selection Screen for Inbound Processing Program RBDAPP01

- Message type.
- Sender partner type, number, and partner function.
- Pack size (number of IDocs sent in a packet).

▶ Object type from the Business Object Repository that links an IDoc to a business document—2032 for a sales order or 2012 for an outbound purchase order or inbound purchase order acknowledgment.

▶ Output list. Triggers creation of a report list of all IDocs selected and exported.

Variants are typically created for RBDAPP01 to focus on particular selection values, such as Sender partner number and Message type. Variants are used to schedule jobs in the SAP Job Scheduler (Transaction SM37) and to control IDoc processing by doing the following, for example:

▶ Limiting execution to a particular range of IDoc numbers, messages, partner or group of partners

▶ Controlling the number of IDocs to be processed in a single batch by a background job

▶ Activating parallel processing to break up large numbers of IDocs into packets that can be processed in separate parallel background tasks

When RBDAPP01 kicks off, the control record table EDIDC is read to get all IDocs at status 64 or 66 that match the selection screen options. In our example, these are message type ORDERS for sender partner type KU (customer), partner GRDY01, and partner function SP (sold-to partner).

The control segments are read into an internal table, which is used to identify all partner profiles for the IDocs and to build another internal table with the structure of EDP21, which stores the inbound partner profile.

This second internal table drives processing of the IDocs identified from EDIDC in batches of common partner types, numbers, and message types.

Function ALE_FTCH_DATA_SEGMENTS_OF_IDOC is called, once for each packet, to get all IDoc data records for the control segments pulled from EDIDC for the partner profile defined batch.

Function APPLICATION_IDOC_POST_IMMEDIAT is called, once for each packet, after the data segments for all control records in the batch are pulled from the database and stored in an internal table with the structure EDIDD.

The IDoc control and data records are then passed to function IDOC_START_INBOUND, which reads the process code for the IDocs. This is linked to the partner profile through the control record.

The process code links the message type to the processing application, which could be a function module or a workflow. The process code and process type is returned by function IDOC_INBOUND_PROCESS_DATA_GET with the control segment passed as the import parameter.

The system then checks for the type of process code identified. If the type is workflow or task, the IDoc is passed to function IDOC_WORKITEM_INBOUND_CREATE. A STATUS IDoc, for example, would be processed by the workflow function.

The ORDERS message is normally processed by a function module linked to process code ORDE.

Function IDOC_INPUT is called when the system determines that the process type is function module. It needs to identify the processing function linked to the process code. It does this by reading table TBD52 with the function code as key.

TBD52 links the process code to both workflow events and a processing function module. Our sales order process code ORDE is linked in TBD52 to function IDOC_INPUT_ORDERS.

Process attributes for the function are read from table TBD51. In this case, IDOC_INPUT_ORDERS is identified as a batch input process that uses a call transaction and allows the display of dialog screens if run in foreground mode.

Assuming no errors, the next step, after the usual round of ABAP checks, is to call function IDOC_INPUT_ORDERS with the IDoc control and data records, along with some flags and message structures required by the system.

The name of the processing function is passed to a field in a string with the structure of TBD52—PIF_EVENT_INFO. It's invoked dynamically through a function call on the variable PIF_EVENT_INFO-FUNCNAME, which holds the function name read from TBD52, as illustrated by the call Listing 7.1.

```
CALL FUNCTION pif_event_info-funcname
  EXPORTING
    input_method        = pi_input_method
    mass_processing     = pi_mass_processing
  IMPORTING
    workflow_result     = pe_workflow_result
    application_variable = pe_application_variable
    in_update_task      = pe_in_update_task
    call_transaction_done = pe_call_transaction_done
```

```
TABLES
  idoc_contrl            = pxt_idoc_control
  idoc_data              = pxt_idoc_data
  idoc_status            = t_appl_idoc_status
  return_variables       = pet_return_variables
  serialization_info     = t_serialization_info
EXCEPTIONS
  wrong_function_called = 1
  OTHERS                = 3.
```

Listing 7.1 The IDoc Processing Function Name Is Determined at Runtime

The parameters of the function call are identical to those of all IDOC_INPUT_<MESSAGE> functions.

This triggers IDOC_INPUT_ORDERS, and the status is updated to 62—*IDoc passed to application.*

IDOC_INPUT_ORDERS loops on the IDoc control records and processes each segment in turn within an END ... WHILE loop in the form routine IDOC_INTERPRET_ORDERS, in the following basic manner:

```
WHEN 'E1EDKA1'.
  MOVE IDOC_DATA-SDATA TO E1EDKA1.
  PERFORM ZUORDNEN_ORDERS_E1EDKA1.
*-additional data is from IDOC (customer exit)--*
  SY-SUBRC = 0.
  PERFORM CUSTOMER_FUNCTION_IDOC USING IDOC_DATA.
```

WHEN determines the segment name. The data record is moved into a string with the field structure of the basic type segment, in this case E1EDKA1, which stores partner identification and address data. A form is then called that handles any processing required from the segment, which ends in the data moved to a structure or internal table based on VBAK, sales order header, VBAP, sales order item, or some other table, structure, or variable associated with the sales order.

If this processing is successful, another form routine is called to invoke a customer function that allows custom processing of the data in the IDoc and the populated structures and segments.

When segment E1EDKA1 is processed, the EDPAR partner conversion logic is applied that we described in our discussion of EDPAR in Section 7.1.4.

After all segments have completed processing, sales organization and order type data are pulled from table EDSDC and the CMIR material number conversion is run if the customer has not sent Acme's item number and if CMIR has been set up.

After all of the checks and house-keeping are done, the data are moved to an internal table with the structure BDCDATA for the call transaction. BDCDATA is a standard batch input processing structure that is very familiar to most ABAP programmers. It contains the following fields:

▶ PROGRAM: Name of dialog program being called for a screen

▶ DYNPRO: Screen number for the dialog program

▶ DYNBEGIN: BDC screen start flag indicates whether the screen being populated is the first screen in the transaction

▶ FNAM: Fully qualified name of field to be populated

▶ FVAL: Used to pass value to field in BDC session, including data and codes to command fields that move processing along or save the record

Finally, the call transaction to VA01 is run in background mode. It mimics the manual entry of all the values in BDCDATA into each field and screen in its normal sequence. If successful, a sales order is created and a success message returned.

IDOC_INPUT_ORDERS then returns control to function IDOC_INPUT, which handles clean-up processing, any messages returned by the call transaction, and the build of the status records.

IDoc control and status records are updated to 53, and the new sales order number is passed to a success message in the status record.

We haven't looked at error trapping throughout this process. At every checkpoint, and at the completion of every process, errors are trapped by checking the internal control field SY-SUBRC. If SY-SUBRC is not equal to 0, an error is returned and a message built and inserted into the status record.

If the call transaction fails, error information is returned from the failed Dynpro and passed back to the IDoc status record with code 51—*Application document not posted*—and a message identifying the nature of the error and where it occurred.

7.2   Outbound Configuration Generates IDocs

Outbound processing is a little more complicated than inbound. It is about generating IDocs from business documents or records. This is done through message control, by an ABAP program, or with change pointers that output an IDoc whenever a master data object is created or changed.

Either way, the end result is that data are collected and an IDoc is built and sent to an external system or partner, in our case Acme's EDI RIM. The EDI RIM, for its part, needs to recognize the transaction and the receiving partner so that it can figure out what to do with the IDoc.

To generate an outbound IDoc for Acme's EDI RIM, the following configuration must be in place:

1. RFC Destination

2. XML File Port

3. Message control for SD and MM documents

4. A unique outbound partner profile with message control

Extending our inbound purchase order example, we'll configure and follow the processing flow for an outbound ORDRSP PO acknowledgment. The IDoc will be generated from the sales order created by Gordy's inbound purchase order.

In addition to the base outbound configuration, we'll also need entries in the following EDI lookup tables:

▶ EDPAR: Conversion of Acme's internal ship-to partner to Gordy's store location numbers

▶ KNMT: CMIR conversion of Acme's internal SAP material to Gordy's own material number

▶ ZEDIXREF: Identification of Gordy's EDI interchange partner ID from Acme's SAP sold-to number, message type, basic type, and direction

Key interface values will be passed to the control segment from the partner profile and the sending SAP system. These keys, listed in listed in Table 7.8, allow the EDI RIM to identify, map, and route the outbound ORDRSP IDoc.

Field	Description	Value
RCVPOR	Receiving port. The outbound XML port set up with Transaction WE21.	XML_IDOC
RCVPRT	Receiving partner type (e.g., customer, vendor, etc.), as configured in Transaction WE44.	KU
RCVPRN	Receiving partner from master data. Sold-to partner for Gordy retail or Klub Kazoo.	GRDY01
MESCOD	Message code. Identifies different use cases for the same partner/logical message. Value can be null or anything else.	
MESFCT	Message function. Same as MESCOD.	
SNDPOR	Sending port. Always a concatenation of SAP+<SystemID>.	SAPDEV
SNDPRT	Sending partner type. Always logical system.	LS
SNDPRN	Sending partner. Always the logical system for the sending SAP client.	DEVCLNT100
MESTYP	Logical message type for IDoc.	ORDRSP
RCVPFC	Receiving partner function. Always null for outbound IDocs.	
SNDPFC	Sending partner function (i.e., sold-to partner). Value can be null or one of a defined list of functions per partner type.	SP
IDOCTP	IDoc basic type.	ORDERS05

Table 7.8 Control Segment Values for the EDI RIM

In addition, the extension will be passed if one has been configured for the IDoc and is present in the partner profile. We'll also add some values of our own to the partner profile for custom processing on the way out SAP and in the EDI RIM.

We'll begin by looking at configuring message control.

7.2.1   Message Control

Message or output control is a way of configuring SAP to automatically generate one or more IDocs under specific conditions for a particular business document. It is similar to setting up print, fax, email, or any other type of output.

Message control is only used to generate IDocs for Sales and Distribution (SD) and Materials Management (MM) documents. Other modules, such as FI, and master data distribution generate IDocs with ABAP programs.

Message control can be confusing and SAP doesn't explain it very clearly. You need to actually do it. Hand-on exposure is the easiest way to learn it, particularly if you can debug the code, follow the processing flow, and understand the lookup tables used to generate an IDoc from a business document.

Message control is tied to the partner profile. It must be unique for each instance of an IDoc message generated for a receiving party through an outbound partner profile.

We'll begin by looking at the different elements of message control and how they tie together to produce an IDoc. At its most basic, message control links a business document for a partner to a partner profile for a message and basic type to the application that will generate and send the IDoc, illustrated in Figure 7.14.

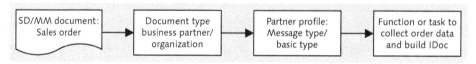

Figure 7.14 Message Control Links a Document to an IDoc Build Function

These links are established through the three major message control settings in the outbound partner profile, all of which can be customized to your heart's content:

▶ **Application code**
   Groups application documents that can generate IDocs through message control. In SD, these include the following:

   ▶ V1: Sales documents, including quotations, contracts, sales orders, confirmations, scheduling agreements, and others

- ▶ V2: Shipping documents, including delivery notes, shipping notifications, shipping orders, packing lists, cross-docking deliveries, and many others

- ▶ V3: Billing documents, including invoices, invoice lists, and others

- ▶ **Message type**
Identifies the business document, the type of output it can generate, and the conditions that apply to its output, such as an order confirmation linked to a particular sales organization, customer, and order type.

- ▶ **Process code**
Links a message type to the function module that reads the business document, builds the IDoc, writes it to the database, and calls export processing to send it to its destination.

For Gordy's Galaxy, five IDoc message types will require message control:

- ▶ **ORDRSP**
Order acknowledgment to the customer created when the sales order is saved

- ▶ **ORDERS**
Purchase order for replication services from a contract supplier output when the PO is saved in Acme's system

- ▶ **DESADV**
Shipping order to the distributor generated when delivery document is saved

- ▶ **DESADV**
Advanced shipping notification to the customer triggered after the post goods issue is posted to the outbound delivery

- ▶ **INVOIC**
Invoice to the customer triggered when the billing document is saved

We'll step through setting up message control to generate an ORDRSP IDoc when a sales order is created from an inbound purchase order from Gordy. Later in this chapter, we step through the processing flow that is called to generate the IDoc when the sales order is saved.

But first a few words about the unique keys that tie message control to the partner profile. These keys control how we apply message control to a partner and an IDoc logical message type.

Message Control Keys

Message control objects assigned to a particular partner profile are stored in table EDP12. The key fields in this table define the message control options for a partner profile. The following fields make up the key for table EDP12:

▸ MANDT: SAP client (mandatory; system assigned)

▸ RCVPRN: Receiving partner (mandatory; links to the same field in the partner profile)

▸ RCVPRT: Partner type (mandatory; links to the same field in the partner profile)

▸ RCVPFC: Partner function or role (optional; links to the same field in the partner profile)

▸ KAPPL: Message control application (mandatory)

▸ KSCHL: Message or output type (mandatory)

▸ AENDE: Change flag in message control (optional)

The first four must match exactly to the outbound partner profile, stored in table EDP13. The last three, which define the message control objects, must not be repeated in any other partner profiles that use the first four key fields.

There are times when we will need to set up message control for more than one partner profile for the same partner, partner type, partner function, and logical message type. In practical terms, this means we need a custom output type when we build different partner profiles for the same partner and logical message to handle different business use cases, such as a PO confirmation with no special processing or one flagged for bundling into an extended IDoc with a custom SDQ segment.

It's generally good practice to use custom output types for all interfaces. But we'll stick to the standards where possible in our examples. Where we need a custom output type, we'll copy the standard and adjust as necessary.

Custom Message Control: Basic Steps

Custom message control is set up with the following steps:

1. Create an output type against an application code and assign it an access sequence.

2. Assign the output type to a procedure within the application.

3. Create condition records for the output type and access sequence.

4. Use the application code and output type in the message control screen of the outbound partner profile.

Figure 7.15 outlines these tasks.

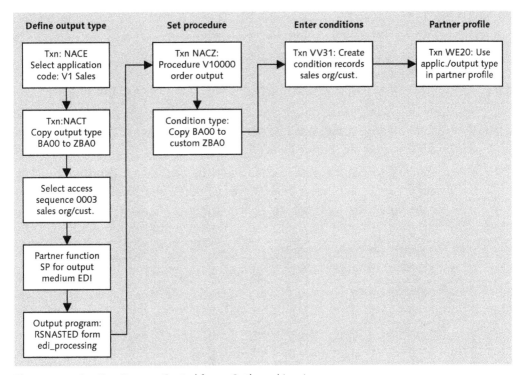

Figure 7.15 Creating Message Control for an Outbound Invoice

7.2.2 Create an Output Type

We'll create a custom output type by copying an existing standard one. Follow these steps:

1. Call Transaction NACE.

2. Select application V1 SALES and click OUTPUT TYPES (see Figure 7.16) to open the OUTPUT TYPES: OVERVIEW in display mode.

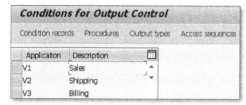

Figure 7.16 Application Codes for Sales Documents in NACE

3. Select menu path TABLE VIEW • DISPLAY • CHANGE or press $\boxed{\text{Ctrl}}$+$\boxed{\text{F1}}$ and then select standard output BA00 (order confirmation). Click COPY AS or press $\boxed{\text{F6}}$.

4. Change the name of the output type to "ZBA0" and enter a description for the PO confirmation. Make sure the ACCESS TO CONDITIONS and MULTIPLE ISSUING checkboxes are both set (see Figure 7.17).

The ACCESS TO CONDITIONS checkbox tells the system to identify output by searching condition records. The MULTIPLE ISSUING checkbox allows us to generate the same output for the same partner more than once.

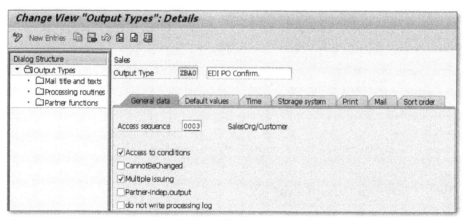

Figure 7.17 Renaming Output Type BA00 to ZBA0

5. Assign the access sequence in the GENERAL DATA tab. We'll keep the standard 0003 for SALESORG/CUSTOMER.

The access sequence is critical to generating IDoc output. It defines the tables that are read to get the conditions that have been defined to build an IDoc, the sequence in which these tables are read at runtime, and the keys that link the output type to the partner and document.

Sequence 0003 will generate an ORDRSP IDoc when any sales order is created against a defined Acme sales organization and Gordy's sold-to partner number. This link will be specified in the condition table.

We can restrict these conditions even further, but this will be worked out by the functional teams as they fine-tune their configuration for sales orders and other documents that support the business relationship between Gordy and Acme Pictures.

6. Select the following in the DEFAULT VALUES screen (see Figure 7.18). Please note that these values are defaults for the output type that can be overridden through configuration and condition records.

   ▶ Choose SEND IMMEDIATELY (WHEN SAVING THE APPLICATION) from the DISPATCH TIME dropdown. This generates an IDoc when the sales order is saved.

   ▶ Choose EDI FROM THE TRANSMISSION MEDIUM dropdown. This generates IDocs for EDI transmission.

   ▶ Choose SP SOLD-TO PARTY from the PARTNER FUNCTION pop-up. This generates an IDoc for the sold-to to party in the sales order. If you enter "AG", it will be converted to SP.

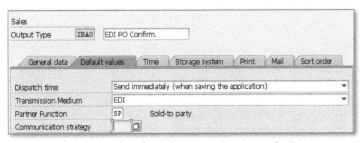

Figure 7.18 Default Values for Output Type Processing Options

7. Press ⌈Enter⌋. A dialog opens to inform you that the entry to be copied has dependent entries. Click ONLY COPY ENTRY to copy only the values in the OUTPUT TYPES: DETAIL screen from BA00 to ZBA0.

If you copy all dependent entries, all configuration options in output type BA00 are copied into ZBA0. But it will not copy the procedure or any conditions records created for BA00.

8. The OUTPUT TYPES: OVERVIEW screen is returned in change view. Select output ZBA0, and double-click the PROCESSING ROUTINES folder to open the PROCESSING ROUTINES: OVERVIEW screen.

9. We'll add the program name and form that will generate the IDoc after the sales order is saved. Click NEW ENTRIES to open the DETAILS OF ADDED ENTRIES screen.

10. Enter the following values into the DETAILS OF ADDED ENTRIES screen (see Figure 7.19):

   ▶ TRANSM.MEDIUM: "EDI"

   ▶ PROGRAM (Processing 1): "RSNASTED" for the standard SAP IDoc output program. You can also use a custom ABAP output program. Use RSNASTED as a model.

   ▶ FORM ROUTINE: "EDI_PROCESSING", which identifies and calls the function that will build the IDoc, writes it the database, sends it to the outbound IDoc processing function, and updates its status record.

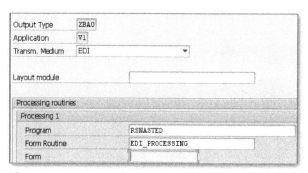

Figure 7.19 Assigning the Processing Program and Form Routine

11. Press [Enter] and double-click the PARTNER FUNCTIONS folder to open the PARTNER FUNCTIONS: OVERVIEW screen.

12. Click NEW ENTRIES and select EDI in the MEDIUM field and SP (sold-to party) in the FUNCT field, as shown in Figure 7.20. Click SAVE.

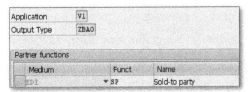

Figure 7.20 Assigning Output Medium to the Sold-To Party for ZBA0

7.2.3 Assign Output Type to a Procedure

Next we will assign the output type to a procedure. Procedures drive the use and function of condition tables, which define output parameters. Procedures also link the output type to a business document such as an order, a contract, or a quotation.

The procedure determines, for example, that an IDoc will be generated from a sales order as a PO confirmation. This can be further refined with standard and custom ABAP rules in a requirement that allows generation of the IDoc only if specific conditions are met within the sales order.

Return to Transaction NACE, select APPLICATION code V1, and click PROCEDURES to open the PROCEDURES OVERVIEW screen, as illustrated in Figure 7.21.

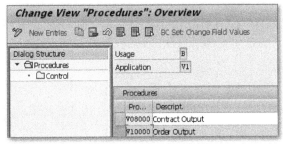

Figure 7.21 Procedures Overview with Order Output Selected

The USAGE field refers to the application functionality that the condition tables are determining. The system supports 28 usages, including pricing, transportation routing, material determination, and so on. B represents output.

1. Select procedure V10000 ORDER OUTPUT, and double-click the control folder to open a list of output types linked to the procedure.

2. Select BA00 ORDER CONFIRMATION, and click the COPY AS icon. All BA00 values are copied into a table control except for the COUNTER.

3. Change the name of the output type in the CTYP column from BA00 to ZBA0. Change the CNTR field value to 0 (see Figure 7.22).

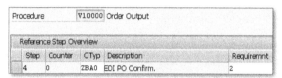

Figure 7.22 Assigning the Output Type to the V10000 Procedure

The column headings in Figure 7.22 refer to the following values:

▶ Step defines the sequence in which conditions are evaluated within the procedure at runtime. A step number is unique.

▶ Counter is the access number of the conditions within the step. This is most relevant for pricing procedures.

▶ CTyp (condition type) is the output type and is used by the procedure to determine the type of document generated, like our PO confirmation.

▶ Requirement is an ABAP rule that defines document conditions for output generation.

Don't forget to save. The output type is assigned to the procedure.

Requirements Defined by ABAP Code

View the ABAP code behind requirement 2 for output type ZBA0 by selecting the requirement and pressing F4 to open the ROUTINES pop-up. Select requirement 2 and click the SOURCE TEXT icon (see Figure 7.23) or press F5 to open the code in the ABAP Editor.

Requirement 2 is an ABAP form routine called just before the sales order is saved. The code is displayed in Listing 7.2.

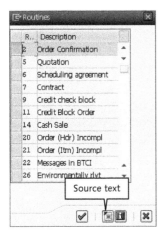

Source text

Figure 7.23 Requirement Code is Read in Routines Pop-Up

```
FORM KOBED_002.
*Create the output if the the sales document is complete.
  SY-SUBRC = 0.
  IF KOMKBV1-UVALL NE 'C'.
    SY-SUBRC = 4.
    EXIT.
  ENDIF.
  IF KOMKBV1-COSTA NE SPACE AND KOMKBV1-COSTA NE 'C'.
    SY-SUBRC = 4.
    EXIT.
  ENDIF.
  IF NOT KOMKBV1-LIFSK IS INITIAL.
    IF KOMKBV1-LIFSK NE TVLS-LIFSP.
      SELECT SINGLE * FROM TVLS WHERE LIFSP = KOMKBV1-LIFSK.
    ENDIF.
    IF SY-SUBRC = 0 AND
       TVLS-SPEDR NE SPACE.
      SY-SUBRC = 4.
      EXIT.
    ENDIF.
  ENDIF.
*No output if the credit block is set.
  IF KOMKBV1-CMGST CA 'BC'.
    SY-SUBRC = 4.
```

```
      EXIT.
    ENDIF.
  ENDFORM.
```

Listing 7.2 Requirement 2 Only Allows Output of Completed Orders

Requirement 2 checks a number of flags in KOMKBV1 to confirm that the order is complete before it allows output to be issued. It begins by setting system variable SY-SUBRC to 0. If SY-SUBRC still equals 0 when the checks are completed, output is issued. If not, no IDoc is generated.

KOMKBV1 is an internal table filled from header, status, and item-level business data from the sales order on save, including all the flags that define order completion status. KOMKBV1 is populated by function KOMKBV1_FILL in function group V61B (output control conditions).

The following flags are checked by requirement 2:

▶ KOMKBV1-UVALL NE 'C': Overall completion status of the sales order header. Value C indicates the order is complete at the header level.

▶ KOMKBV1-COSTA NE 'SPACE' and NE 'C': If space, then the order is not relevant for confirmation and the check is passed. If not space, then it must equal C to pass; all schedule lines must be confirmed by MM.

▶ KOMKBV1-LIFSK NOT INITIAL: Block of code checks that there is no delivery or printing block on the order. From the DELIVERY BLOCK field of the SALES SCREEN at the header level of the sales order.

▶ KOMKBV1-CMGST CA 'BC': Confirms that there is no credit block on the order.

Custom requirements can be created in the IMG with Transaction V/27 or Transaction SPRO and path SALES AND DISTRIBUTION • BASIC FUNCTIONS • OUTPUT CONTROL • DEFINE REQUIREMENTS.

Requirements are numbered. SAP reserves numbers above 900 for customer-coded requirements.

7.2.4   Condition Records

The final step in configuring message control is to enter condition records, which are linked to the output type and access sequence and are used by the system to decide whether, in our example, an ORDRSP IDoc should be generated for a partner when a sales order is saved.

Before we create our condition records, we'll look at the access sequence that we selected for output type ZBA0.

Access Sequence

The access sequence is directly linked to an output type, which assigns it a document type to evaluate for output at runtime. In the case of ZBA0, that document type is a purchase order confirmation to be sent by EDI.

The procedure links that output type to a sales order and to requirements—business rules—for generation of an order confirmation IDoc.

The access sequence takes these links one step further to a trading partner, logical system, or any other partner or document key that specifies who gets a PO confirmation under the business rules defined by the procedure.

The access sequence does this by defining three objects that are critical to output control:

1. The condition tables that are used to store and access condition records
2. The sequence in which those condition tables are read at runtime
3. The fields used to read those tables: the *key combination* or *access* that is similar to options on the selection screen of a program

The access fields for output type ZBA0 are pulled from the Data Dictionary communications structure KOMKBV1, which passes sales document header data to output control when the document is saved.

The access fields are used to read the condition table that stores the output parameters for the document being saved for a trading partner, regardless of partner type. The condition values define output for the document and partner: print, EDI, ALE, fax, and so on.

Output type ZBA0, copied from standard type BA00, has 8 standard access sequences, numbered from 0001 through 0011, as illustrated in Figure 7.24. Access sequences can be customized with Transaction NACX against an application such as V1 for sales.

Figure 7.24 Standard Access Sequences Copied from Output Type BA00

Access sequence 0003, used in our custom output type ZBA0, includes the following key field combination from KOMKBV1:

▶ VKORG: Sales organization

▶ KNDNR: Sold-to party

Return to NACE, select application V1, and click ACCESS SEQUENCES. From the OVERVIEW ACCESS SEQUENCE screen, select access sequence 0003, and double-click the ACCESSES folder to open the ACCESSES: OVERVIEW screen (see Figure 7.25).

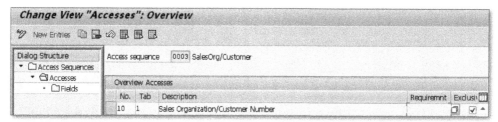

Figure 7.25 Access Sequence 0003 with Table 001

Note that requirements can also be called through an access sequence to further refine conditions for output. These are the same requirements we saw in the procedure. The access sequence applies them more selectively.

Number 1 in the TAB column refers to table B001 that will be used to store condition records for the key combination. The tables can be numbered from 1 to 999, but each application gets its own range. These tables are based on B000, which SAP provides as a template for creating condition tables for message control. B000 provides the following fields that must be present in all condition tables:

▶ MANDT: SAP client.

▶ KAPPL: Application for output type, such as V1 for sales.

▶ KSCHL: Output type, such as our ZBA0.

▶ VAKEY: 100 byte variable key replaced in the condition tables, such as B001, by the access sequence field key. When a condition record is created in the condition table the access sequence values are inserted into VAKEY in table NACH, which stores detailed header information for each condition record for all applications and output types.

▶ KNUMH: Unique output condition record generated when the condition record is created that links NACH to the condition table.

The access sequence completes the key for reading the condition table used for the output type. In the case of access sequence 0003 for output type ZBA0, this is the full key:

▶ MANDT: SAP client

▶ KAPPL: V1

▶ KSCHL: ZBA0

▶ VKORG: Sales organization

▶ KNDNR: Sold-to party

To look at the access sequence, select access 10 in the ACCESSES: OVERVIEW screen, and double-click FIELDS to open the FIELDS: OVERVIEW screen, as displayed in Figure 7.26.

Figure 7.26 The Fields Assigned to Access Sequence 0003

This record describes data flow at the time the sales order is saved and the system begins its evaluation of output possibilities. The document fields VKORG and

KUNNR flow into the access sequence fields VKORG and KNDNR in the sales document communication structure KOMKBV1.

They are then available for use as a key, with the application and output type, to read the record in the condition table—in our case B001—that determines what actually gets output for our sold-to party. The condition record drives the actual output of our IDoc.

To output an order confirmation for Gordy's purchase order by EDI, we will create a condition record against our access sequence using the following key values:

- VKORG: Sales organization 3000 Los Angeles
- KNDNR: Sold-to partner GRDY01 Gordy's Galaxy

Create Condition Records for the PO Confirmation

There are two ways to get at the condition record data entry screen for the PO confirmation.

One is through Transaction NACE. Select application V1 and click the CONDITIONS RECORD button to open the OUTPUT TYPES pop-up listing all output types defined for the application. Select ZBA0 and click the CONDITIONS RECORD button at the bottom of the pop-up (or press F2) to open the CHANGE EDI PO CONFIRM (ZBA0): SELECTION screen, as illustrated in Figure 7.27.

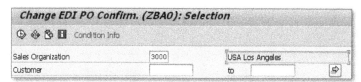

Figure 7.27 Condition Record Selection Screen for Output Type ZBA0

Enter a sales organization (in our example, 3000 for USA Los Angeles) and click EXECUTE or press F8.

You can also use Transaction VV11, which opens the CREATE OUTPUT – CONDITION RECORDS screen. Enter output type ZBA0 and click the KEY COMBINATION button to open the KEY COMBINATION pop-up listing all the accesses available for the access sequence and output type (see Figure 7.28).

Figure 7.28 Select an Access from Key Combination

Either way, you'll land in the CREATE CONDITION RECORDS: FAST ENTRY table control. Enter the following values:

- CUSTOMER: "GRDY01"
- FUNCT (partner function): "SP" or "AG"
- MEDIUM: "6" for EDI
- DATE/TIME: "4" for send immediately
- LANGUAGE: "EN" for English

Click SAVE to create the condition record.

Remember Gordy's club chain Klub Kazoo? We could use a condition record to output a confirmation IDoc from a Klub Kazoo sales order to Gordy's retail sold-to partner. This would mean creating only one outbound partner profile for both sold-to partners and sending the EDI transmission to the one trading partner ID for both organizations.

To do this, enter the following values into the table control:

- CUSTOMER: "GCLB01" for Klub Kazoo
- FUNCT: "SP" or "AG"
- PARTNER: "GRDY01" to map Klub Kazoo to Gordy's sold-to partner for output type ZBA0
- MEDIUM: "6" for EDI
- DATE/TIME: "4" for send immediately
- LANGUAGE: "EN" for English

The entries will look like Figure 7.29.

Create Condition Records (EDI PO Confirm.): Fast Entry								
Communication 🔍 🗑								
Sales Organization 3000		USA Los Angeles						
Condition Recs.								
Customer	Name		Funct	Partner	M.	Date/Time	Language	
GCLB01	Klub Kazoo		SP	GRDY01	6	4	EN	
GRDY01	Gordy's Galaxy of Games & B Flix		SP		6	4	EN	

Figure 7.29 Condition Records for Gordy's Galaxy PO Confirmation

This condition record identifies who gets the EDI PO confirmation, not who created the purchase order and subsequent sales order.

If PARTNER is populated when message control evaluates the condition record, its value is checked against the partner profile and plugged into the RCVPRN (receive partner) field of the IDoc control segment. If it isn't populated, CUSTOMER is used instead.

Save the condition records.

> **A Hint about Loading Condition Records**
>
> Understand the table structure of your condition records and you can write a simple ABAP program to load conditions from a file with an SQL insert. You only need to populate table NACH and the BXXX conditions table for the key combination of your access sequence.

7.2.5   The Outbound Partner Profile with Message Control

Now that we have configured output control, we'll need an outbound partner profile for Gordy's Galaxy and message type ORDRSP.

Like the inbound profile, the outbound partner profile links a trading partner to a logical message and process. The difference is that the outbound partner profile supports identification of the process for generating an IDoc from a business document through message control. An overview of these relationship is displayed in Figure 7.30.

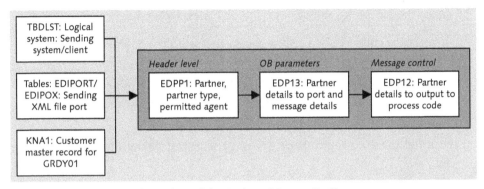

Figure 7.30 Underlying Relationships of the Outbound Partner Profile

A partner profile must be unique for each interface that it will be used for, even if the same message type is used for different purposes.

Outbound partner profile settings are stored in table EDP13. The key fields in this table, listed here, define unique partner profile settings that determine the particular usage of a logical message type for a receiving partner:

▸ MANDT: SAP client (mandatory; system-assigned)

▸ RCVPRN: Receiving partner (mandatory)

▸ RCVPRT: Partner type (mandatory)

▸ RCVPFC: Partner function or role (optional)

▸ MESTYP: Logical message type (mandatory)

▸ MESCOD: Message code (optional)

▸ MESFCT: Message function (optional)

▸ TEST: Test flag indicating IDoc a test message (optional)

The contents of all the key fields will be passed to the corresponding fields of the IDoc control record. Null is an acceptable value for the optional data elements.

The IDoc basic type is not part of the key, but it is a mandatory field in the partner profile and must be populated. The basic type tells the system how to structure the logical message.

IDoc extension and view are also optional fields that are not part of the key. But if either is being used in an IDoc, they must be included in the partner profile; otherwise, the system won't know to call them to refine the structure of the basic type.

To create the partner profile for our ORDRSP message to Gordy:

1. Go to Transaction WE20 and find the partner profile we created for Gordy during inbound configuration.

   The same outbound partner profile will be used for the retail and club chains. The condition record will determine the partner profile to call for the club chain by mapping partner GCLB01 to Gordy's retail GRDY01.

2. Click the CREATE OUTBOUND PARAMETER icon just below the outbound table control.

3. Enter the following values into the OUTBOUND PARAMETERS screen:

   ▶ PARTNER ROLE field: "SP" (sold-to)

   ▶ MESSAGE TYPE field: "ORDRSP"

   ▶ RECEIVER PORT field: "XML_IDOC"

   ▶ OUTPUT MODE area:

     – COLLECT IDOCS option: COLLECT batches IDocs at status 30—*IDoc ready for dispatch*—until program RSEOUT00 runs to export them through the file port.

     – START SUBSYSTEM option: Set to trigger the EDI RIM through the file port and RFC destination.

   ▶ BASIC TYPE: "ORDERS05"

4. Save the partner profile. The OUTBOUND OPTIONS screen should look like Figure 7.31.

5. Click on the MESSAGE CONTROL tab and then the INSERT ROW icon to create a unique message control record, as discussed in Section 7.2.1, Message Control. Enter the following values:

   ▶ APPLICATION: "V1" for sales document

   ▶ MESSAGE TYPE: "ZBA0" for the output type

   ▶ PROCESS CODE: "SD10", which links to IDoc processing function IDOC_OUTPUT_ORDRSP.

   ▶ CHANGE MESSAGE checkbox: Leave null to trigger generation of an IDoc every time the sales order is changed. If it's not set, an IDoc will only be output when the sales order is first created.

Partner profiles: Outbound parameters

Partner No.	GRDY01	Gordy's Galaxy of Games & B Flix
Partn.Type	KU	Customer
Partner Role	SP	Sold-to party

Message Type	ORDRSP	Purchase order / order confirmation
Message code		
Message function		☐ Test

Outbound Options / Message Control / Post Processing: Permitted Agent / Telep... ◄ ► 🖳

Receiver port	XML_IDOC	XML File	Test port for XML IDoc output

Output Mode
- ○ Transfer IDoc Immed.
- ● Collect IDocs
- ● Start subsystem
- ○ Do not start subsystem
- Output Mode   3

IDoc Type

Basic type	ORDERS05	Purchasing/Sales
Extension		
View		

☑ Cancel Processing After Syntax Error

Figure 7.31 Setting Up Message Type ORDRSP in Outbound Options

The system checks that the change flag is null the first time that an IDoc is generated when the business document is created and saved. If you want to also output an IDoc each time the document changes, create another message control entry that includes a checked change flag, as illustrated in Figure 7.32.

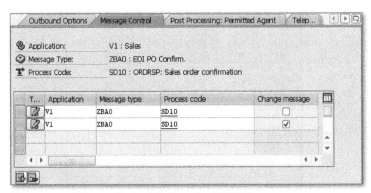

Outbound Options / **Message Control** / Post Processing: Permitted Agent / Telep... ◄ ► 🖳

🏷 Application:	V1 : Sales	
✉ Message Type:	ZBA0 : EDI PO Confirm.	
🛠 Process Code:	SD10 : ORDRSP: Sales order confirmation	

T...	Application	Message type	Process code	Change message	🔲
📝	V1	ZBA0	SD10	☐	
📝	V1	ZBA0	SD10	☑	

Figure 7.32 Message Control Options for ORDRSP

We will also enter EDI-specific values to pass to the IDoc control record. These values will help identify EDI data for the RIM and provide additional EDI-specific search criteria for the IDoc in SAP. Follow these steps.

1. Go to the EDI STANDARD tab at the edge of the message control.

2. Enter the following values in the EDI STANDARD tab:

   ▸ EDI STANDARD: "X" for X12

   ▸ MESSAGE TYPE: "855" for the X12 transaction

   ▸ VERSION: "005010" for the X12 transaction version

   The completed screen should look like Figure 7.33.

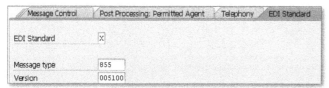

Figure 7.33 EDI Standards Are Passed to the IDoc Control Record

3. Save the partner profile.

Now that output control and a partner profile are set up, the system is ready to generate an ORDRSP IDoc each time Acme creates a sales order for Gordy. We still need to add some reference data to help the process along.

7.2.6 EDI Outbound Reference Data

We looked at the EDI reference tables we need to post SD documents during inbound processing in Section 7.1.4. We'll use two of the same tables for outbound processing of the order confirmation:

▸ EDPAR: Internal to external partner conversion.

▸ ZEDIXREF: Custom table to convert control segment partner number and IDoc message and basic type to the receiving EDI trading partner ID and transaction set.

External to internal material number conversion was done during inbound processing; we don't have to do it outbound. The supplier's material number posted to the sales order so it will be available to the IDoc.

EDPAR

The values we entered into EDPAR for inbound processing for Figure 7.8 will also work for outbound. We have an inbound sold-to and ship-to conversion for Gordy's retail and Klub Kazoo. All are linked to Gordy's retail sold-to number, GRDY01.

Outbound partner processing with EDPAR is a little more restrained than inbound. For the ORDRSP order confirmation IDoc only the sold-to, vendor, personnel, contact person, or unloading point numbers (for the ship-to party) will be converted through EDPAR.

For the purposes of our PO confirmation, the standard EDPAR routine will only return the external sold-to partner for Gordy or Klub Kazoo. If the customer needs to receive his external ship-to number, we have two choices:

1. Store it in the customer master record for the ship-to partner, in the ACCT AT CUST. field in the SALES screen of the SALES AREA DATA.

   The external ship-to number will automatically flow into the IDoc when the order confirmation is generated. This means, of course, that you need to create a sales view by sales organization, distribution channel, and division for each ship-to partner.

2. Write a customer exit to read EDPAR at the end of the XVBPA processing loop for the ship-to partner (PARVW = "WE") using function SD_INT_TO_EXT_PARTNER_NUMBER during the build of segment E1EDKA1, in either CUSTOMER-FUNCTION '002' or GV_BADI_SD_ORDRSP_IDOC_OUTPUT->IDOC_DATA_APPEND.

3. Both exits are called in the form CUSTOMER_FUNCTION at the end of the XVBPA loop. The code would be run for the ship-to party, or for whoever else you wanted to convert to an external number.

The master data option is possible because of how the external conversion is handled during outbound processing.

It begins with a loop on XVBPA, an internal table for VBPA, which stores all partner records for the sales order. In the first pass, it gets the sold-to partner number and passes it to variable KUNAG that's used to read the KUNNR field in EDPAR. KUNAG is never cleared during loop processing of XVBPA. EDPAR is always read with the sold-to party as the KUNNR key.

The next check is for the partner function from the partner profile. This gets the value for the internal partner number key in EDPAR-INPNR. Only the following partner functions are checked:

- ▶ KU: Sold-to partner. Passes `XVBPA-KUNNR` to variable `INT`.

- ▶ LI: Vendor. Passes `XVBPA-LIFNR` to variable `INT`.

- ▶ PE: Personnel number. Passes `XVBPA-PERNR` to variable `INT`.

- ▶ AP: Contact person. Passes `XVBPA-PARNR` to variable `INT`.

- ▶ OTHERS: Passes `XVBPA-ABLAD`, unloading point, to variable `INT`. This only goes to the ship-to party.

Function `SD_INT_TO_EXT_PARTNER_NUMBER` is then called to read EDPAR for the external partner number with parameters:

- ▶ KUNAG: Sold-to partner.

- ▶ INT: Internal SAP partner number for partner type.

- ▶ XVBPA-PARVW: Partner function in the current loop pass.

For the order confirmation the partner function coming out of the sales order is typically:

- ▶ AG (SP): Sold-to party

- ▶ RE (BP): Bill-to party

- ▶ RS (PY): Payer party

- ▶ WE (SH): Ship-to partner

EDPAR is then read by the function with the following SQL statement:

```
SELECT * FROM EDPAR
  WHERE KUNNR = CUSTOMER_NUMBER (KUNAG)
    AND PARVW = PARTNER_ROLE (INT)
    AND INPNR = INTERNAL_PARTNER_NUMBER. (XVBPA-PARVW)
```

If a hit is made—and in our example, only the sold-to partner will return a hit—then a variable is populated with the external partner number and processing returns to the IDoc function.

The external partner number is then passed to `E1EDKA1-LIFNR`.

If nothing is found, an exception is raised, the function terminates, and processing returns to the IDoc function. Another function—`VIEW_KNVV`—is then called with the current partner number in XVBPA-KUNR, regardless of partner type, and the sales organization. It returns table KNVV, which stores sales area data from the customer master record, including the external partner number from field EIKTO.

If the external partner number is in KNVV-EIKTO it will be passed to E1EDKA1-LIFNR.

ZEDIXREF: EDI Trading Partner IDs

Our custom EDI lookup table ZEDIXREF works the same way for outbound processing as inbound, although the values, listed in Table 7.7, are different.

Field	Value	Description
DIRECT	1	Direction outbound
STDMES	855	EDI PO confirmation transaction
MESTYP	ORDRSP	IDoc message type
IDOCTP	ORDERS05	IDoc basic type
CIMTYP		IDoc extension
SNDPRN	DEVCLNT100	SAP logical system: send partner
RCVPRN	GRDY01	SAP receive partner: Gordy's sold-to customer number in Acme's system
SNDLAD	01234567US0	EDI send partner: Gordy's trading partner ID for Acme
RCVLAD	9999999USD	EDI receiver partner: Gordy's trading partner ID for Gordy

Table 7.9 ZEDIXREF Entry for the Outbound 855 to Gordy

The table is read in the same enhancement used for inbound—SIDOC001. The outbound read pulls the SNDLAD and RCVLAD fields from table ZEDIXREF into the same fields in the IDoc using the following key fields from the control record:

- ▶ EDIDC-DIR: Direction
- ▶ EDIDC-STDMES: EDI transaction or message, mapped from the EDI transaction set
- ▶ EDIDC-MESTYP: IDoc logical message type
- ▶ EDIDC-IDOCTP: IDoc Basic type
- ▶ EDIDC-CIMTYP: IDoc extension
- ▶ EDIDC-SNDPRN: SAP sender partner number
- ▶ EDIDC-RCVPRN: SAP receiver partner number

This will then be used by the EDI RIM to identify envelopes and routing for the outbound 855 transmission.

7.2.7 The SAP EDI Outbound Process Flow

Outbound processing for EDI in SD and MM builds an IDoc from a business document using message control, saves it to the application server in an XML file, and then triggers the EDI RIM through an RFC to a listening workflow.

We'll illustrate this process by following the progress of an outbound purchase order confirmation ORDRSP IDoc to Gordy.

To enable outbound processing for Gordy's ORDRSP, we need the following:

▶ RFC destination EDI_DEV_100

▶ XML file port XML_IDOC

▶ Message control configured for output type ZBA0

▶ Condition records entered for sales organization and sold-to partners GRDY01 (Gordy retail) and GCLB01 (Gordy's Klub Kazoo)

In addition, we need a partner profile for Gordy with the following outbound parameters:

▶ OUTBOUND OPTIONS tab:

    ▶ PARTNER FUNCTION: "SP" for sold-to partner

    ▶ MESSAGE TYPE: "ORDRSP"

    ▶ RECEIVER PORT: "XML_IDOC"

    ▶ OUTPUT MODE: COLLECT IDOCS and START SUBSYSTEM (3)

    ▶ BASIC TYPE: "ORDERS05"

▶ MESSAGE CONTROL tab:

    ▶ APPLICATION: "V1"

    ▶ STANDARD MESSAGE TYPE: "ZBA0"

    ▶ PROCESS CODE: "SD10", which links to function `IDOC_OUTPUT_ORDRSP`.

▶ EDI STANDARD tab:

    ▶ EDI STANDARD: "X" for X12

    ▶ MESSAGE TYPE: 855 purchase acknowledgment

    ▶ VERSION: "005010"

Figure 7.34 shows a high-level view of the outbound EDI process flow. These steps are implemented in ABAP code through function modules that access a mix of configured and master data tables. We'll look at some of the key processing points as we step through the flow.

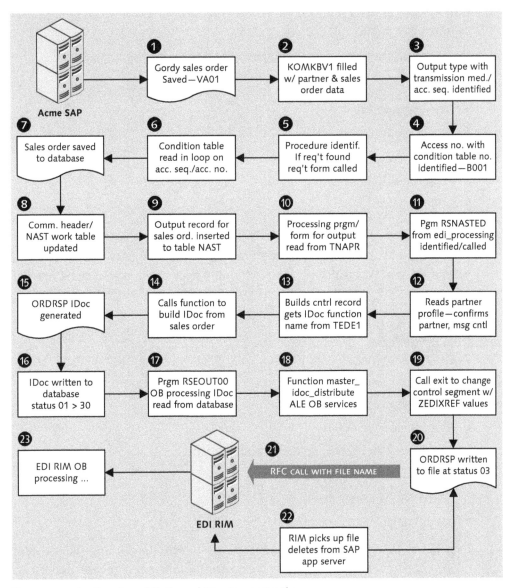

Figure 7.34 An Overview of Outbound IDoc Processing Flow

Building Output

A sales order is created and saved from an incoming purchase order ORDERS IDoc from Gordy with Transaction VA01.

Header and partner data from the sales order are passed to communications structure KOMKBV1, with function COMMUNICATION_AREA_KOMKBV1, which immediately calls function KOMKBV1_FILL.

Communications structure KOMKBV1 includes the following values:

▶ Sales order number

▶ Sales organization

▶ Distribution channel

▶ Division

▶ Partner function

▶ Sold-to party

▶ Ship-to party

The system identifies message control objects through a series of table reads in function MESSAGING, which is called before the sales order is assigned a number and then saved by function RV_SALES_DOCUMENT_ADD. These output objects include the following:

▶ Application: V1

▶ Procedure: V10000. Note that the requirement is identified and called if one exists in the procedure.

▶ Output type: ZBA0

▶ Access sequence: 0003

▶ Access number 10 with key field combination:

   ▶ VKORG: Sales organization

   ▶ KNDNR: Sold-to party

▶ Condition table: 001 (B001)

Function SD_COND_ACCESS called within MESSAGING reads the condition table within a loop on table T682I, which links the application, access sequence, and access number to the condition table number.

The condition table is read in a loop because multiple access numbers within the access sequence for our application could be found in table T682I. The condition records are further broken down by output type, partner number, and partner type. Multiple outputs could be configured for each: print, EDI, fax, and so on.

In our example, the condition record in table B001 determines that output type ZBA0 for application V1 for sold-to partner Gordy (GRDY01) in sales organization 3000 will be output by EDI as soon as the sales order is saved.

If the sales order is for Gordy's Klub Kazoo chain, the condition record will tell the system that sold-to partner GLCB01 is mapped to sold-to partner GRDY01 for generation of an IDoc using output type ZBA0. GRDY01, rather than GLCB01, will be the IDoc receiver checked against the partner profile and mapped to the control segment field RCVPRN.

An output record for the sales order is prepared for table NAST based on the condition record. NAST stores details of output status for each output identified for every business document instance, such as the sales order we just saved, that uses message control. The record prepared for NAST includes such values as:

- KAPPL (Application): V1
- OBJKY: Sales order document number with leading zeroes
- KSCHL (Output type): ZBA0
- PARNR: Message partner
- PARVW: Partner type AG (sold-to)
- NACHA: Output medium 6 for EDI
- VSZTP: Dispatch time (immediately on save or batched)

Writing the IDoc to the Database

The sales order is saved and table NAST is updated. The next major task is to identify and call the processing program and form routine associated with output type ZBA0. For EDI, these were defined as form EDI_PROCESSING in program RSNASTED.

This is done in function RV_MESSAGES_UPDATE by reading table TNAPR with the output type (ZBA0) and transmission medium (6 for EDI).

The NAST record is used to build a key to read the outbound partner profile for Gordy using function EDI_PARTNER_READ_OUTGOING. The read key, in our example, includes the following:

- RCVPRN: GRDY01 (receive partner number)
- RCVPRT: KU (receive partner type)
- RCVPFC: SP (receive partner function)
- KAPPL: V1 (message control application)
- KSCHL: ZBA0 (message or output type)
- AENDE: Change message flag not populated

If the partner profile is found, the system reads table TEDE1 with the process code from the message control table of the partner profile (EDP12).

Table TEDE1 links the process code to the IDoc processing function. In this case, process code SD10, entered into the message control screen of Gordy's outbound partner profile for ORDRSP, links to IDoc function IDOC_OUTPUT_ORDRSP.

The control record of the IDoc is then built from the partner profile and some system values and function IDOC_OUTPUT_ORDRSP is called with the control record and the output record from NAST. IDOC_OUTPUT_ORDRSP takes over processing and begins to build the IDoc data records.

First it reads the sales order tables into internal work tables with the NAST-OBJKY, which stores the sales order number. These tables include the following:

- VBAK: Sales order header
- VBKD: Business data header
- VBPA: Sales order partners
- VBAP: Line item data
- VBEP: Delivery schedule lines

It then pulls the terms of payment and offers a user exit to allow custom reads of additional sales order data into the internal tables already populated.

After some more house-keeping and data reads, including another user exit to update the control segment, it builds the IDoc data records one at a time, beginning with E1EDK01, in the order that the segments appear in the IDoc.

The code steps through each segment in the ORDERS05 basic type through a form routine with the naming convention *fill_<segnam>* (for example, FILL_E1EDKA1).

Each routine hard-codes the segment name to the data record SEGNAM field in the control area and then passes the data values to SDATA field through a string that has the structure of the segment. E1EDKA1, for example, is built using a string with a structure defined by Data Dictionary object E1EDKA1.

The data for each segment are pulled from the internal tables populated when the sales order was read and/or pulled from other sources.

At the end of each segment's form processing, several things happen:

1. The populated string is passed to the SDATA field in an internal table with the data record structure EDIDD: INT_EDIDD-SDATA.

2. The new segment record is appended to INT_EDIDD-SDATA.

3. A customer function is called to allow custom processing of the internal data record table.

After all segments have been populated and appended in their proper order into INT_EDIDD, the business object is identified for message type ORDRSP with function SD_OBJECT_TYPE_DETERMINE based on SD document type—C for a sales order. The business object for ORDRSP is BUS2032.

After a final user exit is hit, IDOC_OUTPUT_ORDRSP is done and processing returns to RSNASTED, where the first task is to update NAST.

Function COMMUNICATION_IDOC_CREATE is then called to create the control segment, apply some ALE house-keeping services, and call function IDOC_CREATE_ON_DATA-BASE, which in turn calls function EDI_DOCUMENT_OPEN_FOR_CREATE.

This last function prepares the IDoc to be written to the database and updates the status record. But first it calls the exit in enhancement SIDOC001. This is where we will read our custom EDI lookup table ZEDIXREF to update the control segment with Gordy's EDI send and receive trading partner numbers.

When the IDoc is written to the database, status records are built with an initial status of 01—*IDoc generated*.

Processing mode is checked for the partner profile. In our example, the IDoc is not going to be kicked out immediately. Status in the control and status records is changed to 30—*IDoc ready for dispatch*. IDoc processing ends.

Logical versus Basic Type

This process of building an outbound IDoc is a good illustration of the difference between a message type and a basic type.

The structure that is being populated is basic type ORDERS05. But the logic that is pulling the data and selecting the segments and fields to populate is the message type ORDRSP, which represents the business object.

The basic type ORDERS05 is the neutral container while the message type ORDRSP is the logic and the data that make the IDoc instance a purchase order confirmation.

Sending the IDoc to the EDI RIM

Program RSEOUT00 (Transaction WE14) will be scheduled to kick batched IDocs out the door. All of Acme's customers are important, but Gordy is more important than all the others because of the volume of business they do every day. That means lots of orders and order confirmations, so it was decided to schedule separate jobs for Gordy's IDocs.

The RSEOUT00 selection screen options that we'll use for Gordy are displayed in Figure 7.35. Most of these fields used to read the control record of the IDoc from table EDIDC IDocs.

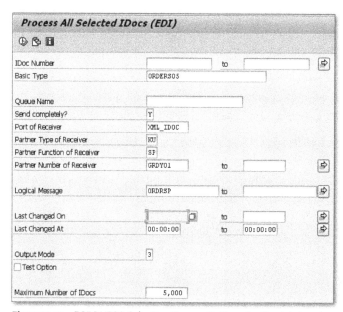

Figure 7.35 RSEOUT00 Selection Screen Options for Gordy's Invoice

1. RSEOUT00 first reads table EDIDC to identify all IDocs at status 30 that match all parameters entered on the selection screen.

2. Found records are inserted into internal table INT_EDIDC with the structure EDIDC and used to read table EDIQO to determine whether any are assigned to a queue. Any IDocs found in the queue table that have not already been processed are processed together. All other IDocs in INT_EDIDC that do not have a corresponding EDIQO record are deleted.

3. If nothing is found in EDIQO, the control records are passed to function IDOC_OUTPUT_NEW for outbound processing.

4. Function EDI_PORT_READ is called to confirm the XML file port in the control segment from table EDIPOX, and then form CF_OUTPUT_XML (called from form GENERAL_OUTPUT) triggers final outbound processing with function IDOCS_OUT- PUT_IN_XML_FORMAT.

5. The XML file port is confirmed again and the IDocs are read one more time from the database. The IDoc records are converted to XML format, beginning with the control segment, and appended to internal table I_XMLOUT. This internal table is then written through a single 1,270 character string to the outgoing XML IDoc file.

6. The path and file names are read from the XML port, and the IDoc file is written to the file path on the SAP application server.

7. The locks on the IDoc database are released, and the status record updated to 03—*Data passed to port OK*.

8. After some additional house-keeping and error checking, form START_TRIG- GER_AND_WRITE_STATUS is called to trigger C function RFC_REMOTE_EXEC using the RFC destination read from the XML file port.

9. The RFC passes to the EDI RIM the full path and file name and the values in the command line that we set up in the XML file port.

10. If the hit to the EDI RIM RFC destination is successful, the C function SY-SUBRC returns a value of 0, and the control and status records of the IDoc are updated with status 18—*Triggering EDI subsystem OK*—and the RFC connection is closed.

11. If it fails, the control and status records of the IDoc are updated to status 20— *Error triggering EDI subsystem*.

Processing is complete, and control is returned to RSEOUT00.

7.3   Summary

The team at Acme Pictures covered a lot of ground here. We've configured inbound and outbound interfaces for a purchase order from Gordy with message type ORDERS and a purchase order confirmation back from Acme with message type ORDRSP.

We went over the inbound and outbound partner profiles we'll need to support these interfaces, and covered EDI configuration tables useful to SD IDocs, including EDPAR, which enables conversion of internal SAP to external partner numbers, and ZEDIXREF, a custom table that we'll build to convert Acme's SAP partner numbers to our customer and supplier's EDI trading partner IDs.

We also went over message control configuration and processing, which generates outbound IDocs from business documents in SD and MM. Both are both heavy consumers of EDI. Our basic philosophy is that the easiest way to understand message control is to do it—and, if you can, debug it.

Once the configuration pieces were place, we followed the processing flow for our inbound PO and outbound PO confirmation, hitting on the key functions and routines that make it all happen.

Of course, we chose the happy path that followed standard IDoc processing. But few people knew better than Acme's legendary founder the great Darryl Q that the path is rarely happy or straight in the real world. We always have our own way of doing things and businesses are no different, especially in Hollywood. And that means we have to consider customization.

"I couldn't build my way out of a paper bag," Darryl Q would tell the carpenters who built his cheesy sets. Acme's legendary founder knew that the success of his films depended on his workers' ability to build. Just as the success of the new SAP EDI system, and the business that relies on it, rests on the ability of the team to build and extend IDocs. So let's delve into this fascinating topic and go over the tools and techniques we use to craft our own custom IDocs.

8 Custom IDocs and IDoc Extensions

Now we're getting to the interesting part: creating, coding, and configuring custom IDocs and extending standard IDocs.

Our custom IDoc will post an X12 846 inventory report to a custom table. Acme will use the data to write custom reports to support inventory balancing.

We'll build our extended IDoc from basic type ORDERS05 for an outbound supplier purchase order using message type ORDERS. We'll add a BOM segment just beneath the E1EDP01 item parent to send the bill of materials associated with a purchase order to Acme's third-party manufacturer, Disc Services International, in the outbound 850 supplier purchase order.

Let's begin by taking a quick tour of the tools that we'll use to develop and configure our IDoc interfaces.

8.1 IDoc Development and Configuration Tools

Our starting point for the development of custom IDocs and extensions is the EDI area menu. You can access it with Transaction WEDI from the SAP EASY ACCESS main menu. WEDI is an area menu and cannot be accessed from other transaction screens.

The key IDoc development tools that we'll be using for our customization are clustered in the DEVELOPMENT folder, illustrated in Figure 8.1.

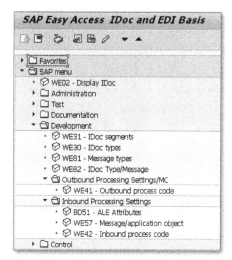

Figure 8.1 IDoc Development Tools in the EDI Area Menu

There are other development tools that we'll be using in addition to those in the EDI area menu. We'll look each tool in the order of use in our development workflow.

8.1.1 Transaction SE11—Data Dictionary

Get to the Data Dictionary with Transaction SE11 through the REPOSITORY INFORMATION SYSTEM (Transaction SE90) in the ABAP DICTIONARY folder, or through SAP menu TOOLS • ABAP WORKBENCH • DEVELOPMENT • ABAP DICTIONARY.

We've touched on the role of the Data Dictionary in defining IDoc syntax and architecture (see Chapter 6, Section 6.2, IDoc Architecture and the Data Dictionary). We'll use the Data Dictionary to create the following objects:

▶ Domains: Tables DD01L and DD01T.

▶ Data elements: Tables DD04L and DD04T. Domains and data elements will be used for custom fields in custom segments.

▶ Structures and transparent tables to store master and transactional data for use in custom programs: Tables DD02L and DD02T.

We'll also use the Data Browser to look at data stored in transparent tables and to do informal extracts for analysis. The Data Browser can be reached with Transaction SE16.

8.1.2 Transaction WE31—Segment Editor

We'll use the segment editor to build and edit segments for custom and extended IDoc basic types. The segments are saved as structures in the Data Dictionary in tables DD02L and DD02T.

As shown in Figure 8.2, the segment editor keeps track of all external names and versions of the segment, along with its string lengths, the number of fields it contains, and the SAP release number current when it was last changed.

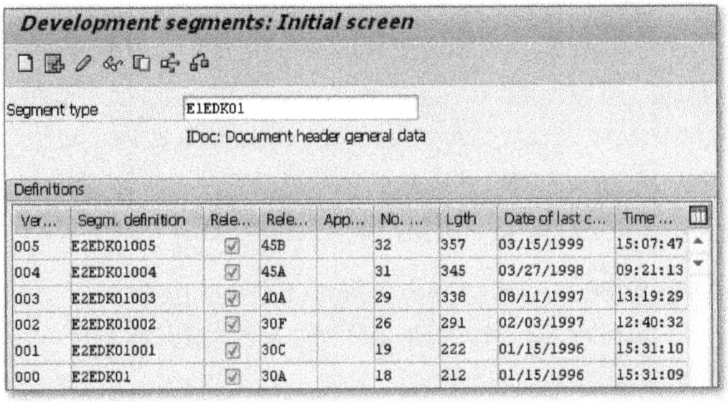

Development segments: Initial screen

Segment type   E1EDK01

IDoc: Document header general data

Definitions

Ver...	Segm. definition	Rele...	Rele...	App... No. ...	Lgth	Date of last c...	Time ...
005	E2EDK01005	☑	45B	32	357	03/15/1999	15:07:47
004	E2EDK01004	☑	45A	31	345	03/27/1998	09:21:13
003	E2EDK01003	☑	40A	29	338	08/11/1997	13:19:29
002	E2EDK01002	☑	30F	26	291	02/03/1997	12:40:32
001	E2EDK01001	☑	30C	19	222	01/15/1996	15:31:10
000	E2EDK01	☑	30A	18	212	01/15/1996	15:31:09

Figure 8.2 Segment Versions in the Initial Screen of the Segment Editor

Double-click any segment definition row to get to its fields, as illustrated in Figure 8.3 for segment type E1EDK01.

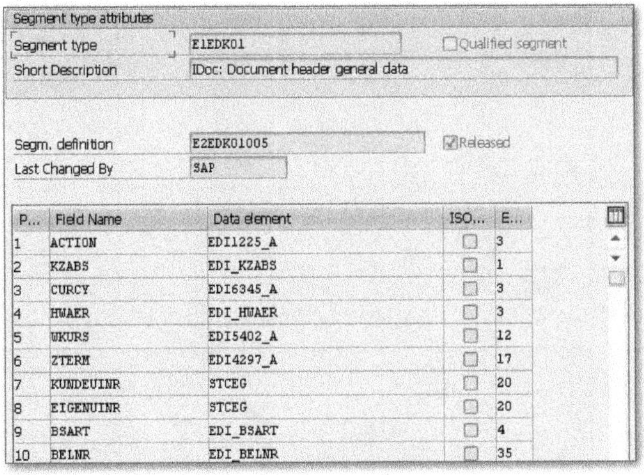

Segment type attributes

Segment type	E1EDK01	☐ Qualified segment
Short Description	IDoc: Document header general data	

Segm. definition	E2EDK01005	☑ Released
Last Changed By	SAP	

P...	Field Name	Data element	ISO...	E...
1	ACTION	EDI1225_A	☐	3
2	KZABS	EDI_KZABS	☐	1
3	CURCY	EDI6345_A	☐	3
4	HWAER	EDI_HWAER	☐	3
5	WKURS	EDI5402_A	☐	12
6	ZTERM	EDI4297_A	☐	17
7	KUNDEUINR	STCEG	☐	20
8	EIGENUINR	STCEG	☐	20
9	BSART	EDI_BSART	☐	4
10	BELNR	EDI_BELNR	☐	35

Figure 8.3 Field List in Segment Editor

Fields are added to this screen during the creation of segments, and data elements are assigned to the fields. The data element is linked to a domain. Double-clicking on the data element name opens the DISPLAY DATA ELEMENT screen. Double-clicking on the domain name opens the DISPLAY DOMAIN screen. If there are qualifiers associated with the domain in a value range, you can click on the VALUE RANGE tab to see them.

The segment is activated after it has been released in the initial screen by selecting menu option EDIT • SET RELEASE. The segment must be released before it can be used in a basic type.

To get to the segment editor, open the DEVELOPMENT folder in the WEDI area menu, and double-click IDOC SEGMENTS, or use Transaction WE31, SAP menu TOOLS • ALE • ALE DEVELOPMENT • IDOC • IDOC TYPE DEVELOPMENT • SEGMENTS.

8.1.3 Transaction WE30—IDoc Type Editor

We use the type editor to assemble segments into custom or extended IDoc basic types. It's also a great way to display the structure and segment attributes of standard IDoc basic types such as ORDERS05.

Double-click on any segment name to open the ATTRIBUTE DISPLAY dialog. It records key parameter values for the segment that controls its place within the IDoc basic type, including the following:

► Segment type name
► Mandatory segment flag
► Minimum and maximum number of occurrences
► Parent segment number
► Hierarchy level

Click the SEGMENT EDITOR button to open the FIELD DISPLAY screen of the segment editor.

The custom or extended IDoc is released after it's been assembled in the initial screen of the type editor with menu option EDIT • SET RELEASE. It must be activated before it can be used in an interface or transported to other SAP clients.

You can get to the type editor by opening the DEVELOPMENT folder in the WEDI area menu, and double-clicking IDOC TYPES, or by using either Transaction WE30 or SAP menu TOOLS • ALE • ALE DEVELOPMENT • IDOC • IDOC TYPE DEVELOPMENT • IDOC TYPES.

IDoc basic and extended types are stored in table IDOCSYN.

8.1.4   Transaction WE81—Logical Messages

Create logical message types when building custom IDoc in the message type editor. To get there, double-click LOGICAL MESSAGES in the DEVELOPMENT folder in the WEDI area menu, use Transaction WE81, or follow menu path TOOLS • ALE • ALE DEVELOPMENT • IDOC • IDOC TYPE DEVELOPMENT • LOGICAL MESSAGES.

Logical message types are stored in tables EDMSG and EDIMSGT.

8.1.5   Transaction WE82—Message to Basic Type Link

This links the message type to the IDoc basic type, providing structure to the logical message. Multiple message types can be linked to one basic type. Transaction WE82 is also used to link IDoc extensions to messages and basic types. Message, basic, and extended types are linked in table EDIMSG.

The relevant menu paths are IDOC TYPE/MESSAGE in the DEVELOPMENT folder of the WEDI area menu or TOOLS • ALE • ALE DEVELOPMENT • IDOC • IDOC TYPE DEVELOPMENT • IDOC TYPE FOR MESSAGE.

8.1.6   Transaction SE37—Function Editor: Function Groups

All function modules are created within a function group. Create function groups in the PROGRAM LIBRARY folder in the Repository Information System (Transaction SE80). Click the EDIT OBJECT button and navigate to the FUNCTION GROUP tab, as illustrated in Figure 8.4.

You can also use Transaction SE37, SAP menu path TOOLS • ABAP WORKBENCH • DEVELOPMENT • FUNCTION BUILDER, or menu path GOTO • FUNCTION GROUPS • CREATE GROUP.

Function groups are programs that logically group related function modules into a common package with global data types, declarations, constants, and so on. The naming convention for the function pool program generated for the function group is always *SAPL<FUNCGRP>*, where FUNCGRP is the name of the function group.

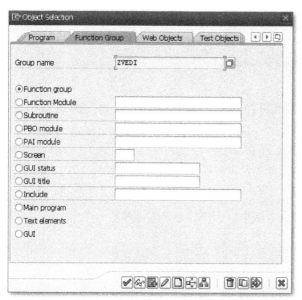

Figure 8.4 Creating a Function Group in the Repository Info System

For example, function group EINM (Figure 8.5), which includes function IDOC_OUT-PUT_ORDERS, has the program name SAPLEINM.

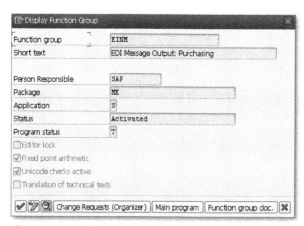

Figure 8.5 Attributes for Function Group EINM

The main function group program always contains the following includes:

▶ L<FUNCGRP>TOP
  Global data declarations for the function group.

▶ L<FUNCGRP>UXX

Stores includes with the function modules.

▶ L<FUNCGRP>FOX

Form subroutines called by the functions. The X character can be a number from 0 to N or a letter to distinguish multiple include programs.

There could also be other includes that do not follow this naming convention with form routines that perform special functions.

We'll create one function group per function module for Acme's custom IDoc development.

8.1.7 Transaction SE37—Function Editor: Function Modules

This is where the code hits the road. Most of our programming in the IDoc interface will be in the Function Builder.

Function modules are created using the same transactions and menu paths as function groups.

Functions are encapsulated programs that perform one function. They have a standard interface with import and export parameters and can transfer internal tables for processing at runtime. They also return error codes that can be trapped for error message processing.

The great bulk of the work of the IDoc interface is done with functions, even with the trend toward object-oriented programming in SAP. Functions are so pervasive throughout the interface that it's highly unlikely they'll be replaced any time soon, although method calls are increasingly being used and exits, in particular, are mirrored by BAdIs.

For example, functions are used to build partner profiles within WE20. This is a three-step process implemented by four function calls that populate the partner profile tables:

1. Build the general view:

   ▶ EDI_AGREE_PARTNER_INSERT: Table EDPP1

2. Build outbound parameters and message control:

   ▶ EDI_AGREE_OUT_MESSTYPE_INSERT: Table EDP13

   ▶ EDI_AGREE_OUT_IDOC_INSERT: Table EDP12

3. Build inbound parameters:

▶ `EDI_AGREE_IN_MESSTYPE_INSERT`: Table EDP21

Functions are also used as customer exits for IDocs and other standard SAP applications. Customer exits allow the user to extend the functionality of standard IDoc functions to accommodate unique business requirements.

IDocs are mostly processed through function modules. Workflow tasks can be used to process some IDocs but we won't be doing this in our Acme implementation except for the standard task that processes the STATUS message type. Our main concern here is with the `IDOC_INPUT` and `OUTPUT` functions, which follow the naming conventions:

▶ `IDOC_INPUT_<MESSAGE>`
The application programming interface (API) for inbound functions is described in the upcoming subsection "API for Inbound IDoc Processing Functions." An example is function `IDOC_INPUT_ORDERS`.

▶ `IDOC_OUTPUT_<MESSAGE>`
The API for outbound functions with message control is described in the upcoming subsection "API for Outbound IDoc Processing Functions." An example is function `IDOC_OUTPUT_INVOIC`.

▶ `MASTER_IDOC_CREATE_<MESSAGE>`
These are standalone IDocs that are not generated by message control. An example is the BOMMAT message that sends bills of material master data with function `MASTER_IDOC_CREATE_BOMMAT`.

The Function Builder is divided into the seven tabs seen in Figure 8.6:

1. ATTRIBUTES: Administrative data for the function:
   ▶ Function group, program names, descriptions, and package
   ▶ Processing type flag, including remote-enabled (RFC) function

2. IMPORT: Structured strings based on Data Dictionary types used to bring data into the function for processing at runtime.

3. EXPORT: Structured strings based on Data Dictionary types used to return data from the function after processing at runtime.

4. CHANGING: Tables or structured strings to carry data that will be changed by the function by runtime processing. Rarely used.

5. TABLES: Internal tables based on Data Dictionary tables or structures that will carry table data for processing at runtime.

6. EXCEPTIONS: String descriptions of error conditions that can be raised at runtime. Exceptions end processing at the point they are raised and return control to the calling program, which can then use them to trigger error message or other processing.

7. SOURCE CODE: Default view where the function's ABAP code is written. The function name at the top of the window is followed by a commented block documenting import and export parameters, tables, and exceptions, as illustrated in Figure 8.6.

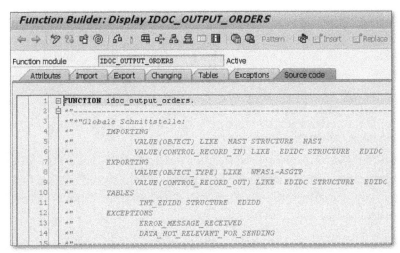

Figure 8.6 Function Builder Source Code Screen

API for Outbound IDoc Processing Functions

The API for outbound IDoc processing functions is standard for all outbound processing actions that use message control. The outbound function is identified and called by form EDI_PROCESSING in program RSNASTED, but can also be used in custom code. Check the Function Builder for the structures of each parameter.

▶ IMPORTING: Parameters passed from RSNASTED.

  ▶ OBJECT: The NAST table record containing the document key and output type for the business document that will be read to build the IDoc.

- ► CONTROL_RECORD_IN: The control record built by RSNASTED from the partner profile read before the IDoc function is called.

- ▶ EXPORTING: Parameters passed back to RSNASTED.

  - ► OBJECT_TYPE: Business object name for the business document. Links the IDoc to the business document.

  - ► CONTROL_RECORD_OUT: Fully populated control record built by the IDoc processing function returned to RSNASTED.

- ▶ TABLES: Internal tables that pass data arrays from the calling function or back to it from the IDoc processing function.

  - ► INT_EDIDD: Output. Returns the data records for the IDoc from the processing function.

- ▶ EXCEPTIONS: Parameters that raise errors in the IDoc processing function. Stop execution of the function at the point the error is trapped and return control to the calling program.

  - ► ERROR_MESSAGE_RECEIVED: Identifies errors called during IDoc processing.

  - ► DATA_NOT_RELEVANT_FOR_SENDING: Added to customer functions and method calls in outbound IDoc processing.

API for Inbound IDoc Processing Functions

The API for inbound IDoc processing functions is standard for all inbound processing actions. Inbound functions are called by the standard IDoc interface function IDOC_INPUT, but you can also call them from custom code. Check the Function Builder for the structure of each parameter.

- ▶ IMPORTING: Parameters passed from the calling function.

  - ► INPUT_METHOD: Used only for call transaction posting. Default is blank for background mode. Other modes are A for All screens in foreground, and E for Display Error screen only.

  - ► MASS_PROCESSING: For workflow processing. Default is blank.

- ▶ EXPORTING: Parameters passed back to the calling function.

  - ► WORKFLOW_RESULT: Workflow error handling. Triggers tasks that pass success or error messages to the SAP workplace inbox or other workflow targets.

- ► APPLICATION_VARIABLE: Advanced workflow programming. Default value is space.

- ► IN_UPDATE_TASK: Triggers a follow-up task to handle database commit. Default value is space for no update task. "X" delays posting until an explicit commit is called.

- ► CALL_TRANSACTION_DONE: Set to "X" if the status record isn't updated in the code of the IDoc processing function. In this case, it is updated within the calling function's processing flow.

- ► DOCUMENT_NUMBER: This is an example of how the standard can vary. IDOC_INPUT_ORDERS uses this parameter to return the sales order number after posting, but not all IDoc functions do this.

► TABLES: Internal tables that pass data arrays from the calling function or back to it from the IDoc processing function.

- ► IDOC_CONTRL: Input. Passes control record data to the processing function.

- ► IDOC_DATA: Input. Passes data records to the IDoc processing function for posting to the document.

- ► IDOC_STATUS: Output. Returns status records indicating success or failure in posting for each IDoc passed to the function. Linked to IDOC_CNTRL and IDOC_DATA through the IDoc number.

- ► RETURN_VARIABLES: Output. Returns additional posting results for each IDoc that are used in workflow processing.

- ► SERIALIZATION_INFO: Output. Used by the IDoc interface to sort a batch of IDocs in a particular order.

8.1.8 Transaction SMOD—SAP Enhancements

Enhancements collect one or more customer exits that are called from strategic points in the code of the IDoc processing function. The customer exits are grouped together in components within each enhancement.

Click on the COMPONENTS button to access the exits. All customer exits that are associated with the component are listed in the CHANGE PROJECT screen.

For example, enhancement SIDOC001 contains one component: customer exit function EXIT_SAPLEDI1_001, used to process the control record of the IDoc before it's created on the IDoc database during inbound and outbound processing (see Figure 8.7). It gives the customer the opportunity to add data to the control record that aren't provided by standard processing.

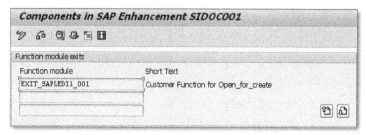

Figure 8.7 Components for Enhancement SIDOC001

This list of functions is our entry point to code the customer exit. Double-click the exit name to open the Function Builder SOURCE CODE window. Note the include statement and program name. We write the code in the include program. But we don't do this through the enhancement object. We first assign the enhancement to a modification project.

Choose ENHANCEMENTS • CUSTOMER EXITS • ENHANCEMENTS in the Repository Information System, use Transaction SMOD, or follow menu path TOOLS • ABAP WORKBENCH • UTILITIES • ENHANCEMENTS • DEFINITION.

Enhancements are stored in tables MODSAP and MODSAPT.

8.1.9 Transaction CMOD—Project Management for SAP Enhancements

We'll use CMOD to create and manage modification to code customer exits for IDoc functions. One or more enhancements can be assigned to each project. For the sake of simplicity, we'll assign only one enhancement per project.

To get to modification projects, use Transaction CMOD, go to ENHANCEMENTS • CUSTOMER EXITS • PROJECTS in the Repository Information System, or follow menu path TOOLS • ABAP WORKBENCH • UTILITIES • ENHANCEMENTS • PROJECT MANAGEMENT.

Modification projects are stored in tables MODACT and MODTEXT.

8.1.10 Transaction WE57—Link Function to Message and Basic Type

This is a key piece of configuration for setting up partner profiles and processing inbound IDocs. It links a processing function, workflow, or task to basic types, extended types, and logical messages.

Different function modules can be assigned to different messages linked to the same basic type. We can add a message code and/or message function and associate different processing functions to the same message and basic type. The message code and function are optional but, if used, become a mandatory part of the partner profile read key.

This gives us tremendous control over how IDocs can be processed under different scenarios and use cases.

The standard link between logical message ORDERS, basic type ORDERS05, and function `IDOC_ORDERS_INPUT` posts a sales order.

We can add a new link for the same message and basic type to a custom function by creating a message code that will be used, for example, to route IDoc data to a custom table for follow-up reporting. The possibilities are limited only by our imagination and our development budget.

These links drive our partner profile. If we were to link ORDERS and ORDERS05 to custom function module `ZSD_INPUT_ORDREPORT` and message code SD0, we would create a partner profile with the following parameters:

▶ Customer number
▶ Partner type KU
▶ Partner function SP
▶ Message type ORDERS
▶ Message code SD0
▶ Custom process code linked to the custom function

Although an optional data element, the message code becomes part of the mandatory key for the partner profile if it is used. It must be present in the control segment field MESCOD to trigger this custom processing.

To get to the link editor, use Transaction WE57, select DEVELOPMENT • INBOUND PROCESSING SETTINGS • MESSAGE/APPLICATION OBJECT from the WEDI area menu, or follow SAP menu path TOOLS • ALE • ALE DEVELOPMENT • IDOC • INBOUND PROCESSING • FUNCTION MODULE • ASSIGN IDOC TYPE AND MESSAGE TYPE.

Table EDIFCT stores these links. Table TOJTB adds a link to the corresponding object in the Business Object Repository (BOR).

8.1.11 Transaction BD51—Define IDoc Attributes

Attributes determine how inbound IDoc functions are processed from the following options:

- **0**

  Mass processing for functions that use direct input to the database to post to a document or other data object.

- **1**

  Individual input for functions that use call transaction to post.

- **2**

  Individual input with a call transaction that locks the IDoc.

- **Dialog allowed**

  Allows screen display during call transactions when IDocs are processed in foreground mode.

To define IDoc attributes, choose DEVELOPMENT • INBOUND PROCESSING SETTINGS • ALE ATTRIBUTES in the WEDI area menu, use Transaction BD51, or follow menu path TOOLS • ALE • ALE DEVELOPMENT • IDOC • INBOUND PROCESSING • FUNCTION MODULE • MAINTAIN ATTRIBUTES.

Attributes for functions are stored in table TBD51.

8.1.12 Transaction WE42—Inbound Process Code

The inbound process code links one IDoc processing function to one or more message types. The process code is required for the inbound partner profile.

Standard process code REMA, for example, is linked to function module IDOC_INPUT_REMADV and to logical messages CREADV, DEBADV, and REMADV.

If a message code and/or message function has been added to the link between the logical message, basic type, and processing function in WE57, then the inbound process code must also contain a record with the link between the message type and the message code and/or message function. This is illustrated in Figure 8.8.

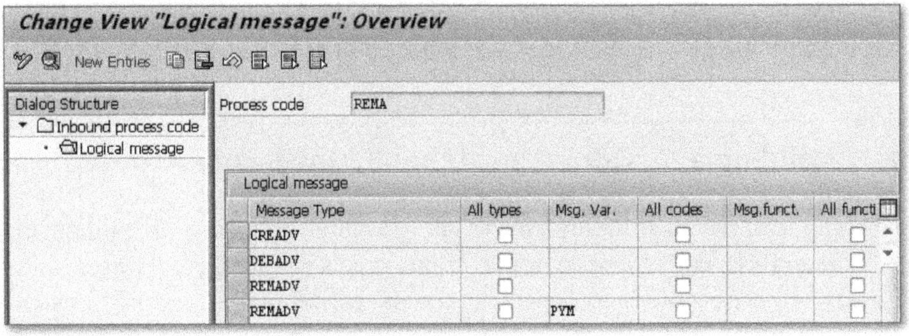

Figure 8.8 Multiple Use Cases Driven by the Process Code

This allows the same function and message to be used in different use cases. You would need to write custom code in a user exit to take advantage of this flexibility.

Use Transaction WE42 to configure the inbound process code or follow menu paths DEVELOPMENT • INBOUND PROCESSING SETTINGS • INBOUND PROCESS CODE in the WEDI area menu or TOOLS • ALE • ALE DEVELOPMENT • IDOC • INBOUND PROCESSING • DEFINE PROCESS CODE IN THE SAP MENU.

The inbound process code is stored in table EDE2T. Its link to the message type key is stored in TMSG2 and to the function module in TEDE2.

8.1.13 Transaction WE41—Outbound Process Code

The outbound process code links one IDoc processing function to one or more message types. Like the inbound, the outbound process code supports multiple use cases through the addition of message codes and/or message functions to the logical message. The configuration screens for the outbound process code are identical to WE41.

The outbound process code is used in the message control screen of the partner profile. It triggers the linked function that reads data from an SAP business document to build and write an IDoc to the database.

Use Transaction WE41 to configure the outbound process code or go to DEVELOPMENT • OUTBOUND PROCESSING SETTINGS/MC • OUTBOUND PROCESS CODE in the WEDI area menu or TOOLS • ALE • ALE DEVELOPMENT • IDOC • OUTBOUND PROCESSING • DEFINE PROCESS CODE in the SAP menu.

The outbound process code is stored in table EDE1T. Its link to the message type key is in TMSG1 and to the message and function module in TEDE1.

8.2 Building a Custom IDoc: Inbound Inventory Report

Now it's time to have a little fun. We're going to build a custom IDoc that maps to an inbound X12 846 inventory report from Acme's vendor Disk Services International (DSI). Before we begin, we'll outline the workflow for creating a custom IDoc from scratch.

8.2.1 Custom IDoc Development Workflow

Figure 8.9 outlines the three steps for building a custom IDoc: develop the IDoc, code the IDoc function, and configure the interface.

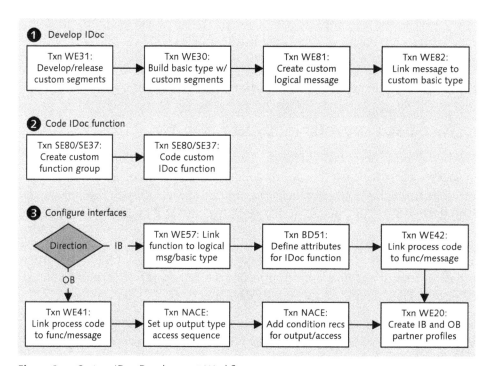

Figure 8.9 Custom IDoc Development Workflow

We'll get into the gritty details as we build our 846 interface. For now, we'll provide a high-level checklist of development tasks:

1. If required, first create domains and data elements in the data dictionary with Transaction SE11.

2. Create segments in the segment editor with Transaction WE31 using standard or custom data elements to create fields.

3. Assemble custom and standard segments into a basic type in the IDoc type editor using Transaction WE30.

4. Create a custom logical message with Transaction WE81.

5. Link the message to the custom basic type with Transaction WE82.

6. Create a new function group for the IDoc processing function with Transaction SE37.

7. Create and code a function module to process the custom IDoc within the new function group with Transaction SE37.

   ▸ Inbound functions post the IDoc to a document or record.

   ▸ Outbound functions extract data to build and distribute an IDoc.

8. For an inbound IDoc, do the following configuration:

   ▸ Link the custom IDoc function to the logical message and basic type with Transaction WE57.

   ▸ Define attributes for the function with Transaction BD51.

   ▸ Create a process code linking the logical message to the custom IDoc function with Transaction WE42.

   ▸ Create an inbound partner profile for the customer, message, and process code with Transaction WE20.

9. For an outbound IDoc, do the following configuration:

   ▸ Create a process code linking the logical message to the custom IDoc function with Transaction WE41.

   ▸ Set up message control: output type, access sequence, and condition record for the output and access with Transaction NACE.

   ▸ Create an outbound partner profile for the customer, message, XML file port, basic type, and message control, including the process code with Transaction WE20.

8.2.2 Building the IDoc Interface

The inbound X12 846 inventory report from DSI carries end-of-day inventory summaries by material for finished movies on DVD and components such as packaging, blank disks, labeling, inserts, stickers, and so on.

Our IDoc will in3sert 846 data into a custom table (ZEDINVRPT) that will be used for daily inventory balancing reports. Table 8.1 list its fields; these are labeled as *M* for mandatory and *O* for optional.

Field	Data Element	Description	Req.
MANDT	MANDT	SAP client	M
INVRPTNO	CHAR10	Unique ID for inventory report rec	M
MATNR	CHAR18	Material number	M
WERKS	CHAR4	Plant/warehouse	M
LGORT	CHAR4	Storage location	O
MENGE	QUAN13	Inventory quantity	M
MEINS	UNIT3	Unit of measure	M
CREDAT	DATS8	Create date	O
CRETIM	TIMS6	Create time	O
UPDAT	DATS8	Date record last changed	O
UPTIM	TIMS6	Time record last changed	O

Table 8.1 Structure of Custom Table ZEDINVRPT

We'll name our message ZINVRPT, which follows the SAP convention of using EDIFACT message names for similar objects. We'll name our basic type ZINVRPT01 and it will have the two segments described in Table 8.2.

Segment	Description	Usage	Repeat
ZIVRPH	Header-level data	M	1
ZIVRPD	Item-level detail	M	N

Table 8.2 Structure of IDoc Basic Type ZINVRPT01

Creating Custom Table ZEDINVRPT

First we create the custom table ZEDINVRPT. The IDoc will post its data to this table and it is a mandatory part of the development cycle.

1. Run Transaction SE11 and enter table name ZEDINVRPT into the DATABASE TABLE field.

2. Click CREATE to open the DICTIONARY: CHANGE TABLE screen in the DELIVERY AND MAINTENANCE tab. Enter a table description in the SHORT DESCRIPTION field and select DELIVERY CLASS A for application data (master and transaction data).

3. In the FIELDS tab, enter the values shown in Figure 8.10.

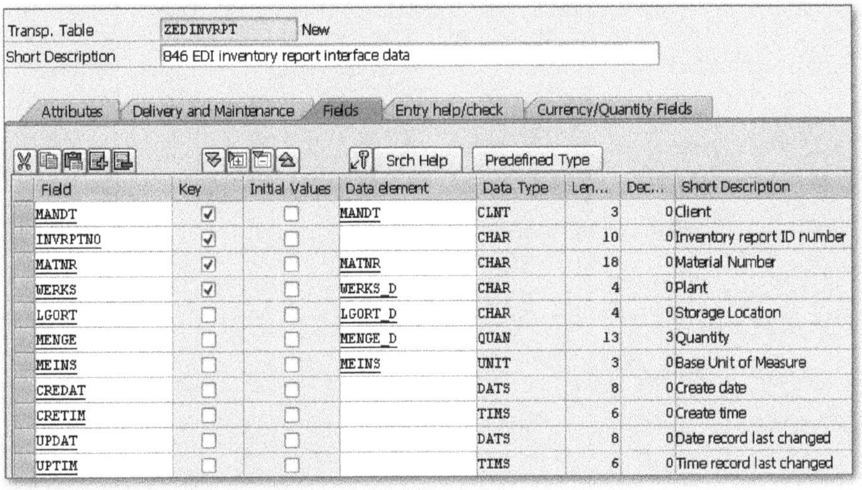

Transp. Table	ZEDINVRPT	New
Short Description	846 EDI inventory report interface data	

Attributes | Delivery and Maintenance | Fields | Entry help/check | Currency/Quantity Fields

Srch Help | Predefined Type

Field	Key	Initial Values	Data element	Data Type	Len...	Dec...	Short Description
MANDT	☑	☐	MANDT	CLNT	3	0	Client
INVRPTNO	☑	☐		CHAR	10	0	Inventory report ID number
MATNR	☑	☐	MATNR	CHAR	18	0	Material Number
WERKS	☑	☐	WERKS_D	CHAR	4	0	Plant
LGORT	☐	☐	LGORT_D	CHAR	4	0	Storage Location
MENGE	☐	☐	MENGE_D	QUAN	13	3	Quantity
MEINS	☐	☐	MEINS	UNIT	3	0	Base Unit of Measure
CREDAT	☐	☐		DATS	8	0	Create date
CRETIM	☐	☐		TIMS	6	0	Create time
UPDAT	☐	☐		DATS	8	0	Date record last changed
UPTIM	☐	☐		TIMS	6	0	Time record last changed

Figure 8.10 Field Structure of Inventory Report Table ZEDINVRPT

4. In the CURRENCY/QUANTITY FIELDS tab a link must be made between the quantity field MENGE and a corresponding unit of measure field in an existing table. Since this is an inventory report, we'll use MSEG-MEINS.

5. Save the table and assign it to a transport. Click TECHNICAL SETTINGS and set DATA CLASS to APPLI (Transaction Data, Transparent Tables) and SIZE CATEGORY to 0 (Data records expected: 0 to 4,300).

6. Save and click REVISED <-> ACTIVATE.

7. Return to the FIELDS tab and click ACTIVATE ($\boxed{\text{Ctrl}}$+$\boxed{\text{F3}}$) in the toolbar above the table name field.

Our custom is ready to accept data.

Creating the Segments

We'll begin by creating the segments. Table 8.3 lists the structure of the header segment ZIVRPH.

Pos	Field	Data Element	Description
01	CREDAT	EDI_CCRDAT	Date IDoc created
02	CRETIM	EDI_CCRTIM	Time IDoc created

Table 8.3 Field Structure of Segment ZIVRPH

Table 8.4 lists the field structure of details segment ZIVRPD.

Pos	Field	Data Element	Description
01	MATNR	MATNR	SAP material number
02	WERKS	WERKS_D	Plant/warehouse
03	LGORT	LGORT_D	Storage location
04	MENGE	MENGE_D	Inventory quantity
05	MEINS	MEINS	Unit of measure

Table 8.4 Field Structure of Segment ZIVRPD

We'll first create ZIVRPH in the segment editor (see Figure 7.13). Go to Transaction WE31, enter "ZIVRPH" into the SEGMENT TYPE field, and click CREATE.

1. The CREATE SEGMENT DEFINITION screen opens. Enter a description in the SHORT DESCRIPTION field:

2. Create the following fields:
   - ▸ Enter "CREDAT" in FIELD NAME and "EDI_CCRDAT" in DATA ELEMENT.
   - ▸ Enter "CRETIM" in FIELD NAME and "EDI_CCRTIM" in DATA ELEMENT.

3. Click SAVE. Assign the segment to a package and a change request. It should like Figure 8.11.

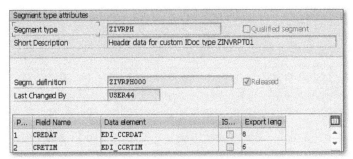

Figure 8.11 Fields Added to the Custom Segment

4. Press F3 to back out to the segment editor's opening screen. Release the segment by selecting menu option EDIT • SET RELEASE. Once released, the initial screen will look like Figure 8.12.

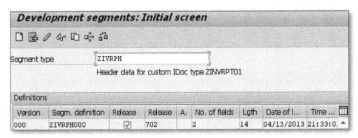

Figure 8.12 Segment ZIVRPH After It's Been Released

5. Follow the same steps to create and release details segment ZIVRPD using the field and data element names in Table 8.4.

Building an IDoc Basic Type

We'll create our custom IDoc basic type with Transaction WE30.

1. Enter "ZINVRPT01" into the OBJ. NAME field, select BASIC TYPE, and click CREATE. The CREATE BASIC TYPE dialog opens after the system informs you that the name is longer than eight characters. The following are radio buttons under New basic IDoc type:

   ▶ CREATE NEW builds a new custom IDoc type.

   ▶ CREATE AS COPY copies an existing IDoc type that we can change.

▶ CREATE SUCCESSOR creates a new release version of an existing custom IDoc type.

2. Select CREATE NEW, and click OK to open the IDoc type editor. We'll assemble our basic type from segments in this screen. To add segments, put the cursor on the IDoc type root name and click CREATE segment, press Shift+F6, or follow the menu path EDIT • CREATE SEGMENT.

3. The MAINTAIN ATTRIBUTES dialog opens, as in Figure 8.13. To add header segment ZIVPRH, do the following:

▶ Enter "ZIVRPH" in the SEGM.TYPE field.

▶ Select the MANDATORY SEG. checkbox.

▶ Enter "1" in MINIMUM NUMBER and "1" in MAXIMUM NUMBER.

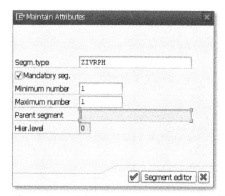

Figure 8.13 Adding a New Segment to the IDoc Type

4. Click OK. ZIVRPH is inserted as a child of the basic type root. Select ZIVRPH and click CREATE SEGMENT to add the details segment.

5. The SEGMENT HIERARCHY dialog opens. Select ADD SEGMENT TYPE AS CHILD.

6. Click OK to open the MAINTAIN ATTRIBUTES dialog. Do the following for the next segment:

▶ Enter "ZIVRPD" in the SEGM.TYPE field.

▶ Select the MANDATORY SEG. checkbox.

▶ Enter "1" in MINIMUM NUMBER and "999999" in MAXIMUM NUMBER.

7. ZIVRPD is added as a child segment to ZIVRPH, as shown in the basic type editor in Figure 8.14.

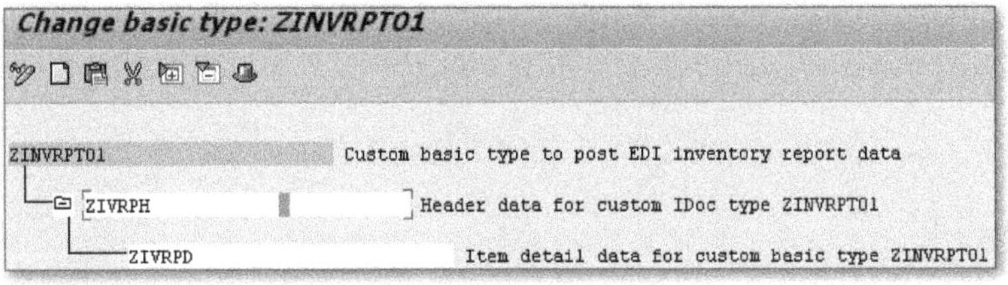

Change basic type: ZINVRPT01

ZINVRPT01   Custom basic type to post EDI inventory report data
    ZIVRPH   Header data for custom IDoc type ZINVRPT01
        ZIVRPD   Item detail data for custom basic type ZINVRPT01

Figure 8.14 Our New IDoc Basic Type ZINVRPT01

8. Double-click ZIVRPD to view the MAINTAIN ATTRIBUTES dialog. The parent segment is ZIVRPH, and the hierarchy level is 2.

9. Save the basic type, and assign it to a package and a change request. Back out of the edit window. Release the IDoc basic type by selecting menu option EDIT • SET RELEASE.

Create a Custom Message Type

Next we create the logical message. Use Transaction WE81, and click DISPLAY CHANGE (menu option TABLE VIEW • DISPLAY -> CHANGE). Click NEW ENTRIES (menu option EDIT • NEW ENTRIES) to open the OVERVIEW OF ADDED ENTRIES screen.

Enter "ZINVRPT" in MESSAGE TYPE and a description of the message in the SHORT TEXT field, as shown in Figure 8.15. Save the message type and assign it to a customizing request.

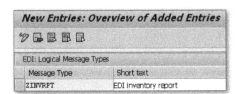

Figure 8.15 Create a Custom Message Type for the IDoc

Link Message to Basic Type

Now we link the logical message to the basic type with Transaction WE82. Click Display Change (menu option TABLE VIEW • DISPLAY -> CHANGE) and then click New Entries (menu option EDIT • NEW ENTRIES) to open the OVERVIEW OF ADDED ENTRIES screen.

Enter the following values into the table control, as illustrated in Figure 8.16:

▶ Enter "ZINVRPT" in the MESSAGE TYPE field.

▶ Enter "ZINVRPT01" in the BASIC TYPE field.

▶ Enter version "702" (your current SAP system release) in the RELEASE field.

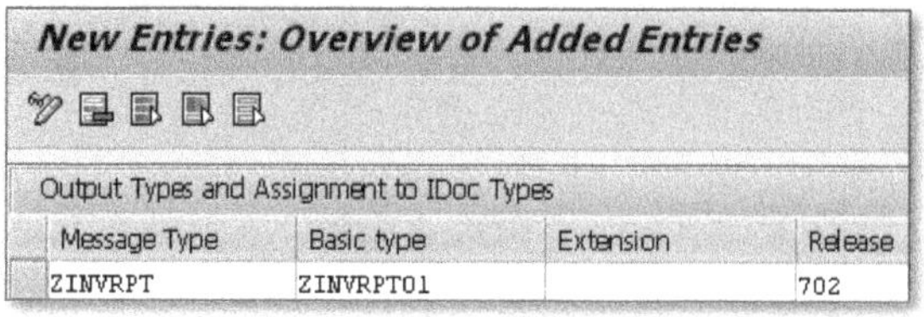

New Entries: Overview of Added Entries

Output Types and Assignment to IDoc Types

Message Type	Basic type	Extension	Release
ZINVRPT	ZINVRPT01		702

Figure 8.16 Linking the Message Type to the IDoc Basic Type

Save the entry and assign it to a customizing request.

Create the Function Group

We'll create the function group in the object navigator.

1. Run Transaction SE80 and click EDIT OBJECT at the top of the OBJECT NAVIGATOR window.

2. Select the FUNCTION GROUP tab, enter "ZEDINVRP" in the GROUP NAME field, and click CREATE.

3. The CREATE FUNCTION GROUP dialog opens. Enter a short description in the SHORT TEXT field, and click SAVE.

4. Assign the function group to a package and a change request.

Function group ZEDINVRP is now ready for coding. It should look like Figure 8.17 in the object navigator.

New Entries: Overview of Added Entries

Output Types and Assignment to IDoc Types

Message Type	Basic type	Extension	Release
ZINVRPT	ZINVRPT01		702

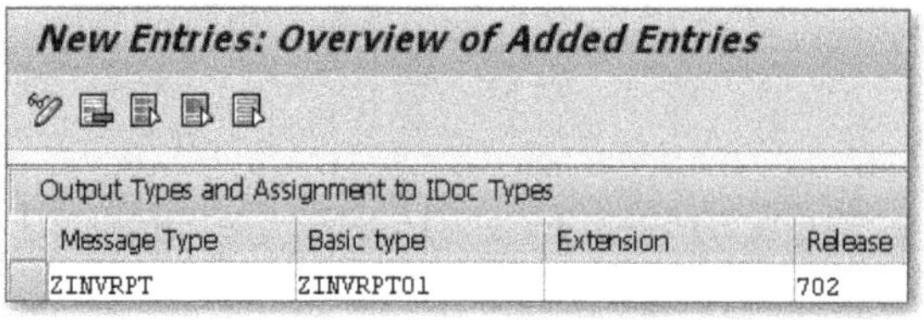

Figure 8.17 Function Group ZEDINVRP is Primed for Coding

Coding the Inbound IDoc Processing Function

We're still in the object navigator:

1. Click EDIT OBJECT, select FUNCTION MODULE in the FUNCTION GROUP tab, and enter the function name "ZIDOC_INPUT_ZINVRPT".

2. Click CREATE. The CREATE FUNCTION MODULE dialog opens.

3. The IMPORT PARAMETERS screen of the Function Builder opens. We'll use standard import parameters that will be passed to the function by the IDoc interface at runtime.

4. Enter the following values illustrated in Figure 8.18.

> **Hint**
>
> Copy and paste standard values for all parameter tabs from any standard inbound processing IDoc function.

Function module	ZIDOC_INPUT_ZINVRPT		Inactive				

Attributes	Import	Export	Changing	Tables	Exceptions	Source code

Parameter Name	Ty...	Associated Type	Default ...	O...	Pass Va...	Short text
INPUT_METHOD	TYPE	BDWFAP_PAR-INPUTMETHD		☐	☑	Inbound method for the IDoc inbound function module
MASS_PROCESSING	TYPE	BDWFAP_PAR-MASS_PROC		☐	☑	Flag: Mass processing

Figure 8.18 Standard Import Parameters for Inbound IDoc Functions

5. Export parameters return workflow and other information to the IDoc interface at runtime. You can also return document numbers and other application data for reporting.

Click the EXPORT tab and enter the values illustrated in Figure 8.19.

Function module	ZIDOC_INPUT_ZINVRPT		Inactive			

Attributes	Import	Export	Changing	Tables	Exceptions	Source code

Parameter Name	Typing	Associated Type	Pass V...	Short text
WORKFLOW_RESULT	TYPE	BDWFAP_PAR-RESULT	☑	Final value of method
APPLICATION_VARIABLE	TYPE	BDWFAP_PAR-APPL_VAR	☑	Variable to be used by application as required
IN_UPDATE_TASK	TYPE	BDWFAP_PAR-UPDATETASK	☑	Flag: Application has triggered update task
CALL_TRANSACTION_DONE	TYPE	BDWFAP_PAR-CALLTRANS	☑	Flag: Application has actually performed call transaction

Figure 8.19 Standard Export Parameters for Inbound IDoc Functions

6. Click the Tables tab and enter the values for the internal tables listed in Figure 8.20.

The tables will pass data in and out of the function. We're most interested in the IDoc control, data, and status records. We won't add any exceptions for this example.

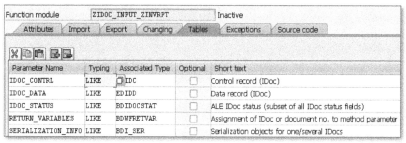

Figure 8.20 Standard Table Parameters for Inbound IDoc Functions

7. Click the Source code tab and enter the function's code as it appears in Listing 8.1.

```
*"----------------------------------------------------------------
FUNCTION ZIDOC_INPUT_ZINVRPT.
*"----------------------------------------------------------------
*"*"Local Interface:
*"  IMPORTING
*"    VALUE(INPUT_METHOD) TYPE  BDWFAP_PAR-INPUTMETHD
*"    VALUE(MASS_PROCESSING) TYPE  BDWFAP_PAR-MASS_PROC
*"  EXPORTING
*"    VALUE(WORKFLOW_RESULT) TYPE  BDWFAP_PAR-RESULT
*"    VALUE(APPLICATION_VARIABLE) TYPE  BDWFAP_PAR-APPL_VAR
*"    VALUE(IN_UPDATE_TASK) TYPE  BDWFAP_PAR-UPDATETASK
*"    VALUE(CALL_TRANSACTION_DONE) TYPE BDWFAP_PAR-CALLTRANS
*"  TABLES
*"    IDOC_CONTRL STRUCTURE  EDIDC
*"    IDOC_DATA STRUCTURE  EDIDD
*"    IDOC_STATUS STRUCTURE  BDIDOCSTAT
*"    RETURN_VARIABLES STRUCTURE  BDWFRETVAR
*"    SERIALIZATION_INFO STRUCTURE  BDI_SER
*"----------------------------------------------------------------
*Data declarations
data: izedinvrpt type standard table of
        zedinvrpt with header line.
```

```
data: gs_zivrph type zivrph,
      gs_zivrpd type zivrpd.
data: gs_last_no like zedinvrpt-invrptno.
*Get last used ID number
clear gs_last_no.
select max( invrptno ) into gs_last_no
    from zedinvrpt.
gs_last_no = gs_last_no + 1.
*process IDoc records and format insert for izedinvrpt
loop at idoc_contrl.
  refresh izedinvrpt. clear izedinvrpt.
  loop at idoc_data where docnum = idoc_contrl-docnum.
    case idoc_data-segnam.
*process header record
      when 'zivrph'.
        gs_zivrph = idoc_data-sdata.
*process detail record
      when 'zivrpd'.
        gs_zivrpd = idoc_data-sdata.
        izedinvrpt-mandt = sy-mandt.
        izedinvrpt-invrptno = gs_last_no.
        izedinvrpt-matnr = gs_zivrpd-matnr.
        izedinvrpt-werks = gs_zivrpd-werks.
        izedinvrpt-lgort = gs_zivrpd-lgort.
        izedinvrpt-menge = gs_zivrpd-menge.
        izedinvrpt-meins = gs_zivrpd-meins.
        izedinvrpt-credat = gs_zivrph-credat.
        izedinvrpt-cretim = gs_zivrph-cretim.
        izedinvrpt-upddat = sy-datum.
        izedinvrpt-updtim = sy-uzeit.
        append izedinvrpt.
        gs_last_no = gs_last_no + 1.
    endcase.
  endloop.
*insert IDoc records to table zedinvrpt
  modify zedinvrpt from table izedinvrpt.
  if sy-subrc = 0.
*success message to status record
    clear idoc_status.
    idoc_status-docnum = idoc_contrl-docnum.
    idoc_status-msgty  = 's'.
    idoc_status-msgid  = 'ZEDI01'.
    idoc_status-msgno  = '001'.
```

```
      idoc_status-status = '53'.
      append idoc_status.
   else.
*verify record count and total before updating.
      clear idoc_status.
      idoc_status-docnum = idoc_contrl-docnum.
      idoc_status-msgty  = 'e'.
      idoc_status-msgid  = 'ZEDI01'.
      idoc_status-msgno  = '002'.
      idoc_status-status = '51'.
      append idoc_status.
   endif.
endloop.

ENDFUNCTION.
```

Listing 8.1 Source Code for Inventory Report IDoc Function

This code is stripped down to its essentials. The control and data records are imported into the function at runtime through the IDOC_CNTRL and IDOC_DATA internal tables. The program logic follows:

1. Gets the last used invoice report ID from ZEDINVRPT-INVRPTNO and increments it for use by the incoming records.
2. Loops through IDOC_CNTRL.
3. Loops through IDOC_DATA at the current IDoc number.
4. Evaluates the SEGNAM field for the current segment name.
5. Moves the SDATA field in the data record to a string structured by the segment type.
6. Moves data from the structured string to an internal table structured by our target database table ZEDINVRPT.
7. When the loops on IDOC_DATA and IDOC_CNTRL are done and internal table IZED-INVRPT is fully populated with all IDoc data, then database table ZEDINVRPT is updated from the internal table.
8. If the update succeeds, the status record is updated with status 53, and a success message pulled from custom message class ZEDI01.
9. If the update fails, the status record is updated with status 51, and an error message pulled from custom message class ZEDI01.

10. Status and message values are passed to internal table `IDOC_STATUS` and returned to the calling IDoc interface function `IDOC_INPUT`, which passes them to routines that update the status records in the database.

All inbound IDoc processing functions work in essentially the same way, with varying levels of complexity for data processing and checks depending on transactional requirements. If you understand this processing approach, you'll understand a lot about the IDoc interface.

Now that the code is written, we'll step through the configuration we need to plug all of our custom objects into the standard IDoc interface.

Link the Function to Message and Basic Type

First up is to link the custom function to our logical message and basic type.

1. Go to Transaction WE57, and click DISPLAY -> CHANGE (menu path TABLE VIEW • DISPLAY -> CHANGE)

2. Click NEW ENTRIES (or press F5) to open the DETAILS OF ADDED ENTRIES screen and enter the following values into it:

   ▸ Enter "ZIDOC_INPUT_ZINVRPT" into the FUNCTION Module field.

   ▸ Select FUNCTION MODULE from the FUNCTION TYPE dropdown.

   ▸ Enter "ZINVRPT01" in the BASIC TYPE field.

   ▸ Enter "ZINVRPT" in the MESSAGE TYPE field.

   ▸ Select INBOUND from DIRECTION dropdown.

Click SAVE and assign the changes to a customizing request. The screen should look like Figure 8.21 after you're done.

Set Attributes for the Function

To set attributes for the function, follow these steps:

1. Go to Transaction BD51 and click NEW ENTRIES.

2. Enter "ZIDOC_INPUT_ZINVRPT" in the FUNCTION MODULE (INBOUND) field and "0" in INPUT T. column for direct input. The function directly inserts IDoc data into the custom table.

Figure 8.21 Linking the Function to the IDoc Basic and Message Types

3. Save and assign the attributes to a transport. The screen should look like Figure 8.22.

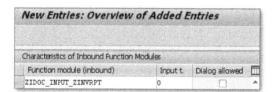

Figure 8.22 Function Attributes for Direct Input

Create a Custom Process Code

The process code ties all the processing pieces together.

1. Go to Transaction WE42, and switch to change mode.

2. Click NEW ENTRIES to open the DETAILS OF ADDED ENTRIES screen, and do the following:

   ▸ Enter "ZINRP" in the PROCESS CODE field.

   ▸ Enter a text description in the DESCRIPTION field. Begin the description with the message name.

   ▸ Set PROCESSING TYPE as the function module.

3. Save the entry and assign it to a transport.

4. A more detailed view of the ADDED ENTRIES screen opens. Select the function "ZIDOC_INPUT_ZINVRPT" from the FUNCTION MODULE dropdown list.

5. Save and add to a transport. After the function has been assigned, back out via F3 to the added entries screen. The function name will be linked to the process code. The screen should look like Figure 8.23.

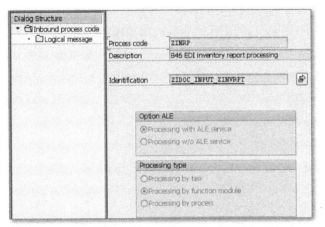

Figure 8.23 The Process Code and Function Module Linked

6. Double-click the LOGICAL MESSAGE folder in the DIALOG STRUCTURE navigation display to open the Logical message overview screen. Click NEW ENTRIES and enter "ZINVRPT" into the MESSAGE TYPE field, as shown in Figure 8.24.

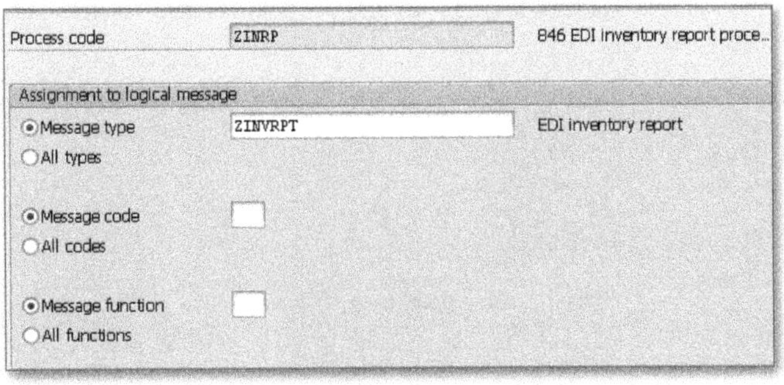

Figure 8.24 Link the Logical Message to the Process Code

Don't forget to save. This completes the link between the process code, the logical message, and the custom function module. All these objects are now ready to be used in a partner profile.

Define the Partner Profile

All that's left is the inbound partner profile. The inventory report is coming from the supplier Disc Services International, entered in Acme's SAP vendor master as DISK01.

So we'll create a partner profile with partner type LI for vendor.

1. Run Transaction WE20, select the PARTNER TYPE LI folder, and create a vendor partner profile header for DSI with partner number DISK01.

2. Save the general view and create inbound parameters to add message type ZIN-VRPT. Enter the following values into the INBOUND PARAMETERS screen:
   - ▸ Enter "VN" in the PARTNER ROLE field.
   - ▸ Enter "ZINVRPT" in the MESSAGE TYPE field.
   - ▸ Enter "ZINRP" in the PROCESS CODE field.
   - ▸ Set TRIGGER IMMEDIATELY as the processing mode. This is a simple table insert that comes in once a day and doesn't involve a lot of processing, so we won't schedule a background job.

3. Save the partner profile. The finished product should look like the inbound partner profile in Figure 8.25.

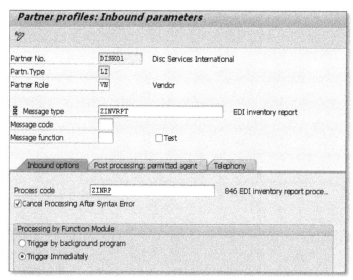

Figure 8.25 Inbound Parameters for DSI Message Type ZINVRP

This interface is now ready to roll—after it goes through the full testing cycle, of course.

8.3   Extending an IDoc: Outbound PO with BOMs

Next we'll try our hand at adding a custom segment to a standard IDoc. Our scenario is pretty simple. DSI needs to receive the bill of materials when Acme sends them a purchase order. They need to know what components Acme expects them to use in manufacturing.

DSI may have the components in inventory or they may need to order from a third-party supplier. The purchase order BOM is key to their manufacturing process.

A custom segment, Z1EDP01, will be created to hold the components just below E1EDP01, the parent for all line item segments, in an extension of IDoc basic type ORDERS05 that we will name ZORDRS01.

The code will be written in a CMOD modification project using enhancement SDEDI001 in component `EXIT_SAPLVEDC_002`.

8.3.1   IDoc Outbound Development Workflow

Extended IDocs are built on existing standard basic types. They are created to send or receive data that are not accommodated in a standard IDoc. Figure 8.26 outlines the workflow for extending an IDoc, which is broken into three main steps: extend the IDoc, code the IDoc enhancement, and configure the interfaces.

To create an extended IDoc type, you insert one or more segments into a standard basic type. The insertion point should make sense in terms of the data the extended segment contains and its semantic context within the IDoc.

We also need custom code to populate and process the extended segments. The code is usually written in a user exit, but sometimes you need a custom IDoc function. For example, message type MBGMCR doesn't have any customer exits, so it would need a custom version of its processing function if it were extended or if you needed to do any non-standard processing.

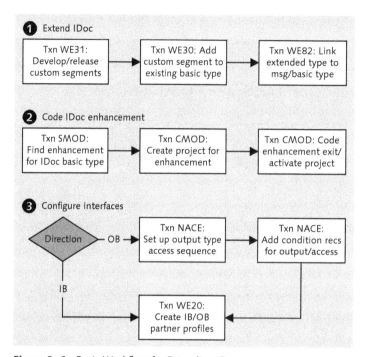

Figure 8.26 Basic Workflow for Extending IDocs

The process for creating and configuring a custom function for an extended IDoc type is the same as for a custom IDoc with the exception that we don't need to create a new message type.

To extend an IDoc by coding a customer exit, follow these steps:

1. Create custom segments in the segment editor with Transaction WE31.

2. Copy an existing standard basic type into an extended type in the IDoc type editor with Transaction WE30.

3. Insert custom segments into the extended type with Transaction WE30.

4. Link the extended type to the logical message and basic type with Transaction WE82.

5. Identify an enhancement with user exits for the extended type with Transaction SMOD.

6. Create a modification project to write and manage the custom code for the exit with Transaction CMOD.

7. Code the customer exit enhancement component in the CMOD project.

8. For an inbound extended IDoc, create inbound partner profile for the customer, message, and process code with Transaction WE20.

9. For an outbound extended IDoc, there are two additional steps:

   ▸ Set up message control (output type, access sequence, and condition record for the output and access with Transaction NACE).

   ▸ Create outbound partner profile for the customer, message, XML file port, basic and extended types, and message control with Transaction WE20.

Identifying Customer Exits

Let's root around the Data Dictionary and consider a simple backend way to identify user exits that we can use in modification projects. First we need to look at the standard frontend approach.

Modification projects organize our user exit work. We can add more than one enhancement to a project allowing it to encompass an entire business process. But at Acme, we'll only create one project per enhancement.

The following process is the typical frontend approach to finding exits:

1. Identify the function for the IDoc that will be extended.

2. Go to the Function Builder in Transaction SE37, enter the function name in the FUNCTION MODULE field, and click DISPLAY.

3. Click ATTRIBUTES to get the package name: VED for all SD EDI development objects and ME for purchasing documents, including EDI and ALE exits.

4. Go to Transaction SMOD, select the input help dropdown (or press F4) and click INFORMATION SYSTEM to open the REPOSITORY INFO SYSTEM: FIND EXITS dialog.

5. Enter the package name in the PACKAGE field of the search help dialog and click EXECUTE.

6. The REPOSITORY INFO SYSTEM: FIND EXITS dialog opens, listing all enhancements in the package.

   For SD package VED, nine hits are returned; for purchasing package ME, 36 hits are returned in ERP 6.0, as shown in Figure 8.27.

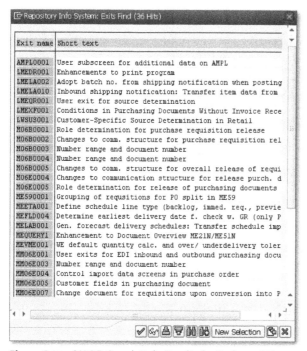

Figure 8.27 SMOD Search Help Results for Package ME

Descriptions of enhancements don't always reveal their purpose or identify their message types. For example, if you search package ME for user exits in PO message ORDERS, you'd have to carefully scan the list of 36 enhancements to learn that MM06E001 is the one you need.

We can use the Data Dictionary backend to refine our search. It takes a couple of steps however. First replicate the SMOD search help results by following these steps:

1. Go to the Data Browser with Transaction SE16.

2. Enter "TADIR" into the TABLE NAME field and press ⌷Enter⌷. TADIR contains all development repository objects in the system.

3. Enter the following values into the selection screen for TADIR.

   ▸ Enter "R3TR" in the PGMID field.

   ▸ Enter "SMOD" in the OBJECT field.

   ▸ Enter "ME" in the DEVCLASS field.

4. Click EXECUTE or press ⌷F8⌷.

A list of every enhancement stored in package VED is returned in the field OBJ-NAME. So what do we need to know to make our job of identifying exits easier?

Focusing on Enhancements

Each enhancement contains all the user exits available to any IDoc function in components that hold a function module with the naming convention EXIT_<PROGRAM>_00X where:

- PROGRAM is the name of the function pool program that contains the IDoc processing function module.
- 00X is the number of the function within the exit function group.

For example, enhancement SIDOC001, which is used to change the control segment just before an IDoc is written to the database, has only one component: function EXIT_SAPLEDI1_001.

Enhancement MM06E001, with purchasing document exits, has 20 components; they are all called during various processing stages of more than one message type, including outbound purchase orders, inbound purchase order change and acknowledgments, and inbound ship notifications.

For processing data in the outbound PO, the key components include the following:

1. EXIT_SAPLEINM_001: Control record changes

2. EXIT_SAPLEINM_002: Data record changes while IDoc is being built

3. EXIT_SAPLEINM_011: Final data changes after the IDoc has been built

Note that EXIT_SAPLEINM_011 is also called for outbound message types ORDCHG (PO change), REQOTE (request for quotation), BLAORD (purchasing contracts), and BLAOCH (purchasing contract change).

The exit names are in function IDOC_OUTPUT_ORDERS. You can find them by going into the code of the function in Transaction SE37 and searching the string CUSTOMER-FUNCTION using the binocular FIND icon at the top of the FUNCTION BUILDER screen. Select IN MAIN PROGRAM.

Every call to a customer function in every message type processed by the main program is listed. The call syntax is CALL CUSTOMER-FUNCTION '00X' where 00X is the number of the exit being called. We're interested in CUSTOMER-FUNCTION '002' for EXIT_SAPLEINM_011.

Click the instance of the customer function call in the GLOBAL SEARCH IN PROGRAMS window, and the system will go to the call point in the code. The customer function is called after each segment has been appended to INT_EDIDD, the internal table used to build the IDoc.

The '002' in single quotes following CALL CUSTOMER-FUNCTION is the function name. Double-click '002' within the single quotes and the system navigates to the exit function. The source code for the function is listed in Listing 8.2.

```
*"----------------------------------------------------------
FUNCTION EXIT_SAPLEINM_002.
*"----------------------------------------------------------
*"*"Global Interface:
*"  IMPORTING
*"     VALUE(XEKKO) LIKE EKKO STRUCTURE  EKKO
*"     VALUE(XLFA1) LIKE LFA1 STRUCTURE  LFA1
*"     VALUE(XLFB1) LIKE LFB1 STRUCTURE  LFB1
*"     VALUE(DOBJECT) LIKE NAST STRUCTURE  NAST OPTIONAL
*"  TABLES
*"     INT_EDIDD STRUCTURE EDIDD
*"     XEKPO STRUCTURE UEKPO OPTIONAL
*"     XEKET STRUCTURE UEKET OPTIONAL
*"     DEKEK_X STRUCTURE EKEK_X OPTIONAL
*"     DEKEH STRUCTURE IEKEH OPTIONAL
*"     DSADR STRUCTURE SADR OPTIONAL
*"     DVBAK STRUCTURE MMVBAK OPTIONAL
*"     DVBAP STRUCTURE MMVBAP OPTIONAL
*"     DVBKD STRUCTURE MMVBKD OPTIONAL
*"  CHANGING
*"     VALUE(ISC_ENHANCEMENT) TYPE ISC_EXIT_SAPLEINM_002 OPTIONAL
*"  EXCEPTIONS
*"     ERROR_MESSAGE_RECEIVED
*"     DATA_NOT_RELEVANT_FOR_SENDING
*"----------------------------------------------------------

  INCLUDE ZXM06U02.

ENDFUNCTION.
```

Listing 8.2 Call to Enhancement Component for Outbound PO

The IMPORTING parameters of the exit are identical to the EXPORTING parameters of the customer function, which is a shell that calls the exit.

Note include program ZXM06U02, which is where the exit code goes. The program doesn't exist until the system creates it when we double-click its name. We can write our code here through the IDoc function, but it is a best practice to code and manage exits in a modification project.

Shortcut to Identifying Enhancements

Let's go back to the ATTRIBUTES screen of IDOC_OUTPUT_ORDERS in Transaction SE37. There are values here that can help us identify our enhancement in the Data Dictionary. Copy the program name SAPLEINM. We can use it to identify which enhancement we need through a table read.

1. Go back to the Data Browser with Transaction SE16.

2. Enter "MODSAP" in the TABLE NAME field, and press ⌜Enter⌝. MODSAP stores SAP enhancements and their components.

3. Enter the program name bracketed by asterisks (*SAPLEINM*) in the MEMBER field. Or, better yet, get the exit name from the IDoc processing function (EXIT_ SAPLEINM_002). Click EXECUTE.

   The enhancement MM06E001 is in the NAME field.

Between the IDoc processing function and table MODSAP, you can quickly identify the enhancement you need to add to your modification project.

Exit Function Groups

The names of exit function groups begin with an X, which can narrow a search for exit functions in Transaction SE37. An open-ended search for function groups that begin with X in ECC 6.0 returns 5,899 exits for all applications.

Function group XM06 contains all 61 user exits for package ME, which contains all development objects for purchasing.

One of the joys of working with SAP is that a little educated poking around goes a long way. And it's fun, too!

It's time to build our extended IDoc. We'll begin with the custom segment.

8.3.2   Create Segment Z1EDP01

The structure of custom segment Z1EDP01 is described in Table 8.5.

Pos	Field	Data Element	Description
01	MATNR	MATNR	SAP component material number
02	MAKTX	MAKTX	Component description

Table 8.5 Structure of BOM Segment Z1EDP01

Build the custom segment in the segment editor with Transaction WE31. Enter "Z1EDP01" in the NAME field and click CREATE to open the CREATE SEGMENT DEFINITION screen.

Enter a description in the SHORT DESCRIPTION field. Add the field and data elements from Table 8.5 into the FIELD NAME and DATA ELEMENT fields in the table control.

Click SAVE and assign the segment to a change request. Press F3 to back out to the segment editor's initial screen. Release the segment by selecting menu option Edit • SET RELEASE.

8.3.3   Build Extension ZORDRS01

Next we extend the standard basic type:

1. Go to the IDoc type editor with Transaction WE30. Enter the name of the IDoc Extension ("ZORDRS01") in the OBJ. NAME field, select EXTENSION, and click CREATE. The CREATE EXTENSION DIALOG opens, as shown in Figure 8.28.

2. Select CREATE NEW and enter "ORDERS05" in the LINKED BASIC TYPE field. Click OK to open the IDoc type editor.

   The structure of basic type ORDERS05 is displayed in the editor with the root name ZORDRS01.

3. Expand the E1EDP01 item group by clicking on the folder icon next to the segment name.

4. To add the custom segment, put the cursor on the E1EDP01 segment name and click CREATE SEGMENT, or press Shift+F6, or choose menu option EDIT • CREATE SEGMENT. A pop-up informs you that the custom segment will be added as a child to E1EDP01. Click OK.

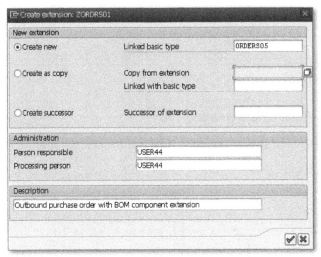

Figure 8.28 Select a Linked IDoc Basic Type to Create an Extension

5. The MAINTAIN ATTRIBUTES dialog opens. Enter the following values to add the Z1EDP01 segment:

   ▸ Enter "Z1EDP01" in the SEGM.TYPE field.

   ▸ Enter "1" in the MINIMUM NUMBER field.

   ▸ Enter "999" in the MAXIMUM NUMBER field.

6. Click OK. Z1EDP01 appears as a child of E1EDP01 (Figure 8.29). Extended type ZORDRS01 now has its custom segment.

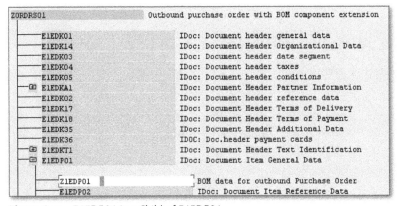

Figure 8.29 Z1EDP01 Is a Child of E1EDP01

7. Save the extension, assign it to a change request, and back out of the edit window.

8. Release the extended type in the initial screen by selecting menu option EDIT • SET RELEASE.

8.3.4 Link Message to Basic and Extended Types

To link the message and basic type to the extended type, follow these steps:

1. Go to Transaction WE82, and click CHANGE • DISPLAY, press [Ctrl]+[F4], or follow menu path TABLE VIEW • DISPLAY -> CHANGE.

2. Click NEW ENTRIES (or press [F5]) to open the OVERVIEW OF ADDED ENTRIES screen. Enter the following values in the table control (see Figure 8.30):

   ▶ Enter "ORDERS" into the MESSAGE TYPE field.

   ▶ Enter "ORDERS05" into the BASIC TYPE field.

   ▶ Enter "ZORDRS01" into the EXTENSION field.

   ▶ Enter version "702" in the RELEASE field.

Output Types and Assignment to IDoc Types				
Message Type	Basic type	Extension	Release	
ORDERS	ORDERS05	ZORDRS01	702	▲

Figure 8.30 Link between the Extension and the Message and Basic Types

3. Save the entry and assign it to a transport request.

8.3.5 Create the Modification Project

Next we'll create the modification project with Transaction CMOD, as shown in Figure 7.35.

1. Enter the project name "ZEDIMPO1" in the PROJECT field and click CREATE. The project attributes screen opens. Enter a description in the SHORT TEXT field (see Figure 8.31).

Attributes of Enhancement Project ZEDIMPO1

Enhancement assignments   Components

Project	ZEDIMP...
Short text	Customer exits for the outbound PO with BOM components

Administrative Data

Package		
Original language	EN	
Created by	USER44	04/17/2013
Last changed on/by		

Figure 8.31 Modification Project ZEDIMPO1 Attributes

2. Save the project and assign it to a change request.

3. Click the ENHANCEMENT ASSIGNMENTS button. Enter "MM06E001" into the ENHANCEMENT field (see Figure 8.32). Save.

Enhancement   Components

Enhancement	Text
MM06E001	User exits for EDI inbound and outbound purchasing documents

Figure 8.32 Our User Exit Is in Enhancement MM06E001

4. Click COMPONENTS to load a list of all exit functions assigned to the enhancements. A partial list is displayed in Figure 8.33.

   The checkmark next to the enhancement means that there is already active code in the exit.

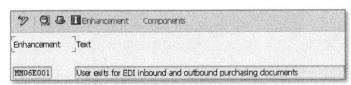

Project				ZMMIDOC
Enhancement	Impl		Exp	MM06E001 User exits for EDI inbound and outbound purchasing documents
Function exit	✓			EXIT_SAPLEINM_001
				EXIT_SAPLEINM_002
				EXIT_SAPLEINM_003
				EXIT_SAPLEINM_004
				EXIT_SAPLEINM_005
				EXIT_SAPLEINM_006

Figure 8.33 Exit Functions Are Components of Enhancements

5. We'll write the code in component EXIT_SAPLEINM_002. Double-click the exit to open the source code window of the Function Builder.

Note the import and table parameters of the exit function in Figure 8.34. We'll read our inputs from the application tables and append our new segment to INT_EDIDD when we write our code.

INT_EDIDD is used to assemble the IDoc segments in the order that they will appear in the finished IDoc.

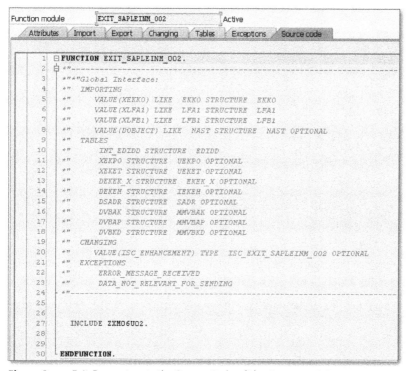

Figure 8.34 Exit Parameters in the Source Code of the Customer Exit

We first need to create the include program ZXM06U02, if it doesn't already exist. When you double-click the include name, SAP returns the following information message:

Program names ZX... are reserved for includes of exit function groups.

Press ⌐Enter⌐ to get past the message and open the CREATE OBJECT dialog informing you of the following:

Include ZSM06U02 does not exist. Create object?

Click YES and assign the include program to a change request. When the ABAP editor loads, we're ready to code.

8.3.6   Coding the Exit

The code for our exit will be called after each instance of segment E1EDP01 is processed and added to the IDoc.

The exit will read the BOM for the purchase order line item material from table MDSB, which stores the material number for the item components against the PO and line item numbers. We can then get the description for each component from table MAKT.

The material number and description for each component will be passed to a separate instance of our custom segment Z1EDP01 and appended to internal table `INT_EDIDD`, which is used to build the IDoc.

The data that we need to identify the BOMs for the finished DVDs in the PO are in the table parameters of `EXIT_SAPLEINM_002`.

The IDoc is built from data in a number of structures and internal tables, including XEKKO (purchase order header) and XEKPO (line item details), which will give us the PO number and line item number to read MDSB. The IDoc build for each segment—and the customer function call for each segment—is in form `FUELLEN_IDOC_INTTAB`.

All line item segments are built within a loop on XEKPO. E1EDP01, the parent segment at the item level, is the first appended to the IDoc within the XEKPO loop. Our code will be called by the exit after E1EDP01 is written to internal table `INT_EDIDD`.

The same exit is called for every segment after it has been written to the IDoc, regardless of level. So we need to check that the current segment name is E1EDP01. This is in field SEGNAM in internal table `INT_EDIDD`.

In addition, we're only doing this for DSI. So we also need to check that the PO is for vendor DISK01. This value will be available to the exit in the import parameter `LFA1-LIFNR`.

This, and the custom segment name, is all we need to get the BOM and append it to the IDoc as a child of E1EDP01. The code is shown in Listing 8.3. Once again, remember that the code is stripped down to its essentials and is really only a starting point for this solution.

```
*&-------------------------------------------------------------*
*&  Include       ZXM06U02                                     *
*&-------------------------------------------------------------*
** Type declarations                                           *
** Component material numbers from MDSB
TYPES: BEGIN OF t_bomrec,
       matnr type matnr,
     END OF t_bomrec.
** Internal table declaration                                 *
** BOM data for custom segment data:
it_pobom type table of t_bomrec.
** Data Declarations                                          *
** Work areas
data: wa_pobom like line of it_pobom,
      ls_z1edp01 type Z1EDP01,
      ls_maktx type maktx.
** Begin processing                                           *
** Restrict processing to segment E1EDP01 and vendor DSI
if xlfa1-lifnr = 'DISK01' and int_edidd-segnam = 'E1EDP01'.
** Get all BOM components and descriptions for finished good
** in current purchase order item.
  select matnr into corresponding fields
       of table it_pobom from mdsb
       where ebeln = xekpo-ebeln
         and ebelp = xekpo-ebelp.
** Get material description by looping on it_pobom and
** reading MAKT by material number
  loop at it_pobom into wa_pobom.
    clear ls_maktx.
    select single maktx into ls_maktx
      from makt where matnr = wa_pobom-matnr.
    if sy-subrc = 0.
** Populate custom segment string
      ls_z1edp01-matnr = wa_pobom-matnr.
      ls_z1edp01-maktx = ls_maktx.
    endif.
** Pass and append data to INT_EDIDD
    int_edidd-segnam = 'Z1EDP01'.
    int_edidd-sdata = ls_z1edp01.
```

```
    append int_edidd.
  endloop.
endif.
```

Listing 8.3 Exit Code Passes BOM Components to Segment Z1EDP01

8.3.7 Customize Message Control

Now we move on to outbound configuration: message control and a partner profile. We'll need a custom output type so that we can enter unique values into the message control screen of our outbound partner profile.

Message type ORDERS will be used in more than one outbound interface for DSI and will require more than one outbound partner profile. We need a unique output type for our BOM ORDERS interface that we will not use in any other partner profile.

Each partner profile must be unique, as we have seen from our discussions of partner profile and message control keys in tables EDP13 and EDP12 in Chapter 7, Section 7.2, Outbound Configuration Generates IDocs.

To create our custom output type ZNEU, we'll copy standard type NEU in application EF (purchase order). We'll only use this custom type to generate an outbound ORDERS IDoc from a PO with the BOM extension.

1. Call Transaction NACE.
2. Select application EF (purchase order) and click OUTPUT TYPES to open the OUTPUT TYPES: OVERVIEW in display mode.
3. Select the menu path TABLE VIEW • DISPLAY • CHANGE (or press $\boxed{\text{Ctrl}}$+$\boxed{\text{F1}}$) and then select standard output NEU. Click COPY AS or press $\boxed{\text{F6}}$.
4. Change the name of the output type to "ZNEU" and enter a description for the extended PO with BOM. Make sure the ACCESS TO CONDITIONS and MULTIPLE ISSUING checkboxes are both set, as in Figure 8.35.
5. Access sequence 0001 (document type, purchasing organization, and vendor) gives us enough granularity to restrict who gets a PO with BOMs from which purchase order.

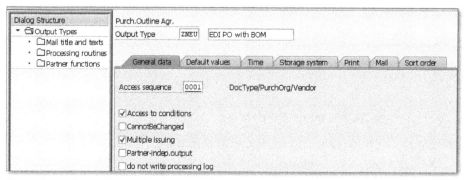

Figure 8.35 CustomOutput Type ZNEU with Access Sequence 0001

6. We'll use a custom PO document type (ZNB) copied for standard PO document type NB to make sure that only some POs are sent to DSI with an extended BOM segment. We'll use ZNB to create purchase orders that will be sent to DSI with the BOM in the extended IDoc type.

Creating a Custom Purchasing Document Type

Not all purchase order IDocs will be sent with a custom BOM segment. We need to distinguish between orders that will generate a BOM segment and those that won't. To do this, we'll create a custom purchase order document type and use this in our condition record.

Functional consultants and business users define custom document types after thorough analysis of how these documents will be used by the business and what data they need to contain in their different use cases.

It's not really the job of the EDI team, but it doesn't hurt to know.

Purchasing document types are configured in the IMG (Transaction SPRO). We'll take the easy road and copy the existing standard PO document type to a custom code.

1. In the IMG, follow menu path SAP CUSTOMIZING IMPLEMENTATION GUIDE • MATERIALS MANAGEMENT • PURCHASING • PURCHASE ORDER • DEFINE DOCUMENT TYPES.

2. In the table control of the DOCUMENT TYPES PURCHASE ORDER CHANGE screen, find and select document type NB (standard PO).

3. Click the COPY AS button (or press F6).

4. Change the document type code to ZNB and add a short description.

5. Press Enter. The SPECIFY OBJECT TO BE COPIED dialog opens with the message that the document type has dependent entries.

6. Click COPY ALL to get an exact copy of the standard document type.

7. Save and assign the custom document type to a transport request.

Our custom purchasing document type can now be used to create purchase orders for whoever needs an EDI PO with the BOM attached.

7. We will select access number 10 in access sequence 0001, which points to condition table 25 (B025) and communications structure KOMKBEA with key fields:

   ▸ BSART: Purchasing document type

   ▸ EKORG: Purchasing organization

   ▸ LIFNR: Vendor

8. Press ⌨Enter. The SPECIFY OBJECT TO BE COPIED dialog opens with the observation that the output type has dependent entries. Click COPY ALL. Another dialog opens with the number of dependent entries.

9. The system returns us to the OUTPUT TYPES: OVERVIEW screen in change view. Select output ZNEU, and double-click the PROCESSING ROUTINES folder to open the PROCESSING ROUTINES: OVERVIEW screen.

10. If there is no program name for medium EDI, add one. Click NEW ENTRIES to open the DETAILS OF ADDED ENTRIES screen.

11. Enter the following values into the added entries details screen:

    ▸ Enter "EDI" in the TRANSM.MEDIUM field.

    ▸ Enter "RSNASTED" in the PROGRAM (Processing 1) field; this is the standard SAP output program. You can also use a custom ABAP output program. Use RSNASTED as a model.

    ▸ Enter "EDI_PROCESSING" in the Form ROUTINE field. This form identifies and calls the function that will build the IDoc, writes it to the database, sends it to the outbound IDoc processing function, and updates its status record.

12. Press ⌨Enter and double-click the PARTNER FUNCTIONS folder to open the PARTNER FUNCTIONS: OVERVIEW screen.

13. Make sure that there's an entry for medium EDI and partner type VN for vendor. If not, click NEW ENTRIES and select EDI in the MEDIUM field and VN in the FUNCT field.

14. Save and assign the new output to a change request. You may need to cycle through several objects to complete the assignment to the request.

Assign ZNEU to a Procedure

1. Back out to the initial output control screen in Transaction NACE. Select application EF and click the PROCEDURES button.

2. There's only one procedure in application EF, and that is RMBEF1. We'll need to assign our custom output type to it.

3. Select the procedure and double-click the CONTROL folder in the navigation pane.

4. Select output type NEU and click the COPY AS button (or press F6). The entry is copied into the CHANGE VIEW CONTROL: OVERVIEW screen.

5. Change the step number to "15" and the output type name to "ZNEU", but leave everything else the same.

6. Press Enter to return to the overview screen. Save the entry and assign it to a change request. The entry should look like Figure 8.36.

Procedure		RMBEF1 Purchase Order			

Reference Step Overview					
Step	C...	C...	Description	Requiremnt	Manual on
10	1	NEU	New PO printout		
15	1	ZNEU	EDI PO with BOM		

Figure 8.36 Assigning ZNEU to the Purchasing Procedure

Create Condition Records

Condition records drive generation of the IDoc for Acme's vendor, DSI. In this case, the IDoc will only be generated for PO document type. Follow these steps:

1. In Transaction NACE, select application EF and click CONDITION RECORDS.

2. Select OUTPUT TYPE "ZNEU". Click the CONDITIONS RECORDS button. The KEY COMBINATION dialog opens. Select the second key combination, as shown in Figure 8.37.

Figure 8.37 Select the Access Sequence in the Key Combination Dialog

3. Press ⌈Enter⌋ or click the green checkmark. The selection screen for the condition record opens. Enter the following values and click EXECUTE to open the condition record table control (see Figure 8.38):

   ▶ Enter "ZNB" for EDI PO with BOM enhancement in the PURCHASE DOC. TYPE field.

   ▶ Enter "3000" (sample) in the PURCH. ORGANIZATION field.

4. In the condition records table control, enter the following:

   ▶ "DISK01" for Acme's vendor Disc Services International

   ▶ "VN" for vendor as the function

   ▶ "6" for EDI as the medium

   ▶ "4" for immediate when the document is saved as the dispatch time

   ▶ "EN" as the language

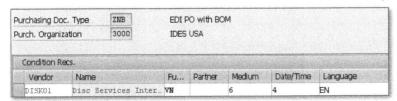

Figure 8.38 Condition Record for Output Type ZNEU in Application EF

Note that the full access key for the condition record is present in the header and table control area of the entry.

8.3.8 Build Outbound Partner Profile

All that's left is to set up a unique outbound partner profile for DSI using our logical message, extended type, and custom message control.

Message code BOM will create the unique key in table EDP12 for our partner profile. The message code links to the logical message and process code. The standard process code for the PO is ME10, which links message type ORDERS to IDoc function IDOC_OUTPUT_ORDERS. And this is where we coded our customer exit to populate the BOM extension.

We have two choices: either create a custom process code or extend the standard to include message code BOM. We'll extend the standard ME10.

Extending the Process Code

We can extend process code ME10 with Transaction WE41 or by following WEDI area menu DEVELOPMENT • OUTBOUND PROCESSING SETTINGS/MC • OUTBOUND PROCESS CODE.

1. Select process code ME10 and double-click the LOGICAL MESSAGE folder in the navigation pane to open the LOGICAL MESSAGE DETAILS screen.

2. Click NEW ENTRIES (or press [F5]) and add the following values to the added entries screen:

   ▶ MESSAGE TYPE: ORDERS

   ▶ MESSAGE CODE: BOM

   We could select the ALL CODES radio button under MESSAGE CODE and the system would pass any value found in the message code field, but being specific gives us better control over our partner profile keys.

3. Save and assign the entry to a change request. The screen should look like Figure 8.39.

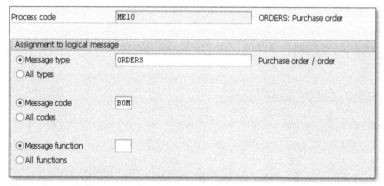

Figure 8.39 Linking Logical Message ORDERS to Message Code BOM

4. There should now be two entries for message ORDERS in the LOGICAL MESSAGE table control in the LOGICAL MESSAGE OVERVIEW screen, as in Figure 8.40.

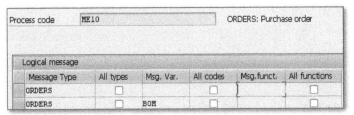

Figure 8.40 Process Code Extended with Multiple Instances of ORDERS

Creating the Partner Profile

Go to Transaction WE20 and create the header level partner profile for DSI in the PARTNER TYPE LI folder in the navigation pane, if one doesn't already exist.

1. Click CREATE OUTBOUND PARAMETER beneath the outbound parameters table control and enter the following values that are shown in Figure 8.41:

   ▸ PARTNER ROLE: "VN"

   ▸ MESSAGE TYPE: "ORDERS"

   ▸ MESSAGE CODE: "BOM"

Partner No.	DISK01	Disc Services International
Partn.Type	LI	Vendor
Partner Role	VN	Vendor

Message Type	ORDERS	Purchase order / order
Message code	BOM	
Message function		☐Test

Outbound Options | Message Control | Post Processing: Permitted Agent | Telep...

| Receiver port | XML_IDOC | XML File | Test port for XML IDoc output |

Output Mode
- ○ Transfer IDoc Immed.
- ⦿ Collect IDocs
- ⦿ Start subsystem
- ○ Do not start subsystem
- Output Mode 3

IDoc Type
Basic type	ORDERS05	Purchasing/Sales
Extension	ZORDRS01	Outbound purchase order wit...
View		
☑Cancel Processing After Syntax Error

Figure 8.41 Outbound Parameters for the BOM PO IDoc

▶ RECEIVER PORT: "XML_IDOC"

▶ OUTPUT MODE: The radio buttons for COLLECT IDocs and START SUBSYSTEM

▶ BASIC TYPE: "ORDERS05"

▶ EXTENSION: "ZORDRS01"

2. Click on MESSAGE CONTROL and add two entries with the following values that are shown in Figure 8.42:

▶ APPLICATION: "EF"

▶ MESSAGE TYPE: "ZNEU"

▶ PROCESS CODE: "ME10"

▶ CHANGE MESSAGE: One checkbox entry null and one checked

Figure 8.42 Message Control Values for the BOM ORDERS

3. We'll also need EDI information for the IDoc control record. All of Acme's IDocs will include this data. Select the EDI STANDARD tab, and enter the following values:

▶ EDI STANDARD: "X" for X12

▶ MESSAGE TYPE: "850" for outbound X12 850

▶ VERSION: "005010"

4. Save the partner profile.

This extended IDoc is now ready to test. Feel free to play with it, tweak it, extend it, and so on. This is only the starting point.

8.4   Summary

Now we've had a brief introduction to building custom and extended IDocs. We've toured the key IDoc development and configuration tools and have seen how they can be used to build a simple custom inbound and an extended outbound IDoc. We've also touched on enhancements and modification projects and have seen how simple it can be to find a specific user exit and enhancement using the Data Dictionary.

But there's so much more to know, so little time, and so few pages to learn it all, which is a major problem in any implementation project. We need to learn enough quickly enough to do the work that needs to be done. So our next step is to put our brief introduction to this material to work. Our legs may still be wobbly, but we'll take the plunge and begin building Acme's new SAP EDI system, at least the order-to-cash cycle of interfaces, beginning with the inbound customer purchase order.

Besides, the great Darryl Q. Fernhausen often began a new picture knowing even less about the plot, the actors, or the writers. So let's open the curtain on Act III and prepare to take the stage.

ACT III
Realizing the Dream – Building Acme's SAP EDI System

"You can't sell what you ain't got," the great Darryl Q would point out to his long-suffering and poorly paid writers when they had no new ideas. Mr. Q knew better than anybody that you can't make a buck if you have no goods to sell. That's why Acme Pictures needs the outbound purchase order interface.

9   Generating the PO for Replication Services

Gordy's Galaxy ordered a batch of movies on DVD from Acme Pictures to stock its over 2,000 stores in North America.

Remember that Acme doesn't actually hold any physical inventory. It's all stored at the warehouse of its supplier and distributor, Disk Services International (DSI), which provides Acme's SAP system with a number of daily inventory interfaces.

This latest order is for a few hot-sellers that just can't seem to stay on the shelves; in fact, when Gordy's purchase order posts and the system checks inventory, SAP finds that there's not enough product to ship everything that Gordy wants.

So since Acme needs the product to sell to Gordy's Galaxy, who is its most important customer, it has to order it from DSI, who will stamp the movies onto DVD, package them, apply all stickers, and ship them out to Gordy's stores and distribution centers.

This is what the outbound purchase order interface is all about. Acme creates a PO in SAP for replication services and generates an ORDERS.ORDERS05 IDoc that instructs DSI how many finished DVDs to produce. The process is completed when DSI sends back a PO acknowledgment that confirms ordered quantities and scheduled delivery dates.

This round trip begins an ordering cycle that ends when DSI moves the finished goods from manufacturing into inventory, invoices Acme for work completed, and Acme pays the invoice. We won't step through the full purchasing cycle, but we will look at a number of its key interfaces.

The bottom line is that you can't make money without spending money, which is something that the great Darryl Q understood. All this activity would bring a huge grin to his face and give him an excuse, if he ever needed one, to pour himself a martini and light up a fat Cuban Cohiba to celebrate the success of his unlikely studio.

9.1 Technical Overview of the Interface

Table 9.1 summarizes the technical information for the outbound purchase order.

Item	Description
Title	Purchase Order for Replication Services
Description	A purchase order is created in Acme's SAP system to order replication services for DVD movies when finished product inventory needs to be replenished. Usually this means that a customer PO has come in and there is not enough on-hand inventory to fulfill the order. Replication and distribution services are purchased from Disk Services International (DSI), who also holds Acme's inventory in their warehouse. The interface is completed when DSI returns an order acknowledgment that updates the purchase order with confirmed quantities and scheduled delivery dates.
Type of interface	Purchasing: IDoc to X12 EDI
Direction	Outbound PO to DSI (vendor) Inbound PO confirmation from DSI
Trading partner	Disk Services International (DSI)
IDoc	Outbound ORDERS.ORDERS05 Inbound ORDRSP.ORDERS05
IDoc extended type	
IDoc function	`IDOC_OUTPUT_ORDERS (PO)` `IDOC_INPUT_ORDRSP (PO confirmation)`
Custom ABAP	
Description	

Table 9.1 Overview of Outbound Replication Services PO Interface

Item	Description
Target file(s)	Outbound X12 850 Inbound X12 855
Source document(s)	Outbound Acme SAP supplier purchase order Inbound DSI sales order
Transaction code	Outbound ME21N Inbound ME22N
Map(s)	ORDERS.ORDERS05 to X12 850 vers. 5010 X12 855 vers. 5010 to ORDRSP.ORDERS05
Custom map logic	
Source system	Acme SAP
Target system	DSI EDI hub via AS2 from Acme EDI RIM
997 acknowledgment	Inbound for OB PO 850 within 24 hours of transmission at the transaction detail level. Function group acknowledgment code: PO. Outbound for IB PO confirmation 855 within 24 hours of transmission from DSI at the transaction detail level. Function group acknowledgment code: PR.
Frequency	Daily, on-demand
Job schedule	Outbound RSEOUT00 for message type ORDERS to DSI Inbound RBDAPP01 for message type ORDRSP from DSI

Table 9.1 Overview of Outbound Replication Services PO Interface (Cont.)

Act III Specification Chapters

All the chapters in Act III have been written as specifications—functional, mapping, and technical. The aim is to present development and configuration requirements for each of Acme's interfaces. All chapters will follow the same rough structure, beginning a summary of the interface requirements in the technical overview.

So let's move on to the functional requirements for the outbound replication purchase order interface.

9.2   Functional Specifications

The purpose of this outbound interface is to order replication services from DSI, Acme's supplier and distributor. Replication services include copying movies to DVD, packaging the disk, and applying cover artwork, shrink wrap, and any labeling and/or stamps that may be required.

Typically, this interface is run after a customer order has been received and an inventory check finds that there is not enough product in stock at DSI to completely fill the order. Acme manually creates a purchase order in SAP with Transaction ME21N for replication services. Existing POs can also be released with Transactions ME28 (collectively) or ME29N (individually). When the PO is saved, an ORDERS. ORDERS05 IDoc is created and sent to DSI.

This interface can also run in an automated workflow process after the system calculates requirements based on the forecast, on-hand inventory, open sales orders, and other calculations. Purchase requisitions are created (Transaction ME51N), released (Transaction ME54N), and purchase orders generated from the requisition with Transactions ME58 (collectively) or ME59N (individually).

The POs are then released by an authorized user with Transactions ME28 or ME29N, and the IDocs generated and sent.

The outbound purchase order for replication services to DSI will not include BOMs for the ordered product. It will be a standard interface with no enhancements or custom programming.

DSI will return an order acknowledgment in an 855 when they receive Acme's PO. DSI's confirmation will update the DELIVERY SCHEDULE and CONFIRMATIONS screens at the line-item level of Acme's purchase order using Transaction ME22N.

9.2.1   Process Overview

The process begins when a supplier purchase order is created or released in Acme's SAP system to order DVD replication services. An ORDERS.ORDERS05 IDoc is parked in the IDoc database until a scheduled program is run to pick it up and send it to the EDI RIM.

The EDI RIM transforms it to an X12 850 purchase order transaction and routes it to DSI's EDI system by AS2 transmission.

When DSI receives the replication PO from Acme, it creates a sales order in their business system. The sales order then generates and sends an X12 855 PO confirmation back to Acme's EDI RIM. The RIM converts this to an ORDRSP.ORDERS05 IDoc and sends it into SAP to update the purchase order.

9.2.2 Requirements

The interface will meet the following functional requirements:

▶ A standard purchase order type NB will be used to generate ORDERS PO messages to DSI and other suppliers.

▶ Each PO can have one or more line items and each can be sent to only one vendor.

▶ The ORDERS.ORDERS05 IDoc is only generated after the PO has been released by an authorized user.

▶ The PO IDoc will contain all purchase order data.

▶ ORDERS IDocs will be generated immediately after the purchase order is released. The IDoc will not be sent immediately but will be parked at status 30—*IDoc ready for dispatch*—until processed by a scheduled job.

▶ Each vendor PO will be acknowledged with an 855-ORDRSP IDoc at the line-item level. The ACKNOWLEDGMENT REQUIRED flag will be set in the CONFIRMATIONS screen for each line item in each PO.

9.2.3 Dependencies

The interface is dependent on the existence of the following objects:

▶ Master data to support creation of purchase orders for replication services to suppliers

▶ Order acknowledgment flag set in the CONFIRMATIONS screen at the item level of the purchase order

▶ DSI receipt of the latest material and BOM master data from Acme's SAP system whenever new records are created or existing records change

▶ Regularly updated inventory levels for Acme-owned stock in DSI storage warehouses

9.2.4 Assumptions

Basic assumptions underlying the replication PO interface include the following:

- DSI and other vendors will be able to exchange a purchase order and PO confirmation by EDI transmission with Acme Pictures.
- An ORDERS IDoc is triggered when the purchase order is completed and released by an authorized business user.
- Only finished goods are sent in the PO transmission.
- The PO confirmation returns only the minimal data required to confirm the purchase order in Acme's SAP system.
- DSI gets Acme's SAP number for all items sent in the PO.
- DSI gets the Global Location Number (GLN) for Acme's sold-to and ship-to partners.
- The IDoc can be regenerated from the purchase order if required.

9.2.5 Data That Will be Passed to an Outbound Purchase Order

The ORDERS PO IDoc is generated when the purchase order is released and saved by Transaction ME29N. Table 9.2 lists fields that may be included in the outbound PO ORDERS IDoc.

Table	Field	Description	Sample Value
Order Header			
EKKO	BSART	Purchasing document type	NB
EKKO	BELNR	Purchase order number	4500016169
EKKO	BEDAT	Purchase order date	20131215
EKKO	EKORG	Purchasing organization; also used to populate sold-to partner	3000
EKKO	EKGRP	Purchasing group	003
EKKO	BUKRS	Company code	3000
EKKO	CURCY	Purchase order currency	USD

Table 9.2 Purchase Order Data That Will Be Sent in the ORDERS IDoc

Table	Field	Description	Sample Value
EKKO	LIFNR	Vendor partner number	5595
Order Items			
EKPO	EBELP	Line item number	00010
EKPO	MATNR	SAP Material number	500210
EKPO	MENGE	Order quantity	26.000
EKPO	MEINS	Unit of measure	EA
EKPO	NETWR	Net order value in PO currency	2600
EKPO	MATKL	Material group	004
EKPO	WERKS	Plant at item level and also used to populate ship-to partner at IDoc header, one per PO; address in E1EDKA1 pulled from address database.	3100
EKPO	LGORT	Storage location	0001
EKET	EINDT	Scheduled delivery date	20140115
EKET	MENGE	Scheduled delivery quantity	26.000

Table 9.2 Purchase Order Data That Will Be Sent in the ORDERS IDoc (Cont.)

Data That Will Post to a Purchase Order Confirmation

Table 9.3 outlines the data that is required to confirm the purchase order.

Table	Field	Description	Sample Value
Order Header			
EKKO	BELNR	Acme purchase order number	4500016169
Order Items			
EKPO	MATNR	SAP material number	500210
EKPO	MENGE	Confirmed order quantity	26.000
EKPO	MEINS	Unit of measure	EA

Table 9.3 Data from DSI to Confirm Acme's PO

373

Table	Field	Description	Sample Value
EKPO	BELNR	Acme purchase order number	4500016169
EKPO	EBELP	Acme PO line item number	000010
EKPO	LABNR	Order acknowledgment ID: DSI sales order number	008872158
EKET	EINDT	Confirmed delivery date	20140115

Table 9.3 Data from DSI to Confirm Acme's PO (Cont.)

9.2.6 Custom Enhancements

There are no custom enhancements in this interface.

9.2.7 Reconciliation Procedure

Data in the ORDERS IDoc will be monitored and checked against the purchase order. IDoc data will also be validated against the translated 850 by the EDI team.

For the inbound ORDRSP, confirmation data in the PO will be checked against the inbound 855 and ORDRSP IDoc.

9.2.8 Errors and Error Handling

Failures in outbound or inbound IDoc processing are tracked by the EDI support team using standard IDoc monitoring tools such as BD87 and WE05. Application errors are reported to the business users immediately.

Confirmations must be returned to Acme from the vendor within 12 hours. The EDI team will monitor inbound traffic through the RIM and identify late confirmations based on aging reports of outbound POs. Late confirmations and other errors will be addressed by the interface owner immediately.

9.3 Generating the ORDERS PO with Message Control

The outbound vendor purchase order is generated by message control when the PO is released and saved.

Let's look at message control configuration for the ORDERS message type and then outline the path of the IDoc from the purchase order outbound to the EDI RIM.

9.3.1 Message Control Configuration for the ORDERS Message

We'll use standard message control configuration to output the ORDERS message type that includes the following objects:

▶ Application EF for purchase order

▶ Output type NEU with access sequence 0001: Document type, purchasing organization, and vendor number

▶ Access number 11 for condition table B025

▶ Communications structure KOMKBEA with fields:

  ▶ BSART: Purchasing document type

  ▶ EKORG: Purchasing organization

  ▶ LIFNR: Vendor

▶ Condition records

▶ Process code ME10 linked to function `IDOC_OUTPUT_ORDERS`

▶ Partner profiles for message type ORDERS

Output Control Setup

We will make some adjustments to output type NEU. Standard output type NEU is configured only for print output. We'll add EDI.

1. Run Transaction NACE.

2. Select APPLICATION EF (purchasing) and click OUTPUT TYPES. Click the pencil icon (or press Ctrl + F4) to switch to change mode.

3. Select output type NEU and double-click it to open the OUTPUT TYPE DETAILS screen for editing.

4. We'll keep ACCESS SEQUENCE 0001 with access number 11 and condition table B025. Set the MULTIPLE ISSUING checkbox. The completed screen should look like Figure 9.1.

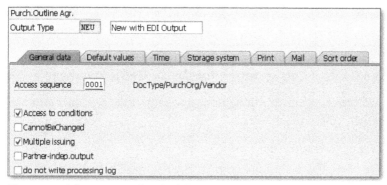

Figure 9.1 Adjustments to Standard Output Type NEU

5. Save output type NEU and assign it to a change request.

6. Double-click the PROCESSING ROUTINES folder in the OUTPUT TYPES navigation panel. Add the EDI program and form to the PROCESSING ROUTINES table control.

7. Click the NEW ENTRIES button and enter the following values:

   ▸ TRANSM. MEDIUM: "EDI"

   ▸ PROGRAM in PROCESSING 1: "RSNASTED"

   ▸ FORM ROUTINE: "EDI_PROCESSING"

8. Save any changes. Double-click the PARTNER FUNCTIONS folder and click NEW ENTRIES to add the following values to the partner functions table control:

   ▸ MEDIUM: "EDI"

   ▸ FUNCT.: "VN" for vendor

9. Save the changes and back out to the CONDITIONS FOR OUTPUT CONTROL screen of Transaction NACE. Select APPLICATION EF and click PROCEDURES. Output type NEU is assigned to procedure RMBEF1 PURCHASE ORDER.

10. Select procedure RMBEF1 and double-click the CONTROL folder in the navigation panel. We'll keep the standard settings.

Condition Record

Now we'll add condition records for Disk Services International using Transaction MN04 or NACE by following these steps:

1. Select application EF and click CONDITION RECORDS. Select output type NEU from the dialog that pops up and click CONDITION RECORDS.

2. Select access sequence DOCTYPE/PURCHORG/VENDOR, which is the second key combination, and click OK (Figure 9.2).

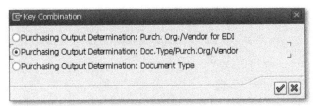

Figure 9.2 Access Sequence 0001 in the Key Combination Dialog

3. Enter the following values into the selection screen of the condition record and click EXECUTE (or press F8):

   ▶ PURCHASING DOC. TYPE: "NB" (standard purchase order)

   ▶ PURCH. ORG: "3000"

4. Enter the following values into the condition records table control in the CREATE CONDITION RECORDS screen:

   ▶ VENDOR: "DISK01" (Disk Services International vendor number)

   ▶ FUNCT: "VN"

   ▶ MEDIUM: "6"

   ▶ DATE: "4"

   ▶ LANGUAGE: "EN"

5. Save the record. Confirm the condition record entries in table B025 in the data browser, Transaction SE16. It should look something like the table in Figure 9.3.

Table: B025
Displayed Fields: 7 of   7   Fixed Columns:

MANDT	KAPPL	KSCHL	BSART	EKORG	LIFNR	KNUMH
800	EF	NEU	NB	3000	DISK01	0000004070

Figure 9.3 Condition Record for Output Type NEU in Table B025

9.3.2 Overview of the End-to-End Process Flow

Figure 9.4 outlines the end-to-end process flow for generating and sending a standard purchase order for replication services to Disk Services International.

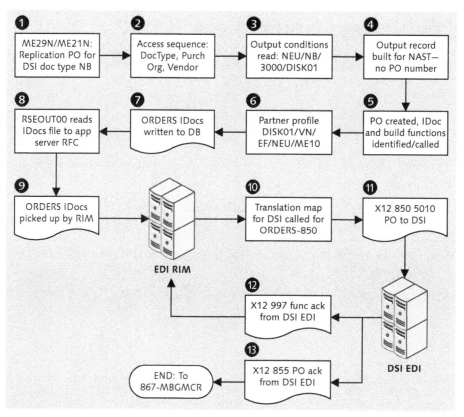

Figure 9.4 The Outbound Purchase Order Process Flow

The process begins when a standard purchase order for replication services from DSI is created with Transaction ME21N or released with Transaction ME29N for document type NB and purchasing organization 3000.

The three values that make up the access sequence—document type, purchasing organization, and vendor—are passed from the purchase order to communications structure KOMKBEA with function COMMUNICATION_AREA_KOMKBEA.

Structure KOMKBEA is used to help identify the application, procedure, output type, and access sequence. These in turn help identify the condition records table, which is read with function SD_COND_ACCESS in function group V61Z with the help of a number of tables that link together all the message control configuration objects that we've looked at.

One of the key links is table T681Z. Table T681Z ties together the header structure of the business document—EKKO for the purchase order—to the application (EF) and the communications structure (KOMKBEA).

Another table—T681—links the application to the conditions table; for our PO, that is linking EF to table B025.

The system link between the PO and application EF is through the purchase document header field EKKO-BSTYP. If EKKO-BSTYP equals F, then the document is a purchase order and application is always EF.

With the condition record from B025 safely in hand, the system begins to build an output record for table NAST. This record drives output processing for the IDoc when the PO has been verified, assigned a PO number, and written to the database but before it has been committed.

The key data elements that drive output in NAST include the following:

- KAPPL: Application
- OBJKY: Document number (in this case, the PO, which is not available when the NAST entry is initially assembled)
- KSCHL: Output type
- SPRAS: Language for the output message
- PARNR: Message partner
- PARVW: Message partner type
- NACHA: Message medium (i.e., an IDoc)
- VSZTP: Dispatch time for message (in this case, immediately upon save)

You'll note that these values include the access sequence, which defines the type of document and partner that will generate the output, and the condition record, which links the access sequence values to the type of output that will be generated: an IDoc in English to be output as soon as the PO is saved.

The missing link at this stage is the PO number. It is assigned just before the PO is completed and posted in form routine BUCHEN called from function group MEPO for Transaction ME21N. The NAST record, still without a PO number, is carried into form BUCHEN.

Following the Call Stack of ME21N

To trace the call stack for Transaction ME21N, go to the Repository Browser (Transaction SE80) and look at function group MEGUI (user interface for purchasing documents). It begins in the PAI modules of screen 0014 and runs through a series of modules, methods, functions, and subroutines to form BUCHEN in function group MEPO.

MEGUI begins the process flow at runtime. The real work is mostly done by functions, forms, and classes in function group MEPO.

The easiest way to follow the call stack is to create a new PO with Transaction ME21N, set the debug switch (/h) in the command field, and save. And then step through each of the PAI modules. Have fun!

Once all the data have been collected to build, verify, and post the purchase order, and before it is committed to the database, function ME_MESSAGES_UPDATE in function group EINV is called to process the IDoc.

ME_MESSAGES_UPDATE updates the NAST record with the new purchase order number and then calls another function (RV_MESSAGES_UPDATE, through form UPDATE_NACH-RICHTEN_EF with an ON COMMIT statement) to identify and call the IDoc build function and insert the output record into table NAST.

The ON COMMIT means that the form doesn't actually run until after the purchase order has been posted (also with an ON COMMIT) and an explicit COMMIT WORK statement has been called.

Yet another function is called to process the IDoc: WFMC_MESSAGE_SINGLE in function group V70A with the NAST record, updated with the PO number, as input.

It doesn't waste any time and immediately calls form EINZELNACHRICHT in program RSNAST00, which identifies the program and form we selected to process EDI output in our message control configuration: RSNASTED with form EDI_PROCESSING. This is stored in table TNAPR and is read with the output type, output medium, and application.

This is then called through a function that is dynamically named at runtime with the form name and program. The first order of business is to establish the partner type and look up the partner profile.

This lookup returns the process code. Table TEDE1 is then read with the process code to get the name of the IDoc processing function — IDOC_OUTPUT_ORDERS, which is confirmed in table TFDIR.

Once we have all this, the system builds the control record and preps the IDoc for editing by calling function IDOC_CCMS_OPEN.

Next, it calls the IDoc processing function IDOC_OUTPUT_ORDERS through the dynamic function call in Listing 9.1.

```
CALL FUNCTION TEDE1-ROUTID
  EXPORTING
    CONTROL_RECORD_IN      = EDIDC
      OBJECT               = NAST
  IMPORTING
    CONTROL_RECORD_OUT     = EDIDC
    OBJECT_TYPE            = HELP_OBJECT_TYPE
  TABLES
    INT_EDIDD              = INT_EDIDD
  EXCEPTIONS
    DATA_NOT_RELEVANT_FOR_SENDING = 01
    OTHERS                 = 04.
```

Listing 9.1 Dynamic Function Call to Build the ORDERS IDoc

TEDE1-ROUTID has the name of the function module to call. Function IDOC_OUT-PUT_ORDERS takes over and builds the IDoc from the new purchase order. It is can be used to process any outbound IDoc generated through message control.

Once this function finishes its work, the IDoc is closed, table NAST is updated with an Output Complete flag and a date and time stamp, and a communications IDoc is created and written to the database at status 01 IDoc generated.

Then function EDI_OUTPUT_NEW in function group EDI7 is called to convert the IDoc into XML format and trigger distribution to the EDI RIM through the partner profile, XML file port, and RFC destination. The status is first updated to 30—*IDoc ready for dispatch*—and then to 03—*Data passed to port OK*—when the IDoc successfully triggers the EDI RIM to pick it up.

This is assuming, of course, that the output mode in the partner profile is set to transfer IDocs immediately and trigger subsystem. If the partner profile is set to collect IDocs, then processing halts at status 30 and the IDocs wait in the database until program `RSEOUT00` runs to pick them up and send them out to the EDI RIM by calling function `EDI_OUTPUT_NEW`.

When the IDoc is successfully translated by the map in the EDI RIM, a STATUS IDoc is created and sent back into SAP to update the status of the outbound ORDERS. ORDERS05 IDoc to 06—*Translation OK for ISA [interchange control number] for TP [receiving partner EDI ID]*.

The process comes full circle when DSI sends back two transmissions:

1. An X12 997 functional acknowledgment within six hours reporting that the 850 transaction has been accepted by DSI's EDI system, updating the outbound IDoc's status to 16—*997 OK*.

2. An X12 855 purchase order confirmation mapped to an inbound ORDRSP. ORDERS05 IDoc that updates the CONFIRMATIONS tab at the line-item level of the purchase order with confirmed quantities and delivery dates and DSI's sales order number.

9.4 Technical Specifications

This technical specification describes the SAP configuration and EDI development required to support the ORDERS.ORDERS05 to X12 850 purchase order for replications services interface to DSI.

There are no custom enhancements to this interface.

9.4.1 Technical Requirements

The generated IDoc will be populated with standard data from the purchase order. DSI will flag their acceptance of the order by returning a confirmation that will update the CONFIRMATIONS tab at the item level of the PO with confirmed delivery dates and quantities.

9.4.2 Dependencies

Message control configuration is complete and conditions records have been entered. Other dependencies include the following:

▸ Outbound partner profile created for DSI with message type ORDERS, basic type ORDERS05, and message control

▸ Inbound partner profile created for DSI with message type ORDRSP

▸ Acme custom cross-reference table ZEDIXREF populated in SAP for DSI to read EDI send and receiving trading partner IDs for the outbound 850 PO and SAP send and receive partners for the inbound 855 PO confirmation

▸ Program variant created for SAP job scheduler (SM36) to run `RSEOUT00` for DSI ORDERS.ORDERS05 PO IDocs

▸ Program variant created for SAP job scheduler (SM36) to run `RBDAPP01` for DSI inbound ORDRSP.ORDERS05 PO confirmation

▸ Outbound envelopes created in the EDI RIM for DSI X12 850 version 5010 EDI purchase order

▸ Inbound envelopes set up for 997 functional acknowledgments from DSI for outbound 850

▸ Inbound envelopes set up for X12 855 purchase order confirmation from DSI

▸ Outbound envelopes set up for 997 functional acknowledgments to DSI for inbound 855 EDI purchase order confirmation from DSI

▸ EDI maps for the outbound ORDERS IDoc to X12 850 purchase order and the inbound X12 855 to ORDRSP IDoc PO confirmation

▸ Business process workflow in the EDI RIM to pick up ORDERS IDocs, convert them to X12 850 POs, and send them to DSI

9.4.3 Assumptions

The EDI RIM gets EDI sending and receiving trading partner IDs from the IDoc control record fields SNDLAD and RCVLAD. The following are other important assumptions:

▸ DSI will return an X12 997 functional acknowledgment within 24 hours of receiving the 850 PO transmission.

▶ If there are any errors posting the 850 PO to DSI's system, Acme will be notified immediately through an X12 864 text message describing the error.

▶ DSI will return an X12 855 confirmation within 48 hours of receiving and successfully posting Acme's 850 PO.

▶ EDI errors will be tracked and addressed in the EDI system by Acme's EDI monitoring team.

▶ Technical errors in the IDoc interface, such as syntax or partner profile errors, will be tracked and corrected in SAP by the EDI team.

9.5   Mapping Specifications

A map will be developed in the EDI RIM to map the ORDERS.ORDERS05 XML IDoc to the X12 850 purchase order to DSI.

Table 9.4 details the mapping requirements for our outbound purchase order scenario.

Mapping Specification Basics

Mapping specifications in Act III of our exploration of Acme Picture's SAP EDI implementation will focus on the key pieces of application data that will post to or be generated from our business documents and will not include the control record.

Common usage for EDI mapping specifications is to map the X12 data from the left, whether it's the source or target structure. We will focus instead on the IDoc. In Table 9.4, the IDoc segment name will occupy a full line in the table and be set in italics while the fields will be in the left-most column.

The target EDI data elements fields will follow, identified by their segment name and position number. The VALUE column contains sample data that will map to or from the IDoc. These data, especially configuration data, will vary from system to system and are presented here only for illustration purposes.

Also, specific mappings to or from IDocs or X12 transactions will also vary from system to system and partner to partner. Many mapping choices made in the specifications that follow in Act III are arbitrary and are meant only as suggestions, not recommendations. Remember that EDI usage in the real world is governed by relationships developed or agreed to by trading partners.

When mapping to an XML IDoc, the SEGMENT attribute must be set to 1 each time a new instance of any segment is mapped to the target IDoc otherwise the IDoc will fail. We will follow this requirement and set the segment attribute in mapping specifications for inbound interfaces only: IDocs going into Acme's SAP system.

The good news with XML IDocs is that you don't have to map any of the key fields of the data record that are normally mapped for an ASCII IDoc, not even the segment name or IDoc number. Everything the IDoc needs is defined in the schema. All the map needs to provide is the data.

ORDERS	850	Value	Comments
E1EDK01—Header—Min 1, Max 1			
CURCY	CUR01	USD	PO currency
BSART	BEG01	NB	If BSART = NB, return 00
BELNR	BEG03	4500017707	Purchase order number
E1EDK03—Header dates—Min 0, Max 10			
IDDAT	DTM01	002	Identifies requested delivery
DATUM	DTM02	20140115	Delivery requested date
E1EDKA1—Partners—Min 1, Max 99—Loop 1 Sold-to			
PARVW	N101	AG	Sold-to party: convert to BY
NAME1	N102	Acme Pictures	Name of buyer party
	N103	UL	Hard code. ID type qualifier: GLN
LIFNR	N104	0999999999999	Acme's sold-to GLN from EDPAR
STRAS	N301	2100 Melrose Ave	Sold-to partner street address
ORT01	N401	Los Angeles	Sold-to partner city
PSTLZ	N403	CA	Sold-to partner postal code
LAND1	N404	91936	Sold-to partner country
REGIO	N402	US	Sold-to partner region
E1EDKA1—Partners—Loop 2 Supplier			
PARVW	N101	LF	Supplier: convert to SU
	N103	UL	Hard code. ID type qualifier: GLN
LIFNR	N104	0999999998888	DSI GLN

Table 9.4 Mapping the Order Confirmation IDoc to the X12 855

ORDERS	850	Value	Comments
NAME1	N102	Disk Services International	DSI the supplier
E1EDKA1—Partners—Loop 3 Ship-to			
PARVW	N101	WE	Ship-to partner: convert to ST
NAME1	N102	Acme Pictures	Name of Acme Pictures ship-to
	N103	UL	Identifies Acme ship-to location as GLN code
LIFNR	N104	01254863254898	Acme ship-to location GLN
STRAS	N301	2100 Melrose Ave	Acme street address
ORT01	N401	Los Angeles	City name
REGIO	N402	CA	State, province, or region code
PSTLZ	N403	91936	Postal code
LAND	N404	US	Country code
E1EDK02— Header documents—Min 0, Max 10			
QUALF		001	Identifies PO number and date
BELNR	BEG03	4500017707	Map if E1EDK01-BELNR null
DATUM	BEG05	20131215	Purchase order date
E1EDP01—Item level details group—Min 1, Max N 1 instance of E1EDP01 per group loop			
POSEX	PO101	000010	Line item number
MENGE	PO102	100	Quantity ordered
MENEE	PO103	EA	Unit of measure for ordered item
VPREI	PO104	12.50	Unit price
E1EDP19—Materials—Min 1, Max 10			
QUALF	PO106	002	Identifies Acme's item number: convert to IN for buyer's number
IDTNR	PO107	985674	Customer material number

Table 9.4 Mapping the Order Confirmation IDoc to the X12 855 (Cont.)

Map Specifications for the X12 855 to ORDRSP PO Confirmation

Table 9.5 details mapping requirements for the inbound purchase order confirmation from DSI in response to the outbound PO.

ORDRSP	855	Value	Comments
E1EDK01— Header—Min 1, Max 1			
@SEGMENT		1	Hard code segment attribute to 1
ACTION		000	Hard code 000
BELNR	BAK03	4500017707	Purchase order number
E1EDK02—Header documents—Min 1, Max 10—Loop 1 PO number			
@SEGMENT		1	Hard code segment attribute to 1
QUALF		001	Identifies Acme PO number
BELNR	BAK03	4500017707	Purchase order number
E1EDK02—Header documents—Loop 2 Supplier sales order			
@SEGMENT		1	Hard code segment attribute to 1
QUALF		002	Identifies DSI sales order number
BELNR	BAK03	00014031	DSI sales order number
E1EDP01— Line item level details group—Min 1, Max N 1 instance of E1EDP01 per group loop			
@SEGMENT		1	Hard code segment attribute to 1
POSEX	PO101	000010	Line item number of PO confirmation
MENGE	PO102	100	Line item order quantity
MENEE	PO103	EA	Base unit of measure
POSEX	PO101	000010	Line item number of PO confirmation
E1EDP02—Item document—Min 1, Max 10			
@SEGMENT		1	Hard code segment attribute to 1
QUALF		001	Identifies Acme PO number
BELNR	BAK03	4500017707	Purchase order number

Table 9.5 Mapping the X12 855 to the Order Confirmation IDoc

387

ORDRSP	855	Value	Comments
ZEILE	PO101	000010	PO line item number
E1EDP20—Delivery schedule—Min 1, Max 10			
@SEGMENT		1	Hard code segment attribute to 1
WMENG	PO102	100	Confirmed delivery quantity
EDATU	DTM02	20140115	Confirmed delivery date
E1EDP19—Material numbers—Min 1, Max 10			
@SEGMENT		1	Hard code segment attribute to 1
QUALF	PO106	002	Customer material number (convert to IN for buyer's number)
IDTNR	PO107	2567898	Acme SAP item number

Table 9.5 Mapping the X12 855 to the Order Confirmation IDoc (Cont.)

9.6 EDI Configuration in SAP

We'll add an entry to our custom EDI mapping table ZEDIXREF to support EDI partner number conversion and two partner profiles for DSI: one for the outbound PO and the other for the inbound order confirmation.

9.6.1 EDPAR Entries: Transaction VOE4

There are no EDPAR entries for the outbound ORDERS.ORDERS05 to X12 850 purchase order for replication services interface.

9.6.2 ZEDIXREF Entries

Table ZEDIXREF maps the IDoc sender and receiving partners—the SAP logical system ID and DSI's vendor number—to the receiving party's sending and receiving EDI trading partner IDs.

We'll use the values in Table 9.6 for the outbound ORDERS.ORDERS05 PO to DSI.

Field	Value	Description
DIRECT	1	Direction outbound
STDMES	850	EDI PO transaction
MESTYP	ORDERS	IDoc message type outbound PO
IDOCTP	ORDERS05	IDoc basic type
CIMTYP		IDoc extension, none for this interface
SNDPRN	DEVCLNT100	SAP send partner: Acme SAP logical system
RCVPRN	DISK01	SAP receive partner: DSI's vendor number in Acme's system
SNDLAD	99999998889	EDI sender partner: DSI trading partner ID for Acme
RCVLAD	99934567999	EDI receiver partner: DSI trading partner ID for DSI

Table 9.6 ZEDIXREF Entries for the Outbound 850 to DSI

We also need an entry for the inbound 855 order confirmation from DSI using the ORDRSP.ORDERS05 IDoc, detailed in Table 9.7.

Field	Value SDQ	Description
DIRECT	2	Direction inbound
STDMES	855	EDI PO confirmation transaction
MESTYP	ORDRSP	IDoc message type
IDOCTP	ORDERS05	IDoc basic type
CIMTYP		IDoc extension, none for this interface
SNDPRN	DISK01	SAP send partner: DSI's vendor number in Acme's system
RCVPRN	DEVCLNT100	SAP receive partner: Acme SAP logical system
SNDLAD	99934567999	EDI sending partner: DSI trading partner ID for DSI
RCVLAD	99999998889	EDI receiving partner: DSI trading partner ID for Acme

Table 9.7 ZEDIXREF Entries for the Inbound 855 from DSI

9.6.3 Partner Profiles: Transaction WE20

We'll need to define one outbound and one inbound partner profile for DSI partner number DISK01, partner type LI (vendor), and partner role VN (vendor).

Outbound Partner Profile: Message Type ORDERS

In the outbound parameters table control of the partner profile for DSI, click the CREATE OUTBOUND PARAMETERS button and enter the following values in the OUTBOUND PARAMETERS screen (Figure 9.5):

▶ PARTNER ROLE: "VN"

▶ MESSAGE TYPE: "ORDERS"

▶ RECEIVER PORT: "XML_IDOC"

▶ OUTPUT MODE area: COLLECT IDOCS and START SUBSYSTEM options

▶ BASIC TYPE: "ORDERS05"

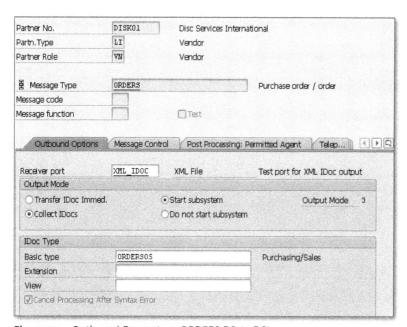

Figure 9.5 Outbound Parameters, ORDERS PO to DSI

Click MESSAGE CONTROL and enter the following values (Figure 9.6):

▶ APPLICATION: "EF"

▶ MESSAGE TYPE: "NEU"

▶ PROCESS CODE: "ME10"

▶ CHANGE MESSAGE checkbox: One entry null and one entry checked

Figure 9.6 Message Control Configuration for the ORDERS PO

The last step is to select the EDI STANDARD tab from the flyout menu at the upper far right of the screen tabs and enter the following values:

▶ EDI STANDARD: "X" for X12

▶ MESSAGE TYPE: "850"

▶ VERSION: "00510"

Don't forget to save. The EDI screen should look like Figure 9.7.

| Message Control | Post Processing: Permitted Agent | Telephony | EDI Standard | ◀ ▶ ⊡ |

EDI Standard	X
Message type	850
Version	005010

Figure 9.7 EDI Standard Values for all ORDER PO IDocs

Inbound Partner Profile: Message Type ORDRSP

In the inbound parameters table control of the partner profile for DSI, click the Create inbound parameters button and enter the following values in the Inbound Parameters screen:

- ▶ Partner Role: "VN"

- ▶ Message Type: "ORDRSP"

- ▶ Process Code: "ORDR" (links to function IDOC_INPUT_ORDRSP)

- ▶ Processing by Function Module: Trigger by background program option

The completed screen should look like Figure 9.8.

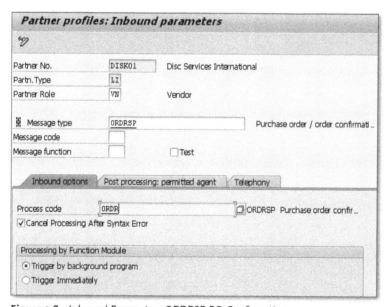

Figure 9.8 Inbound Parameters ORDRSP PO Confirmation

9.7 Summary

We can now order replication services from Disk Services International. This is a crucial piece of the overall order-to-cash process. After all, we can't sell what we don't have in stock and this process fills Acme's shelves with saleable product. The great Darryl Q would be pleased with how straightforward this all is.

The supplier purchase order process is about contract manufacturing. Acme doesn't have the facilities to produce its movies on DVD or to store them in inventory. It is a movie studio after all, and its business is to make movies and sell them. To take advantage of the home entertainment market for its movies, it must buy manufacturing, packaging, and even distribution services from DSI and other suppliers.

The supplier purchase order process begins with the purchase order for replication services, created when inventory levels of saleable finished goods fall below the actual and planned order levels from customers.

Message control is a critical part of generating the IDoc from the purchase order. We've stepped through the configuration required to enable message control and have followed the run-time process flow of generating an IDoc from a purchase order through to transmission of the IDoc to DSI and receipt of the purchase order acknowledgment.

The next step is to receive the ordered goods into Acme's inventory so that they can be sold to their customers. It's time once again to advance our processes and move on to the next interface.

"Just gimme the goods," the great Darryl Q would tell his directors when they started a new project. "I want what I paid for!" This is Buying and Selling 101: When the goods are ready, they need to be received. In Acme's SAP system, this means a goods receipt against the PO that ordered them. Since manufacturing and inventory are outsourced to DSI, this introduces some minor wrinkles.

10 The Inbound Goods Receipt

In the last chapter, Acme Pictures sent a purchase order to Disk Services International (DSI) for production of movies on DVD for sale to such retail outlets as the more than 2,000 stores run by its most important customer, Gordy's Galaxy of Games & B Flix.

Acme outsources production of all its DVD movie products, mostly to DSI. DSI also takes care of packaging, distribution, and inventory. Acme-owned saleable products and raw materials for manufacturing are stored in DSI warehouses.

As we have already noted, the business of Acme Pictures is to make movies, not manufacture and distribute DVD product for sale in stores. But the home entertainment business is too good to pass up, and nobody would have understood that better than Acme's legendary founder, Darryl Q. Fernhausen.

When DSI receives a manufacturing PO from Acme, the raw materials are already in inventory to issue to production. If they're short, they have authorization from Acme to order whatever they need.

These items are all stored in DSI-owned warehouses that are tracked through plants and storage locations set up in Acme's SAP system.

Whenever DSI changes inventory by issuing raw materials to production or receiving finished goods from manufacturing, they generate a feed that updates inventory in Acme's SAP system.

The EDI transaction and IDocs used are the same for both inventory movement types. What's different is the nature of the inventory change, which is defined in the data sent by the transmission.

We're most interested in the goods received from production against an Acme purchase order here, since they are saleable goods and since this ends the manufacturing process. But Acme also needs to know how much it costs to produce a saleable batch of movies on DVD from raw materials that it owns. So let's look at the contents of both interfaces here.

10.1 Technical Overview of Interface

Table 10.1 summarizes the inbound goods issue/goods receipt interface.

Item	Description
Title	Inbound Goods Issue and Goods Receipt from Contract Supplier
Description	DSI keeps Acme-owned raw materials and finished goods in inventory at its locations, which are mirrored by plants and storage locations in Acme's SAP system.
	Inventory management in Acme's SAP system must be kept informed of all changes to Acme-owned inventory held by DSI. This is especially true when DSI produces saleable DVD product against an Acme purchase order.
	The solution is for DSI to generate an EDI feed to Acme when it issues raw materials to production and when it receives saleable product from any of its manufacturing lines against an Acme purchase order.
	These feeds will update inventory in Acme's SAP system with the goods issue and the goods receipt.
	In addition, purchase order history is updated with the details of the goods receipt.
Type of interface	Inventory Management: X12 EDI to IDoc
Direction	Inbound
Trading partner	Disk Services International (vendor)

Table 10.1 Overview of Inbound EDI Goods Receipt and Issue Interfaces

Item	Description
IDoc	MBGMCR.MBGMCR03
IDoc extended type	
IDoc function	`IDOC_INPUT_MBGMCR`
Custom ABAP	
Description	
Source file(s)	867 product transfer and resale report
Target document(s)	Material document in SAP inventory management recording a goods issue or goods receipt against an Acme purchase order.
Transaction codes	MB01 (goods receipt), MB1A (goods issue), and MB03 to view the material document
Map(s)	X12 867 vers. 5010 to MBGMCR.MBGMCR03
Custom map logic	
Source system	DSI EDI via AS2
Target system	Acme SAP via EDI RIM
997 acknowledgment	Outbound at transaction detail level. Function group acknowledgment code: PT
Frequency	Batched once a day at night
Job schedule	`RBDAPP01`: Nightly post of all MBGMCR message types to inventory for all trading partners

Table 10.1 Overview of Inbound EDI Goods Receipt and Issue Interfaces (Cont.)

We have a choice of two IDocs for this interface: MBGMCR.MBGMCR03 and WMMBXY.WMMBID02. Both have more or less the same fields and both will post a goods movement to inventory with the same function module used by Transactions MB01 and MB1A.

But MBGMCR includes the date of manufacture, which we need to post the goods receipt at Acme. WMMBXY has everything else except the date of manufacture.

Another difference is that MBGMCR is generated from a BAPI and has no user exits. WMMBXY does offer user exits.

10.2 Functional Specifications

The purpose of this interface is to update inventory management with goods issue and goods receipt movement types for product that Acme owns but that is held in DSI warehouses and storage locations.

The goods receipt is for finished saleable goods produced by DSI against purchase orders sent by Acme.

The goods issued are raw materials consumed in production of the finished goods ordered by Acme.

10.2.1 Process Overview

Acme sends DSI a purchase order for replication services of saleable movies on DVD. DSI creates a sales order from the PO, which is used to generate a production order.

Raw materials, owned by Acme but held in DSI warehouses, are issued to the production order, creating a link between production, the sales order, and the purchase order number.

When the raw materials are issued to production an X12 867 EDI feed that includes the PO number is generated and sent to Acme's EDI RIM. This 867 is translated to an MBGMCR.MBGMCR03 IDoc, which posts to Transaction MB1A in Acme's SAP system.

When production is completed and the finished goods are ready to sell to a customer, DSI receives them into inventory from the production order and generates another X12 867 feed to Acme's EDI RIM. This feed also includes the Acme PO number.

The 867 is converted to another MBGMCR.MBGMCR03 IDoc that posts the goods receipt against the purchase order in Acme's SAP system.

10.2.2 Requirements

Purchase orders for replication services have been created and sent to DSI, manufacturing of the ordered goods has been completed, and DSI inventory has been updated. Other requirements include the following:

▶ The goods issue is sent as soon as raw materials are issued to a production order by DSI.

▶ The goods receipt is sent as soon as the finished goods have been received into DSI inventory.

▶ The warehouse and storage locations used by DSI to store raw materials and finished goods must match plants and storage locations in Acme's SAP system.

▶ Acme's purchase order number must be present in both feeds from DSI.

▶ The goods receipt must include the date of manufacture.

10.2.3 Dependencies

The 867-MBGMCR inventory update interface is dependent on master data, configuration, and development objects in SAP and the EDI RIM. These include the following:

▶ Master data objects required to support inventory management, including (but not restricted to) the following:

  ▶ GL chart of accounts, profit centers, costing, controlling, special purpose ledgers, and all supporting master data and configuration in the accounting system set up to support inventory

  ▶ Material master consumable raw materials and finished goods

  ▶ Bills of materials: Identifying components in finished goods

  ▶ Plants and storage locations that mirror DSI warehouse and storage locations

  ▶ Inventory management configured for usage of movement types and supporting indicators

▶ Acme sends daily feeds of its material master, BOM, and other relevant master data to DSI whenever a new material is added or an existing one is changed.

▶ IDoc configuration completed in SAP to support inbound MBGMCR goods issue/goods receipt for DSI, including the following:

  ▶ Custom EDI trading partner mapping table ZEDIXREF

  ▶ Inbound partner profile for DSI with message type MBGMCR

▶ EDI map for X12 867 to MBGMCR translations.

▶ Business process workflows built in the EDI RIM to process and route incoming X12 867 goods issue and goods receipt transactions and MBGMCR.MBGMCR03 IDocs.

10.2.4 Assumptions

Goods issue and goods receipt material movements are posted to Acme inventory by MBGMCR.MBGMCR03 IDocs against an Acme purchase order. The IDocs are processed nightly by a scheduled job in SAP.

Each goods issue or goods receipt that posts to Acme's system will create one material document that can be viewed with Transaction MB03.

The following are other key assumptions:

- Acme's plants and storage locations have the same identifiers as the warehouses and storage locations set up in DSI system for Acme-owned materials.
- DSI sends Acme's internal SAP material numbers for all goods issued or received.
- The following transactions and material movement types are used to post to Acme's SAP system:
  - Goods receipt: Transaction MB01 and movement types 101 and 102 (reversal of 101)
  - Goods issue: Transaction MB1A and movement types 261 and 262 (reversal of the 261)
- DSI will only send data required to post the goods issue or goods receipt.
- DSI will accumulate and sum goods issue and goods receipt transactions by production lot number and send one feed per day per batch.
- Each production batch is assigned to only one purchase order.
- Business users will address any application errors in the IDocs.
- All EDI system errors are handled by the EDI team.
- EDI and VMI orders are sent into SAP immediately, and the IDocs are posted to sales orders within no more than an hour.
- EDI errors or issues that may affect the timeliness of order creation are communicated to the business users immediately.

10.2.5 Data That Will Post to a Material Document

Table 10.2 lists the data required to post a goods issue with Transaction MB1A or a goods receipt with Transaction MB01. Inventory movement data are posted to material documents, which are stored in tables MKPF (header level) and MSEG (item details).

Table	Field	Description	Sample value
MKPF	BLDAT	Document date: (can be date of document created at vendor site)	20131215
MKPF	BUDAT	Document posting date	20131215
MSEG	BWART	Material movement type: ▶ Goods receipt = 101, 102 ▶ Goods issue = 261, 262	101
MSEG	MATNR	Acme's SAP material number	500210
MSEG	WERKS	Acme plant, equals DSI warehouse of plant where inventory recorded	3000
MSEG	LGORT	Acme storage location equals DSI storage location	0003
MSEG	CHARG	Production batch number	Q10578
MSEG	ERFMG	Quantity in unit of entry of material issued or received	10.000
MSEG	ERFME	Entry unit of measure	EA
MSEG	EBELN	Acme purchase number	4500016169
MSEG	EBELP	Acme PO line item number	00010

Table 10.2 Fields Populated When a Material Document is Created

10.2.6 Reconciliation Procedure

Successful import of the MBGMCR IDoc is confirmed through any of the standard IDoc monitoring tools, such as BD87 or WE05.

IDoc status should be *64—IDoc ready to be transferred to application*—before the scheduled processing job is kicked off and *53—Application document posted*—after.

The EDI team confirms the data in the IDoc against the data in the X12 867 transaction sent from the supplier. The users validate that the goods issue or goods receipt posted successfully by confirming that the material documents were created and that they posted against the correct PO, material, and quantities, and to the correct GL account.

10.2.7 Enhancements to the Process

No custom programming is required for this interface.

10.2.8 Errors and Error Handling

Errors that may occur during processing of the inbound 867-MBGMCR goods issue or goods receipt interface include the following:

▶ The IDoc will fail if the purchase order number is incorrect or missing. If this error occurs, the PO number can be entered and the IDoc rerun.

▶ The IDoc will fail if the material number is incorrect or missing. If this error occurs, the material number can be entered and the IDoc rerun.

▶ A goods receipt will fail if the full quantity against a purchase order has already been received. Either the quantity needs to be backed out with a 102 reversal or the transaction was sent in error.

Goods issue or goods receipt errors will be communicated to the responsible business user immediately. If there is a data issue with DSI, they will be contacted immediately and the issue will be addressed. If necessary, postings will be backed out with a 102 or 262 reversal and resent by DSI.

10.3 End-to-End Process Flow

Figure 10.1 outlines the end-to-end process flow for posting goods issue or goods receipt in Acme's SAP system from EDI transmissions.

It all begins when DSI receives a purchase order from Acme Pictures and posts it to a sales order in their business system. One or more production orders are generated from the sales order (one for each batch of finished goods) and raw materials are issued.

When production is completed, the finished goods are received from the production orders.

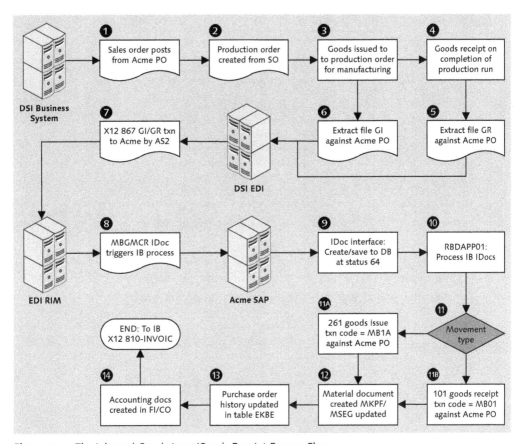

Figure 10.1 The Inbound Goods Issue/Goods Receipt Process Flow

Meanwhile, once a day, an extract program is run to pull all goods issued and received from production against the production order, batch, and Acme purchase order and line item numbers. The PO number and line item are read through the link between the production orders and DSI's sales orders.

The extract produces a file that is sent to DSI's EDI system, where it is converted to an X12 867 transmission file, with one transaction set per PO, line item, material, and production batch number.

The 867 is sent to Acme's EDI RIM, where it is mapped to an MBGMCR.MBGMCR03 XML IDoc file. The map handles two important conversions based on codes in the

PTD segment of the 867, which identify the type of inventory movement recorded in the EDI transaction, as shown in Listing 10.1.

```
If PTD01 = BH and PTD06 = AI (adjustment in),
  then transaction = MB01 and movement type = 101

If PTD01 = BH and PTD06 = AO (adjustment out),
  then transaction = MB01 and movement type = 101

If PTD01 = BC and PTD06 = AI,
  then transaction = MB1A and movement type = 261

If PTD01 = BC and PTD06 = AO,
  then transaction = MB1A and movement type = 262
```

Listing 10.1 Logic for Identifying Material Movement Type and Transaction

The transaction is stored in the IDoc as a two-character code in field GM_CODE in segment E1BP2017_GM_CODE. This code is mapped to the transaction in SAP in table T158G, which supports the following transaction code:

- ▶ 01: MB01 goods receipt (101, 102)
- ▶ 02: MB31 goods receipts
- ▶ 03: MB1A goods issue (261, 262)
- ▶ 04: MB1B transfer posting
- ▶ 05: MB1C other goods receipt
- ▶ 06: MB11 goods movement
- ▶ 07: MB04 subsequent adjustment

Each of these transactions supports a range of movement types specific to its functionality.

Together the transaction code from GM_CODE and the movement type determine whether a goods issue or goods receipt posts to Acme's inventory management system in SAP.

Once the 867 has been converted, the XML IDoc file is sent to the SAP application server and the IDoc adapter makes an RFC through the JCo connector into SAP to trigger function EDI_DATA_INCOMING.

The IDoc file is picked up by EDI_DATA_INCOMING, validated, deleted from the application server, and converted from XML to ASCII before each IDoc is written to the database at status 50—*IDoc added*—and then at status 64—*IDoc ready to be transferred to application.*

The IDocs sit in the database until a scheduled job for program RBDAPP01 runs to pick up all MBGMCR message types at status 64. RBDAPP01 reads the IDocs and partner profiles, and identifies and calls the inbound processing function—IDOC_INPUT_MBGMCR.

IDoc MBGMCR and function IDOC_INPUT_MBGMCR were generated from a BAPI: BAPI_GOODSMVT_CREATE. IDOC_INPUT_MBGMCR is a wrapper for a call to the BAPI that populates its import and table parameters. It also reads table T158G to check that a valid transaction code is coming in.

The actual inventory posting is handed by function MB_CREATE_GOODS_MOVEMENT, which is also used by Transactions MB01, MB1A, MIGO, and most other inventory transactions in SAP. It's also called by the processing function for message type WMMBXY.

The other thing to note about the goods receipt posting is that the purchase order history is updated in table EKBE with complete details of the goods receipt. It shows up in the purchase order at the line-item level in the PURCHASE ORDER HISTORY tab.

Figure 10.2 illustrates the following details that post to purchase order history:

▸ Movement type

▸ Material document number and posting date

▸ Quantity and unit of measure

▸ Dollar amount

Figure 10.2 Posted Goods Receipts Are Listed in Purchase Order History

This provides a record of all postings against the purchase order, regardless of movement type. In addition, the material document number is a link that that will take you directly to the document so you can view the details of the goods receipt.

You should also note that `IDOC_INPUT_MBGMCR` has no user exits, BAdIs, or even enhancement points. If you need to write custom code, create a z-version of the function. You would then create a custom process code linked to MBGMCR and the z-function. Use the custom process code in your inbound partner profile to post the MBGMCR message.

10.4 Technical Specifications

This technical specification section describes the SAP interface configuration and EDI development required to support the X12 867 to MBGMCR.MBGMCR03 goods issue and goods receipt interface from DSI into Acme's SAP system.

There are no custom enhancements to this interface.

10.4.1 Technical Requirements

DSI will send one cumulated X12 867 transaction for each Acme purchase order, line item, and batch number every night for goods issued to, or goods received from, production.

The EDI map will identify goods issued or goods received from the contents of the X12 transaction and map accordingly to the MBGMCR message.

The EDI RIM and SAP will be configured to support inbound MBGMCR messages and outbound 997 functional acknowledgments at the transaction level.

10.4.2 Dependencies

The 867-MBGMCR interface is dependent on a number of development and configuration objects in SAP and the EDI RIM:

▶ Inbound envelopes set up in the RIM for DSI's X12 867 version 5010 transactions

▶ Outbound envelopes for 997 acknowledgments to be created in the RIM for DSI during de-enveloping of inbound 867 transactions

- Custom cross-reference table ZEDIXREF populated in SAP to convert EDI trading partner IDs to the SAP send and receive partner numbers for the inbound 867 from DSI

- Inbound partner profile set up for DSI message type MBGMCR

- Job to be set up in the SAP Job Scheduler (Transaction SM36) to run once a night to post MBGMCR.MBGMCR03 IDocs with program RBDAPP01 with a variant to select for all message types MBGMCR at status 64

10.4.3 Assumptions

The EDI RIM will identify the correct transaction type (either goods issue or goods receipt) from data in the body of the X12 867 transaction. The following are other key assumptions:

- DSI accumulates goods issue and goods receipt transactions and sends only one each day per purchase order, PO line item, material, and batch.

- Identified by movement type, reversals and postings are handled. Goods receipt reversal is a 101 and goods issue is a 262.

- The RIM maps the EDI send and receive trading partner IDs to the IDoc control record fields SNDLAD and RCVLAD. These fields are read by an exit in the IDoc interface to identify the SAP sold-to partner for field EDIDC-SNDPRN and the SAP receiving logical system for field EDID-RCVPRN.

- The RIM will return an X12 997 functional acknowledgment within 24 hours of receiving the X12 867 transmission.

- EDI errors are tracked and addressed in the EDI system. Technical errors in the IDoc interface, such as syntax or partner profile errors, are tracked and corrected by the EDI team.

10.5 Mapping Specifications

A map will be developed in the EDI RIM to map the X12 867 goods issue or goods receipt from DSI to the MBGMCR.MBGMCR03 XML IDoc to send to Acme's SAP system.

Mapping requirements for the inbound goods issue/goods receipt scenario are outlined in Table 10.3. Please note that plant and storage location EDI source fields are only suggested mappings.

MBGMCR	867	Value	Comments
E1BP2017_GM_HEAD_01—Header—Min 1 Max 1			
@SEGMENT		1	Hard-code segment attribute to 1
PSTNG_DATE	DTM02	20131215	Posting date where DTM01 = 007
DOC_DATE	BPT03	20131215	Document date
REF_DOC_NO	PTD05	4500016169	Reference document number where PTD04 = PO. Acme PO. Posts to header of material document.
E1BP2017_GM_CODE—Transaction Code—Min 1 Max 1			
@SEGMENT		1	Hard-code segment attribute to 1
GM_CODE	PTD01	01	Transaction code from T158G. Derived value. Logic: If PTD01 = BH, GM_CODE = 01 (Transaction MB01) If PTD01 = BC, GM_CODE = 03 (Transaction MB1A)
E1BP2017_GM_ITEM_CREATE— Item Details—Min 1 Max N			
@SEGMENT		1	Hard-code segment attribute to 1
MATERIAL	LIN03	500210	Acme SAP material number where LIN02 = BP (customer item).
PLANT	N104	3000	Plant where N101 = 16
STGE_LOC	N104	0003	Instance 2 of N1: storage location where N101 = RL.
BATCH	LIN05	20140115	Acme SAP material number where LIN04 = LT (lot number).

Table 10.3 Mapping Specifications for X12 867 to MBGMCR.MBGMCR03 IDoc

MBGMCR	867	Value	Comments
MOVE_TYPE	PTD01 PTD06	101	Movement type. Derived value. Logic: If PTD01 = BH and PTD06 = AI, MOVE_TYPE = 101 If PTD01 = BH and PTD06 = AO, MOVE_TYPE = 102 (reversal) If PTD01 = BC and PTD06 = AI, MOVE_TYPE = 261 If PTD01 = BC and PTD06 = AO, MOVE_TYPE = 262 (reversal)
ENTRY_QNT	QTY02	10.000	Quantity in entry unit
ENTRY_UOM	QTY03	EA	Unit of measure
PO_NUMBER	REF02	4500016169	Acme purchase order number where REF01 = PO. Inventory movement posts against this PO number.
PO_ITEM	LIN01	00010	Acme PO line item number
PROD_DATE	DTM02	20131130	Date of production where DTM01 = 094. Goods receipt only.

Table 10.3 Mapping Specifications for X12 867 to MBGMCR.MBGMCR03 IDoc (Cont.)

10.6   EDI Configuration in SAP

Let's take a look at IDoc configuration settings in SAP for the inbound MBGMCR message for Disk Services International.

10.6.1   EDPAR Entries: Transaction VOE4

There are no EDPAR entries for the X12 867 to MBGMCR interface.

10.6.2   ZEDIXREF Entries

Table ZEDIXREF maps the sender's send and receive EDI trading partner IDs to the SAP partner numbers—DSI's vendor number in Acme's system and the receiving SAP logical system ID.

Table 10.4 lists the values that we'll enter into custom table ZEDIXREF for the inbound 867 interface from DSI.

Field	Value	Description
DIRECT	2	Direction inbound
STDMES	867	EDI PO transaction
MESTYP	MBGMCR	IDoc message type
IDOCTP	MBGMCR03	IDoc basic type
CIMTYP		IDoc extension, none for this interface
SNDPRN	DISK01	SAP send partner: DSI's customer number in Acme's system
RCVPRN	DEVCLNT100	SAP receive partner: Acme SAP logical system
SNDLAD	99934567999	EDI send partner: DSI trading partner ID for DSI
RCVLAD	99999998889	EDI receive partner: DSI trading partner ID for Acme

Table 10.4 ZEDIXREF Entry for the Inbound 867 from DSI

10.6.3 Partner Profile: Transaction WE20

The inbound partner profile links DSI to the incoming message type and the process code that will trigger the processing function that will post the goods issue or goods receipt.

We'll need one inbound partner profile for DSI partner type LI (vendor) with message type MBGMCR.

In the inbound parameters table control, click CREATE and add the following values to the inbound parameters screen:

▶ PARTNER ROLE: "VN" (vendor)

▶ MESSAGE TYPE: "MBGMCR"

▶ PROCESS CODE: "BAPI"

▶ PROCESSING BY FUNCTION MODULE: TRIGGER BY BACKGROUND PROGRAM option

The finished inbound parameters should look like Figure 10.3. Don't forget to save.

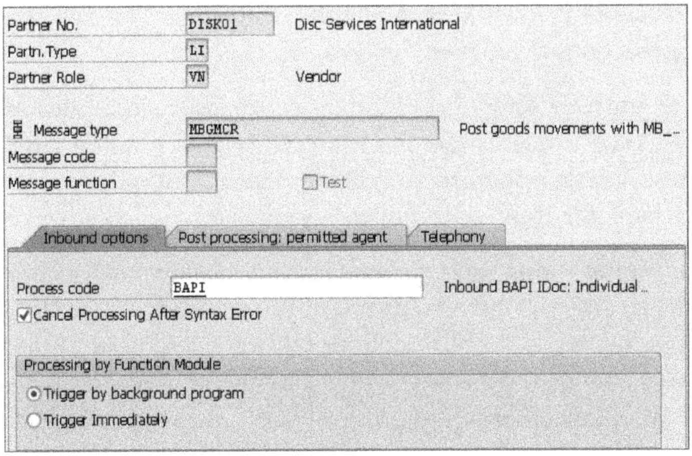

Figure 10.3 Inbound Partner Profile for DSI Message MBGMCR

Process code BAPI links the partner profile to function module `BAPI_IDOC_INPUT1`.

This function is a little different from the ones we've been looking at so far. It's not linked to a specific message type but can process over 800 different messages, mostly IDocs generated from BAPIs.

The first thing `BAPI_IDOC_INPUT1` does when it's called is read the message type from the incoming IDoc field EDIDC-MESTYP and then check table TBDBE (BAPI-ALE Interface for Inbound Processing) for its processing function.

If it gets a hit, the BAPI calls the function and IDoc processing proceeds normally. If it doesn't get a hit, the BAPI returns an error.

10.7 Summary

The goods issue/goods receipt feed is really two interfaces for the price of one, driven by the data contents of the incoming EDI transaction. It illustrates an important fact about EDI and B2B in general: decisions often have to be made at runtime based on the contents of the data.

That means writing rules that can evaluate the data and trigger different processing paths based on the results—in this case, identifying the transaction code and movement type that will post either a goods issue or goods receipt.

This is handled by the map in the EDI RIM and by the IDoc processing function in SAP that calls the transactions fed to it by the IDoc.

We'll need to do this extensively across the EDI architecture, as we have seen in our discussion of the STATUS IDoc interface in Chapter 5, Section 5.5, Reporting EDI Status to SAP, where we run a number of evaluations in custom code, including reads from the database, the IDoc, and runtime system data.

The other point this illustrates is that while we may convert incoming data in our EDI system to ensure that they are processed correctly, we never change their nature. The EDI team is the post office that identifies the mail and ensures that it's delivered to the correct address. We never change the contents of the business data through calculations or any other means.

Technically, this is a fairly simple interface once inventory management in SAP is set up by the business and functional teams to update inventory by IDoc. The most critical problem you're likely to encounter in production is bad data. One or two incorrect feeds (or correct feeds coming in the wrong order) can throw your inventory completely out of whack.

Generating the feeds, running them through the EDI system, and posting them to SAP is the easy part. Making sure the inventory is correct and remains in balance is out of the hands of the EDI team.

Now that Acme has received its newly manufactured goods into inventory, DSI can send its invoice. While the great Darryl Q hated to part with his money, he knew that to sell his product, he needed to pay his suppliers' invoices. We'll end our brief tour of the purchasing process by looking at how supplier invoices are received in Acme's SAP system.

As much as the great Darryl Q hated to part with his money, he knew a simple truth: "You can't make without spending money." But he always insisted on seeing every bill and examining it carefully before shelling out a penny. And that will be our approach in Acme's new SAP system: pay but verify. So let's see how that's done.

11   Processing the Incoming Supplier Invoice

It can be said that the inbound invoice interface from the supplier is truly the child of the interfaces that preceded it. This is true on two levels.

First, before we can receive the invoice from DSI for services rendered, specific processes must have been successfully completed, including the following:

1. An outbound purchase order from Acme to DSI to order replication services for movies on DVD

2. An inbound order acknowledgment from DSI confirming the PO, the materials, quantities, and delivery dates for the order

3. An inbound goods receipt from DSI detailing the quantities of finished product received from production

As we saw in the last chapter, the goods receipt posts against the purchase order used to order the goods and services from DSI. The goods receipt also moves the finished goods into inventory and updates accounting in Acme's SAP system, prepping it for receipt of the invoice.

On the second level, once we get the invoice from our supplier, we must verify it against the purchase order and the goods receipt.

This is handled by Logistics Invoice Verification, a wordy moniker for checking the bill to make sure that it is correct.

After all, the MM invoice closes the purchasing cycle and posts to accounts payables in the finance system. The numbers must match up with what we promised—and what we expected—to pay.

This is all standard stuff supported by an IDoc, a process code, and a little configuration under the hood in the IMG. Let's look at how this is done as we explore the inbound invoice from DSI for goods produced against an Acme purchase order.

11.1 Technical Overview of Interface

Table 11.1 summarizes the inbound invoice interface from the supplier.

Item	Description
Title	Inbound MM Invoice from Supplier Invoice with Invoice Verification.
Description	Acme orders saleable movie titles on DVD from its contract manufacturer and distributor, DSI. DSI completes production and sends Acme a goods receipt that updates inventory and accounting with the items and quantities produced against the purchase order.
	The supplier's invoice follows when the purchasing cycle has been successfully completed. The MM invoice will post to accounting, but first it must verify the following values against the purchase order, PO history, and goods receipt:
	▶ Purchase order number
	▶ Line item number
	▶ Material number
	▶ Quantity ordered and received
	▶ Dollar amount invoiced
	Once verified, the invoice posts and updates the finance system and accounts payables.
Type of interface	Purchasing: X12 EDI to IDoc
Direction	Inbound
Trading partner	Disk Services International (vendor)
IDoc	INVOIC.INVOIC02
IDoc extended type	
IDoc function	`IDOC_INPUT_INVOIC_MRM`

Table 11.1 Overview of Inbound EDI Invoice from Supplier

Item	Description
Custom ABAP	
Description	
Source file(s)	810 supplier invoice
Target document(s)	MM invoice in in SAP referencing purchase order number and GL accounts
Transaction code	MIRO enter incoming invoice by company code
Map(s)	X12 810 vers. 5010 to INVOIC.INVOIC02
Custom map logic	
Source system	DSI EDI via AS2
Target system	Acme SAP via EDI RIM
997 acknowledgment	Outbound at transaction detail level; function group acknowledgment code: IN
Frequency	Batched once a day at night
Job schedule	RBDAPP01: Nightly post of all INVOIC message types for all suppliers

Table 11.1 Overview of Inbound EDI Invoice from Supplier (Cont.)

There are two ways to post the inbound invoice from the supplier. One is directly to accounting and the other is through invoice verification. Both are driven by process codes that trigger different function modules.

One process code posts directly to accounting and does not pass the purchase order number nor verify purchase order data.

The other, which we'll be configuring for Acme, passes the PO number and verifies the purchase order and goods receipt data. We'll touch on the differences between the two in this chapter, but our focus is on logistic invoice verification.

11.2   Functional Specifications

The purpose of this interface is to verify and post an incoming invoice from DSI for sales DVD titles that Acme ordered against a purchase order for replication services.

The goods receipt must be successfully posted and purchase history updated before the invoice can be posted.

11.2.1 Process Overview

After DSI completes production of finished movie product on DVD against an Acme purchase order, the goods are received into inventory and a goods receipt transmission sent to Acme.

The goods receipt posts a 101 movement type (or 102 reversal) against the purchase order that Acme issued to order production of the goods by DSI, creating a material document for each posting.

Accounting documents are also created that post the financial details of the 101 goods receipt to GL accounts that are directly linked to the purchase order and line item number for each material document.

When these documents are in place, Acme can process invoices from DSI. After the goods receipt posts, DSI generates and sends its invoice to Acme by EDI. The invoice must reference the purchase order and line item number. The PO and line item numbers—with the material, order quantity, and dollar amount—are verified against the PO and PO history when the invoice is processed in Acme's system.

If verification succeeds, the incoming invoice posts with Transaction MIRO against Acme's company code and the purchase order items. An accounting document is created and accounts payable prepped for payment.

11.2.2 Requirements

Saleable movies on DVD have been produced by DSI against an Acme purchase order. Goods receipts have posted in Acme's system against the purchase order and inventory updated. The following other requirements must be met:

▶ EDI supplier invoices post through logistics invoice verification against a purchase order and goods receipt.

▶ Supplier, material, and accounting data are pulled from the purchase order in Acme's SAP system.

▶ All charges for goods and services ordered through the purchase order are on the invoice. The invoice only references charges on the PO.

- Invoice quantities and amounts must match the quantities and amounts posted to purchase order history through the goods receipt, within a tolerance limit of five percent.

- If the invoice amount is less than or equal to the amount on the purchase order, the invoice will post and be paid within the payment terms.

- If the invoice amount is higher than the purchase order amount but within the tolerance limit, the invoice will post.

- The invoice will be blocked if the amount exceeds the tolerance limit. The discrepancies will be worked out by the purchasing department.

- If Acme accepts the discrepancies, the PO amount is updated to match the invoice amount and the invoice is posted. If Acme does not accept the discrepancies, the issue is resolved between the parties and an invoice entered manually.

- The payment due date will be calculated by the system based on the invoice date in the IDoc and the payment terms in the purchase order.

11.2.3 Dependencies

The 810-INVOIC supplier invoice interface is dependent on master data, configuration, and development objects in SAP and the EDI RIM:

- Master data objects required to support purchasing, inventory, and supplier invoices including (but not restricted to) the following:
  - GL chart of accounts, profit centers, costing, controlling, special purpose ledgers and all supporting master data and configuration in the accounting system
  - Material master and bills of materials master data for items ordered from Acme's suppliers
  - Vendor master data for Acme's suppliers
  - Plants and storage locations, movement types, and other configuration to support goods receipt and update of accounting

- Configuration completed for logistics invoice verification for EDI for MM invoices including:
  - US and Canadian tax codes set for vendor
  - Vendor linked to Acme company code

▸ Program parameters identifying the invoice document type to be verified and checks to be made when it is processed

▸ Confirmed purchase orders to Acme's suppliers for production of saleable movies on DVD

▸ Goods receipts posted to material documents in Acme's SAP system for the quantity of goods produced by DSI from the replication PO

▸ Accounting documents created when the goods receipt posts detailing the GL account, posting key, and dollar amount for the goods received

▸ IDoc configuration completed in SAP to support inbound INVOIC supplier invoices for DSI, including the following:

    ▸ Custom EDI trading partner mapping table ZEDIXREF

    ▸ Inbound partner profile for DSI configured for logistics invoice verification with message type INVOIC and process code INVF

11.2.4 Assumptions

Incoming invoices from the supplier post from the INVOIC.INVOIC02 IDoc against an Acme purchase order that has been updated with goods receipts from DSI for the full quantity of materials ordered in all items, within the tolerance limit of five percent. The following are other key assumptions:

▸ Invoices will post to the correct period.

▸ Invoices will not be accepted for partial completion of a purchase order.

▸ Units of measure must agree with the purchase order.

▸ Invoices cannot post for blocked purchase order items.

▸ Price variances and tolerance levels have been configured.

▸ All charges, including sales taxes, will be pulled from the purchase order, not the IDoc.

▸ Pricing for the invoice will be pulled from the pricing conditions in the purchase order not from the IDoc.

▸ The invoice will post as an open item against the vendor's account. At the same time, the invoice posting will clear the accrual account that was updated by the goods receipt.

11.2.5 Data That Will Post to an Inbound Supplier Invoice

When the inbound supplier invoice posts with Transaction MIRO, the data are written first to MM tables RBKP (header level) and RSEG (item details) and then copied to the financial accounting tables BKPF (header level) and BSEG (item level).

Table 11.2 details a typical data set that will post to an inbound supplier invoice as it is stored in tables RBKP and RSEG.

Table	Field	Description	Sample value
RBKP	GJAHR	Fiscal year	2013
RBKP	BLDAT	Document date	20131215
RBKP	BUDAT	Posting date of document	20131215
RBKP	XBLNR	Reference document number: supplier billing document	0005000020
RBKP	BUKRS	Company code	3000
RBKP	LIFNR	Invoicing party: supplier	DISK01
RBKP	WAERS	Currency key	USD
RBKP	RMWWR	Total amount of invoice	$1,194.88
RBKP	WMWST1	Dollar amount of tax in document currency at header level	94.88
RBKP	MWSKZ1	Tax code at header level	I1
RBKP	ZBD1T	Cash discount days 1	14
RBKP	ZBD1P	Cash discount percentage 1	3.0
RBKP	ZBD2T	Cash discount days 2	30
RBKP	ZBD2P	Cash discount percentage 2	2.0
RBKP	ZBD3T	Terms of payment in days	45
RBKP	XRECH	Message indicator: post invoice	INVO
RBKP	ZFBDT	Baseline data for payment	20131214
RSEG	EBELN	Acme purchase number	4500016169

Table 11.2 Data That Posts to an Inbound Supplier Invoice

Table	Field	Description	Sample value
RSEG	EBELP	Acme PO line item number	00010
RSEG	MATNR	Acme's SAP material number	500210
RSEG	WRBTR	Line item amount in document currency	$1,100.0
RSEG	MWSKZ	Tax code at item level	I1
RSEG	MENGE	Quantity	10.000
RSEG	BSTME	Unit of measure	EA
RSEG	XBLNR	Delivery document if present is used to identify goods receipt	4000023

Table 11.2 Data That Posts to an Inbound Supplier Invoice (Cont.)

The following are mandatory data elements:

▸ Purchase order and line item numbers

▸ Vendor number

▸ Company code

▸ Tax code

▸ Quantities and dollar amounts

If these values are not in the IDoc, it will fail.

In addition, if the goods receipt posted against a delivery document, the system will identify the material documents by the delivery number. The delivery number is the first check for the goods receipt.

If no delivery number is sent in the IDoc, the system looks at purchase order history at the PO order line item level to identify the goods receipt. This is how our incoming invoice will be processed, since DSI is producing our saleable movies on DVD and receiving them into their finished good storage location for fulfillment of future customer orders.

The goods receipt is key to processing the invoice. It provides both the quantity and dollar amounts to be invoiced; these must match the quantity and amounts in the incoming EDI invoice within the five percent variance or the IDoc will fail.

11.2.6 Reconciliation Procedure

Successful import of the INVOIC IDoc is confirmed through any of the standard IDoc monitoring tools, such as BD87 or WE05.

IDoc status should be 64—*IDoc ready to be transferred to application*—before the scheduled processing job is kicked off and 53—*Application document posted*—after.

After the IDoc posts, the MM invoice can be displayed with Transaction MIR4 or by following SAP menu path LOGISTICS • MATERIALS MANAGEMENT • LOGISTICS INVOICE VERIFICATION • FURTHER PROCESSING • DISPLAY INVOICE DOCUMENT.

The invoice number will be recorded in the status segment for status 53 with the message: *Document no. [Invoice Number] created*.

The EDI team confirms the data in the IDoc against the data in the X12 810 invoice from the supplier. The business users validate that the invoice posted successfully and that the accounting tables BKPF and BSEG were updated.

11.2.7 Configuring Logistics Invoice Verification

Before we can begin receiving invoices from our suppliers, the system needs some additional information:

▶ A link between your supplier's tax codes and yours if they are different

▶ The company code that the supplier's invoice will post to

▶ Program parameters for your partner's invoice, by partner type, partner number, and company code:

  ▸ Invoice and credit memo document types

  ▸ Variance processing parameters, if relevant

  ▸ Additional checks

This is provided through IMG configuration with Transaction SPRO or menu path MATERIALS MANAGEMENT • LOGISTICS INVOICE VERIFICATION • EDI, AS SHOWN IN Figure 11.1.

First, let's look at the tax code. Acme and DSI are in different states and have different tax codes, so we must map them to properly process their invoices.

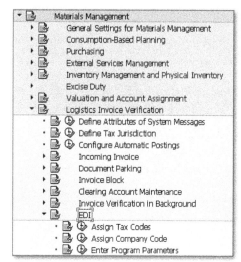

Figure 11.1 IMG Menu Path to Logistics Invoice Verification

Click ASSIGN TAX CODES to open the tax codes mapping screen. Click NEW ENTRIES (or press F5) and enter the following values for DSI into the table control (see Figure 11.2):

▶ PARTN.TYPE: "LI" for vendor

▶ PARTNERNO: "DISK01"

▶ TAX TYPE: "ST" for external X12 EDI code for state sales tax

▶ Tx: "I1" for Acme's internal tax code identifying sales tax payable (rates are defined by jurisdiction in SAP)

Partn.Type	PartnerNo	Tax type	Tax rate	C..	Tx
LI	DISK01	ST			I1

Figure 11.2 Tax Code Mapping Between DSI and Acme

Save the entry. The tax code mappings are stored in table T076M, which is read during inbound processing of the IDoc to get the mapping between the incoming external tax code and the internal code used by Acme.

The tax codes are standard SAP codes stored in table T700A against a country-specific procedure. The external code under TAX TYPE could be anything, as long as it matches the tax code sent in the IDoc segments E1EDK04 and E1EDP04.

You can also enter the external tax rate in the TAX RATE column. When the IDoc is processed, the system compares the rate entered here with the tax rate in the IDoc. If there is a discrepancy the IDoc will fail.

Next we assign the vendor to the Acme company code that will process the incoming supplier invoice.

You need to go back to the IMG and click ASSIGN COMPANY CODE. The company code overview screen opens. Click NEW ENTRIES (or press F5). Enter the following values into the table control (Figure 11.3):

▶ PARTN.TYPE: "LI" for vendor

▶ PARTNERNO: "DISK01"

▶ COCD: "3000" for Acme's company code

Partn.Type	PartnerNo	Comp.code name in the invoice	CoCd
LI	DISK01		3000

Figure 11.3 Assigning the Company Code

Save the entry. The company code name in the invoice can be entered into the table control. But any name entered in this column must match exactly the name of the invoice recipient in the INVOIC IDoc in E1EDKA1-PARTN or NAME1 (if PARTN is null) where PARVW = RE.

Last but not least, enter program parameters. Go back to the IMG and click ENTER PROGRAM PARAMETERS to open the overview screen. Click NEW ENTRIES (or press F5) to open the DETAILS OF ADDED ENTRIES screen. Enter the following values:

▶ PARTN.TYPE: "LI" for vendor

▶ PARTNERNO: "DISK01"

▶ COCD: "3000" for Acme's company code

▶ INVOICE DOC.TYPE: "RE" for gross receipt invoice

▶ CRED.MEMO DOC.TYPE: "RE"

▶ PROCESSING: "3" to enforce vendor-specific tolerances

Leave the rest blank. We won't be using conventional invoice verification, and the rest are checks that we don't need. Save the entry and assign it to a change request.

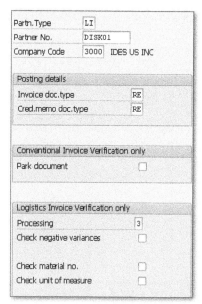

Figure 11.4 Program Parameters Assigned to the Supplier

It would be more accurate to label PROCESSING as the correction indicator for variances. It tells the system what to do if it encounters a variance in the quantity or amount between the invoice data in the IDoc and the data the system expects from the purchase order and purchase order history.

There are five options for variance processing:

▶ Null = No error reported if there's a variance. The EDI invoice is posted without any changes.

▶ 1 = Unclarified error: park invoice. An invoice is created and parked using system data, not IDoc data. Business users can then make changes after consulting the supplier or accept the invoice that was created.

▶ 2 = Vendor error: reduce invoice. System data are accepted and the supplier invoice is reduced by the amount of the variance.

▶ 3 = Vendor-specific tolerances. The system checks tolerance levels set for specific vendors and posts the invoice in one of two ways:

▶ The EDI invoice posts if the total variance with the purchase order is less than the allowed variance levels set for the vendor. If the variance is five percent and the EDI invoice is within that five percent, the supplier's invoice will post.

▸ The EDI invoice will not post if the total variance with the purchase order is greater than the allowed variance set for the vendor. The purchase order data are used to create an invoice, which is then parked. The business can then resolve the issue with the supplier and either edit the IDoc and reprocess or the parked invoice and post.

▸ 4 = Tolerances correspond to those for online processing. Tolerances are the same as those used in manual invoice creation, which are maintained by company code.

Vendor-specific tolerances are configured in the IMG using menu path MATERIALS MANAGEMENT • LOGISTICS INVOICE VERIFICATION • INCOMING INVOICE • CONFIGURE VENDOR-SPECIFIC TOLERANCES.

The details of this configuration will be worked out by the business users and the functional team. We've discussed the topic here because this verification is critical to successfully posting the inbound supplier invoice and it is useful for the EDI team to know what's happening under the hood.

A Word about Process Codes

The other key piece of configuration is the partner profile, which we look at later in this chapter. The key point here is that there are two processing choices for message INVOIC that are driven by different process codes:

▸ INVF: Posts invoice directly to FI as an accounting document. Does not reference the purchase order number. Linked to IDoc function `IDOC_INPUT_INVOIC_FI` that posts the invoice with function `PROCESS_IDOC_INVOIC_FI`.

▸ INVL: Logistics invoice verification. Verifies data against purchase order, PO history, and goods receipt. Calls IDoc function `IDOC_INPUT_INVOIC_MRM` that posts the invoice with function `MRM_INVOICE_CREATE`.

There is a third process code but it is obsolete: INVM. It posts the invoice by calling Transaction MR01, which has been replace by MIRO.

Because we have more than one process code for the same message type, it is conceivable that we will need to use both in future.

To distinguish the supplier invoice from the accounting invoice, we will extend process code INVL with message code MM, which we will use in the inbound parameters of the partner profile.

11.2.8 Enhancements to the Process

No custom programming is required for this interface.

11.2.9 Errors and Error Handling

The following are errors that may occur during processing of the inbound 810-INVOIC supplier invoice interface that will cause the IDoc to fail:

▶ The purchase order and/or line item numbers are incorrect or missing.

▶ The supplier's SAP vendor number is incorrect or missing.

▶ The material number in the invoice does not match the purchase order material.

▶ The dollar amount or quantities are outside the configured five percent variance.

In most cases, the IDoc can be edited and reposted. If the amounts or quantities exceed the variance, the issue will be resolved by the business and if necessary DSI. Once resolved, the IDoc can be edited and reposted or the parked invoice can be edited or recreated manually and posted. This is dependent on how we configure variance processing.

11.3 End-to-End Process Flow

Figure 11.5 outlines the end-to-end process flow for posting an inbound MM supplier invoice to SAP from an X12 810 transmission from DSI.

It all begins with the purchasing process. Acme orders replication of saleable movies on DVD from DSI using an ORDERS.ORDERS05 IDoc and an X12 850 customer PO. DSI confirms the order with an X12 855, which updates the PO in Acme's SAP system with confirmed quantities and delivery dates, and begins producing the finished goods by issuing Acme-owned raw materials from inventory to production orders. Remember that DSI holds both raw material and finished goods inventory for Acme.

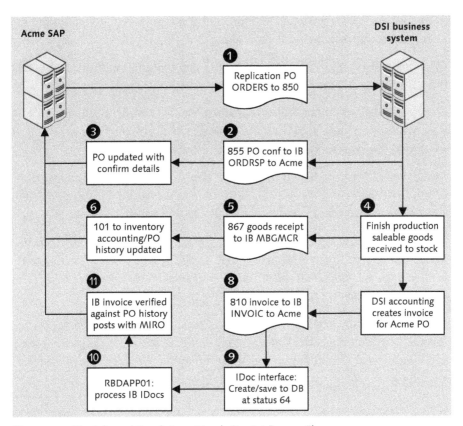

Figure 11.5 The Inbound Goods Issue/Goods Receipt Process Flow

When production is completed, DSI receives the DVD movies from the production order into finished goods inventory. DSI then generates an X12 867 transaction with details of the goods receipt, including the PO and line item numbers, Acme material number, production batch number, quantity produced, and the date of production.

The 867 is converted by the EDI RIM into an MBGMCR.MBGMCR03 IDoc, which posts a 101 goods receipt movement type with Transaction MB01 against the purchase order and line item number into inventory management in Acme's SAP system.

The goods receipt creates a material document with full details of the item received. Accounting is also updated with debit and credit postings to the G/L accounts recording raw materials consumed and finished goods received linked to the purchase order line item and material document.

The G/L entries also pull in unit pricing for the raw materials and finished goods and the total dollar value for both, which must match.

Accounting is now prepped to receive an invoice for the goods produced. DSI issues an invoice and sends it to their EDI system, which converts it to an X12 810 invoice transaction and sends it to Acme's EDI RIM by AS2.

The RIM converts it to an INVOIC.INVOIC02 IDoc in XML format and saves it in a file on the SAP application server. The RIM then makes an RFC through its IDoc adapter and the JCo Connector into SAP to trigger RFC function EDI_DATA_INCOMING.

The IDoc file is picked up by EDI_DATA_INCOMING, validated, deleted from the application server, and converted from XML to ASCII before each IDoc is written to the database at status 50 — *IDoc added* — and then status 64 — *IDoc ready to be transferred to application.*

A scheduled job for program RBDAPP01 kicks off to pick up all INVOIC message types at status 64. RBDAPP01 reads the IDocs and partner profiles, and uses process code INVL to identify and call inbound processing function IDOC_INPUT_INVOIC_MRM.

The function makes a number of checks, including the following:

▶ E1EDKA1 where PARVW = LF: the supplier in table LFB1

▶ E1EDKA1 where PARVW = RE: the company code in table T076B

▶ EDI_DC40: the external tax code in table T076M based on the send partner type and send partner number, and the program parameters in table T076S based on the send partner type, send partner number, and company code

If any of these values from the IDoc do not match their corresponding values in SAP, an error is returned and the IDoc fails.

If all these checks pass, purchase order and purchase order history data is pulled from SAP based on the PO and line item number in the E1EDP02 segment of the INVOIC IDoc. If there is no matching purchase order and line item number, an error is returned and the IDoc fails.

If all these checks pass, data are passed from the IDoc segments to internal tables with the structure of tables RBKP (invoice header), RSEG (line item details), and RBTX (tax data).

These internal tables are then passed to function `MRM_INVOICE_CREATE`, which verifies the supplier invoice data from the IDoc and either parks or posts the invoice, depending on our supplier invoice configuration.

This work is done through function modules on the data collected from the IDoc, the purchase order, and the goods receipt.

The goods receipt is key to verifying the quantities and dollar amounts in the incoming invoice against the PO. It's critical for the system to identify it from IDoc data. If the system cannot identify a goods receipt, an error will be returned and the IDoc will fail.

If the goods receipt posted against a delivery, the delivery document number is sent in the IDoc and used to identify the goods receipt. The delivery document is the system's first choice for identifying the goods receipt.

In fact, the system can identify the goods receipt with a delivery document number, even if the purchase order number is not included in the IDoc, if the delivery number exits only once for the sending supplier.

If there is no delivery document number in the IDoc, the system checks the PO and PO line item numbers and reads the open goods receipts through purchase order history at the line-item level.

Function `MRM_INVOICE_CREATE` runs the critical verification checks through function `MRM_INVOICE_CHECK`. Function `MRM_INVOICE_PARK` is called if the invoice is configured to be parked and approved before posting and function `MRM_INVOICE_POST` if the invoice is to be posted directly.

When the supplier invoice posts, its data are stored in tables RBKP (header), RSEG (line item details), and RBTX (tax data). Accounting documents are created almost immediately and the invoice stored tables BKPF (header) and BSEG (item details).

Accounting is now ready to pay the invoice.

11.4 Technical Specifications

This technical specification section describes the SAP IDoc configuration and EDI development to support the X12 810 to INVOIC.INVOIC02 supplier invoice interface from DSI into Acme's SAP system.

11.4.1 Enhancements to the Process

There are no custom enhancements to this interface.

11.4.2 Technical Requirements

DSI will send one X12 810 invoice transaction for each purchase order from Acme for replication services that has been fully manufactured and the finished goods received into inventory.

The 810 will include all data required to post an inbound supplier invoice in Acme's SAP system after goods receipts have successfully posted against the full quantity of a purchase order and accounting has been updated, including all relevant G/L accounts.

The EDI RIM and SAP will be configured to support inbound supplier invoice INVOIC messages and outbound 997 functional acknowledgments at the transaction level.

11.4.3 Dependencies

The 810-INVOIC interface is dependent on a number of development and configuration objects in SAP and the EDI RIM:

▶ Logistical invoice verification configuration completed in SAP

▶ Process code INVL extended with message code MM for logical message INVOIC

▶ Inbound envelopes set up in the RIM for DSI's X12 810 version 5010 transactions

▶ Outbound envelopes for 997 acknowledgments to be created in the RIM for DSI during de-enveloping of inbound 810 transactions

- Custom cross-reference table ZEDIXREF populated in SAP to convert EDI trading partner IDs to the SAP send and receive partner numbers for the inbound 810 from DSI

- EDI map for X12 810 to INVOIC translations

- Business process workflows built in the EDI RIM to process and route the incoming X12 810 and INVOIC.INVOIC02 IDocs

- Message code MM defined for process code INVL

- Inbound partner profile set up for DSI message type INVOIC with message code MM and process code INVL

- Job set up in the SAP Job Scheduler (Transaction SM36) to run twice a day to post INVOIC.INVOIC02 IDocs with program RBDAPP01 with a variant to select for all suppliers and all messages at status 64

11.4.4 Assumptions

The EDI RIM will not validate any of the mandatory data elements in the incoming 810 supplier invoice. It will simply map the transaction to the IDoc and SAP will handle validation. The following are additional technical assumptions:

- The RIM will map the EDI send and receive trading partner IDs to the IDoc control record fields SNDLAD and RCVLAD. These fields will be read by an exit in the IDoc interface to identify the SAP sold-to partner for EDIDC-SNDPRN and the SAP logical system for EDID-RCVPRN.

- The RIM will return an X12 997 functional acknowledgment during de-enveloping of the inbound X12 810 transaction.

- EDI errors are tracked and addressed in the EDI system. Technical errors in the IDoc interface, such as syntax or partner profile errors, are tracked and corrected by the EDI team.

11.5 Mapping Specifications

A map will be developed in the EDI RIM to map the X12 810 supplier invoice from DSI to the INVOIC.INVOIC02 XML IDoc to send to Acme's SAP system.

Table 11.3 outlines mapping requirements for the inbound supplier invoice for our DSI to Acme Pictures scenario.

INVOIC	810	Value	Comments
E1EDK01—Header—Min 1, Max 1			
@SEGMENT		1	Hard-code segment attribute to 1
CURCY	CUR02	USD	Document currency
BSART	BIG06	INVO	Document type. Tells system to post invoice. If BIG06 = FD, BSART = INVO. If BIG06 = CR, BSART = CRME, Credit Memo.
E1EDKA1—Partners—Min 1, Max 99—Loop 1 company code			
@SEGMENT		1	Hard-code segment attribute to 1
PARVW	REF01	RE	Acme company code handling purchasing and payments for DSI where REF01 = DP. Checked during verification.
PARTN	REF02	3000	Acme company code.
E1EDKA1—Partners—Loop 2 supplier			
@SEGMENT		1	Hard-code segment attribute to 1
PARVW	N101	LF	Customer vendor number, where N101 = SU
PARTN	N104	23568	Acme SAP partner number for DSI. First priority in check.
LIFNR	N104	0008888888899	GLN for Acme supplier number. Checked if PARTN not populated.
E1EDK02—Documents—Min 0, Max 10—Loop 1 supplier invoice			
@SEGMENT		1	Hard-code segment attribute to 1
QUALF		009	Identifies supplier invoice. Hard code to IDoc where BIG02 is not null.
BELNR	BIG02	0005000020	Supplier invoice number
E1EDK03—Dates—Min 0, Max 10—Loop 1 invoice date			
@SEGMENT		1	Hard-code segment attribute to 1
IDDAT		012	Invoice document date
DATUM	BIG01	20140115	Supplier invoice date

Table 11.3 Mapping Specification for X12 810 to INVOIC.INVOIC02 IDoc

INVOIC	810	Value	Comments
E1EDK03—Dates—Min 0, Max 10 — Loop 2 posting date			
@SEGMENT		1	Hard-code segment attribute to 1
IDDAT		024	Identifies baseline date for valuation
DATUM	BIG01	20140115	Supplier invoice posting date
E1EDK04—Taxes—Min 0, Max N			
@SEGMENT		1	Hard-code segment attribute to 1
MWSKZ	TXI01	ST	EDI tax code identifying sales tax to be converted to internal SAP tax code. From summary level of TX1.
MWSBT	TXI02	94.88	Total amount of tax at header pulled from summary level of TX1
E1EDK18—Terms of payment—Min 0, Max 10—Cash discount			
@SEGMENT		1	Hard-code segment attribute to 1
QUALF	ITD01	001	Payment terms 1: cash discounts, if applicable. Cash discount terms where ITD01 = 22.
TAGE	ITD05	10	Cash discount if invoice paid within number of days
PRZNT	TX103	3.0	Percentage of cash discount. Additional cash discounts or other terms may be applied dependent on business agreements with supplier.
E1EDP01—Item-level details group—Min 1, Max N 1 instance of E1EDP01 per group loop			
@SEGMENT		1	Hard-code segment attribute to 1
POSEX	IT101	000010	Invoice line item. Same as PO line item number.
MENGE	IT102	100.000	Quantity invoiced
MENEE	IT103	EA	Unit of measure

Table 11.3 Mapping Specification for X12 810 to INVOIC.INVOIC02 IDoc (Cont.)

INVOIC	810	Value	Comments
E1EDP02—Item level documents—Min 1, Max N—Loop 1 Acme PO			
@SEGMENT		1	Hard-code segment attribute to 1
QUALF		001	Identifies PO number
BELNR	BIG04	4500016169	Purchase order number pulled from BIG04 at header level of 810.
ZEILE	IT101	000010	PO line item number pulled from invoice line item which is from the PO.
E1EDP02—Item-level documents—Min 1, Max N—Loop 2 delivery			
@SEGMENT		1	Hard-code segment attribute to 1
QUALF	REF01	016	Identifies delivery number if available from line item level where REF01 = DO (delivery order), if available.
BELNR	REF02	4000023	Delivery order number.
E1EDP19—Material numbers—Min 1, Max 10—Loop 2 delivery			
@SEGMENT		1	Hard-code segment attribute to 1
QUALF	IT106	001	Identifies customer material number where IT106 = IN (buyer's item number).
IDTNR	IT107	9999888	Acme material number
BELNR	REF02	4000023	Delivery order number
E1EDP26—Amount—Min 1, Max 20			
QUALF		003	Identifies line item amount in document currency.
BETRG	IT102 IT104	1000.00	Multiply quantity (IT102) by unit price (IT104)
E1EDS01—IDoc summary totals—Min 1, Max 30			
SUMID		011	Identifies total billed value of invoice
SUMME	TDS01	1094.88	Total gross invoice dollar amount, including tax

Table 11.3 Mapping Specification for X12 810 to INVOIC.INVOIC02 IDoc (Cont.)

11.6   EDI Configuration in SAP

Let's walk through IDoc configuration settings in SAP for the inbound INVOIC supplier invoice message from Disk Services International.

11.6.1   Extending Process Code INVL

Process code INVL will be extended with message code MM to provide a unique key for the inbound partner profile for logical message INVOIC when used as an inbound supplier invoice.

1. Go to Transaction WE42 or the WEDI area menu Development • Outbound Processing Settings M/C • Outbound process code.

2. Click the Display • Change pencil icon (or press Ctrl+F1), select process code INVL, and double-click folder Logical message folder in the navigation pane.

3. Click New Entries (or press F5) to open the Details of Added Entries screen. Add the following values:

   ▸ Message type: "INVOIC"

   ▸ Message code: "MM"

4. Save and assign the entries to a change request. The finished screen should look like Figure 11.6.

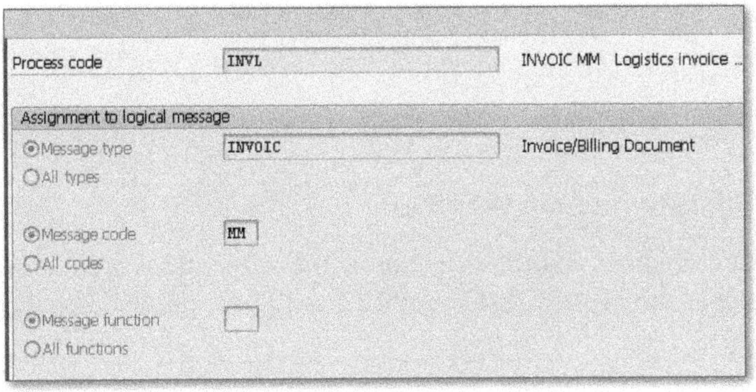

Figure 11.6   Process Code INVL Extended for the Supplier Invoice

435

11.6.2 EDPAR Entries: Transaction VOE4

There are no EDPAR entries for the 810 to INVOIC interface.

11.6.3 ZEDIXREF Entries

Table ZEDIXREF maps the sender's send and receive EDI trading partner IDs to the SAP partner numbers; these are DSI's vendor number in Acme's system and the receiving SAP logical system ID.

Table 11.4 lists the values that we'll enter into custom table ZEDIXREF for the inbound 810 supplier invoice interface from DSI.

Field	Value	Description
DIRECT	2	Direction inbound
STDMES	810	X12 supplier invoice transaction
MESTYP	INVOIC	IDoc invoice message type
IDOCTP	INVOIC02	IDoc basic type
CIMTYP		IDoc extension, none for this interface
SNDPRN	DISK01	SAP send partner: DSI's customer number in Acme's system
RCVPRN	DEVCLNT100	SAP receive partner: Acme SAP logical system
SNDLAD	99934567999	EDI send partner: DSI trading partner ID for DSI
RCVLAD	99999998889	EDI receive partner: DSI trading partner ID for Acme

Table 11.4 ZEDIXREF Entry for the Inbound 810 from DSI

11.6.4 Partner Profile: Transaction WE20

The inbound partner profile links DSI to the incoming message type and the process code that will trigger the processing function that will post the goods issue or goods receipt.

We'll need one inbound partner profile for DSI partner type LI (vendor) with message type INVOIC. We'll also add a message code to distinguish the inbound supplier invoice with logistics invoice verification from any other inbound invoice we may need in future.

Remember that second process code for logical message INVOIC? INVF posts an invoice directly to accounting without a purchase order number. We may need to use it in future, so it's important to ensure that our partner profile is unique.

In the inbound parameters table control, click CREATE and add the following values to the inbound parameters screen (see Figure 11.7):

- ▶ PARTNER ROLE: "VN" for vendor
- ▶ MESSAGE TYPE: "INVOIC"
- ▶ MESSAGE CODE: "MM"
- ▶ PROCESS CODE: "INVL" for logistics invoice verification
- ▶ PROCESSING BY FUNCTION MODULE: Choose either TRIGGER BY BACKGROUND PROGRAM or TRIGGER IMMEDIATELY.

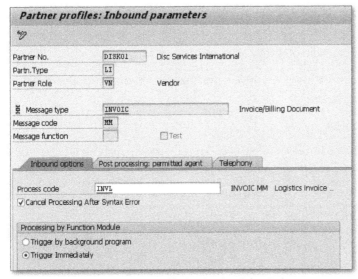

Figure 11.7 Inbound Partner Profile for Gordy's Sales Orders

Don't forget to save. As we have seen, process code INVL links the partner profile to function module `IDOC_INPUT_INVOIC_MRM`.

11.7   Summary

This closes our little tour of Acme's purchasing cycle. We've touched on three of its key interfaces: the outbound purchase order (and inbound order confirmation), inbound goods receipt, and the inbound supplier invoice.

We've seen that the invoice is dependent on the purchase order and the goods receipts that have posted against that PO. The purchase order tells DSI what to produce and the goods receipts describe what was actually produced for each line item in the PO.

The quantities and dollar amounts in both must either match the quantities and dollar amounts billed in the invoice, or at least fall within a set tolerance limit, which is plus or minus five percent between Acme and DSI.

The purchase order and line item numbers are critical keys that must be returned in the invoice. Purchase order history, created when goods are received against a PO line item with either a 101 or 102 movement type, links to both the material and accounting documents created by the goods receipts.

At its most basic, logistics invoice verification for an inbound supplier invoice involves the following steps:

▶ Determine the invoicing party

▶ Convert the incoming company code, tax code, and program parameters through mapping tables set up in configuration

▶ Verify the invoice against the purchase order and goods receipt

▶ Post the invoice and the follow-up accounting documents

The other requirement is a unique partner profile for the INVOIC message that triggers logistics invoice verification for the supplier invoice with process code INVL to distinguish it from an accounting invoice that does not reference a PO number and uses process code INVF.

In the real world, purchasing is a lot more complicated than what we've outlined in these interfaces. We haven't even touched on processes such as requirements and resource planning, raw materials acquisition, inventory management, the production life cycle, delivery, payments, and many more, that stretch across Acme, DSI, and third party suppliers.

But we needed to get a feel for how Acme gets the goods that it sells to its customers. Nobody understood the complexity of the business better than Acme's legendary founder, Darryl Q. Fernhausen, who knew that you have to buy before you can sell.

The interfaces flowing back and forth may have confused him, but the great Darryl Q would have been the first to break out into a big smile as he realized how much money these automated processes could save him in processing costs, time, and reduced employee error.

And that means greater profit margins from what he sells to his customers, which was his real passion. So now we will follow the trail of that passion as we address the order-to-cash cycle: sales, distribution, invoicing, and—our legendary founder's greatest joy—payment from the customer.

Moving product is the heart of the business, and the great Darryl Q knew that it's all about selling stuff. But there's a long way to go before the customer gets what he wants. And the first step is the inbound 850 PO. So let's look at the specs and go over the business process and consider what else we need to do to make it work.

12 The Inbound Customer Purchase Order

We've already been through the blueprint phase and looked at Acme's business and legacy systems. We have a design for our new SAP EDI system and have learned a little about EDI and the IDoc interface.

Now we're going to build some interfaces.

The chapters in Act III are written as functional and technical specifications for the key interfaces in the order-to-cash cycle between Acme Pictures, its most important customer, Gordy's Galaxy of Games & B Flix, and its third-party contract manufacturer, Disc Services International (DSI).

In this chapter we look at the requirements for building the interfaces, map the IDocs to the EDI transaction, and go over any custom code or configuration we may need to be develop.

Because Acme and Gordy are VMI (vendor-managed inventory) partners, they exchange two types of purchase orders:

1. Direct EDI for new release: X12 850 to ORDERS.ORDERS05

2. VMI PO's for replenishment and catalog sales

VMI is a two-step process:

▶ X12 852 daily sales and weekly inventory feeds to Acme's VMI system that supports calculation of suggested customer orders

▶ VMI flat file with suggested PO to ORDERS.ORDERS05

The end result is the same for both: Sales orders are created in SAP by an ORDERS. ORDERS05 IDoc and the order-to-cash processing cycle begins. So let's look at both types of order.

12.1 Technical Overview of Interface

The inbound purchase order interface is summarized in Table 12.1.

Item	Description
Title	Sales order from customer PO–VMI and EDI
Description	VMI orders are suggested customer POs created in the VMI system based on store level daily sales, weekly on-hand inventory, and other calculations. EDI sales orders are converted from inbound X12 850 POs sent by the customer to order new release DVDs. Both types of order create a sales order in SAP.
Type of interface	Sales: X12 EDI or VMI flat file to IDoc
Direction	Inbound
Trading partner	Gordy's Galaxy (customer)
IDoc	ORDERS.ORDERS05
IDoc extended type	
IDoc function	`IDOC_INPUT_ORDERS`
Custom ABAP	User exit in enhancement VEDA0001 in modification project ZEDISOO1
Description	Duplicate PO number check on customer PO number, ship-to partner, and material number
Source file(s)	850 (PO), 852 (VMI), VMI suggested orders flat file
Target document(s)	SAP sales order
Transaction code	VA01
Map(s)	X12 850 vers. 5010 to ORDERS.ORDERS05 VMI orders FF to ORDERS.ORDERS05

Table 12.1 Overview of Inbound EDI and VMI PO Interfaces

Item	Description
Custom map logic	One-to-many mapping; unbundle store order quantity per material in SDQ segments into one IDoc per store
Source system	Gordy's Galaxy EDI via AS2
Target system	Acme SAP via EDI RIM
997 acknowledgment	Outbound at transaction detail level. Function group acknowledgment code: PO
Frequency	Daily, on demand
Job schedule	RBDAPP01: Every hour, posts all ORDERS message types to sales orders

Table 12.1 Overview of Inbound EDI and VMI PO Interfaces (Cont.)

12.2 Functional Specifications

The purpose of this interface is to create sales orders in SAP for Gordy's Galaxy to order a defined quantity of DVD product by a particular date. This is the first step in the order-to-cash cycle; all subsequent steps are dependent on the sales order posting successfully.

When the sales order is saved, it generates an acknowledgment to Gordy. It is also used to feed requirement calculations for the outbound replication PO to the contract manufacturer DSI and to generate outbound deliveries.

12.2.1 Process Overview

It begins with an EDI transmission—either an 852 POS to VMI or an 850 customer purchase order that is translated to an ORDERS.ORDERS05 IDoc.

The 852 sends VMI daily sales and weekly inventory data at the store level. Other feeds provide such detailed store level information as shelf layout and dimensions. This all feeds into calculations that generate suggested purchase orders for Gordy's Galaxy, which are output in a custom flat file format.

Like the 850 PO, the VMI orders are mapped to an ORDERS.ORDERS05 IDoc and sent to SAP to create sales orders.

12.2.2 Requirements

SAP sales orders are created for one sold-to and one ship-to partner and will be identified by order type:

- ZEDI for EDI orders with no SDQ
- ZEDS for EDI orders with SDQ
- ZVMI for VMI orders

The following are additional requirements:

- There can be no duplicate posting of customer PO numbers except where an 850 with SDQ segments at the item level uses one PO number to order product for multiple ship-to partners.
- The order type will post to the sales order from the IDoc rather than from table EDSDC.
- Delivery dates and plants for VMI orders are sent from the VMI system. They can be changed after the sales order is created but before the delivery generated.
- An order acknowledgment is created when the sales order is saved and is sent to the EDI RIM as an ORDRSP IDoc, unless there is a credit or other hold on the customer.
- Only completed sales orders generate delivery documents. Incomplete orders can still be saved, but they'll require follow-up processing and release before delivery can be generated. Two conditions can lead to an incomplete order:
  - The customer credit check fails.
  - The ATP (item availability) check fails to find sufficient inventory to fill the order. The sales order can still generate an acknowledgment, but the delivery document is not generated. The order instead feeds into requirements planning for a replication PO.

12.2.3 Dependencies

The 850-ORDERS interface is dependent on master data, configuration, and development objects in SAP and the EDI RIM:

- ▶ Master data objects required to create sales orders, including the following:
  - ▶ GL chart of accounts: Assigned to the company code to record dollar values for costs and revenues for the accounting system
  - ▶ Customers: For sold-to and ship-to partners, payment terms, shipping conditions, and credit checks, assigned to Acme sales organization, distribution channel, and division
  - ▶ Delivery plants: For assignment of vendor plants for shipping
  - ▶ Materials: For finished DVD movies and component materials
  - ▶ Bills of materials: Identifying components in finished goods
  - ▶ Customer material info records (table KNMT): for conversion of external customer to internal Acme SAP material number
  - ▶ Pricing conditions: For header-level and item-level standard prices, taxes, discounts, credits, promotions, freight charges, and so on
  - ▶ EDPAR: Partner mapping from external to internal customer numbers ensuring identification of SAP sold-to and ship-to partners
  - ▶ EDSDC: Sales organization data for the SAP sold-to partner and the customer's vendor number
  - ▶ Partner profiles: To identify the sold-to partner for the incoming IDoc order. Partner profiles will be at the sold-to partner level; there will be only one partner profile per EDI customer
- ▶ IDoc configuration completed in SAP to support inbound ORDERS for Gordy's Galaxy, including custom EDI trading partner mapping table ZEDIXREF
- ▶ EDI maps for 852 VMI and 850 order translations
- ▶ Business process workflows built in the EDI RIM to process incoming 850 POs and route ORDERS.ORDERS05 IDocs to SAP

12.2.4 Assumptions

Sales orders are created from ORDERS.ORDERS05 IDocs that have been processed by a scheduled job in SAP. There is only one sold-to and ship-to partner for each sales order, although one customer PO can be linked to multiple sales orders. The following are additional key assumptions:

- Gordy's Galaxy sends GLNs for its sold-to and ship-to partners.
- Gordy sends UPC numbers and Acme's internal SAP material numbers for all goods ordered.
- VMI order pricing is determined by pricing conditions for the customer and material called when the order is created.
- Pricing for EDI orders is determined when the sales order is created in SAP by comparing the prices sent in Gordy's PO to the price proposed by the pricing conditions configured for the material ordered.
  - If the two match or are within a tolerance limit, Gordy's price posts to the sales order.
  - If the difference between the two prices exceeds tolerance, the reason for the difference is identified, and the correct price is used.
- The base unit of measure for items ordered is EA (eaches).
- All data that must be returned to the customer in the invoice must post to the sales order from the IDoc. Data that can't be accommodated in a standard field in the order go into a text element.
- Business users are responsible for addressing application errors in the IDocs.
- All EDI system errors are handled by the EDI team.
- EDI and VMI orders are sent into SAP immediately, and the IDocs are posted to sales orders within no more than an hour.
- EDI errors or issues that may affect the timeliness of order creation are communicated to the business users immediately.

12.2.5 Data That Will Post to an Inbound Sales Order

SAP sales orders are created with Transaction VA01. At a minimum, the fields listed in Table 12.2 must be populated to create a sales order.

Table	Field	Description	Sample Value
VBAK	AUART	Order type	ZEDI
VBAK	VKORG	Sales organization	0010
VBAK	VTWEG	Distribution channel	10

Table 12.2 Fields That Are Populated When a Sales Order Is Created

Table	Field	Description	Sample Value
VBPA	PARVW	Partner qualifier—sold-to	AG
VBAK	KUNNR	Sold-to partner	GRDY01
VBPA	PARVW	Partner qualifier—ship-to	WE
VBPA	KUNNR	Ship-to partner	GRDY01001
VBKD	BSTKD	Customer PO number	9997895
VBKD	BSTDK	Customer PO date	20081202
VBAK	VDATU	Requested delivery date	20081204
VBAP	MATNR	SAP material number	999284
VBAP	KWMENG	Order quantity	230
VBAP	VRKME	Sales unit of measure	EA

Table 12.2 Fields That Are Populated When a Sales Order Is Created (Cont.)

12.2.6 Reconciliation Procedure

Successful import of the ORDERS IDoc is confirmed through any of the IDoc monitoring tools, such as BD87 or WE05.

IDoc status should be 64—*IDoc ready to be transferred to application*—before the scheduled processing job is kicked off and 53—*Application document posted*—after.

The EDI team confirms the data in the IDoc against the data in the X12 850 transaction set sent from the customer, and the users validate that the sales order was created against the data sent in the IDoc.

12.2.7 Enhancements to the Process

An enhancement is required during sales order creation to ensure that a customer PO posts only once. This may be a little like squaring the circle. Each PO can contain product ordering information for multiple store locations at the line-item level, whereas each SAP sales order only carries ordering information for one store.

This means that we must be able to create multiple sales orders for each PO while ensuring that the same customer PO number for the same ship-to partner doesn't post again.

Double-posting can result in double-ordering and duplicate shipments to the customer, leading to unnecessary costs, returns, and customer dissatisfaction with Acme's service.

The duplicate PO check occurs in code during IDoc processing and is transparent to the user. It checks PO number and date, sold-to, and ship-to partner numbers.

If an existing sales orders is found against PO number, the enhancement checks whether it uses the same material number as the incoming. If it does, it's most likely a duplicate posting and an error is returned. IDoc processing is terminated and the responsible user investigates.

12.2.8 Errors and Error Handling

The following errors may occur during processing of the inbound 850-VMI-ORDERS interface:

▶ The IDoc will fail if the sold-to or ship-to partners don't exist in SAP, or if the sales organization can't be determined. If these errors occur, the customer or sales organization data are entered, and the IDoc is rerun.

▶ The IDoc will fail if SAP can't identify the material number from the item number sent in the EDI transaction. The customer is asked to resend the PO, or the IDoc is edited and reprocessed.

▶ A customer PO that has already posted will trigger an error in the IDoc if tries to post it again. If the PO needs to be reposted, the sales orders that posted in the initial run are deleted.

▶ If there isn't enough inventory to fulfill an order when the sales order is created, it will be put on hold and deliveries won't be generated until inventory is entered and the sales order completed. The product will be ordered from DSI through a replication PO.

▶ If a customer credit check fails during sales order creation, the order will be put on hold until the credit department releases it.

Sales order or IDoc errors will be communicated to the responsible business user immediately. There is a service-level agreement with the partner mandating how quickly shipments need to be sent after orders are received.

Standard IDoc monitoring programs such as WE05 or B87 will be used to track and monitor IDocs.

12.3 End-to-End Process Flow

Figure 12.1 gives an overview of the end-to-end process flow for creating SAP sales orders from EDI transmissions.

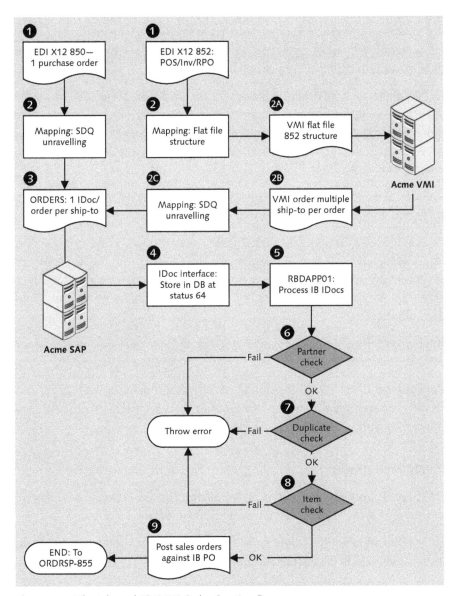

Figure 12.1 The Inbound EDI/VMI Order Creation Process

Two processes are at work here for Gordy's Galaxy: new release orders with EDI and replenishment and catalog orders with VMI. The two merge with the creation of one ORDERS message instance for each sales order that will post to SAP.

This is easier said than done because the 850 PO and the VMI order file include all ordering data for each of Gordy's 2,000 store locations at the item level. Ordering quantity for each store in the 850 is in one or many SDQ segments that occur as children of item-level parent segment PO1, which contains the item numbers and total item quantity for the product being ordered.

The SDQ segment can hold order quantities for up to 10 stores. The VMI order file is structured in a similar manner. But an SAP sales order can only be created for one sold-to and one ship-to store location. We need to build one ORDERS IDoc for each store that includes each DVD product ordered by that store, with its quantity, in a separate line item.

This can be handled in an ABAP program if we build an ORDERS05 basic type with an SDQ segment to bring the PO data into SAP.

We'll look at the logic for doing this, whether in a map through a Java exit, a script, or ABAP. The logical problem is the same, but the specifics of doing it vary from tool to tool. Many mapping tools have robust programming or rules languages that allow conditional processing, looping, indexing, and also support arrays and even Java objects.

Some mapping tools natively support splitting out multiple sales by ship-to partner from SDQ segments in one 850 PO.

But Acme's doesn't, so we have to code it. As long as our mapping tool has access to all of the source structures and data, we should be able to unravel the SDQ into multiple orders with the help of a little creative code.

12.3.1 VMI Processing

The VMI process flow begins with an 852 transmission from Gordy's Galaxy by AS2 into the EDI RIM. The 852 carries three types of data:

▸ Nightly point of sale (POS) data from each store that consolidates check-out scans of items sold in each store throughout the day

▸ Weekly on-hand inventory levels in every store

▶ Intermittent open reserved PO numbers (RPOs), before Acme runs out of valid PO numbers for VMI orders.

The 852 is mapped to an internal flat file with a structure similar to the 852 and is sent into the VMI system. This file is also sent to the legacy StoreData system for use in store-level replenishment calculations that include such esoteric values as floor size, shelf location, shelf dimensions, title order history, minimum and maximum order levels, and so on, for each store.

The results of these calculations are sent to VMI in a flat file. The final order calculations include the StoreData feed, additional algorithms on the POS and weekly inventory data, and a number of daily feeds from SAP, including the following:

▶ Customer store locations

▶ Finished goods master data

▶ BOMs and BOM changes since the last feed

▶ Inventory levels at the vendor's warehouse

▶ Open and changed sales orders

▶ Open deliveries

▶ Returns

▶ Open vendor POs for manufacture of finished goods

The result of all this activity is a suggested PO that aggregates item orders for each of Gordy's stores. The PO number is pulled from a table populated by the RPO feed. The selected number is then marked consumed and is no longer available for use.

The VMI order is extracted to an ASCII file by VMI. The file has a flatter structure than an 850 PO, but it includes an SDQ-like record with order item quantity for up to six stores in each segment that is a child to an item header that identifies the product being ordered.

The following key values are mapped to the IDoc:

▶ The SAP sold-to partner number for Gordy to the send partner field in the control record EDIDC-SNDPRN

▶ Order type ZVMI for VMI order to field E1EDK14-ORGID with qualifier 012 in field QUALF

▶ The RPO number to field E1EDK02-BELNR with qualifier 001 in field QUALF

▶ Gordy's store location GLN to E1EDKA1-LIFNR with qualifier WE in field PARVW

▶ The quantity to be ordered for each item in field E1EDP01-MENGE

▶ The SAP material number for each movie ordered in field E1EDP19-IDTNR with qualifier 002 in field QUALF

▶ The item's UPC code in field E1EDP19-IDTNR with qualifier 003 in field QUALF

▶ Gordy's item number in field E1EDP19-IDTNR with qualifier 001 in field QUALF

The VMI order file is exported to the EDI RIM, where it is identified as a VMI order for Gordy's Galaxy. RIM calls a map that unravels the store-level data and builds one ORDERS IDoc for each store and each product being ordered by that store.

The IDocs are batched together into a file and, at this point, the VMI process ends and the IDoc is sent into SAP through the IDoc adapter.

12.3.2 EDI 850 Processing

The EDI processing flow begins with the receipt of an 850 PO transmission from Gordy's Galaxy by AS2 into the EDI RIM. The RIM identifies the 850 from Gordy, strips away envelope, and calls the map to translate it.

Gordy uses the SDQ segment at the item level to identify each store and the quantity of product being ordered. As with the VMI file, the map unravels order data from the item level and builds one XML ORDERS IDoc for each store ship-to party.

The same key values are mapped to the IDoc as for the VMI order.

The IDocs are batched into a file and sent by the RIM into SAP through the IDoc adapter by calling function `EDI_DATA_INCOMING`.

12.3.3 VMI and EDI Processes Merge

At this point, the VMI and EDI processes merge. The SAP IDoc interface kicks in, confirms that the file contains IDocs, converts the XML to ASCII, checks that there are matching partner profiles, and writes the IDocs to the database at status 64.

The IDocs are processed by program `RBDAPP01`, which is scheduled to pick up Gordy's orders every hour. `RBDAPP01` reads the IDoc database and identifies all ORDERS IDocs at status 64 where EDIDC-SNDPRN equals Gordy's SAP sold-to partner.

It then identifies the IDoc function—`IDOC_INPUT_ORDERS`—from the process code ORDE in the inbound partner profile for Gordy's Galaxy message type ORDERS and calls it to post the IDocs to sales orders. `IDOC_INPUT_ORDERS` takes over and loops through the IDoc.

When it hits segment E1EDKA1, it reads EDPAR to convert Gordy's GLN to the SAP ship-to partner number. If the EDPAR read fails, an error is thrown, IDoc processing stops, and a status 51 application error is added to the IDoc status record. The conversion can't be made because it's not there.

If the read succeeds and the conversion is made, the system checks that the ship-to partner is valid for the sales organization against which the order is being posted.

If this check fails, an error is returned. The ship-to partner may need to be extended to the sales organization reported or the sales organization may be wrong. The sold-to partner is checked during creation of the sales order.

After the ship-to partner is validated, a duplicate order check is run to ensure that the customer PO hasn't already posted a sales order for the current sold-to and ship-to partners.

Table VBAK is read for the sales organization, order type, SAP sold-to partner, customer PO number, and date, and material number. If there's no hit, there's no duplicate, and IDoc processing continues to the next check.

If there is a hit, table VBPA is read with the sales order number and sold-to partner to identify the ship-to. VBPA stores complete partner data for all sales documents. If there's no hit, the ship-to party is different, and PO duplicate check processing exits.

If there is a hit, we have a possible duplicate. The final check is on the material number. If they are the same in the sales order as in the posting IDoc, then we have a duplicate. We do this by reading table VBAP with the sales order and material numbers.

Fun with Sales Document Data

In a typical system, VBAK and VBAP can grow to be extremely large tables. There may be times that you need to identify one or more sales orders for a sold-to partner or material but have no sales order number to go by.

SAP's sales document index tables speed searches across sales, delivery, and billing document tables, even if you do not have a document number. The index tables have a consistent format and offer a variety of selection options, including creation dates, document types, sales organizations, and so on.

Index table names always begin with a V and include two characters from the main header or item table name of the sales document:

▶ VAK (header) or VAP (item level) for sales orders

▶ VLK (header) or VLP (items) for delivery docs

▶ VRK (header) or VRP (items) for billing documents

The last two characters identify the key selection option used in the index:

▶ VAKPA: sales orders by sold-to partner

▶ VAPMA: sales orders items by material number

▶ VLKPA: delivery documents by ship-to partner

▶ VLPMA: delivery items by material number

▶ VRKPA: billing documents by payer partner

▶ VRPMA: billing document items by material number

Perhaps your code needs to identify all IDocs generated from a sales order. Function `NREL_GET_NEIGHBOURHOOD` links the sales order number (the object key) and its business object type (BUS2032) to all IDocs that were created or generated from it.

You only need to populate the `IS_OBJECT` import parameter with the sales order number with all leading zeroes into the `OBJKEY` field and the business object into the `OBJTYPE` field.

The function returns a list of all IDoc numbers in the `OBJKEY_B` field for IDocs generated from the sales order. Of course, this not restricted to sales orders: you can do the same for any document that has a business object.

If the material number is the same, an error is returned and IDoc processing ends. The responsible user checks the sales order and confirms. If it's a duplicate, either the IDoc or the posted sales order is marked for deletion. If the sales order is deleted, the IDoc is reprocessed.

If the PO number is incorrect, it's corrected in the IDoc and reprocessed.

The next check is on the item with the SAP material number checked first. If there's no SAP material number in the IDoc, the customer info record (CMIR) is read from table KNMT with the customer number, sales organization, and Gordy's UPC number.

If there's a hit, the SAP material number is pulled into the IDoc and material check processing ends. If it fails, an error is returned. Either the customer material number is incorrect or the CMIR record hasn't been maintained in KNMT.

If all checks are passed, or errors are corrected and the IDoc reprocessed, the function passes data from the IDoc to an internal table referencing Data Dictionary structure BDCDATA. These data are used to create the sales order through a call to Transaction VA01. As the order is saved, the system does its ATP, credit check, and other checks.

The process ends when output control kicks in and generates an ORDRSP IDoc to send to Gordy to acknowledge posting of its PO or VMI order. The acknowledgment is especially important for VMI orders, because the PO was created by Acme's systems. Gordy uses the acknowledgment to create the purchase order in their own business system.

12.4 Technical Specifications

This technical specification describes interface configuration and custom program support in the EDI RIM and SAP for the delivery, translation, and creation of EDI and VMI sales orders in SAP.

12.4.1 Technical Requirements

One ORDERS.ORDERS05 IDoc is generated by the translation map for each store location ship-to party and all items ordered by that location for order types ZVMI (VMI), ZEDI (EDI no SDQ), or ZEDS (EDI with SDQ).

Custom coding in user exits blocks posting of duplicate customer POs to SAP sales orders.

Configuration in the EDI RIM and SAP supports inbound orders and outbound 997 acknowledgments.

12.4.2 Dependencies

The 850-VMI-ORDERS interface is dependent on a number of development objects in SAP and the EDI RIM:

▶ Inbound envelopes set up in the RIM for Gordy's 850 and 852 version 5010 EDI transactions

▶ Outbound envelopes for 997 acknowledgments to be created in the RIM for Gordy's Galaxy during de-enveloping of inbound 850 and 852 transactions

▶ Custom cross-reference table ZEDIXREF populated in SAP to convert EDI trading partner IDs to the SAP send and receive partner numbers for the inbound 850 from Gordy

▶ Job to be set up in the SAP Job Scheduler (SM36) to run once an hour to post ORDERS.ORDERS05 IDocs with program `RBDAPP01` with variants to select for Gordy's Galaxy and status 64

12.4.3 Assumptions

Purchase orders from Gordy's Galaxy post from to Acme sales orders from 850 EDI transactions and VMI suggested orders. Gordy sends both SDQ and non-SDQ POs. The following are additional technical assumptions:

▶ The map, a script, or a custom external or ABAP program will extract store-level item ordering data in the SDQ segment into an indexed array and build one ORDERS.ORDERS05 IDoc for each store location.

▶ The RIM maps the EDI send and receive trading partner IDs to the IDoc control record fields SNDLAD and RCVLAD. These fields are read by an exit in the IDoc interface to identify the SAP sold-to partner for field EDIDC-SNDPRN and the SAP receiving logical system for field EDID-RCVPRN.

▶ The RIM will return an X12 997 functional acknowledgment during de-enveloping of the inbound X12 850 transaction.

▶ During the EDPAR check on partner segment E1EDKA1, the SAP sold-to partner is read from EDIDC-SNDPRN and used to convert Gordy's GLN for the ship-to partner.

▶ EDI errors are tracked and addressed in the EDI system. Technical errors in the IDoc interface, such as syntax or partner profile errors, are tracked and corrected by the EDI team.

12.5 Mapping Specifications

SDQ segments at the item level of the VMI order and the EDI 850 PO contain order quantities for each store. The product and total order quantity for the line item are identified in the parent line-item segment.

The map, with a little custom coding, extracts the line-item material and SDQ quantity data for each location, identified by GLN in the SDQ record, and builds one ORDERS.ORDERS05 IDOC for each store.

GLN for the store is inserted into field E1EDKA1-LIFNR with qualifier WE at the header level of the ORDERS IDoc. The basic principle is that each SAP sales order includes all DVD movies ordered by one sold-to partner (Gordy's Galaxy) for one ship-to partner (Gordy's store location).

The map has a one-to-many relationship between the input and the output. In addition, it moves the store's GLN from the item level of the input to the header level of the output.

This is a common issue in EDI implementations. SDQ is widely used in the 850 PO, 852 POS, and 855 confirmation. Most mapping tools that handle this do so with custom code. We'll look at a logical process that uses an indexed array and some looping that can be used to build one IDoc for each store in an SDQ segment.

To better understand where we're coming from and where we want to go, we need to look at our mapping specifications for the 850 SDQ PO to the ORDERS IDoc, which are outlined in Table 12.3.

ORDERS	850	Value	Comments
E1EDK01 — General header—Min 1, Max 1			
@ SEGMENT		1	Hard-code segment attribute to 1.
CURCY	CUR02	USD	Document currency
BELNR	BEG03	990012	Customer PO number.
E1EDK14— Org data—Min 0, Max 12			
@ SEGMENT		1	Hard-code segment attribute to 1.
QUALF		012	Order type. Hard code.
ORGID		ZEDS	EDI with SDQ with QUALF 012. Hard code.

Table 12.3 Mapping Specification for EDI 850 PO to ORDERS.ORDERS05 IDoc

ORDERS	850	Value	Comments
E1EDK03—Header Dates—Min 0, Max 10			
@ SEGMENT		1	Hard-code segment attribute to 1.
IDDAT	DTM01	002	Identifies requested delivery date where DTM01 = 010
DATUM	DTM01	20140115	Customer requested delivery date
E1EDKA1—Partners—Min 1, Max 99—Loop 1 Sold-to			
@ SEGMENT		1	Hard-code segment attribute to 1.
PARVW	REF01	AG	Sold-to partner where REF01 = DP. Department code. Gordy purchasing department responsible for Acme.
LIFNR	REF02	0001	Gordy's internal purchasing department number to be converted by EDPAR to Acme SAP number
E1EDKA1—Partners—Loop 2 Supplier			
@ SEGMENT		1	Hard-code segment attribute to 1.
PARVW	N101	LF	Customer vendor number, where N101 = SU
PARTN	N104	23568	Acme SAP partner number for DSI
E1EDKA1—Loop 3 Ship-to—Non-SDQ			
@ SEGMENT		1	Hard-code segment attribute to 1.
PARVW	N101	WE	Customer ship-to number where N101 = ST
LIFNR	N104	0008888888888	GLN for Gordy's store number

Table 12.3 Mapping Spec for EDI 850 PO to ORDERS.ORDERS05 IDoc (Cont.)

ORDERS	850	Value	Comments
E1EDKA1—Partners—Loop 3 Ship-to—SDQ			
@ SEGMENT		1	Hard-code segment attribute to 1.
PARVW		WE	Hard-code WE
LIFNR	SDQ03 – SDQ21		GLN for Gordy's store number from SDQ segment at line-item level. Odd number SDQ fields have store numbers that will be split out to multiple IDocs, one per ship-to partner.
E1EDK02—Documents—Min 0, Max 10			
@ SEGMENT		1	Hard-code segment attribute to 1.
QUALF	BEG01	001	Customer PO qualifier
BELNR	BEG03	999999	Customer PO number (repeated)
DATUM	BEG05	20131215	PO date in format YYYYMMDD
E1EDP01—Item level details group—Min 1, Max N 1 instance of E1EDP01 per group loop			
@ SEGMENT		1	Hard-code segment attribute to 1.
POSEX	PO101	000010	Line item number
MENGE	PO102	500	Total quantity ordered for item. For SDQ, quantity will come from the even numbers SDQ04 to SDQ22 paired with the store number, split into one ORDERS IDoc per ship-to partner and quantity pair.
MENEE	PO103	EA	Unit of measure for total quantity
VPREI	PO104	9.485	Unit price

Table 12.3 Mapping Spec for EDI 850 PO to ORDERS.ORDERS05 IDoc (Cont.)

ORDERS	850	Value	Comments
E1EDP19—Materials—Group Min 1, Max 5 per E1EDP01 loop			
@ SEGMENT		1	Hard-code segment attribute to 1.
QUALF	PO106	003	Customer material number where PO106 = IN. Gordy uses GTIN code.
IDTNR	PO107	9999999	Customer's product number

Table 12.3 Mapping Spec for EDI 850 PO to ORDERS.ORDERS05 IDoc (Cont.)

12.5.1 Structure of the 850 to IDoc Build Array

We'll take a two-step approach. First we'll loop through the 850 input data and map it to a build array with two segments that flatten the IDoc header and item records, as illustrated in Table 12.4. The build array segment and field names are in the BUILD ELEMENTS column.

Build Elements	Value	Comments
IDOC_HDR Record Line—Header Level Data—Mandatory—Max 1		
STOREIDX	5	Store index for GLN
DC4_MANDT	100	SAP target client
DC4_DOCREL	702	SAP version
DC4_DIRECT	2	Inbound
DC4_IDOCTYP	ORDERS05	Basic type
DC4_MESTYP	ORDERS	Message type
DC4_STD	X	EDI standard
DC4_STDVRS	005010	EDI version
DC4_STDMES	850	EDI transaction
DC4_SNDPOR	XML_IDOC	Sender file port

Table 12.4 IDoc Build Array With 2 Flattened Header and Item Segments

Build Elements	Value	Comments
DC4_SNDPRT	KU	Customer
DC4_SNDPFC	AG	Sold-to partner
DC4_SNDPRN	0001	Gordy's sold-to (department no.)
DC4_SNDLAD		Gordy's EDI sender partner ID
DC4_RCVPOR	SAPDEV	Receiver port
DC4_RCVPRT	LS	Logical system
DC4_RCVPRN	SAPDEV100	Logical client
DC4_RCVLAD		Gordy's EDI receiver partner ID for Acme
DC4_REFINT		ISA Ctrl number
DC4_REFGRP		GS Grp Ctrl number
DC4_REFMES	850	ST Txn ID
K01_BELNR	990012	Customer PO no.
K14_QUALF	12	Order type
K14_ORGID	ZEDS	EDI SDQ order
K03_IDDAT	002	Req. delivery date
K03_DATUM		Date
KA1AG	AG	Sold-to customer
KA1AG_LIFNR	0001	Gordy's sold-to (department no.)
KA1LF	LF	Cust. vendor number
KA1LF_LIFNR		Acme GLN
KA1WE	WE	Cust. ship-to number
KA1WE_LIFNR		Gordy ship-to from SDQ segment
K02_QUALF	001	Customer PO
K02_BELNR	990012	PO number

Table 12.4 IDoc Build Array With 2 Flattened Header and Item Segments (Cont.)

461

Build Elements	Value	Comments
K02_DATUM	20131215	PO date
IDOC_ITEM Record Line—Item details 1 to N looping group		
P01_POSEX	0001	Item number
P01_MENGE	50.000	SDQ qty
P01_MENEE	EA	UOM
P01_VPREI		Unit price
P19_ QUALF_001	001	Customer item
P19_IDTNR	9999999	Material number

Table 12.4 IDoc Build Array With 2 Flattened Header and Item Segments (Cont.)

These two segments mimic and simplify the ORDERS05 IDoc structure. We also have an index at the header level that will be used to identify the IDoc being assembled in the build array for a particular store location.

This IDoc build array is where our custom code will collect and assemble the data that we need to built one IDoc for each SDQ store location. Each IDoc will be identified by an index that links the common header data from the 850 to the store location number from the SDQ and all materials it may be ordering in all P01 segments.

The code will unravel the SDQ segments by store and quantity pair into an array that will be used to pass the store's GLN number to the header level E1EDKA1-LIFRN field with PARVW WE. A store level index will be set that will map material and quantity data to an item details segment for every instance of that store GLN ID that occurs throughout the 850 loop.

Each time a new store is encountered in the SDQ, a new header will be created, and a new store index linked to the transaction index.

In addition, a third index will keep track of the total number of records recorded for each store location, including the header record. This will allow us to get the index for the last record stored in the IDoc build array.

12.5.2 Mapping the Build Array to the Target IDoc

Once the 850 has been completely looped through, the IDoc build array will be mapped to the IDoc target structure. There should be one flattened header and one-to-many item detail records for each store location in the build array. Each of these will create one IDoc in the target ORDERS05 structure as the code loops through each build array record.

Whether you can do this in your mapping tool depends on how it processes source and target files, its rules language, and/or ability to call external exits from the map. You can follow the same logic in an ABAP program (or a script) but would need to build an extended IDoc with an SDQ segment.

Table 12.5 details the mapping specifications for the IDoc build to IDoc target array.

Input	IDoc Target	Value	Comments
IDOC_HDR Record Line—Header Level Data—Mandatory—Max 1			
DC4_MANDT	EDI_DC40-MANDT	100	SAP target client
DC4_DOCREL	EDI_DC40-DOCREL	702	SAP version
DC4_DIRECT	EDI_DC40-DIRECT	2	Inbound
DC4_IDOCTYP	EDI_DC40-IDOCTYP	ORDERS05	Basic type
DC4_MESTYP	EDI_DC40-MESTYP	ORDERS	Message type
DC4_STD	EDI_DC40-STD	X	EDI standard
DC4_STDVRS	EDI_DC40-STDVRS	005010	EDI version
DC4_STDMES	EDI_DC40-STDMES	850	EDI transaction
DC4_SNDPOR	EDI_DC40-SNDPOR	XML_IDOC	Sender file port
DC4_SNDPRT	EDI_DC40-SNDPRT	KU	Customer
DC4_SNDPFC	EDI_DC40-SNDPFC	AG	Sold-to partner
DC4_SNDPRN	EDI_DC40-SNDPRN	0001	Gordy's sold-to (department no.)
DC4_SNDLAD	EDI_DC40-SNDLAD		Gordy's EDI sender partner ID

Table 12.5 Arrays to Build and Bundle IDocs in SDQ Process

Input	IDoc Target	Value	Comments
DC4_RCVPOR	EDI_DC40-RCVPOR	SAPDEV	Receiver port
DC4_RCVPRT	EDI_DC40-SNDPRT	LS	Logical system
DC4_RCVPRN	EDI_DC40-SNDPRN	SAPDEV100	Logical client
DC4_RCVLAD	EDI_DC40-RCVLAD		Gordy's EDI receiver partner ID for Acme
DC4_REFINT	EDI_DC40-REFINT		ISA Ctrl number
DC4_REFGRP	EDI_DC40-REFGRP		GS Grp Ctrl number
DC4_REFMES	EDI_DC40-REFMES	850	ST Txn ID
K01_BELNR	E1EDK01-BELNR	990012	Customer PO no.
K14_QUALF	E1EDK14-QUALF	12	Order type
K14_ORGID	E1EDK14-ORGID	ZEDS	EDI SDQ order
K03_IDDAT	E1EDK03-IDDAT	002	Req. delivery date
K03_DATUM	E1EDK03-DATUM		Date
KA1AG	E1EDKA1-PARVW	AG	Sold-to customer
KA1AG_LIFNR	E1EDKA1-LIFNR	0001	Gordy's sold-to (department no.)
KA1LF	E1EDKA1-PARVW	LF	Cust. vendor number
KA1LF_LIFNR	E1EDKA1-LIFNR		Acme GLN
KA1WE	E1EDKA1-PARVW	WE	Cust. ship-to number
KA1WE_LIFNR	E1EDKA1-LIFNR		Gordy ship-to from SDQ segment
K02_QUALF	E1EDK02-QUALF	001	Customer PO
K02_BELNR	E1EDK02-BELNR	990012	PO no.
K02_DATUM	E1EDK02-DATUM	20131215	PO date
IDOC_ITEM Record Line—Item Details 1 to N Looping Group			
P01_POSEX	E1EDPO1-POSEX	0001	Item number

Table 12.5 Arrays to Build and Bundle IDocs in SDQ Process (Cont.)

Input	IDoc Target	Value	Comments
P01_MENGE	E1EDP01-MENGE	50.000	SDQ qty
P01_MENEE	E1EDP01-MENEE	EA	UOM
P01_VPREI	E1EDP01-VPREI		Unit price
P19_QUALF_001	E1EDP19-QUALF	001	Customer item
P19_IDTNR	E1EDP19-IDTNR	9999999	Material number

Table 12.5 Arrays to Build and Bundle IDocs in SDQ Process (Cont.)

So let's give it a try.

12.6 SDQ Processing Program Logic

Our basic working assumption is that the entire 850 input file is available for processing before we map to the ORDERS.ORDERS05 IDoc target file. We also assume that we can declare and loop through indexed arrays in our mapping tool rules or at least that we can call an external program, class file, or script from a user exit in the map.

We'll process the 850 file in three loops with the help of a number of key indexes: one on the transaction, another on each P01 item, and the third on an array created from the SDQ segment within each P01 loop.

The IDocs are built in the flattened build array during the deepest loop, at the SDQ level within each item, after the store location and quantity pairs in the SDQ segments have been moved into an indexed array.

The logical processing flow for creating one ORDERS IDoc for each store in an SDQ 850 PO is outlined in Figure 12.2. Though it seems that there's a lot of stuff happening here, it's not as complex as it might seem.

The code loops through the input one 850 transaction at a time, setting the transaction-level index (TXNIDX) to 1. All other indexes are reset to 0 with each 850 transaction loop. TXNIDX identifies common header data pulled from the current 850 that will be written to the IDOC_HDR record for each IDoc that we build for each store in our SDQ segments.

465

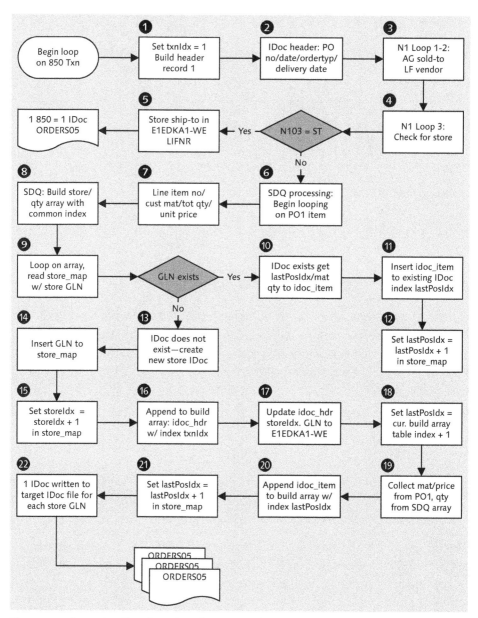

Figure 12.2 Processing Flow for Unbundling SDQ Orders

The BEG segment is read first. Base PO data are moved into the K01 and K02 fields of the IDOC_HDR record using index TXNIDX:

- ▶ BELNR: Customer PO number from BEG03
- ▶ DATUM: PO date from BEG05
- ▶ QUALF: PO qualifier 001

Constant IDoc header values are also passed to the header records:

- ▶ EDI_DC40: All known IDoc control record fields
- ▶ K14: QUALF 012 and ORGID ZEDS

The DTM segment is read next. DTM01 is checked for qualifier 010. If it's found, the following values are written to the K03_002 fields with index TXNIDX:

- ▶ IDDAT: Qualifier 002 identifying the requested delivery date
- ▶ DATUM: Date from DTM02

A translation error is thrown if qualifier 010 isn't found in DTM01. The delivery date is a mandatory field in Acme's SAP system.

The N1 looping group is read next. N103 is checked for qualifiers AG and SU. If found, the sold-to number is passed to KA1AG_LIFNR and the vendor to KA1LF_LIFNR. AG is passed to KA1AG_PARVW and LF to KA1LF-PARVW.

During loop read 3 of the N1 group, N103 is checked for qualifier ST store location. If qualifier ST is found in N103, there are no SDQ segments and standard processing proceeds. One IDoc is generated for each 850 transaction.

If the ST qualifier is not found, loop processing exits and SDQ processing proceeds.

Another loop is kicked off when PO1 is hit. PO1 is the first segment read in the group. The following values are passed from the PO1 segment to the P01 fields of the IDOC_ITEM record:

- ▶ POSEX: Item number from PO101
- ▶ VPREI: Unit price from PO104

The ordered items are passed next to the P19 fields of the IDOC_ITEM record from the PO1 segment of the 850:

- ▶ QUALF_001: Qualifier 001 where PO106 = IN
- ▶ IDTNR: Gordy's material number from PO107

The values that we've collected into our temporary IDoc so far serve as the template that we'll use to build each IDoc for each store and quantity pair in the SDQ segment within the current item loop. These values will be common to all IDocs that we create from this 850 for each store regardless of items and quantity ordered.

Reading the SDQ Segments

Now we come to the fun part. The SDQ segments are read, one at a time. They hold the store locations as GLNs paired with an order quantity for the material in the parent PO1 segment.

Each store location and quantity pair is moved into an indexed array (or an internal table if you're doing this in ABAP) that we'll loop through to create one IDoc for each store. The array could look something like Table 12.6.

Index	GLN	Qty
1	9997495958768	23
2	9997495959876	12
3	9997495960786	6
4	9997495961986	45
5	9997495962686	20

Table 12.6 Indexed Array with Store Order Quantity Pairs

This unravels the SDQ into a tabular structure with one record per store and quantity pair.

We can now loop through this array within our current loop on the 850 PO1 item and match the store and quantity to the material being ordered for it.

All SDQ segments within the PO1 group are processed one at a time during execution in the order they appear in the group. The logic to build the SDQ array would look something like this in pseudo code:

```
IF SDQON IS NOT NULL THEN
  MOVE SDQON TO SDQ_ARRAY COL2
  MOVE SDQONN TO SDQ_ARRAY COL3
  SDQIDX = SDQIDX + 1
  MOVE SDQIDX TO SDQ_ARRAY COL1
```

```
   STORECNT = SDQIDX.
ENDIF.
```

Each store location and quantity pair in each SDQ segment is treated in the same way. SDQ0N is the number of the location-quantity data pairs, beginning with SDQ03 for the store and SDQ04 for the quantity, and ending with SDQ21 for the store and SDQ22 for the quantity.

After all SDQ segments have been read, and the SDQ array built with all store-quantity pairs for the current item, the PO1 loop ends. Before we begin to loop on the next PO1 group, another loop is kicked off on the SDQ array.

This is where we build our IDocs, one for each store, regardless of the number of items ordered by each store.

At the top of each loop of the SDQ array, a Java hash map object or other array or internal table (STORE_MAP) is searched for the store GLN being processed by the current loop pass. STORE_MAP has the GLN number for the store, its STOREIDX, and a LASTPOSIDX that identifies the last row in the IDoc build array that a store record was appended to.

If the store GLN is not found in STORE_MAP, no IDoc exists yet for that store and a new IDoc will be appended to the IDoc build array for the store. But first the GLN is appended to STORE_MAP and a unique STOREIDX assigned to it.

We build the new IDoc by appending every field of IDOC_HDR at index TXNIDX to the IDoc build array. We then move the store's GLN into the KA1WE_LIFNR field and its STORE_MAP index to the STOREIDX field in the new IDOC_HDR. This links the new IDoc to the store location.

Next the item data that were collected from the current 850 PO1 group are written to a new IDOC_ITEM record and the row number of the insert is moved into STORE_MAP-LASTPOSIDX.

The order quantity for that store is then moved from the SDQ array to the PO1_MENGE field and the material number to P19_IDTNR and 001 to P19_QUALF_001.

Each GLN in the current SDQ array is processed in the same way until the last record is reached. If no matching record is found in STORE_MAP, a new IDoc is appended for each GLN. At the end of the PO1 loop, the SDQ array is cleared.

The next PO1 is then read in a loop, if it exists, and a new SDQ array built. If a store GLN is found in STORE_MAP, then an IDoc already exists for that store. We'll append our new IDOC_ITEM data—material number, quantity and unit price—to the existing IDoc in the IDoc build array, identifying the insertion point with the LASTPOSIDX index from STORE_MAP.

The order quantity for the store is then read from the SDQ array and written to the PO1_MENGE field in the IDOC_ITEM record being appended to the existing IDoc with write index LASTPOSIDX.

Listing 12.1 shows pseudo code for this loop. This code is called after the PO1 segment has been processed.

```
loop at sdq_array.
  read store_map for key store_GLN
  if exists get storeIdx lastPostIdx from store_map
    append current idoc_item_p01 fields to existing IDoc
      using index lastPostIdx
    move quantity from SDQ array to
      idoc_item-p01_menge using index lastPostIdx
    lastPostIdx = lastPostIdx + 1
    move lastPostIdx to store_map-lastPostIdx
  else does not exist create new IDoc
    move store GLN to store_map-GLN
    move storeIdx to store_map-storeIdx
    store_map-storeIdx = store_map-storeIdx + 1
    append idoc_hdr fields to build IDoc array

      using index txnIdx
    move store_map-storeIdx to idoc_hdr-storeIdx
    move WE to IDOC_HDR-KA1_WE in new IDoc
      using index current table index
    move store GLN from current SDQ array to
      idoc_hdr-kai_we_lifnr in new IDoc
      using index current IDoc build array index
    append current idoc_item_p01 fields to new IDoc
    move quantity from current SDQ array to
      idoc_item-p01_menge using index
      current IDoc build array index
    copy current idoc_item_p19_002 fields to new IDoc
      using index current IDoc build array index
    copy current idoc_item_p19_001 fields to new IDoc
```

```
      using index current IDoc build array index
    copy current idoc_item_p19_003 fields to new IDoc
      using index current IDoc build array index
    move current IDoc build array index
      to store_map-lastPosIdx
  end if.
endloop
```

Listing 12.1 SDQ Array Loop to Build One IDoc per Store Location

One IDoc for each store location is being assembled in the IDoc build array in memory. All that's left to do is map it to the target ORDER.ORDERS05 structure.

12.7 Duplicate Checking Enhancement

The enhancement for checking duplicates is a straightforward user exit that prevents duplicate custom POs from posting to sales orders in SAP.

The issue here is that if the same PO posts twice for the same store location, double the number of goods that were ordered would be shipped, resulting in higher shipment costs, increased returns, and poor customer service.

There are times when we need to post a customer PO a second time because of errors in an initial transmission that have been fixed. But this scenario will be known in advance, and all sales orders that posted against the initial transmission will be deleted.

The basic rule is that no customer PO should be allowed to post twice to an SAP sales order for the same ship-to partner.

The code will be written in CUSTOMER-FUNCTION '011' in the IDoc processing function IDOC_INPUT_ORDERS.

We'll need to create two objects to enable this enhancement:

▶ Error message flagging the duplicate PO, ship-to partner, and sales order number

▶ CMOD modification project to code the exit

Let's look at each of these.

12.7.1 Create Error Message

We previously created our custom messages in the 900 and above range in standard message class IDOC_ADAPTER. To create our new message, follow these steps:

1. Go to the SAP Repository with Transaction SE80 and click REPOSITORY INFORMATION SYSTEM.

2. Open the folder OTHER OBJECTS.

3. Double-click MESSAGE CLASSES, and enter "IDOC_ADAPTER" in the MESSAGE CLASS field of the STANDARD SELECTIONS screen. Execute.

4. The REPOSITORY INFO SYSTEM: MESSAGE CLASSES FIND screen loads listing the message class.

5. Double-click IDOC_ADAPTER to load the MESSAGE MAINTENANCE screen and click the MESSAGES tab.

6. Click DISPLAY <-> CHANGE (or press [Ctrl]+[F1]) and scroll down to message 904, which should be blank.

7. Enter the following message into 902:

   Duplicate PO & for ship-to & in sales order &.

8. Save the message and assign it to a change request.

12.7.2 Create Modification Project

To create the modification project, follow these steps:

1. Go to CMOD and enter project name "ZEDISOO1". Click CREATE.

2. Enter a description in the SHORT TEXT field of the ATTRIBUTES screen. Save the project and assign it to a change request.

3. Click ENHANCEMENT ASSIGNMENTS to open the enhancements screen. Enter VEDA0001 in the ENHANCEMENT column.

4. Click COMPONENTS and select function set EXIT_SAPLVEDA_011 with function CUSTOMER-FUNCTION '011'.

5. Double-click the exit name to open the exit in the source code editor of the function builder (see Figure 12.3).

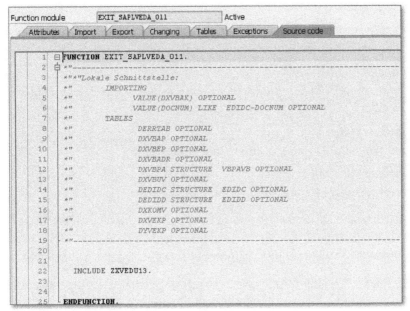

Figure 12.3 EXIT_SAPLVEDA_011 in the Source Code Editor

Notice the import parameters and tables. `CUSTOMER-FUNCTION '011'` is called near the end of `IDOC_INPUT_ORDERS` processing, after all the data required to post the sales order have been extracted from the IDoc and the system, just before the call transaction is executed.

Everything that is going into the sales order is available to the code in the exit.

6. Double-click `ZXVEDU13` to create the include program we'll use to write the code. The system will throw up the message:

Program names ZX... are reserved for includes of exit function groups

7. Press Enter to bypass the message and create the program. You'll be prompted to assign it to a change request.

The ABAP Editor opens to a blank screen.

12.7.3 Program Flow

`CUSTOMER-FUNCTION '011'` has two import and eleven table parameters. For the purposes of this example we are only interested in the following:

- Import parameter `DXVBAK`
  Imports sales order header data into the exit with the structure VBAK, the sales order header table, with a number of additional fields

- Table parameter `DXVBAP`
  Brings sales order item data into the exit with the structure VBAP, including the material number

- Table parameter `XVBPA`
  SAP partner type and ID for all partners in the sales order

- Table parameter `DERRTAB`
  Collects error messages to pass to the IDoc status record

The sold-to partner and customer PO number are pulled from fields KUNNR and BSTKD in XVBAK. The ship-to partner is pulled from field KUNNR in XVBPA where the qualifier PARVW = WE. The material number is pulled from XBAP-MATNR.

The exit reads sales index table VAKPA with the sold-to partner, sales organization, and PO number as the key. The SQL will look like Listing 12.2, where `S_VBELN` is a variable to hold the sales order number.

```
select single vbeln into s_vbeln from vakpa
    where kunde = xvbak-kunnr
      and parvw = AG
      and vkorg = xvbak-vkorg
      and vtweg = xvbak-vtweg
      and spart = xvbak-spart
      and bstnk = xvbak-bstdk.
if sy-subrc <> 0.
  exit. * No dupe end processing.
else.
  check for ship-to partner.
endif.
```

Listing 12.2 Selecting Sales Order from VBAK for Duplicate PO Exit Check

If there is no hit, the PO has not posted for the sold-partner and sales organization, exit processing ends, control returns to the IDoc function, and the call transaction proceeds.

If there is a hit, table VBPA is read with the sales order number pulled from VAKPA and the ship-to number from XVBPA. The code will look something like Listing 12.3.

```
read table xvbpa with key parvw = 'WE'.
if sy-subrc = 0.
  s_kunnr = xvbpa-kunnr
  select single kunnr into s_kunnr from vbpa
      where vbeln = s_vbeln
        and parvw = 'WE'
        and kunnr = s_kunnr.
  if sy-subrc <> 0.
    exit. * No dupe end processing.
  else.
    write error message to derrtab.
  endif.
else.
  exit. * No dupe end processing.
endif.
```

Listing 12.3 Reading the Ship-To Partner for the Sales Order

If there is no hit, the incoming PO has not yet posted for that ship-to partner. There is no duplicate and exit processing ends.

If there is a hit, the customer PO has already posted for that ship-to partner. Next we check whether it posted with the same material number by reading table VBAP with the sales order number, item number, and material number from XVBAP. The SQL will look like Listing 12.4, where S_MATNR is a variable to hold the material number.

```
select single matnr into s_matnr from vbap
    where vbeln = xvbap-vbeln
      and posnr = xvbap-posnr
      and matnr =.xvbap-matnr.
if sy-subrc <> 0.
  exit. * No dupe end processing.
else.
  Error. Dupe PO posting.
endif.
```

Listing 12.4 If the Material Is the Same, It's a Duplicate

If there's no hit, we have no duplicate, and exit processing ends. If we have a hit, however, the PO is treated as a duplicate, and an error is raised. Error message variables are written to internal table DERRTAB, and exit processing ends. The values in Listing 12.5 are passed.

```
DERRTAB-ARBGB = 'IDOC_ADAPTER'.
DERRTAB-CLASS = 'E'.
DERRTAB-MSGNR = '904'.
DERRTAB-MSGV1 = xvbak-bstdk.
DERRTAB-MSGV2 = s_kunnr.
DERRTAB-MSGV3 = s_vbeln.
append DERRTAB.
```

Listing 12.5 Writing the Error Message to DERRTAB

The following happens in Listing 12.5:

- ▸ ARBGB identifies our message class.

- ▸ CLASS identifies the error type.

- ▸ MSGNR is our custom message number.

- ▸ MSGV1 passes the customer PO number to our message.

- ▸ MSGV2 passes the customer SAP ship-to partner from VBPA.

- ▸ MSGV3 passes the sales order number.

12.8   EDI Configuration in SAP

Let's look at configuration settings for the inbound ORDERS message for Gordy's Galaxy.

12.8.1   EDPAR Entries: Transaction VOE4

We'll enter one record for each of Gordy's stores and distribution centers that will send Acme EDI orders into EDPAR, as illustrated in Table 12.7.

Field	Value	Description
KUNNR	GRDY01	Gordy sold-to partner from IDoc
PARVW	WE	Partner function ship-to
EXPNR	0999999999999	External partner for ship-to—Gordy's GLN
INPNR	GRDY010098	Internal SAP ship-to partner number

Table 12.7   One EDPAR Entry for Each of Gordy's Stores

This maps Gordy's sold-to partner, from the control segment of the IDoc to Gordy's store GLN from the N1 or SDQ segments of the 850, to the SAP ship-to partner number in Acme's system.

Because EDPAR isn't linked to any other tables or programs, it can be safely loaded with a custom ABAP that inserts data directly into it. It can also be loaded through an LSMW project or CATT script on Transaction VOE4.

12.8.2 EDSDC Entry: Transaction VOE2

Enter the following record into table EDSDC for Gordy, as in Table 12.8.

Field	Value	Description
KUNNR	GRDY01	Gordy sold-to partner from IDoc
LIFNR	564567	Acme vendor number in Gordy's system
VKORG	3000	Acme sales organization
VTWEG	10	Distribution channel
SPART	00	Division
AUART		Sales order type; ZEDI or ZEDS or ZVMI passed in E1EDK14 (IDoc feeds the document type)

Table 12.8 EDSDC Entry for Gordy's Galaxy

LIFNR is Gordy's number for Acme Studios, although it doesn't have to be. It *does* need to be a number that always comes in the ORDERS IDoc translated from Gordy's 850 PO.

This table entry maps Gordy's sold-to partner to the SAP sales organization that will be used to create the sales order.

12.8.3 ZEDIXREF Entries

We don't need to populate ZEDIXREF for the 852 because it doesn't post to SAP, but we do need to add the information from Table 12.9 to custom table ZEDIXREF for the inbound 850 interface from Gordy.

Field	Value	Description
DIRECT	2	Direction inbound
STDMES	850	EDI PO transaction
MESTYP	ORDERS	IDoc message type
IDOCTP	ORDERS05	IDoc basic type
CIMTYP		IDoc extension, none for this interface
SNDPRN	GRDY01	SAP send partner: Gordy's customer number in Acme's system
RCVPRN	DEVCLNT100	SAP receive partner: Acme SAP logical system
SNDLAD	99934567999	EDI send partner: Gordy's trading partner ID for Gordy
RCVLAD	99999998889	EDI receive partner: Gordy's trading partner ID for Acme

Table 12.9 ZEDIXREF Entry for the Inbound 850 from Gordy

12.8.4 Partner Profile: Transaction WE20

We'll need one inbound partner profile for message type ORDERS for Gordy's Galaxy partner type KU (customer).

In the inbound parameters table, control click CREATE and add the following values to the inbound parameters screen:

► PARTNER ROLE: "SP" for sold-to partner

► MESSAGE TYPE: "ORDERS"

► PROCESS CODE: "ORDE"

► PROCESSING BY FUNCTION MODULE: TRIGGER BY BACKGROUND PROGRAM option

Process code ORDE links to processing function IDOC_INPUT_ORDERS and message type ORDERS.

Don't forget to save. The finished inbound parameters should look like Figure 12.4.

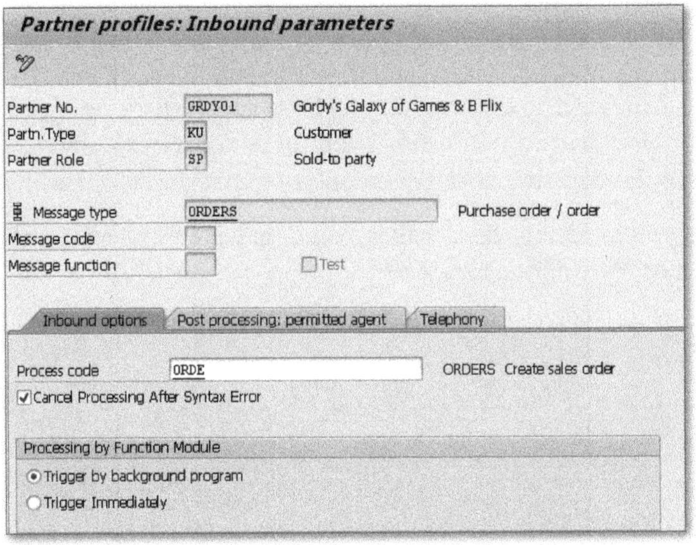

Figure 12.4 Inbound Partner Profile for Gordy's Sales Orders

12.9 Summary

So we've been through the first interface in the order-to-cash sales cycle. We still have miles to go before we can bank the cash for the saleable goods that Gordy's Galaxy of Games & B Flix ordered from us.

The key wrinkle that we had to iron out is common to EDI ordering, at least in the X12 world, which is that a large customer such as Gordy's Galaxy—with its more than 2,000 North American stores—orders for every store that needs product with one purchase order.

The quantity ordered is paired up the store number in an SDQ segment at the line-item level. But to post the sales order in SAP, our basic rule is one sold-to and one ship-to partner.

So we had to look at code that would unravel the single purchase order sent by Gordy into one sales order for each store location. One important lesson from our approach to unbundling Gordy's purchase order is that EDI is an integrated ecosystem with multiple parts, and each one plays its role. We could have just as easily mapped the SDQ purchase order to an extended IDoc and then unraveled the SDQ with an ABAP program. But we chose to do it by writing code in the map in the EDI system. The complexity and effort involved is about the same. It's just different.

Of course, there are many ways to do everything. Please consider the approach we take for any of our interfaces only a starting point for your own explorations. There are no answers, only suggestions. And questions, of course, just like real life.

So with that thought, let's tackle our next challenge and move this cycle one step further: the outbound order confirmation.

"You don't know what you don't know," the great Mr. Q used to say. And that's true for Gordy's Galaxy when Acme posts a VMI order. Whether VMI or not, the customer needs to know that his order will be delivered by a particular date. And that's the job of the ORDRSP order confirmation interface. But this one has an interesting twist.

13   Building the Outbound Order Confirmation

In the previous chapter, we saw that two types of customer purchase orders (VMI and non-VMI) post to Acme's SAP system and that both types of PO post to sales orders in SAP, one for each store receiving product.

The customer needs confirmation when his purchase order posts to a sales order in the supplier's system. The confirmation tells him whether the supplier can provide the ordered product (or offers an alternative) by a target delivery date. This is done by transmitting an X12 855 EDI transaction.

Although the technical process for the acknowledgment is the same for both types of orders, the 855 is particularly critical for a VMI customer such as Gordy's Galaxy of Games & B Flix. It's the only way that Gordy knows what has been ordered for his stores.

The 855 confirmation for a VMI order creates the purchase order in Gordy's system. As far as VMI is concerned, there is no order in the customer system until the 855 is received. So it's critical that Gordy, Acme's most important customer, get his 855.

This is generally a straightforward process, but here we have an interesting issue with SDQ orders that provides us an opportunity to think creatively and gives us further insight into how EDI and the IDoc interface works.

So let's proceed with development of Acme's 855 order confirmation interface with Gordy.

13.1   Technical Overview

Table 13.1 summarizes the outbound purchase order acknowledgment.

Item	Description
Title	Purchase Order Confirmation
Description	A purchase order confirmation is generated after a customer PO has been received and posted to a sales order. It includes all the data in the sales order, including any changes that may have been made to the order materials, quantities, or delivery dates. SDQ orders that create multiple sales orders will be bundled into a single PO confirmation.
Type of interface	Sales: IDoc to X12 EDI
Direction	Outbound
Trading partner	Gordy's Galaxy (customer)
IDoc	ORDRSP.ORDERS05
IDoc extended type	ORDRSP.ZORSDQ01
IDoc function	`IDOC_OUTPUT_ORDERS`
Custom ABAP	`ZEDI_ORDRSPSDQ`
Description	Bundles all IDocs with message code SDQ into one extended IDoc with an SDQ segment and sends them to the EDI RIM
Target file(s)	X12 855 no SDQ, 855 with SDQ
Source document(s)	SAP sales order
Transaction code	VA01
Map(s)	ORDRSP.ORDERS05 to X12 855 vers. 5010 ORDRSP.ZORSDQ01 to X12 855 vers. 5010
Custom map logic	
Source system	Acme SAP
Target system	Gordy's Galaxy EDI via AS2 from Acme EDI RIM

Table 13.1   Overview of Outbound PO Confirmation Interface

Item	Description
997 acknowledgment	Inbound within 24 hours of transmission at the transaction detail level. Function group acknowledgment code: PR.
Frequency	Daily, on demand
Job schedule	RSEOUT00: Every hour, sends all non-SDQ ORDRSP message types to Gordy ZEDI_ORDRSPSDQ: Every hour, bundles and sends all SDQ ORDRSP

Table 13.1 Overview of Outbound PO Confirmation Interface (Cont.)

13.2   Functional Specifications

Sales orders are created manually or through EDI transmission from VMI and non-VMI partners. EDI and VMI orders must be acknowledged through X12 855 EDI transmissions back to the customer's system.

When a sales order is created and saved in SAP, an ORDRSP.ORDERS05 IDoc is generated with all the data in the sales order. The IDoc is then mapped to an X12 855 transaction in the EDI RIM.

Customers that send POs in 850 transactions with their store location and quantity data in SDQ segments receive only one 855 with SDQ segments that bundle all sales orders for all ship-to partners, not one confirmation for each sales order.

A custom ABAP will bundle all sales orders created from an SDQ order into one IDoc with a custom SDQ segment. Gordy's Galaxy sends both SDQ and non-SDQ orders, so it gets both types of acknowledgment.

13.2.1   Process Overview

The process begins when a sales order is created in SAP. An order response message type ORDRSP with basic type ORDERS05 is generated and parked in the IDoc database.

Two types of IDocs are generated:

▶ ORDRSP message type with no message code. One 855 is created for one sales order and ORDRSP IDoc.

- ORDRSP message type with message code SDQ. A custom ABAP report collects SDQ IDocs and bundles them into one ORDRSP IDoc against one customer PO number with SDQ segments. The program then sends the bundled extended IDoc to the EDI RIM.

13.2.2 Requirements

The interface will meet the following functional requirements:

- Several order types are created in the IMG for EDI sales orders that will be acknowledged with an ORDRSP message:
  - ZEDI: EDI orders with no SDQ in the inbound 850
  - ZEDS: EDI orders with SDQ store locations in the inbound 850
  - ZVMI: VMI suggested orders from the VMI system
- Sales orders for Gordy's Galaxy are created in SAP from POs sent in 850 EDI transactions or suggested orders from the VMI system using one of the custom EDI order types.
- Order acknowledgments are generated as ORDRSP IDocs by message control when the sales order has been created.
- The sales order must pass a credit check on the customer before the confirmation is output.
- The order confirmation IDoc will contain all the data in the sales order. One ORDRSP will be created for each sales order.
- ORDRSP IDocs will be parked and processed by scheduled jobs.
- The message code field in the control segment determines what happens next. ORDRSP IDocs with no message code were created by inbound orders without SDQ segments. They are sent directly to the EDI system by running program RSEOUT00 by a scheduled job.
- ORDRSP IDocs with message code SDQ in the control record are picked up by a custom ABAP that does the following:
  - Selects IDocs by SAP sold-to partner, PO number, and message code
  - Creates one new ORDRSP IDoc of extended type ZORSDQ01 with SDQ segments per sold-to partner and PO number
  - Moves all ordered quantities for each store into multiple line items by material in the SDQ segments

- ► Sends the consolidated ORDRSP SDQ IDoc to the EDI RIM for mapping to an 855 X12 transaction and transmission to Gordy
  - ► Marks the original ORDRSP IDocs with the SDQ message code in the control segment for deletion by changing their status to 31
- ► Deliveries are generated by the delivery due list after sales orders are created and acknowledgments are sent to the customer.

13.2.3 Dependencies

The interface is dependent on the existence of the following objects:

- ► Master data to support creation of sales orders plus EDPAR mapping from SAP ship-to to Gordy's GLN store numbers
- ► IDoc extension ZORSDQ01 with an SDQ segment at the item level is created
- ► IDoc configuration in SAP to support generating and sending outbound acknowledgments for Gordy's Galaxy, including the following:
  - ► Linking extended type ZORSDQ01 to ORDRSP.ORDERS05
  - ► Copy process code SD10 to ZD10 and add an entry for message type ORDRSP with message code SDQ
  - ► Message control configured to generate IDoc output for SDQ and non-SDQ ORDRSP from sales orders
  - ► Outbound partner profiles for message type ORDRSP
- ► EDI map for the 855 and ORDRSP message type that can handle SDQ and non-SDQ IDocs
- ► Business process workflow in the EDI RIM that will pick up ORDRSP IDocs, convert them to 855s, and send them to Gordy's Galaxy

13.2.4 Assumptions

The following basic assumptions apply:

- ► All customers who send EDI or VMI purchase orders receive an 855 order acknowledgment.
- ► Only finished goods are sent in the ORDRSP.

▶ Gordy's gets GLNs for all sold-to and ship-to locations in the 855.

▶ The IDoc can be regenerated from the sales order if required.

13.2.5 Data That Will Pass to an Outbound Order Confirmation

The ORDRSP IDoc is generated when the sales order is created and saved by Transaction VA01. Table 13.2 displays some of the many fields in the sales order that are passed to the ORDRSP IDoc.

Table	Field	Description	Sample Value
Order Header			
VBAK	VBELN	Sales order number	0000012780
VBAK	AUART	Order type	ZEDI
VBAK	WAERK	Document currency	USD
VBAK	VKORG	Sales organization	0010
VBAK	VTWEG	Distribution channel	10
VBAK	SPART	Division	00
VBKD	ZTERM	Terms of payment key	Z123
VBPA	PARVW	Sold-to partner function	AG
VBPA	KUNNR	Sold-to partner	GRDY01
VBPA	PARVW	Ship-to partner function	WE
VBPA	KUNNR	Ship-to partner	GRDY01001
VBPA	PARVW	Bill-to partner	RE
VBPA	KUNNR	Bill-to partner	GRDY01
VBPA	PARVW	Payer partner function	RG
VBPA	KUNNR	Payer partner	GRDY01001
VBKD	BSTNK	Customer PO number	989898
VBKD	BSTDK	PO date	20131215
VBAK	AUDAT	Sales order document date	20131215

Table 13.2 Sales Order Data That Will Pass to the ORDRSP IDoc

Table	Field	Description	Sample Value
VBKD	PRSDT	Pricing date	20131215
VBAK	VDATU	Requested delivery date	20140115
VBAK	VSBED	Shipping conditions	03
VBKD	INCO1	Inco terms 1	PPD
VBKD	INCO2	Inco terms 2	Destination
Order Items			
VBAP	KWMENG	Order quantity	1
VBAP	MEINS	Unit of measure	EA
KOMP	NETWR	Item net price	12.50
KOMV	KBETR	Unit price	12.50
VBAP	MATKL	Material group	001
VBAP	ANTLF	Maximum no. partial deliveries	9
VBKD	FKDAT	Billing date	20131215
VBEP	EDATU	Scheduled delivery date	20140115
VBEP	WMENG	Scheduled delivery quantity	6
VBAP	MATNR	SAP material number	2356784
VBAP	EAN11	UPC item number	799142939512

Table 13.2 Sales Order Data That Will Pass to the ORDRSP IDoc (Cont.)

Almost everything in the sales order ends up in the IDoc, but not all values are mapped to the 855 sent to Gordy.

13.2.6 Custom Enhancements

Two key enhancements are required to complete the interface:

▶ Extended basic type ZORSDQ01 to IDoc basic type ORDERS05 with an SDQ segment at the line-item level below E1EDP01.

The custom SDQ segment will follow the same structure for the store number quantity pairs as the standard EDI 855 SDQ segment.

▶ A custom ABAP report will read parked ORDRSP IDocs with message code SDQ, group them by SAP sold-to partner and customer PO number, and bundle them into one outbound ORDRSP IDoc for translation to one 855 order confirmation.

Custom Report to Build and Output ORDRSP with SDQ

The custom IDoc bundling report is called ZEDI_ORDRSPSDQ and will be accessed by Transaction ZSDQ. The following are selection options for the program:

▶ IDoc number

▶ IDoc receive partner (SAP sold-to)

▶ IDoc create date and time

▶ IDoc change date and time

The program collects IDocs at status 30 — *IDoc ready for dispatch* — with message code SDQ in EDIDC-MESCOD.

When all selected IDocs have been collected and bundled into the new SDQ ORDRSP by sold-to partner and purchase order number, the program returns an ABAP List Viewer list (ALV) report with all bundled SDQ IDocs. The report has a header and records linked by the SDQ IDoc number.

The report header fields include the following:

▶ IDoc number of bundled SDQ ORDRSP

▶ SAP receive partner

▶ IDoc output date (change date at time of output)

▶ Customer PO number

The report detail record fields include the following:

▶ IDoc number of individual IDocs generated from each sales order

▶ SAP ship-to partner

▶ SAP sales order number

▶ IDoc status code and message

ZEDI_ORDRSPSDQ will be run by the SAP Job Scheduler every half hour throughout the day. Users will also be able to run it on-demand through Transaction ZSDQ.

13.2.7   Reconciliation Procedure

Data in the ORDRSP IDoc will be validated against the sales order. Store item order quantities will be validated in the bundled SDQ IDoc against the item data in the single IDocs that were generated from each sales order.

IDoc data will also be validated against the translated 855. Data in the outbound 855 will be validated against the original inbound PO, whether it is an 850 or a VMI order.

The EDI team will confirm that the 855 was sent to the correct customer.

13.2.8   Errors and Error Handling

Failures in outbound IDoc processing are tracked by the EDI support team using standard IDoc monitoring tools such as BD87 and WE05. Application errors are reported to the business users immediately.

Custom code will trap all relevant errors by checking SY-SUBRC after each operation that can change the return value. Critical errors will return meaningful messages identifying the condition that terminated processing.

Sales orders that do not successfully pass all checks can be manually posted to generate an order acknowledgment.

Confirmations must be sent within a very tight time frame. Errors will be addressed by the interface owner immediately.

13.3   Generating the ORDRSP with Message Control

The outbound PO confirmation is generated by message control when the sales order is created. Before we can outline the path of the IDoc from the sales order outbound, we'll look at the message control configuration that we need for both standard and SDQ order confirmations.

13.3.1   Message Control Configuration for the ORDRSP

The good news is that we use essentially the same output configuration for the SDQ and non-SDQ IDocs, although we do need a custom output type. We'll also make some adjustments to the standard output type and extend the process to include message codes SDQ and 855.

The non-SDQ ORDRSP order confirmation is a standard IDoc generated with standard message control configuration and no customization.

The SDQ order confirmation process, on the other hand, uses two IDocs:

▶ A standard ORDRSP IDoc identified by message code SDQ

▶ An extended IDoc that will be processed and distributed by a custom ABAP program, not by message control

We'll need the following message control objects:

▶ Output type BA00 with a new access sequence and all supporting configuration and condition records to output confirmations from one sales order to one purchase order

▶ Custom output type ZBA0 copied from BA00 and all supporting configuration and condition records to support output of confirmations from multiple sales orders to one purchase order with SDQ segments

▶ Process code SD10 extended for ORDRSP with MESCOD SDQ

▶ Three partner profiles for Gordy's Galaxy and message type ORDRSP:

    ▶ One with standard message control for the confirmation from one sales order to one PO

    ▶ One with MESCOD SDQ and with a custom output type to identify multiple confirmations from multiple sales orders for one PO

    ▶ One with MESCOD 855 and no message control to identify the bundled sales orders IDoc extended with an SDQ segment that will be distributed by a custom program

Setting up Output Control: BA00

1. Run Transaction NACE.

2. Select Application V1 Sales, and click Output types. Click the pencil icon (or press [Ctrl]+[F4]) to switch to change mode.

3. Select output type BA00 and double-click to open the Output Type Details screen for editing.

4. Change the ACCESS SEQUENCE to 0009: Sales organization, customer, and order type.

5. Access number is 1 for condition table B150 and communications structure KOMKBV1 with key fields:

  ▶ AUART: Sales document type

  ▶ VKORG: Sales organization

  ▶ KUNNR: Sold-to customer party

6. Set the MULTIPLE ISSUING flag, which allows you to resend the same output. The completed screen should look like Figure 13.1.

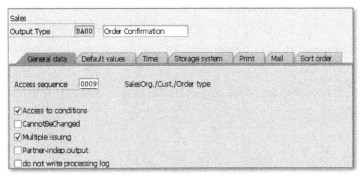

Figure 13.1 Changes to Standard Output Type BA00

7. Click the DEFAULT VALUES tab and enter the following values. Default values entered in this tab can be overridden. You can still generate print or any other type of output with BA00 (Figure 13.2).

Figure 13.2 Changes to the Default Values Subscreen

  ▶ DISPATCH TIME field: SEND IMMEDIATELY (WHEN SAVING THE APPLICATION) option

▶ TRANSMISSION MEDIUM field: EDI option

▶ PARTNER FUNCTION field: "SP"

8. Save output type BA00 and assign it to a change request.

9. Double-click the PROCESSING ROUTINES folder in the OUTPUT TYPES navigation panel. Confirm that EDI with program RSNASTED is entered in the PROCESSING ROUTINES table control.

10. If it is not, click the NEW ENTRIES button and enter the following values:

▶ TRANSM. MEDIUM: "EDI"

▶ PROGRAM in PROCESSING 1: "RSNASTED"

▶ FORM ROUTINE: "EDI_PROCESSING"

11. Save any changes. Double-click the PARTNER FUNCTIONS folder and confirm that the PARTNER FUNCTIONS table control has an entry for EDI with partner function SP.

12. If it does not, click NEW ENTRIES and add the following values to the table control:

▶ MEDIUM: "EDI"

▶ FUNCT.: "SP" for sold-to partner

13. Save any changes. Back out to the CONDITIONS FOR OUTPUT CONTROL screen of Transaction NACE. Select APPLICATION V1 and click PROCEDURES. Output type BA00 is assigned to procedure V10000 ORDER OUTPUT.

14. Select procedure V10000 and double-click the CONTROL folder in the PROCE-DURES navigation panel. We'll use the standard settings.

Copy BA00 to ZBA0

Once we've configured output type BA00, we'll copy to our custom output ZBA0. This will ensure a unique message control entry in the partner profile for ORDRSP with MESCOD SDQ.

1. In the initial screen for output control, select application V1 and click OUTPUT TYPES.

2. Select menu path TABLE VIEW • DISPLAY • CHANGE (or press `Ctrl`+`F1`) and then select output BA00. Click COPY AS or press `F6`.

3. Change the name of the output type to ZBA0 and enter a description for the SDQ order confirmation.

4. Press ⌜Enter⌝. The SPECIFY OBJECT TO BE COPIED dialog opens with the observation that the output type has dependent entries. Click COPY ALL. Another dialog opens with the number of dependent entries.

5. The system returns to the OUTPUT TYPES: OVERVIEW screen. You've copied all dependent entries from BA00 so you don't have to do anything further here. Check to confirm that EDI processing routines and partner functions are set up.

6. Back out to the initial screen for output control. Next, assign the custom output type to the procedure. Select application V1 and click PROCEDURES.

7. Select procedure V10000 and double-click the control folder in the navigation pane.

8. Select BA00 and click the COPY AS button (or press ⌜F6⌝). Change the step number to 15 and the output type name to ZBA0, but leave everything else the same.

9. Press ⌜Enter⌝ to return to the overview screen. Save the entry and assign it to a change request.

We now have our two output types and will need to create condition records against each one.

Condition Records: BA00

We can add the condition records for Gordy with Transaction VV11 or directly within NACE. In VV11:

1. Enter "BA00" into OUTPUT TYPE and click KEY COMBINATION.

2. Select the radio button for the DOCTYPE./SALESORG/CUSTOMER access sequence and click OK (see Figure 13.3).

Figure 13.3 Access Sequence 0001 in the Key Combination Dialog

3. Enter three records for Gordy into the CREATE CONDITION RECORDS screen, one for each EDI order type. Enter the following values for the first (these will differ from organization to organization):
   - SALES DOCUMENT TYPE: "ZEDI"
   - SALES ORGANIZATION: "3000"
   - SOLD-TO PT: "GRDY01"
   - FUNCT: "SP"
   - MEDIUM: "6"
   - DATE: "4"
   - LANGUAGE: "EN"
4. Save the record. The last two records are the same except for the document types ZEDS and ZVMI.
5. Confirm the condition record entries in table B150 in the data browser, Transaction SE16. It should look something like Figure 13.4.

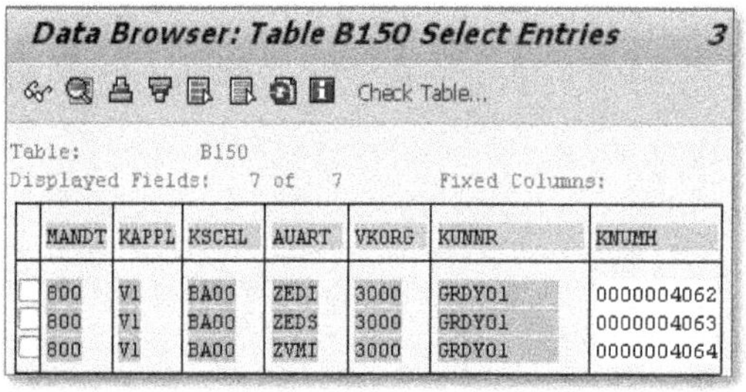

MANDT	KAPPL	KSCHL	AUART	VKORG	KUNNR	KNUMH
800	V1	BA00	ZEDI	3000	GRDY01	0000004062
800	V1	BA00	ZEDS	3000	GRDY01	0000004063
800	V1	BA00	ZVMI	3000	GRDY01	0000004064

Figure 13.4 Condition Records in Table B150 for BA00 by Order Type

Repeat this process for output type ZBA0. The condition records are the same except for the output type.

Extending Process Code SD10

We'll extend process code SD10 to handle ORDRSP messages with SDQ and 855 in the MESCOD field to give us unique partner profile keys for both of our special case order confirmations.

1. Go to Transaction WE41 or through the WEDI area menu DEVELOPMENT • OUTBOUND PROCESSING SETTINGS M/C • OUTBOUND PROCESS CODE.

2. Click the Display • Change pencil icon (or press `Ctrl`+`F1`), select process code SD10, and double-click the Logical message folder in the navigation pane.

3. Click the New Entries button (or press `F5`) to open the Details of Added Entries screen. Add the following values:

   ▶ Message type: "ORDRSP"

   ▶ Message code: "SDQ"

4. Save and assign the entries to a change request.

5. Back in the initial change view screen, select ZD10 and double-click the Logical message icon. Click New Entries (or press `F5`) to open the Details of Added Entries screen.

6. Enter the following values and save process code ZD10. Assign it to a change request.

   ▶ Message type: "ORDRSP"

   ▶ Message code: "SDQ"

7. Back out of the added entries screen and repeat the process to add MESCOD 855 to logical message ORDRSP. The finished screen should look like Figure 13.5.

Process code	SD10						
Logical message							
Message Type	All types	Msg. Var.	All codes	Msg.funct.	All functions		
ORDRSP	☐		☐		☐		
ORDRSP	☐	855	☐		☐		
ORDRSP	☐	SDQ	☐		☐		

Figure 13.5 Process Code ME10 Extended for All Three IDocs

13.3.2 Overview of the End-to-End Process Flow

Figure 13.6 outlines the end-to-end process flow for generating and sending a purchase order confirmation to Gordy's Galaxy.

The process begins when an ORDERS IDoc creates a sales order in SAP against sales organization 3000 (USA Los Angeles) and order type ZEDI (non-SDQ), ZEDS, or ZVMI (both SDQ). The SAP sold-to partner is the third critical key; in this case, that is Gordy's Galaxy, or customer GRDY01.

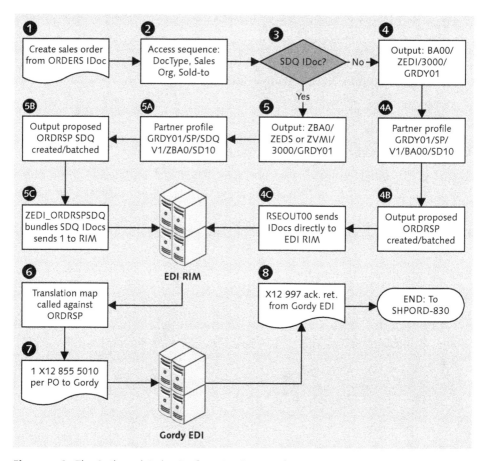

Figure 13.6 The Outbound Order Confirmation Process Flow

All output control keys, including application, procedure, output type, and access sequence, are determined before the sales order is created by the IDoc's call to Transaction VA01 (program SAPMV45A).

Output control keys are identified and an output record prepared for table NAST by the functions COMMUNICATION_AREA_KOMKBV1 and MESSAGING that are called before the sales order is posted by function RV_SALES_DOCUMENT_ADD.

The following are the output control keys for the order confirmation:

▸ Application V1: Sales document

▸ Output type BA00 or ZBA0: Order confirmation for standard or SDQ purchase orders

- Access Sequence 0009: Sales organization, order type, and sold-to partner number
- Access number 1: SD document type, sales organization, and customer number in condition table B150
- Procedure V10000: Order output linked to output type BA00 and ZBA0
- Requirement 2: Order confirmation

The access key—that is, the sales document type, sales organization, and sold-to partner—is passed to communications structure KOMKBV1 from the sales order.

The condition table is read with the output type, BA00 or ZBA0, and the access keys. Since we've entered one condition record for each output and order type, we'll get a hit if the sales order was created against one of our document types.

Gordy's outbound partner profile is then checked by a call to function EDI_PART-NER_READ_OUTGOING through the key fields in structure EDK12:

- RCVPRN: Receiver partner sold-to number: GRDY01
- RCVPRT: Receiver partner type: KU (customer)
- RCVPFC: Receiver partner function: SP (AG—sold-to partner)
- KAPPL: Message control application: V1
- KSCHL: Message type: BA00 or ZBA0

Two partner profiles are set up with message type ORDRSP for the IDocs coming out of the sales order. The difference is the MESCOD key in table EDP13. MESCOD values are null for orders with no SDQ processing and SDQ for orders with SDQ processing (Figure 13.7).

Figure 13.7 Message Code SDQ Triggers SDQ Processing

Both message types are linked to the same function module through the same process code—IDOC_OUTPUT_ORDRSP. Both will be recognized and generated from the sales order in the same way, although using different output types, via the following process:

1. IDoc output is proposed and saved in an output record in table NAST.

2. An ORDRSP.ORDERS05 IDoc is created immediately and batched in the IDoc database at status 30 — *IDoc ready for dispatch.*

3. If the IDoc is generated from a sales order of order type ZEDS or ZVMI, then EDIDC-MESCOD is set to SDQ.

4. Likewise, if the IDoc is generated from a sales order of order type ZEDI, then EDIDC-MESCOD remains null.

The control segments must match the key values in the partner profile.

If EDIDC-MESCOD is null, then the IDoc is processed by standard output program RSEOUT00, which runs every half hour, collects all of Gordy's outbound ORDRSP IDocs at status 30, and sends them to the EDI RIM.

If EDIDC-MESCOD equals SDQ, then the following actions are triggered by a scheduled job that runs every half hour:

1. Custom program ZEDI_ORDRSPSDQ picks up all of Gordy's outbound ORDRSP IDocs at status 30 where EDIDC-MESCOD equals SDQ and EDIDC-SNDPRN equals GRDY01.

2. Gordy's PO number is read from each IDoc. Regardless of whether the PO number exists in only one or more IDocs, all are bundled into one ORDRSP IDoc with extension ZORSDQ01 for each sold-to-PO number combination.

3. Store order quantity information for each material is bundled into one or more SDQ segments at the E1EDP01 item group level, and the new IDoc is written to the IDoc database at status 30.

4. The old IDocs are marked for deletion by changing their status to 31 — *Error, no further processing.*

5. The MESCOD of the control record in the new IDoc is set to 855.

6. Function MASTER_IDOC_DISTRIBUTE is called to send the new bundled SDQ IDoc to the EDI RIM.

7. The IDoc is saved as an XML file on the SAP application server. The system then makes an RFC through the JCo connector to the receiving business process in the EDI RIM.

8. The IDoc file is picked up and moved to the translation process, which identifies the envelopes from the EDI send and receive trading partner IDs and the EDI transaction and version in the IDoc control segment.

9. The ST envelope identifies and calls the translation map, which converts the SDQ IDoc is then converted to an X12 855 version 5010 transaction set with an ST envelope.

10. The ST transaction set is bundled into a group with a GS envelope. The group is then bundled into an interchange with an ISA envelope.

11. The X12 interchange is passed to the communications process, which sends it to Gordy's EDI system through an AS2 call, and waits for the MDN acknowledgment, which comes immediately.

12. The process ends when Gordy sends back a 997 FA, which generally happens within an hour.

13. If there's an application error in the 855, Gordy immediately sends back X12 824 application advice with information about the issue. Fixing the issue in the order usually involves some communication between the two partners and regenerating the confirmation.

No shipping orders are sent to Disc Services International until all issues are resolved.

13.4   Technical Specifications

This technical specification describes an IDoc extended type with custom processing program, function, and configuration to support generation of non-SDQ and SDQ ORDRSP message types for transmission to customers as confirmation of purchase orders posted.

13.4.1   Technical Requirements

The following objects must be developed to support this interface:

▶ IDoc Extension ZORSDQ01 for message type ORDRSP and basic type ORDERS05 with a custom X12 SDQ segment

- ABAP program `ZEDI_ORDRSPSDQ` to select and bundle all ORDERSP IDocs at status 30 where EDIDC-MESCOD equals SDQ into one ZORSDQ01 extended IDoc type by sold-to partner and customer PO for transmission to the EDI RIM

13.4.2 Dependencies

This interface is dependent on the following:

- Message control configuration is complete and condition records have been created.

- An outbound partner profile is created for each of Gordy's ORDRSP message types with MESCOD values null, SDQ, and 855.

- Outbound envelopes set up in the EDI RIM for Gordy's 855 version 5010 EDI order confirmation.

- Inbound envelopes set up for 997 functional acknowledgments from Gordy

- Custom cross-reference table ZEDIXREF populated in SAP to get the EDI send and receiving trading partner IDs for the outbound 855 to Gordy

- Variants created for jobs in the SAP Job Scheduler (Transaction SM36) to run:

  - `RSEOUT00` to export non-SDQ ORDRSP IDocs to the EDI RIM

  - `ZEDI_ORDRSPSDQ` to bundle SDQ IDocs into a single extended IDoc by sold-to partner and PO number with store location and order quantity data in an SDQ segment, and to send them to the EDI RIM

13.4.3 Assumptions

The following assumptions are behind this interface:

- All SDQ processing will done in SAP by a custom ABAP program. The map in the EDI RIM will not do SDQ processing except to map the SDQ values from the IDoc to the 855.

- EDI errors will be tracked and addressed in the EDI system.

- Technical errors in the IDoc interface, such as syntax or partner profile errors, will be tracked and corrected by the EDI team.

13.4.4 Extended IDoc Type ZORSDQ01

The IDoc extended type ZORSDQ01 will be created and linked to message type ORDRSP and basic type ORDERS05.

ZORSDQ01 will be copied from basic type ORDERS05 and extended with a custom SDQ segment immediately below, and as a child to, line-item level parent segment E1EDP01.

13.4.5 Creating the Extended IDoc Type

Creating our extended IDoc type ZORSDQ01 is a three-step process:

1. Create and release the custom segment.
2. Create and release the extended type with the custom segment as a child of E1EDP01.
3. Link the new extended type to message type ORDRSP and basic type ORDERS05.

In addition, we'll take a fourth optional step and create a view that restricts the segments used in the extended type.

Let's walk through all of these steps.

Creating Custom Segment Z1PSDQ

The first step is create our custom SDQ segment in the Segment Editor.

1. Use Transaction WE31 to get to the Segment Editor or follow WEDI area menu path DEVELOPMENT • IDOC SEGMENTS.
2. Enter the name of the custom segment Z1PSDQ in the SEGMENT TYPE field and click CREATE (or press F5).
3. When the CREATE SEGMENT DEFINITION screen opens, enter a description of the new segment in the SHORT DESCRIPTION field.
4. The structure of the IDoc SDQ segment will mirror the structure of the standard X12 SDQ segment, with ten pairs of store location order quantity data. Enter the fields from Table 13.3 into the Segment Editor table control.

Pos	Field	Data Element	Description
01	MENEE	EDI_MENEE	Order unit of measure
02	QUALF	EDI_QUALFI	Location type qualifier (UL for GLN)
03	EXPNR1	EDI_EXPNR	Customer store number (GLN)
04	MENGE1	EDI_MENGE	Order quantity
05	EXPNR2	EDI_EXPNR	Customer store number (GLN)
06	MENGE2	EDI_MENGE	Order quantity
07	EXPNR3	EDI_EXPNR	Customer store number (GLN)
08	MENGE3	EDI_MENGE	Order quantity
09	EXPNR4	EDI_EXPNR	Customer store number (GLN)
10	MENGE4	EDI_MENGE	Order quantity
11	EXPNR5	EDI_EXPNR	Customer store number (GLN)
12	MENGE5	EDI_MENGE	Order quantity
13	EXPNR6	EDI_EXPNR	Customer store number (GLN)
14	MENGE6	EDI_MENGE	Order quantity
15	EXPNR7	EDI_EXPNR	Customer store number (GLN)
16	MENGE7	EDI_MENGE	Order quantity
17	EXPNR8	EDI_EXPNR	Customer store number (GLN)
18	MENGE8	EDI_MENGE	Order quantity
19	EXPNR9	EDI_EXPNR	Customer store number (GLN)
20	MENGE9	EDI_MENGE	Order quantity
21	EXPNR10	EDI_EXPNR	Customer store number (GLN)
22	MENGE10	EDI_MENGE	Order quantity

Table 13.3 Custom Segment Z1PSDQ Exactly Mirrors the X12 SDQ

The unit of measure will always be EA (eaches) and the location type qualifier for Gordy's stores is always UL for GLN.

5. Save the custom SDQ segment, and assign it to a change request. The completed table control should look like Figure 13.8.

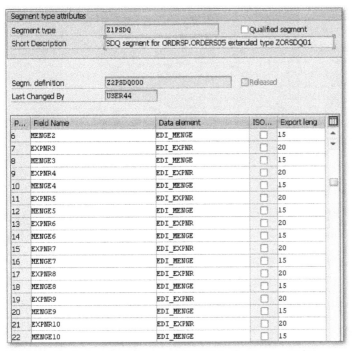

Figure 13.8 Custom SDQ Segment Z1PSDQ in the Segment Editor

6. Back out of the Segment Editor to the initial screen and release the new SDQ segment by selecting menu option EDIT • SET RELEASE.

Extending a Basic Type with a Custom Segment

We're ready to build our extended type in the IDoc type editor.

1. To get to the IDoc type editor, use Transaction WE30 or follow WEDI area menu path DEVELOPMENT • IDOC TYPES.

2. Enter the name of extended type ZORSDQ01 in the OBJ. NAME field and select EXTENSION in the DEVELOPMENT OBJECT group. Click CREATE (or press F5).

3. Select CREATE NEW in the NEW EXTENSION area and enter "ORDERS05" in the LINKED BASIC TYPE field.

4. Enter a short description in the DESCRIPTION field. When the screen looks like Figure 13.9, click OK.

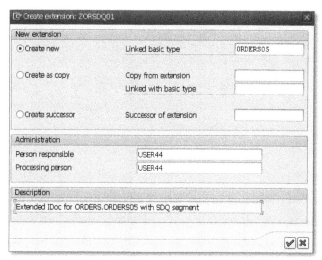

Figure 13.9 Create Extension Screen for Extended Type ZORSDQ01

5. The main screen of the IDoc type editor opens. Select segment E1EDP01. Move the cursor to the folder and it will turn into a hand pointer. Click on the folder to expand the group.

6. Click CREATE segment. The system informs you that the new segment will be inserted as a child of E1EDP01.

7. Click OK to open the MAINTAIN ATTRIBUTES screen. Enter the following values, as shown in Figure 13.10.

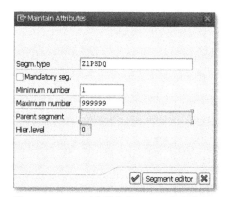

Figure 13.10 Add SDQ Segment Z1PSDQ to Extended Type ZORSDQ01

- Enter "Z1PSDQ" in the SEGM.TYPE field. Do not check MANDATORY SEG. checkbox.

- Enter "1" in the MINIMUM NUMBER field.

- Enter "999999" in the MAXIMUM NUMBER field.

8. Click the OK green checkmark in the MAINTAIN ATTRIBUTES screen above to add the segment. The new segment is shown as a child of E1EDP01, as shown in Figure 13.11.

ZORSDQ01	Extended IDoc for ORDERS.ORDERS05 with SDQ segment
E1EDK01	IDoc: Document header general data
E1EDK14	IDoc: Document Header Organizational Data
E1EDK03	IDoc: Document header date segment
E1EDK04	IDoc: Document header taxes
E1EDK05	IDoc: Document header conditions
E1EDKA1	IDoc: Document Header Partner Information
E1EDK02	IDoc: Document header reference data
E1EDK17	IDoc: Document Header Terms of Delivery
E1EDK18	IDoc: Document Header Terms of Payment
E1EDK35	IDoc: Document Header Additional Data
E1EDK36	IDOC: Doc.header payment cards
E1EDKT1	IDoc: Document Header Text Identification
E1EDP01	IDoc: Document Item General Data
Z1PSDQ	SDQ segment for ORDRSP.ORDERS05 extended type ZORSDQ01
E1EDP02	IDoc: Document Item Reference Data
E1CUREF	CU: Reference order item / instance in configuration
E1ADDI1	IDoc: Additionals
E1EDP03	IDoc: Document Item Date Segment

Figure 13.11 Extended Type ZORSDQ01 in the IDoc Type Editor

9. Save the extension and assign it to a change request.

10. Back out of the IDoc type editor to the initial screen and release the extended type with menu option EDIT • SET RELEASE.

11. The system throws up an information dialog with the message:

   Extension types cannot be changed after being released. Release extension?

   Click YES to release the extension.

Linking ZORSDQ01 to the Message and Basic Types

We can't do anything with our new IDoc extension until it has been linked to the message and basic types. Without this step, our extension is no more than a structure without a home or purpose.

To link the extended type to the message and basic types:

1. Use Transaction WE82 or follow WEDI area menu path DEVELOPMENT • IDOC TYPE/MESSAGE.

2. Click the pencil icon to switch to change mode (or press ⌃Ctrl+F1).

3. Click the POSITION button and enter "ORDRSP" in the MESSAGE TYPE field and "ORDERS05" in the BASIC TYPE field.

4. Click the OK green checkmark to navigate to the existing entry.

5. Select the entry and click COPY AS at the top of the screen, or press F6.

6. Enter "ZORSDQ01" in the EXTENSION column and change the RELEASE number to 702 (or your current SAP release). Press Enter. Two entries now exist for ORDRSP-ORDERS05, as shown in Figure 13.12.

Output Types and Assignment to IDoc Types				
Message Type	Basic type	Extension	Release	
ORDRSP	ORDERS05		46A	▲
ORDRSP	ORDERS05	ZORSDQ01	702	▼

Figure 13.12 Linking the Extension to the Message and Basic Types

7. Click SAVE and assign the change to a workbench request.

Creating a View for the Extended IDoc Type

We won't use every segment in the standard ORDERS05 basic type. Acme doesn't send its customers all of the data in the sales order. We only map a few segments to the outbound 855:

▶ E1EDK01: Header general data

▶ E1EDK03: Document dates

▶ E1EDKA1: Partner information

▶ E1EDK02: Document numbers

▶ E1EDP01: Item-level base data

▶ Z1PSDQ: SDQ segment with store order quantities

▶ E1EDP19: Material identification

We can't delete standard ORDERS05 segments from the extended IDoc, but we can select only the segments that we want to include by creating a view in the IDoc view editor.

1. To get to the view editor, use Transaction WE32 or follow the WEDI area menu CONTROL • IDOC VIEWS.

2. In the VIEW NAME field, enter "ZORSDQ01_BAS" 01 and click CREATE.

3. Enter the following values in the CREATE VIEW dialog (Figure 13.13):

   ▶ BASICTYP: "ORDERS05"

   ▶ EXTENSION: "ZORSDQ01"

   ▶ LOGICAL MESSAGE: "ORDRSP"

   ▶ DESCRIPTION: A brief description of the view

Figure 13.13 Creating a View for the SDQ Extended Type

4. Click OK to open the CREATE VIEW editor.

   Note the list of segments in the opening screen. E1EDK01 is the only segment included in the view by default. Every other segment that will be part of the view must be specifically included (Figure 13.14).

```
Create view: ZORSDQ01_BAS

ZORSDQ01_BAS                    Base view of ZORSDQ01 SDQ extended type

        E1EDK01          IDoc: Document header general data
        E1EDK14          IDoc: Document Header Organizational Data
        E1EDK03          IDoc: Document header date segment
        E1EDK04          IDoc: Document header taxes
        E1EDK05          IDoc: Document header conditions
        E1EDKA1          IDoc: Document Header Partner Information
        E1EDK02          IDoc: Document header reference data
        E1EDK17          IDoc: Document Header Terms of Delivery
        E1EDK18          IDoc: Document Header Terms of Payment
        E1EDK35          IDoc: Document Header Additional Data
        E1EDK36          IDOC: Doc.header payment cards
        E1EDKT1          IDoc: Document Header Text Identification
        E1EDP01          IDoc: Document Item General Data
        E1CUCFG          CU: Configuration data
        E1EDL37          Handling unit header
        E1EDS01          IDoc: Summary segment general
```

Figure 13.14 E1EDK01 is Included By Default in the View

5. To include a segment in the view, click on the segment name and then click the INCLUDE IN VIEW black arrow icon next to the pencil icon at the top of the view editor or press ⌐F8⌐.

6. Include the following segments in the view:

   ▶ E1EDK03

   ▶ E1EDKA1

   ▶ E1EDK02

   ▶ E1EDP01

   ▶ Z1PSDQ

   ▶ E1EDP19

The completed view is displayed in Figure 13.15.

ZORSDQ01_BAS	Base view of ZORSDQ01 SDQ extended type
E1EDK01	IDoc: Document header general data
E1EDK14	IDoc: Document Header Organizational Data
E1EDK03	IDoc: Document header date segment
E1EDK04	IDoc: Document header taxes
E1EDK05	IDoc: Document header conditions
E1EDKA1	IDoc: Document Header Partner Information
E1EDK02	IDoc: Document header reference data
E1EDK17	IDoc: Document Header Terms of Delivery
E1EDK18	IDoc: Document Header Terms of Payment
E1EDK35	IDoc: Document Header Additional Data
E1EDK36	IDOC: Doc.header payment cards
E1EDKT1	IDoc: Document Header Text Identification
E1EDP01	IDoc: Document Item General Data
Z1PSDQ	SDQ segment for ORDRSP.ORDERS05 extended type ZORSDQ01
E1EDP02	IDoc: Document Item Reference Data
E1CUREF	CU: Reference order item / instance in configuration
E1ADDI1	IDoc: Additionals
E1EDP03	IDoc: Document Item Date Segment
E1EDP04	IDoc: Document Item Taxes
E1EDP05	IDoc: Document Item Conditions
E1EDP20	IDoc schedule lines
E1EDPA1	IDoc: Doc.item partner information
E1EDP19	IDoc: Document Item Object Identification

Figure 13.15 The Completed View with All Included Segments

7. Save the view and assign it to a change request.

The view will be included as an outbound parameter in the partner profile for the extended type, just below the basic type and extension fields.

13.4.6 SDQ Bundling and IDoc Output Program

`ZEDI_ORDRSPSDQ` addresses a common issue in EDI implementations: the need to send one 855 order confirmation in response to a customer PO that recorded order quantity data for multiple store locations at the line-item level, and that may have generated hundreds or even thousands of SAP sales orders.

Custom program `ZEDI_ORDRSPSDQ` is supported by a number of custom development objects and configuration, including the following:

▶ IDoc extension ZORSDQ01 for message type ORDRSP and basic type ORDERS05 with custom segment Z1PSDQ beneath item-level parent E1EDP01

▶ View ZORSDQ01_BAS for IDoc extension ZORSDQ01

▶ Output type BA00 linked to Gordy's order through condition records in table B150

▶ Process codes SD10 and ZD10 for message type ORDRSP linking to function `IDOC_OUTPUT_ORDRSP`

▶ An outbound partner profile to identify the SDQ order confirmations before they are bundled into one IDoc:

  ▶ Message type ORDRSP

  ▶ Basic type ORDERS05

  ▶ Message function (MESCOD) SDQ

  ▶ No extended type

  ▶ Standard BA00 message control

▶ Another outbound partner profile to send the SDQ IDoc after it has been bundled by the customer program:

  ▶ Message type ORDRSP

  ▶ Basic type ORDERS05

  ▶ Extended type ZORSDQ01

  ▶ View ZORSDQ01_BAS

  ▶ No value in message function (MESCOD)

  ▶ No message control

`ZEDI_ORDRSPSDQ` collects all ORDRSP IDocs by sold-partner where the MESCOD field in the control segment EDIDC equals SDQ. It groups them by customer PO number, which it reads from the E1EDK02 segment in the IDoc, loops through them, and builds a single ORDRSP IDoc using extended type ZORSDQ01 and the other segments in view ZORSDQ01_BAS.

The program builds a common control and header data records by sold-to partner and PO number before assembling line items by material number. It collects up to 10 pairs of store order quantity fields by material into each SDQ segment and inserts the completed SDQ just below the E1EDP01 item detail header segment.

The SDQ ORDRSP IDoc built with this program contains only data that needs to be sent to the customer in the 855 confirmation. There's no need to map every field that comes out of the sales order.

After the consolidated ORDRSP SDQ IDoc is written to the IDoc database, it is sent to the EDI system through a standard function call. The original ORDRSP IDocs generated from the sales orders with SDQ in the MESCOD field are then marked for deletion and an ALV list report is output.

The ALV report header identifies the IDoc extension and its PO number. The report detail lists all IDocs and their corresponding sales order numbers used to build the extension.

Sales Order to SDQ IDoc Mapping

We need to map the one-to-many confirmation IDocs that will be generated from our sales orders for our SDQ PO from Gordy to one IDoc of extended type ZORSDQ01. So let's begin by outlining the mapping between the two IDocs in Table 13.4.

IDoc Element	Mapping Instructions to Target
IDoc Header Data Records—Mandatory—Max 1	
EDIDC	▸ Map entire control segment except MESCOD SDQ. Target MESCOD is null. ▸ Only one instance of segment mapped. ▸ Move ZORSDQ01 to CIMTYP.

Table 13.4 Mapping the Extended IDoc Type ZORSDQ01

IDoc Element	Mapping Instructions to Target
E1EDK01	▸ Map entire segment. ▸ Only one instance of segment mapped. ▸ An instance of the PO number should be stored here.
E1EDK03	▸ Map entire segment. ▸ Up to 10 instances of segment may be mapped.
E1EDKA1	▸ Map each instance of E1EDKA1 where PARVW not equal to WE. This should include AG (Customer), RE (Bill-to), RG (Payer). ▸ Up to 99 instances of segment may be mapped. ▸ The sold-to number is one of the two header keys that will be used to consolidate the many sales order confirmation IDocs into one SDQ extended IDoc. ▸ Ship-to, where PARVW = WE, is mapped to custom segment Z1PSDQ at item level.
E1EDK02	▸ Map entire segment. ▸ Up to 10 instances of segment may be mapped. ▸ The PO number is stored here. This is the second header key used to consolidate the many sales order IDocs into one.
E1EDP01—Line Item Level Data Group—Mandatory—Min 1/Max N	
E1EDPO1	▸ Loop through all source E1EDP01 group segments linked to sold-to and PO number. ▸ Map one instance of entire segment to target E1EDP01 except MENGE (quantity) and MENEE (unit of measure). ▸ Sum source MENGE for each instance of E1EDP01 in all IDocs for sold-to, ship-to, PO number, and current material, and map to target E1EDP01-MENGE. ▸ Only one instance of segment mapped to target.
Z1PSDQ	▸ 0 to N instances can be populated. ▸ Move E1EDP01-MENEE to Z1PSDQ-MENEE. ▸ Hard code UL (GLN) to ZIPSDQ-QUALF. ▸ Pass each value once each time a new instance of ZIPSDQ is created.

Table 13.4 Mapping the Extended IDoc Type ZORSDQ01 (Cont.)

IDoc Element	Mapping Instructions to Target
Z1PSDQ	▶ Ship-to number/quantity pair comes from sales order confirmation IDoc for sold-to, ship-to, PO number, and current material.
	▶ Up to 10 pairs from 10 sales order IDocs can be passed to one ZIPSDQ segment.
	▶ Move store GLN from E1EDKA1-LIFNR where PARVW = WE to Z1PSDQ-EXPNR1
	▶ Move E1EDPO1-MENGE to Z1PSDQ-MENGE1 from the same IDoc
	▶ The next pair is mapped to Z1PSDQ-EXPNR2 and Z1PSDQ-MENGE2, and the next to Z1PSDQ-EXPNR3 and Z1PSDQ-MENGE3 and so on, until either there are no more pairs or all ten pairs are populated.
	▶ If all ten pairs are populated, another instance of Z1PSDQ is created, and so on, until all the store location/quantity pairs for each ship-to sales order for the PO, sold-to, and current material have been processed.
E1EDP19	▶ Map entire segment once for current material, regardless of how many ship-to/quantity pairs mapped to Z1PSDQ.
	▶ 1 to 5 instances are possible.

Table 13.4 Mapping the Extended IDoc Type ZORSDQ01 (Cont.)

Program Structure

Our custom ABAP program ZEDI_ORDRSPSDQ includes the following elements:

▶ Table declarations

▶ Selection screen definition

▶ Type, internal table, string, and field variable declarations

▶ ALV list report data declarations, including the following:

  ▶ Type pools

  ▶ Work area definitions for structured strings and internal tables for the ALV list report function

  ▶ ALV list report work fields or variables

- An include program for the report header form routine called by the ALV list report function
- An ABAP INITIALIZATION event
- A START-OF-SELECTION event that groups all data selection and processing in discrete form routines, including the following:
  - FORM_000_READ_IDOC_DATA: Select all IDocs at status code 30 with MESCOD SDQ using select options entered into selection screen.
  - FORM_010_BUILD_SDQ_IDOC: SDQ IDoc processing. Group selected IDocs by sold-to partner and PO number, build extended IDoc with SDQ segment, write to IDoc database, and send to EDI system.
  - FORM_020_BUILD_ALV_REPORT: Build internal tables for report header and detail data.
  - FORM_030_ALV_SETUP: Handle ALV data house-keeping, including defining keys and sort order.
  - FORM_040_BUILD_SEL_FIELDCAT: Build the ALV field catalog, identifying the internal table, its fields, and field lengths that contain the report data.
  - FORM_050_WRITE_REPORT: Call ALV list report function to output report.

Create Program ZEDI_ORDRSPSDQ

To create the custom program ZEDI_ORDRSPSDQ, follow these steps:

1. Go to the ABAP Editor with Transaction SE38 or the Object Navigator with Transaction SE80. Click EDIT OBJECT and navigate to the PROGRAM tab. Enter the program name ZEDI_ORDRSPSDQ and click CREATE (or press F5).

2. Fill out the ATTRIBUTES dialog area as indicated in Figure 13.16 by entering the following values:
   - Select EXECUTABLE program in the TYPE field.
   - Select CUSTOMER PRODUCTION PROGRAM in the STATUS field.
   - Select CROSS-APPLICATION in the APPLICATION field.
   - Select the FIXED POINT ARITHMETIC and UNICODE CHECKS ACTIVE checkboxes.

3. Click SAVE and assign the program to a change request.

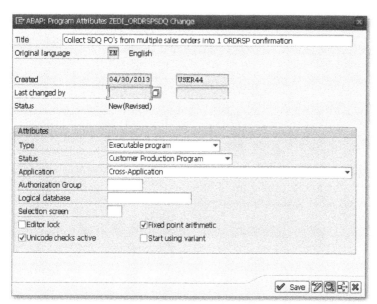

Figure 13.16 Attributes for Program ZEDI_ORDRSPSDQ

Program Code

Before we step through the logic and its supporting variables, remember that this is just a starting point, not a complete solution.

We begin by declaring our tables:

- ▸ EDIDC, EDID4, and EDIDS: IDoc database
- ▸ VBAK and VBAP: Sales order data

The main IDoc processing internal tables and work areas will reference our declared database objects, defined in Listing 13.1 and listed after.

```
data: gt_control_in type table of edidc, ,"Control rec in
      gt_control_out type table of edidc, "Control rec out
      gs_control_in type edidc, "Control rec in work area
      gs_control_out type edidc, "Control rec out work area
      gt_comm_idocs type edidc, "Communications idoc
                          "returned by ALE services
      gt_data_in type table of edidd,    "Data records in
      gt_data_out type table of edidd,  "New records out
      gs_data type edidd,           "Data work area
```

```
        gt_status type table of edids,      "Status record
        gs_status type edids,               "Status work area.
```

Listing 13.1 Internal Tables and Work Areas for IDoc Processing

▸ GT_CONTROL_IN will read the control records for all IDocs generated from sales orders for one PO and one sold-to where MESCOD = SDQ.

▸ GT_CONTROL_OUT will store the control record for the consolidated IDoc with the custom SDQ segments for store location and ordering quantity that will be sent to the EDI system for mapping to the 855.

▸ GT_DATA_IN will load the data records for all sales order SDQ IDoc.

▸ GT_DATA_OUT will carry the data records, including all SDQ segments, for the consolidated IDoc to the EDI system.

We'll need types for internal tables and work areas to group IDocs by PO, sold-to, material, and ship-to partner numbers. We'll also need types for an ALV list report that will identify all sales order IDocs bundled into our extended SDQ IDoc. All of our internal tables and work areas will reference a type.

The types, internal tables, and work areas that we'll use to group and sort our sales order IDocs are defined in Listing 13.2.

```
****   Types for PO grouping   ***
types: begin of t_po,
        bstnk type bstnk,           "PO number
      end of t_po.

types: begin of t_po_idoc,
        docnum type edi_docnum,     "Idoc no.
        rcvprn type edi_rcvprn,     "Sold-to partner
        vbeln type vbeln,           "Sales order number
        bstnk type bstnk,            "PO number
      end of t_po_idoc.

****   Type for PO material groupings   ***
types: begin of t_matnr,
        bstnk type bstnk,           "PO number
        matnr type matnr,           "Material number
        kunnr_we type lifnr_edi,    "Ship-to partner
        menge type edi_menge,       "Item quantity
        menee type edi_menee,       "Unit of measure
```

```
        end of t_matnr.

types: begin of t_item,
        matnr type matnr,
        end of t_item.

types: begin of t_store,          "Store no/qty pairs
        matnr type matnr,         "Material number
        kunnr_we type lifnr_edi,  "Ship-to partner
        menge type edi_menge,     "Item quantity
        end of t_store.

****   PO grouping tables and work areas   ***
data: gt_po_idoc type table of t_po_idoc,
      gt_po type table of t_po,
      gs_po_idoc type t_po, gs_po type t_po.
      gs_po type t_po, gs_po type t_po.

****   Material grouping tables and work areas   ***
data: gt_matnr type table of t_matnr,
      gt_item type table of t_item,
      gs_matnr type t_matnr,
      gs_item type t_item.

****   Store quantity pair table and work areas   ***
data: gt_store type table of t_store,
      gs_store type t_store.
```

Listing 13.2 PO and Material Grouping Internal Tables

For the ALV list processor, we need to reference a standard type pool and define types and internal tables to structure and output a report (Listing 13.3).

```
*Reference to ALV type pool

type-pools: slis.

****   Type for Report Header   ***
types: begin of t_header,
        docnum type edi_docnum,   "Idoc no.
        rcvprn type edi_rcvprn,   "Sold-to partner
        upddat type edi_upddat,   "IDoc Output date
        bstnk  type bstnk,        "Customer PO no.
        msg(30) type c,           "Status and msg
```

```
          end of t_header.

****  Type for Report Details  ***
types: begin of t_out,
          docnum type edi_docnum,     "t_header Idoc no.
          bstnk  type bstnk,          "t_header PO no.
          so_docnum type edi_docnum,  "sales order Idoc no.
          vbeln type vbeln,           "sales order no.
        end of t_out.

****  Report output tables and work areas  ***
data: ihead type table of t_header,  "Report header
      shead type t_header,           "Header work area
      iout type table of t_out,      "Report detail
      sout type t_out.               "Detail work area
```
Listing 13.3 Report Header and Detail Type Declarations

Report fields DOCNUM (the final bundled extended SDQ IDoc number) and BSTNK (the PO number) in IHEAD link to the same fields in IOUT. The ALV list processor uses this key to create a relationship between the single bundled IDoc with the custom SDQ segment in the IHEAD header table and the IDocs generated from the sales orders with MESCOD SDQ in the IOUT details level of the report.

We also need the following internal tables and strings that reference type pool SLIS. Each of these will pass key data about the report to function REUSE_ALV_HIERSEQ_LIST_DISPLAY to generate the hierarchical ALV list report.

▶ IFIELDCAT TYPE SLIS_T_FIELDCAT_ALV and SFIELDCAT LIKE LINE OF IFIELDCAT: Passes the catalog of fields in IHEAD and IOUT to the ALV list report.

▶ ISORTCAT TYPE SLIS_T_SORTINFO_ALV and SSORTCAT LIKE LINE OF ISORTCAT: Defines report data sort order.

▶ SLAYOUT TYPE SLIS_LAYOUT_ALV: Defines layout parameters for the report such as minimum line size.

▶ IEVENTCAT TYPE SLIS_T_EVENT and SEVENTCAT LIKE LINE OF IEVENTCAT: Identifies ALV report events defined in type pool SLIS, such as SLIS_EV_TOP_OF_PAGE, which points to a form used to process the top of the report event. Our top of form is embedded in an include program that provides a standard format for the report header.

▶ `SKEYINFO TYPE SLIS_KEYINFO_ALV`: Defines the key fields that link the ALV list report header and detail output tables.

Next we declare variables to parse and process each segment in the source ORDRSP and target ZORSDQ01 extended IDoc. The variables are strings with the data structure of each segment type. We'll also define constants to name unchanging values such as message, type, and segment names, status codes, and so on Listing 13.4.

```
*Structures to parse and process IDoc data segments
data: gs_eledk01 type eledk01,
      gs_eledk02 type eledk02,
      gs_eledka1 type eledka1,
      gs_eled103 type eledk03,
      gs_eledp01 type eledp01,
      gs_z1psdq type z1psdq,
      gs_eledp19 type z1psdq.

constants: c_ordrsp type c value 'ORDRSP',
           c_orders05 type c value 'ORDERS05',
           c_zorsdq01 type c value 'ZORSDQ01',
           c_eledk01 type c value 'E1EDK01',
           c_30 type c value '30',
           c_sdq type c value 'SDQ',
           c_855 type c value '855'
           c_dir_out type c value '1'
```

Listing 13.4 Segment Type Structures and Constants

Of course, we need selection options to identify SDQ IDocs generated by the sales orders. We'll keep it simple for this example:

▶ `s_docnum`: Returns a range of IDoc numbers

▶ `p_kunnr`: Identifies one SAP sold-to partner

▶ `s_upddat`: Date range for the last update to the IDocs

▶ `p_bstnk`: Identifies one customer PO number

Control segment selection parameters passed to the SQL read of the IDoc database include status, message and basic type, and MESCOD SDQ.

Processing Flow

When the start of selection event kicks off, the first step is to identify all IDoc control records at status 30 with message code SDQ from table EDIDC that meet the criteria entered in our selection screen. This is done in FORM 000_READ_IDOC_DATA. RCVPRN is the sold-to partner for Gordy's Galaxy.

```
select * into table gt_control_in from edidc
        where docnum in s_docnum
          and status = c_30
          and direct = c_dir_out
          and rcvprn = p_kunnr
          and mescod = c_sdq
          and mestyp = c_ordrsp
          and upddat in s_upddat.
```

Listing 13.5 gives the SQL code to pull these records.

```
select * into table gt_control_in from edidc
        where docnum in s_docnum
          and status = c_30
          and direct = c_dir_out
          and rcvprn = p_kunnr
          and mescod = c_sdq
          and mestyp = c_ordrsp
          and upddat in s_upddat.
```

Listing 13.5 Get All SDQ IDocs Generated from Sales Orders

An unsuccessful read returns an error and IDoc processing terminates.

A successful read populates an internal table with all the control records for each confirmation ORDRSP IDoc generated from every sales order created by one VMI or one 850 SDQ PO for Gordy's Galaxy.

We will group these IDocs by PO number and build our SDQ extension in FORM 010_BUILD_SDQ_IDOC.

Loop through GT_CONTROL_IN and pull all instances of segment E1EDK02, which stores the customer PO number against qualifier 001. To do this, we call three functions:

▶ EDI_DOCUMENT_OPEN_FOR_READ passing the IDoc number in the current loop pass. This confirms that the IDoc exists and has no foreign locks against it.

▶ `EDI_SEGMENT_GET` for the current IDoc number and segment E1EDK02. This returns all E1EDK02 segments in the IDoc, including control and `SDATA` fields. We'll pass this to internal table `GT_DATA_IN`.

▶ `EDI_DOCUMENT_CLOSE_READ` for the current IDoc number. We need to make more than one segment call for each IDoc, so we won't close the read until all of our segments have been retrieved.

There will likely be more than one E1EDK02 segments per IDoc. The PO confirmation includes the customer PO number (if it posted to the sales order) and the sales order number. We need both.

Loop on `GT_DATA` and move `SDATA` into string variable `GS_E1EDK02`. If the qualifier equals 001, move `GS_E1EDK02` to our `GT_PO_IDOC` internal table:

▶ `GT_CONTROL_IN-DOCNUM` to `GT_PO_IDOC-DOCNUM`

▶ `GT_CONTROL_INC-RCVPRN` to `GT_PO_IDOC-RCVPRN`

▶ `GS_E1EDK02-BELNR` to `GT_PO_IDOC-BSTNK`

If the qualifier equals 002, move the sales order number from `GS_E1EDK02-BELNR` into `GT_PO_IDOC-VBELN`. Then append `GS_E1EDK02` to `GT_PO_IDOC-BSTNK`.

As we build `GT_PO_IDOC`, we'll also collect `BSTNK` into internal table `GT_PO`, which only stores the purchase order number. This will give us a list of unique PO numbers across all the IDocs we read, which tells us how many consolidated IDocs we need to build.

Next we group our order materials by PO and ship-to partner. These data are in three segments:

▶ `E1EDKA1` with qualifier `WE` for the ship-to store location. This will go into the custom SDQ segment of the consolidated IDoc.

▶ `E1EDP01` for the order quantity for the store location, unit of measure, and unit price ordered. The quantity will go into the custom SDQ segment. It will also be summed with all other quantities for all ship-to partners using the same PO number.

▶ `E1EDP19` with qualifier `003` for the material number in the customer's system.

Refresh and clear table `GT_DATA_IN`. The current IDoc is still open for reading until the end of the `GT_CONTROL_IN` loop. Call `EDI_SEGMENT_GET` once for each of the three segments that we will process.

Refresh and clear `GT_DATA_IN` and `GS_DATA_IN` before each call to function `EDI_SEG-MENT_GET`. Then loop at `GT_DATA_IN` to read our segment data and build our internal tables, just as we did for `E1EDK02`.

For `E1EDKA1`, move `GS_DATA_IN-SDATA` to `GS_E1EDKA1` where the partner type qualifier in `PARVW` equals `WE`. Move:

▶ `GS_E1EDK02-BELNR` to `GT_MATNR-BSTNK`

▶ `GS_E1EDKA1-LIFNR` to `GT_MATNR-KUNNR_WE`

For `E1EDP01` move `GS_DATA_IN-SDATA` to `GS_E1EDP01`. Then move:

▶ `GS_E1EDP01-MENGE` to `GT_MATNR-MENGE`

▶ `GS_E1EDP01-MENEE` to `GT_MATNR-MENEE`

▶ `GS_E1EDP01-VPREI` to `GT_MATNR-VPREI`

For `E1EDP19`, move `GS_DATA_IN-SDATA` to `GS_E1EDP19`. The function pulls all instances of the segment in the current IDoc but we only care about the customer's external material number, which is stored against qualifier `003`. The logic would be similar to Listing 13.6:

```
if gs_e1edp19-qualf = '003'.
  gs_matnr-matnr = gs_e1edp19-idtnr.
endif.
append gs_matnr to gt_matnr.
```

Listing 13.6 Collecting the Customer Material Number

After we're finished processing all our segments, we call function `EDI_DOCUMENT_CLOSE_READ` at the bottom of the `GT_CONTROL_IN` loop.

When the `GT_CONTROL_IN` loop completes, we are left with the following:

▶ Internal table `GT_PO` with a list of all unique PO numbers. Each consolidated IDoc we build will be associated with one PO number.

▶ Internal table `GT_PO_IDOC` linking the POs to IDocs, sales orders, and sold-to partner numbers. This identifies the ORDRSP IDocs and sales orders created from one customer PO that we'll use to build our consolidated SDQ IDoc.

▶ Internal table `GT_MATNR` linking PO numbers to the store location, material, quantity ordered, and unit price. This identifies the product order data that will be used to build our E1EDPO1 item-level detail group in our consolidated IDoc.

> ### More Than One Way to Read an IDoc
>
> The logic for reading each segment of an IDoc is fundamentally the same. The call to `EDI_SEGMENT_GET` should be encapsulated in a form routine that passes the segment name, segment structure, and internal tables for processing each time that it's called.
>
> And, of course, there's more than one way to get your IDoc data. We can do a direct SQL read of table EDIDD by IDoc number and move all segments into an internal table. We can also call function `IDOC_READ_COMPLETELY` in function group EDI1 that will do the direct read for you.
>
> Function groups EDI1 and EDI5 contain a number of very useful functions for reading, editing, and processing IDocs.

Building the SDQ

We are now ready to build our ORDRSP SDQ IDoc based on the structure of the view that we created for our extension.

The segments in our target IDoc will be identical to the same segments in the source IDocs generated from the same PO number. The changes to the segments in the consolidated IDoc include the following:

▶ E1EDK02 where `QUALF` equals `002`: The sales order number is not copied across. There is one sales order for each ship-to, which could amount to thousands of them for a customer as large as Gordy's Galaxy.

▶ E1EDKA1 where `PARVW` equals `WE`: This is not mapped to the SDQ IDoc.

▶ E1EDP01: Data changes. Item quantity in `E1EDP01-MENGE` is the sum of the quantity ordered by each store in the SDQ segment.

▶ Z1PSDQ: Up to 10 store quantity pairs per custom SDQ segment for the item ordered in the E1EDP01 looping group.

▶ E1EDP19: The customer material number is mapped once for each PO item grouped by product ordered, not for each sales order item.

We begin with a sort and a loop on internal table `GT_PO`. The SDQ IDoc build takes place entirely within this loop and its list of unique PO numbers. `GT_PO` has the PO number for each bundled SDQ IDoc that we will build.

Our first step is to collect all our order materials into an internal table. We'll use this table later within the current loop on GT_PO to collect order item details into E1EDP01 item level groups.

```
refresh: gt_item.
clear : gt_item, gs_item.
loop at gt_matnr into gs_matnr where
          bstnk = gs_po-bstnk.
  gs_item-matnr = gs_matnr-matnr.
  collect gs_item into gt_item.
endloop.
```

Next we build the control and header data records for our ZORSDQ01 extension from one of the IDocs associated with the current PO number. It doesn't matter which one because the control and header data records for each IDoc generated for the same PO will be identical, except for the IDoc number and ship-to partner. We'll use the IDoc number from the model IDoc as a key to link the control segment to the header and details data segments of our new consolidated IDoc.

We will pull all data records from the IDoc with function IDOC_READ_COMPLETELY, as in Listing 13.7.

```
***   Clear IDoc control structures ***
clear: gt_control_in, gs_control_in,
       gt_data in, gs_data_in,
       gt_control_out, gs_control_out,
       gt_data out, gs_data_out.


***   Get an IDoc number for current PO   ***
read gt_po_idoc into gs_po_idoc with key
        bstnk = gs_po-bstnk.
  if sy-subrc <> 0. exit.
  else.


***   Get control and data records for first IDoc ***
***   in gt_po_idoc loop   ***
    call function 'idoc_read_completely'
      exporting
        document_number = gs_po_idoc-docnum
      importing
        idoc_control    = gt_control_in
      tables
        int_edidd = gt_data_in.
  endif.
```

Listing 13.7 Get an IDoc to Use as a Model for the Bundled SDQ IDoc

The complete IDoc is returned. GT_CONTROL_IN has the control segment and GT_ DATA_IN all the data records for the model IDoc. We'll copy GT_CONTROL_IN to GT_CONTROL_OUT with some modifications to the control record of the new consolidated ZORSDQ01 IDoc, as detailed in Listing 13.8.

```
***  Copy control segment into ZORSDQ01  ***
loop at gt_control_in into gs_control_out.
  clear gs_control_out-status.
  clear gs_control_out-mescod.
  gs_control_out-cimtyp = 'ZORSDQ01'.
  append gs_control_out to gt_control_out.
endloop.

*** Copy header segments into ZORSDQ01  ***
loop at gt_data_in into gs_data_out.
  case gs_data_out-segnam.
    when c_eledk01 or c_eledk03.
      append gs_data_out to gt_data_out.
      clear gs_data_out.
    when c_eledk02.
      clear gs_eledk02.
      gs_eledk02 = gs_data_out-sdata.
      if gs_eledk02 = '002'.    "PO number only
        append gs_data_out to gt_data_out.
        clear gs_data_out.
      endif.
    when c_eledka1.
      clear gs_eledka1.
      gs_eledka1 = gs_data_out-sdata.
      if gs_eledka1-parvw <> 'WE'.  "All except store number
        append gs_data_out to gt_data_out.
        clear gs_data_out.
      endif.
    endcase.
  endloop.
```

Listing 13.8 Building Control and Header Data Records for the New IDoc

The control and header data records are now appended to the new IDoc being built in GT_DATA_OUT.

Next we build the item group by looping on GT_ITEM with its unique list of all materials ordered in the current PO. Each line in GT_ITEM represents one E1EDP01 group within the new consolidated SDQ IDoc.

The data we need to build segments E1EDP01, Z1PSDQ, and E1EDP19 (in that order) will be read from internal table GT_MATNR. The order quantity will be accumulated during the build of all SDQ segments within the item group and inserted into field E1EDP01-MENGE.

The SDQ segments are assembled through the dynamic assignment of store and quantity field names to field symbols at runtime. The base names—EXPNR and MENGE—are incremented with an index that resets to 1 when it hits 10. This allows us to populate up to 10 pairs of store location and quantity fields for each SDQ segment and to begin building a new SDQ segment when we hit 10.

We declare the following field symbols and variables in the declarations header area of our program to build store location and quantity field pairs for assembling each SDQ segment (Listing 13.9):

▶ Field symbol <EXPNR> passes store location values to the SDQ segment work area.

▶ Field symbol <MENGE> passes order quantity values to the SDQ segment work area.

▶ String variable GS_EXPNRVAR builds SDQ segment field names for store location dynamically at runtime.

▶ String variable GS_MENGEVAR builds SDQ segment field names for store quantity dynamically at runtime.

▶ Integer SDQ_INDX counts the number of instances of store location and quantity pairs per SDQ segment. Begins at 0, increments by 1 until it hits 10 then resets to 0.

▶ String variable STR_SDQ_INDX appends SDQ_INDX to GS_EXPNRVAR and GS_MENGE-VAR to dynamically build field names at runtime.

```
****  Field symbols for store location and qty ***
field-symbols: <expnr>,    "Store location number
               <menge>.    "Store order qty

****  Variables to build SDQ field names ***
data: gs_expnrvar type edi_expnr,   "Store field name
```

```
        gs_mengevar type edi_menge,    "Qty field name
        sdq_indx type p value 0,   "Store count per segment
        gs_sdq_indx type c.  "Passes count to field names
```

Listing 13.9 SDQ Field Names Built by Field Symbols and Index

Listing 13.10 shows the code for the item-level detail segment builds.

```
***   Initialize segment work areas   ***
sort: gt_item, gt_matnr by matnr ascending.
clear: gs_eledp01, gs_z1psdq, gs_eledp19,
       str_expnrvar, _mengevar.
***   Index  keeps track of SDQ fields ***
sdq_indx = 0, posex_cnt = 0.

*** Begin loop on gt_item ***
loop at gt_item into gs_item.

***   Read item data from GS_MATNR   ***
  loop at gt_matnr into gs_matnr
            where matnr = gs_item-matnr
              and bstnk = gs_po-bstnk.

    if gs_eledp01 is initial.
***   Build segment string E1EDP01 one time***
      gs_eledp01-posex = posex_cnt + 10.
      gs_eledp01-menee = gs_matnr-menee.
      gs_eledp01-vprei = gs_matnr-vprei.
    endif.

***   Build segment strings E1EDP19 only one time ***
    if gs_eledp19 is initial.
      gs_eledp19-qualf = '003'.
      gs_eledp19_01-idtnr = gs_item.
    endif.

***   Build SDQ segment Z1PSDQ ***
***   Set SDQ index   ***
    sdq_indx = sdq_indx + 1.
    if sdq_indx < 11.
      clear: str_sdq_indx, str_expnrvar, str_mengevar.
      sdq_indx_str = sdq_indx.
      condense sdq_indx_str.
```

```
***   Concatenate strings to create variable field names  ***
      concatenate 'gs_z1psdq-expnr' sdq_indx_str
                into str_expnrvar.
      concatenate 'gs_z1psdq-menge' sdq_indx_str
                into str_mengevar.

***   Assign variable field names to field symbols ***
***   Identifies fields for update  ***
      assign (str_expnrvar) to <expnr>.
      assign (str_mengevar) to <expnr>.
***   Update gs_z1psdq store and quantity fields ***
***   with dynamically assigned field symbols  ***
      <expnr> = gs_matnr-kunnr_we.
      <menge> = gs_matnr-menge.
***   Cumulate order quantity for item  ***
      gs_e1edp01-menge = gs_e1edp01-menge +
                       gs_matnr-menge.
    endif

***   reset sdq index & write SDQ segment to SDQ itab  ***
    if sdq_indx = 10.
      gs_z1psdq-menee = gs_matnr-menee.
      gs_z1psdq-qualf = 'UL'.
      append gs_z1psdq to gt_z1psdq.
      clear gs_z1psdq.
      sdq_indx = 0.
    endif.
  endloop.

***   Append all item segments to SDQ IDoc  ***
***   Append E1EDP01 to SDQ IDoc  ***
  clear gs_data.
  gs_data-mandt = sy-mandt.
  gs_data-docnum = gs_po_idoc-docnum.
  gs_data-segnam = 'E1EDP01'.
    gs_data-hlevel = '2'.
  gs_data-sdata = gs_e1edp01.
  append gs_data to gt_data.

***   Append z1psdq to SDQ IDoc  ***
  clear gs_z1psdq.
  loop at gt_z1psdq into gs_z1psdq.
    gs_data-mandt = sy-mandt.
```

```
      gs_data-docnum = gs_po_idoc-docnum.
      gs_data-segnam = 'Z1PSDQ'.
      gs_data-hlevel = '3'.
      gs_data-sdata = gs_z1psdq.
      append gs_data to gt_data.
      Clear: gs_data , gs_z1psdq.
    endloop.

*** Append E1EDP19 to SDQ IDoc ***
    clear gs_data.
    gs_data-mandt = sy-mandt.
    gs_data-docnum = gs_po_idoc-docnum.
    gs_data-segnam = 'E1EDP19'.
    gs_data-hlevel = '3'.
    gs_data-sdata = gs_e1edp19.
    append gs_data to gt_data.
endloop.
```

Listing 13.10 Assembling the Consolidated SDQ IDoc

After the consolidated SDQ IDoc has been assembled, it needs to be written to the IDoc database and sent to the EDI RIM. One function module takes care of both jobs: MASTER_IDOC_DISTRIBUTE. We'll distribute one IDoc at a time. The call parameters are displayed in Listing 13.11.

```
  call function 'master_idoc_distribute'
    exporting
      master_idoc_control         = gs_control_out
    tables
      communication_idoc_control = gt_comm_idocs
      master_idoc_data            = gt_data_out
    exceptions
      error_in_idoc_control       = 1
      error_writing_idoc_status   = 2
      error_in_idoc_data          = 3
      others                      = 4.
  if sy-subrc <> 0.
    message id sy-msgid type sy-msgty number sy-msgno
         with sy-msgv1 sy-msgv2 sy-msgv3 sy-msgv4.
  endif.
```

Listing 13.11 Triggering IDoc Interface Services and Distribution

We pass the control segment in GS_CONTROL_OUT and all data segments in GT_DATA_OUT. A new IDoc number will be assigned when the IDoc is written to the database. The new number will be returned in GT_COMM_IDOCS.

The status of the new SDQ IDoc is set to 18 — *Triggering EDI subsystem OK* — when it triggers the EDI RIM through the file port in the outbound partner profile. After successful translation, the EDI RIM updates the status through the STATUS IDoc interface to 06 — *Translation OK*.

Next we change the status of the original ORDRSP IDocs generated when the sales orders for our PO were saved.

To do this, we need the IDoc numbers of the IDocs used to build the consolidated SDQ segments. The control segments of the original IDocs are in internal table GT_CONTROL_IN and the data segments in GT_DATA_IN.

We've declared internal table GT_STATUS and a work area GS_STATUS with the structure BDIDOCSTAT, which has the key fields for the IDoc status record in table EDIDS.

Change the status of all ORDRSP IDocs with MESCOD SDQ that created the bundled confirmation with the SDQ segment to 31 — Error, no further processing. Then return a custom message from message class IDOC_ADAPTER for the status 31 IDocs — *Confirmation IDoc & has been written to outbound IDoc &*. The first "&" will be replaced with the original IDoc number, the second with the bundled IDoc number. The standard function in

Listing 13.12 writes the new status to the IDoc database.

```
***   Build status record with message for each IDoc   ***
***   gt_control_in has original IDoc number ***
***   gt_comm_idocs has new IDoc number  ***
clear gs_control_out.
loop at gt_comm_idocs into gs_control_out.
  loop at gt_control_in into gs_control_in.
    gs_status-docnum = gs_control_in-docnum.
    gs_status-status = '31'.
    gs_status-msgty = 'S'.
    gs_status-msgid = 'IDOC_ADAPTER'.
    gs_status-msgno = '001'.
    gs_status-msgv1 = gs_control_in-docnum.
    gs_status-msgv2 = gs_control_out-docnum.
    gs_status-repid = sy-cprog.
    append gs_status into gt_status.
```

```
***  Standard function to change IDoc status  ***
   call function 'idoc_status_write_to_database'
      exporting
         idoc_number              = gs_status-docnum
      tables
         idoc_status              = gt_status
      exceptions
         idoc_foreign_lock        = 1
         idoc_not_found           = 2
         idoc_status_records_empty = 3
         idoc_status_invalid      = 4
         db_error                 = 5
         others                   = 6.
   endloop.
endloop.
```

Listing 13.12 Changing the Status of Each Original IDoc

Our IDoc processing is now complete. The last job is to build the report header and detail output tables for the ALV list report.

The report header data for internal table IHEAD comes from here:

▶ GT_COMM_IDOCS-DOCNUM: Consolidated IDoc number

▶ GT_COMM_IDOCS-RCVPRN: Receiving sold-to partner

▶ GT_COMM_IDOCS-UPDDAT: IDoc change date

▶ GT_PO_IDOC-BSTNK: Customer PO number

▶ GT_COMM_IDOCS-STATUS: Bundled IDoc status

The report detail data for internal table IOUT comes from here:

▶ GT_COMM_IDOCS-DOCNUM: Consolidated IDoc number links to IHEAD (will not display at details level of report)

▶ GT_PO_IDOC-BSTNK: Customer PO number links to IHEAD (will not display at details level of report)

▶ GT_CONTROL_IN-DOCNUM: Sales order ORDRSP IDoc

▶ GT_PO_IDOC-VBELN: Sales order number

After we've populated our report header and item details internal tables, we build an ALV list field catalog for IHEAD and IOUT with the bundled IDoc number and PO number fields linking the two. The keys are the final bundled SDQ IDoc number and customer PO number and are identified by their field names in IHEAD and IOUT. The keys are passed in a structure string defined by a type from the SLIS type pool: SLIS_KEYINFO_ALV, which is shown in Listing 13.13.

```
clear skeyinfo.
skeyinfo-header01 = 'DOCNUM'.
skeyinfo-item01 = 'DOCNUM'.
skeyinfo-header02 = 'BSTNK'.
skeyinfo-item02 = 'BSTNK'.
```

Listing 13.13 Defining the Key between Report Header and Details

The field catalog is defined in an internal table that references SLIS type pool type SLIS_T_FIELDCAT_ALV. It identifies internal tables and fields that will be displayed in the ALV list report and it defines how they will be displayed: field labels, output lengths, data dictionary type, check boxes, and so on. It is typically populated in blocks of code that can be modularized into a form and called each time a new field is declared. Listing 13.14 gives an example.

```
***  Pass bundled SDQ IDoc IDoc number  ***
clear sfieldcat.
sfieldcat-fieldname    = 'DOCNUM'.
sfieldcat-tabname      = 'IHEAD'.
sfieldcat-reptext_ddic = 'OB IDoc no'.
sfieldcat-outputlen    = '0016'.
append sfieldcat to ifieldcat.

***  Pass Sales order number  ***
clear sfieldcat.
sfieldcat-fieldname    = 'VBELN'.
sfieldcat-tabname      = 'IOUT'.
sfieldcat-reptext_ddic = 'Sales order no'.
sfieldcat-outputlen    = '0010'.
append sfieldcat to ifieldcat.
```

Listing 13.14 Building the ALV Field Catalog One Field at a Time

Once these house-keeping chores are done, we display the report by calling function REUSE_ALV_HIERSEQ_LIST_DISPLAY in function group SALV, which is filled with ALV functions. The function call passes everything the ALV processor needs to output a nicely formatted standard ALV list report.

```
call function 'REUSE_ALV_HIERSEQ_LIST_DISPLAY'
  EXPORTING
    i_callback_program = sy-cprog
    is_layout          = slayout
    it_fieldcat        = ifieldcat
    it_sort            = isortcat
    i_save             = 'A'
    it_events          = ieventcat
    i_tabname_header   = 'IHEAD'
    i_tabname_item     = 'IOUT'
    is_keyinfo         = skeyinfo
  TABLES
    t_outtab_header    = ihead
    t_outtab_item      = iout
  EXCEPTIONS
    program_error      = 1
    others             = 2.
```

Listing 13.15 Calling a Hierarchical ALV List Report

Assign Transaction Code ZSDQO

Finally, we need a transaction code to run our custom SDQ bundling program.

1. Go to MAINTAIN TRANSACTION with Transaction SE93 or through Transaction SE80 and the Repository Browser.

2. Click the EDIT OBJECT button and select the MORE SCREEN tab.

3. Enter the transaction code "ZSDQ0" and click CREATE.

4. In the CREATE TRANSACTION dialog, enter a description of the transaction in the SHORT TEXT field.

5. Select the PROGRAM AND SELECTION SCREEN (REPORT TRANSACTION) radio button in the START OBJECT area (Figure 13.17).

6. Click OK to open the CREATE REPORT TRANSACTION screen.

7. Enter "ZEDI_ORDRSPSDQ" in the PROGRAM field. The SELECTION SCREEN value should be "1000".

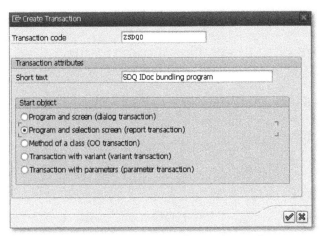

Figure 13.17 Creating a Transaction for our Custom Program

8. Select whatever SAPGUI you need in the GUI SUPPORT area.

9. Save the transaction code and assign it to a change request. The transaction screen should look like Figure 13.18.

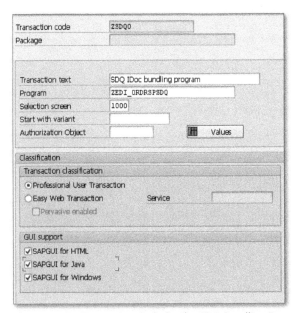

Figure 13.18 Transaction Code for the SDQ Bundling Program

13.5   Mapping Specifications

We'll create one map in the EDI RIM to translate both the ORDERS05 basic type and the ZORSDQ01 extended type to Gordy's 855 X12 version 5010 order confirmation.

Table 13.5 details the mapping requirements for the outbound ORDRSP-855 transaction for Gordy's Galaxy. This is not a complete mapping for the order confirmation, and the details will vary from site to site.

ORDRSP	855	Value	Comments
E1EDK01— Header—Min 1, Max 1			
ACTION	BAK01	000	Original document. Convert to 00.
	BAK02	AP	Identifies type of PO confirmation. Set to AP if EDIDC-MESTYP = ORDRSP.
CURCY	CUR02	USD	Document currency
BELNR		999999	Gordy purchase order number. Mapped from E1EDK02.
E1EDK03—Header dates—Min 0, Max 10			
IDDAT	DTM01	002	Delivery requested date qualifier. Convert to 002 in EDI.
DATUM	DTM02	20140115	Confirmed delivery date
E1EDKA1—Partners—Min 1, Max 99—Loop 1 Sold-to			
PARVW	N101	AG	Sold-to qualifier. Convert to BY.
	N103	UL	Hard-code. Identifies GLN.
LIFNR	N104	0999999999999	Gordy sold-to GLN from EDPAR
NAME1	N102	Gordy's Galaxy	Sold-to partner name
STRAS	N301	2356 Halsted St	Sold-to partner street address
ORT01	N401	Chicago	Sold-to partner city
PSTLZ	N403	60601	Sold-to partner postal code
LAND1	N404	US	Sold-to partner country

Table 13.5   Mapping the Order Confirmation IDoc to the X12 855

ORDRSP	855	Value	Comments
REGIO	N402	IL	Sold-to partner region
E1EDKA1—Partners—Loop 2 Bill-to			
PARVW	N101	RG	Invoice recipient. Convert to BT.
LIFNR	N104	0999999999999	Acme location GLN from EDPAR
NAME1	N102	Gordy's Galaxy	Gordy's Galaxy payer party
	N103	UL	Hard-code. Identifies GLN.
LIFNR	N104	0999999999999	Gordy sold-to GLN from EDPAR
NAME1	N102	Gordy's Galaxy	Bill-to partner name
STRAS	N301	2356 Halsted St	Sold-to partner street address
ORT01	N401	Chicago	Bill-to partner city
PSTLZ	N403	60601	Bill-to partner postal code
LAND1	N404	US	Bill-to partner country
REGIO	N402	IL	Bill-to partner region
E1EDKA1—Partners—Loop 3 Ship-to location			
PARVW	N101	WE	Invoice recipient. Convert to ST.
	N103	UL	Hard code. Identifies GLN.
LIFNR	N104	0999999999888	Acme location GLN from EDPAR
NAME1	N102	Gordy Store 001	Store location name
STRAS	N301	265 Orange Ave	Sold-to partner street address
ORT01	N401	West Lafayette	Store location city
PSTLZ	N403	47906	Store location postal code
LAND1	N404	US	Store location country
REGIO	N402	LA	Store location region
E1EDKA—Partners—Loop 4 Supplier name			
	N102	Acme Pictures	Supplier partner name. Hard code.

Table 13.5 Mapping the Order Confirmation IDoc to the X12 855 (Cont.)

535

ORDRSP	855	Value	Comments
E1EDK02—Documents—Min 1, Max 10			
QUALF		001	PO number where E1EDK02-QUALF = 001
BELNR	BAK03	999999	Gordy's PO number
DATUM	BAK04	20131215	Purchase order date
E1EDPO1—Item level details group—Min 1, Max N 1 instance of E1EDP01 per group loop			
POSEX	PO101	000010	Item number
MENGE	PO102	100	Total sum of quantity ordered for all stores in item
MENEE	PO103	EA	Base unit of measure
VPREI	PO104	12.50	Unit price
MENEE	SDQ01	EA	Base unit of measure for all stores
	SDQ02	UL	ID type qualifier: Store GLN E1EDKA1-PARVW = WE
Z1PSDQ—Custom IDoc SDQ Segment—Min 1, Max N			
EXPNR1	SDQ03	0999999999999	Store location GLN 1 from IDoc 1 used to build SDQ IDoc.
MENGE1	SDQ04	10	Confirmed quantity ordered store 1
EXPNR2	SDQ05	0999999999990	Store location GLN 2 from IDoc 2 used to build SDQ IDoc.
MENGE2	SDQ06	10	Confirmed quantity ordered store 2
EXPNR3	SDQ07	0999999999991	Store location GLN 3 from IDoc 3 used to build SDQ IDoc.
MENGE3	SDQ08	10	Confirmed quantity ordered store 3
EXPNR4	SDQ09	0999999999992	Store location GLN 4 from IDoc 4 used to build SDQ IDoc.
MENGE4	SDQ10	10	Confirmed quantity ordered store 4

Table 13.5 Mapping the Order Confirmation IDoc to the X12 855 (Cont.)

ORDRSP	855	Value	Comments
EXPNR5	SDQ11	0999999999993	Store location GLN 5 from IDoc 5 used to build SDQ IDoc.
MENGE5	SDQ12	10	Confirmed quantity ordered store 5
EXPNR6	SDQ13	0999999999994	Store location GLN 6 from IDoc 6 used to build SDQ IDoc.
MENGE6	SDQ14	10	Confirmed quantity ordered store 6
EXPNR7	SDQ15	0999999999995	Store location GLN 7 from IDoc 7 used to build SDQ IDoc.
MENGE7	SDQ16	10	Confirmed quantity ordered store 7
EXPNR8	SDQ17	0999999999996	Store location GLN 8 from IDoc 8 used to build SDQ IDoc.
MENGE8	SDQ18	10	Confirmed quantity ordered store 8
EXPNR9	SDQ19	0999999999997	Store location GLN 9 from IDoc 9 used to build SDQ IDoc.
MENGE9	SDQ20	10	Confirmed quantity ordered 9
EXPNR10	SDQ21	0999999999998	Store location GLN 10 from IDoc 10 used to build SDQ IDoc.
MENGE10	SDQ22	10	Confirmed quantity ordered store 10
E1EDP19—Materials—Min 1, Max 10			
QUALF	PO106	002	Customer material number. Convert to IN for buyer's number.
	PO108	EN	Product type qualifier: GTIN code
IDTNR	PO109	799142939512	Gordy material number
E1EDS01—Materials—Min 1, Max 10			
SUMID		001	Qualifier identifies number of line items in PO confirmation
SUMME	CTT01	1	Total number of line items

Table 13.5 Mapping the Order Confirmation IDoc to the X12 855 (Cont.)

13.6   EDI Configuration in SAP

We need entries in the EDPAR partner-mapping table that will be used by both standard and custom SDQ ORDRSP output processing. We also need separate partner profiles to support the output of standard and custom SDQ ORDRSP message types for Gordy's Galaxy.

13.6.1   EDPAR Entries: Transaction VOE4

During outbound interface processing, the EDPAR read uses the SAP ship-to partner from the sales order to check KUNNR and pull the external partner GLN from EXPNR. The sold-to partner isn't used in the outbound read.

Go to Transaction VOE4 and enter one record for each of Gordy's stores and distribution centers that will be receiving product from Acme Studios.

Make sure the sold-to partner number is in field KUNNR, the SAP ship-to in INPNR, and the partner type WE in PARVW. Gordy's GLN will be in EXPNR. The data should look like Table 13.6.

Field	Value	Description
KUNNR	GRDY01	Gordy sold-to partner from sales order
PARVW	WE	Partner function ship-to
EXPNR	0999999999999	External partner for ship-to (Gordy's GLN)
INPNR	GRDY01001	Internal SAP ship-to partner number

Table 13.6   Outbound EDPAR Ship-To Mapping

GLN is then mapped to the N1 or SDQ segments of the outbound 855, with qualifier UL (N103 or SDQ02). If it's a non-SDQ IDoc, the N1 segment is further identified with an ST—ship-to—qualifier in N101.

13.6.2   ZEDIXREF Entries

Our custom table ZEDIXREF maps the IDoc sender and receiving partners—the SAP logical system ID and Gordy's sold-to—to the receiving party's send and receive EDI ID numbers. We'll use the values in Table 13.7 for the outbound ORDRSP confirmation to Gordy's Galaxy, for both bundled SDQ and standard non-bundled IDocs.

Field	Value SDQ	Value Non-SDQ	Description
DIRECT	1	1	Direction outbound
STDMES	855	855	EDI PO confirmation transaction
MESTYP	ORDRSP	ORDRSP	IDoc message type
IDOCTP	ORDERS05	ORDERS05	IDoc basic type
CIMTYP	ZORSDQ01		IDoc extension
SNDPRN	DEVCLNT100	DEVCLNT100	SAP send partner: Acme SAP logical system
RCVPRN	GRDY01	GRDY01	SAP receive partner: Gordy's customer number in Acme's system
SNDLAD	99999998889	99999998889	EDI send partner: Gordy's trading partner ID for Acme
RCVLAD	99934567999	99934567999	EDI receiver partner: Gordy's trading partner ID for Gordy

Table 13.7 ZEDIXREF Entries for the Outbound 855 to DSI

13.6.3 Partner Profiles: Transaction WE20

We'll need to define three outbound partner profiles for message ORDRSP for Gordy's Galaxy partner number GRDY01 partner type KU (customer) and partner role SP (sold-to):

1. With null MESCOD and message control to support output of a standard ORDRSP IDoc generated from one sales order referencing one purchase order that is not referenced by any other sales orders

2. With MESCOD SDQ and message control to output standard ORDRSP IDocs from multiple sales orders that reference one purchase order and sold-to partner

3. With MESCOD 855, extended basic type with SDQ segment and view but no message control to support output of one bundled order confirmation that references one purchase order at the header and multiple ship-to partners at the item details level.

All partner profiles are configured with Transaction WE20.

Partner Profile: No SDQ

To create the standard partner profile with message control, enter the following values into the OUTBOUND PARAMETERS screen:

- MESSAGE TYPE field: "ORDRSP"
- RECEIVER PORT field: "XML_IDOC"
- OUTPUT MODE area: COLLECT IDocs and START SUBSYSTEM checkboxes (3)
- BASIC TYPE field: "ORDERS05"

The finished outbound parameters should look like Figure 13.19.

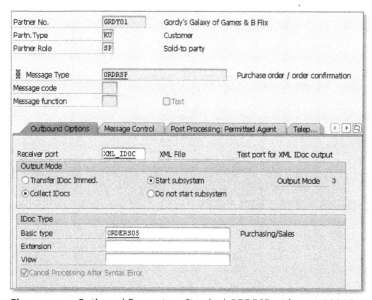

Figure 13.19 Outbound Parameters, Standard ORDRSP with no MESCOD

Click MESSAGE CONTROL and create two entries with the following values into the table control (Figure 13.20):

- APPLICATION: "V1"
- MESSAGE TYPE: "BA00"
- PROCESS CODE: "SD10" (links to function IDOC_OUTPUT_ORDRSP)
- CHANGE MESSAGE checkboxes: One entry null and one entry checked

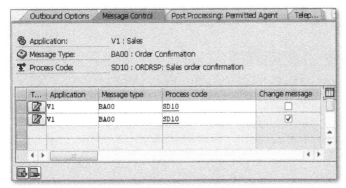

Figure 13.20 Message Control ORDRSP Without SDQ MESCOD

Finally, go to the EDI STANDARD tab by selecting it from the far right of the screen tabs and enter the following values:

▶ EDI STANDARD: "X" for X12

▶ MESSAGE TYPE: "855"

▶ VERSION: "00510"

Don't forget to save. The EDI screen should look like Figure 13.21.

Figure 13.21 EDI Standard Values for all ORDRSP IDocs

Partner Profile: With SDQ MESCOD

These IDocs will be read by custom program ZEDI_ORDRSPSDQ for bundling into extended type ZORSDQ01 against one purchase order and sold-to partner.

To create a partner profile with MESCOD SDQ and message control, enter the following values into the OUTBOUND PARAMETERS screen:

▶ MESSAGE TYPE: "ORDRSP"

▶ MESSAGE CODE: "SDQ"

▶ RECEIVER PORT: "XML_IDOC"

▸ OUTPUT MODE area: COLLECT IDOCS and DO NOT START SUBSYSTEM checkboxes (4)

▸ BASIC TYPE in IDOC TYPE area: "ORDERS05"

The finished outbound parameters should look like Figure 13.22.

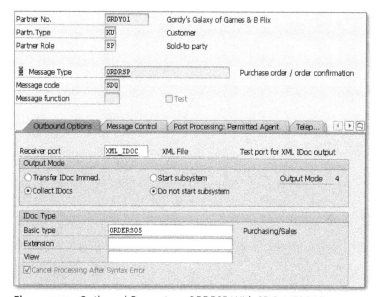

Figure 13.22 Outbound Parameters, ORDRSP With SDQ MESCOD

The only difference in message control configuration is the process code. We can't use the same application, message type, and process code twice for the same partner and message type. Process code ZD10 is a copy of SD10 extended to include message code SDQ.

Click MESSAGE CONTROL and create two entries with the following values into the table control (Figure 13.23):

▸ APPLICATION: "V1"

▸ MESSAGE TYPE: "ZBA0"

▸ PROCESS CODE: "SD10"

▸ CHANGE MESSAGE checkbox: One entry null and one entry checked

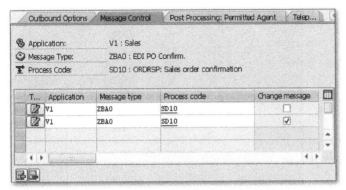

Figure 13.23 Message Control ORDRSP With SDQ MESCOD

We'll also populate the EDI STANDARD tab with the same X12 855 version 005010 values, as for the standard IDoc with no SDQ MESCOD.

Partner Profile: Extended Type ZORSDQ01

This partner profile will support export to the EDI RIM of the extended IDoc basic type ZORSDQ01 by custom program ZEDI_ORDRSPSDQ.

We'll enter the following values into the OUTBOUND PARAMETERS screen:

▶ MESSAGE TYPE: "ORDRSP"

▶ MESSAGE CODE: "855"

▶ RECEIVER PORT: "XML_IDOC"

▶ OUTPUT MODE: COLLECT IDocs and START SUBSYSTEM checkboxes (3)

▶ BASIC TYPE: "ORDERS05"

▶ EXTENSION: "ZORSDQ01"

▶ VIEW: "ZORSDQ01_BAS"

The finished outbound parameters should look like Figure 13.24.

Because the extended type will be processed and sent by a custom ABAP and not generated from a document, we do not configure message control. We will, however, add the X12 855 values to the EDI STANDARD tab.

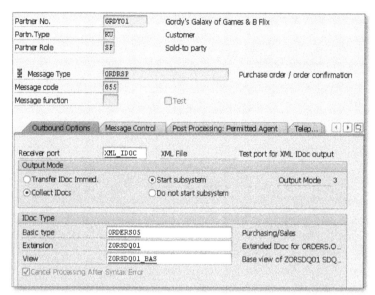

Figure 13.24 Outbound Parameters, ORDRSP with SDQ Extension

13.7 Summary

We're well on our way now. The order confirmation is a key piece of our order-to-cash cycle. It confirms to our customer that we have received their purchase order and that we can deliver their product by a scheduled date.

In the case of VMI orders, the confirmation gives our customer the data they need to post a purchase order in their own system so they can approve and begin tracking the goods that we will ship to them.

We've also seen that this can be a complex interface, particularly if one PO is used to order goods for multiple store locations, creating one sales order in SAP for each ship-to partner. VMI ordering works the same way for Acme's biggest customers, like Gordy's Galaxy of Games & B Flix with its more than 2,000 store locations across North America.

The problem, of course, is that the customer sent one PO and expects one PO confirmation back. So we need to customize our outbound confirmation to support bundling of multiple sales orders against one PO into a single IDoc with an SDQ segment with order quantities for each store location.

We looked at all the pieces of the puzzle that we need to support this: an extended IDoc, custom and standard configuration, message control, and ABAP logic that could serve as a starting point to bundle our multiple ship-to partners into a single PO confirmation.

The great Darryl Q, who was all about the customer, would have been pleased. Assuming that Acme's third-party contract manufacturer, DSI, who also provides warehousing and delivery services, has the ordered saleable items in inventory, we're ready to ship the order to the customer's distribution centers and stores. That process begins with the shipping order.

"Just deliver the goods," Darryl Q often fumed at his writers and directors when a bump was encountered in their creative process. That's exactly what the ship order interface does: It tells the distributor what goods to deliver to whom, against what purchase order, and when. In this chapter we check out the ship order interface and see how it delivers the goods.

14 Sending a Shipping Order to the Supplier

After the order confirmation has been sent, and the customer knows that his order is being processed, Acme's supplier Disc Services International (DSI) steps up to the plate.

The first thing DSI does is check the finished goods inventory it keeps for Acme. Does it have enough of the ordered product in stock to put together a delivery and ship it?

In this chapter we take the happy path and assume that they do. We look at what happens if they *don't* have enough stock in the next chapter.

As we've seen, DSI provides Acme Pictures the full range of manufacturing and distribution services for its movies on DVD: replication, cover art, packaging, warehousing and inventory management, delivery, and even ordering raw materials for manufacturing finished product.

When it comes to shipping an Acme order, DSI needs to know the five Ws:

1. Who ordered the goods?
2. What did they order?
3. Where does the order ship from?
4. Where is the order being shipped to?
5. When does the order have to ship?

This is what the outbound message type SHPORD to X12 830 ship order interface does: It is triggered by creation of an outbound delivery in Acme's SAP system and sent to a third-party warehouse to kick off the shipping process of an order to a customer.

The 830 posts to DSI's business system and creates a pick list. DSI then retrieves the ordered DVDs from inventory, packs them into boxes, moves the boxes to a loading area, and then loads them into trucks for delivery to Gordy's Galaxy of Games & B Flix.

This is a critical piece of the order-to-cash cycle. Without the 830 to DSI, nothing gets shipped, and the customer doesn't get his goods.

14.1 Technical Overview of Interface

Table 14.1 summarizes the outbound purchase order acknowledgment.

Item	Description
Title	Ship Order to Third Party Warehouse
Description	The ship order interface is sent to a third-party warehouse that has been contracted to ship and deliver ordered product for Acme.
	It is triggered after the sales order has been completed and the order confirmation sent. It is generated either by creating an individual outbound delivery document from a sales order or by running the delivery due list in Acme's SAP system.
	When the delivery is completed and saved, a SHPORD message is generated and sent to the EDI RIM where it will be converted to an outbound X12 830 ship order.
	The 830 is then routed to DSI's EDI system by AS2. It posts to their business system and begins the shipping process to the customer. Ordered goods are picked, packed, organized into shipments, and loaded onto trucks for delivery.
Type of interface	Distribution: IDoc to X12 EDI
Direction	Outbound
Trading partner	Disk Services International (vendor)
IDoc	SHPORD.DELVRY03

Table 14.1 Overview of Outbound PO Confirmation Interface

Item	Description
IDoc extended type	
IDoc function	`IDOC_OUTPUT_DELVRY`
Custom ABAP	
Description	
Target file(s)	X12 830 ship order to third-party warehouse
Source document(s)	SAP outbound delivery document
Transaction code	VL01N, VL10
Map(s)	SHPORD.DELVRY03 to X12 830 vers. 5010
Custom map logic	
Source system	Acme SAP
Target system	DSI EDI via AS2 from Acme EDI RIM
997 acknowledgment	Inbound within 24 hours of transmission at the transaction detail level. Function group acknowledgment code: PS.
Frequency	Every 30 minutes throughout the day, on demand
Job schedule 1	`RVV50R10C` (VL10). Six times daily to run the delivery due list.
Job schedule 2	`RSEOUT00`: Every hour, sends all SHPORD message types to DSI.

Table 14.1 Overview of Outbound PO Confirmation Interface (Cont.)

14.2 Functional Specifications

The purpose of this interface is to order shipping and delivery of product in inventory in DSI's warehouse against Acme sales orders.

DSI is Acme's one-stop shop for manufacturing, packaging, warehousing, and shipping to customers of its movies on DVD. Through an ongoing process of planning and ordering by Acme, DSI maintains enough finished product in its inventory that it can deliver on almost any shipping order that comes its way.

The shipping order interface typically runs after the order confirmation has been generated from the completed sales order and acknowledged with a 997 by the customer. Any issues that may exist with the customer over the sales order must first be resolved.

The outbound delivery is created from one or more completed sales orders against one of DSI's warehouses set up as a shipping point and plant in Acme's SAP system. It can be generated either from the delivery due list or directly from a sales order.

The sales order is linked to the delivery document at the line-item level. The delivery document can accommodate one or more sales orders, which means that it can also be linked to multiple customer purchase orders. But at Acme Pictures, we're keeping it simple. One of the early design decisions was to create only one delivery document per sales order.

The outbound delivery is also a key element of the order-to-cash document flow in SAP. It follows the sales order and must be confirmed before Acme can issue an invoice to the customer.

Sales document flow is stored table VBFA.

14.2.1 Process Overview

The delivery documents is created from one sales order using transaction VL01N (create single) or from multiple sales orders with Transaction VL10 from the delivery due list. Either way, one delivery document is created per sales order.

Creation of the outbound delivery reserves the ordered goods for shipment in Acme inventory and triggers generation of an IDoc using message type SHPORD and basic type DELVRY03.

The IDoc is parked in the IDoc database at status 30—*IDoc ready for dispatch*—until it's picked up and exported to the EDI RIM by a scheduled job that runs every 15 minutes.

The RIM converts the SHPORD message to an X12 830 transaction and sends it to DSI by AS2, where it posts to their shipping system and generates a picking list. DSI then picks the ordered goods from their warehouse storage location, transfers them to a loading area, packs them into cartons and pallets, and loads them onto trucks for shipment to Gordy's distribution center, which in turn sends them on to the ordering stores.

14.2.2 Requirements

Customers order goods for delivery on a particular date, so shipping orders must be dropped to the third-party distributor's warehouse (DSI) as quickly as possible. There are a few other business requirements:

▶ All deliveries for catalog and new release titles are created by running the delivery due list with Transaction VL10 after the sales order has been successfully confirmed and completed.

▶ When required, one-off deliveries can be created with Transaction VL01N or directly within a sales order that is ready for delivery with Transaction VA02.

▶ The delivery due list is run for a number of key options:

  ▶ Shipping plant

  ▶ Delivery date

  ▶ Sold-to and ship-to partners

  ▶ Sales order numbers

▶ One outbound delivery is issued per shipping plant and sales order.

▶ EDI ship order delivery documents are created for sales orders of sales document type:

  ▶ ZEDI for EDI orders with no SDQ

  ▶ ZEDS for EDI orders with SDQ

  ▶ ZVMI for VMI orders

▶ The delivery document inherits all data from the sales order, including item-level sales BOMs for multi-packs.

▶ No partial deliveries are allowed for Gordy's Galaxy.

▶ The outbound delivery is created, and the IDoc generated, only if there is enough available stock in inventory to cover the order. That stock is reserved and put on hold for the delivery.

▶ Sticker information is included in text elements at the item level of the sales order and delivery document and is sent to DSI in the IDoc.

▶ The sales BOM for multi-pack items is included in the delivery at the standard line-item level. The sales BOM will be sent by EDI for the supplier's information. It must also be listed on the shipping and billing documents sent to Gordy.

Multi-Pack Items at Acme Pictures

A multi-pack is a freestanding corrugate display with multiple DVD titles packaged for the retailer as a single product. The consumer buys discs individually from the display.

Material master records are created in SAP for the corrugate display item and for each component DVD title included within it.

The multi-pack has a sales and a production BOM associated with the material number for the corrugate display. The sales BOM consists of each DVD title and a separate entry for the corrugate display, which is the last item listed. The production BOM includes text descriptions for each component DVD title and a separate entry for the corrugate material number.

Each component title in the multi-pack has its own production BOM, which includes the raw materials required to assemble the finished DVD title.

Gordy's Galaxy orders multi-packs through the high-level corrugate item in its 850 EDI PO. When the ORDERS IDoc posts to an SAP sales order, each sales BOM component DVD title is pulled in immediately after the multi-pack item—which posts as item 10—in the order that each appears in the BOM. Each component title has a line item number, beginning with 20, and refers back to the corrugate as its parent.

This is standard SAP practice and is driven by data in the material master, including the material group and item category. The item category for the corrugate material at Acme is ZTAP, and the category for each component item is ZAQ.

Pricing is accumulated at the multi-pack level, but each component DVD title has its own pricing. The sum of the price of the components must equal the total price of the multi-pack.

The sales BOM explosion is triggered from the posting of the sales order by the ORDERS IDoc. It is then passed to each subsequent document in the sales document flow and to each outbound IDoc generated.

DSI only cares about the multi-pack shipping item, but Gordy wants to see each component DVD title in the sales BOM in its delivery and billing documents.

The sales BOM is passed to IDocs generated from both of these documents, and it's included in the 830 transmission to DSI.

14.2.3 Dependencies

The SHPORD-830 interface is dependent on master data, configuration, and development in SAP and the EDI RIM, including everything required to support sales orders and confirmations. The following are additional dependencies:

▸ A vendor master record for DSI exists flagged for goods receipt-based invoicing.

▸ Material master data for standalone and multi-pack shipping finished goods is assigned to DSI warehouses as ship plants and storage locations and to Acme sales organization and distribution channels.

▸ Production and sales BOMs exist in SAP for multi-pack materials and component DVD titles.

▸ The full sales BOM is pulled in orders for multi-pack items when the sales order is created by a customer PO in an ORDERS IDoc.

▸ IDoc configuration in SAP supports outbound deliveries to DSI for Gordy's Galaxy, including output control to generate SHPORD IDocs from deliveries and partner profiles with message control that link the vendor to the outbound SHPORD message type.

14.2.4 Assumptions

SHPORD IDocs are automatically generated when delivery documents are created. One delivery document and one SHPORD IDoc are output for each sales order and shipping point—which is defined at Acme as a shipping plant at the vendor location.

There are a few other key assumptions about the SHPORD-830 interface:

▸ The sales order has been completed in Acme's SAP system, and the 855 confirmation has been sent and confirmed by a return 997 to Acme before the delivery document is generated.

▸ The sales order contains all customer- and material-related data.

▸ All relevant sales order data are passed to the delivery document during output processing, including the following:

  ▹ Customer PO and SAP sales order numbers

  ▹ Relevant partner numbers and addresses for sold-to, ship-to, payer, and invoice recipient

  ▹ All ordered finished goods that will be shipped

  ▹ Sales BOMs for multi-pack items ordered by Gordy's Galaxy

▸ Sales order pricing, however, is not included. Pricing is not maintained in the delivery document and is not sent to DSI in the IDoc.

▸ Inventory contains sufficient stock to cover order requirements for the delivery.

- The SHPORD IDoc contains all data in the delivery document.

- The IDoc is sent as an X12 830 shipping order to DSI, the contract distributor, who is set up as a vendor in Acme's SAP system.

- The SHPORD IDoc can be regenerated from the delivery if required.

- DSI receives Acme's SAP partner and material numbers. All of DSI's interfaces are supported by daily extracts, both full and delta, of master and transactional data from Acme's SAP system that include the following:

  - Customer master sold-to and ship-to partners

  - Material master finished goods and components

  - Production BOMs

  - Customer material info records

  - Inventory levels for finished goods

  - Open sales orders and deliveries

- DSI also receives the GTIN number for ordered goods, which is printed on the packing labels and other paperwork sent to Gordy with the delivery.

  The GTIN number is stored in the EAN/UPC field of the Sales A subscreen at the item level of the delivery document. It passes to the IDoc in the EAN11 field of line item segment E1EDL24.

- Packaging data for the ordered items can pass to the IDoc, but we won't look at that in this specification.

14.2.5 Data That Will Pass to an Outbound Ship Order

Table 14.2 displays the source for key data passed to the SHPORD IDoc from the delivery document.

Table	Field	Description	Sample Value
Delivery Header			
LIKP	VBELN	Delivery number	0816160750
LIKP	VSTEL	Shipping point (DSI ship plant)	0015
LIKP	VKORG	Sales organization	0010

Table 14.2 Key Delivery Document Data That Pass to the SHPORD IDoc

Table	Field	Description	Sample Value
LIKP	WADAT	Planned goods issue date	20081220
LIKP	LFDAT	Delivery date	20081220
LIKP	INCO1	Inco terms 1	PPD
LIKP	INCO2	Inco terms 2	Destination
VBPA	KUNNR	PARVW = AG: Sold-to partner	GRDY01
VBPA	KUNNR	PARVW = WE: Ship-to partner	GRDY01001
VBPA	KUNNR	PARVW = RE: Bill-to party	GRDY01
VBPA	KUNNR	PARVW = RG: Payer	GRDY01
LIKP	BTGEW	Total gross weight of all items	128.750
LIKP	NTGEW	Net weight of all items	128.750
STXH	TDID	Text ID for delivery texts sent to DSI	Z005
STXL	CLUSTR	Header text from delivery	Delivery text
Delivery Items			
LIPS	POSNR	Item number	000010
LIPS	PSTYV	Delivery item category. Identifies top-level and component items in a multi-pack sales BOM.	ZTAP
LIPS	MATNR	Order item (SAP)	2356784
LIPS	WERKS	Shipping plant	0015
LIPS	LGORT	Storage location in plant	0010
LIPS	KDMAT	Customer material number	799142939512
LIPS	LFIMG	Delivery quantity for item	4
LIPS	MEINS	Unit of measure for quantity	EA
LIPS	NTGEW	Net weight for item	1
LIPS	BRGEW	Gross weight for item	1
LIPS	VGBEL	Delivery item sales order number	0021611916
VBKD	BSTKD	Customer PO number	292259
LIPS	EAN11	GTIN global item number	799142939512

Table 14.2 Key Delivery Document Data That Pass to the SHPORD IDoc (Cont.)

Delivery item category field LIPS-PSTYV identifies whether the material is a standard shipping item, the top-level shipping item from a multi-pack item sales BOM, or a component title within the sales BOM.

The item category for the top-level shipping unit of a sales BOM is ZTAP, always in line item 10. DVD title components of the multi-pack sales BOM have item category ZAQ and are numbered sequentially from line item 20, in the same order that they appear in the sales BOM.

The customer PO number is pulled from sales document table VBKD using the sales order number from LIPS-VGBEL.

A lot of data passes to the SHPORD IDoc from the delivery and related documents and records. Only the values that will be sent to DSI are mapped to the 830.

14.2.6 Enhancements to the Process

There are no custom enhancements in this interface.

14.2.7 Reconciliation

Data in the SHPORD IDoc will be validated against the delivery document. IDoc data will also be validated against the translated 830.

The EDI team will confirm that the 830 was sent to the correct customer.

Output of the SHPORD IDoc can be confirmed by checking the output screen of the delivery document in Transaction VL03N menu option EXTRAS • DELIVERY OUTPUT HEADER, which should display an output record with a green traffic light for output type ZSH1, partner type SH (ship-to), and partner DISK01. The PROCESSING LOG button will return the IDoc number.

14.2.8 Errors and Error Handling

If the SHPORD IDoc fails to generate, confirm that message control is correctly configured for the message type and that there is no credit or delivery block against the customer.

Failures in outbound IDoc processing are tracked by the EDI support team using standard IDoc monitoring tools such as BD87 and WE05. Application errors are reported to the business users immediately.

14.3 Generating a SHPORD IDoc with Message Control

The outbound ship order to DSI is generated by message control when the delivery document is created. We'll cover the message control settings to automatically output the IDoc in this section.

The outbound delivery is a funny kind of document. It can be used to generate more than one type of outbound IDoc. Here we're creating a ship order that goes to a third-party distributor. But later, in Chapter 16, we generate an advanced ship notification which goes to a customer.

Both can be generated from the same outbound delivery and use the same application and output type in message control, the same process code, and more or less the same IDoc basic type. But they generate different logical messages, support different points in the delivery process, and have different business meaning, so we need a unique custom output type for each process.

We will create the following configuration objects to support generation of the SHPORD IDoc to DSI:

▶ Custom output type ZSH1 copied from standard output LAVA with access sequence 0010 (for delivery type and shipping point) and supporting configuration

▶ Condition record mapping vendor DSI to the Acme shipping point set up for the DSI warehouse

▶ One partner profile with message control for DSI with the ship order message type SHPORD

14.3.1 Configuring Message Control

To create our custom output type ZSH1, we'll copy standard type LAVA in application V2 (shipping) using Transaction NACE. Follow these steps:

1. Select application V2 and click Output types to open the Output Types: Overview in display mode.

2. Select menu path Table View • Display • Change (or press Ctrl+F1) and select standard output LAVA. Click Copy as or press F6.

3. Change the output type name to ZSH1 and enter a description for the ship order to the supplier. Make sure Access to conditions and Multiple issuing are both set (as shown in Figure 14.1).

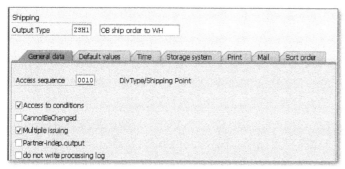

Figure 14.1   Custom Output Type ZSH1 with Access Sequence 0010

4. Keep access sequence 0010 for delivery type and shipping point.

   The shipping point will be unique to DSI. We can further control who gets this IDoc by mapping the vendor number to the shipping point in the condition record.

5. The access number is 10 and the condition table is 21 (B021) with communications structure KOMKBV2 with two key fields:

   ▶ LFART: Delivery type

   ▶ VSTEL: Shipping point

6. Press Enter. The Specify object to be copied dialog opens, noting that the output type has dependent entries. Click Copy all. Another dialog opens with the number of dependent entries.

7. The system returns us to the Output types: Overview screen in change view. Save the new output type and assign to a change request.

8. Select output ZSH1 and double-click the Processing routines folder to open the Processing routines: Overview screen.

9. If there is no program and form routine for medium EDI, add one. Click NEW ENTRIES to open the DETAILS OF ADDED ENTRIES screen. Enter the following values:

    ▶ TRANSM.MEDIUM: "EDI"

    ▶ PROGRAM (Processing 1): "RSNASTED" for the standard SAP output program

    ▶ FORM ROUTINE: "EDI_PROCESSING", which identifies and calls the function that generates and sends the IDoc

10. Press ⎡Enter⎤ and double-click the PARTNER FUNCTIONS folder to open the PARTNER FUNCTIONS: OVERVIEW screen.

11. Make sure that there's an entry for medium EDI and partner type VN for vendor. If not, click NEW ENTRIES and select EDI in the MEDIUM field and VN in the FUNCT field.

12. Save any changes since your last save.

Assign ZSHI1 to a Procedure

Follow these steps:

1. Back out to the output control initial screen in Transaction NACE. Select application V2 and click PROCEDURES.

2. Select procedure V10000 (header output) and double-click CONTROL in the navigation pane.

3. Select output type LAVA and click the COPY AS button (or press ⎡F6⎤). The entry is copied into the CHANGE VIEW CONTROL: OVERVIEW screen.

4. Change the step number to 35, the counter to 1, and the output type name to ZSH1. Change the requirement from 1 to 3.

    Requirement 1 issues output only after goods issue has posted against the outbound delivery. The goods issue will be posted by the ship confirmation after DSI has loaded the ordered goods onto a truck and shipped them to Gordy's Galaxy. It's still too soon in the process for this. The ship order interface tells DSI what to ship.

    Requirement 3 checks that there's no credit block on the delivery. This is a reasonable output check for our ship order.

5. Press ⎡Enter⎤ to return to the overview screen. Save the entry and assign it to a change request. The entry should look like Figure 14.2.

Procedure	V10000	Header Output			

Reference Step Overview					
Step	Counter	CTyp	Description	Requiremnt	Manual o
30	3	LAVA	Outg. ship.notifica.	1	
35	1	ZSH1	OB ship order to WH	1	

Figure 14.2 ZSH1 Assigned to Outbound Delivery Header Output Procedure

Create Condition Records

As we have seen, condition records drive generation of the IDoc for Acme's vendor DSI. For the ship order, the IDoc will be generated by delivery document type and shipping point, which mirrors DSI's shipping point.

We can create the condition records directly in Transaction NACE by selecting application V2, clicking CONDITION RECORDS, and selecting output type ZSH1, or directly with Transaction VV21.

1. Using Transaction VV21, enter output type ZSH1 and click the KEY COMBINATION button. Then select DLVTYPE/SHIPPING POINT and press ⌈Enter⌋.

2. Enter "LF" for standard delivery in the DELIVERY TYPE field and the following values in the condition records table control (see Figure 14.3):

   ▶ SHIP POINT: "3100"

   ▶ FUNCTION: "VN" FOR VENDOR

   ▶ PARTNER: "DISK01"

   ▶ MEDIUM: "6" for EDI

   ▶ DISPATCH TIME: "4" for immediately when the document is saved

   ▶ LANGUAGE: "EN"

Delivery Type	LF	Delivery					

Condition Recs.							
Ship Point	Name		Funct	Partner	Medium	Date/Time	Language
3100	Shipping Point Chicago		VN	DISK01	6	4	EN

Figure 14.3 Condition Record for Output Type ZSH1 Application V2

14.3.2 Overview of the End-to-End Process Flow

Figure 14.4 gives an overview of the end-to-end process flow for generating and sending EDI ship orders to DSI for a Gordy's Galaxy order.

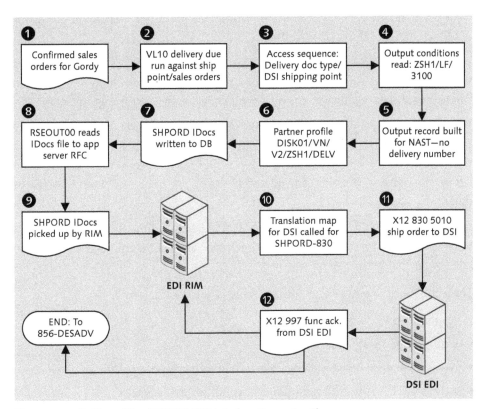

Figure 14.4 Outline of the SHPORD-830 Interface Processing Flow

Outbound SHPORD Processing

The SHPORD-830 interface kicks off after the 997 functional acknowledgment has been received from Gordy's Galaxy for the outbound 855 order confirmation. Delivery documents are generated from completed but not yet shipped sales orders by running the delivery due list using Transaction VL10.

Two critical keys are read from the sales order after the delivery is built and just before it is saved:

- **Shipping point**
  The DSI plant set up in Acme's SAP system used to deliver product to Gordy's Galaxy

- **Delivery document type**
  LF for standard deliveries generated from sales order types ZEDI and ZEDS for all EDI and ZVMI for all VMI orders

Function SHP_EXTENDED_DUE_LIST_VIEW in function group V50R_VIEW is called by the VL10 delivery due list program RVV50R10C to collect data from eligible sales orders and to create delivery documents by calling Transaction VL01 (program SAPMV50A).

All output control keys (including application, procedure, output type, and access sequence) are identified. An output record is prepared for table NAST by functions COMMUNICATION_AREA_KOMKBV2 and MESSAGING in function group V61B. This is done before the delivery document is posted by BAPI SHP_BAPI_DELIVERY_REPLICA in function group V50K.

SHP_BAPI_DELIVERY_REPLICA also updates the document flow for sales documents in table VBFA to include the outbound delivery as a follow-up document for the sales order that generated it.

These are output control keys for the delivery document:

- Application V2: Shipping
- Output type ZSH1: Shipping request
- Access sequence 0010: Delivery document type, shipping point
- Access 10: DlvType/shipping point in condition table B021
- Procedure V10000: Header output linked to output type ZSH1

The fields that make up the access are from communications structure KOMKBV2: VSTEL (shipping point) and LFART (delivery type).

The condition record is entered through Transaction VV21. It links the delivery document type to the shipping plant and vendor number for DSI in Acme's SAP system.

The condition tables are read with the access keys, the DSI shipping plant is hit, and the vendor number returned.

DSI's outbound partner profile is then checked by calling function EDI_PARTNER_READ_OUTGOING through the key fields in structure EDK12:

► RCVPRN: Receive partner sold-to number: DISK01

► RCVPRT: Receive partner type: LI (vendor)

► RCVPFC: Receipt partner function: VN (vendor)

► KAPPL: Message control application: V2

► KSCHL: Message type: ZSH1

► AENDE: Change message flag

One partner profile is set up for DSI with outbound message type SHPORD. It links to output control through the Message Control subscreen, which includes three values:

► Application V2 for shipping messages

► Output (or message) type ZSH1

► Process code DELV that links message type SHPORD to standard IDoc processing function module IDOC_OUTPUT_DELVRY

As the delivery document is saved, the IDoc output is proposed and generated.

The output proposal is saved in an output record in table NAST. IDoc processing program RSNASTED and form routine EDI_PROCESSING are identified from a read of table TNAPR.

The partner profile is read, the control record assembled, and the IDoc build function identified from table TFDIR.

The function IDOC_OUTPUT_ORDERS is called, and the IDocs are built and written to the database at status 30—*IDoc ready for dispatch*.

The partner profile was set to batch the SHPORD IDocs and send them by running program RSEOUT00 every 30 minutes to pick up all outbound SHPORD IDocs at status 30 for DSI, convert them to XML format, and send them to the EDI RIM.

The XML IDocs are saved in a file on the SAP application server and an RFC is made through JCo to the receiving business process workflow in the EDI RIM.

The IDoc file is picked up and moved to the translation process, which identifies the envelopes from the EDI send and receive trading partner IDs and the EDI transaction and version in the IDoc control segment.

The ST envelope identifies and calls the translation map.

The IDoc is translated to an X12 830 version 5010 transaction set with an ST-SE envelope. It is bundled into a group defined by a GS-GE envelope with any other IDocs in the file.

When all IDocs have been translated and the group completed, it is bundled into an interchange with an ISA-IEA envelope.

The X12 interchange is passed to a communications workflow, which sends it to DSI's EDI system through an AS2 call. The process waits for the MDN acknowledgment, which comes immediately.

The cycle ends when DSI returns a 997 acknowledgment for the 830 transactions. This generally happens within minutes or an hour at most.

If it takes longer than 24 hours to receive the 997, Acme's EDI team contacts the DSI EDI team to find out whether there are any issues.

At the Warehouse

Upon receipt of the shipping orders, DSI posts them to their business system. This drives follow-up processes:

1. Picking goods for shipment from storage locations in DSI's warehouse

2. Applying customer-specific stickers to the product for Gordy's Galaxy

3. Packing the delivery goods into cartons and onto pallets and moving them all into a loading area

4. Attaching labels to the containers and pallets in human-readable and barcode format that identify:

   ▸ The delivery store, address, and postal code

   ▸ Sold-to GLN identification code and name

   ▸ Purchase order number and GTIN codes for the delivery items with packing, dimension, and weight information

   ▸ Tracking number for the shipment

5. Printing and attaching packing lists to the shipment (for Gordy's Galaxy, this includes the sales BOM explosion for multi-pack shipping goods, with each title in the display pack identified)

6. Loading the pallets of packaged delivery items onto trucks for shipment to Gordy's distribution center

7. Generating a ship confirmation for return to Acme by EDI as the truck pulls away from the dock

14.4 Technical Specifications

This technical specification describes the SAP configuration and EDI development required to support the SHPORD to X12 830 EDI interface to DSI to trigger shipment processing of ordered items to Gordy's Galaxy.

14.4.1 Technical Requirements

The generated IDoc will store all standard data from the outbound delivery.

For multi-pack orders, the EDI map passes the shipping unit and all of the components of the sales BOM to the 830 EDI transaction at the standard line-item level.

14.4.2 Dependencies

Message control configuration is complete, and condition records have been entered. There are a few other dependencies:

▶ Outbound partner profile created for DSI with message type SHPORD

▶ Acme custom cross-reference table ZEDIXREF populated in SAP for DSI to read EDI send and receive trading partner IDs for the outbound 830 ship order

▶ Program variants created for jobs in the SAP Job Scheduler (Transaction SM36) to run:

▶ RVV50R10C for generating delivery documents from sales orders for all customers using the delivery due list

▶ RSEOUT00 for exporting SHPORD IDocs to DSI (receiver partner type LI and partner DISK01)

- Outbound envelopes created in the EDI RIM for DSI's 830 version 5010 EDI transmissions, including the following:

  - ISA: IEA interchange control

  - GS: GE group control

  - ST: SE transaction set

- Inbound envelopes set in the RIM to receive 997 version 5010 FAs from DSI for the outbound 830

- Translation maps created in the EDI RIM for SHPORD IDoc to 830 X12 version 5010 ship order

- Business process workflows existing in the EDI RIM to pick up IDoc files from the SAP application server, convert them to X12 830 ship orders, and send them to DSI

14.4.3 Assumptions

The EDI RIM gets EDI sending and receiving trading partner IDs from the IDoc control record fields SNDLAD and RCVLAD. The following are additional key assumptions:

- DSI will return an X12 997 functional acknowledgment within 24 hours of receiving the 830 ship order transmission.

- If there are any errors posting the 830 ship order to DSI's system, the EDI team at Acme will be notified immediately by phone or email.

- All IDoc errors are monitored by the EDI team in SAP.

- Technical errors in the IDoc interface, such as syntax or partner profile errors, are documented and corrected by the EDI team.

- All IDoc application errors are handled by the business users and backed up by the EDI team where appropriate.

- The EDI team communicates IDoc application errors to the business users immediately.

- EDI errors are tracked and addressed in the EDI system.

14.5   Mapping Specifications

A map will be developed in the EDI RIM to translate the SHPORD IDoc to an 830 X12 5010 transaction to DSI. All deliveries for all customers who are handled by DSI will flow through the same map.

Table 14.3 details the mapping requirements for the outbound SHPORD-830 transaction for DSI.

SHPORD	830	Value	Comments
E1EDL20—Header—Min 1, Max 1			
	BFR01	00	Hard-code. Original message.
VBELN	BFR02	0080016843	Delivery number
VSBED	TD505	02	Routing code
E1EDL21—Additional header data—Min 0, Max 1			
LPRIO	REF02	02	Priority code. Maps to REF segment where REF01 = PH priority rating.
E1ADRM1— Delivery partner—Min 1, Max 99, Loop 1 Ship-from			
PARTNER_Q	N101	OSP	Convert to SF for shipping plant ID qualifier.
PARTNER_ID	N104	3100	DSI shipping point ID
NAME1	N102	New York Shipping Point	Shipping point name
STREET1	N301	2100 Grant	Shipping point street address
POSTL_COD1	N403	17789	Shipping point postal code
CITY1	N401	New York City	Shipping point city name
COUNTRY1	N404	US	Shipping point country code
REGION	N402	NY	Shipping point region country code

Table 14.3   Map Specification for the Ship Order IDoc to the X12 830

SHPORD	830	Value	Comments
E1ADRM1—Partners—Loop 2 Ship-to			
PARTNER_Q	N101	WE	Convert to ST for ship-to qualifier.
PARTNER_ID	N104	GRDY01001	Customer ship-to location
NAME1	N102	Gordy store 1213	Ship-to location name
STREET1	N301	2300 Colonel Rd	Ship-to location street address
POSTL_COD1	N403	07960	Ship-to location postal code
CITY1	N401	Morristown	Ship-to location city name
COUNTRY1	N404	US	Ship-to location country code
REGION	N402	NJ	Ship-to location region code
E1ADRM1— Partners—Loop 3 Sold-to			
PARTNER_Q	N101	AG	Convert to BT for bill-to qualifier.
PARTNER_ID	N104	GRDY01	Customer sold-to location
NAME1	N102	Gordy's Galaxy	Sold-to partner name
STREET1	N301	2356 Halsted St	Sold-to partner address
POSTL_COD1	N403	60642	Sold-to partner postal code
CITY1	N401	Chicago	Sold-to partner city name
COUNTRY1	N404	US	Sold-to partner country code
REGION	N402	IL	Sold-to partner region code
E1EDT13—Delivery dates—Min 0, Max 99—Loop 1 Requested delivery			
QUALF	DTM01	007	Convert to 002 requested delivery.
NTANF	DTM02	20140115	Requested delivery date
E1EDT13— Delivery dates—Loop 2 Requested ship date			
QUALF	DTM01	006	Convert to 010 requested ship date.
NTANF	DTM02	20140115	Requested delivery date

Table 14.3 Map Specification for the Ship Order IDoc to the X12 830 (Cont.)

SHPORD	830	Value	Comments
E1EDL24—Line-item level details group—Min 1, Max N 1 instance of E1EDL24 per group loop			
POSNR	LIN01	000010	Line item number
	LIN02	MG	Hard-code MG to identify supplier (Acme) material number.
MATNR	LIN03	2567898	Acme SAP item number
	PID01	F	Hard-code F for free form description.
ARKTX	PID05		Material description
	LIN06	IN	Hard-code IN identifying customer material number.
KDMAT	LIN07	799142939512	Customer material number
LFIMG	QTY02	100.000	Delivery item quantity
VRKME	QTY03	EA	Unit of measure
	LIN04	UP	Hard-code UP to identify GTIN code in EAN11 following.
EAN11	LIN05	02563587889125	GTIN code
Hard code	SLN09	MG	Vendor (Acme) part number
E1EDL43—Reference documents—Min 1, Max 99—Loop 1 sales order			
QUALF	REF01	C	Convert to VN for vendor order. Acme sales order.
BELNR	REF02	00014031	Acme sales order number
E1EDL43—Reference documents—Loop 2 customer purchase order			
QUALF	REF01	V	Convert to PO for customer purchase number.
BELNR	REF02	4500017707	Gordy purchase order number

Table 14.3 Map Specification for the Ship Order IDoc to the X12 830 (Cont.)

This is a simplified specification that doesn't take either the sales BOM for multi-pack items or the packaging hierarchy (handling units) into account.

Sales BOM components for multi-pack orders would be mapped to the SLN group within one LIN item group that stores the highest level shipping item.

In the IDoc, the shipping item and the sales BOM components are stored as sequential items. The sales BOM components are identified by fields:

▶ E1EDL24-HIPOS: Points to the parent item number for the component of a sales BOM.

▶ E1EDL24-HIEVW: Code identifying usage of a component item: 2 = BOM item.

The packaging hierarchy, if defined in the delivery document, would be stored in a separate group of segments under parent E1EDL37 following the E1EDL24 line item group.

14.6   EDI Configuration in SAP

Let's add an entry to our custom EDI mapping table ZEDIXREF to support outbound EDI trading partner number conversion and an outbound partner profile for DSI.

14.6.1 EDPAR Entries: Transaction VOE4

There are no EDPAR entries for the outbound SHPORD.DELVRY03 to X12 830 shipping order interface.

14.6.2 ZEDIXREF Entries

We'll map the IDoc sender and receiver partner numbers—the SAP logical system ID and DSI's vendor number—to the receiving party's send and receive EDI trading partner IDs.

Table 14.4 lists the ZEDIXREF values for the outbound SHPORD.DELVRY03 interface to DSI are listed in.

Field	Value	Description
DIRECT	1	Direction outbound
STDMES	830	EDI transaction
MESTYP	SHPORD	IDoc message type

Table 14.4   ZEDIXREF Entry for the Outbound 830 to DSI

Field	Value	Description
IDOCTP	DELVRY03	IDoc basic type
CIMTYP		IDoc extension, none for this interface
SNDPRN	DEVCLNT100	SAP send partner: Acme SAP logical system
RCVPRN	DISK01	SAP receive partner: DSI's vendor number in Acme's system
SNDLAD	99999998889	EDI send partner: DSI trading partner ID for Acme
RCVLAD	99934567999	EDI receiver partner: DSI trading partner ID for DSI

Table 14.4 ZEDIXREF Entry for the Outbound 830 to DSI (Cont.)

14.6.3 Partner Profiles: Transaction WE20

We'll define one outbound partner profile for DSI partner number DISK01, partner type LI (vendor), and partner role VN (vendor).

In the outbound parameters table control of the partner profile for DSI, click the CREATE OUTBOUND PARAMETERS button and enter the following values in the OUT-BOUND PARAMETERS screen, as shown in Figure 14.5.

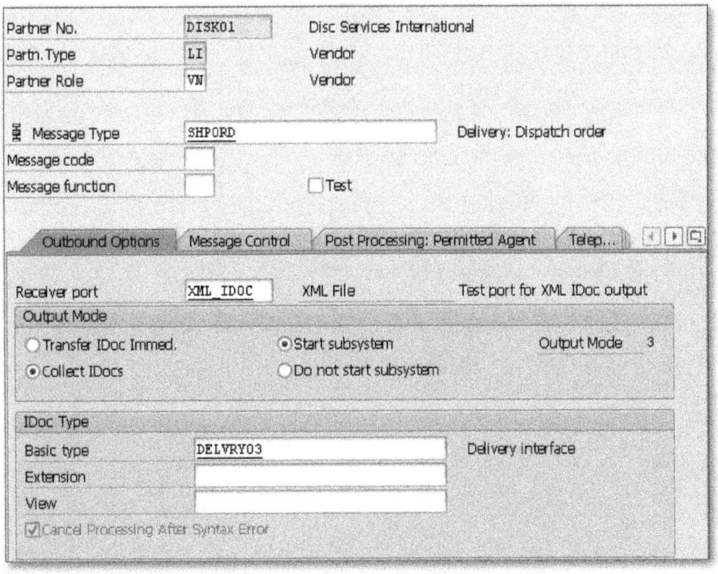

Figure 14.5 Outbound Parameters, SHPORD Ship Order to DSI

- PARTNER ROLE: "VN"
- MESSAGE TYPE: "SHPORD"
- RECEIVER PORT: "XML_IDOC"
- OUTPUT MODE area: COLLECT IDocs and START SUBSYSTEM checkboxes
- BASIC TYPE: "DELVRY03"

Click MESSAGE CONTROL and enter the following values, which are shown in Figure 14.6:

- APPLICATION: "V2"
- MESSAGE TYPE: "ZSH1"
- PROCESS CODE: "DELV"
- CHANGE MESSAGE checkbox: One entry null and one checked

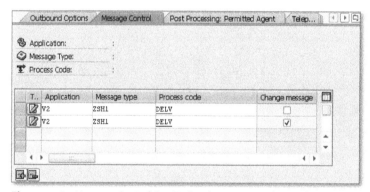

Figure 14.6 Message Control Set Up for the SHPORD Ship Order

Process code DELV links to function module `IDOC_OUTPUT_DELVRY`, which builds the IDoc from the delivery document and sales order.

The last step is to select the EDI STANDARD tab from the upper far right of the screen tabs and enter the following values, as shown in Figure 14.7:

- EDI STANDARD: "X" for X12
- MESSAGE TYPE: "830"
- VERSION: "005010"

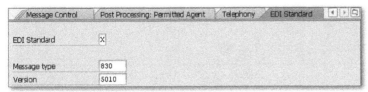

Figure 14.7 EDI Standard Values for the SHPORD Ship Order

Don't forget to save the partner profile.

14.7 Summary

Acme Pictures is now ready to send shipping orders by EDI transmission to their contract distributor, Disk Services International.

For its part, DSI will receive these messages and kick off the shipping process so that goods ordered by Gordy's Galaxy of Games & B Flix are delivered and shelves continue to be stocked with Acme product.

This makes everybody happy because they all make money.

As we've seen, this is a standard and not overly complex process. The sales order is completed, outbound delivery documents are issued, and IDocs are generated using standard message control configuration.

We did need to create custom output type because the delivery document will generate another IDoc to the customer as an advanced shipping notification later in the process. But we'll get to that later.

The only wrinkle—and it's a minor one—is with multi-pack items that will sit on Gordy's floor as displays featuring multiple DVD movie titles. These will appear in the IDoc as regular line items beneath the multi-pack container, linked to it through a reference to the parent item.

So now the ball is in DSI's court. Once they ship the ordered product, they'll let Acme know that those DVDs are winging their way to the customer by sending a ship confirmation as soon as the truck leaves their loading dock. We look at the ship confirmation, which is the next logical interface in the order-to-cash cycle.

While the great Mr. Q trusted his writers and directors to deliver the movies, he wanted confirmation at every key stage of a project. It's the same thing with the shipping confirmation interface: It confirms to Acme that DSI did its job and shipped the customer order to Gordy. So let's see how this works. It all begins with a truck.

15 The Inbound Shipping Confirmation

We've seen that the ship order provides Disc Services International (DSI) with the five Ws of DVD distribution: who, what, where from, where to, and when to ship the ordered goods.

DSI, in turn, needs to tell Acme when the order has been fulfilled and the goods picked, packed, and shipped to Gordy's Galaxy of Games & B Flix.

This is a key piece of the puzzle for Acme Pictures. Until Acme knows that the goods are out the door and on their way to Gordy, the delivery document won't be closed, and inventory won't be relieved of the saleable finished goods received when DSI produced them.

The shipping confirmation completes the delivery by updating the quantity of goods picked for shipment and by posting the goods issue, which creates material and accounting documents recording the quantity and dollar value for the inventory released against the appropriate G/L accounts.

This provides accounts receivable with the information it needs to invoice Gordy's Galaxy for the order. But Acme must first send Gordy an advanced shipping notification before the shipment arrives from DSI. Then Gordy must receive and accept the goods against the ASN, which preps their accounts payable to receive an invoice from Acme.

We'll go over these processes in the next two chapters. Before we can get there, Acme must receive the shipping confirmation and that's we're going to look at in this chapter.

15.1   Technical Overview of the Interface

Table 15.1 summarizes the inbound invoice interface from the supplier.

Item	Description
Title	Inbound Ship Confirmation from Supplier
Description	Acme has sent a shipping order to DSI with details of finished movies on DVD that have been ordered by Gordy's Galaxy through a purchase order. The shipping order was generated from as sales created by an EDI purchase order sent by Gordy.
	The shipping order tells DSI what to pick, pack, and deliver. DSI checks their inventory for the finished product in the ship order. The full order quantity is picked and moved to a packing location where they are put into cases and the cases onto pallets for shipping.
	Stickers may also be put on the packages if required by the customer or local regulations in the state or province where the goods are being shipped.
	When the goods are fully packed, and the paperwork is settled—bills of lading, packing lists and so on—the truck pulls away from the loading dock, and an X12 856 transaction is generated confirming that the order has been shipped and detailing the pick quantity and inventory transfers just completed. Acme's outbound delivery document number must be included in this transmission.
	The 856 shipping confirmation is sent to Acme's EDI RIM where it is converted to a SHPCON.DELVRY03 IDoc and sent into SAP to update the picking quantity in the outbound delivery and trigger the post goods issue relieving inventory and updating accounting.
Type of interface	Delivery: X12 EDI to IDoc
Direction	Inbound
Trading partner	Disk Services International (vendor)
IDoc	SHPCON.DELVRY03
IDoc extended type	

Table 15.1   Overview of Inbound EDI Ship Confirmation

Item	Description
IDoc function	`IDOC_INPUT_DELVRY`
Custom ABAP	
Description	
Source file(s)	X12 856 ship confirmation
Target document(s)	SAP outbound delivery document
Transaction code	VL02N: update outbound delivery with pick quantities and post goods issue
Map(s)	X12 856 vers. 5010 to SHPCON.DELVRY03
Custom map logic	
Source system	DSI EDI via AS2
Target system	Acme SAP via EDI RIM
997 acknowledgment	Outbound at transaction detail level; function group acknowledgment code: SH
Frequency	Batched once a day at night, on demand
Job schedule	`RBDAPP01`: Seven times a day at 5 a.m., 8 a.m., 11 a.m., 2 p.m., 6 p.m., 9 p.m., and 1 a.m. to post all SHPCON message types for all suppliers

Table 15.1 Overview of Inbound EDI Ship Confirmation (Cont.)

15.2   Functional Specifications

The 856-SHPCON interface is the second of three steps in the delivery processing cycle. It follows successful completion of the outbound ship order to the supplier. All three steps must be successfully completed before invoicing can run.

Delivery documents are generated in Acme's SAP system from completed sales orders and are sent to DSI. The sales orders were created from customer purchase orders sent by EDI.

DSI's business system outputs shipping paperwork and its warehouse picks and packs the DVD titles in the shipping order.

The shipping confirmation is created by DSI's business system after the order ships to Gordy. The shipping confirmation updates the delivery document in Acme's SAP system with the picked quantity and closes it with a post goods issue (PGI).

15.2.1 Process Overview

The process begins when DSI receives a ship order from Acme and picks, stickers, and packs the order into cartons for shipment. Once the cartons are loaded onto trucks, the trucks pull away from the dock. DSI generates a shipping confirmation referencing the delivery document number in the shipping order. It sends the confirmation to Acme as an 856 EDI transmission.

The 856 is converted to an IDoc with message type SHPCON and basic type DELVRY03 in Acme's EDI RIM.

The IDoc is parked in the IDoc database until it's picked up and posted against the outbound delivery by a scheduled job that runs four times a day.

When the delivery is completed with the picking quantity update and the PGI, a DESADV IDoc is generated and sent to Gordy as an ASN, ending the delivery processing cycle.

15.2.2 Requirements

The delivery document has been generated in Acme's SAP system from the completed sales order, and the shipping order was successfully sent to DSI, who shipped the order to Gordy.

One delivery document exists in SAP per shipping plant and sales order. The shipping confirmation updates the outbound delivery in Acme's SAP system with the total quantity picked and shipped, the number of packages used, and the PGI. There are a few other business requirements:

▶ The 856 shipping confirmation from DSI uses the outbound delivery document and line item numbers from the shipping order to update the delivery in Acme's SAP system.

▶ No tolerance levels are set for picking quantities. The item must be picked and delivered in full with no overages or partial deliveries.

- Goods issue is only posted when all items have been fully picked, packed, and shipped from DSI's warehouse.

- Inventory is decremented by the goods issue. It generates the following documents that become part of the sales order and delivery document flow recorded in table VBFA:

  - A picking request recording the quantities of each item picked

  - A material document with movement type 601 (goods issue) that records the reduction in inventory

  - Accounting documents that record the inventory movements for each item against the bill-to customer and posts them to a G/L account and profit center

- Updating the delivery document with the PGI triggers output of an ASN in a DESADV IDoc that will be sent to Gordy's Galaxy to describe the shipment sent from DSI.

- Pricing data is not included in the delivery or the ship confirm.

Picking

In SAP, picking is a process where a quantity of goods is moved from one storage location to another staging location to be prepared for shipping.

At Acme Pictures, the storage location is in a DSI warehouse. The DSI warehouse is set up as a plant and a shipping point in Acme's SAP system, and the storage location is defined against that plant.

The finished goods are DVD movie titles or multi-pack corrugate displays composed of DVD movie titles. Preparing them for shipping involves (but isn't restricted to) the following steps:

- Applying customer or regional-specific stickers to the packaging (such as the infamous Régie classification sticker for the Canadian province of Quebec) that generates a lot of custom development work at every studio that sells DVD movies into that small market

- Putting the goods into cartons

- Printing and applying shipping labels to the cartons

- Stacking the cartons onto palettes for loading onto specific trucks traveling a particular route

- Printing and attaching paperwork, such as bills of lading, to the cartons or palettes

The current picking status is recorded in the delivery document against each item in the PICKING subscreen. The pick quantity must equal the actual delivery quantity for all items in the delivery document before the goods issue can be posted.

> **Post Goods Issue**
>
> Post goods issue is an inventory movement that, in the business relationship between Acme and DSI, reflects the real-world movement of ordered saleable product from DSI's warehouse to the customer.
>
> The PGI is triggered in the delivery by the incoming ship confirmation, which updates the quantity of goods picked and shipped and identifies the date they were shipped as the actual goods issue date.
>
> The goods issue is applied against the delivery document as a whole so all items must be fully picked and shipped. The goods issue creates one material document—linked to the delivery through the delivery document number—that records an inventory movement for each shipped item with movement type 601 (goods issue: delivery). This movement subtracts the shipped quantity of the saleable item from inventory.
>
> The customer invoice generated after the delivery closes must correspond to these inventory movements.

15.2.3 Dependencies

The 856-SHPCON interface is dependent on master data, configuration, and development in SAP and the EDI RIM, including everything required to support sales orders and outbound deliveries. There are a few other dependencies:

▶ DSI warehouses, storage locations, and shipping docks are set up as plants, storage locations, and shipping points in Acme's SAP system.

▶ The carrier—the trucking firm, railroad, courier, or other shipper—that will ship the order is set up in Acme's SAP system with a vendor master record.

▶ Item categories identifying the components of sales BOMs for multi-pack items aren't flagged as relevant to picking.

▶ If packing hierarchies (handling units, in SAP) are to be tracked in deliveries, packaging materials must be set up in the material master.

▶ Inbound IDoc configuration, including partner profile, is completed to link DSI to message type SHPCON.

15.2.4 Assumptions

The incoming SHPCON IDoc includes all fields required to identify the SAP delivery document and item, update the picked quantity, and post the goods issue. Consider these additional key assumptions:

▶ The shipping order to DSI has been sent, and the order gets picked and put on the truck en route to the customer before the 856-SHPCON interface updates the delivery document in Acme's SAP system.

▶ Data sent by DSI in the 856 ship confirm shall match data in Acme's outbound delivery document.

▶ The quantity picked shall not exceed the item quantity in the delivery document.

▶ Partial deliveries will not allowed.

▶ DSI sends Acme's SAP material numbers in the 856 for all materials in the delivery.

▶ The bill of lading (BOL) number is included in the 856 if available. It will update the delivery document.

▶ If the delivery is for a multi-pack order, picking quantity isn't updated for the components, only for the top-level corrugate item.

▶ When the delivery is completed by the post goods issue, an outbound DESADV IDoc is triggered and sent as an advanced ship notification to Gordy's Galaxy.

▶ Post goods issue is with movement type 601 or 602 for reversal.

▶ The ship confirmation process is the same for EDI and VMI purchase orders, regardless of delivery document type, customer, or item.

15.2.5 Delivery Document Data after Ship Confirm Update

The delivery document in SAP is updated with Transaction VL02N. Table 15.2 lists some key fields and tables in a standard delivery document after update by an inbound shipping confirmation.

Table	Field	Description	Sample Value
Delivery Header			
LIKP	VBELN	Delivery order number	0816160750
LIKP	VSTEL	Shipping point (DSI ship plant)	0015
LIKP	VKORG	Sales organization	0010
LIKP	LFART	Delivery type	LF

Table 15.2 Updated Delivery Document by Shipping Confirmation

Table	Field	Description	Sample Value
LIKP	LFDAT	Delivery date	20081220
LIKP	KODAT	Picking date	20081220
LIKP	INCO1	Inco terms 1	PPD
LIKP	INCO2	Inco terms 2	Destination
LIKP	BTGEW	Total gross weight of all items	128.750
LIKP	ANZPK	Total number of packages shipped	20
LIKP	LGNUM	Warehouse number	012
LIKP	WADAT_IST	Actual goods issue date	20081219
VBPA	KUNNR	PARVW = AG: Sold-to partner	GRDY01
VBPA	KUNNR	PARVW = WE: Ship-to partner	GRDY01001
VBUK	WBSTK	Goods issue status	C
VBUK	KOQUK	Status of pick confirmation	C
VBPA	KOSTK	Overall pick status	C
Delivery Items			
LIPS	POSNR	Item number	000010
LIPS	PSTYV	Delivery item category	TAP
LIPS	MATNR	Material ordered (SAP number)	2356784
LIPS	WERKS	Shipping plant	0015
LIPS	LGORT	Storage location in plant	0010
VBUP	KOSTA	Picking status	C (complete)
VBUP	WBSTA	Goods issue status	C (complete)
LIPS	KDMAT	Customer material number	0999429395121
LIPS	EAN11	UPC item number	0999429395121
LIPS	LFIMG	Delivery quantity for item	4
VBFA	RFMNG	Referenced qty = pick qty	4

Table 15.2 Updated Delivery Document by Shipping Confirmation (Cont.)

Table	Field	Description	Sample Value
LIPS	MEINS	Unit of measure for quantity	EA
LIPS	NTGEW	Net weight for item	1
LIPS	BRGEW	Gross weight for item	1
LIPS	VGBEL	Delivery item sales order number.	0021611916
VBKD	BSTKD	Customer PO number	292259

Table 15.2 Updated Delivery Document by Shipping Confirmation (Cont.)

The pick quantity that displays in the delivery document item-level picking screen (field LIPSD-PIKMG) is a dynamic value that references the actual quantity shipped. This comes in through the IDoc field E1EDL24-LFIMG and updates inventory through the goods issue 601 movement type.

The shipped quantity appears in the picking request document in table VBFA (document flow), with the sales order number referencing the material document number created by the PGI, the delivery item material number, and the 601 movement type.

Like the purchase order acknowledgment, the shipping confirmation confirms an existing document and updates only a handful of its fields, although these updates are critical to completing delivery processing.

15.2.6 Enhancements to the Process

No custom programming is required for this interface.

15.2.7 Reconciliation

Successful import of the SHPCON IDoc is confirmed through any of the standard IDoc monitoring tools such as BD87 or WE05.

IDoc status should be *64—IDoc ready to be transferred to application—*before the scheduled processing job is kicked off, and *53—Application document posted—*after.

Other validations can be performed:

▶ The pick quantity for each item in the delivery was the same as the shipping quantity in the IDoc field E1EDL24-LFIMG.

- The delivery document was updated with a post goods issue.

- Material and accounting documents were created for the post goods issue with movement type 601.

- Picking and goods issue dates are updated in the delivery.

- Picking and goods issue status at header and item levels are marked "C" for complete.

- The document flow (delivery document menu option ENVIRONMENT • DOCUMENT FLOW or table VBFA) includes relevant warehouse transfer, or picking, and material documents for the 601 movement type.

- The EDI team confirms the data in the SHPCON IDoc against the 856 ship confirm transaction set.

15.2.8 Errors and Error Handling

If the IDoc fails to update the delivery, the EDI team and the business users work together to identify and correct the error. Application errors must be corrected immediately. It is critical that the confirmation posts successfully and the ASN is sent to Gordy's Galaxy before the shipment arrives at their receiving dock.

The following application errors can occur during inbound SHPCON IDoc processing:

- A delivery number is missing or incorrect. Contact DSI and request a resend with the correct delivery number.

- An item number is missing or doesn't match the item in the delivery. If the number of IDocs is small, the IDoc can be edited and reprocessed; otherwise, DSI will resend.

- A material number is missing or doesn't match the material in the delivery item. If there is only a small number of IDocs, assuming everything else (including the pick quantity) is correct, edit and reprocess the IDoc; otherwise, DSI will resend.

- The picking quantity is less than the delivery quantity. Confirm with DSI whether a partial shipment was sent. If so, the remainder of the product must be shipped and another shipping confirmation sent with the pick quantity equal to the delivery quantity. If it is an error, edit the IDoc and reprocess.

- The delivery is already picked and the goods issue posted. Mark the IDoc for deletion.

▶ The delivery is locked and can't be updated. Reprocess the IDoc when the lock is released. This can occur when a lot of shipping confirmations are being processed, particularly if RBDAPP01 is running in parallel mode.

15.3 End-to-End Process Flow

Figure 15.1 gives an overview of the end-to-end process flow for updating the delivery document with the 856-SHPCON ship confirmation interface.

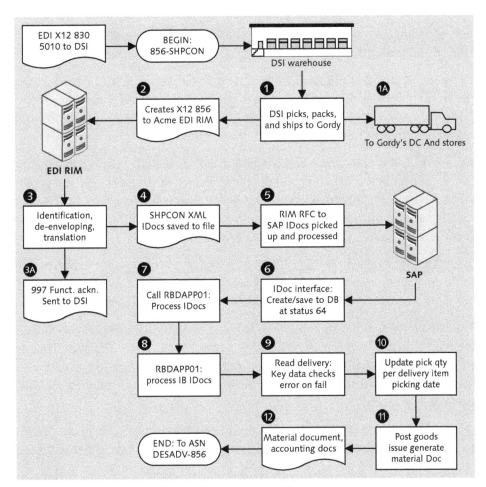

Figure 15.1 Acme's Inbound Ship Confirmation Process Flow

The 856 to SHPCON ship confirmation kicks off after the SHPORD to 830 interface posts a shipping order to DSI's business system.

It all happens in the DSI warehouse. Picking lists are printed and the ordered goods are pulled from inventory and scanned into DSI's system, recording the storage locations and the quantities picked.

The ordered items are moved into staging locations for shipping. Stickers are applied to the packaging, and the DVDs are loaded into cartons with packing lists. Shipping labels are applied to the cartons and the cartons are stacked onto palettes that are wrapped up for shipping.

Bills of lading and other shipping documents are printed, and the palettes are labeled and loaded onto trucks bound for Gordy's distribution centers.

Every step is recorded and scanned into DSI's business system. As the truck leaves the loading dock, a ship confirmation is generated as an ASCII file and sent to DSI's EDI system. There the file is translated to an 856 EDI ship confirmation and transmitted by AS2 to Acme's EDI RIM.

Acme's AS2 server picks it up and passes it to a de-enveloping process that identifies the sender and transaction, checks the syntax of the interchange, and generates a 997 functional acknowledgment that is immediately sent back to DSI. The map is also identified and called and each 856 transaction set in the interchange is converted to one SHPCON.DELVRY03 XML IDoc.

The IDocs are batched into one file that is sent to an inbound directory on the SAP application server. The RIM's SAP adapter then triggers an RFC to function EDI_DATA_INCOMING, which kicks off IDoc interface processing in SAP.

The IDoc interface confirms that the file contains IDocs, checks that the XML is well-formed, and confirms that the IDoc structure is correct. The XML IDoc is then converted to ASCII and the partner profile read and confirmed using values from the control record. If everything checks out, each IDoc is written to the IDoc database at status 64.

A job to run program RBDAPP01 is set up in the SAP job scheduler (Transaction SM36) to run seven times a day to pick up and process all SHPCON messages at status 64.

RBDAPP01 identifies the application function (IDOC_INPUT_DELVRY) from the process code DELV in the inbound partner profile for DSI message type SHPCON.

The IDoc is parsed and posted in IDOC_INPUT_DELVRY by two performs:

▶ DELVRY_IDOC_PARSE

▶ DELIVERY_UPDATE

The first, DELVRY_IDOC_PARSE, loops through the IDoc data in an internal table. It first checks field VBELN in segment E1EDL20 to confirm that a delivery document number is present. It also checks POSNR and MATNR in each instance of E1EDL24 to confirm that an item and material number exist.

If any of these values are missing, an error is returned, IDoc processing ends, and the status is updated to 51 — *Application document not posted*.

If the checks pass, the loop builds internal tables, strings, and flags that pass to function WS_DELIVERY_UPDATE_2 in form DELIVERY_UPDATE, which, as its name implies, updates the delivery document with the pick quantities and PGI. At the header level, that means passing the following values:

▶ Delivery number

▶ Picking date

▶ Warehouse number

▶ Post goods issue indicator

▶ Post goods issue and other key dates

▶ Global weights and volumes

▶ Processing flags

▶ Bill of lading number

▶ Number of packages in delivery

At the item level, the following values are passed:

▶ Delivery and line item numbers

▶ SAP material number

▶ Plant

▶ Pick quantity and unit of measure

▶ Packaging hierarchies (handling units) if present

WS_DELIVERY_UPDATE_2 uses the delivery number to confirm the delivery document, update the picking quantity, and post the goods issue.

When the delivery document is saved, another DESADV IDoc is generated and batched at status 30—*IDoc ready for dispatch*—for outbound processing to Gordy's Galaxy as an ASN.

15.4 Technical Specifications

This technical specification section describes the SAP configuration and EDI development required to support the X12 856 to SHPCON.DELVRY03 interface from the DSI third-party warehouse, confirming that orders have been shipped to Gordy's Galaxy.

15.4.1 Technical Requirements

DSI will send one X12 856 transaction for one outbound delivery from Acme. The transaction will be sent only when the truck pulls away from the loading dock, and it will have the outbound delivery document number.

The 856 will have all the data it needs to update pick quantities and post the goods issue in Acme's SAP system.

Component titles in multi-pack orders, however, will not update the pick quantity in Acme's delivery document. The EDI map will not pass pick quantities for multi-pack component titles to the IDoc if they are present in the 856 interchange.

Development and configuration in the EDI RIM must support routing and conversion of inbound 856 to SHPCON.DELVRY03 shipping confirmation IDocs and generation of outbound 997 functional acknowledgments.

SAP configuration must support update of the outbound delivery document through posting of SHPCON messages.

15.4.2 Dependencies

The 856 to SHPCON shipping confirmation interface is dependent on inbound IDoc configuration in SAP and several development objects in the EDI RIM:

▶ Outbound delivery document exists in SAP and an outbound SHPORD IDoc sent to DSI

▶ Outbound delivery number present in the inbound X12 856 and passed to the IDoc

▶ Inbound envelopes set up in the RIM for DSI's X12 856 version 5010 transaction

▶ Outbound envelopes for 997 acknowledgments set up in the RIM for generation during de-enveloping of inbound 856 transactions from DSI

▶ Translation map built in the EDI RIM for the 856 X12 version 5010 to SHPCON. DELVRY03 IDoc conversion

▶ Custom cross-reference table ZEDIXREF populated in SAP to read the SAP send and receive partners for the inbound 856 from DSI

▶ Business process workflows built in the EDI RIM to process and route the incoming X12 856 and SHPCON.DELVRY03 IDocs

▶ Inbound partner profiles set up in SAP for DSI message type SHPCON

▶ Job created in the SAP Job Scheduler (Transaction SM36) to run seven times a day to post SHPCON.DELVRY03 IDocs with program `RBDAPP01` with a variant to select for all suppliers and all messages at status 64

15.4.3 Assumptions

The RIM sends EDI send and receive trading partner IDs in the IDoc control segment fields SNDLAD and RCVLAD which used to read the SAP partner numbers in a customer exit during IDoc processing in SAP. There are a few other key assumptions:

▶ The EDI RIM will return an X12 997 during de-enveloping of the inbound 867 transaction.

▶ All IDoc errors are monitored by the EDI team in SAP. EDI errors are tracked and addressed in the EDI system.

▶ Technical errors in the IDoc interface, such as syntax or partner profile errors, are documented and corrected by the EDI team.

▶ All IDoc application errors are handled by the business users, backed up by the EDI team where appropriate.

▶ The EDI team communicates IDoc application errors to the business users immediately.

15.5   Mapping Specifications

A map will be developed in the EDI RIM to translate the X12 856 version 5010 from DSI to a SHPCON.DELVRY03 shipping confirmation IDoc. All deliveries for all customers who are handled by DSI flow through the same map.

Table 15.3 outlines mapping requirements for the inbound 856-SHPCON transaction for DSI. This mapping assumes shipment by truck.

SHPCON	856	Sample Value	Comments
E1EDL20—Delivery header—Min 1 Max 1			
@SEGMENT		1	Hard-code segment attribute to 1.
VBELN	BSN02	0080016843	Acme outbound delivery number. Delivery document to be confirmed. Mandatory value.
BTGEW	TD107	280.000	Gross weight where TD106 = G (weight qualifier) and HL01 = 1 and HL03 = S for shipment level. Instance 1 of TD01. Segment repeated for each shipment-level total weight, quantity, or volume.
NTGEW	TD107	250.000	Net weight where TD106 = N (weight qualifier) and HL01 = 1 and HL03 = S for shipment level. Instance 2 of TD01.
GEWEI	TD108	KGM	Weight unit for header weights
BOLNR	REF02	9874785900	Bill of lading number where REF01 = BM
TRAID	TD303	999999	Trailer ID number where TD01 = TL for standard truck trailer
LIFEX	PRF01	060598-1400	Customer purchase order number at header level
E1EDL18—Control codes—Min 1, Max 99—Loop 1 change flag			
@SEGMENT		1	Hard-code segment attribute to 1.
QUALF		CHG	Hard-code change flag. Tells system to update delivery document.

Table 15.3 Mapping the 856 Shipping Confirmation to the SHPCON IDoc

SHPCON	856	Sample Value	Comments
E1EDL18—Control codes—Loop 2 pick flag			
@SEGMENT		1	Hard-code segment attribute to 1.
QUALF		PIC	Hard-code picking flag. Tells system to update picking quantity.
E1EDL18—Control codes—Loop 3 PGI flag			
@SEGMENT		1	Hard-code segment attribute to 1.
QUALF		PGI	Hard-code post goods issue flag. Tells system to post goods issue against delivery when all updates complete. E1EDL18 can also flag change to gross or net weight, volume, or delete delivery.
E1EDT13—Dates—Min 1, Max 99—Loop 1 goods issue date			
@SEGMENT		1	Hard-code segment attribute to 1.
QUALF	DTM01	006	Identifies goods issue where DTM01 = 011 date shipped and HL03 = S for shipment
IEDD	DTM02	20140115	Actual date of goods issue
E1EDT13—Dates—Loop 2 Delivery date			
@SEGMENT		1	Hard-code segment attribute to 1.
QUALF	DTM01	007	Identifies delivery date where DTM01 = 010 delivery date and HL03 = S for shipment
NTANF	DTM02	20140114	Delivery date
E1EDT13—Date—Loop 3 Picking date			
@SEGMENT		1	Hard-code segment attribute to 1.
QUALF	DTM01	010	Identifies picking date where DTM01 = 011 date shipped and HL03 = S for shipment
IEDD	DTM02	20140115	Picking date

Table 15.3 Mapping the 856 Shipping Confirmation to the SHPCON IDoc (Cont.)

SHPCON	856	Sample Value	Comments
E1EDL24—Item level details group—Min 1, Max N—1 instance of E1EDL21 per group loop			
@SEGMENT		1	Hard-code segment attribute to 1.
POSNR	LIN03	000010	Delivery line item number. Pull from LIN03 where HL03 = I for looping packing hierarchy item level of 856 shipment. Segment LIN will appear once for every instance where looping segment HL03 = I. Mandatory value.
MATNR	LIN05	0005000020	Acme material number fully expanded to 18 characters, including all leading zeroes. Take from LIN05 where LIN04 = IN (buyer's item number) and HL103 = I (item level of packing hierarchy) and HLI01 = HLI01 (hierarchy level number) for LIN03 (current) line item number. Mandatory value.
CHARG	LIN07	458248	Batch number if present. Take from LIN07 where LIN06 = LT (lot number) and HL103 = I (item level of packing hierarchy) for current line item.
LFIMG	SN102	100.000	Number of units shipped. Updates picking quantity. Pull from SN102 where HL103 = I (item level of packing hierarchy) for current line item.
VRKME	SN103	EA	Unit of measure for LFIMG quantity
LGMNG	SN105	100.000	Delivery quantity. Pull from SN105 where HL103 = I (item level of packing hierarchy) for current line item.
MEINS	SN106	EA	Unit of measure for LGMNG quantity
NTGEW	TD107	250.000	Net weight of item where TD106 = N and HL103 = I (item level of packing hierarchy) for current line item. TD1 is a looping group: one instance per type of weight.

Table 15.3 Mapping the 856 Shipping Confirmation to the SHPCON IDoc (Cont.)

SHPCON	856	Sample Value	Comments
BRGEW	TD107	280.000	Gross weight of item where TD106 = G and HL103 = I (item level of packing hierarchy) for current line item.
GEWEI	TD108	KGM	Unit of measure for weight
E1EDL43—Item-level sales documents—Min 1, Max 99—Loop 1 Acme Sales Order			
@SEGMENT		1	Hard-code segment attribute to 1.
QUALF	REF01	C	Identifies Acme sales order. Map to C where REF01 = CO (customer order). Acme is the customer for DSI.
VGBEL	REF02	00014031	Purchase order number pulled from BIG04 at header level of 810
VGPOS	REF05	000010	Sales order line item number where REF04 = LI (line item)

Table 15.3 Mapping the 856 Shipping Confirmation to the SHPCON IDoc (Cont.)

In addition, serialized deliveries can be confirmed at the line-item level using segment E1EDL11. Packaging hierarchies (in SAP, handling units) can be communicated back to update the outbound delivery using segment E1EDL37 and its children.

These are the basic segments and data elements processed by function `IDOC_INPUT_DELVRY`. If you need to include other values in your ship confirm, two exits are available after all segments have been parsed:

▶ `CUSTOMER-FUNCTION` `'001'`: Enhancement V55K0001, component `EXIT_SAP-LV55K_001`.

▶ `CUSTOMER-FUNCTION` `'002'`: Enhancement V55K0002, component `EXIT_SAP-LV55K_002`.

Everything you need to update the header or line-item level of the outbound delivery is available to both exits.

We wrote rules to identify the shipment or item level of data elements through the HL segment. This is critical to the organization of the 856 (and to mapping), so it's useful to look at how this works.

15.5.1 Hierarchical Structure of the 856

Hell hath nine circles of suffering, according to Dante Alighieri's sublime poem *The Inferno*. But the 856 has many more potential hierarchical levels that have wrought their own special brand of grief to countless EDI mappers, even if these torments haven't been described by Dante.

The 856 is a beast with multiple personalities and a flexible hierarchical structure. We're using it here as an inbound shipping confirmation, a relatively simple usage—assuming the packaging hierarchy isn't included and that we're not dealing with a serialized shipment where every individual item, including packing cartons and pallets, is assigned a serial number.

Regardless of how complex or simple the data set, the basic structural rules for its use are the same. So we'll keep it simple here and try to understand its organization. We use it again in the next chapter as an outbound advanced shipping notification (in the EDIFACT world, a dispatch advice), which is the last critical step before Acme can invoice Gordy for its order.

As ordered by the HL looping group, its hierarchy is the key to understanding the 856, regardless of its usage or the data it carries. The HL loop defines the hierarchical levels of the shipment and its parent-child relationships.

Figure 15.2 shows the segment structure of the 856 that we will map for the shipping confirmation or the ASN in the next chapter.

BSN	0200	Beginning Segment for Ship Notice		Mandatory
DTM	0400	Date/Time Reference	10	Optional
HL	0100	Hierarchical Level	200000	Mandatory
HL	0100	Hierarchical Level		Mandatory
LIN	0200	Item Identification		Optional
SN1	0300	Item Detail (Shipment)		Optional
SLN	0400	Subline Item Detail	1000	Optional
PRF	0500	Purchase Order Reference		Optional
MEA	0800	Measurements	40	Optional
PKG	1000	Marking, Packaging, Loading	25	Optional
TD1	1100	Carrier Details (Quantity and Weight)	20	Optional
TD5	1200	Carrier Details (Routing Sequence/Transit Time)	12	Optional
TD3	1300	Carrier Details (Equipment)	12	Optional
REF	1500	Reference Information	>1	Optional
MAN	1900	Marks and Numbers Information	>1	Optional
DTM	2000	Date/Time Reference	10	Optional
N1	2200	Party Identification	200	Optional
N1	2200	Party Identification		Optional
N3	2400	Party Location	2	Optional
N4	2500	Geographic Location		Optional

Figure 15.2 Simplified Structure of an X12 856 Transaction

Like most EDI transactions, the 856 has header and details sections. The header only has two segments, only one of which (BSN) is mandatory. BSN provides a document number that identifies the whole shipment.

In Acme's SAP system, this could be a delivery or shipment document number from transport planning. If it's a shipment document, it may include one or more deliveries in the HL looping group.

As defined by the 856, a shipment can include multiple deliveries, each identified by its own delivery number within the HL looping group. The 856 is closer to SAP's SHPMNT message, which is generated from the shipment document in transport planning and can include multiple delivery documents representing multiple sales and customer purchase orders.

But the 856 can also map to logical message DESADV with its one delivery document. So if we're mapping the 856 to DESADV, the shipment identifier in BSN02 is Acme's delivery document number.

If, however, we're mapping to a SHPMNT IDoc, BSN02 stores the shipping document number from transport planning while the delivery document number is in one or more HL looping groups, depending on the number of deliveries per shipment.

The key to all this is the HL looping segment, which can repeat up to 200,000 times. All detail section segments are children of HL.

For such an important segment, HL has a modest structure: only four data elements, but we only care about the first three, described in Table 15.4.

Pos	Field	Description	Data
HL01	0628	Hierarchical ID number. Identifies sequential occurrence of HL group with child segments.	1
HL02	0734	Hierarchical parent ID number. Used by a child HL group to identify the sequential occurrence ID number (HL01) of its parent HL group. ▶ If the HL01 parent = 1, then HL02 = 0 ▶ If the HL01 parent = 2, then HL02 = 1	0

Table 15.4 Defining 856 Hierarchy with the HL Segment

Pos	Field	Description	Data
HL03	0735	Hierarchical level object code. Qualifier that identifies type of object reported in child segments. Includes values such as the following: ▶ S: Shipment ▶ O: Order or other shipping document ▶ T: Shipping tare or pallet ▶ P: Pack ▶ I: Item	S

Table 15.4 Defining 856 Hierarchy with the HL Segment (Cont.)

There are hundreds of potential qualifiers for HL03, although not all are relevant to a shipment. These qualifiers determine what segments follow HL within each HL loop, including additional HL looping groups.

For example, qualifier "P" refers to a pack filled with saleable items or to a pack filled with smaller packs. Each of these contains items or smaller packs with items, like a Russian doll.

These hierarchical relationships are enforced by the combination of HL01 and HL02. HL01 always begins with 1 and is incremented sequentially each time an HL segment is encountered throughout the transaction. HL02 always refers to its immediate HL01 parent, regardless of how many HL segments precede it and regardless of what they reference as their parent HL01.

The top level of the hierarchy is the shipment, which stores data that affects all documents and objects to be delivered in the same shipment, identified by qualifier "S" in HL03 of sequence 1 in HL01 and a parent of 0 in HL02.

For a shipping confirmation or other 856 instance referencing an SAP delivery document, the key identifiers in this HL loop are the carrier's reference or the bill of lading (BOL) number, or another document identifier for the load carried by the shipment, stored in data element REF02 qualified by REF01.

The shipment level includes the following segments that provide data for the shipment as a whole, although they won't all necessarily be present, particularly for our simple shipping confirmation:

- TD1: Carrier details—quantity and weight
- TD5: Carrier details—routing sequence and transit time
- TD3: Carrier details—transport equipment
- REF: Reference document numbers (i.e., BOL)
- DTM: Scheduled delivery, ship, and other relevant dates
- N1: Ship-to and ship-from partners (addresses can also be included in N3 and N4)

Child segments follow, with the order level next. HL01 will be incremented to 2 and HL02 will equal 1, pointing to its parent HL01 segment.

This can be a customer purchase order or a delivery document if we were mapping a SHPMNT IDoc. In the case of our ship confirmation from DSI to Acme (or our outbound ASN to Gordy), this will be the customer purchase order. The following segments will be present:

- PRF: Purchase order reference
- TD1: Carrier details (quantity and weight for the recorded order)

  In our example of one shipping confirmation per delivery, which was generated for one sales order and one purchase order, this would be a repeat of TD1 above. In other words, this quantity and weight reflects the purchase order, not the shipment as a whole, which could include multiple purchase orders.

Because this is a simple example focused on the ship confirmation without packaging hierarchy, the next child HL group is for the delivery item. HL01 is incremented to 3 and HL02 equals 2, because the item is being delivered against the purchase order. The following segments can be present:

- LIN: Material item identification number
- SN1: Quantities and units of measure for ordered item
- P04: Physical details of item (i.e., weight, volume, length, width, units of measure, and other characteristics)

The easiest way to see how this works is by looking at a sample transaction. An example of a simple shipping confirmation without packaging hierarchies or serial numbers is displayed in Listing 15.1.

```
BSN*00*0080016843*20140115*09404267*0001~
HL*1*0*S~
TD1*CTN25*14****G*9774*LB~
TD5****ZZ*GROUND 5 DAYS~
TD3*TL**999999~
REF*BM*9878~
REF*CN*9787~
DTM*011*20140115~
DTM*002*20140115~
N1*ST**92*5293E~
N1*SF**91*0015~
HL*2*1*O~
PRF*99334330~
TD1*CTN25*14****G*9774*LB~
HL*3*2*I~
LIN*001*IN*0005000020~
SN1**2520*EA**16290*EA~
PO4*2520~
```

Listing 15.1 Sample 856 with No Packing Hierarchy

This example only goes directly to the saleable item level for one item in the delivery document and does not display any packing hierarchies. It includes the data that we need to update the picking quantity and post the goods issue against Acme's delivery document.

The key is the HL segment, which defines the shipment, identifies the object in the shipment that it is describing, determines the data it needs to return for that object, and defines that object's relationship to its immediate parent and, through the parent, to the shipment as a whole.

That's a whole lot of stuff in anybody's book. If you need to define mapping specifications, remember to keep your eye on the ball: that HL segment. And trace it back to the HL segment(s) that it references.

In the real world, the 856 will get a lot more complicated, whether for a shipping confirmation or an ASN, particularly if we throw packaging and/or serial numbers into the mix. But the HL looping group is flexible enough to transmit a vast array of data about a shipment and each of its objects.

For mapping, the trick is to understand how to move data from a deeper looping hierarchical level in the 856 to either the header, line item, or packaging hierarchy levels of the IDoc.

So let's briefly go over the structure of the DELVRY03 basic type to give us an idea of the mapping challenges we may face with the 856.

15.5.2 The DELVRY03 IDoc

The DELVRY03 basic type is just as flexible as the 856 and it stores potentially even more data, including packaging hierarchies and serial numbers, if these are present in the EDI transaction. The IDoc is organized differently, as is readily apparent from the simplified structure of basic type DELVRY03 in Figure 15.3.

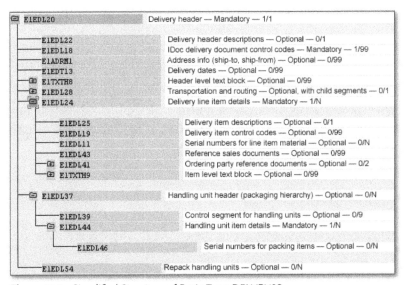

Figure 15.3 Simplified Structure of Basic Type DELVRY03

A number of segments that won't be used in Acme's implementation have been deleted from the IDoc in Figure 15.3. But as it stands, the IDoc retains the segments that we'll need for both the shipping confirmation and the ASN that we look at it in the next chapter.

The IDoc and the 856 take different approaches to the same problem. The basic approach of the 856 is to begin with the shipment and work its way down through the document and the highest level packaging item, whether that's a container or a pallet or a pack, down through subsequent packaging layers into the saleable item being delivered.

The IDoc begins with the delivery document and works its way first through the saleable items, in segment E1EDL24 and its children, and then to the packaging hierarchy beginning with E1EDL37 and its children, particularly E1EDL44, which stores the line-item level of the packaging hierarchy.

E1EDL44 is where the full packaging hierarchy (again, handling units in SAP) is stored. In order to be used in the delivery, each packaging item, whether a pallet or a carton or a pack of any type, must exist in SAP with a material master record.

The DELVRY03 basic type is designed to fit into a shipment message in a SHPMNT IDoc at the line-item level. DELVRY03 segment E1EDL20 becomes the line item details parent of the shipment and can be repeated multiple times to accommodate multiple complete deliveries in one shipment.

The SHPMNT IDoc is generated from the transport planning system and includes more data about transportation, routing, and equipment than is typically found in a delivery document.

The IDoc approach to structuring the delivery and its packaging hierarchy is almost identical to the approaches taken by EDIFACT, OAGIS, xCBL, and other XML B2B message formats that support shipping and delivery.

15.6   EDI Configuration in SAP

Let's walk through configuration settings for the inbound SHPCON message type from DSI.

15.6.1 EDPAR Entries: Transaction VOE4

There are no EDPAR entries for the 856-SHPCON interface.

15.6.2 ZEDIXREF Entries

Custom table ZEDIXREF maps the sender's sending and receiving EDI trading partner IDs to the SAP partner numbers—DSI's vendor number in Acme's system and the receiving SAP logical system ID.

Table 15.5 lists the values that we'll enter into custom table ZEDIXREF for the inbound 856 ship confirmation from DSI.

Field	Value	Description
DIRECT	2	Direction inbound
STDMES	856	EDI transaction
MESTYP	SHPCON	IDoc message type
IDOCTP	DELVRY03	IDoc basic type
CIMTYP		IDoc extension
SNDPRN	DISK01	SAP send partner
RCVPRN	DEVCLNT100	SAP receive partner
SNDLAD	99934567999	EDI send trading partner ID
RCVLAD	99999998889	EDI receive trading partner ID

Table 15.5 ZEDIXREF Entries for the Inbound 856 from DSI

15.6.3 Partner Profiles: Transaction WE20

The inbound partner profile links DSI to the incoming message type and the process code that will trigger the processing function that will post the incoming ship confirmation.

We'll need one inbound partner profile for DSI partner type LI (vendor) with message type SHPCON.

In the inbound parameters table control, click CREATE and add the following values to the inbound parameters screen (Figure 15.4):

► PARTNER ROLE: "VN" for vendor

► MESSAGE TYPE: "SHPCON"

► PROCESS CODE: "DELV"

► PROCESSING BY FUNCTION MODULE: TRIGGER BY BACKGROUND PROGRAM option

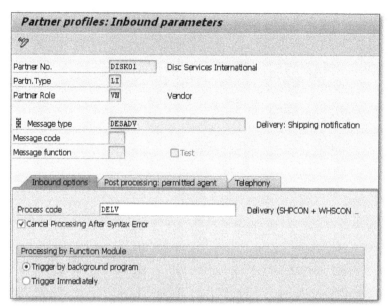

Figure 15.4 Inbound Partner Profile for Ship Confirmation from DSI

Process code DELV links to function `IDOC_INPUT_DELVRY`, which posts the IDoc against Acme's outbound delivery document and updates pick quantity and posts the goods issue.

Don't forget to save.

15.7   Summary

The shipping confirmation is an important step along Acme's road to invoicing. It confirms that DSI shipped an order of saleable movies on DVD to Gordy's Galaxy of Games & B Flix, Acme's most important customer.

DSI generates an 856 ship confirmation and sends it to Acme when the truck leaves the shipping dock with a load bound for Gordy's distribution center.

The shipment was picked, packed, and shipped after Acme sent DSI a shipping order through an X12 830 transaction with details of what saleable items to deliver to Gordy against what purchase order.

The shipping order to DSI was generated from an outbound delivery document in Acme's SAP system. The 856 shipping confirmation sent by DSI to Acme references the outbound delivery, as well as the saleable material shipped, its quantity, and ship dates. It can also include details of packaging hierarchies, if DSI provides them and Acme needs them to update the delivery.

The shipping confirmation updates the pick quantity for the saleable item and triggers the post goods issue in the outbound delivery, which relieves inventory of the finished goods and the raw materials used to produce them.

We looked at the structure of the 856 and the DELVRY03 IDoc and noted the differences between the looping, hierarchical, top-down organization of the 856 versus the more traditional, flatter header-detail levels structure of the IDoc.

Mapping the 856 can be difficult, but the key is understanding how the HL segment is used to organize the different hierarchical levels of each object in the delivery, from the shipment through the order and the packaging levels from the top down to the saleable item.

So now the DVDs that Gordy ordered are loaded onto a truck and safely on their way. Acme's legendary founder Darryl Q. Fernhausen would be smiling in anticipation of what follows: the customer receives delivery and Acme issues an invoice and gets paid for its efforts.

Before that happy moment can arrive, however, there are still steps that must be completed, beginning with telling Gordy's that the stuff they ordered is on its way. And that's what we'll look at next.

"Let 'em know what they're getting," Darryl Q would tell his writers when they got stumped by a script. It's no different for Gordy, who needs to know what he's getting when his order has been shipped. And that's what the outbound ASN does: It tells the customer what he is going to receive in his order. It's also the last step before Acme can invoice. So let's see how it's done.

16 The Advanced Shipping Notice to the Customer

This is where the rubber begins to meet the road. The delivery has been issued and the shipping order dropped to the third-party warehouse Disc Services International (DSI). The order has been picked and shipped, and DSI has confirmed the shipment, completing Acme's delivery document with the pick quantity and post goods issue.

Each step has been documented and enabled by an EDI transmission: the outbound SHPORD to X12 830 interface for the shipping order and the inbound X12 856 to SHPCON for the ship confirmation.

All that's left is to provide Gordy's Galaxy of Games & B Flix, Acme's most important customer, with over 2,000 store locations, with its own version of the five Ws of DVD distribution:

▶ What order is on its way? "Order" refers to Gordy's customer purchase order not Acme's sales or delivery order.

▶ Which of Gordy's distribution centers is it being sent to?

▶ When will the order get there?

▶ Which of Gordy's stores are receiving product in the order?

▶ What products are being shipped to what stores?

Gordy needs to receive this information in an outbound X12 856 advanced ship notification (ASN) and post it to their business system before the delivery arrives at their receiving dock.

When the order arrives, Gordy must then confirm that all the goods in the delivery are recorded on the ASN before they can receive them into their business system against their purchase order.

If the ASN arrives after the delivery, or if there are discrepancies between the ASN and the items received in the delivery, Gordy will not authorize Acme to issue an invoice. It simply has to be right.

So let's consider this critical interface, the last obstacle to overcome before we can invoice.

16.1 Technical Overview of Interface

Table 16.1 summarizes the outbound ASN interface.

Item	Description
Title	Advanced Shipping Notification to the Customer
Description	The ASN is the third interface in the shipping cycle triggered when an outbound delivery document is created in SAP from a completed sales order against a purchase from Gordy's Galaxy of Games & B Flix. The first is the outbound ship order to the third-party warehouse (DSI) with details of the order to be delivered to the customer. The second is the ship confirmation returned from DSI with details of the order that was picked, packed, loaded onto a truck, and shipped to Gordy. The shipping confirmation updates the outbound delivery with the pick quantity and post goods issue. The ASN is generated from the outbound delivery after the post goods issue closes the delivery. A DESADV IDoc is populated with the details of the delivery as confirmed by DSI and sent to Gordy so that they can receive the delivery against it when it arrives at their distribution center. The goods received on the dock must match the goods described in the ASN or Gordy will reject the delivery.

Table 16.1 Overview of Outbound DESADV ASN Interface

Item	Description
	If Gordy rejects the delivery, they immediately send an X12 824 text report describing the error. The EDI RIM converts the 824 to an email and routes it to the business users for correction. If Gordy receives the goods successfully against the ASN, Acme can issue its invoice for the order.
Type of interface	Distribution: IDoc to X12 EDI
Direction	Outbound
Trading partner	Gordy's Galaxy (customer)
IDoc	DESADV.DELVRY03
IDoc extended type	
IDoc function	`IDOC_OUTPUT_DELVRY`
Custom ABAP	
Description	
Target file(s)	X12 856 advance ship notification to the customer
Source document(s)	Completed SAP outbound delivery document
Transaction code	VL02N
Map(s)	DESADV.DELVRY03 to X12 856 vers. 5010
Custom map logic	
Source system	Acme SAP
Target system	Gordy's Galaxy EDI via AS2 from Acme EDI RIM
997 acknowledgment	Inbound within 24 hours of transmission at the transaction detail level; function group acknowledgment code: SH
Frequency	Every 15 minutes throughout the day, on demand
Job schedule 1	`RSEOUT00`: Every hour, sends all DESADV message types to DSI

Table 16.1 Overview of Outbound DESADV ASN Interface (Cont.)

16.2   Functional Specifications

The DESADV-856 ASN to the customer is the last of three steps in the delivery processing cycle.

The first is the ship order from an outbound delivery that tells DSI what to pick, pack, and ship to Gordy's Galaxy against a particular purchase order.

The second is the ship confirmation from DSI after the shipment has left their loading dock that updates the outbound delivery with the pick quantity and post goods issue.

The ASN is generated when the post goods issue completes the outbound delivery document. After the ASN has been successfully received into Gordy's business system and the goods delivered and confirmed against the ASN, Acme can issue an invoice against the customer PO.

16.2.1   Process Overview

The process begins after the order ships from DSI and an 856 ship confirm is sent back to Acme to update the delivery document with the pick quantity and the post goods issue.

When the delivery is saved and completed, output control generates a DESADV. DELVRY03 IDoc, which is parked in the IDoc database until it is picked up and exported to the EDI RIM by a scheduled job that runs every 15 minutes.

The IDoc pulls all the data in the outbound delivery, including all transport and saleable item data and the full packing hierarchy if packaging has been set up for the delivery.

The RIM converts the DESADV.DELVRY03 IDoc to an 856 advanced ship notification and sends it to Gordy's EDI system. This ASN posts to Gordy's business system against the purchase order number and is used on the receiving dock to confirm receipt of all items in the delivery against the PO when the shipment arrives.

Gordy's purchase order is closed with a goods receipt (GR) after all of the items in the order have been confirmed and scanned into its system. The saleable items are received into Gordy's inventory and eventually distributed to all stores that ordered product for sale.

16.2.2 Requirements

Gordy has only two requirements for the DESADV-856 ASN interface:

▶ It must be 100 percent accurate 100 percent of the time and must do the following:

    ▶ Report exactly how many units of what products were shipped against what Gordy purchase order number

    ▶ Match the physical contents of the shipment, including component items of multi-pack displays

    ▶ Include codes to track items down to the carton level that match barcoded labels on cartons and palettes in the physical shipment

▶ It must be on time. The ASN shall always post to Gordy's business system before the shipment arrives at the receiving dock.

    ▶ Gordy must validate the ASN data against its purchase order in its business system before the delivery arrives.

    ▶ Gordy must confirm every physical item in the delivery at the receiving point against the ASN and its purchase order, including saleable items and packaging materials if sent.

    ▶ The goods must post successfully to Gordy's inventory before signing off on the ASN.

If these requirements are not fulfilled, Gordy will not accept receipt of an invoice, let alone pay for it. This makes the ASN an interface of "musts."

There are a few other requirements:

▶ Picking quantities in the delivery have been updated from the DSI warehouse through the 856-SHPCON interface.

▶ Post goods issue has completed the delivery, which means that two things have happened:

    ▶ Material documents have been created for the inventory posting with movement type 601 or 602 for reversals.

    ▶ Finance has been updated through account postings reflected in the material and accounting documents.

- The IDoc is generated as soon as the delivery is closed and the ASN is sent to the customer immediately. Jobs to export DESADV IDocs are to be scheduled every 15 minutes.

- ASN references key document numbers:

  - Gordy's purchase order number

  - DSI's bill of lading (BOL)

  - Acme's delivery document

- All ASNs associated with a customer purchase order are bundled together into a single interchange for transmission by the EDI system.

16.2.3 Dependencies

The DESADV to 856 ASN interface is dependent on master data, configuration, and development in SAP and the EDI RIM, including all data required to support sales orders, acknowledgments, shipping orders, and inbound ship confirmations.

Other dependencies include (but are not restricted to) the following:

- Material master records for all packaging materials that may be sent in the ASN.

- Shipping conditions, routes, and schedules are set up.

- Message control is configured to support output of DESADV ASN IDocs from outbound deliveries once post goods issue is saved.

- Outbound partner profile set up for DSI for message type DESADV with the configured message control settings.

- External partner conversion table PUMA populated with Gordy's internal and external ship-to partner.

16.2.4 Assumptions

The ASN is output from the outbound delivery so all base assumptions for the SHPORD to 830 interface are also true for the DESADV to 856.

IDocs are automatically generated when the delivery document is updated with the pick quantity and post goods issue. One DESADV IDoc is output for each delivery document and sales order.

The following are additional key assumptions:

▸ All previous documents and updates in the sales and delivery cycle are completed, and inventory has been updated and posted to FI.

▸ Pick quantities in the delivery document represent the quantity that was actually shipped.

▸ Billing has not yet been run.

▸ Relevant customer purchase order and delivery data are passed to the ASN during output processing, including the following:

  ▹ Purchase order, delivery, and BOL numbers

  ▹ The vendor number that Gordy uses for Acme Pictures

  ▹ Gordy's store location ship-to number and address

  ▹ Relevant dates, particularly ship date

  ▹ All ordered items and shipped quantities

  ▹ Sales BOMs for multi-pack items ordered by Gordy's Galaxy

▸ Pricing isn't included in the ASN.

▸ Gordy uses GLNs for its store location ship-to numbers and GTINs for the items it orders.

▸ The IDoc is sent as an 856 ASN to Gordy's Galaxy, where it is used in the business system and the warehouse to manage transportation, distribution, and receiving of goods ordered from Acme.

▸ If there are errors posting the 856 ASN to Gordy's business system, an error report is returned to Acme in a separate X12 824 transmission. The error report is distributed by email to the responsible business users.

▸ The DESADV IDoc can be regenerated from the outbound delivery if required.

16.2.5 Data That Pass to the IDoc from the Delivery

Table 16.2 lists source tables and fields for some of the delivery document data that may be passed to the DESADV IDoc ASN to Gordy's Galaxy.

Table	Field	Description	Sample Value
Delivery Header			
VBPA	KUNNR	PARVW = WE: ship-to partner	GRDY010987
VBPA	LIFNR	PARVW = SP: forwarding agent	FEDEX01
LIKP	VBELN	Delivery number	0816160750
VBKD	BSTNR	Customer PO number	292259
LIKP	BOLNR	BOL number	1Z492Y660133495
LIKP	VSTEL	Shipping point (DSI ship plant)	0015
LIKP	VSART	Shipment type — truck	01
LIKP	VSBED	Shipping conditions	04
LIKP	ROUTE	Route	21
LIKP	LFDAT	Delivery date	20081220
LIKP	LDDAT	Load date	20081220
LIKP	BTGEW	Gross weight	10128.750
LIKP	ANZPK	Number of packages	20
LFA1	SCACD	SCAC code—vendor master	FDEG
STXH	TDID	Header text ID; custom text ID for SCAC code	ZSCA
STXL	TDLINE	Text—SCAC code	FDEG
VEPK	VHILM	Packing material number. Corresponds to a material master item number in SAP.	PK-096
VEKP	EXIDV	SSCC-18 barcode on pallet or other top level packaging item label where EXIDA = C or D	000353003016674769
Delivery Items			
LIPS	POSNR	Item number	000010
LIPS	PSTYV	Delivery item category	TAP

Table 16.2 Delivery Data That May Pass to the DESADV ASN IDoc

Table	Field	Description	Sample Value
LIPS	MATNR	Order item (SAP)	2356784
LIPS	ARKTX	Material description	I Married an Alien
LIPS	LFIMG	Delivery quantity for item	4
LIPS	MEINS	Unit of measure for quantity	EA
LIPS	BRGEW	Gross weight	1
LIPS	GEWEI	Weight unit of measure	LB
LIPS	KDMAT	Customer material number	799142939512
LIPS	EAN11	UPC item number	799142939512
VEPO	MATNR	SAP material master number for packaging item at item details level of packaging hierarchy (handling units)	P-102

Table 16.2   Delivery Data That May Pass to the DESADV ASN IDoc (Cont.)

The Standard Carrier Alpha Code (SCAC) is a two- to four-digit code used by the transportation industry to identify freight carriers. The standard delivery doesn't have a field for the SCAC, so Acme stores it in a header text element with text ID ZSCA. Gordy requires the code in its ASN because it tells Gordy who's shipping the order.

FDEG is the SCAC code for FedEx Ground. FedEx is set also up in Acme's SAP system as a vendor.

The SCAC code can be stored in the vendor master for the forwarding party, in field LFA1-SCACD. It's read during outbound partner processing by function IDOC_ OUTPUT_DELIVRY, which builds the DESADV IDoc. For this to work, the forwarding agent must be in the PARTNER tab at the header level of the delivery document.

The route at Acme is used to define both the delivery carrier and conditions of shipment, in this case, FedEx Ground collect overnight. The BOL number came into the delivery from the ship confirmation from DSI.

16.2.6   Enhancements to the Process

There are no custom enhancements in this interface.

16.2.7 Reconciliation

Output of the DESADV IDoc is confirmed by checking the output screen of the delivery document in Transaction VL03N with menu option Extras • Delivery Output • Header.

Confirm that an output record with a green traffic light exists for output type LAVA, partner type SH (ship-to), and partner number GRDY01001. Click the Processing log button to get the IDoc number.

There are a few other validations that we can perform:

▶ Data in the IDoc match the delivery document:
  ▶ Delivery number
  ▶ Ship-to partner and address
  ▶ Customer PO number
  ▶ BOL number
  ▶ Picking and packing quantities
▶ The DESADV IDoc sent to the EDI RIM and successfully translated to an outbound X12 856
▶ The data in the 856 match the IDoc and conform to Acme's EDI mapping specifications and Gordy's 856 EDI guidelines
▶ DSI successfully receives and acknowledges the 856 and does not send an 824 text report with application errors within 24 hours

16.2.8 Errors and Error Handling

If the outbound delivery fails to generate a DESADV IDoc when the post goods issue is saved, the EDI team and business users will work together to identify and correct the error.

If the delivery document is properly updated and completed, then any errors involve output control or the partner profile. If the IDoc doesn't generate, the following checks are required:

▶ Transaction VV23 to confirm that the condition table is populated for output type LAVA for the sales organization and ship-to partner mapped to the sold-to partner

▶ Transaction WE20 to confirm that the outbound partner profile for Gordy's Galaxy sold-to partner with message type DESADV is correctly set up

16.3 Generating an ASN IDoc with Message Control

The outbound ASN to Gordy's Galaxy is generated by message control when the shipping confirmation successfully completes the outbound delivery with the post goods issue. We'll cover message control settings to automatically output the DESADV IDoc in this section.

In the shipping order interface in Chapter 14, we generated the outbound SHPORD IDoc by creating a custom version of standard output type LAVA. Output type LAVA can generate both the SHPORD and DESADV messages. Both use the same process codes and come out of the same outbound delivery document.

But the processes are very different and come at different points in the shipping cycle. The shipping order goes to the supplier and tells him what to ship to the customer, while the ASN goes to the customer and tells him what to expect to receive from the supplier. This goes back to the flexible nature of the delivery document and its critical role in the document flow in the overall order-to-cash process.

We need to set up the following message control configuration to output the ASN to the customer:

▶ Standard output type LAVA with access sequence 0005 (sales organization and customer, which will be the ship-to partner) and supporting configuration

▶ Condition record mapping the sales organization and ship-to partner to Gordy's sold-to customer

▶ One partner profile with message control for Gordy's Galaxy sold-to partner with the ASN message type DESADV

16.3.1 Configuring Message Control

We shouldn't need to change anything in the output type, but we will confirm that all the pieces are in place.

Output of the DESADV ASN is restricted to an outbound delivery that has been completed by a post goods issue through a requirement linked to the output type procedure mapping.

To confirm message control configuration, use Transaction NACE and follow these steps:

1. Select application V2 SHIPPING, and click OUTPUT TYPES. Select OUTPUT TYPE LAVA, and double-click to open the OUTPUT TYPE DETAILS screen.

2. Confirm that the ACCESS SEQUENCE field contains 005 and that the ACCESS TO CONDITIONS and MULTIPLE ISSUING checkboxes are both checked. The screen should look like Figure 16.1.

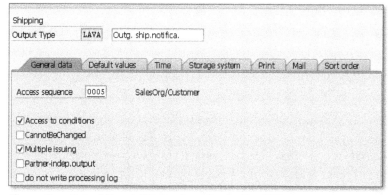

Figure 16.1   Output Type LAVA Configuration for the ASN

3. Access number is 1 for condition table 1 (B001) and communications structure KOMKBV2 with key fields:

   ▸ VKORG: Sales organization

   ▸ KNDNR: Ship-to party

4. Double-click the PROCESSING ROUTINES folder in the navigation panel to open the PROCESSING ROUTINES: OVERVIEW screen and confirm that there is an EDI entry in the table control.

5. If there is no program and form routine for medium EDI entered in the table control, click NEW ENTRIES to open the DETAILS OF ADDED ENTRIES screen. Enter the following values:

   ▸ TRANSM.MEDIUM: "EDI"

   ▸ PROGRAM (Processing 1): "RSNASTED" for the standard SAP output program

   ▸ FORM ROUTINE: "EDI_PROCESSING", which identifies and calls the function that generates and sends the IDoc

6. Press ⌈Enter⌉ and double-click the PARTNER FUNCTIONS folder to open the PART-NER FUNCTIONS: OVERVIEW screen.

7. Confirm that there's an entry for medium EDI and partner types SH (ship-to) and SP (sold-to partner).

8. The screen should look like Figure 16.2. If it doesn't, click NEW ENTRIES and select EDI in the MEDIUM field and KU in the FUNCT field.

| Application | V2 | Shipping |
| Output Type | LAVA | Outg. ship.notifica. |

| Partner functions | | |
Medium	Funct	Name
EDI	▼ SP	Sold-to party
EDI	▼ SH	Ship-to party
Distribution (ALE)	▼ SH	Ship-to party

Figure 16.2 Partner Functions for Output Type LAVA

9. SAVE any changes since your last save.

Confirm the Procedure and Requirement

Next we'll confirm that output type LAVA is linked to procedure V10000 and that there is a requirement to generate output only if a post goods issue against the delivery document has been completed.

1. Return to the main screen of Transaction NACE.

2. Select APPLICATION V2. Click PROCEDURES. The PROCEDURES OVERVIEW screen opens.

3. Select procedure V10000 header output, and double-click the CONTROL folder in the navigation panel.

4. Confirm that output type LAVA is assigned to the procedure and that requirement 1 is assigned to LAVA.

   The ABAP code in requirement 1 ensures that an IDoc is generated only if post goods issue has been completed against the delivery document.

   This is determined by reading the PGI completed flag in field WBSTK in communication structure KOMKBV2. If WBSTK equals C, then the post goods issue is done, the delivery is complete, and the IDoc can be generated. If not, output is blocked.

Condition Record

The condition record drives generation of the IDoc by sales organization and ship-to partner. But because the partner profile for Gordy is defined by sold-to partner, we must also map the ship-to partner from the delivery document to the sold-to partner.

We can create the condition record with Transaction NACE by selecting application V2, clicking CONDITION RECORDS, and selecting output type LAVA, or with Transaction VV21.

1. Call Transaction VV21, enter output type LAVA, and click the KEY COMBINATION button. The pop-up has only option: SALES ORGANIZATION/CUSTOMER NUMBER. Press [Enter] or click the green arrow icon.
2. Enter "3000" in the SALES ORGANIZATION field and the following values in the condition records table control, as shown in Figure 16.3:
   - CUSTOMER: "GRDY01001" for Gordy ship-to partner
   - FUNCTION: "SH" for ship-to partner
   - PARTNER: "GRDY01" for Gordy sold-to partner
   - MEDIUM: "6" for EDI
   - DISPATCH TIME: "4" for immediately when the document is saved
   - LANGUAGE: "EN"

Sales Organization 3000 Apple USA

Condition Recs.

Customer	Name	Funct	Partner	Medium	Date/Time	Language
GRDY01001	Gordy Store 001	SH	GRDY01	6	4	EN

Figure 16.3 Condition Record for ASN Output Type LAVA

This maps the sold-to partner to the RCVPRN field of the IDoc control segment, rather than the ship-to partner. We need to do this because the outbound partner profile is set up for the sold-to, not the ship-to partner.

If we did not enter the sold-to partner in the PARTNER field, the ship-to would be mapped to the RCVPRN filed of the IDoc control segment.

Output type LAVA is now ready for use in the message control screen of the outbound partner profile.

16.3.2 Overview of the End-to-End Process Flow

Figure 16.4 outlines the end-to-end process flow for generating and sending an ASN with a DESADV IDoc and an 856 to Gordy's Galaxy.

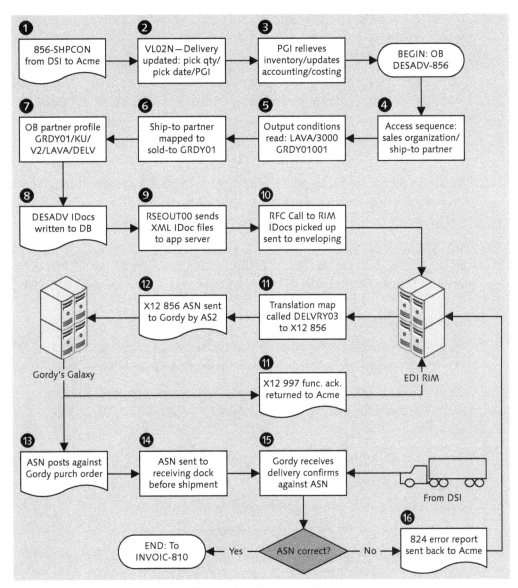

Figure 16.4 Outline of the DESADV-856 Interface Processing Flow

The outbound DESADV to 856 ASN interface kicks off after the delivery has been completed by the post goods issue triggered by a SHPCON IDoc translated from an inbound 856 ship confirmation sent from DSI after the shipment left for Gordy's Galaxy.

The ASN must be in Gordy's system before the shipment arrives at its receiving point. Gordy uses it to confirm the contents of the shipment and to close its purchase order with a goods receipt.

The post goods issue to Acme's delivery creates follow-up material documents that record the inventory change against movement type 601 (602 for reversals) and update the relevant G/L account. Follow-up accounting and costing documents are also created that prepare the system for generation of an invoice against the sales (and purchase) order and receipt of its payment.

The SD document flow table VBFA is updated to include a link between the new inventory and accounting documents and the delivery, which is already linked to the sales order and through it to the customer's purchase order.

The accounting document is not part of the SD document flow. It is recorded in the accounting database in table BKPF (document header) and table BSEG (item details) with a link to both the delivery and material document for the 601 PGI.

Message Control Processing

The system is now primed to issue an invoice, but we can't do that until the ASN process runs its course. And that begins with generating the IDoc.

Just before the delivery is saved, output control keys are identified, and an output record is created for table NAST by functions COMMUNICATION_AREA_KOMKBV2 and MESSAGING.

The following are output control keys for the outbound delivery ASN:

- ▶ Application V2: Shipping
- ▶ Output type LAVA: Outgoing ship notification
- ▶ Access sequence 0005: Sales organization/ship-to partner
- ▶ Access 1: Sales organization/ship-to partner number in condition table B001
- ▶ Procedure V10000: Header output linked to output type LAVA
- ▶ Requirement 1: Post goods issue completed in delivery document

The following access fields are from communication structure KOMKBV2:

- VKORG: Sales organization
- KNDNR: Ship-to party

The condition record is created through Transaction VV21. It links the SAP sales organization and ship-to number to Gordy's sold-to partner, which becomes the receiver partner in the IDoc control segment and identifies the outbound partner profile (always created against the sold-to partner).

Condition table B001 and output table NACH are read with the access keys from table LIKP, the delivery document header. The Acme sales organization and Gordy ship-to store location are hit and the condition record is pulled, along with Gordy's sold-to partner number.

Function `EDI_PARTNER_READ_OUTGOING` is called to get the partner profile using the key fields in structure EDK12:

- RCVPRN: Receive partner sold-to number: GRDY01
- RCVPRT: Receive partner type: KU (Customer)
- RCVPFC: Receipt partner function: SP (Sold-to Partner)
- KAPPL: Message control application: V2
- KSCHL: Message type: LAVA

The outbound partner profile is set up for Gordy with message type DESADV. It links to output control through the MESSAGE CONTROL tab, which includes three values:

- Application V2: Shipping
- Output (or message) type: LAVA
- Process Code: DELV

Process code DELV links message type DESADV to the standard IDoc processing function `IDOC_OUTPUT_DELVRY`, which is kicked off to build the IDoc.

Building the IDoc

`IDOC_OUTPUT_DELVRY` first confirms that it is processing the right IDoc, initializes all work areas, and takes care of some housekeeping tasks.

The delivery number is passed from the NAST output record key and is used to read all delivery and sales order document data into internal tables and strings from the relevant database tables:

- LIKP: Delivery header
- LIPS: Delivery item details
- VBUK: Delivery status
- VBFA: SD document flow
- VBPA: Delivery partners
- VBAK: Dales order header
- VBAP: Sales order item details
- VBKD: Sales order business data
- VEKP: Handling units (packing hierarchy) header level, if present in the delivery document
- VEPO: Handling units (packing hierarchy) details level, if present in the delivery document

These data build the IDoc, one segment at a time, beginning with E1EDL20, in the sequence in which each segment appears in the finished IDoc.

Each segment is built within its own process perform that does the following:

- Checks that the segment is active and has not been excluded through IDoc reduction
- Fills a string that has the structure of the IDoc segment with data from the delivery and sales order data work areas
- Performs relevant checks
- Populates a string (IDOC_DATA with structure EDIDD) with the segment name (to field SEGNAM) and application data (to field SDATA) for the segment
- Appends IDOC_DATA to the internal table INT_EDIDD, which also has the structure EDIDD
- Calls CUSTOMER-FUNCTION '002' for custom processing of the current segment or to add additional segments immediately after it

Partner data are treated a little differently. They use two segments: E1ADRM1 and its child segment E1ADRE1, which is populated with a variety of extended data, including SCAC for the carrier and the external partner number conversion.

The two segments are processed in a loop on table VBPA delivery partner data. The partner type and SAP partner numbers are passed to E1ADRM1, followed by full contact and address information from the address database.

E1ADRE1 is processed after E1ADRM1 and appended to `INT_EDIDD` within the same loop through VBPA.

There is also an external partner number mapping table similar to EDPAR handled by function `PARTNER_CONVERSION_INT_TO_EXT`. Acme would use the following parameters to convert the ship-to partner:

▶ NAST-PARVW: Partner type AG, sold-to, pulled from the output record table NAST. This is the receive partner in the IDoc control record that identifies the partner profile.

▶ NAST-PARNR: Sold-to partner number that was mapped from our condition record.

▶ VBPA-PARVW: Ship-to partner type WE, pulled from the delivery document.

▶ VBPA-KUNNR: Ship-to partner number.

These keys are used to read table PUMA, which maps an internal SAP partner number to an external ID such as a GLN or whatever the external partner needs. PUMA is only used to convert partner numbers for outbound deliveries.

`PARTNER_CONVERSION_INT_TO_EXT` will return the GLN for Gordy's ship-to partner. This will be stored in field E1ARDE1-EXTEND_D. Multiple instances of E1ARDE1 can be appended as children of E1ADRM1 so we can send multiple external partner numbers.

Segment processing for E1ADRE1 also identifies the SCAC code if it is maintained in field SCACD in the carrier or forwarding agent's vendor master record. The SCAC code is read from vendor master table LFA1.

When all segments have been built and assembled in the correct sequence in `INT_EDIDD`, function `IDOC_OUTPUT_DELVRY` exits and returns processing to the standard IDoc interface. The standard interface writes the IDoc to the database at status 01 —*IDoc generated*—and then status 30—*IDoc ready for dispatch*.

Sending the IDoc

Program `RSEOUT00` runs every 15 minutes to pick up all outbound DESADV IDocs at status 30 for Gordy's Galaxy and send them to the EDI RIM.

`RSEOUT00` reads the DESADV IDocs from the database and calls function `EDI_OUTPUT_NEW`, which converts the ASCII IDocs to XML format and saves them to a file on the SAP application server.

It then makes an RFC through the JCo connector to a listening workflow process in the EDI RIM that picks up the IDoc file with an FTP service and passes it to an enveloping process.

The envelopes are identified from the send and receive trading partner IDs in the IDoc control segment: SNDLAD and RCVLAD. Control segments fields are also used to identify the EDI standard (STD), the transaction (STDMES), and the version (STDVRS). The IDocs are grouped and a translation loop runs based on EDI partner, transaction, and X12 version.

The ST envelope identifies and calls the translation map for each IDoc in the file. The XML IDoc is converted to an X12 856 transaction set and wrapped in an ST envelope. The translation loop continues until each IDoc in the file is converted and wrapped in an ST envelope.

The converted transactions are then bundled into a group with a GS-GE envelope by function—SH for the 856—and trading partner and assigned a group control number. The group is bundled into an ISA interchange envelope by send and receive trading partner ID and assigned an interchange control number.

If any translation errors occur, the failed IDoc is moved to a workflow that maps it to a STATUS IDoc and sends it back into SAP to update the failed IDoc with an error status and message.

Assuming a best case scenario with no errors, the interchange is passed to a communications process and sent to DSI's EDI system through an AS2 call. The process waits for an MDN acknowledgment, which comes immediately, and a STATUS IDoc is sent back to SAP updating all the outbound IDocs in the interchange with a transmission OK status.

Gordy sends back a 997 acknowledgment for the 856 ASN group, ending the EDI transmission. The 997 is generated as soon as the interchange passes the technical checks in Gordy's EDI system, generally within seconds of importing the file.

If it takes longer than 24 hours to receive the 997, Acme's EDI team contacts Gordy's EDI team to find out whether there are any issues.

At Gordy's Receiving Point

A number of checks are made before the ASN posts to Gordy's business system:

▸ To verify the structure of the 856 ASN, particularly the sequencing, parentage, and relationships of the HL looping groups

▸ That Acme is a valid vendor authorized to send ASNs

▸ That the purchase order number matches an existing PO to Acme and the PO date is correct

▸ That the GLN for the ship-to location is a valid store number

▸ That the GTIN numbers for the ordered items are valid and the quantities ordered for each ship-to match the purchase order

If there are issues with any of these validations, an 824 text report is immediately sent to Acme, identifying errors against the purchase order and delivery numbers. Acme must correct 824 issues within 24 hours.

If the validations pass, or all errors are corrected, the ASN posts to Gordy's business system and is available at the receiving point. The receiving point must be able to access the ASN before the truck pulls into the receiving dock with the shipment from DSI.

When the shipment arrives at the receiving point, the ordered goods, their store locations, and quantities are scanned into Gordy's system and compared to the ASN. If everything checks out and there are no errors, the items are received into inventory with a goods receipt, updating and completing the purchase order.

If there are any issues with the postings, an 824 error report is immediately generated and sent to Acme and the issues addressed by the business. Errors must be addressed within 24 hours.

If no 824 is sent, the ASN process is complete. Gordy's accounts payable is updated and ready to accept and pay Acme's invoice.

16.4   Technical Specifications

This technical specification section describes the SAP configuration and EDI development required to support the DESADV to 856 advanced ship notification EDI interface to Gordy's Galaxy.

16.4.1 Technical Requirements

The outbound ASN is sent to Gordy's Galaxy within 15 minutes of the ship confirm and post goods issue in Acme's system. It must hit Gordy's system before the shipment arrives at their receiving point.

The ASN passes Gordy's purchase order number, DSI's bill of lading, pick quantities, and date the order was shipped.

For multi-pack orders, the EDI map passes to the 856 EDI transaction the shipping unit and all component items of the sales BOM.

16.4.2 Dependencies

The DESADV to 856 ASN interface to Gordy's Galaxy is dependent on outbound IDoc configuration in SAP and on several development objects in the EDI RIM:

▶ External partner mapping table PUMA populated with sold-to, ship-to, and supplier conversions from SAP to GLN ID numbers

▶ Custom table ZEDIXREF populated with mappings between SAP sending and receiving partners and EDI sending and receiving trading partner IDs for Acme and Gordy

▶ Outbound partner profile for Gordy with message type DESADV

▶ Batch job set up in the SAP Job Scheduler for program RSEOUT00 with variant to output DESADV IDocs at status 30 for all customers once every hour throughout the day

▶ A full set of outbound envelopes created in the EDI RIM for Gordy's Galaxy 856 X12 version 5010 transmissions

▶ A full set of inbound envelopes created in the EDI RIM to process X12 997 version 5010 functional acknowledgments from Gordy's Galaxy for the outbound 856 ASN

- Translation map created in the EDI RIM for DESADV IDoc to X12 856 ASN version 5010

- Business processes in the EDI RIM to do the following:

  - Pick up IDoc files from the SAP application server

  - Run map to convert the IDoc file to an EDI with one group and one or more outbound 856 transaction sets

  - Transmit the 856 interchange to Gordy by AS2

  - Receive an X12 824 ASN error report, translate it to a human readable PDF format, and attach the report to an email routed to the responsible business users

16.4.3 Assumptions

IDoc errors are monitored by the EDI team in SAP using standard IDoc monitoring tools, such as BD87 and WE09. This includes technical errors, such as incorrect syntax or missing partner profile, and application errors.

Technical errors are corrected by the EDI team. With the support of the EDI team, business users tackle application errors.

All errors in the EDI system are corrected by the EDI team. Any issue that might impact the application is communicated to the appropriate business user immediately.

Application errors from Gordy are sent to Acme in an X12 824 text message and routed to the responsible business users from the EDI RIM in an error report attached to an email.

The IDoc control record fields SNDLAD and RCVLAD pick up the EDI sending and receiving trading partner IDs through a customer exit called before the IDoc is written to the database during outbound processing. The EDI RIM identifies the EDI trading partner IDs from the control segment fields.

16.5 Mapping Specifications

One map is developed in the EDI RIM to translate the DESADV IDoc to an 856 X12 5010 ASN transaction to Gordy's Galaxy.

Table 16.3 outlines the mapping requirements for the outbound DESADV to 856 ASN for Gordy's Galaxy. This is by no means a complete mapping. We are not, for example, including the packaging hierarchy in handling unit segment E1EDL37 and its children.

DESADV	856	Value	Comments
	BSN03	20131215	IDoc Date from EDIDC-CREDAT
	BSN04	133908	IDoc time from EDIDC-CRETIM
E1EDL20—Delivery header—Min 1 Max 1			
VBELN	BSN02	0080016843	Acme outbound delivery number. Delivery document to be confirmed. Mandatory value.
	REF01	DO	Hard-code delivery order where HL03 = O (order level).
VBELN	REF02	0080016843	Delivery number also mapped here where HL03 = O and REF01 = DO
VSBED	TD504	02	Transportation method code where HL03 = S (shipment level). Convert to J (Motor).
	TD106	G	Hard-code gross weight qualifier where HL03 = S. Instance 1 of TD1.
BTGEW	TD107	280.000	Gross weight where HL03 = S and TD106 = G. Instance 1 of TD01. Segment repeated for each shipment-level total weight, quantity, or volume. Instance 1 of TD1.
	TD106	N	Hard-code net weight qualifier where HL03 = S. Instance 2 of TD1.
NTGEW	TD107	250.000	Net weight where HL03 = S and TD106 = N. Instance 2 of TD01.

Table 16.3 Mapping Specifications for the DESADV IDoc to ASN X12 856

DESADV	856	Value	Comments
GEWEI	TD108	KGM	Weight unit for header weights
	REF01	BM	Hard-code BOL qualifier where HL03 = S
BOLNR	REF02	9874785900	Bill of lading number where HL03 = S and REF01 = BM
	TD303	TL	Hard-code standard truck trailer ID qualifier where HL03 = S
TRAID	TD303	999999	Trailer ID number where HL03 = S TD01 = TL
E1EDL18—Control codes—Min 1, Max 99			
QUALF	BSN01	ORI	Convert to 00 original document.
E1ADRM1—Delivery partner—Min 1, Max 99, Loop 1 Ship-from			
PARTNER_Q	N101	OSP	Convert to SF for shipping point ID qualifier where HL03 = S.
	N103	91	Hard-code to 91 seller's ID where HL03 = S and N101 = SF.
PARTNER_ID	N104	3100	DSI shipping point ID where HL03 = S and N101 = SF and N103 = 91.
E1ADRM1—Delivery partner—Loop 2 Ship-to			
PARTNER_Q	N101	WE	Convert to ST for ship-to receiving point ID qualifier where HL03 = S.
	N103	92	Hard-code to 92 seller's ID where HL03 = S and N101 = ST.
NAME1	N102	Gordy's Galaxy	Gordy's ship-to location name. See E1ARDE1 for the ship-to ID.
E1ARDE1—Delivery partner extension—Ship-to GLN			
EXTEND_Q		100	Identifies ILN or GLN number. Convert to 92 for buyer's number where HL03 = S and N101 = ST and N103 = 92.

Table 16.3 Mapping Specifications for the DESADV IDoc to ASN X12 856 (Cont.)

DESADV	856	Value	Comments
EXTEND_D	N104	01254863254898	Identifies ILN or GLN number. Converted from Table PUMA.
E1ADRM1—Delivery partner—Loop 3 Sold-to partner			
PARTNER_Q	REF01	AG	Convert to DP for sold-to department number qualifier where HL03 = O.
E1ARDE1—Delivery partner extension—Sold-to department number			
EXTEND_Q		300	Identifies partner's ID number in extension
EXTEND_D	REF02	1005	Gordy's purchasing department number where HL03 = O and REF01 = DP. Converted from PUMA.
E1EDT13—Dates—Min 1, Max 99—Loop 1 Shipping date			
QUALF	DTM01	011	Map to DTM01 (shipped date) where HL03 = S
ISDD	DTM02	20140115	Actual shipping date where HL03 = S and DTM01 = 011
E1EDT13—Dates—Loop 2 Delivery date			
QUALF	DTM01	007	Convert to 010 for requested ship date where HL03 = S for shipment.
ISDD	DTM02	20140114	Actual delivery date where HL03 = S and DTM01 = 010
E1EDL24—Item-level details group—Min 1, Max N—1 instance of E1EDL21 per group loop			
POSNR	LIN01	000010	Delivery line item number where HL03 = I. Segment LIN will appear once for every instance where looping segment HL03 = I.
	LIN02	BC	Hard-code supplier's brand code for Acme's material number where HL03 = I.

Table 16.3 Mapping Specifications for the DESADV IDoc to ASN X12 856 (Cont.)

DESADV	856	Value	Comments
MATNR	LIN03	0005000020	Acme material number where HL03 = I and LIN03 = BC.
	LIN04	LT	Hard-code lot number for batch where HL03 = I if batch number present.
CHARG	LIN05	458248	Batch number where HL103 = I and LIN04 = LT
	LIN06	IN	Hard-code buyer's catalog number where HL03 = I for Gordy's material number.
KDMAT	LIN07	9999999	Customer's material number (Gordy) where HL03 = I and LIN06 = IN
LFIMG	SN102	100.000	Number of units shipped. Updates picking quantity. Pull from SN102 where HL103 = I (item level of packing hierarchy) for current line item.
VRKME	SN103	EA	Unit of measure for LFIMG quantity.
LGMNG	SN105	100.000	Delivery quantity. Pull from SN105 where HL103 = I (item level of packing hierarchy) for current line item.
MEINS	SN106	EA	Unit of measure for LGMNG quantity
NTGEW	TD107	250.000	Net weight of item where TD106 = N and HL103 = I (item level of packing hierarchy) for current line item. TD1 is a looping group: one instance per type of weight.
BRGEW	TD107	280.000	Gross weight of item where TD106 = G and HL103 = I (item level of packing hierarchy) for current line item.

Table 16.3 Mapping Specfications for the DESADV IDoc to ASN X12 856 (Cont.)

DESADV	856	Value	Comments
GEWEI	TD108	KGM	Unit of measure for weight
E1EDL41—Customer purchase order			
QUALI		001	Identifies Gordy's purchase order where HL03 = O
BSTNR	PRF01	32112	Customer purchase order number where HL03 = O
BSTDT	PRF04	20131215	Customer purchase order date

Table 16.3 Mapping Specifications for the DESADV IDoc to ASN X12 856 (Cont.)

This specification is for a simple ASN that includes only shipment, order, and item hierarchies. In the real world, the ASN will likely be much more complex and could include sales BOMs and multiple levels of packing and repacking hierarchies, not to mention different mappings for different trading partner relationships.

After all, every business relationship is different and EDI at its heart is the expression of a business relationship in data.

16.6   EDI Configuration in SAP

We need the following configuration settings to support our outbound DESADV to X12 856 ASN interface to Gordy's Galaxy:

▶ Entries in SAP standard external partner conversion table PUMA for the sold-to and ship-to partners

▶ An entry in custom EDI mapping table ZEDIXREF to support outbound trading partner number conversion

▶ An outbound partner profile for customer Gordy with message type DESADV and output control

16.6.1 EDPAR Entries

There are no EDPAR entries for the outbound DESADV.DELVRY03 to X12 856 ASN interface.

16.6.2 PUMA Entries: Transaction VNPU

Outbound external partner conversion tale PUMA is read during population of segment E1ARDE1 by function `IDOC_OUTPUT_DELVRY`. It maps the SAP partner to the external partner number in a variety of formats for the EDI receiver of the outbound DESADV ASN IDoc.

In our case, it will link sold-to and ship-to partner numbers for Gordy in SAP to its internal system numbers. Use Transaction VNPU to enter the data in Table 16.4 into PUMA.

Field	Value	Description
Sold-to partner mapping		
REC.FUNC.	AG	Recipient sold-to partner
RECPARTNO	GRDY01	Recipient sold-to partner number
CONV.FUNC	AG	Partner function to be converted
PARTNOCONV	GRDY01	Partner number to be converted
EXTERNAL PARTNER NO.	1005	Gordy's external purchasing organization
Ship-to partner mapping		
REC.FUNC.	WE	Recipient ship-to partner function
RECPARTNO	GRDY01001	Recipient ship-to partner number
CONV.FUNC	WE	Partner function to be converted
PARTNOCONV	GRDY01001	Partner number to be converted
EXTERNAL PARTNER NO.	0999857055556	External partner number (GLN) for Gordy's ship-to store location

Table 16.4 PUMA Entries for Gordy's Sold-to and Ship-to Partners

Don't forget to save your entries and assign them to a change request. The finished result in Transaction VNPU should look like Figure 16.5.

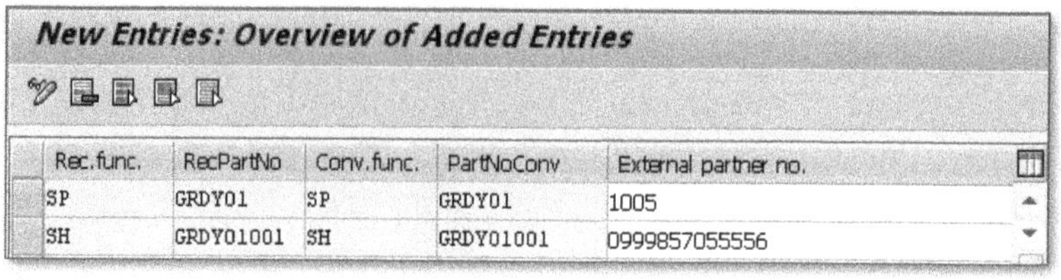

Figure 16.5 PUMA Partner Mapping Entries for Gordy's Galaxy

16.6.3 ZEDIXREF Entries

IDoc sender and receiver partners (the SAP logical system ID and Gordy's customer number) will be mapped to Gordy's EDI sender and receiver trading partner IDs.

The ZEDIXREF values for the outbound DESADV.DELVRY03 interface to Gordy's Galaxy are listed in Table 16.5.

Field	Value	Description
DIRECT	1	Direction outbound
STDMES	856	856 EDI ASN transaction
MESTYP	DESADV	IDoc message type
IDOCTP	DELVRY03	IDoc basic type
CIMTYP		IDoc extension, none for this interface
SNDPRN	DEVCLNT100	SAP send partner: Acme SAP logical system
RCVPRN	GRDY01	SAP receive partner: DSI's vendor number in Acme's system
SNDLAD	9999999USD	EDI send partner: Gordy's EDI trading partner ID for Acme
RCVLAD	01234567US0	EDI receiver partner: Gordy's EDI trading partner ID for Gordy

Table 16.5 ZEDIXREF Entries for Gordy's Outbound 856 ASN

16.6.4 Partner Profiles: Transaction WE20

We'll need one outbound partner profile for Gordy's Galaxy partner number GRDY01, partner type KU (customer), and partner role SP (sold-to) with message type DESADV.

In the outbound parameters table control of the partner profile for Gordy's Galaxy, click the CREATE OUTBOUND PARAMETERS button and enter the following values in the OUTBOUND PARAMETERS screen, as shown in Figure 16.6.

▸ PARTNER ROLE: "SP"

▸ MESSAGE TYPE: "DESADV"

▸ RECEIVER PORT: "XML_IDOC"

▸ OUTPUT MODE area: COLLECT IDOCs and START SUBSYSTEM radio buttons

▸ BASIC TYPE: "DELVRY03"

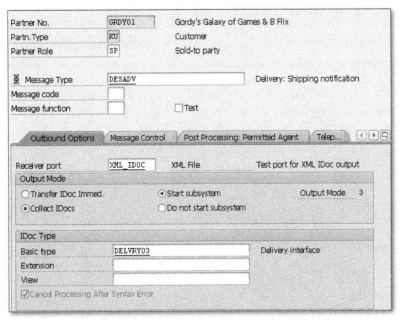

Figure 16.6 Outbound Parameters DESADV ASN to Gordy's Galaxy

Click the MESSAGE CONTROL tab and enter the following values, as in Figure 16.7.

▸ APPLICATION: "V2"

▸ MESSAGE TYPE: "LAVA"

▸ PROCESS CODE: "DELV"

▸ CHANGE MESSAGE checkboxes: One entry null and one checked

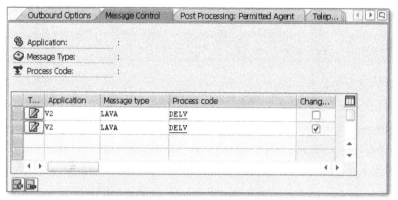

Figure 16.7 Message Control Setup for the DESADV ASN

Process code DELV links to function module `IDOC_OUTPUT_DELVRY`, which builds the IDoc from the delivery document and sales order.

The last step is to select the EDI STANDARD tab at the upper far right and enter the following values, as in Figure 16.8:

▶ EDI STANDARD: "X" for X12

▶ MESSAGE TYPE: "856"

▶ VERSION: 005010

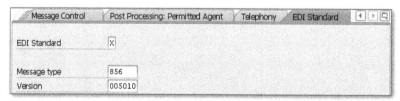

Figure 16.8 EDI Standard Values for the DESADV ASN

Don't forget to save the partner profile.

16.7 Summary

We have seen that Acme generates the advanced shipping notification (ASN) in a SHPCON.DELVRY03 IDoc after its outbound delivery has been updated with the pick quantity, shipping date, and post goods issue from its third-party distributor, Disc Services International.

The update comes from a shipping confirmation in an X12 856 sent by DSI as soon as the truck carrying Gordy's goods leaves the shipping point.

Gordy's Galaxy expects the ASN to hit their business system through a DESADV. DELVRY03 IDoc converted to an X12 856 transmission before the shipment arrives at the receiving dock in their distribution center.

This is a critical transaction for Gordy's Galaxy. The ASN must match the purchase order (or purchase orders) in their system for Acme Pictures. They check the purchase order numbers, the materials and quantities ordered, and the ship-to location, among other data to confirm that the ASN is correct.

If there are any discrepancies, an error report is generated and fired off to Acme in an X12 824 transmission. The issue must be resolved immediately or Gordy won't be able to receive the goods.

Assuming no errors, when the shipment arrives the workers at the receiving dock scan each carton as it comes off the truck and the system compares it to the accepted ASN. As long as everything matches up, the goods are received into inventory.

When all items in a purchase order have been confirmed against the ASN and received into inventory, the PO is closed and accounting updated. Any errors are reported back to Acme with an 824 and dealt with immediately.

Until the ASN is clear, Gordy's system will not accept an invoice.

We've gone over the data and the process flows and have configured the key pieces of this interface. And if we tried to explain all this mumbo-jumbo to the great Darryl Q, the legendary founder of Acme Pictures, his eyes would glaze over and his mind wander to a refreshing, pool-side martini.

But what comes next would bring a happy spring to his step because it's why he got into this crazy business in the first: the invoice. So without further ado, let's turn our attention to generating the invoice for the DVD movies ordered by our favorite customer, Gordy's Galaxy of Games & B Flix.

"Put it on my tab" was one of Darryl Q's signature lines. But before he paid, he went over that tab carefully. It's the same with the customer invoice, one of Acme's signature documents. The customer needs to receive it before he can pay it. And that's what we'll do now as we go over the INVOIC interface — make sure Acme's customer gets the tab for the goods they ordered.

17 Generating the Outbound Customer Invoice

We're near the end of the road for our order-to-cash cycle of interfaces between Acme Pictures, its contract manufacturer and distributor, Disc Services International, and its most important customer, Gordy's Galaxy of Games & B Flix.

To use the vernacular so loved by Darryl Q. Fernhausen, the unlikely Hollywood mogul who founded Acme Pictures, the time has come to bring home the dough.

Acme's 856 advanced shipping notification posted to Gordy's business system before the delivery arrived, and every item was received successfully into inventory against the purchase order without any errors.

Gordy got its goods and is now ready to send them to the stores, line them up on shelves, and make a ton of money selling Acme's artistic creations.

Meanwhile, back at Acme Pictures, the 997 acknowledgment for the ASN was successfully received, and there was no follow-up 824 error report.

The post goods issue, triggered by the earlier 856 shipping confirmation, updated FI with a material document that records what was sold and shipped to Gordy against a GL account and profit center for the sold-to partner and item.

Conditions are ripe in Acme's SAP system for issuing a customer invoice, and Gordy is ready to authorize payment. All Gordy needs is an invoice that accurately describes what was received and how much it cost, against the purchase order and line item numbers.

As soon as Gordy gets its invoice, the clock starts ticking: Gordy must send the money within 60 days, the time frame agreed to in the terms of payment. We're now entering the mysterious realm of the accountants and book-keepers: payables at Gordy and receivables at Acme.

It's time, then, to consider the functional and technical requirements for our outbound INVOIC.INVOIC02 to X12 810 interface to Gordy's Galaxy.

17.1   Technical Overview of Interface

Table 17.1 summarizes the outbound customer invoice interface.

Item	Description
Title	The Customer Invoice
Description	The customer invoice interface is generated from the SAP billing document. It can be created manually or through a batch job by the billing due list or individually directly by creating or changing a billing document.
	The immediate trigger for creation of the billing document is the post goods issue against the outbound delivery from DSI in the ship confirm interface.
	After this is done, a scheduled job to run the billing due list generates billing documents from deliveries that have been completed.
	INVOIC IDocs are issued from the billing document if there are no errors or blocks, and the IDocs sit at status 30 until RSEOUT00 is run to send them to Gordy as 810 X12 customer invoices.
	Timing here is critical. Gordy will accept the invoices only if the ASN generated from the Acme's outbound delivery has posted against their PO to their business system and successfully verified all items received into inventory from the delivery when the shipment arrives.
	If all the pieces are in place correctly, Gordy will post the invoice to its accounts payable and pay within the agreed terms of payment.

Table 17.1 Overview of Outbound INVOIC Customer Invoice Interface

Item	Description
	Errors in the invoice in Gordy's system will generate an X12 864 error report back to Acme. Until the errors are corrected, the invoice won't be processed. A custom ABAP will allow users to change the purchase order number in the INVOIC IDoc if it is incorrect because of faulty data entry in a manually created sales order or some other error in processing.
Type of interface	Distribution: IDoc to X12 EDI
Direction	Outbound
Trading partner	Gordy's Galaxy (customer)
IDoc	INVOIC.INVOIC02
IDoc extended type	
IDoc function	`IDOC_OUTPUT_INVOIC`
Custom ABAP	`ZSDCHINVOIC`
Custom transaction	ZEDINV
Description	ALV grid report with data entry functionality for mass change of customer PO in INVOIC IDocs
Target file(s)	X12 810 customer invoice
Source document(s)	SAP billing document
Transaction code	VF01 (single), VF04 (billing due list), and VF06 (billing due list in background mode)
Map(s)	INVOIC.INVOIC02 to X12 810 vers. 5010
Custom map logic	
Source system	Acme SAP
Target system	Gordy's Galaxy EDI via AS2 from Acme EDI RIM
997 acknowledgment	Inbound within 24 hours of transmission at the transaction detail level; function group acknowledgment code: IN
Frequency	Twice daily, on demand

Table 17.1 Overview of Outbound INVOIC Customer Invoice Interface (Cont.)

Item	Description
Job schedule 1	RV60SBAT: once daily (at 9 p.m.) runs the billing due list in background mode for all completed deliveries that have been shipped to the customer
Job schedule 2	RSEOUT00: twice daily (at 8 a.m. and 8 p.m.) sends all INVOIC message types to all customers at status 30

Table 17.1 Overview of Outbound INVOIC Customer Invoice Interface (Cont.)

17.2   Functional Specifications

The INVOIC to X12 810 interface is the second to last step in the order-to-cash processing cycle. And it one of the most critical. Without an accurate invoice, Gordy won't pay Acme for their order.

The invoice tells the bill-to partner (Gordy's purchasing department and accounts receivable) how much money the company owes against the delivered purchase order.

After the invoice has been successfully received and validated in Gordy's business system, accounts payable steps in to process the payment and cut a check—or better yet, trigger an electronic payment—within the time frame defined in Gordy's terms of payment with Acme.

There will also be a custom ALV grid report that allows us to correct some errors in the IDoc and to either reprocess it or mark it for deletion.

17.2.1   Process Overview

The process begins after Gordy receives the shipment from DSI and confirms its contents against the 856 ASN received from Acme. The shipment must match exactly the items and quantities listed in the ASN.

Errors in ASN processing result in generation of an X12 824 error report back to Acme.

When the ASN is validated against the shipment, Gordy moves the goods received into inventory and updates accounts payable. Acme then runs the delivery due list in a batch job once a night to generate billing documents in SAP against completed deliveries.

INVOIC IDocs are generated and parked in the IDoc database at status 30 when the billing documents are saved, assuming there are no errors, blocks, or other issues.

RSEOUT00 runs twice a day to pick up all INVOIC IDocs at status 30 and sends them to the EDI RIM, where they are converted to an X12 810 EDI customer invoices and transmitted to Gordy's EDI system.

The invoice posts to Gordy's business system. Assuming there are no unresolved issues with the ASN, or the goods received, or errors in the invoice, accounts payable is updated and the clock starts ticking on the 60-day payment period agreed to in the terms of payment.

If there are any issues, an X12 864 text message is generated by Gordy and sent to Acme with an error report detailing the issues. These must be fixed before the invoice can post to Gordy's system and the clock can start ticking on the payment.

17.2.2 Requirements

Billing documents are generated from completed deliveries, which means the delivery has been updated with a post goods issue from an inbound 856 shipping confirmation, has posted inventory and accounting documents, and has generated an outbound ASN that was sent to Gordy in the DESADV to x12 856 interface.

Although the system may be ready to generate billing documents after the delivery is complete, Gordy won't accept an invoice until the ASN posts to its system and until it receives the shipment and validates the delivery items against the ASN and receives the goods against the purchase order.

So there is potential lag time between sending the ASN and generating the invoice in SAP. This is usually taken care of by running the billing due list in batch once a day—at 9:00 p.m., giving Gordy and Acme the whole day to validate and receive the goods against the ASN and correct any issues that may arise.

One billing document is generated for each completed delivery. The billing document is defined by the following data:

▸ Billing type, which is ZEDI for EDI customer invoices

▸ Customer purchase order number and date

- Billing data, including bill-to partner, material, profit center, quantity, currency, and terms of payment
- Pricing conditions, recording prices, costs, discounts, promotions, taxes, and so on

INVOIC IDocs are generated when the billing document is saved only if it is complete—that is, when the following has happened:

- A material document recording the goods movements triggered by the post goods issue on the outbound delivery is posted to inventory against the GL account and profit center.
- The post goods issue against the delivery triggered creation of an accounting document. The accounting document is linked to the delivery and material documents, and records debit and credit account postings for the materials.
- The billing document header and item details data are complete.
- Pricing is complete.
- Two acccounting documents have posted for the billing document:
    - An FI invoice that posts to accounts receivable each pricing and cost element in the billing document against its relevant GL account (accounts receivable clears this document when the payment posts)
    - A controlling document recording primary costs against the billing

The billing document is issued for the bill-to partner. For Gordy, and most of Acme's big customers, this is the same as the sold-to partner, although it has its own partner function.

The INVOIC IDoc references key document numbers:

- Gordy's purchase order
- Acme's SAP sales order
- Acme's SAP outbound ASN delivery
- Acme's billing document

17.2.3 Dependencies

The INVOIC to X12 810 invoice interface is dependent on master data, configuration, and development in SAP and the EDI RIM, including everything that is required to support sales orders, confirmations, shipping orders, and inbound ship confirmations.

Other dependencies include (but aren't restricted to) the following:

▶ General ledger accounts, profit centers, and billing document types

▶ Blocking reasons are defined and assigned to billing document types

▶ Bill-to partner exists for Gordy's Galaxy and is associated with the sold-to partner in the customer master record

▶ Billing data in the customer master are complete, including incoterms, terms of payment, account assignment group, and tax classifications

▶ The internal SAP sold-to, bill-to, and ship-to partner numbers for Gordy are mapped to their GLN in EDPAR

▶ Message control is configured to support output of INVOIC IDocs from billing documents (custom output type ZD00 will be copied from standard billing document output type ED00)

▶ Outbound partner profile set up for Gordy's Galaxy for message type INVOIC with the configured message control settings

17.2.4 Assumptions

INVOIC IDocs are automatically generated when the billing document is saved. One INVOIC IDoc is output for each billing document containing all billing document data, including pricing conditions at the item level only.

Any pricing conditions that won't be sent to the customer aren't mapped to the 810 invoice in the EDI RIM. This is true for all data that the customer doesn't need to receive.

Other key assumptions about the INVOIC-810 interface include the following:

▶ An EDI invoice is sent to all EDI customers.

▶ We could theoretically bundle multiple sales orders and deliveries into one invoice, but Acme will generate only one billing document for one delivery and one sales order.

▶ The INVOIC IDoc can be regenerated from the billing document using Transaction VF31 if necessary.

- ► The INVOIC IDoc is sent to the customer as an X12 810 EDI invoice.
- ► Gordy expects to receive the GLN for its sold-to, bill-to, and ship-to partner numbers in its invoice.
- ► Gordy expects all items invoiced to be identified by their own material number.
- ► Relevant customer purchase order, sales order, and delivery data are passed to the EDI invoice, including the following:
  - ► Customer purchase order and billing document numbers
  - ► Gordy's sold-to, bill-to, and store ship-to GLNs
  - ► All ordered items, quantities, prices, and costs
  - ► Sales BOMs for multi-pack items ordered by Gordy's Galaxy, with pricing and costs reflected only for the top-level corrugate item, not for the component titles
- ► If Gordy records any errors against the 810 invoice in its business system, it returns an error report within 24 hours in a separate X12 864 error report EDI transmission. The 864 will be mapped to a report in PDF format and immediately emailed to the relevant business users.

17.2.5 Data That Pass to the IDoc from the Billing Document

Table 17.2 displays the source for some of the key data that are passed to the INVOIC IDoc from the billing, delivery, and sales order documents for the outbound invoice to Gordy's Galaxy.

Table	Field	Description	Sample Value
Billing Header			
VBRK	VBELN	Invoice number	0906524859
VBRK	FKART	Billing type invoice	F1
VBAK	BSTKD	Customer purchase order number	292259
VBRK	BUKRS	Company code	3000
VBRK	VKORG	Sales organization	0010
VBRK	VTWEG	Distribution channel	0010

Table 17.2 Billing Data That Pass to the Outbound Invoice IDoc

Table	Field	Description	Sample Value
LIKP	VBELN	Delivery number	816160750
VBRK	WAERK	Document currency	USD
VBRK	FKDAT	Billing date (invoice date)	20081222
VBRK	FKDAT	Due date: Calculated	20081223
LIKP	LFDAT	Delivery date	20081220
VBAK	BSTDK	Customer PO date	20081219
VBRK	ZTERM	Terms of payment	ZT60
LIKP	BTGEW	Gross weight	10128.750
LIKP	NTGEW	Net weight	10128.750
LIKP	GEWEI	Weight unit of measure	LB
VBPA	KUNNR	PARVW = AG: Sold-to	GRDY01
VBPA	KUNNR	PARVW = RE: Bill-to	GRDY01
VBPA	KUNNR	PARVW = WE: Ship-to partner	GRDY01001
Billing Items			
VBRP	POSNR	Item number	000010
VBRP	FKIMG	Invoiced quantity	4
VBRP	VRKME	Unit of measure for quantity	EA
VBRP	PRSDT	Pricing date	20131215
VBRP	NETWR	Net value of billing item	47968.00
VBRP	MWSBP	Tax amount for billing item	7195.20
KONP	KSCHL	Pricing condition type	PR00
KONP	KBETR	Unit price, taxes, allowances, subtotals, and other pricing conditions	11.23
VBRP	MATNR	Order item (SAP)	2356784
VBRP	ARKTX	Material description	I Married an Alien
VBRP	KDMAT	Customer material number	799142939512

Table 17.2 Billing Data That Pass to the Outbound Invoice IDoc (Cont.)

Table	Field	Description	Sample Value
VBKD	BSTKD	Customer purchase order number at line item level	799142939512
VBAP	POSEX	Purchase order line item number	000010
VBAP	VBELN	Supplier sales order number	00014031
VBAP	POSNR	Supplier sales order line item number	000010

Table 17.2 Billing Data That Pass to the Outbound Invoice IDoc (Cont.)

The billing document and IDoc are populated with a great deal of data that won't be sent to Gordy's Galaxy in the X12 810 invoice. Banking information, such as Acme's bank key, name, account number, and address may show up in the IDoc but won't be sent to Gordy.

Many of the data in the billing document are already in Gordy's system in the purchase order, ASN, and their own master data. The IDoc, for example, pulls the bill-to, payer, invoiced party, sold-to, and ship-to parties. But we only need to send the sold-to and ship-to numbers. Gordy already knows who's paying the bill and they have all the addresses they need.

17.2.6 Enhancements to the Process

Business users need an enhancement that allows them to change the customer purchase order number field in INVOIC IDocs when it has been entered incorrectly. This can happen when a sales order is created or updated manually.

The business was able to do this in the X12 810 transaction in legacy and wants to continue doing it in SAP, particularly for Gordy's Galaxy.

17.2.7 Enhancement Details

The INVOIC editing program is run after IDocs have been generated for the billing documents using custom transaction ZEDINV. The following are options for the program:

- IDoc number
- IDoc send partner (SAP sold-to)

- IDoc status
- EDI ISA interchange control number
- IDoc change date and time
- Invoice number

IDocs are listed in one or more single-line record displays in an ALV grid report in the lower portion of the screen with the following fields:

- IDoc number
- IDoc change date
- SAP sold-to and ship-to partners
- Invoice number
- Customer purchase order number and date
- Error message

Each IDoc line has a checkbox to allow individual or batch selection of IDocs for editing or other processing. Only the line selected is changed and written to the IDoc for reprocessing.

A data entry field in the upper portion of the report screen allows changing of the customer purchase order number. The report display is updated after the edit but before the IDoc is updated. Changes made to the displayed data can be reversed or changed again before posting to the IDoc.

Buttons are provided to update and reprocess one or more changed IDocs with the new customer purchase order number in the data entry screen and to mark the IDoc for deletion by changing its status to 31—*Error, no further processing*.

Users can also branch to a tree display view of the IDoc by double-clicking an IDoc or by clicking a button.

17.2.8 Reconciliation

Generation of the IDoc can be confirmed within the billing document in Transaction VF03 by selecting menu option GoTo • HEADER • OUTPUT. Look for output type ZD00 for medium EDI, partner function BP (bill-to), and partner number GRDY01 for Gordy's Galaxy.

The IDoc can be called up and analyzed using any of the standard IDoc monitoring tools, including Transactions WE05 and BD87.

Data in the INVOIC IDoc will be validated against the billing document, particularly the following items:

- ▶ Invoice number
- ▶ Billing date
- ▶ Sold-to, bill-to, and ship-to partners with the correct GLNs
- ▶ Payment terms
- ▶ Customer PO, delivery, and sales order numbers
- ▶ Invoiced material number and text description
- ▶ SAP and UPC item numbers
- ▶ Quantity and dollar amount
- ▶ Pricing conditions

There are a few other things to validate here:

- ▶ The INVOIC IDoc was sent to the EDI system and was successfully translated to an outbound 810.
- ▶ The data in the 810 matches the IDoc and conforms to Acme's EDI mapping specifications and to Gordy's 810 EDI guidelines.
- ▶ Gordy receives and acknowledges the 810 with a 997 within 24 hours.
- ▶ Gordy does not return an X12 864 error report detailing invoice issues within 24 hours.

17.2.9 Errors and Error Handling

If an INVOIC IDoc fails to generate when the billing document is created, the EDI team and business users work together to identify and correct the errors. The following checks can be made:

- ▶ The billing document is released to accounting. Click the ACCOUNTING button in the billing document screen. A list of accounting documents should appear.
- ▶ Transaction NACE to confirm that message control for custom output type ZD00 has been completed correctly.

- Transaction VV33 to confirm that condition records have been entered for output type ZD00.

- Transaction WE20 to confirm that the outbound partner profile for Gordy's Galaxy message type INVOIC is set up with the correct output type and process code.

In addition, IDoc data issues could cause the map to fail in the EDI RIM without triggering an error in SAP. These are identified by the EDI team and communicated to the business users:

- Missing customer material number

- Missing customer purchase order number

Another set of data issues could trigger a failure in Gordy's business system. These errors will generate an X12 864 error report that will be sent back to Acme by EDI transmission:

- The invoice posting to Gordy's system before the ASN is validated against the purchase order

- The invoice posting before all delivery items have been confirmed against the ASN and received into inventory

- Incorrect purchase order number

- Incorrect customer material number

- Incorrect GLN for Gordy's sold-to or ship-to

- Mismatch between the shipment received and the invoice

Until the errors are addressed by the business, the clock won't start ticking on payment of the invoice.

17.3 Generating an INVOIC IDoc with Message Control

Before we get into the details of the outbound process flow and the custom code we'll write for this interface, we'll configure our message control.

The outbound invoice to Gordy's Galaxy is generated by message control when the billing document is created after the outbound delivery has been saved with the post goods issue.

We will create the following configuration objects to support generation of the INVOIC IDoc to Gordy's Galaxy:

▶ Custom output type ZD00, with supporting configuration, copied from standard output RD00 with access sequence 0003: sales organization, distribution channel, division, and bill-to customer number

▶ Condition record mapping the sales organization keys to the bill-to and sold-to partner for customer Gordy's Galaxy

▶ One outbound partner profile with message control for Gordy with invoice message type INVOIC

17.3.1 Configuring Message Control

We'll copy standard output type RD00 in application V3 (billing) to create custom output type ZD00 using Transaction NACE. Follow these steps:

1. Select application V3 and click OUTPUT TYPES to open the OUTPUT TYPES: OVERVIEW in display mode.

2. Select menu path TABLE VIEW • DISPLAY • CHANGE (or press Ctrl+F1) and select standard output RD00. Click COPY AS OR PRESS F6.

3. Change the output type name to ZD00 and enter a description for the EDI invoice. Make sure ACCESS TO CONDITIONS and MULTIPLE ISSUING are both set.

4. Change the sequence to "0003" for sales organization, distribution channel, division, and customer, as shown in Figure 17.1.

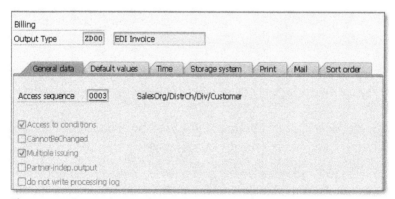

Figure 17.1 Custom Invoice Output Type ZD00 with Access Sequence 0003

5. Access number is 10, condition table 6 (B006), communications structure KOMKBV3 with key fields:

   ▸ VKORG: Sales organization

   ▸ VTWEG: Distribution channel

   ▸ SPART: Division

   ▸ KNDNR: Bill-to partner

6. Press ⌑Enter⌑. The SPECIFY OBJECT TO BE COPIED dialog opens, noting that the output type has dependent entries. Click COPY ALL. Another dialog opens with the number of dependent entries.

7. The system returns us to the OUTPUT TYPES: OVERVIEW screen in change view. Save the custom output type and assign all copied objects to a change request.

8. Select output ZD00 and double-click the PROCESSING ROUTINES folder to open the PROCESSING ROUTINES: OVERVIEW screen.

9. If there is no program and form routine for medium EDI, add one. Click NEW ENTRIES to open the DETAILS OF ADDED ENTRIES screen and enter the following values:

   ▸ TRANSM.MEDIUM: "EDI"

   ▸ PROGRAM (Processing 1): "RSNASTED" for the standard SAP output program

   ▸ FORM ROUTINE: "EDI_PROCESSING", which identifies and calls the function that generates and sends the IDoc

10. Press ⌑Enter⌑ and double-click the PARTNER FUNCTIONS folder to open the PARTNER FUNCTIONS: OVERVIEW screen.

11. Make sure that there's an entry for medium EDI and partner type BP for bill-to partner. If not, click NEW ENTRIES and select EDI in the MEDIUM field and BP in the FUNCT field.

12. SAVE any changes since your last save.

Assign ZD00 to a Procedure

Back out to the output control initial screen in Transaction NACE. Select application V2 and click PROCEDURES. Then follow these steps:

1. Select procedure V10000 (billing output) and double-click CONTROL in the navigation pane.

2. Select output type RD00 and click the Copy as button (F6). The entry is copied into the Change View Control: Overview screen.

3. Keep the step number at 10, change the counter to 2 (or whatever else works for you), and change the output type name to "ZD00".

4. Select requirement 62. This checks flags in communications structure KOMKBV3 to confirm that the billing document is complete and accounting documents have posted before generating an output.

5. Press Enter to return to the overview screen. Save the entry and assign it to a change request. The entry should look like Figure 17.2.

Procedure		V10000	Billing Output			
Reference Step Overview						
Step	Counter	CTyp	Description	Requiremnt	Manual only	
10	1	RD00	Invoice		☐	☐
10	2	ZD00	EDI Invoice	62	☐	

Figure 17.2 ZD00 Assigned to the Billing Output Procedure

Create Condition Records

We need a condition record to drive generation of the IDoc for the invoice to Gordy. An IDoc will be generated from the billing document when the sales organization keys and bill-to partner match the condition record.

We can create the condition records directly in Transaction NACE by selecting application V3, clicking Condition records, and selecting output type ZD00—or directly with Transaction VV31.

1. Using Transaction VV31, enter output type ZD00 and click the Key combination button. Select Sorg./Distrib.Ch/Division/Customer and press Enter.

2. Enter the following values into the header fields and the condition records table control (see Figure 17.3):

   ▸ Sales Organization: "3030" (Acme sales organization for Gordy)

   ▸ Distribution Channel: "10"

   ▸ Division: "00"

   ▸ Customer: "GRDY01"

   ▸ Funct: "BP" for bill-to party

- MEDIUM: "6" for EDI

- DISPATCH TIME: "4" for immediately when the document is saved

- LANGUAGE: "EN"

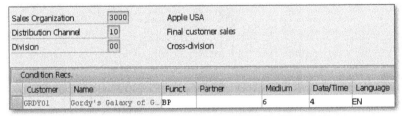

Figure 17.3 Condition Record for Output Type ZSH1 Application V2

We don't need to map the bill-to to the sold-to partner for generation of the IDocs. The output type is set to partner function BP (bill-to) and the partner profile will key to partner role BP.

The sold-to and bill-to numbers are the same at any rate. The link is maintained in the sold-to partner customer master record, in the PARTNER FUNCTIONS screen of SALES AREA DATA.

17.3.2 Overview of the End-to-End Process Flow

Figure 17.4 gives an overview of the end-to-end process flow for generating and sending EDI invoices to Gordy's Galaxy.

The outbound INVOIC to X12 810 interface kicks off when the billing due list is run for completed deliveries. The shipment has already been delivered, and the 856 ASN sent to Gordy after the post goods issue is saved.

An X12 997 acknowledgment has been received for the ASN, the shipment has been successfully received into Gordy's inventory, and no 824 error reports have been returned. This should all happen before the next scheduled run of the billing due list.

We'll be looking at running the billing due list online, rather than through the scheduled background job for Transaction VF06 program RV60SBAT, which uses much of the same processing but doesn't produce a billing due list report to use to select and generate billing documents. Rather, it will generate them directly.

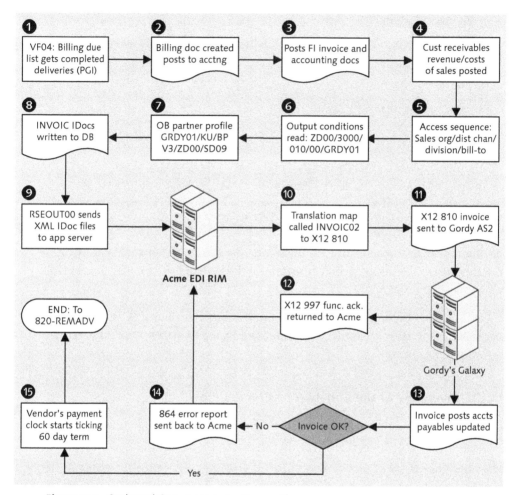

Figure 17.4 Outbound Customer Invoice Process Flow

The online billing due list program `SDBILLDL` is run with Transaction VF04 and kicked off with the following parameters:

▶ BILLING DATE FROM is blank, and To is the current date to cover every possible completed delivery document to date

▶ BILLING TYPE includes all EDI and non-EDI billing document types

▶ SALES ORGANIZATION

▶ SOLD-TO PARTNER

EDI customer invoices are generated from delivery documents for both EDI and non-EDI output. Output control determines whether an invoice outputs hard copy to a printer, generates an IDoc, or does both.

Generating the Invoices

After a little house-keeping, `SDBILLDL` reads invoice index table VKDFS by calling function `RV_READ_INVOICE_INDEX`. VKDFS keeps track of delivery documents that are ready for invoicing, making it a very useful table to know.

The full read key for table VKDFS is detailed in Table 17.3. All of these keys are available from the selection screen of the billing due list as either a select option or selection parameter.

Field	Value	Description
FKTYP	L	Billing category: Delivery related
VKORG	3000	Acme sales organization
FKDAT	20131215	Billing date
KUNNR	GRDY01	Sold-to customer
FKART	LF	Billing type: EDI customer invoice
LLAND		Country
VBELN		Delivery document number
VBTYP	J	SD document category for delivery
SORTKRI		Sort criteria (for user exit custom sort criteria)
VTWEG	0010	Distribution channel
SPART	00	Division
VSTEL	0015	Shipping point

Table 17.3 Read Key for Invoice Index Table VKDFS

Using this read key, VKDFS returns a list of deliveries that are ready to be invoiced—the billing due list—and passes it to the screen in an ALV grid list report. Three processing choices are offered in the report:

- INDIVIDUAL BILLING DOCUMENT: Runs for one delivery. Returns the billing document for online review before saving. Calls Transaction VF01 to create the billing document.

- COLLECTIVE BILLING DOCUMENT: Runs for more than one delivery document in batch. Saves the billing document in the background. Calls function SD_COLLEC-TIVE_RUN_EXECUTE to create batch billings.

- COLLECTIVE BILLING DOC/ONLINE: Returns multiple deliveries for online review before saving. Calls Transaction VF01 to create the billing documents.

All three options collect data from the sales order and delivery document, including dates, partners, items, quantities, pricing, shipping, and more. They then call function RV_INVOICE_CREATE (function group V60A) to post the billing document.

RV_INVOICE_CREATE calls RV_INVOICE_DOCUMENT_ADD to get the next available billing number, post accounting documents, update the delivery and billing document status in table VBUK, call output control, and save the billing document to the database.

At the same time, the posting of the FI invoice and accounting documents updates accounts receivable and posts both the revenues and costs of the sale represented by the shipped order.

Message Control Processing

Just before the billing document is saved, an output record is created for table NAST with the following output keys:

- Application V3: Billing
- Output type ZD00: Invoice
- Access sequence 0003: SalesOrg/DistrCh/Div/Customer (bill-to)
- Access 10: SOrg./Distrib.Ch/Division/Customer, condition table B006
- Procedure V10000: Billing (EDI) output

The access fields from communications structure KOMKBV3 include the following:

- VKORG: Sales organization
- VTWEG: Distribution channel

- SPART: Division
- KNDNR: Bill-to partner

The access keys are populated from the billing document header table VBRK. They are used to read condition tables B006 and NACH for Gordy's bill-to partner. The output type links to, and calls, the output processing form routine EDI_PROCESS-ING in program `RSNASTED`, which first calls function `EDI_PARTNER_READ_OUTGOING` to get the partner profile using the key fields in structure EDK12:

- RCVPRN: Receive partner number: GRDY01
- RCVPRT: Receive partner type: KU (customer)
- RCVPFC: Receive partner function: BP (bill-to partner)
- KAPPL: Message control application: V3
- KSCHL: Message type: ZD00

Gordy's outbound partner profile for message type INVOIC is linked to the output record for NAST through the message control subscreen, which includes three values:

- Application V3: Billing
- Output (or message) type ZD00: Invoice
- Process code SD09: Invoice

Process code SD09 links message type INVOIC to the function module `IDOC_OUT-PUT_INVOIC`, which is kicked off to build the IDoc.

Building the IDoc

The IDoc function collects the data it needs in form `LESEN_FAKTURA`, which initializes all internal tables and work areas, calls a data extraction routine, and ends with a customer function that allows custom processing of billing document data in the internal tables and strings that are used to assemble the IDoc.

The data are extracted mostly by function calls from the billing, delivery, and sales order documents and supporting tables. The billing document number is passed from the NAST output record.

The IDoc is built in form `FUELLEN_IDOC_INTTAB` one segment at a time, in an internal table (`INT_EDIDD`) with the structure EDIDD, using the document data just collected as the starting point.

Beginning with E1EDK01, each segment is laid down in the order that it appears in the IDoc. It's a straightforward process. A string that has the structure of the current segment is cleared and populated with the document data that will be stored in that segment.

Any additional data that need to be retrieved are pulled while the segment is being built. For example, pricing conditions for the invoice header are extracted by function RV_PRICE_PRINT_HEAD during the build of segments E1EDK05 and E1EDK04.

Item-level pricing conditions are read by a routine that calls function RV_PRICE_ PRINT_ITEM just before the item segments are built within a loop on internal table TVBDPR (structure VBDPR). TVBDR holds item-level data from the billing, delivery, and sales order documents.

When the segment string is fully populated, it is moved into the SDATA field of INT_EDIDD, the segment name is moved into INT_EDIDD-SEGNAM, and the internal table is appended.

Segment processing ends with a call to CUSTOMER-FUNCTION '002' for custom processing of the current loop segment or to add additional segments immediately following it.

A partner conversion is called during the build of the E1EDKA1 segments. This is done within a loop on internal table XVBPA (structure VBPA), which stores all of the SAP partners used in the billing document.

Gordy needs to see the GLNs for its sold-to and ship-to partners. These are stored in EDPAR as external partners linked to the SAP partner. Function SD_INT_TO_ EXT_PARTNER_NUMBER is called to read EDPAR and get the external partner number.

The current partner number in VBPA-KUNNR is passed to a variable — KUNRE — and then the partner type is determined. For customer partner type KU, VBPA-KUNNR is moved into another variable. The function is then called as shown in Listing 17.1.

```
CALL FUNCTION 'SD_INT_TO_EXT_PARTNER_NUMBER'
  EXPORTING
    customer_number         = kunre
    internal_partner_number = int
    partner_role            = xvbpa-parvw
  IMPORTING
```

```
    external_partner_number = ext_partner_number
  EXCEPTIONS
    partner_not_found        = 1.
```
Listing 17.1 Function Call Returns External Partner Number

It has three exporting parameters:

▶ `CUSTOMER_NUMBER = KUNRE`: This is the SAP partner number from VBPA-KUNNR.

▶ `INTERNAL_PARTNER_NUMBER = INT`: For partner type customer, this a second instance of the SAP partner number from VBPA-KUNNR.

▶ `PARTNER_ROLE = XVBPA-PARVW`: Partner type for the current partner.

This is being read in a loop on VBPA so all partners in the billing document can be processed if they have corresponding entries in EDPAR. The external partner number, in our example, Gordy's GLN, is returned in the import parameter `EXTERNAL_PARTNER_NUMBER`.

The function does a simple select on EDPAR, as shown in Listing 17.2.

```
SELECT * FROM EDPAR
  WHERE KUNNR = CUSTOMER_NUMBER
    AND PARVW = PARTNER_ROLE
    AND INPNR = INTERNAL_PARTNER_NUMBER
ENDSELECT.
IF SY-SUBRC <> 0.
  RAISE PARTNER_NOT_FOUND.
ENDIF.
EXTERNAL_PARTNER_NUMBER = EDPAR-EXPNR.
```
Listing 17.2 EDPAR Read in External Conversion Function

To pull GLN for Gordy's ship-to, we would use the following variables:

▶ `CUSTOMER_NUMBER = GRDY01001`

▶ `PARTNER_ROLE = SH`

▶ `INPNR = GRDY01001`

GLN for the ship-to would be read from EDPAR-EXPNR and passed to the `EXTERNAL_PARTNER_NUMBER` variable.

The expectation is that these values have been entered into EDPAR along with the external partner number. If not, the external partner won't be found. But the function will still be called, regardless of whether or not we want to pull the external partner number.

The SAP customer number will be moved to E1EDKA1-PARTN whether or not an external partner is found. The external customer number will be moved to E1EDKA1-LIFNR.

Partner processing for all E1EDKA1 segment builds also includes getting full address data for each partner, including ISO country codes and properly formatted postal codes. But we won't be mapping the addresses.

After all segments have been built and assembled in their proper sequence in internal table `INT_EDIDD`, function `IDOC_OUTPUT_INVOIC` hands off to the standard IDoc interface, and the IDoc is written to the database at status 30—*IDoc ready for dispatch*.

Sending the IDoc

Program `RSEOUT00` runs twice a day to pick up all outbound INVOIC IDocs at status 30 for all customers and send them to the EDI RIM.

`RSEOUT00` reads the INVOIC IDocs from the database and calls function `EDI_OUTPUT_NEW`, which converts the ASCII IDocs to XML format and saves them to a file on the SAP application server.

The system then makes an RFC through the JCo connector to a listening workflow process in the EDI RIM that picks up the IDoc file with an FTP service and passes it to an enveloping process.

The IDoc file is picked up and moved to the translation process, which identifies the envelopes from the EDI sending and receiving trading partner IDs and the EDI transaction and version in the IDoc control segment.

The translation map is identified and called, and the IDoc is converted to an X12 810 version 5010 invoice transaction set defined by an ST-SE envelope.

The transaction set is appended to a functional group delimited by a GS-GE envelope with the other translated transactions sets from the IDoc file.

When all IDocs have been translated and appended to the group, the group is bundled into an interchange with an ISA-IEA envelope. The interchange is passed to a communications workflow, which sends it to Gordy's EDI system through an AS2 call.

An MDN acknowledgment is returned by Gordy immediately. MDN is followed by a 997 acknowledging the 810 functional group, ending the EDI transmission cycle.

The 997 is received within minutes, or an hour at the most. If it takes longer than 24 hours, Acme's EDI team contacts Gordy's EDI team to find out whether there are any issues.

Translation, transmission, and acknowledgment status, whether success or failure, is reported back to SAP in STATUS IDocs that update the original outbound IDocs with the milestone results.

When the invoice posts to Gordy's system, it is validated against the ASN and the purchase order. If there are any errors Gordy sends back to Acme's EDI RIM an error report in an X12 864 text message.

The EDI RIM converts the 864 to a human readable report in PDF format listing the errors. The PDF report is attached to an email and sent to the responsible business users who must fix the errors and regenerate and resend the INVOIC IDoc before Gordy will accept it.

Once the invoice posts successfully to Gordy's system, the clock begins ticking on payment.

17.4   Technical Specifications

This technical specification describes development and configuration in SAP and the EDI RIM to support the INVOIC to X12 810 customer invoice interface to Gordy's Galaxy.

17.4.1   Technical Requirements

The outbound customer invoice is sent twice a day after Gordy receives its order and validates Acme's ASN against DSI's shipment.

For multi-pack orders, the shipping unit and component items of the sales BOM are sent. Pricing is at the shipping unit level, not the component item.

A custom ABAP ALV grid report is provided to allow editing of customer purchase order numbers in INVOIC IDocs before sending them to Gordy.

17.4.2 Dependencies

The INVOIC to X12 810 customer invoice interface to Gordy's Galaxy is dependent on outbound IDoc configuration in SAP and on several development objects in the EDI RIM:

▶ Message control configuration for output type ZD00 and a condition record populated for Gordy's bill-to partner

▶ Outbound partner profile for Gordy with message type INVOIC and partner function bill-to

▶ Cross-reference table ZEDIXREF entry mapping SAP send and receive partner numbers to Gordy's EDI trading send and receive trading partner IDs for themselves and for Acme

▶ Batch job set up in the SAP Job Scheduler for program RSEOUT00 with a variant to output INVOIC IDocs at status 30 INVOIC for all customers twice daily at 8:00 a.m. and 8:00 p.m.

▶ A full set of outbound envelopes created in the EDI RIM for Gordy's Galaxy 810 X12 version 5010 transmissions

▶ A full set of inbound envelopes created in the EDI RIM to process X12 997 version 5010 functional acknowledgments from Gordy's Galaxy for the outbound 810 customer invoice

▶ Translation map built in the EDI RIM for the IDoc to X12 810 customer invoice conversion for Gordy's Galaxy

▶ Business processes in the EDI RIM to do the following:

  ▷ Pick up IDoc files from the SAP application server

  ▷ Run map to convert IDoc files to an EDI with one group and one or more outbound 810 transaction sets

  ▷ Transmit the X12 810 interchange to Gordy by AS2

  ▷ Receive an X12 864 invoice error report, translate it to a human readable PDF format, and attach the report to an email routed to the responsible business users

17.4.3 Assumptions

All EDI customers receive an EDI invoice. IDoc errors are monitored by the EDI team in SAP using standard IDoc monitoring tools such as Transactions WE05,

BD87, and WE09. This includes technical errors, such as incorrect syntax or missing partner profile, and application errors.

Technical errors are corrected by the EDI team. Business users, with the support of the EDI team, tackle application errors.

All errors in the EDI system are handled by the EDI team. Any issue that might impact on the application is communicated to the appropriate business user immediately.

The IDoc control segment fields SNDLAD and RCVLAD pick up the EDI send and receive trading partner IDs through a customer exit called before the IDoc is written to the database during outbound processing. The EDI RIM identifies the EDI trading partner IDs from the control segment fields.

17.4.4 Purchase Order Number IDoc Edit Report

ZSDCHINVOIC is an ABAP ALV grid report with a custom screen, one data entry field, and a table object to hold a list of selected INVOIC IDocs in a single-line display with one entry for each one. Each entry sports a checkbox to select the IDoc for editing, reprocessing, or deletion.

A data entry field at the top of the screen enables editing of the customer purchase order number in a selected IDoc. The field has a checkbox next to it to tell the program that it has been selected for editing. Changes are written to the IDoc database and users can post the edited IDocs.

SAP keeps the original IDoc at status 33—*Original of an IDoc which was edited*. It creates a copy of this IDoc with the edited data and stores it at status 32—*IDoc was edited*. A copy of the original IDoc is always available, regardless of how it was edited.

ZSDCHINVOIC also allows selected IDocs to be marked for deletion so that they can no longer be processed. This changes the status of the IDoc to 31—*Error, no further processing*.

Additional fields for editing and the code that processes them can be added in the future. We're only doing one to illustrate the development flow.

This report, with its IDoc display, editing, and reprocessing functionality, introduces key functions used in the IDoc interface. Understanding these functions will give you a better understanding of how SAP processes IDocs.

ALV Grid Characteristics and Template Coding

As an ALV grid report, ZSDCHINVOIC takes advantage of standard ABAP objects, events, and methods in class CL_GUI_ALV_GRID and its predecessor ALV and GUI classes:

- ▶ CL_GUI_ALV_GRID_BASE
- ▶ CL_GUI_CONTROL
- ▶ CL_GUI_OBJECT

ZSDCHINVOIC is a hybrid of object-oriented and more traditional ABAP programming. It has a simple, consistent, and repeatable structure that is well suited to cookie-cutter programming and can serve as a template for any other ALV grid report program you may need to write.

ZSDCHINVOIC is presented here as a starting point for your own explorations, not as a complete solution. Key elements of the program are presented to illustrate the process flow but you'll have to work out the gaps on your own.

Program Structure

The structure of the program is composed of the following elements:

- ▶ Table declarations
- ▶ Selection screen definition
- ▶ Type, internal table, string, and field variable declarations
- ▶ ALV grid-specific data declarations, including type pools, work areas for structured strings and internal tables to feed the ALV grid display object, and ALV grid variables
- ▶ Declaration, definition, and implementation of a local custom class with two methods for ALV grid report event handling
- ▶ Include programs for the report header form routine called by the ALV engine and for PBO and PAI modules to process ALV grid output to custom screen 100
- ▶ An ABAP INITIALIZATION event that creates the report title for the header form and builds a table of ALV grid menu objects to exclude from the report display using standard line type UI_FUNC
- ▶ An ABAP START-OF-SELECTION event that groups all data selection and processing in discrete form routines, including the following:

- ▶ Form 000: Get all relevant IDocs
- ▶ Form 010: Build an internal table to hold report data
- ▶ Form 020: ALV data housekeeping, including defining sort order
- ▶ Form 030: Build the ALV field catalog identifying the internal table, its fields, and field lengths that contain the report data
- ▶ Call custom screen 100, where all display and processing functions are handled through the screen's flow logic and GUI status

Custom Objects

We'll need to create the following custom objects:

- ▶ ABAP Data Dictionary structure ZEDI_UPD to define fields that will be selected for editing in screen 100
- ▶ ALV grid report ZSDCHINVOIC
- ▶ Custom screen 100 with data entry fields at top of screen and a table control below to hold the report list
- ▶ Custom GUI status MAIN100 with title bar MAIN100
- ▶ Include program ZSDCHINVOIC_PBO to set up GUI status MAIN100 and the ALV grid, and to populate the table control for custom screen 100
- ▶ Include program ZSDCHINVOIC_PAI to read input events from custom screen 100 and to determine appropriate response
- ▶ Transaction code ZEDINV to run custom ALV grid report ZSDCHINVOIC

Create Data Dictionary Structure ZEDI_UPD

Structure ZEDI_UPD is used to provide fields to custom screen 100.

Go directly to the Data Dictionary with Transaction SE11 and follow these steps.

1. Select DATA TYPE, enter "ZEDI_UPD", and click CREATE.
2. Select STRUCTURE from the CREATE TYPE dialog.
3. Enter a description of the screen structure in the SHORT TEXT field.
4. Enter the following values into the COMPONENTS screen table control:
   - ▶ COMPONENT: "BSTKD"
   - ▶ COMPONENT TYPE: "BSTKD"
   - ▶ DESCRIPTION: 35-character customer PO number

The description is returned by the system. If additional fields need to be added to our screen in future, they will first be added to ZEDI_UPD.

5. Save structure ZEDI_UPD. Assign it to a package and change request.

6. Activate structure ZEDI_UPD by clicking the activate icon, or selecting menu option STRUCTURE • ACTIVATE.

Create Program ZSDCHINVOIC

To create the program, go to Transaction SE80, and follow these steps:

1. Click EDIT OBJECT. Select the PROGRAM tab. Enter "ZSDCHINVOIC" in the PROGRAM NAME field and click CREATE.

2. Uncheck the TOP INCL option in the CREATE PROGRAM dialog, and either press ⌷Enter⌷ or click the green checkmark.

3. The PROGRAM ATTRIBUTES screen opens as shown in Figure 17.5.

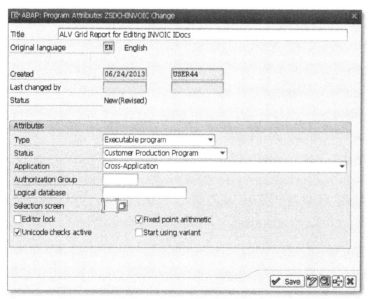

Figure 17.5 Program Attributes Screen for ALV Grid Report ZSDCHINVOIC

Enter a text description in the TITLE field, and select the following:

▸ EXECUTABLE PROGRAM from the TYPE dropdown

▸ CUSTOMER PRODUCTION PROGRAM from the STATUS dropdown

▸ CROSS-APPLICATION from the APPLICATION dropdown

4. Save the program and assign it to a change request. The ABAP editor opens ready for coding.

Program Flow and Pseudo Code

The table declaration points to the following tables and structures:

▸ EDIDC, EDID4, and EDIDS: The IDoc database

▸ VBRK and VBRP: Sales order data

▸ ZEDI_UPD: Screen 100 field structure

▸ E1EDK01: IDoc header general data for INVOIC02

▸ E1EDKA1: Header partner identification data

▸ E1EDK02: Customer PO data

Selection options include the following:

▸ IDoc number

▸ SAP receive partner (customer bill-to partner)

▸ EDI ISA interchange control number

▸ IDoc last change date

▸ Customer purchase order number

We'll structure our internal tables by declaring types and referencing them in data declarations.

Type T_IDOCS provides the structure for an internal table and string to select and process IDoc messages from the IDoc database, as declared in Listing 17.3.

```
types: begin of t_idocs,
        docnum type edi_docnum,      "Idoc no.
        refint type idoccrfint,      "ISA cnt no
        stamid type edi_stamid,      "Msg class
        stamno type edi_stamno,      "Msg no.
        stapa1 type edi_stapa1,      "Msg variable 1
```

```
        stapa2 type edi_stapa2,      "Msg variable 2
        stapa3 type edi_stapa3,      "Msg variable 3
        stapa4 type edi_stapa4,      "Msg variable 4
        upddat type edi_upddat,      "IDoc Change date
     end of t_idocs.
```

Listing 17.3 Type Declaration for t_idocs

An internal table and string are then declared using T_IDOCS with the syntax:

```
data: iidocs type standard table of t_idocs,
      sidocs type t_idocs.
```

The same goes for the internal table used to output the report list. Type T_OUT is first declared and then followed by the internal table and string declaration, as shown in Listing 17.4.

```
types: begin of t_out,
        docnum type edi_docnum,      "Idoc no.
        rcvprn type edi_rcvprn,      "Receive partner
        refint type idoccrfint,      "ISA cnt no
        upddat type edi_upddat,      "IDoc Change date
        segnum type edi_segnum,      "Segment no.
        psgnum type edi_psgnum,      "Parent seg. no.
        segnam type edilsegtyp,      "Segment name
        bstkd type bstkd,            "Cust. PO no.
        datum type edidat8,          "PO date
        kunnr_bp type kunnr,         "Bill-to partner
        kunnr_we type kunnr,         "Ship-to partner
        errmsg(130) type c,          "Error msg
     end of t_out.

****  Report output table:  ***
data: iout type table of t_out,
      sout type t_out.
```

Listing 17.4 Report Output Type and Internal Table

We'll declare another internal table and string referencing type T_OUT to process IDocs selected for change or delete from the ALV grid report listing:

```
****  Select IDocs for change/delete ***
data: isel type standard table of t_out,
      ssel type t_out.
```

Additional internal tables for IDoc processing include:

▸ GT_EDIDC referencing the full structure of table EDIDC

▸ GT_EDIDD referencing the full structure of table EDIDD

▸ IDOC_PROCESS referencing type BDIDOCS, which contains only one field (IDoc number)

For ALV grid setup and data processing, we'll require the following internal tables and strings:

▸ Internal table IFIELDCAT referencing table type LVC_T_FCAT and string sfieldcat reference structure LVC_S_FCAT. It is used to build the field catalog passed to the ALV processor when the table control is populated with the report during PBO processing of screen 100.

▸ Internal table ISORTCAT referencing table type LVC_T_SORT and string SSORTCAT referencing structure LVC_S_SORT. These objects are used to define the sort order for the report data passed to the ALV processor during PBO processing of screen 100.

▸ String SLAYOUT referencing structure LVC_S_LAYO. It is used to define the layout of the ALV grid report and is passed to the ALV processor during PBO processing of screen 100.

▸ Internal table IROWS referencing table type LVC_T_ROW and string SROW referencing structure LVC_S_ROW for grid row selection by the index number of the selected rows.

▸ IFUNCTION referencing type UI_FUNCTIONS to build a table of standard ALV functions to exclude from the report display.

Declare the local class LCL_EVENT_RECEIVER for event handling like this:

```
class lcl_event_receiver definition deferred.
```

Definition of the local event handler class is deferred because we need to declare a work field that references it. The code in the two methods that implement the class references this work field.

Next we add variables that we'll use to create the grid display and to enable event handling when the screen is called or refreshed. These variables reference ABAP objects classes that will create our custom ALV screen grid display and are invoked using the CREATE keyword:

▶ G_CONTAINER: References data element SCRFNAME with a default value of SELECT-GRID. This object is used to name the parent container the first time the screen is called. This variable must be set to the name of the custom control that we'll create when we design the report screen. In our example, the control name will be GRID1.

▶ G_PARENT: References class CL_GUI_CUSTOM_CONTAINER. This is created with the screen name in G_CONTAINER the first time screen 100 is called. This object builds the container for the custom controls in GUI status MAIN100 and screen 100.

▶ GRID1: References class CL_GUI_ALV_GRID. This object builds the ALV grid control that nests within the custom container created by G_PARENT. It must have the same name as the custom control that will be added to the screen to hold the ALV grid list report.

▶ EVENT_RECEIVER: References local class LCL_EVENT_RECEIVER. Used to create and register (keyword SET) event handling during PBO processing of screen 100.

Listing 17.5 shows the local class definition for LCL_EVENT_RECEIVER with two event handlers declared.

```
class lcl_event_receiver definition.
public section.

  methods:

*** Handle Call Back
    handle_call_back
      for event delayed_changed_sel_callback
        of cl_gui_alv_grid,

*** Handle double click
    handle_double_click
      for event double_click of cl_gui_alv_grid
        importing e_row.

endclass.              "lcl_event_receiver DEFINITION
```
Listing 17.5 Local Event Handler Classes

The next step is to implement the local class with the following line:

```
class lcl_event_receiver implementation.
```

Method HANDLE_CALL_BACK is triggered when the user selects one or more rows. It counts the number of rows selected and then passes that count back to the title, as shown in Listing 17.6.

```
method handle_call_back.
  data prev_count(3) type n.
  prev_count = title_count.

*** Get the index of all selected rows
  refresh irows.
  call method grid1->get_selected_rows
    IMPORTING
      et_index_rows = irows.

*** Update the title with the new number of selected rows
  describe table irows lines rows_sel.
  describe table iout lines title_count.
  if prev_count ne title_count.
    concatenate 'Number of returned IDocs -'title_count
      into layout-grid_title separated by space.

*** Refresh the table layout for the new title.
    call method grid1->set_frontend_layout
      EXPORTING
        is_layout = layout.
  endif.
endmethod.                        "handle_call_back
```

Listing 17.6 Counting the Number of Rows Selected by the User

The HANDLE_CALL_BACK method works in a straightforward manner:

1. A call to method GET_SELECTED_ROWS returns all selected rows to internal table IROWS.

2. The title text is updated with the row count and passed to the field GRID_TITLE in structure LAYOUT if the row count is different from the previous count.

3. Method SET_FRONTEND_LAYOUT refreshes the layout of the grid with the new title.

Method HANDLE_DOUBLE_CLICK is triggered when the user double-clicks any part of a report line.

The current line is read and passed to form CALL_LINE_TCODE, which then calls the IDoc tree display mentioned in Listing 17.7. This form is also called during PAI input processing for GUI functions in screen 100.

```
method handle_double_click.
*** Read current line
  g_row = e_row.
  read table iout into sout index e_row-index.
*Call IDoc tree display.
  perform: call_line_tcode using sout-docnum.
endmethod.                          "handle_double_click
```
Listing 17.7 Double-Click Event Calls an External Transaction

The local class implementation for the two event handlers ends with an ENDCLASS statement after the methods have been defined.

The next part is some house-keeping with an INITIALIZATION event. The key piece is to build a table of standard menu functions that will be excluded from the ALV grid display during PBO processing of screen 100. The excluded functions are appended to internal table IFUNCTION, which has only one field. Take a look at the syntax for this:

```
append cl_gui_alv_grid=>mc_fc_sum to ifunction.
```

This excludes from the ALV grid menu a button that would return a total for a selected column. Explore the available standard functions by double-clicking structure cl_gui_alv_grid in the ABAP Editor. Every function that is not excluded will appear in the ALV grid when the report is run. All this free standard functionality that you don't have to code is one of the beauties of the ALV grid.

Start of Selection

The first step in the start of selection event is to read IDoc tables EDIDC and EDIDS for all INVOIC IDocs that meet the criteria entered in the selection screen. The SQL code to access these tables uses an inner join to link the two, as shown in Listing 17.8.

```
select distinct a~docnum a~rcvprn a~refint
    b~stamid b~stamno b~stapa1 b~stapa2
    b~stapa3 b~stapa4 a~upddat
  into table iidocs
  from edidc as a join edids as b on
```

```
  ( a~docnum = b~docnum and
    a~status = b~status and
  a~upddat = b~credat )
where a~docnum in so_doc
  and a~status in so_status
  and a~sndprn in so_prn
  and a~refint in so_isa
  and a~upddat in so_updat
  and a~mestyp = 'INVOIC'.
```

Listing 17.8 Reading INVOIC IDoc Messages by Status

If there's a hit, our internal table IIDOCS is populated with a few things:

► The IDoc number, ISA interchange control ID, and the last change date from the IDoc control record table EDIDC.

► Message class, message number, and variables from the IDoc status record table EDIDS.

Next we assemble data for the report table IOUT. This is done within a loop on IDOCS into the structured string SDOCS. IDoc control record data are passed from SDOCS into structured string SOUT, including the following:

► DOCNUM: IDoc number to SOUT-DOCNUM

► SNDPRN: SAP sold-to partner to SOUT-KUNNR_BP (bill-to and sold-to are the same for Gordy)

► REFINT: ISA interchange control ID to SOUT-REFINT

► UPDDAT: IDoc change date to SOUT-UPDDAT

Data records are read in the IDOC loop with a three-step process. First, open the current IDoc. Next, get the segments and pass them to an internal table with the structure EDIDD (GT_EDIDD). Finally, after all segments have been read, close the IDoc. The three function calls are illustrated in Listing 17.9.

```
*** Open the IDoc for the read
call function 'EDI_DOCUMENT_OPEN_FOR_READ'
  EXPORTING
    document_number        = p_docnum
  IMPORTING
    idoc_control           = gs_edidc
  EXCEPTIONS
    document_foreign_lock  = 1
```

```
      document_not_exist     = 2
      document_number_invalid = 3
      others                 = 4.
if sy-subrc <> 0.
  message id sy-msgid type sy-msgty number sy-msgno
    with sy-msgv1 sy-msgv2 sy-msgv3 sy-msgv4.
endif.

*** Read all segments
call function 'EDI_SEGMENTS_GET_ALL'
  EXPORTING
    document_number         = p_docnm
  TABLES
    idoc_containers         = p_data
  EXCEPTIONS
    document_number_invalid = 1
    end_of_document         = 2
    others                  = 3.
if sy-subrc <> 0.
  message id sy-msgid type sy-msgty number sy-msgno
    with sy-msgv1 sy-msgv2 sy-msgv3 sy-msgv4.
endif.

*** Close the IDoc
  call function 'EDI_DOCUMENT_CLOSE_READ'
    EXPORTING
      document_number    = p_docnum
    EXCEPTIONS
      document_not_open = 1
      parameter_error   = 2
      others            = 3.
if sy-subrc <> 0.
  message id sy-msgid type sy-msgty number sy-msgno
    with sy-msgv1 sy-msgv2 sy-msgv3 sy-msgv4.
endif.
```

Listing 17.9 Reading IDoc Data Records

The pattern is the same for reading, editing, or creating IDocs. The only change is the second function called to match the process.

1. Call EDI_DOCUMENT_OPEN_FOR_READ for the current IDoc number within the loop on internal table IIDOCS.

- This function first appends the IDoc number to internal table `DOCUMENT_IN_READ`.

- It confirms that the IDoc control and data records exist and passes the control record to internal table `LIST_CONTROL_READ` and the data records to internal table `LIST_CONTAINER_READ`.

- It can return the IDoc control segment in a structured string.

2. Call function `EDI_SEGMENTS_GET_ALL` for the current IDoc number. The internal table `GT_DATA` is populated with all IDoc data records.

- The function loops through internal table `DOCUMENT_IN_READ` to confirm that the IDoc has been opened. An error is returned if the internal table is empty.

- Then it loops on `LIST_CONTAINER_READ` and moves all of the IDoc's data records into internal table `IDOC_CONTAINERS`.

- This internal table exports the IDoc data, including the segment control fields, to the calling program as an internal table with the structure EDIDD through the table parameter `P_DATA`.

3. Call `EDI_DOCUMENT_CLOSE_READ` for the current IDoc number, which is deleted from internal table `DOCUMENT_IN_READ`. This closes the IDoc and returns control to the calling program.

Now we need to filter our IDocs by the purchase order numbers entered into the selection screen, if any. If a PO number was entered, we only return IDocs with that purchase order number.

We begin by reading internal table `GT_EDIDD` for segment E1EDK02 with qualifier 001, which holds the purchase order number. There will be only one entry for this segment value in `GT_EDIDD`. The code for this internal table read is illustrated in Listing 17.10.

```
*** read the internal table with a search key
read table gt_edidd into gs_edidd
     with key segnam = 'E1EDK02'.
*** Segment found, check qualifier
if sy-subrc = 0.
  gs_e1edk02 = sdata-sdata.
  if qualf = '001'.
*** Confirm PO number matches PO select option
    check gs_e1edk02-belnr in so_bstkd.
  endif.
```

```
else.
  exit.
endif.
```
Listing 17.10 Reading the PO Number Select Option from the IDoc

If there is a hit, the SDATA field is moved into a structured string and BELNR is checked to see if it matches SO_BSTKD.

If there is no matching value in GS_E1EDK02-BELNR, the current loop on IDOCS is exited, SDOCS is cleared, and the next IDoc read.

If there is a hit, the following report header values are moved:

▶ SDOCS-SEGNAM: Segment name to SOUT-SEGNAM

▶ SDOCS-SEGNUM: Segment number to SOUT-SEGNUM

▶ GS_E1EDK02-BELNR: PO number to SOUT-BSTKD

▶ GS_E1EDK02-DATUM: PO date to SOUT-DATUM

Next we assemble the IDoc status record error message into field SOUT-ERRMSG. This is done in a form routine that calls a standard function. The form call is shown in Listing 17.11.

```
perform build_msg using sdocs-stamid sdocs-stamno
                        sdocs-stapa1 sdocs-stapa2
                        sdocs-stapa3 sdocs-stapa4
                        sout-errmsg.
```
Listing 17.11 IDoc Status Message Build Form

Let's walk through it:

▶ SDOCS-STAMID is the message class from the IDoc status record.

▶ SDOCS-STAMNO is the message number.

▶ SDOCS-STAPA1 through SDOCS-STAPA4 holds the variables that are fed to the message.

▶ SOUT-ERRMSG is the field that will be populated with the message built by the routine.

Form BUILD_MSG passes these variables to standard function RPY_MESSAGE_COMPOSE that assembles the full text message and passes it to field SOUT-ERRMSG.

We now need to get the rest of our report data from GT_EDIDD. Loop on GT_EDIDD into GS_EDIDD, restricting the segment reads to the partner data segment E1EDKA1, for the SAP ship-to number:

▶ Move GS_EDIDD-SDATA to string GS_E1EDKA1 with the structure E1EDKA1.

▶ If GS_E1EDKA1-PARVW doesn't equal WE, exit the current loop, and read the next E1EDKA1 segment.

▶ If GS_E1EDKA1-PARVW equals WE, the Gordy's store is in field PARTN. Move it to SOUT-KUNNR_WE.

Now that we've collected all of our report data, append SOUT to IOUT.

Next we need to set up parameters and internal tables for the ALV grid report. For this report, that means defining the sort order and populating the field catalog. These values are then passed to the ALV processor during PBO processing of screen 100.

The sort order is defined by populating internal table ISORTCAT. We'll hard-code this:

```
ssortcat-spos = '1'.
ssortcat-fieldname = 'DOCNUM'.
ssortcat-up = 'X'.
append ssortcat to isortcat.
```

This append block defines the IDoc number in field DOCNUM as the sort field for our report. We won't be using any other field.

The field catalog identifies fields from internal table IOUT that will be used in the ALV list report. It also defines the order in which the fields appear in the report, their column headings, and their widths. We'll use the following very simple syntax:

```
clear sfieldcat.
sfieldcat-fieldname = 'DOCNUM'.
sfieldcat-tabname    = 'IOUT'.
sfieldcat-reptext_ddic  = 'IDocNo'.
sfieldcat-outputlen     = '0010'.
append sfieldcat to ifieldcat.
```

This block of code adds the IDoc number field DOCNUM to the field catalog for inclusion in the list report. It identifies the report column label as IDocNo and the width of the column as 10 characters.

This is a simple approach that can be easily repeated for each field that needs to be added to the report. Conditions can also be set and evaluated to add or suppress fields from appearing in the report.

Everything has now been done to collect the data and set up ALV data and parameters to run the report. Now we need to pass all of these data to our custom screen to trigger output of the report. We do this using the statement:

```
call screen 100.
```

Now we build the objects that will host the report: custom screen 0100, GUI status MAIN100, and title bar MAIN100.

Create Custom Screen 100

SAP provides a graphical screen painter that we'll use to create screen 0100. There are a number of ways to create the screen.

▶ If you created ZSDCHINVOIC in the repository browser (Transaction SE80). Select the program name in the navigation pane and right-click to open a context menu. Select CREATE • SCREEN. The system will prompt for a screen number. Enter "0100".

▶ Use Transaction SE51 or follow menu path TOOLS • ABAP WORKBENCH • DEVELOPMENT • USER INTERFACE • SCREEN PAINTER. Enter the program name and screen number "0100" and click CREATE.

▶ Enter the call to screen 100 in program code in the ABAP Editor and double-click the 100. If the screen doesn't exist, a dialog will open, asking if you want to create it.

Any one of these steps opens the ATTRIBUTES screen of the Screen Painter. Follow these steps:

1. Enter a description in the SHORT DESCRIPTION field and save the screen.

2. Click the ELEMENT LIST tab, and enter "OK_CODE" under NAME in the GENERAL ATTR tab. This holds the function code returned when a GUI object (a menu option or button) is selected.

3. Click the LAYOUT button to load the graphical Screen Painter. We'll begin by adding two screen elements to organize the layout.

4. From the element palette to the left of the screen, click on the box element. The arrow turns into an upside-down L. Drag this icon from the upper-left corner across the blank screen down to less than a third of the screen. We'll lay out our data entry fields to edit the IDoc in this box.

5. Double-click the box to open the ELEMENT ATTRIBUTES dialog. Enter "BOX_ CNTRL" in the NAME field and "Select_Fields_for_Editing" in the TEXT field. The text appears in the top-left corner of the box to identify the function of the group of fields it contains.

6. Click CUSTOM CONTROL on the element palette, and draw the control to fill the rest of the blank screen. The custom control contains the ALV grid list objects and data at runtime. We'll write code to pass this stuff to the control in the flow logic of the screen.

7. Enter "GRID1" in the NAME field at the top of the Screen Painter editor. This name must match the value in the g_container variable we set up in our data declarations. At this point, the screen should look like Figure 17.6.

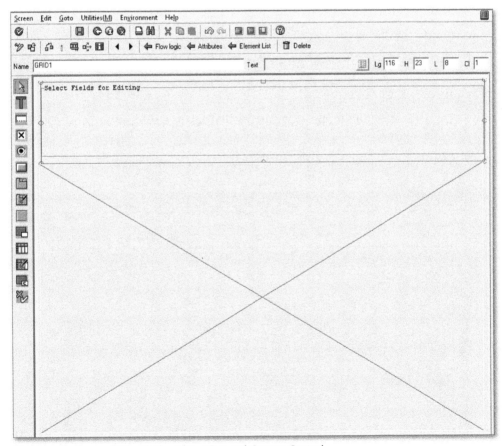

Figure 17.6 Screen 100 with the Editing Box and Custom Control

We'll add our edit field to the box element next. The attributes for the data entry field come from Data Dictionary structure ZEDI_UPD. We'll also add a checkbox next to the field to tell the code which IDoc field is being edited.

1. Select the TEXT FIELD tool from the element palette. Position the cursor within the box control and click to place the text field. This holds the description of the data entry field.

2. Enter "LBL_PO" in the NAME field at the top of the work area. Enter "Customer_PO_no:" in the TEXT field.

3. Click the CHECKBOX tool in the element palette. Position the cursor in the box control and click to place the checkbox.

4. Enter the checkbox name "CHECK_PO" in the NAME field.

5. Click the INPUT/OUTPUT FIELD tool in the element palette. Position the cursor next to the checkbox, and click to place the field.

6. Enter "ZEDI_UPD-BSTKD" in the NAME field at the top of the work area. The system opens a dialog to ask if you want the element to refer to a Data Dictionary object. Click YES.

   This pulls attributes for the data entry field from the custom structure ZEDI_UPD that we just created.

7. Save and activate the completed screen. It should like Figure 17.7.

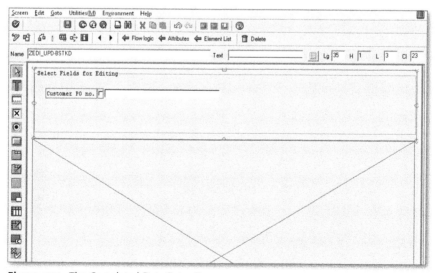

Figure 17.7 The Completed Data Entry Screen

8. Click the ELEMENT LIST button to go to the general attributes tab of the elements list. This screen details properties for all objects and data elements used on the screen. Figure 17.8 shows where we stand so far.

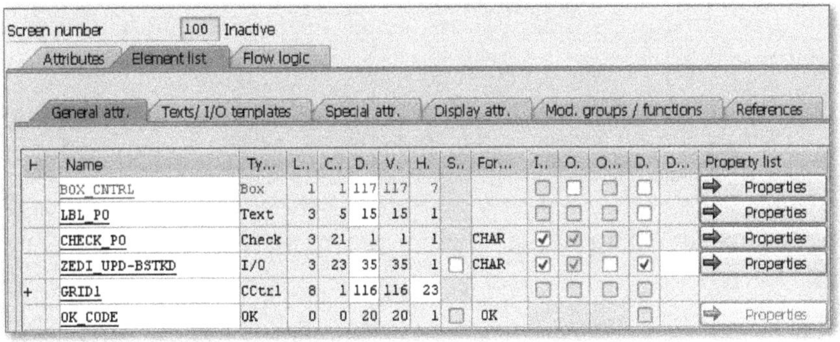

Screen number	100	Inactive												

Attributes | Element list | Flow logic

General attr. | Texts/ I/O templates | Special attr. | Display attr. | Mod. groups / functions | References

⊢	Name	Ty...	L..	C..	D.	V.	H.	S..	For...	I..	O.	O...	D.	D...	Property list
	BOX_CNTRL	Box	1	1	117	117	7			☐	☐	☐	☐		➡ Properties
	LBL_PO	Text	3	5	15	15	1			☐	☐	☐	☐		➡ Properties
	CHECK_PO	Check	3	21	1	1	1		CHAR	☑	☑	☐	☐		➡ Properties
	ZEDI_UPD-BSTKD	I/O	3	23	35	35	1	☐	CHAR	☑	☑	☐	☑		➡ Properties
+	GRID1	CCtrl	8	1	116	116	23			☐	☐	☐	☐		
	OK_CODE	OK	0	0	20	20	1	☐	OK				☐		➡ Properties

Figure 17.8 Objects and Data Elements on the Data Entry Screen

Create GUI Status and Title Bar

Menus, icons, buttons, and function key assignments will be added to the screen through a GUI status. This is more than just eye candy! These objects link to function codes that trigger program responses in the screen's flow logic. They tell our program what the user wants it to do next.

The function codes we add to our GUI status will offer the user a number of report and IDoc processing options when a menu option is selected, an icon or button clicked, or a function key pressed, including the following:

▸ UPDT: Update all selected IDocs with values entered in a data entry field.

▸ REST: Restore the original values to one or more selected IDocs.

▸ POST: Save edits to the selected IDocs and reprocess them.

▸ DEL: Mark selected IDocs for deletion by changing their status to 31.

▸ TREE: Trigger the IDoc tree display for one selected IDoc or by double-clicking its report line.

The title bar sets up the title that runs across the top of the report window. We'll name the GUI status and title bar MAIN100. To create a GUI status, you can do any of the following:

683

▶ If you're in the repository browser (Transaction SE80), select the program name in the navigation pane and right-click to open a context menu. Select CREATE • GUI STATUS. The system will prompt you for a status name and description.

▶ Run Transaction SE41 or follow menu path TOOLS • ABAP WORKBENCH • DEVELOPMENT • USER INTERFACE • MENU PAINTER. Enter the program and status name and click CREATE.

▶ Enter the call to GUI status "MAIN100" in the program code anywhere in the ABAP Editor, and double-click the name. If the screen doesn't yet exist, a dialog opens that asks if you want to create it.

The CREATE STATUS pop-up opens with the program name filled out. Now follow these steps:

1. Enter "MAIN100" into the STATUS field, add a description into the SHORT TEXT field, and select the NORMAL SCREEN radio button as the status type (see Figure 17.9).

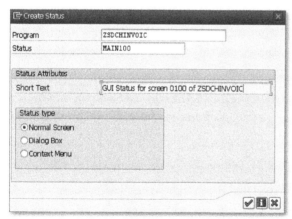

Figure 17.9 The Create Status Pop-Up

2. Click the green checkmark to open the MAINTAIN STATUS editor.

3. Open the menu bar by clicking the expand tree sign and then click the DISPLAY STANDARDS button.

4. Change the name of the Extras menu to IDOC PROCESSING and press `Enter`. Click OK in the CHANGE MENU TEXT dialog.

5. We're only using the IDOC PROCESSING menu in our current example, so delete all the others.

6. Double-click the IDoc Processing menu to open it. Enter the function codes and text descriptions in the Code and Text columns that are shown in Figure 17.10.

7. Don't forget to save.

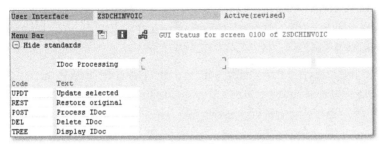

Figure 17.10 Function Codes in the IDoc Processing Menu

Next we add the function codes to the Application toolbar. Follow these steps:

1. Collapse the menu bar and expand the Application toolbar.

2. Type the function codes into the design grid, and press [Enter] to open the Assign Function to Function Key dialog. The function codes won't be saved to the Application toolbar until they have been assigned to a function key.

3. Assign the following function keys to each function code:

   ▶ UPDT: Press [F2].

   ▶ REST: Press [F5].

   ▶ POST: Press [F6].

   ▶ DEL: Press [F7].

   ▶ TREE: Press [F8].

The application toolbar should look like Figure 17.11. Text descriptions from the IDoc Processing menu will appear as buttons on the report screen when the GUI status is called. Save and activate the GUI status.

Figure 17.11 Custom Application Toolbar Assignments

Next we'll create a title bar. We have two options:

▶ In the navigation pane of the repository browser, select the program name and right-click to open the context menu. Select CREATE • GUI TITLES.

▶ Use Transaction SE41, select TITLE LIST, enter the program name, and click CREATE.

▶ Set the title bar in the program code with the statement SET TITLEBAR 'MAIN100', and double-click its name.

However you do it, the CREATE TITLE dialog will pop-up. The title code is the GUI status name. Enter a text description for the title as in Figure 17.12 and click the green checkmark. We now have our GUI status and title bar.

Figure 17.12　Creating the GUI Status Title Bar

Testing the Screen and GUI

We can do a test run of our screen, GUI status, and title bar in the status edit window by clicking the wrench-like TEST STATUS button (or press [F8]) in the toolbar above the navigation pane.

The STATUS SIMULATION dialog opens with the status name. Enter the screen number, select the new title, and click EXECUTE (see Figure 17.13).

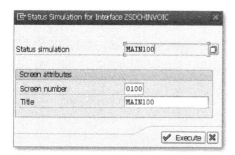

Figure 17.13　Testing the GUI and Screen

If you click through the test screen dialog that pops up, a simulation of our data entry screen with the application tool bar and IDoc processing menu opens with the custom menu, the application tool bar, and the data entry fields (see Figure 17.14).

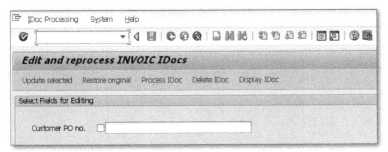

Figure 17.14 Editing Screen Simulation for ALV Grid IDoc Edit Report

Flow Logic

The flow logic has two ABAP events to set up the report screen and GUI with all of its objects and data and to respond to onscreen events like double-clicking a line, selecting a menu option, or clicking a button or icon:

▶ PROCESS BEFORE OUTPUT (PBO): Initial setup and refresh of the screen display with its GUI menus, icons, and functions. It also returns and formats the report data in the ALV grid list report custom control.

▶ PROCESS AFTER INPUT (PAI): Responds to onscreen events triggered by selecting menu options, buttons, function keys, or double-clicking a line.

From within the screen editor, click the FLOW LOGIC button to open the flow logic editor. You'll see the following code template:

```
PROCESS BEFORE OUTPUT.
* MODULE STATUS_0100.
*
PROCESS AFTER INPUT.
* MODULE USER_COMMAND_0100.
```

Before we begin looking at each, we'll change the module template to this:

```
PROCESS BEFORE OUTPUT.
MODULE PBO_100.
*
PROCESS AFTER INPUT.
MODULE PAI_100.
```

Follow these steps:

1. Double-click MODULE PBO_100. A dialog opens offering to create the module. Click YES to open the CREATE PBO MODULE dialog. The code for the PBO and PAI modules is written in two include programs inserted into ZSDCHINVOIC, as shown in Figure 17.15.

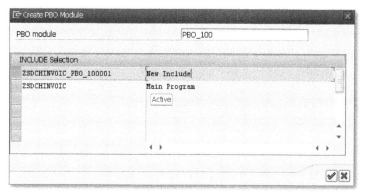

Figure 17.15 Inserting the Include Program for the PAI Module

2. Click the OK button to open the ABAP Editor. Our first job is to set the GUI status and title bar that we just created with two statements:

```
set pf-status 'MAIN100'.
set titlebar  'MAIN100'.
```

Next we check whether the ALV grid custom container that holds the report data has been created.

▶ If they have not been created, the program is running for the first time and we need to create them.

▶ If they already exist, then the program is already running and the objects have been created, and we need to refresh the table display with the results of any processing that may have been completed.

To create the ALV Grid custom container, we use the following code:

```
create object g_parent
    exporting container_name = g_container.
create object grid1
    exporting i_parent = g_parent.
```

This code creates the parent container to hold the custom GUI control using the name of the custom control that we defined in the screen editor and the grid object with reference to the parent container.

We'll also get a count of the number of rows in the report and append this with some text to the titles table.

After the container and grid objects are ready, we can populate them with the report data and GUI controls. We do this with the following method call from class CL_GUI_ALV_GRID:

```
call method grid1->set_table_for_first_display
  EXPORTING
    i_save                        = 'X'
    is_layout                     = layout
    it_toolbar_excluding          = ifunction
  CHANGING
    it_outtab                     = iout
    it_fieldcatalog               = ifieldcat
    it_sort                       = isortcat
  EXCEPTIONS
    invalid_parameter_combination = 1
    program_error                 = 2
    too_many_lines                = 3
    others                        = 4.
```

Let's walk through this:

▶ LAYOUT allows us to control the look of the report.

▶ IFUNCTION excludes ALV grid functions from the report's GUI.

▶ IOUT contains the report data.

▶ IFELDCAT holds the field catalog that the ALV processor will use to return and format the report.

▶ ISORTCAT holds the sort key for display of the report.

Next we need to set our event handlers for the grid. These are the two methods that we defined and implemented in the declarations block of our program. We first create the event receiver object that we declared and then link it to our methods, using the following statements:

```
create object event_receiver.
set handler event_receiver->handle_call_back for grid1.
set handler event_receiver->
    handle_double_click for grid1.
```

If this isn't the first time the program runs, this work has already been done. We refresh the grid control with the following statement:

```
call method grid1->refresh_table_display.
```

If everything is working as it should, and all the IDoc selection and report build bugs have been ironed out, the ALV grid list report screen should look Figure 17.16 when the program is run.

Edit and reprocess INVOIC IDocs

Update selected   Restore original   Process IDoc   Delete IDoc   Display IDoc

Select Fields for Editing

Customer PO no.

Number of returned IDocs - 0000000036

IDoc no.	Changed on	Segment	PO no.	PO date	Bill-to	Message
539774	02/11/2003	E1EDK02	4500015082	20030210	T90CLNT090	We have a report!
539775	02/11/2003	E1EDK02	4500015082	20030210	T90CLNT090	We have a report!
539776	02/11/2003	E1EDK02	4500015082	20030210	T90CLNT090	We have a report!
539777	02/11/2003	E1EDK02	4500015082	20030210	T90CLNT090	We have a report!
539778	02/11/2003	E1EDK02	4500015082	20030210	T90CLNT090	We have a report!
539779	02/11/2003	E1EDK02	4500015082	20030210	T90CLNT090	We have a report!
539780	02/11/2003	E1EDK02	4500015082	20030210	T90CLNT090	We have a report!
539781	02/11/2003	E1EDK02	4500015082	20030210	T90CLNT090	We have a report!
539787	02/11/2003	E1EDK02	4500015094	20030211	T90CLNT090	We have a report!

Figure 17.16   ALV Grid List Report with Data Entry Field

The buttons above the report title in the custom control don't need to be coded. This is one of the beauties of ALV Grid report programming. With a little of effort, you get a lot of functionality, most of it baked in by SAP.

GUI functions, on the other hand, do need to be coded. This is done in the PAI module, which responds to the function codes generated by the buttons when we clicked that we created in the GUI status.

PAI processing is straightforward. It evaluates the function code in the screen variable OK_CODE within a CASE ... ENDCASE statement and triggers one or more form routines to handle processing for each case (Listing 17.12).

```
case ok_code.
  when 'UPDT'.
    perform update_rows.
  when 'REST'.
    iout[] = iorg[].
  when 'POST'.
    perform update_idocs.
    if not iidocs[] is initial.
      perform process_idocs.
    endif.
  when 'DEL'.
    perform change_idoc_status.
  when 'TREE'.
    perform call_line_tcode using ''.
  when 'EXIT'.
    leave to screen 0.
endcase.
clear ok_code.
```

Listing 17.12 Evaluating Function Codes from the GUI in the PAI

Each OK_CODE triggers a different processing block, including the following:

► UPDT

Updates selected rows with values entered into one or more selected data entry fields:

  ► Call method GRID1->GET_SELECTED_ROWS to get the index for all report lines selected and pass them to an internal table.

  ► Loop through the index table and read report table IOUT to find the indexed entry.

  ► Determine which checkbox next to the data entry fields is selected.

  ► Whenever a checkbox equals X, pass the new value in the data entry field to report table IOUT.

Technically, we don't need to test for the checkbox because we have only one edit field. But if we were to add fields in the future, we would at least have the code in place.

▶ REST

Restores the original report values to IOUT from backup report table IORG, which is never changed.

▶ POST

Writes updated values from edited report lines to the selected IDocs and then posts them:

▶ Call method GRID1->GET_SELECTED_ROWS to get the index for all report lines selected and pass them to an internal table.

▶ Loop through the index table and read report table IOUT to find the indexed entry and append it to internal selections table ISEL.

▶ Loop through ISEL.

▶ Call function EDI_DOCUMENT_OPEN_FOR_EDIT for each new IDoc number in ISEL. This returns all IDoc data records to internal table GT_EDIDD.

▶ Identify changed IDoc segments from the report in table ISEL.

▶ Read table GT_EDIDD for the changed segment record.

▶ Copy changed values from ISEL to the IDoc segment through the GT_EDIDD entry.

▶ Call function EDI_CHANGE_DATA_SEGMENT with the updated records in GT_EDIDD after all of the edits have been recorded.

This writes changes to the database and saves a copy of the original IDoc at status 32—*IDoc was edited*, which can then be reprocessed. The original IDoc is stored at status 33—*Original of an IDoc which was edited*.

Next we call function EDI_DOCUMENT_CLOSE_EDIT after all edited segments in all selected IDocs have been written to the database. This appends the IDoc number of the edited IDoc to internal table IPROCESS.

We then call function MASTER_IDOC_DISTRIBUTE and pass the edited IDocs from GT_EDIDC and GT_EDIDD to export them to the EDI RIM.

▶ DEL

Changes the status of the selected IDocs to 31—*Error, no further processing*, marking it for deletion:

▶ Call method GRID1->GET_SELECTED_ROWS to get the index for all report lines selected and pass them to an internal table.

- ▶ Loop through the index table and read report table `IOUT` to find the indexed entry and append it to internal selections table `ISEL`.
- ▶ Loop through `ISEL`.
- ▶ The message from the new status is passed to `IOUT` and the report.

▶ TREE

Calls the tree display of a selected IDoc from the report. The functionality is also triggered by the double-click event handler.

- ▶ Check that the IDoc number for the current row has not been passed by the form call. The event handler for the double-click has the IDoc number that was passed to it from the form call.
- ▶ Call method `GRID1->GET_SELECTED_ROWS` to get the index for the selected report line and pass it to the internal index table if the IDoc number has not been passed in the form call.
- ▶ Read table `IOUT` with the index number of the selected report line and append it to internal selections table `ISEL`.
- ▶ Loop through `ISEL` and confirm that only one line has been selected.
- ▶ Call function `EDI_DOCUMENT_TREE_DISPLAY` and pass the current IDoc number.
- ▶ The IDoc is displayed in a tree view with the control, data, and all status records, similar to the IDoc views in Transactions BD87 or WE05. One interesting difference is that it includes a button that will toggle between displaying all segments or only those with errors, if the errors have been flagged in the segments.
- ▶ Get back to the report window by pressing [F3] or clicking the green return arrow icon.

Create Transaction Code

The final step is to create a transaction code for our new program. We'll do this in the repository information system since we're already there.

1. Right-click the program name in the navigation pane of the repository browser to open the context menu. Select CREATE • TRANSACTION.

2. Enter "ZEDINV" in the TRANSACTION CODE field and a description in the SHORT TEXT field.

3. In the START OBJECT area, select PROGRAM AND SELECTION SCREEN (REPORT TRANS-ACTION) to set the transaction code for an ABAP.

4. Click OK to open the CREATE REPORT TRANSACTION screen. Enter "ZSDCHINVOIC" in the PROGRAM field. The SELECTION SCREEN value is 1000.

5. In the GUI SUPPORT area, select SAPGUI FOR WINDOWS (and/or HTML and Java, depending on your environment).

6. Save the transaction code and assign it to a package and change request.

17.5   Mapping Specifications

One map will be developed in the EDI RIM to translate the INVOIC IDoc to an 810 X12 5010 transaction to Gordy's Galaxy.

Table 17.4 outlines the mapping requirements for the outbound INVOIC-810 for Gordy's Galaxy.

INVOIC	810	Value	Comments
E1EDK01—Header—Min 1, Max 1			
CURCY	CUR01	USD	PO currency
BSART	BIG06	INVO	Invoice document type. Convert to FD in target.
	BIG08	00	Hard-code original
E1EDKA1—Partners—Min 1, Max 99—Loop 1 Sold-to			
PARVW	N101	AG	Sold-to party: convert to BY
	N103	UL	Hard-code. ID type qualifier: GLN
LIFNR	N104	0999999999999	Gordy sold-to GLN from EDPAR
NAME1	N102	Gordy's Galaxy	Name of buyer party
STRAS	N301	2356 Halsted St	Sold-to partner street address
ORT01	N401	Chicago	Sold-to partner city
PSTLZ	N403	60601	Sold-to partner postal code
LAND1	N404	US	Sold-to partner country

Table 17.4   Map Specifications for the INVOIC to X12 810 Invoice Interface

INVOIC	810	Value	Comments
REGIO	N402	IL	Sold-to partner region
E1EDKA1—Partners—Loop 2 Invoicing party (supplier)			
PARVW	N101	BK	Supplier: convert to SU
NAME1	N102	Acme Pictures	Invoicing party (supplier) name: Acme Pictures
E1EDKA1—Partners—Loop 3 Ship-to			
PARVW	N101	WE	Ship-to partner: convert to ST
	N103	UL	Identifies Gordy's ship-to partner
LIFNR	N104	01254863254898	Gordy ship-to partner GLN
NAME1	N102	Gordy Store 00118	Name of Gordy's ship-to party
E1EDK02—Header docs—Min 0, Max 10—Loop 1 Purchase order			
QUALF		001	Identifies PO number and date
BELNR	BIG04	4500017679	Purchase order number
DATUM	BEG03	20131215	Purchase order date
E1EDK02—Header docs—Loop 2 Invoice			
QUALF		009	Identifies invoice number and date
BELNR	BIG02	0090038759	Invoice number
DATUM	BEG01	20131215	Invoice date
E1EDK03—Header dates—Min 0, Max 10			
IDDAT	DTM01	011	Identifies delivery date
DATUM	DTM02	20140115	Shipping date for order
E1EDK18—Terms of payment—Min 0, Max 10			
QUALF	ITD01	001	Payment term 1. Convert to 05 in target for discount not applicable.
	ITD02	3	Hard-code 3 for invoice date.

Table 17.4 Map Specifications for the INVOIC to X12 810 Invoice Interface (Cont.)

INVOIC	810	Value	Comments
DATUM	ITD06	20140115	Invoice date from E1EDK02 where QUALF = 009
TAGE	ITD07	30	Number of days for payment
E1EDP01—Item level details group— Min 1, Max N 1 instance of E1EDP01 per group loop			
POSEX	IT101	000010	Line item number
MENGE	IT102	100.000	Quantity ordered
MENEE	IT103	EA	Unit of measure for ordered item
MENGE	ISS01	100.000	Sum E1EDP01-MENGE to get total quantity ordered in invoice and move into X12 shipment summary segment ISS
MENEE	ISS02	EA	Unit of measure for sum quantity
E1EDP19—Materials—Min 1, Max 10			
QUALF	IT106	001	Identifier's Gordy's material number. Convert to IN for buyer's material number.
IDTNR	IT1107	985674	Customer material number
KTEXT	PID05	I Married an Alien	Material description
E1EDP05—Pricing conditions—Min 1, Max 99			
KRATE	IT104	25.890	Unit price where WHERE condition type in KSCHL identifies price
IDTNR	PO107	985674	Customer material number
E1EDS01—IDoc Summary—Min 1, Max 30—Loop 1 Total amount			
SUMID		011	Identifies total billed value for invoice
SUMME	TDS01	2589.000	Total billed value in invoice
E1EDS01—IDoc Summary Loop 2 Number of line items			
SUMID		001	Identifies total number of lines in invoice
SUMME	ISS01	1	Number of lines in invoice

Table 17.4 Map Specifications for the INVOIC to X12 810 Invoice Interface (Cont.)

17.6   EDI Configuration in SAP

We'll add mapping entries to EDPAR and our custom EDI trading partner mapping table ZEDIXREF. And, of course, we need an outbound partner profile for Gordy's Galaxy with message type INVOIC and message control.

17.6.1   EDPAR Entries: Transaction VOE4

The GLNs for the sold-to and ship-to partners for Gordy's Galaxy are read from EDPAR during outbound processing of the INVOIC IDoc. EDPAR support these reads. We need the values in Table 17.5.

Field	Value	Description
Sold-to partner mapping		
KUNNR	GRDY01	Gordy sold-to partner from sales order
PARVW	WE	Partner function ship-to
EXPNR	0999999999999	External partner for ship-to (Gordy's GLN)
INPNR	GRDY01	Internal SAP sold-to partner number
Ship-to partner mapping		
KUNNR	GRDY01	Gordy sold-to partner from sales order
PARVW	WE	Partner function ship-to
EXPNR	0999999999999	External partner for ship-to (Gordy's GLN)
INPNR	GRDY01001	Internal SAP ship-to partner number

Table 17.5   EDPAR Mapping for Invoice Sold-to and Ship-to

17.6.2   ZEDIXREF Entries

We map the SAP sender and receiver partner numbers to Gordy's Galaxy EDI send and receive trading partner IDs for Acme and Gordy. Enter the values in Table 17.6.

Field	Value	Description
DIRECT	1	Direction outbound
STDMES	810	EDI customer invoice transaction
MESTYP	INVOIC	IDoc message type
IDOCTP	INVOIC02	IDoc basic type
CIMTYP		IDoc extension
SNDPRN	DEVCLNT100	SAP send partner: Acme SAP logical system
RCVPRN	GRDY01	SAP receive partner: Gordy's customer number in Acme's system
SNDLAD	9999999USD	EDI send partner: Gordy's trading partner ID for Acme
RCVLAD	01234567US0	EDI receiver partner: Gordy's trading partner ID for Gordy

Table 17.6 Trading Partner Mapping for the 810 Customer Invoice

17.6.3 Outbound Partner Profile: Transaction WE20

We need an outbound partner profile for Gordy's Galaxy partner number GRDY01, partner type KU (customer), and partner role BP (bill-to) with message type INVOIC.

We use bill-to because our output type and condition record are both set to partner type BP.

In the outbound parameters table control of the partner profile for Gordy's Galaxy, click CREATE OUTBOUND PARAMETERS and enter the following values in the OUTBOUND PARAMETERS screen, as shown in Figure 17.17.

▶ PARTNER ROLE: "BP"
▶ MESSAGE TYPE: "INVOIC"
▶ RECEIVER PORT: "XML_IDOC"
▶ OUTPUT MODE area: COLLECT IDocs and START SUBSYSTEM radio buttons
▶ BASIC TYPE: "INVOIC02"

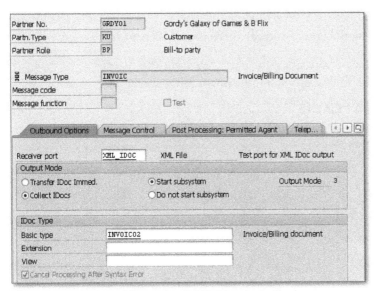

Figure 17.17 Outbound Parameters INVOIC Invoice to Gordy

Click on the MESSAGE CONTROL tab and enter the following values shown in Figure 17.18.

▶ APPLICATION: "V3"

▶ MESSAGE TYPE: "ZD00"

▶ PROCESS CODE: "SD09"

▶ CHANGE MESSAGE checkbox: One entry null and one checked

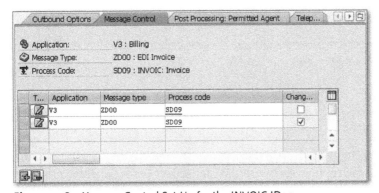

Figure 17.18 Message Control Set Up for the INVOIC IDoc

Process code SD09 links to function module `IDOC_OUTPUT_INVOIC`, which builds the IDoc from the billing document and the delivery and sales order.

The last step is to select the EDI STANDARD tab from the upper far right of the screen and enter the following values, as shown in Figure 17.19:

▶ EDI STANDARD: "X" for X12

▶ MESSAGE TYPE: "810"

▶ VERSION: "005010"

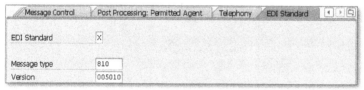

Figure 17.19 EDI Standard Values for the 810 Invoice

Don't forget to save the partner profile.

17.7 Summary

And that wraps up the invoice interface. We've run the billing due list and generated our billing documents from completed outbound deliveries.

Assuming the order has been delivered and the customer has received the finished goods into his inventory without issuing any error messages, we will generate an IDoc from the billing document when it is saved.

The INVOIC is generated from the billing document but also pulls its data from both the outbound delivery and sales order.

We chose to set up a custom output type to generate the invoice and have followed its progress from the billing document through the IDoc interface out to the EDI RIM and Gordy's business system.

We also created a custom ALV grid report program to allow the users to edit the customer purchase order number in the INVOIC IDoc if for some reason it was entered into the sales order incorrectly.

This was an opportunity to explore some of the features of standard ALV grid programming, especially functionality that can be used over and over again in different programs. The standard elements provided by SAP are so consistent that we can reuse any ALV grid program we create as a template for just about any ALV grid report we may need in future.

The other thing the custom program stepped us through was reading, editing, and displaying IDocs using a number of standard function modules.

The great Darryl Q. Fernhausen would no doubt appreciate the economy of all this standard reusability. He was no programmer, and didn't know an IDoc from a hole in the head, but he did appreciate both efficiency and the money it could save him.

And this whole invoicing process would just whet his appetite for the main course: the payment, which we will look at next. The end point for our order-to-cash cycle beckons.

"Show me the money!" was one of Darryl Q's favorite expressions. Mr. Q never lost sight of the fact that his business was to make money. So he would have loved the 820 payment interface, which tells Acme that the customer paid his bill. It can be complex and data-rich, but it records every penny of the final bill, and the bottom line is that it's money in the bank for goods sold.

18 Processing the Inbound Payment Advice

Gordy has its invoice. Everything has been validated. Goods were ordered, delivered, and billed. Creation of the billing document in SAP updated accounts receivable at Acme Pictures, while receipt of the invoice updated accounts payable at Gordy's Galaxy of Games & B Flix.

The 997 acknowledgment for the outbound 810 customer invoice was received by Acme and no follow-up error reports were sent in an 864 text message.

All that's left for the entire order-to-cash cycle to come to a close is for Gordy to pay up. Gordy has committed to pay within 60 days of receipt of the invoice.

That payment will be made electronically directly into Acme's bank account and then reported to Acme's SAP system in an 820 remittance advice and an REMADV IDoc. Accounts receivable will use the data brought in by the IDoc to clear all of the invoices, and any credit and debit memos or other adjustments covered by Gordy's payment.

The X12 820 to REMADV payment interface must reference every detail of every one of these items for all invoices paid by the customer in one payment. For a customer as large as Gordy, this adds up to a whole lot of data, particularly during the busy Christmas shopping season. Data volumes from Gordy alone can exceed 100,000 line items per month for sales made during the holidays.

Payment processing is the one EDI interface that senior management really cares about. The failure to properly process a payment jeopardizes period-end closing, leads to inaccurate customer statements resulting in damaged customer relations, and can trigger audit issues.

In our final exploration of the order-to-cash cycle, we'll work through the functional and technical details of Acme's X12 820 to REMADV interface and consider an approach to handling the massive files that Gordy sends during the holidays. So let's show the great Darryl Q the money!

18.1 Technical Overview of the Interface

Table 18.1 summarizes the inbound REMADV to X12 820 payment interface from the customer.

Item	Description
Title	Inbound Payment or Remittance Advice
Description	The payment advice is sent by the customer to Acme Pictures when an electronic payment has been made on one or more invoices.
	The 820 payment advice is generated from the customer's business system when the electronic payment hits Acme's bank account. It identifies the bank and account number and every invoice paid.
	It also provides details of all taxes, discounts, surcharges, penalties, and any other credit or debit that impacted the final amount paid.
	All of these debits or credits are recorded in accounting documents. Some are in the invoice itself, and others in credit and debit memos sent by Gordy to Acme in separate X12 812 debit/credit memo transmissions before the payment. These documents all post to Acme's accounting system and must be included in the X12 820 sent with the payment for clearing.
	Very large payments result in extremely large datasets transferred in the 820. These datasets can be so large that if they were directly mapped to the REMADV IDoc, they could trigger an application dump in SAP.
	There is a need for a process in the EDI RIM to split very large 820s into smaller transactions. The trick is to ensure that the sum total of each of these transaction equals the sum total of the original 820.

Table 18.1 Overview of the Inbound EDI Payment Interface

Item	Description
	The 820 will map to a REMADV IDoc that will be used to provide the data needed for clearing the payment in accounts receivable in SAP.
	The REMADV IDoc posts its data to holding tables in accounting with a payment advice number that are then used to clear the payments.
	The clearing process can only handle up to 999 line items at a time. Payments that exceed the 999 line item limit will be split by a standard SAP program into multiple payment advices.
Type of interface	Delivery: X12 EDI to IDoc
Direction	Inbound
Trading partner	Gordy's Galaxy (customer)
IDoc	REMADV.PEXR2003
IDoc extended type	
IDoc function	`IDOC_INPUT_REMADV`
Custom ABAP	
Description	
Source file(s)	X12 820 payment advice
Target document(s)	SAP payment advice note
Transaction code	FBE1: Create payment advice
Map(s)	X12 820 vers. 5010 to REMADV.PEXR2003
Custom map logic	
Source system	Gordy's Galaxy EDI via AS2
Target system	Acme SAP via EDI RIM
997 acknowledgment	Outbound at transaction detail level; function group acknowledgment code: RA
Frequency	Once a day on demand
Job schedule	`RBDAPP01`: Daily, at noon, to post all REMADV message types for all customers

Table 18.1 Overview of the Inbound EDI Payment Interface (Cont.)

18.2   Functional Specifications

The X12 820 to REMADV IDoc remittance advice interface is the last step in the order-to-cash cycle. It reports details of Gordy's payments to Acme's bank account.

Gordy makes one or more payments a month on every payment document received from Acme or sent to Acme in a separate X12 812 debit/credit memo adjustment EDI transmission. On a very large payment, these adjustments could include a range of debits or credits, such as allowances, returns, discounts, penalty charges, and so on.

All these adjustment documents plus the invoices represent open items in Acme's accounts receivable system in SAP. All of these open items will be cleared by the payment advice document posted to Acme's SAP system by the REMADV IDoc.

18.2.1   Process Overview

The process begins when Gordy makes a payment to Acme by electronic funds transfer. The payment covers all items in Gordy's accounts payable that have hit their 60-day terms of payment limit.

Gordy typically makes five payments to Acme each month, four of which are relatively small. The exception can get very large, particularly during and immediately after the Christmas holiday shopping season. In a good year, Acme can receive monthly payments as large as $25 million or more.

After the funds are sent, a remittance advice is generated in Gordy's system with details of every invoice and adjustment included in the payment. This document is exported to Gordy's EDI system where it is converted to an X12 820 remittance advice and transmitted to Acme's EDI system.

Large payments create extremely large and complex X12 820 interchanges that can reference thousands of invoices and credit and debit memos. This must be successfully translated to a REMADV IDoc in Acme's EDI RIM and sent into SAP to post a payment advice with transaction FBE1.

Accounts receivable takes over and the process ends. The payment advice is used to automatically identify and clear customer open items in accounts receivable using Transaction F-28.

18.2.2 Requirements

Gordy issued a payment on aged open invoices and adjustments. An X12 820 transmission is sent to Acme and converted to an IDoc with message type REMADV and basic type PEXR2003.

The data in the 820 have details of all of Gordy's open items and invoices covered by the current payment. Adjustments are sent by Gordy to Acme in a separate X12 812 debit/credit memo advice and these are also included, with their document numbers, as line items in the 820.

Gordy sends up to five X12 820 transmissions a month, including one very large transaction on the 15th. Gordy's 820s normally arrive in the mid-morning and must be available for clearing by accounts receivable users early the next morning at the latest. A job is set up in the SAP Job Scheduler to process Gordy's REMADV IDocs every day at noon.

The REMADV IDoc posts to a payment advice with Transaction FBE1 in accounts receivable in Acme's SAP Financial Accounting (FI) module. The SAP payment advice is created against the following:

► Company code: 3000 for Acme Pictures

► Account type: Customer account (D)

► Account number: Gordy SAP customer number = GRDY01

The payment advice is used by the business users to select open items on Gordy's account and clear them when the amounts match exactly, using SAP incoming payments Transaction F-28.

Where the payment amount doesn't match the open item, a partial payment posts with the reason code sent by Gordy in the 820. The reason code posts to the payment advice from the IDoc, which contains the external EDI reason code sent by Gordy. The external reason code is converted to Acme's internal SAP reason code for posting to the payment advice.

There is no limit on the number of line items that can post to the payment advice in SAP. Very large payments from Gordy might result in an 820 transaction with more than 100,000 line items.

Data volume is an issue both in the EDI RIM and SAP. Two issues need to be addressed:

▶ The EDI RIM must be able to process very large 820 transactions from Gordy that could range in size from 4MB to as much as 30MB.

▶ IDocs sent into SAP from the EDI RIM must not be so large that they overload background processes, which have a practical limit of 2GB, depending on how your system is set up. Very large 820 payments are split before they are converted to an IDoc, a common issue and approach on sites that process 820s.

The SAP clearing programs can only process payment advices of 999 line items or less. A payment advice that exceeds this must be split into multiple documents before accounts receivable can run the clearing programs.

When clearing is run, and the open items in the payment advice cleared, its data are deleted. The payment advice acts as a holding document for clearing and has no other purpose in Acme's SAP system.

18.2.3 Dependencies

The X12 820 to REMADV payment interface is dependent on master data, configuration, and development in SAP and the EDI RIM, including all data and configuration required to support all documents and interfaces covered so far:

▶ Customer master data:
  ▶ Bank data maintained in the PAYMENT TRANSACTIONS screen under GENERAL DATA
  ▶ RSN CODE CONVN. field in the PAYMENT TRANSACTIONS screen in COMPANY CODE DATA populated with a reason code conversion version value

▶ Business documents generated or manually created in SAP:
  ▶ Customer SD invoice
  ▶ FI invoice and other accounting documents posted by the SD invoice
  ▶ Credit and debit memos from Gordy's Galaxy for adjustments sent in earlier X12 812 credit/debit memo interfaces

▶ Inbound IDoc configuration, including a partner profile to link Gordy's Galaxy to message type REMADV

▸ EDI related configuration in accounts receivable in the IMG:

   ▸ Link the sold-to partner who will send payment advices to the Acme company code

   ▸ Maintain SAP reason codes for payment adjustments and the external to internal reason code conversion table

18.2.4 Assumptions

The sum of all line items must be equal to the total amount submitted as the payment at the header level of the incoming 820 interchange. The same is true for the IDoc.

Each line item in the X12 820 presents an amount added to or subtracted from the payment, either through an invoice paid or an adjustment made to what was owed through a claim or deduction. These amounts must add up to the total payment recorded by the 820.

There are a few other key assumptions about the 820-REMADV interface:

▸ The customer's reason codes for adjustments in the 820 are converted to Acme's internal SAP reason codes before posting the payment advice. The SAP reason code conversion table is kept up to date.

▸ The 820 transaction identifies both the paying customer and the Acme company code that will post the payment.

▸ The IDoc won't automatically run clearing when it posts a payment advice. AR business users will run clearing separately after payment advices have been posted by the IDoc.

▸ When a payment advice posts in SAP with more than 999 line items, it is split into multiple documents with fewer than 999 lines each using standard SAP program SPLIT_PAYMENT_ADVICE.

18.2.5 Payment Advice Note Data

The payment advice note is created in SAP with Transaction FBE1 with data from the REMADV IDoc. It is used to clear open items in accounts receivable, including any number of credits and debits, that have been accommodated by a payment. The data detailed in Table 18.2 are relevant for clearing the payment by accounts receivable.

Table	Field	Description	Sample Value
Payment Advice Header			
AVIK	BUKRS	Company code	0010
AVIK	KOART	Account type – D = Customer	D
AVIK	KONTO	Customer account number	GRDY01
AVIK	AVSID	Payment advice number	040034038180
AVIK	RWBTR	Total payment amount	15,492,341.23
AVIK	RWSKT	Cash discount	0.00
AVIK	VBLNR	Payment document number	1245879
AVIK	ZALDT	Payment date	20090108
AVIK	AVTXT	Payment advice header text	Notes on payment
AVIK	XBENR	Object key	34038180
AVIK	XBTYP	Reference procedure	IDOC
Payment Advice Line Items			
AVIP	AVSID	Payment advice item number	00001
AVIP	NBETR	Net payment for item	100,289.90
AVIP	WRBTR	Gross payment for item	100,525.26
AVIP	ABBTR	Total amount of all deductions for item	235.36
AVIP	WSKTO	Discount amount + or -	235.36
AVIP	RSTGN	Reason code for adjustment	017
AVIP	BELNR	Accounting document number	906524859
AVIP	GJAHR	Fiscal year	2009
AVIP	BUZEI	Line item within accounting doc	1
AVIP	ABWKO	Alternate account number	GRDY01
AVIP	VBELN	Billing document number	906524859
VBUP	XBLNR	Reference document	0906524859

Table 18.2 Payment Advice Note Fields Used in Clearing

Table	Field	Description	Sample Value
VBUP	XREF1	Reference key 1	816160750
AVIP	ZUONR	Assignment number	816160750
AVIP	SWERT	Document number—selection field	906524859

Table 18.2 Payment Advice Note Fields Used in Clearing (Cont.)

You can display a payment advice note with Transaction FBE3, which is made up of three tables:

▶ AVIK: Payment advice header

▶ AVIP: Payment advice line item

▶ AVIR: Subitems referencing AVIP items (not used at Acme Pictures)

These are temporary holding tables for payment data until clearing runs. After the payment has been applied against the corresponding open items in accounts receivable payment data in all three tables are deleted by SAP.

You can write pre-clearing reports against these tables. For example, an IDoc cash receipts report could identify and summarize all payments that posted through a REMADV message rather through a spreadsheet update or manual entry. Another report could identify payments that exceed 999 lines for splitting by program SPLIT_PAYMENT_ADVICE.

It's easy to identify payments that posted with an IDoc. Reference procedure field AVIK-XBTYP is populated with "IDOC" and object key field XBENR has the IDoc number for the REMADV message that posted the payment.

Another interesting factoid is that the IDoc number is embedded in the last eight digits of the payment advice number.

18.2.6 Enhancements to the Process

There won't be any custom ABAP programming, but we will create a user transaction code (ZSPLIT) to run the standard program SPLIT_PAYMENT_ADVICE that splits a payment advice with more than 999 lines into multiple payments for clearing.

We'll also need a process in the EDI RIM that will split very large X12 820 transactions into smaller transaction sets to ensure that there are no memory overruns when the IDocs come into SAP.

18.2.7 Reconciliation

Successful import of the REMADV IDoc is confirmed through any of the IDoc monitoring tools such as Transactions BD87 or WE05.

IDoc status should be 64—*IDoc ready to be transferred to application*, before the scheduled processing job is kicked off, and 53—*Application document posted*, after. The following other validations can also be performed:

▶ Check that the payment advice includes all line items in the IDoc.

▶ Spot-check line item amounts in the payment advice to confirm that they are the same as in the IDoc.

▶ Confirm that the sum of all items in an IDoc equals the total payment reported at the header level.

▶ Confirm that the sum of all of the items in an 820 equal the total payment reported at the header level of the transaction. This must be confirmed for both whole and split 820s.

▶ For split 820s, confirm that the header total for all transactions split off equal the header total for the original undivided 820.

▶ While not strictly the responsibility of EDI, the total amount of the payment advice that comes into SAP through the IDoc must equal the total amount of the electronic payment sent to the bank.

The business will confirm this; if there are issues, the payment advice in SAP may be deleted and the 820 resent by Gordy.

18.2.8 Errors and Error Handling

Aside from missing data in the transaction, the key error that can occur in posting the payments from the REMADV IDoc is that the line item amounts don't equal the header totals. This is validated in two places:

▶ When large 820 transactions are split into smaller ones

▶ In the EDI map when the 820 is converted to an IDoc

If the error occurs, the EDI team sums the line item amounts of the 820, pre-split and post-split where relevant. If the line item amounts equal the header total, the problem is in the map.

18.3 End-to-End Process Flow

Figure 18.1 gives an overview of the end-to-end process flow for the inbound X12 820 to REMADV IDoc interface.

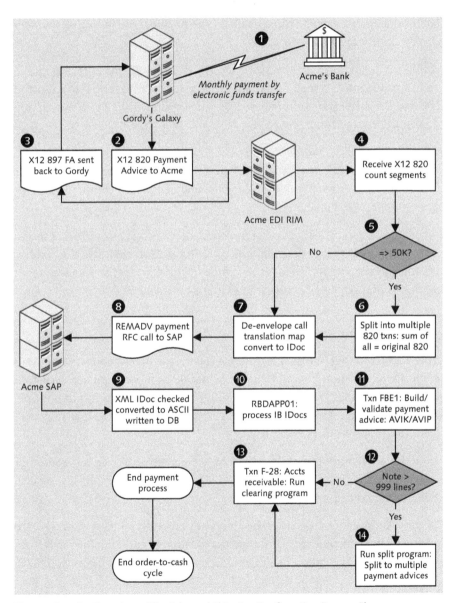

Figure 18.1 An Overview of the Inbound Shipping Confirmation Process Flow

18.3.1 Following the 820 Flow

The X12 820 to REMADV payment advice interface kicks off when Gordy makes a monthly payment by electronic transfer directly into Acme's bank account.

As soon as the payment is made Gordy's accounts payable system kicks out a remittance advice document that contains details of the payment, including all invoices and debit or credit adjustments paid.

One remittance document is created for each electronic payment, referencing the check or electronic funds transfer number. The document is exported to a file and transferred to Gordy's EDI system where it is translated to an X12 820 transaction set and bundled into an interchange.

Each payment advice is converted to one X12 820 transaction set. With only four or five payments a month, the number of 820 transactions received by Acme is small. But if business is good, they can be extremely large and complex, perhaps exceeding 100,000 line items.

The interchange is encrypted and sent by AS2 to Acme's EDI RIM. Acme's AS2 server picks it up and passes it to a de-enveloping workflow that identifies the sender, receiver, and the transaction; checks the syntax of the message; and generates an X12 997 that is immediately sent back to Gordy's EDI system.

18.3.2 An Intelligent Split

The map is identified, but before it is called, a separate process counts the number of segments in the 820 transaction. If there are 50,000 or more segments, a custom program is triggered that loops through the interchange and splits it into multiple X12 820 transactions that are bundled into a new interchange with the same ISA and GS control numbers as the original.

The transaction set control IDs of the split 820s are incremented from the number of the original. If the original transaction set ID is 1, the newly split transaction sets are incremented beginning with 2.

The 820 must be split intelligently. The line item amounts in each split 820 are summed and the total moved into the transaction header. In addition, the totals from all of the split transactions must equal the total payment in the original unsplit 820.

The splitting is necessary because a REMADV IDoc could be more than 10 times larger than the 820 that it was translated from. A 20MB 820 transaction for a $20 million payment with more than 800,000 segments could be translated to a REMADV IDoc with more than double the number of segments exceeding 200MB.

An IDoc this large overwhelms the memory limits for background processes in SAP, triggering a short dump before the IDoc is written to the database. This is a common problem on all sites that receive large 820s with many adjustments and is almost always addressed by splitting the 820 into multiple transaction sets before translating it and sending it into SAP.

After the split runs, or if the transaction set is smaller than 50,000 segments, the map is called, and the 820 translated to a REMADV XML IDoc. Split 820s are converted to multiple IDocs that are batched into one IDoc file.

The XML IDocs are saved to an inbound folder on the SAP application server. The SAP adapter in the EDI RIM triggers an RFC to function EDI_DATA_INCOMING, which kicks off IDoc interface processing in SAP.

The IDoc interface confirms that the file contains valid XML IDocs and checks that their structure is correct. The IDoc file is deleted from the application server and the XML IDocs converted to ASCII. The partner profile is read and confirmed using values from the control segment and, if everything checks, each IDoc is written to the database at status 64.

18.3.3 Posting the Payment

Program RBDAPP01 is set up in the SAP Job Scheduler (Transaction SM36) to run once a day to pick up and process all REMADV IDocs at status 64. It identifies the application function (IDOC_INPUT_REMADV) from process code REMA in the inbound partner profile for Gordy with message type REMADV.

IDOC_INPUT_REMADV loops through internal tables IDOC_CONTROL and IDOC_DATA and builds the payment advice by inserting the data into tables AVIK (header level) and AVIP (line-item level).

Qualifiers, date formatting, and amounts are all validated before it is moved into table AVIK or table AVIP. If any of these values are missing, an error is returned, IDoc processing ends, and the status is updated to 51 — *Application document not posted*.

The system does not confirm the validity of document numbers in the IDoc, nor does it confirm the validity of reason codes; it only checks that they are present.

Two customer functions are available after the internal tables used to build AVIK and AVIP have been fully populated. Both allow additional custom processing on AVIK and AVIP and provide complete IDoc control and data records. The second is called after a function that determines whether a partial payment is allowed on the current account.

When all checks and validations pass, the function reads AVIK to determine if the current payment exists. If it does, a change payment function is called.

Because we're dealing with a new payment, function REMADV_INSERT is called to create the payment advice. This is done by calling Transaction FBE1, passing AVIK and AVIP data directly into the screen fields, calculating header totals, and saving the document.

After the payment advice is created, a success message is sent back to the IDoc interface. The status record is updated with 51 and the new payment advice number.

Next, accounts receivable users evaluate the size of the payment advice. If it exceeds 999 lines, program SPLIT_PAYMENT_ADVICE is run with custom Transaction ZSPLIT to create multiple documents of 900 lines or less. The selection screen for SPLIT_PAY-MENT_ADVICE would look something like Figure 18.2.

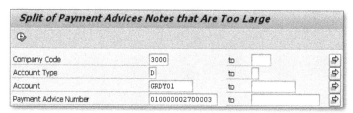

Figure 18.2 Selecting a Payment Advice to Split

The payment process ends when accounts receivable clears all items in the payment advices using Transaction F-28. Items cleared included credit and debit memos created during earlier transmissions of X12 812 from Gordy with credit and debit adjustments to outstanding invoices.

18.4 Technical Specifications

This technical specification section describes SAP configuration and EDI development required to support the X12 820 to REMADV IDoc payment advice interface from Gordy's Galaxy that reports details of a monthly electronic payment to Acme's bank account.

18.4.1 Technical Requirements

Very large payments from Gordy's Galaxy are split into multiple 820 transaction sets before being converted to IDocs in the EDI RIM to improve mapping performance and avoid memory overruns and program dumps in SAP.

The split process in the EDI RIM must ensure that the sum of all line items in these multiple transactions must equal the total payment recorded in the header of the original 820 transaction. This will ensure that the sum of all line items in the converted REMADV IDoc will equal the header total, assuming the map works correctly.

A user transaction will be created for program `SPLIT_PAYMENT_ADVICE` that splits payment advices with 999 lines or more into multiple documents for clearing.

18.4.2 Dependencies

The X12 820 to REMADV IDoc interface is dependent on standard and custom development and configuration in the EDI RIM and SAP:

▶ A program, script, or process to count the number of segments in an incoming X12 820 transaction

  ▶ If the count exceeds 50,000 lines, split the 820 into multiple smaller transaction sets.

  ▶ During the split, validate that the sum total of all line item amounts equals the header total of the original single 820.

▶ Business process workflows built in the EDI RIM to process and route the incoming X12 810 and REMADV.PEXR2003 IDocs

▶ Inbound envelopes set up in the RIM for Gordy's X12 820 version 5010 transaction

▶ Outbound envelopes for 997 acknowledgments set up in the EDI RIM for generation during de-enveloping of inbound 820 transactions from Gordy's Galaxy

▸ Translation map in the EDI RIM for the inbound 820 X12 version 5010 to REMADV IDoc conversion, including validation that the sum of items in the converted IDoc equals the header total in the transaction

▸ FI configuration in SAP linking Acme's company code to Gordy for the EDI payment advice

▸ Custom cross-reference table ZEDIXREF populated in SAP to convert the EDI trading partner numbers to the SAP send and receive partners for the inbound 820 from Gordy

▸ Inbound partner profile for Gordy with message type REMADV

▸ Variant created for a job in the SAP Job Scheduler (Transaction SM36) for program `RBDAPP01` to post status 64 REMADV IDocs for all partners

▸ Workflows in the EDI RIM and configuration in SAP to support posting of credit and debit memos from Gordy using X12 transaction 812 and messages CREADV (credit memo) and DEBADV (debit memo) with IDoc basic type PEXR2003.

These interfaces will run before the payment advice posts and will create credit and debit memo documents in accounts receivable that will be cleared by the payment advice.

18.4.3 Assumptions

Only 820 transactions with fewer than 50,000 segments are mapped to REMADV IDocs for Gordy's Galaxy.

The split is run by a script, program, or process that validates that the amounts recorded at the item level of the split 820 transactions equal the sum total recorded at the header of the original unsplit 820.

The REMADV IDoc posts to a payment advice in SAP. Posting of the IDoc to a payment won't trigger automatic clearing. AR clears the payment after the remittance advice posts and after ensuring that the document does not exceed 999 lines.

There are a few other key assumptions:

▸ An X12 812 credit and debit interface has been configured and that credit and debit memos are being sent by Gordy's Galaxy recording adjustments to their final payment.

- ► The EDI RIM sends EDI send and receive trading partner IDs in the IDoc control segment fields SNDLAD and RCVLAD to identify SAP partner numbers through a customer exit in the IDoc interface before the partner profile is read.

- ► All IDoc errors are monitored by the EDI team in SAP.

- ► Technical errors in the IDoc interface are documented and corrected by the EDI team.

- ► All IDoc application errors are handled by business users, backed up by the EDI team where appropriate.

- ► EDI errors are tracked and addressed in the EDI system.

18.4.4 EDI Process to Split Very Large 820s

A custom program, script, or process runs on all incoming 820s before they are translated in the EDI RIM. This is a common EDI issue where very large payments with numerous adjustments can be received. Scripts, java exits, or classes called from a map or executed at the operating system level can all be used to run the split logic. Your environment and available skill set will dictate your own approach.

Acme's custom process counts the number of segments in the transaction, and if the total exceeds 50,000, it splits the 820 into multiple transaction sets of around 50,000 segments each.

The multiple transaction sets are bundled into a single interchange and group with the same ISA and GS envelopes that bundled the original unsplit 820 transaction set.

The control IDs for the split interchange and group are the same as the original. The ST control IDs for the split transaction sets are incremented by 1, beginning with the control ID of the original 820, for each split 820 in the group. If the original 820 control ID is 1, then the first split 820 is 2 and so on for all the split transaction sets in the group.

After the split run is complete the 820 is passed back to the EDI RIM for translation and routing to SAP.

The splitting is necessary because the translated REMADV IDocs are more than 10 times the size of the X12 820. IDocs that can exceed 200MB trigger short dumps when they hit SAP. These are caused by overruns in roll, heap, and extended memory in background work processes before the IDoc is written to the database.

If you want to learn more about this, butter up your friendly local Basis team. It's always a good idea for a developer to be on good terms with Basis.

Structural Issues that Affect the 820 Split

Before we can split the 820, Acme's SAP EDI team must understand the structure of the transaction. You can't just split it any which way. The basic rule is that line items must be kept intact, which means that the split can only occur after the last line of either the RMR or ADX looping group.

The RMR looping group (the remittance advice accounts receivable open item reference) reports details of invoices paid in the current remittance.

The ADX looping group (the adjustment) provides details of the customer's adjustments to the current payment, including any debit or credit memos generated by the customer.

These adjustments should have been reported to Acme by the separate transmission of an X12 812 credit/debit adjustment advice. But in the real world, this doesn't always happen, so standard EDI reason codes are used to provide some explanation for any adjustments. Reason codes are included even when there is no debit or credit memo to report.

From the point of view of the split, understanding the structure of each group and how each occurs within a typical transaction is critical. The good news is that there is consistency to these looping groups. The bad news is that this consistency can fluctuate. And because each customer is different, it can implement the rules, or not, differently.

The structure of each group is consistent...to a degree. Gordy is very good about group occurrence. A typical 820 from Gordy always includes a block of data that has nothing but RMR invoice groups followed by a block that is all ADX adjustments, if there are any adjustments to report.

The two line item detail groups have three different structures:

- ▶ Standalone ADX only: Adjustment amount and details
- ▶ Standalone RMR only: Invoice amount and details
- ▶ RMR with ADX subgroup: Invoice amount and details with adjustments to the invoice payment

Let's look at a few data samples to help clarify what this means.

Adjustments Block

The standalone ADX looping group always begins with an ADX and ends with an REF segment, as in the line item sample in Listing 18.1.

```
ADX*-124.24*RL*CM*999401~
REF*ST*0999653098076~
REF*60*694~
REF*BP*999510922~
```

Listing 18.1 Standalone ADX Payment Adjustment Looping Group

The data elements of the ADX segment identifies the following values:

- ADX01: The amount of the adjustment.

- ADX02: EDI reason code (RL for *Freight on Returned Merchandise*) identifying the purpose for the payment adjustment.

- ADX03: Adjustment document type: CM for credit memo or DM for debit memo

- ADX04: Adjustment document number (sent to Acme in an earlier 812 transmission)

Gordy's ADX group includes three REF segments that are always in the same order and provide supporting information for the adjustment, including:

- REF01 = ST: Ordering store location GLN

- REF01 = 60: Qualifier identifying Gordy's internal reason code for the adjustment

- REF01 = BP: Qualifier identifying Gordy's internal adjustment control number

Invoice Payment Block

Gordy's standalone RMR looping group always begins with an RMR and ends with a DTM segment, as in the sample in Listing 18.2.

```
RMR*IV*0090000763*PO*1924.52*1924.52~
REF*PO*0000000805~
REF*MR*0077~
REF*TN*001230453~
REF*19*13~
```

```
REF*ST*0999653098076~
DTM*097*20090120~
```

Listing 18.2 Standalone RMR Invoice Payment Looping Group

The data element of the RMR segment identifies the following values:

- ▶ RMR01: Payment document qualifier: IV for customer invoice
- ▶ RMR02: Payment document number (Acme's invoice number)
- ▶ RMR03: Payment action code: PO = Payment on account
- ▶ RMR04: Actual payment amount, including all adjustments taken
- ▶ RMR05: Invoiced amount

Gordy's standalone RMR group includes four or five REF segments that are always in the same order and provide supporting data for the payment document, including:

- ▶ REF01 = PO: Qualifier identifying customer PO number
- ▶ REF01 = MR: Qualifier identifying merchandise type code for the ordered product (can be omitted from the RMR group)
- ▶ REF01 = TN: Qualifier identifying Gordy's internal payment transaction reference number
- ▶ REF01 = 19: Qualifier identifying Gordy's division or department
- ▶ REF01 = ST: Qualifier identifying Gordy's store location GLN

The DTM date segment holds the payment transaction date identified by qualifier 097. This is the date that the payment was sent to Acme's bank.

Adjusted Invoice Payments — Defining the Split

The RMR looping group with an ADX subgroup is a little more complicated. It always begins with an RMR and ends with an REF segment as in the data sample in Listing 18.3.

```
RMR*IV*0090000764*PO*655.4*671.3~
REF*PO*0000000806~
REF*MR*0077~
REF*19*13~
REF*ST*0999653098076~
DTM*097*20090120~
ADX*-15.9*01*CM*09991131~
```

```
REF*60*611~
REF*BP*999510922~
```

Listing 18.3 RMR Payment Looping Group with Reported Adjustment

The qualifiers for the RMR main and ADX subgroup are the same as for the stand-alone RMR and ADX groups.

The issue is how we split. We know that we can always split a standalone RMR or ADX group where the next segment equals RMR or ADX *except* where there is an ADX group within an RMR group.

The structure of the ADX group is the key: Gordy only sends two REF segments qualifying the ADX adjustment to the invoice payment when the ADX occurs within an RMR group. They identify Gordy's internal reason code and adjustment control number and are always present in that order. So the split logic should follow the code in Listing 18.4.

```
If next segment = RMR then
  Split before the next RMR segment
Elseif the next segment = ADX
  Count the following ref segments
  If ref segment count > 2 then
    Split before next ADX segment
  Else
    Split after ADX segment but
      before next ADX or RMR segment
  endif
endif
```

Listing 18.4 Logic for Split of Large 820s at ADX or RMR Item Level

Of course, the logic would change if your customer did not follow the same structural approach in their 820s as Gordy's Galaxy. The key to the logic is to identify the structural pattern in your customer's usage.

The split process leaves us with two or more 820 transactions that are around 50,000 segments in size.

We'll also keep running totals for all line item amounts. This amount comes from data elements ADX01 in the standalone ADX group and RMR04 for the standalone RMR and combined RMR-ADX line item groups.

The total for each split 820 will be saved in the `BPR02` amount data element in the header of the new transaction. Another running total will be kept for all split 820s and this will be compared to the total of the original unsplit 820. If there is a discrepancy, an error will be raised, the split and unsplit transactions will be analyzed manually, and the error will be identified.

If the totals match, the header segments of the original 820 are copied into each new 820 transaction and the `BP02` amount updated with the running total for the split. The item groups are transferred as is from the original and the ST-SE envelopes are applied. SE01 is updated with the number of segments in the new transaction set. So a count is also kept of the number of segments, including ST-SE envelopes, moved into the split transaction.

When all split transactions have been built, transaction sets are bundled into one file, and the GS-GE and ISA-IEA group and interchange envelopes are applied. The 820s are then handed off to the de-enveloping and translation workflows and the IDocs sent into SAP.

18.4.5 User Transaction Code for the SAP Split Program

Even though `SPLIT_PAYMENT_ADVICE` is a standard SAP program, it does not provided a transaction code. The only way that we can allow business users to run it is by creating a custom transaction code for them. Follow these steps:

1. Go to MAINTAIN TRANSACTION using Transaction SE93.

2. Enter transaction code "ZSPLIT" and click CREATE.

3. In the CREATE TRANSACTION dialog, do the following:

   ▶ Enter a description of the transaction in the SHORT TEXT field.

   ▶ Select PROGRAM AND SELECTION SCREEN (REPORT TRANSACTION) in the START OBJECT area.

4. Click OK to open the CREATE REPORT TRANSACTION screen. Enter "SPLIT_PAY-MENT_ADVICE" in the PROGRAM field. The selection screen should be 1000.

5. Save the transaction code and assign it to a change request.

18.5   Mapping Specifications

One map will be developed in the EDI RIM to translate the X12 820 remittance advice from Gordy's Galaxy to the REMADV.PEXR2003 IDoc. Mapping specifications for our example are detailed in Table 18.3.

REMADV	820	Sample Value	Comments
E1IDKU1—Payment header—Min 1, Max 1			
@SEGMENT		1	Hard-code segment attribute to 1.
BGMTYP	BPR01	REM	Qualifier identifies remittance advice where BPR01 = I
BGMNAME		REMITTANCE ADVICE	Hard-coded. Document name.
BGMREF	TRN02	89587458952	Document reference. Gordy's electronic payment or check number as reference.
BGMLEV		ORG	Hard-code. Document type reference.
E1IDK03—Payment header dates—Min 0, Max 3			
@SEGMENT		1	Hard-code segment attribute to 1.
IDDAT		017	Qualifier identifies payment date
DATUM	BPR16	20140315	Date of payment
E1IDK02—Payment header documents—Min 0, Max 1			
@SEGMENT		1	Hard-code segment attribute to 1.
QUALF		022	Qualifier identifies payment document number
BELNR	TRN02	89587458952	Payment document number such as EFT ID or check number

Table 18.3   Mapping the X12 820 to the REMADV.PEXR2003 IDoc

REMADV	820	Sample Value	Comments
E1IDKU3—Payment instructions—Min 0, Max 1			
@SEGMENT		1	Hard-code segment attribute to 1.
PAIMED	BPR04	003	Identifies payment method: SWIFT electronic transfer if BPR04 = ACH
E1IDKU5—Header level amounts—Min 1, Max 1			
@SEGMENT		1	Hard-code segment attribute to 1.
MOAQUAL		001	Identifies header level payment applied to remittance advice
MOABETR	BPR02	5007089.34	Total amount of payment
	CUR01	PR	Qualifier identifies payer's currency for payment currency
CUXWAERZ	CUR02	USD	Payment currency
E1IDB02—Bank details—Min 0, Max 4—Loop 1 Payer's bank			
@SEGMENT		1	Hard-code segment attribute to 1.
MOAQUAL	BPR06	BA	Identifies the sending bank of the sold-to party where BPR06 = 01 for ABA transit routing number of paying bank
FIIBKENN	BPR07	895474124255	Bank ID of paying bank
	CUR01	PR	Qualifier identifies payer's currency for payment currency
CUXWAERZ	CUR02	USD	Payment currency
E1IDB02—Bank details—Loop 2 Acme's bank			
@SEGMENT		1	Hard-code segment attribute to 1.

Table 18.3 Mapping the X12 820 to the REMADV.PEXR2003 IDoc (Cont.)

REMADV	820	Sample Value	Comments
MOAQUAL	BPR10	BB	Identifies Acme's bank that received the payment where BPR10 = 01 for transit routing number of receiving bank
FIIBKENN	BPR11	912141111588	Bank ID of receiving bank
E1IDKA1—Partner info—Min 0, Max 4—Loop 1 Payer party			
@SEGMENT		1	Hard-code segment attribute to 1.
PARVW	N101	RG	Identifies payer party where N101 = PR
PARTN	N104	0999999999999	Gordy's GLN number where N103 = UL
E1IDKA1—Partner info—Loop 2 Beneficiary (payee)			
@SEGMENT		1	Hard-code segment attribute to 1.
PARVW		BE	Identifies payer party where N101 = PE
NAME1	N102	Acme Pictures	Payee's name in payer's system
E1IDPU1—Line item details—Min 1, Max N—1 instance for each line item detail group— RMR payments			
@SEGMENT		1	Hard-code segment attribute to 1.
DOCNAME	RMR01	REM	Identifies remittance advice (payment) where RMR01 = INV (invoice paid)
DOCNUMMR	RMR02	0090038759	Acme invoice number
E1IDPU5—Line item level amounts—Min 1, Max 10—Loop 1 Actual amount of payment			
@SEGMENT		1	Hard-code segment attribute to 1.

Table 18.3 Mapping the X12 820 to the REMADV.PEXR2003 IDoc (Cont.)

REMADV	820	Sample Value	Comments
MOAQUAL		006	Hard-code. Identifies net actual amount paid on invoice, including all credit and debit adjustments.
MOABETR	RMR04	2400.00	Net amount of payment (position of net from trading partner guidelines)
CUXWAERZ	CUR02	USD	Pull from header level payment currency for payer
E1IDPU5—Line item level amounts—Min 1, Max 10			
MOAQUAL		004	Identifies amount on invoice
MOABETR	RMR05	3400.00	Invoiced amount
CUXWAERZ	CUR02	USD	Header level payment currency
E1EDP03—Line item level dates—Min 0, Max 4			
@SEGMENT		1	Hard-code segment attribute to 1.
IDDAT		017	Hard-code. Qualifier identifies payment date.
DATUM	DTM02	20140315	Date invoice paid
E1EDP02—Line item level documents—Min 0, Max 4—Loop 1			
@SEGMENT		1	Hard-code segment attribute to 1.
QUALF		009	Hard-code. Qualifier identifies Acme invoice number.
BELNR	RMR02	0090038759	Acme invoice number
E1EDP02—Line item level documents—Loop 2			
@SEGMENT		1	Hard-code segment attribute to 1.
QUALF	REF01	001	Hard-code. Qualifier identifies Gordy's PO number where REF01 = PO.

Table 18.3 Mapping the X12 820 to the REMADV.PEXR2003 IDoc (Cont.)

REMADV	820	Sample Value	Comments
BELNR	REF02	4500017679	Gordy's purchase order number
E1EDPU2—Line item level deductions—Min 0, Max 100 (only populated if RMR group has ADX adjustments)			
@SEGMENT		1	Hard-code segment attribute to 1.
AJTGRUND	ADX02	06	EDI reason code. Will map to SAP code during IDoc processing in table T053E: by company code, external reason code, and internal SAP reason code.
MOABETRG	ADX01	-18.09	Deduction amount
MOAWAERS	CUR02	USD	Header level payment currency
E1IDPU1—Line item details—ADX adjustments payment only			
@SEGMENT		1	Hard-code segment attribute to 1.
DOCNAME	ADX03	CRM	Qualifier identifying credit memo where ADX03 = CM. IDoc debit memo would be DBM and ADX03 would = E2.
DOCNUMMR	ADX04	1865151339	Gordy's credit memo number
E1IDPU5—Line item level amounts—Min 1, Max 10			
@SEGMENT		1	Hard-code segment attribute to 1.
MOAQUAL		007	Qualifier identifies deduction amount
MOABETR	ADX01	-180.09	Amount of deduction from payment
CUXWAERZ	CUR02	USD	Header level payment currency
E1EDP02—Line item level documents—Min 0, Max 4—Loop 1			
@SEGMENT		1	Hard-code segment attribute to 1.

Table 18.3 Mapping the X12 820 to the REMADV.PEXR2003 IDoc (Cont.)

REMADV	820	Sample Value	Comments
QUALF		014	Qualifier identifies accounting document in customer's system
BELNR	RMR02	1865151339	Credit memo number
E1EDPU2—Line item level deductions—Min 0, Max 100			
@SEGMENT		1	Hard-code segment attribute to 1.
AJTGRUND	ADX02	RL	EDI reason code. Will map to SAP reason code during IDoc processing.
MOABETRG	ADX01	-18.09	Deduction amount
MOAWAERS		USD	Hard-code
E1EDLU5—Total Amounts—Min 0, Max 10			
@SEGMENT		1	Hard-code segment attribute to 1.
MOAQUAL		002	Qualifier identifying sum total payment amount for remittance
MOABETR	BPR02		Total amount of payment from X12 header level
CUXWAERZ	CUR02		Payment currency of payer

Table 18.3 Mapping the X12 820 to the REMADV.PEXR2003 IDoc (Cont.)

Running totals of the item-level amounts within the interchange, whether split or unsplit, are kept during mapping. This is the syntax for this accumulation:

```
PU1_TOTAL = PU1_TOTAL + RMR04 OR ADX01
```

At the end of the mapping loop for each transaction set, the running total for the items is compared to the header total for the transaction in BPR02. If there's a discrepancy, a transaction-level error is returned, and the map fails.

The running total in PU1_TOTAL is then cleared for the next transaction in the interchange.

For split interchanges, additional running totals are kept for all header-level and item level totals across the entire interchange. This is the correct syntax:

```
KU1_TOTAL = KU1_TOTAL + BPR02
SPLIT_PU1_TOTAL = SPLIT_PU1_TOTAL + RMR04 OR ADX01
```

At the end of the mapping loop on the interchange, `SPLIT_PU1_TOTAL` is compared to `KU1_TOTAL`. If there is a discrepancy, a split interchange error is thrown, and the map fails.

We can also, if needed at the summary level of the IDoc, keep running totals for discounts, deductions, taxes, credit memos, debit memos, and so on.

The sold-to partner posts to the account field of the payment advice in SAP. It is identified from the SNDPRN field of the IDoc control segment. There are no partner mappings from the 820 N1 segment, and there is no external partner conversion read of EDPAR for the REMADV IDoc in SAP.

The external payment adjustment reason code is mapped to the IDoc and passed to function `REMADV_INSERT`, which posts the payment advice. The external reason code is converted to the internal SAP reason code during IDoc processing by reading table T053E (the reason code conversion table) before the payment advice is posted. Both the external and internal SAP reason codes are posted to the payment advice. Table T053E is maintained in the IMG.

18.6   EDI Configuration in SAP

We have some additional configuration in the IMG for the REMADV IDoc that we did not have for other IDocs, including linking the sold-to partner to Acme's company code and maintaining the external to internal reason code mapping table.

18.6.1 EDPAR Entries

There are no EDPAR entries for the 820-REMADV interface.

18.6.2 Company Code to Sold-to Party Transaction OCBA

Each sold-to party who will send an EDI payment must be linked to Acme's company code in table T076B.

Table T076B is read for the company code mapping during processing of the E1EDKA1 partner segment using the SNDPRN value from the IDoc control segment. If there is no hit, the control segment field RCVPRN, which stores the logical system for the receiving SAP system, will be used to read the company code in table T001. If there is no hit in T001, an error is returned and IDoc processing stops.

Call Transaction OBCA, click NEW ENTRIES, and enter the following values:

▶ PARTN.TYPE: "KU" for customer

▶ PARTNERNO: "GRDY01" for Gordy's sold-to

▶ COCD: "3000" for Acme's company code

We won't enter a value into the company code name field. If we do, it must exactly match the name sent by Gordy in E1EDKA1-NAME1 where PARVW = RE.

Save the entry. The completed entry should look like Figure 18.3.

Partn.Type	PartnerNo	Comp.code name in the invoice	CoCd
KU	GRDY01		3000

Figure 18.3 Linking the Sold-to Partner to Acme's Company Code

18.6.3 Reason Code Conversion

Reason codes tell us why a payment was adjusted. They describe over- or underpayments and can be used in clearing when no adjustment document is referenced, such as a credit memo.

There are 481 standard reason codes in X12 version 005010 in ADX02 (data element 0426). Whatever reason codes Gordy is using in their own system will map to the X12 codes.

We can define as many reason codes as we need in SAP and then map them to any external codes. The contents and configuration of the reason codes is for the business users and functional consultants. Our job is to map reason codes we'll be receiving from Gordy to reason codes set up for payment processing in SAP.

Reason codes are created against a company code in the IMG (Transaction SPRO) using menu path FINANCIAL ACCOUNTING • ACCOUNTS RECEIVABLE AND ACCOUNTS

PAYABLE • BUSINESS TRANSACTIONS • INCOMING PAYMENTS • INCOMING PAYMENTS GLOBAL SETTINGS • OVERPAYMENT/UNDERPAYMENT • DEFINE REASON CODES. They are stored in tables T053R (Classification of Payment Differences) and T053S, which stores the text descriptions.

We'll assume that the reason codes have already been created. Users must also define a version for the reason code conversion. The version allows for multiple reason code mappings within the same company code. The menu path is the same except the activity at the end, which is DEFINE REASON CODE CONVERSION VERSION.

We'll assume that this has also been done. The reason code mapping is done by activity Define Conversion of Payment Difference Reason Codes and stored in table T053E.

Click the activity and the DETERMINE WORK AREA: ENTRY dialog pops up. Enter company code "3000" and click the green check mark to open the overview screen.

Click the NEW ENTRIES button and enter the following values:

▶ VERSION: "CUS"

▶ EXT.REASN CODE: 06 = X12 quantities contested

▶ REASON CODE: "CT", which was configured by our finance team earlier for contested quantities.

Save the entry. The completed screen should look like Figure 18.4.

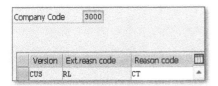

Figure 18.4 Reason Code Mapping in SAP

18.6.4 ZEDIXREF Entries

Custom EDI trading partner cross-reference table ZEDIXREF is populated with the entries shown in Table 18.4 for the inbound 820 interface from Gordy's Galaxy.

Field	Value	Description
DIRECT	2	Direction inbound
STDMES	820	EDI transaction
MESTYP	REMADV	IDoc message type
IDOCTP	PEXR2003	IDoc basic type
CIMTYP		IDoc extension
SNDPRN	GRDY01	SAP send partner
RCVPRN	DEVCLNT100	SAP receive partner
SNDLAD	99934567999	EDI send trading partner ID
RCVLAD	99999998889	EDI receive trading partner ID

Table 18.4 Trading Partner Mapping for Gordy's 820 Payment Advice

18.6.5 Inbound Partner Profile Transaction WE20

We'll need an inbound partner profile for Gordy's Galaxy partner number GRDY01, partner type KU (customer), and partner role BP (bill-to) with message type REMADV.

In the inbound parameters table control of the partner profile for Gordy's Galaxy, click CREATE OUTBOUND PARAMETERS and enter the following values in the OUT-BOUND PARAMETERS screen, as shown in Figure 18.5.

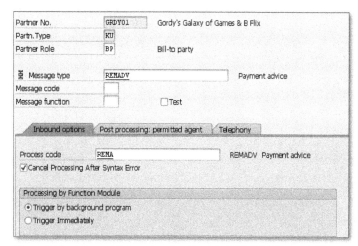

Figure 18.5 Inbound Parameters for Gordy's REMADV Payment IDoc

- Partner Role: "BP"

- Message Type: "INVOIC"

- Process Code: "REMA"

- Processing by Function Module area: Trigger by background program radio button

Don't forget to save the partner profile.

Process code REMA posts to a payment advice without triggering clearing. It links to function module `IDOC_INPUT_REMADV`. Clearing is done later by accounts receivable using Transaction F-28.

Process code REMC creates the payment advice and automatically triggers follow-up clearing. It links to function `IDOC_INPUT_REMADV_CTR`.

18.7 Summary

Right about now the great Darryl Q. Fernhausen would be smiling happily and ordering a second martini at the perennially film noir Formosa Café, his favorite Hollywood watering hole.

The money is in the bank, accounts receivable have been cleared, and the profits on his sales have been posted to his books. You wouldn't blame him for thinking that the world is his oyster.

Let's review. The overall process is fairly straightforward. An X12 820 interchange is sent when an electronic payment is made to Acme's bank. It is translated to a REMADV.PEXR2003 IDoc that posts to a payment advice in SAP. The payment advice is then used to clear accounts receivable.

Of course, there were some knotty issues to unravel before the remittance could post and receivables clear, mostly having to do with size.

Though Acme's most important customer Gordy's Galaxy of Games & B Flix only sends about four or five payments a month, one of these 820s can be very large, especially around the holiday shopping season—so large that it could trigger a program dump in SAP if it were converted directly to an IDoc.

We handled this issue by describing the logic for a script that would count the number of segments in each incoming 820. If this number equaled 50,000 or more, the script would split the interchange into multiple 820 transaction sets of less than 50,000 segments each.

We also saw that payment advice notes with more than 999 line items had to be split by a standard SAP program into multiple smaller documents before they could be cleared.

We noted the extra configuration steps for the inbound REMADV message. These include linking the sold-partner for the customer sending an 820 to the Acme company code and mapping external to internal SAP reason codes for payment adjustments.

All in all this is a very interesting interface that poses stimulating challenges for the EDI developer both in and out of SAP. And it's one that has a very high profile so it's important to get it right.

The inbound remittance advice closes the order-to-cash cycle and ends our exploration of Acme's key EDI interfaces. It's time now to move on and look at extending the IDoc interface with some custom utilities in Act IV.

ACT IV
Finishing Touches

"Work with me, baby!" Darryl Q would plead with his actors when they couldn't feel his vision for a role. We all need a helping hand sometimes — and it's no different for Acme's SAP system. Luckily the IDoc interface provides plenty of opportunity to help us help ourselves. So let's look at some useful utilities that will shed light on how to extend the IDoc interface with a little bit of creative ABAP.

19 Extending the Interface: Custom IDoc Tools

Developers love their tools. We build them in response to needs that crop up during the course of a project. Our toolkits are more than just a collection of programming tools, utilities, and processes: They are memories of people, projects, and challenges that were met with persistence and creativity.

SAP provides particularly rich opportunities to build custom solutions to our own unique problems. ABAP is a simple and elegant programming language with powerful data-processing capabilities. The SAP Data Dictionary is a cornucopia of business, application, and programming data and metadata.

The IDoc interface is a sublime and consistent development platform largely implemented through standard function and method calls that are easy to use in our own programs. All it takes is a little time and effort to understand how it all works together.

Darryl Q. Fernhausen, the legendary founder of Acme Pictures, may not have been a programmer, but he knew that we are only limited by our imagination. And the requirements of the project.

So let's roll up our sleeves and step through four solutions that we may find useful during implementation and production support:

▸ EDI to IDoc trading partner conversion with custom table ZEDIXREF

▸ Partner profile mass upload

▸ Mass transfer of IDocs from one SAP client to another

▸ Sending IDoc status from SAP to an external system

We'll end our exploration by briefly stepping into the realm of XML schema development to add qualifiers to an IDoc XSD exported from SAP.

And once again, please remember that nothing is presented here as a final solution—only as a starting point for your own explorations.

19.1   EDI to IDoc Trading Partner Conversion

Tinkering with the code deep inside the IDoc interface has led to countless hours spent figuring out how to use the IDoc control segment to meet different needs in different places.

That's how we ran into enhancement SIDOC001. It has only one exit—EXIT_ SAPLEDI1_001—called from a strategic location during inbound and outbound processing: just before the IDoc is written to the database.

SIDOC001 provides a last-chance opportunity to add custom values to the control record before the IDoc is written to the database and prepped either for export (outbound) or for inbound application processing.

19.1.1   The Issue

The issue is about different systems and different needs. SAP can only process an IDoc if the SAP partner number is in the SNDPRN (inbound) or RCVPRN (outbound) fields of the control segment.

The EDI RIM can't identify, translate, or route IDocs and EDI messages unless it has the EDI sending and receiving trading partner IDs.

On the inbound, the EDI RIM can't pass the SAP partner number to the SNDPRN field unless it's hard-coded in the map or stored in a custom cross-reference table and accessed by a process before the IDoc is sent into SAP. The RIM stores partner information by EDI trading partner ID, not SAP customer or vendor numbers.

On the outbound, SAP can't pass the EDI trading partner IDs unless they are stored in a custom cross-reference table, accessed by a user exit and inserted into the control segment before the IDoc is sent to the EDI RIM.

So we need a cross-reference table and custom code to read it, either in the RIM or in SAP. Acme Pictures decided to keep these data and development in SAP.

19.1.2 The Solution

Build and populate table ZEDIXREF to link the SAP EDI partner number to the EDI trading partner ID and transaction for both inbound and outbound interfaces. We will enter one record for each interface.

ZEDIXREF will have a maintenance dialog for data entry with Transaction SM30.

The table will be read in a custom modification project—ZEDITPXR—in EXIT_ SAPLEDI1_001 from enhancement SIDOC001. The user exit code runs during both outbound and inbound processing, so we need to determine the direction of the IDoc at runtime.

During outbound processing, the SAP send and receive partners and the message type are used to get the EDI trading partner IDs from ZEDIXREF and insert them into the RCVLAD and SNDLAD fields of the control record before the IDoc is written to the database and exported to the EDI RIM.

The RIM then uses the EDI trading partner IDs and message type in the control segment to identify the envelopes, translation map, and the target destination for the converted X12 transaction.

During inbound processing, the EDI partner IDs in RCVLAD and SNDLAD and the message type are used to get the SAP send and receive partners from ZEDIXREF and insert them into SNDPRN and RCVPRN of the control record before the partner profile is checked and the IDoc written to the database.

The structure of table ZEDIXREF and the read keys for outbound and inbound processing are detailed in Chapter 7, Section 7.4.4, subsection ZEDIXREF: Custom EDI SAP Trading Partner ID Conversion.

19.1.3 Development Work Flow

We will need to create the following objects to implement this exit:

▶ Custom EDI to SAP partner conversion table ZEDIXREF

▶ Custom function group ZVEDI for the maintenance screen that we will also use for other custom EDI functions

- Maintenance screen for table ZEDIXREF

- Modification project ZEDITPXR using enhancement SIDOC001

- User exit code in include program `ZXEDIU01` for `EXIT_SAPLEDI1_001`.

We will create table ZEDIXREF in the Data Dictionary either with Transaction SE11 or the Object Navigator, with Transaction SE80, or by clicking EDIT OBJECT • DICTIONARY • DATABASE TABLE.

1. Enter "ZEDIXREF" into the DATABASE TABLE field, and click CREATE to open the MAINTAIN TABLE screen.

2. Enter a text description in the SHORT DESCRIPTION field.

3. In the DELIVERY AND MAINTENANCE tab, enter the following:

   - DELIVERY CLASS: "A" for Application table

   - DATA BROWSER/TABLE VIEW MAINT.: DISPLAY/MAINTENANCE ALLOWED to generate a maintenance screen for data entry with Transaction SM30 for the custom table

4. Type the field and data element names in the FIELDS tab displayed in Figure 19.1.

5. Save the table and assign it to a package and a change request.

Transp. Table	ZEDIXREF	Active				
Short Description	EDI to SAP trading partner mapping table					

Attributes / Delivery and Maintenance / Fields / Entry help/check / Currency/Quantity Fields

Srch Help   Predefined Type   1 / 10

Field	K..	I...	Data element	Data Type	Len...	Dec...	Short Description
MANDT	✓	✓	MANDT	CLNT	3	0	Client
DIRECT	✓	✓	EDI_DIRECT	CHAR	1	0	Direction for IDoc
STDMES	✓	✓	EDI_STDMES	CHAR	6	0	EDI message type
MESTYP	✓	✓	EDI_MESTYP	CHAR	30	0	Message Type
IDOCTP	✓	✓	EDI_IDOCTP	CHAR	30	0	Basic type
CIMTYP	☐	☐	EDI_CIMTYP	CHAR	30	0	Extension
SNDPRN	☐	☐	EDI_SNDPRN	CHAR	10	0	Partner Number of Sender
RCVPRN	☐	☐	EDI_RCVPRN	CHAR	10	0	Partner Number of Receiver
SNDLAD	☐	☐	EDI_SNDLAD	CHAR	70	0	Logical address of sender
RCVLAD	☐	☐	EDI_RCVLAD	CHAR	70	0	Logical address of recipient

Figure 19.1 Field and Data Elements for Table ZEDIXREF

6. Click the TECHNICAL SETTINGS button. In the MAINTAIN TECHNICAL SETTING screen, enter the following values:

   ▶ DATA CLASS: "APPL1" for transaction data

   ▶ SIZE CATEGORY: "0" for 0 to 2,300 records

   ▶ Default for all other options

7. Activate the technical settings by clicking the activate icon.

8. Return to the MAINTAIN TABLE screen and activate table ZEDIXREF.

Create Function Group ZVEDI

Our custom table is ready to be populated. Next we'll create a custom function group that we will use for the maintenance screen and for other EDI utilities that we will put into function modules.

Function groups can be created with Transaction SE37, menu option GOTO • FUNCTION GROUPS • CREATE GROUP or in the repository information system with Transaction SE80 by clicking button EDIT OBJECT and selecting the FUNCTION GROUP tab.

We'll use a slightly different, more direct, technique.

1. Go to the repository information system with Transaction SE80.

2. Select FUNCTION GROUP from the dropdown list in the navigation panel and enter the name of a custom function group: "ZVEDI".

3. Press ⌊Enter⌋. A pop-up will point out that function group ZVEDI does not exist and will ask to create the object. Click Yes.

4. The CREATE FUNCTION GROUP dialog will pop up. Enter a text description and click SAVE (as shown in Figure 19.2).

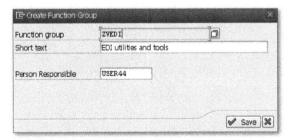

Figure 19.2 Custom Function Group for EDI Utilities

5. Assign the object to a change request when prompted and the function group will be created.

6. Note that the function group has two include programs: `LZVEDITOP` and `LZVE-DIUXX`. Never change the names of either of these includes.

   ▸ If we create a function module in our custom function group, all data declarations and global variables will go into `LZVEDITOP`.

   ▸ `LZVEDIUXX` will hold the parameters and main code for all function modules created in generated include programs.

We will leave the function group for now. We are ready to generate a maintenance screen.

Create Maintenance Screen

Meanwhile, back at the Data Dictionary, the maintenance screen for table ZEDIXREF is waiting to be created.

1. Select menu option UTILITIES • TABLE MAINTENANCE GENERATOR in the MAINTAIN TABLE screen.

2. The GENERATE MAINTENANCE DIALOG screen opens. Enter the following values:

   ▸ In the AUTHORIZATION GROUP field, enter either a custom or standard group name, depending on your security requirements and policies.

   ▸ In the FUNCTION GROUP field, enter the custom function group `ZVEDI` that we just created.

   ▸ In the MAINTENANCE TYPE field, choose the TWO STEP radio button, which provides an overview and details data entry screen.

   ▸ MAINT. SCREEN NO.: Enter "100" and "200".

The default selections are fine for the rest. The screen should look like Figure 19.3.

3. Select menu path GENERATED OBJECTS • CREATE. The system prompts you to assign the maintenance screen to a change request. After this is done, the screen is created and a generation log is returned.

4. Confirm that the maintenance screen exists with Transaction SM30. Enter the table name and click MAINTAIN. The OVERVIEW screen appears first.

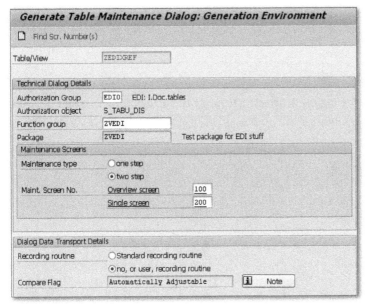

Figure 19.3 Generating the Data Entry Screens for ZEDIXREF

5. Click NEW ENTRIES, and the data entry detail screen will open, as displayed in Figure 19.4.

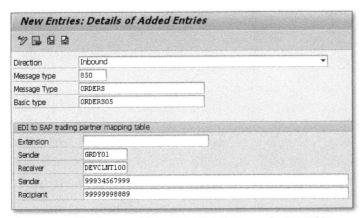

Figure 19.4 The Generated Data Entry Details Screen for ZEDIXREF

6. Begin entering SAP-EDI trading partner cross-reference data. Save each record entered.

Now that we have the table and a maintenance screen, we can move on to the exit code.

19.1.4 Writing the Code

Figure 19.5 outlines the logical processing flow for the EDI and SAP partner updates to the IDoc control segment in the exit code in modification project ZEDITPXR.

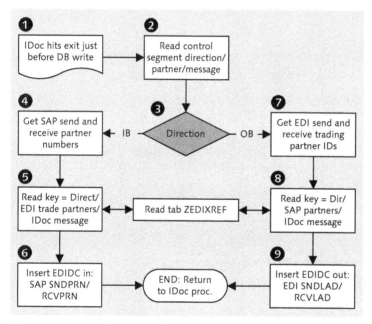

Figure 19.5 Logical Processing Flow for Modification Project ZEDITPXR

It is a pretty straightforward piece of code, regardless of direction. The exit is called just before the IDoc is written to the database. During inbound processing, the partner profile has not been read yet. An SQL statement reads the table and, if there's a hit, the IDoc control segment is updated.

There are a couple of gotchas that we need to be aware of. This exit is called for every inbound or outbound IDoc. Processing should be restricted to the messages and partners that we want to call it. We should not return a fatal error if the SQL read of ZEDIXREF fails.

We begin by creating modification project ZEDITPXR in CMOD. Don't forget to save the project and assign it to a package and a change request. We use enhancement SIDOC001 with component `EXIT_SAPLEDI1_001`. Double-click the component, and then double-click `INCLUDE ZXEDIU01` in the function builder to create the exit program and assign it to a package and a change request.

Before we begin coding, let's look at how our exit is used. It's called by function `EDI_DOCUMENT_OPEN_FOR_CREATE`, which itself is one of the first tasks invoked by function `IDOC_CREATE_ON_DATABASE` before the IDoc has been checked, assigned a number, and written to the database.

`EDI_DOCUMENT_OPEN_FOR_CREATE` calls the exit immediately, before it does anything else. The function call is in Listing 19.1.

```
CALL CUSTOMER-FUNCTION '001'
     EXPORTING CONTROL_IN = IDOC_CONTROL
     IMPORTING CONTROL_OUT = IDOC_CONTROL.
```

Listing 19.1 Call Syntax for EXIT_SAPLEDI1_001

It has only two parameters: control segment in and control segment out. The current control segment is passed in and out, allowing us to add or change any value in the control record.

After the exit completes its work, `EDI_DOCUMENT_OPEN_FOR_CREATE` checks the control segment to ensure that all mandatory fields, including MESTYP, IDOCTP, SNDPRT, SNDPRN, RCVPRT, RCVPRN, and others, are populated with valid values. Errors are returned, and the IDoc fails if any are empty or invalid.

The initial IDoc status record is also created, and the status set to 01—*IDoc generated*—for outbound or 50—*IDoc added*—for inbound.

When processing is returned to `IDOC_CREATE_ON_DATABASE`, the IDoc data segments are built, status records are assembled, an IDoc number is assigned, additional syntax checks are run, and the control, data, and status records are written to the IDoc database.

During inbound processing, the partner profile is checked after the IDoc has been written to the database by `IDOC_CREATE_ON_DATABASE`. We can add the SAP partner numbers to SNDPRN and RCVPRN through our exit and they will pass all checks in the IDoc interface, including the partner profile.

Our first logical requirement is to restrict the control records updated to our EDI IDocs. We can use the EDI transaction field in STDMES, since we'll be populating it only for EDI IDocs:

```
*Only change control segment for EDI IDocs
IF NOT CONTROL_IN-STDMES IS INITIAL.
ENDIF.
```

Processing will immediately end for any IDoc that does not pass this check and control returned to the calling function.

We also need to distinguish between inbound and outbound interfaces, as shown in Listing 19.2.

```
*IDENTIFY IDOC DIRECTION -- 1 = OUTBOUND PROCESSING
  IF CONTROL_IN-DIRECT = '1'.
*INBOUND PROCESSING
  ELSE.
  ENDIF.
```

Listing 19.2 Distinguishing between Inbound and Outbound Interfaces

For inbound processing, we pull the SAP partner numbers from ZEDIXREF and put them into the SNDPRN and RCVPRN fields of the CONTROL_OUT export parameter. We do this with the SQL statement in Listing 19.3.

```
*GET SAP PARTNER NUMBERS FOR INBOUND IDOCS

SELECT SINGLE RCVPRN SNDPRN INTO (CONTROL_OUT-RCVPRN,
                                  CONTROL_OUT-SNDPRN)
    FROM ZEDIXREF WHERE DIRECT = CONTROL_IN-DIRECT
                  AND STDMES = CONTROL_IN-STDMES
                  AND MESTYP = CONTROL_IN-MESTYP
                  AND IDOCTP = CONTROL_IN-IDOCTP
                  AND CIMTYP = CONTROL_IN-CIMTYP
                  AND SNDLAD = CONTROL_IN-SNDLAD
                  AND RCVLAD = CONTROL_IN-RCVLAD.
```

Listing 19.3 Reading SAP Partner Numbers during Inbound Processing

During outbound processing we read the EDI trading partner IDs into the RCVLAD and SNDLAD fields of the CONTROL_OUT export parameter using the SQL statement in Listing 19.4.

```
*GET EDI TRADING PARTNER ID'S FOR OUTBOUND IDOCS
SELECT SINGLE RCVLAD SNDLAD INTO (CONTROL_OUT-RCVLAD,
                                  CONTROL_OUT-SNDLAD)
      FROM ZEDIXREF WHERE DIRECT = CONTROL_IN-DIRECT
                      AND STDMES = CONTROL_IN-STDMES
                      AND MESTYP = CONTROL_IN-MESTYP
                      AND IDOCTP = CONTROL_IN-IDOCTP
                      AND CIMTYP = CONTROL_IN-CIMTYP
                      AND SNDPRN = CONTROL_IN-SNDPRN
                      AND RCVPRN = CONTROL_IN-RCVPRN.
```

Listing 19.4 Getting EDI Trading Partner IDs during Outbound Processing

There's another very important gotcha. Even if nothing is changed in this code—even if the exit function in INCLUDE ZXEDIU01 is activated but no code is written—control_in must be copied to control_out; otherwise the control segment will be initialized and the IDoc will fail at status 56—*IDoc with errors added*.

The calling program uses control_out to complete the control segment that is written to the IDoc database *if the exit is active*. If control_in is not copied to it, control_out will be blank and the IDoc will fail with no control segment.

Save and activate the code. Navigate back to the selection screen of the modification project and activate it by selecting menu option PROJECT • ACTIVATE PROJECT.

19.2 Mass Upload of Partner Profiles to SAP

Like many ABAP programmers, we started out writing batch data communications (BDC) programs to load master data into SAP from ASCII flat files.

Our next ABAP utility (ZEDI_UPLDPP) isn't all that different from these old-fashioned BDCs. You load a file, fill internal tables with data, and then pass the populated tables to an application.

Instead of calling a transaction or creating and running a batch input session, we will pass our internal tables to the same standard function modules that SAP uses to create or change partner profiles with Transaction WE20.

The program behind Transaction WE20, `SAPMSEDIPARTNER`, is old-school ABAP, with some object-oriented event handling, that builds its internal tables and calls the following functions in function group `EDI6` to create or change partner profiles:

- `EDI_AGREE_PARTNER_INSERT`: Inserts new partner profile header in table EDPP1

- `EDI_AGREE_OUT_MESSTYPE_INSERT`: Creates outbound partner profile in table EDP13.

- `EDI_AGREE_OUT_IDOC_INSERT`: Inserts message control record for outbound partner profile in table EDP12

- `EDI_AGREE_IN_MESSTYPE_INSERT`: Inserts new inbound partner profile in table EDP21

- `EDI_AGREE_OUT_MESSTYPE_UPDATE`: Changes an existing outbound partner profile

- `EDI_AGREE_OUT_IDOC_UPDATE`: Updates existing message control record for outbound partner profile

- `EDI_AGREE_IN_MESSTYPE_UPDATE`: Changes existing inbound partner profile

Our custom ABAP utility only adds the ability to create or change more than one partner profile at a time.

This utility takes advantage of standard IDoc interface functionality and is a great way to learn more about how SAP processes partner profiles.

19.2.1 The Issue

Partner profiles can't be transported from one client to another. On a typical project they are created or changed manually every time there is a move to a new client or environment. This happens frequently during a project lifecycle, particularly as we gear up for multiple rounds of integration and performance testing and for cutover to the production system.

So this task can be tedious and time-consuming, particularly if a large number of partners are set up each time. Life would be simpler if we could just run a program that would upload our partner profiles from stable text files each time we needed to rebuild them.

19.2.2 The Solution

We will write an ABAP program (ZEDI_UPLDPP) to load partner profiles from three text files that will be maintained in a Microsoft Access database, along with other EDI trading partner data collected from spreadsheets and other sources.

The text files provide the data feed needed to populate the following partner profile master tables in SAP:

- EDP13: Outbound
- EDP12: Outbound message control
- EDP21: Inbound

The structure of the outbound partner profile text load file for EDP13 is detailed in Table 19.1.

Field Name	Length	Value	Description
RCVPRN	10	GRDY01	SAP receive partner
RCVPRT	2	KU	Receive partner type: customer
RCVPFC	2	BP	Receive partner function: bill-to
MESTYP	30	INVOIC	IDoc message type: Invoice
MESCOD	3		Message code
MESFCT	3		Message function
OUTMODE	1	3	Output mode: Collect IDocs, transfer, and start external subsystem
RCVPOR	10	XML_IDOC	Receive port: EDI file port
IDOCTYP	30	INVOIC02	IDoc basic type
CIMTYP	30		IDoc extension
STD	1	X	EDI standard: X12
STDVRS	6	005010	Version of EDI standard
STDMES	6	810	EDI transaction/message type
EDIVIEW	30		IDoc view

Table 19.1 Outbound Partner Profile File Structure with Sample Value

Table 19.2 details the structure of the outbound partner profile message control configuration text load file for EDP12.

Field Name	Length	Value	Description
RCVPRN	10	GRDY01	SAP receive partner
RCVPRT	2	KU	Receive partner type: Customer
RCVPFC	2	BP	Receive partner function: Bill-to
KAPPL	2	V3	Application: Billing
KSCHL	4	ZD00	Message (output) type
EVCODA	30	SD09	Process code
MESTYP	30	INVOIC	IDoc message type: Invoice
MESCOD	3		Message code
MESFCT	3		Message function

Table 19.2 Outbound Partner Profile Message Control File Structure

Table 19.3 details the structure of the inbound partner profile text load file for EDP21.

Field Name	Length	Value	Description
SNDPRN	10	GRDY01	SAP send partner
SNDPRT	2	KU	Send partner type: Customer
SNDPFC	2	SP	Receive partner function: Sold-to
MESTYP	30	ORDERS	IDoc message type: Invoice
MESCOD	3		Message code
MESFCT	3		Message function
EVCODE	30	ORDE	Process code
INMODE	1	3	Processing mode: Trigger by background program

Table 19.3 Inbound Partner Profile Text File Structure

The program can load partner profiles for all partner types but we'll only use it for customers and vendors.

19.2.3 Dependencies

Customer and vendor master records for all EDI partners must be loaded into SAP before we can build partner profiles.

Output control must be configured and condition tables populated for all output types and EDI partners.

A table is built in the external database to hold partner profile data for each of the load files. The structure of each table mirrors the structure of its corresponding load file as detailed in the tables above.

An extract of all EDI vendors and sold-to partner numbers is pulled into an ASCII file from table KNA1 (customer master) and table LFA1 (vendor master).

The partner number extract is imported into the access database and stored in a table that is updated with partner types KU for customers and LI for vendor. An extract is also pulled from each output type condition table with the following values:

- Application
- Output type
- Partner number

The two SAP extracts provide the feed data to begin building the partner profile extract tables for EDP13, EDP12, and EDP21. The three tables can be populated through a mix of update queries on the SAP extracts and manual data entry to capture all the gaps.

After the partner profile tables have been populated, a query is created for each to sort and export the partner profile table data to three ASCII flat files for use by our load utility.

Changes to partner profiles can be maintained in the local database and loaded to SAP by ZEDI_UPLDPP, at least through the development and test phases of the project.

19.2.4 Coding ZEDI_UPLDPP

At its most basic, ZEDI_UPLDPP loads three text files from a local PC directory (or the application server) and moves them into internal tables that have the structure of the partner profile tables in SAP. These internal tables drive creation or change of the partner profiles by the program.

It loops on the partner number at the header level and first checks if the partner profile already exists. If it does not, it creates a new partner profile by calling the relevant create functions for the inbound (EDP21) or outbound (EDP13 and EDP12) tables.

If the partner profile exists, it calls change functions for the partner profiles and updates them with the internal table values.

Once the partner profiles are created or any errors are identified, it builds an internal table for a report and outputs it as an ALV list report.

Figure 19.6 outlines the processing flow for the partner profile upload program ZEDI_UPLDPP.

ZEDI_UPLDPP has a simple structure composed of the following elements:

▶ Table declarations

▶ Selection screen definition

▶ Type, internal table, string, and field variable declarations

▶ ALV list report data declarations, including type pools, internal table, string, and variable definitions

▶ A report header include program for the ALV list report

▶ An ABAP INITIALIZATION event

▶ A START-OF-SELECTION event that modularizes program functions in discrete form routines:

   ▶ Form 000: Initialize internal tables and strings

   ▶ Form 010: Upload input files and pass to internal tables

   ▶ Form 020: Build internal tables used to load the partner profiles

   ▶ Form 030: Create partner profiles and build a status report table

▶ Form 040: ALV report housekeeping, including defining sort order and appending report titles

▶ Form 050: Build ALV list report field catalog

▶ Form 060: Call the ALV list report function to output report

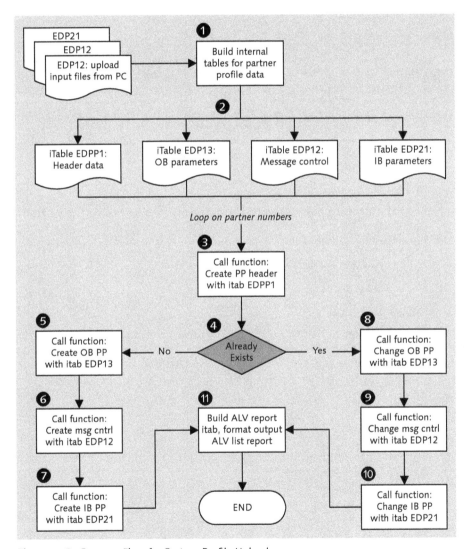

Figure 19.6 Program Flow for Partner Profile Upload

The selection screen for `ZEDI_UPLDPP` in Figure 19.7 points to the input files that will be used to load the partner profiles.

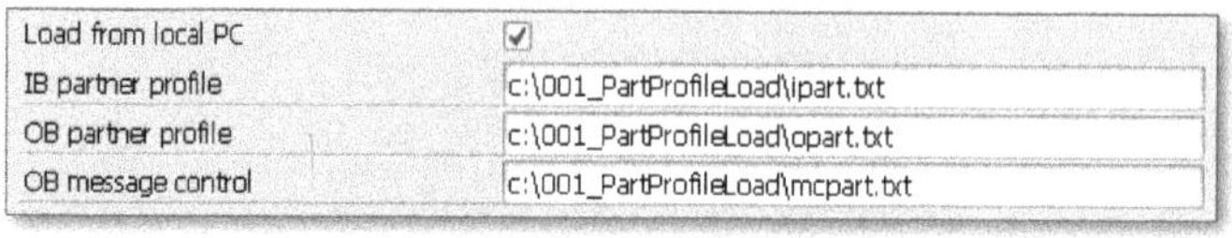

Load from local PC	☑
IB partner profile	c:\001_PartProfileLoad\ipart.txt
OB partner profile	c:\001_PartProfileLoad\opart.txt
OB message control	c:\001_PartProfileLoad\mcpart.txt

Figure 19.7 Selection Screen for ZEDI_UPLDPP

First we create `ZEDI_UPLDPP` using Transaction SE38 or, from the Object Navigator SE80, the path EDIT OBJECT • PROGRAM • CREATE. We'll use the following attributes:

▶ TITLE: Partner profile upload utility

▶ TYPE: Executable program

▶ STATUS: Customer production program

▶ APPLICATION: Cross-application

The table declaration points to the key partner profile tables:

▶ EDPP1: Partner profile header

▶ EDKP1: Key structure for EDPP1

▶ EDP12: Message control

▶ EDP13: Outbound profile

▶ EDP21: Inbound profile

Types are declared for each of the three input files matching the structures in Table 19.1, Table 19.2, and Table 19.3. Listing 19.5 declares the structure of the status report.

```
*** Type for output of report detail
types: begin of t_out,
       parnum type edipparnum,
       partyp type edippartyp,
       direct(03) type c,
       parfunc type ediprcvpfc,
       mescod type edipmescod,
       mesfct type edipmesfct,
       mestyp type edipmestyp,
       stdmes type edi_pvstdm,
       msg(70) type c,
```

```
      ok_flg(01) type c,
    end of t_out.
```
Listing 19.5 Status Report Type Structure

Internal tables are declared to load the partner profiles, read the data from the three input files, and output the status report, as described in Listing 19.6.

```
*** Partner profile load tables
data: gt_edpp1 type standard table of edpp1
        with header line,
      gt_edp12 type standard table of edp12
        with header line,
      gt_edp13 type standard table of edp13
        with header line,
      gt_edp21 type standard table of edp21
        with header line,
      gt_parnum type standard table of t_parnum
        with header line.
*** Partner profile retrieval tables
data: gt_ifile type standard table of t_ifile
        with header line,
      gt_ofile type standard table of t_ofile
        with header line,
      gt_mcfile type standard table of t_mcfile
        with header line.
*** ALV report output table
data: iout type standard table of t_out with header line.
```
Listing 19.6 Partner Profile and Report Internal Tables

Next we declare tables and strings for our ALV list report referencing type pool SLIS to pass report data to function REUSE_ALV_LIST_DISPLAY, which outputs the ALV list report:

▶ IFIELDCAT TYPE SLIS_T_FIELDCAT_ALV and SFIELDCAT LIKE LINE OF IFIELDCAT: Passes the field catalog for the header and details tables used in the ALV list report

▶ ISORTCAT TYPE SLIS_T_SORTINFO_ALV and SSORTCAT LIKE LINE OF ISORTCAT: Defines ALV list report data sort order

▶ SLAYOUT TYPE SLIS_LAYOUT_ALV: Defines layout parameters for the report such as minimum line size

- ▶ IEVENTCAT TYPE SLIS_T_EVENT and SEVENTCAT LIKE LINE OF IEVENTCAT: Identifies ALV report events defined in type pool SLIS

START-OF-SELECTION processing begins. After all internal tables are initialized, form 010_GET_INPUT_FILES is called three times (once for each input file) to load the file with function GUI_UPLOAD.

The internal table name and the path and file name for each input file is passed to the routine. This is the call syntax:

```
perform: 000_get_input_files tables gt_ifile
                             using gs_filename rc.
```

RC returns the status of the upload from return code SY-SUBRC.

If GUI_UPLOAD successfully loads all input files into their internal tables, form 005_BUILD_DATA_TABS is called to build the tables that will be used to load the partner profiles.

First, all partners are identified from the input files and passed to internal table GT_PARNUM, which holds only the partner number and partner type. The build of each partner profile table then proceeds through a loop on GT_PARNUM, beginning with the build of EDPP1, which creates the partner profile header. The code to build EDPP1 is in Listing 19.7.

```
*** Collect partner profile header data in gt_edpp1
loop at gt_parnum.
  gt_edpp1-mandt = sy-mandt.
  gt_edpp1-parnum = gt_parnum-parnum.
  gt_edpp1-partyp = gt_parnum-partyp.
  gt_edpp1-matlvl = 'A'.
  gt_edpp1-usrtyp = 'US'.
  gt_edpp1-usrkey = sy-uname.
  gt_edpp1-usrlng = sy-langu.
  append gt_edpp1.
endloop.
```

Listing 19.7 Building the Partner Profile Header

Each subsequent partner profile table is built by looping on the internal table that holds the input file data, as in the code in Listing 19.8.

```
*** Collect inbound partner profile data in gt_edp21
Loop at gt_ifile.
```

```
  move-corresponding gt_ifile to gt_edp21.
  gt_edp21-mandt = sy-mandt.
  gt_edp21-synchk = 'X'.
  collect gt_edp21.
endloop.
sort gt_edp21 ascending.
```

Listing 19.8 Template for Building Partner Profile Internal Tables

Now comes the *pièce de résistance*, as they say: inserting or updating the partner profiles in form 010_CREATE_PARTNERS through another loop on GT_PARNUM. Each pass also builds the status report internal table IOUT.

This is a two-step process, as displayed in the code in Listing 19.9.

```
*** Loop thru partners, build report output tab
refresh: iout.
loop at gt_parnum.
  clear: iout.
  iout-parnum = gt_parnum-parnum.
  iout-partyp = gt_parnum-partyp.

*** create partner profile at header level
  perform create_header using iout-parnum
                              iout-partyp
                              pp_rc.
  if pp_rc = 0 or pp_rc = 2.

*** create partner profile detail
    perform create_parameters using pp_rc.
  endif.
endloop.
```

Listing 19.9 Two-Step Partner Profile Build Process

First form CREATE_HEADER is called to insert the partner profile header by calling function EDI_AGREE_PARTNER_INSERT using a string populated by internal table GT_EDPP1, as illustrated in Listing 19.10.

```
*** Move current record in itab gt_eddp1 to string
clear gs_edpp1.
move-corresponding gt_edpp1 to gs_edpp1.
call function 'EDI_AGREE_PARTNER_INSERT'
```

```
EXPORTING
  rec_edpp1             = gs_edpp1
EXCEPTIONS
  db_error              = 1
  entry_already_exist   = 2
  parameter_error       = 3
  others                = 4.
```

Listing 19.10 Calling the Partner Profile Header Function

If the partner profile doesn't exist, the record is inserted, and SY-SUBRC returns 0. This is passed to a variable (PP_RC) which drives the call to the insert functions to create the subsequent partner profile records for the current partner in GT_EDP21, GT_EDP13, and GT_EDP12.

If the partner profile exists, SY-SUBRC updates variable PP_RC with 2, which then drives the call to the update functions for the subsequent partner profile records for our current partner.

If SY-SUBRC returns an error code, an error message is appended to the status report table IOUT, and loop processing on the current partner in GT_PARNUM ends and the next partner, if present, is processed.

If PP_RC equals 0 or 2, the program creates or updates partner profiles by calling the appropriate function module.

Outbound records are processed first with a loop on GT_EDP13 into string GS_EDP13 for the current partner and partner type in GT_PARNUM. PP_RC is evaluated if 0 (the create function) is called or if 2 (the change function) is called with import parameter string GS_EDP13:

EDI_AGREE_OUT_MESSTYPE_INSERT where PP_RC = 0

EDI_AGREE_OUT_MESSTYPE_UPDATE where PP_RC = 2

If the insert or the update is successful, message control is processed by looping on GT_EDP12 into GS_EDP12 if the table is not null where:

RCVPRN = GS_EDP13-RCVPRN AND
RCVPRT = GS_EDP13-RCVPRT AND
RCVPFC = GS_EDP13-RCVPFC AND
MESTYP = GS_EDP13-MESTYP

String GS_EDP12 is passed as the import parameter to the relevant function:

```
EDI_AGREE_OUT_IDOC_INSERT where PP_RC = 0

EDI_AGREE_OUT_IDOC_UPDATE where PP_RC = 2
```

If the insert or update is successful, a success message is passed to IOUT in variable GS_MSG by calling form UPDATE_STATUS_REPORT along with the following values:

```
OUT
GS_EDP13-RCVPRN
GS_EDP13-MESCOD
GS_EDP13-MESFCT
GS_EDP13-MESTYP
GS_EDP13-STDMES
Y for success
```

If it fails, an error is passed to IOUT using the same form and variables except success, which is set to N.

The inbound partner profiles are processed in the same way: with a loop on GT_EDP21 into GS_EDP21 for the current partner and partner type in GT_PARNUM and a call to either:

```
EDI_AGREE_IN_MESSTYPE_INSERT where PP_RC = 0

EDI_AGREE_IN_MESSTYPE_UPDATE where PP_RC = 2
```

GS_EDP21 is passed to the function as the import parameter.

Success or failure is reported in the same way—by writing the message and calling form UPDATE_STATUS_REPORT with all relevant report values.

So now our partner profile is done, and the output report table is populated. It is a simple status report with a flat rather than hierarchical structure, so we don't need to set up a header and details table.

We do our ALV setup, build the field catalog, and write the report with a call to function REUSE_ALV_LIST_DISPLAY:

```
*** Call report display function
call function 'REUSE_ALV_LIST_DISPLAY'
  EXPORTING
    i_callback_program = repid
    is_layout          = layout
    it_fieldcat        = ifieldcat
```

```
    it_sort          = isortcat
    i_save           = 'A'
    it_events        = ieventcat
  TABLES
    t_outtab         = iout
  EXCEPTIONS
    program_error    = 1
    others           = 2.
```

Assign Transaction Code ZEDIPP

Last but not least, we will create a transaction code (ZEDIPP) for our new program.

1. Go to Maintain Transaction with Transaction SE93.

2. Enter transaction code "ZEDIPP" and click Create. Do the following in the Create Transaction dialog:

   ▶ Add a description of the transaction in the Short text field.

   ▶ Select Program and selection screen (report transaction) under Start Object.

3. Click OK to open the Create Report transaction screen. In the Program field, enter "ZEDI_UPLDPP".

4. Save the transaction code and assign it to a change request.

19.2.5 Further Automating Partner Profile Processing

It's not exactly accurate to say that partner profiles can't be transported from client to client. There is a feature in Transaction WE20 that allows export of a single partner profile to an IDoc under menu option Utilities • IDoc output.

This option exports one partner profile from a sending system in message type SYPART with basic type SYPART01, which was designed specifically to send partner profiles.

It calls function EDI_PARTNER_CREATE_SYPART01, which collects key data for the selected partner profile into structure EDK13 and then calls another function, EDI_PARTNER_SEND_IDOC, to get partner profile data for the key, populate the IDoc, and then send it to an external system by calling function MASTER_IDOC_DISTRIBUTE.

There are two problems: function `EDI_PARTNER_CREATE_SYPART01` will not send a partner profile to another SAP client, and there is no function to process and post an inbound SYPART IDoc.

In other words, you can send a partner profile in an IDoc in SAP but you cannot receive one.

For mass transfer of partner profiles between SAP clients, you could write send and receive code. It is not that difficult, but we would need to set up partner profiles in each system for message type SYPART.

The send program would run from the sending system. It would call function `EDI_PARTNER_SEND_IDOC` to identify and collect all selected partner profiles, build the SYPART.SYPART01 IDoc, and then send it to a file on the application server destined for the external system.

You would need an outbound partner profile in the sending system for the target system and message type SYPART. The partner type would be LS and the partner number would be the receiving logical system name. Point to a file or XML file port on the application server that can be reached by the receiving system and do not trigger the EDI sub-system.

The receiving process would be a little more complex, but not much. You could write a program that sweeps the application server directory for the SYPART file and calls function `EDI_DATA_INCOMING` if one were found. This imports the IDoc into the receiving system and writes it to the database.

We would then call a custom function to create the partner profiles from the IDoc. It would move partner profile data out of the IDoc into internal tables for EDPP1, EDP13, EDP12, and EDP21. The internal tables would then be used to call the partner profile functions we described for `ZEDI_UPLDPP`.

We would create an inbound partner profile for partner type LS and message type SYPART. The partner number would be the logical system name for the sending SAP system. We would also need a custom process code linked to our custom IDoc function and message type SYPART.

There would be some effort up front, but the pay-off is that we would only create partner profiles once in the development system and then cleanly transport them every time we needed to move to another system or client. Furthermore we would be able to track movement of our partner profiles through standard IDoc monitoring tools.

We could do this in a single step if we use a transactional RFC (tRFC) port and included a selection option for a target system's logical system name in our program code. Let's look at how this might work for a different IDoc transfer in the next section.

19.3 Mass Transfer of IDocs between Systems

Once upon a time there was a problem. The problem began with a question: How do you debug an unexpected error in custom IDoc code after it has been moved to production?

Security folks are notorious for frowning on developers rooting around in the guts of the production system. Luckily, most SAP sites maintain a QAS test client that is fairly regularly refreshed from PRD, providing a production-like environment for testing and debugging.

But we still don't have the IDoc that failed. This utility will move it for us.

19.3.1 The Issue

During test phases of project implementation and in production support, you may need to transfer one or more failed IDocs from a production client to QAS or DEV for debugging, break-fix development, and testing.

This is especially useful where unexpected errors occur in production in one or more IDocs and you have to recreate the error for debugging in a production-like QAS environment.

19.3.2 The Solution

Build an IDoc mass transfer utility — `ZEDI_TRNSFIDOCS` with Transaction ZEDIXFR — that allows development and support teams to select IDocs by IDoc number in one client for transfer to another client.

The program rebuilds the control segments of the selected IDocs in the source system, converts them into outbound IDocs, and sends them to a target client using standard Application Link Enabling (ALE) functionality.

19.3.3 Dependencies

The ALE transfer is done through an asynchronous call through a tRFC port that points to an RFC destination with the IP address and login settings for the target client. It is dependent on the following configuration:

▸ Logical systems defined for all clients that will exchange IDocs

▸ One RFC destination for each client that will exchange IDocs with its IP address and login settings configured; RFC destinations will have the logical system names for the participating clients

▸ One transactional RFC port created for each transfer client pointing to its RFC destination

▸ One outbound partner profile in the source system for all target systems:

　▸ Partner number: Logical system name of the target client

　▸ Partner type: LS (logical system)

　▸ Message: All messages that may be transferred to target client

　▸ Receiver port: tRFC port of the target client with its RFC destination

▸ Inbound partner profiles set up for customers and vendors in the target clients will support receiving IDocs from the source systems

The target client will treat the IDocs as if they had been sent by the partner. We do a little editing of the control record in code to make this happen.

19.3.4 Program ZEDI_TRNSFIDOCS

Figure 19.8 outlines the logical processing flow for the IDoc mass transfer utility.

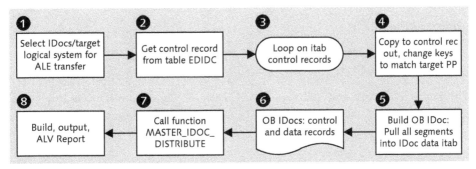

Figure 19.8 Logical Processing Flow for Program ZEDI_TRNSFIDOCS

The key select options for the program is one or more IDoc numbers and the target SAP system selected from table TBDLS, which stores logical system master data.

The control records for the selected IDocs are retrieved into an internal table, which is copied to a control record out. The control record out is then changed, as illustrated in the pseudo code in Listing 19.11.

```
SNDPRN = customer or vendor number for the selected IDoc.
If IDoc inbound
  move RCVPRN to SNDPRN
  RCVPRT to SNDPRT
  and RCVPFC to SNDPFC.
If outbound
  no change to these fields.

SNDPOR = concatenate SAP + send EDI system    "ie, SAPE82.
RCVPRN = logical system name for target client
  from selection screen.
RCVPRT = LS
RCVPFC = null.
RCVPOR = tRFC port for target SAP system
  from the outbound partner profile.
```
Listing 19.11 Pseudo Code with Control Record Population Logic

The goal is to match control record out values to the inbound partner profile in the target client.

The next step is to pull the IDoc data records from the database using standard functions, build the outbound IDoc, and call function MASTER_IDOC_DISTRIBUTE (also used for EDI output) to send it to the target client by ALE transfer through the tRFC port.

Program Structure

ZEDI_TRNSFIDOCS uses the same template as all of our other standalone ABAP programs that output an ALV list report.

The key selection screen values for ZEDI_TRNSFIDOCS are the IDoc number and target SAP system, as shown in Figure 19.9; these are mandatory fields.

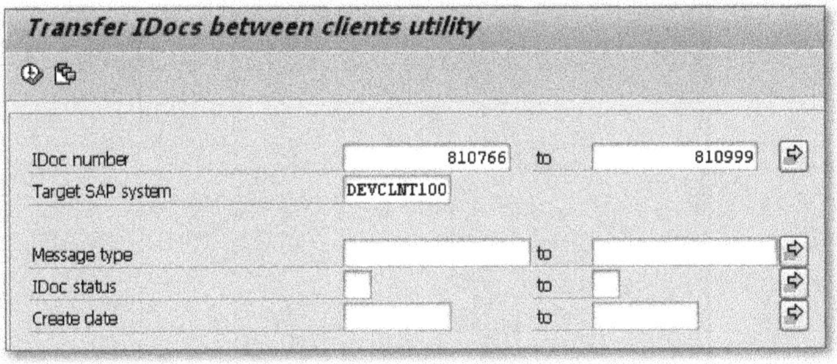

Figure 19.9 Selection Screen for ZEDI_TRNSFIDOCS

First we create the program in the ABAP editor using Transaction SE38 or the Object Navigator (SE80) with the following attributes:

▶ PROGRAM NAME: ZEDI_TRNSFIDOCS

▶ TITLE: Utility to *Transfer IDocs between SAP clients*

▶ TYPE: Executable program

▶ STATUS: Customer production program

▶ APPLICATION: Cross-application

Save and assign the program to a package and a change request.

We begin by declaring our tables, selection screen, types, internal tables, strings, variables, and constants. Our only table declarations are EDIDC and EDIDD, which are the IDoc control and data records, respectively.

Our key type declaration is T_OUT, which provides the structure for an ALV list report that will output the results of IDoc transfer processing, detailed in Listing 19.12.

```
*** Type for output of report detail
types: begin of t_out,
        from_logsys type logsys,     "Source system
        to_logsys type logsys,       "Target system
        from_mandt type sy-mandt,    "Source client
        docnum type edi_docnum,      "Source IDoc no.
        com_docnum type edi_docnum,  "Target IDoc no.
        mestyp type edi_mestyp,      "Message type
        stdmes type edi_stdmes,      "EDI txn
        partn type edi_partn,        "Source partner no.
      end of t_out.
```

Listing 19.12 ALV Output Report Structure for ZEDI_TRNSFIDOCS

Internal tables and structured strings are declared to read the selected IDocs, rebuild the control segment, get the partner profile for the outbound IDoc, transfer the IDoc, and output the status report. These tables are described in Listing 19.13.

```
*** IDoc transfer processing itabs
data: gt_control_in type standard table of edidc,
      gs_control_in type edidc
        "Source IDoc control record
      gt_control_out type standard table of edidc,
      gs_control_out type edidc,
        "Target IDoc control record
      gt_control_com type standard table of edidc,
      gs_control_com type edidc,
        "Communications IDoc created by ALE services
      gt_data_out type standard table of edidd
      gs_data_out type edidd,
        "Target IDoc data record
      gt_edk13 type standard table of edk13,
      gs_edk13 type edk13,
        "Partner Profile read key

*** ALV list output report itab
data: iout type standard table of t_out with header line.
```

Listing 19.13 Internal Tables for the IDoc Transfer Utility

Variables and constants are added for source and target logical systems while tables and strings are declared for ALV list reporting—the same ones we declared for earlier programs including ZEDI_UPLDPP in this chapter.

Our first job in START-OF-SELECTION processing is to get the control record for all selected IDocs, read in a form routine using the logic in Listing 19.14.

```
form 000_get_idocs.

data: ls_mess_txt(70) type c.

select * into table gt_control_in from edidc
        where docnum in so_docnm
          and status in so_stat
          and mestyp in so_mstyp
          and credat in so_crdat.
if sy-subrc <> 0.
```

```
  message i005 with so_docnm-low.   "Error message
  exit_flg = 'X'.
endif.

endform.                      " a000_read_data
```

Listing 19.14 Reading IDoc Control Records for Transfer

If the selected IDocs aren't found, a message is returned, and an exit flag is set to end program processing.

Assuming the IDocs *are* found, an outbound control record is built for each one, data records are pulled and IDocs are assembled and distributed, and the status report is written to table IOUT.

This is all very straightforward. It is done one step at a time within a loop on GT_CONTROL_IN into string GS_CONTROL_IN.

We build the outbound control record with a series of statements that copies the current control segment and adds—or deletes—values for the target logical system, as shown in Listing 19.15. This includes reading the outbound partner profile to get the receiver port.

```
*** Build OB control record for transfer IDoc
gs_control_out = gs_control_in.    "Copy current control
gs_control_out-rcvprn = gs_logsys_out. "Target LS
gs_control_out-rcvprt = 'LS'.       "Partner Type LS
gs_control_out-rcvpfc = space.      "Delete any values
*** SNDPRN changed only for OB IDocs in sending system
if gs_control_out-direct = '1'.    "Outbound IDoc
  gs_control_out-sndprn = gs_control_in-rcvprn.
     "OB receive partner becomes IB send partner
     "Else no change to SNDPRN
endif.
*** Build sender port SAP + system ID
concatenate 'SAP' sy-sysid  into gs_control_out-sndpor.
gs_control_out-arckey = space.     "Delete any values
gs_control_out-refint = space.     "Delete any values
gs_control_out-refmes = space.     "Delete any values

*** Build OB partner profile read key
gs_edk13-mandt = sy-mandt.
gs_edk13-rcvprn = gs_control_out-rcvprn.
```

```
gs_edk13-rcvprt = 'LS'.
gs_edk13-mestyp = gs_control_out-mestyp.
append gs_edk13 to gt_edk13

*** Read OB partner profile get tRFC port
call function 'edi_partner_appl_read_out'
  exporting
    rec_edk13            = gs_edk13
  importing
    rec_edp13            = gs_edp13
  exceptions
    partner_is_inactive = 1
    partner_is_template = 2
    partner_not_found   = 3
    others              = 4.
if sy-subrc = 0.
  gs_control_out-rcvpor = gs_edp13-rcvpor.
        "tRFC receiver port
endif.
```

Listing 19.15 Building the Outbound Control Record

The important thing to remember here is that we are transferring an IDoc that may be inbound or outbound in the sending system to a target client, where it becomes an inbound IDoc—as if we were the sending trading partner transmitting an IDoc to a receiving SAP system.

After we build the outbound control record, form GET_IDOC_DETAILS is called to pull data records for the current IDoc. This is done by calling three functions:

▶ EDI_DOCUMENT_OPEN_FOR_READ: Reads IDoc data

▶ EDI_SEGMENTS_GET_ALL: Returns IDoc data records

▶ EDI_DOCUMENT_CLOSE_READ: Clears internal read tables used by the previous functions

All IDoc data records are passed to internal table GT_DATA_OUT.

We're now ready to distribute our IDocs by ALE. All it takes is a function call like the one shown in Listing 19.16.

```
*** pass control to ALE services layer for export
*** to target logical system (client)
call function 'master_idoc_distribute'
```

```
  exporting
    master_idoc_control          = gs_control_out
  tables
    communication_idoc_control = gt_control_com
    master_idoc_data             = gt_data_out
  exceptions
    error_in_idoc_control        = 1
    error_writing_idoc_status    = 2
    error_in_idoc_data           = 3
    others                       = 4.
if sy-subrc <> 0.
  message id sy-msgid type sy-msgty number sy-msgno
      with sy-msgv1 sy-msgv2 sy-msgv3 sy-msgv4.
endif.
commit work.
```

Listing 19.16 Exporting the Transfer IDoc by ALE

The outbound control record is read in string GS_CONTROL_OUT with the data records in GT_DATA_OUT. A communication IDoc is created and written to the database, so a COMMIT WORK is also required. This is a new outbound IDoc that will be sent to the target client, after passing through all of the standard ALE services, checks, and validations.

The key is the outbound partner profile and the tRFC port with the RFC destination for the target client. The system will use it to send the IDoc by an ALE call to function IDOC_INBOUND_ASYNCHRONOUS in the target client.

IDOC_INBOUND_ASYNCHRONOUS is the ALE equivalent of function EDI_DATA_INCOMING. It kicks off inbound IDoc processing in the target client.

If the transfer succeeds, MASTER_IDOC_DISTRIBUTE returns 0 in SY-SUBRC and the control record for the communications IDoc. We can now build our status report in table IOUT with the communications IDoc control record and format and prep it in the normal manner for the ALV report.

Assign Transaction Code ZEDIXFR

The final step is to create transaction code ZEDIXFR in Transaction SE93 for program and selection screen for report ZEDI_TRNSFIDOCS. Don't forget to save the transaction code and assign it to a change request.

19.4 Sending IDoc Status to an External System

You may need to send the status of inbound IDocs to an external EDI or SAP system for reporting in a dashboard or some other reason. It could be to the system that sent them originally, or it could be to a system that's keeping track of data flows and other activity.

We used the STATUS IDoc to report back to SAP processing milestones in the EDI system. But STATUS is only an inbound IDoc, and without writing a custom program we can't send it to any external system.

SAP provides another IDoc to report the status of inbound IDocs sent from external systems: ALEAUD with basic type ALEAUD01 run by Transaction BDM8 (ABAP program RBDSTATE).

ALEAUD is very similar to STATUS in structure and functionality except that it is designed to be sent by ALE transmission to an external logical system.

We won't do any custom programming here but we do need to configure the interface. This introduces us to some basic ALE concepts.

19.4.1 The Issue

The external EDI system needs to receive a message reporting status of IDocs it sent into our SAP system. It uses these data in a dashboard report that tracks errors in its data traffic with SAP and other systems.

19.4.2 The Solution

SAP provides a standard program and IDoc to send these data. RBDSTATE—Transaction BDM8—identifies IDocs by sending system, message type, and date of change. It then extracts the status record from these IDocs and uses it to build an ALEAUD.ALEAUD01 IDoc, which is then sent to the selected external system by ALE transmission.

19.4.3 Dependencies

The ALE transfer of message ALEAUD is dependent on the following configuration:

- Logical systems defined for all external systems that will receive an IDocs. At Acme, the EDI RIM has been set up with the following logical system names:
  - EDIRIMD100: Dev client 100
  - EDIRIMQ100: QA client 100
  - EDIRIMP100: Prod client 100.
- A distribution model in the ALE IMG that documents the transfer of message ALEAUD between sending logical system DEVCLNT100 and target logical system EDIRIMD100
- An outbound partner profile for partner type LS (logical system) and partner number EDIRIMD100 with the following parameters:
  - MESSAGE: "ALEAUD"
  - RECEIVER PORT: "XML_IDOC"
  - OUTPUT MODE: COLLECT IDOCS and START SUBSYSTEM options
  - BASIC TYPE: "ALEAUD01"
  - No message control

We'll assume that the logical systems are already defined.

19.4.4 Defining the Distribution Model

The distribution model is defined in the ALE IMG. Call Transaction SALE and follow menu path IDOC INTERFACE/APPLICATION LINK ENABLING (ALE) • MODELLING AND IMPLEMENTING BUSINESS PROCESSES • MAINTAIN DISTRIBUTION MODEL AND DISTRIBUTE VIEWS.

1. Switch from display to change mode in the distribution model edit screen by clicking the pencil icon at the top or pressing F9.
2. Click CREATE MODEL VIEW to set up the ALEAUD transmission from the Acme logical system. Enter the following values, which are shown in Figure 19.10:
   - In the SHORT TEXT field, enter a description of the distribution model.
   - In the TECHNICAL NAME field, enter "STATUSOUT" to identify the distribution model.

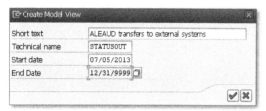

Figure 19.10 Creating the Distribution Model

3. Click OK. The new model will appear at the bottom of the list of distribution models.

4. Select the model we just created and click ADD MESSAGE TYPE. The technical name of the model will appear in the MODEL VIEW field. Enter the following values, which are shown in Figure 19.11:

   ▶ SENDER: "DEVCLNT100", the logical system for the IDoc sender

   ▶ RECEIVER: "EDIRIMD800"

   ▶ MESSAGE TYPE: "ALEAUD"

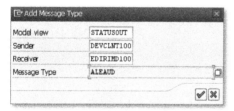

Figure 19.11 Adding the Message Type to the Model

5. Click OK. Don't forget to save the distribution model. The finished model will look like Figure 19.12.

ALEAUD transfers to external systems	STATUSOUT
Dev client 100 LS	DEVCLNT100
EDI RIM logical system 100	EDIRIMD100
ALEAUD	ALE: Confirmations for Inbound IDocs
No filter set	

Figure 19.12 Distribution Model STATUSOUT

This view illustrates the basic nature of the distribution model. It first defines a sending system—Acme's DEV client logical system—and then assigns one or more receiving systems to it. In this case, the receiving system is the EDI RIM.

At the lowest level is the message (or BAPI) transmitted by the sending to the receiving system.

Any number of receiving systems and messages can be added to the sending system. Each receiving system is identified separately with its own messages below the sender.

For interfaces back to Acme's DEV client, you would add messages for the external sender. Acme's DEV client would be entered as the receiver.

RBDSTATE checks for the distribution model after it has pulled IDocs that it will report status for. It uses the distribution model to confirm the selected receiving logical system is set up for message type ALEAUD. It also identifies and applies any filters that may be defined for the ALEAUD message for the sender and receiver in the distribution model.

Outbound Partner Profile

We need to set an outbound partner profile to support sending the ALEAUD IDoc to the EDI RIM.

1. Run Transaction WE20 and open the Partner Type LS folder.

2. Click the CREATE button or press [F5] to create a new partner profile.

3. Enter the following values into the general level of the partner profile:

   ▶ PARTNER NO. field: "EDIRIMD100" for the RIM's logical system

   ▶ PARTN.TYPE field: "LS"

   ▶ TY. field: "O" for organizational unit (or as required by your team)

   ▶ AGENT field: An organization number, such as 50010120 for EDI department

   ▶ LANG. field: "EN" or your preferred language

4. Save the partner profile.

5. Enter the following outbound parameters (see Figure 19.13) and save the partner profile:

   ▶ MESSAGE TYPE field: "ALEAUD"

   ▶ RECEIVER PORT field: "XML_IDOC"

   ▶ OUTPUT MODE area: COLLECT IDOCS and START SUBSYSTEM options

   ▶ BASIC TYPE field: "ALEAUD01"

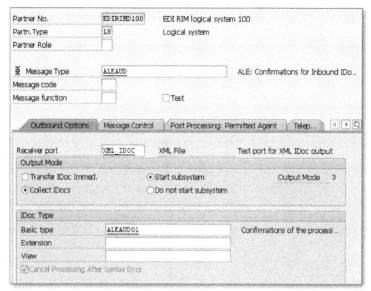

Figure 19.13 Outbound Parameters for ALEAUD to the EDI RIM

Running Program RBDSTATE

Get to the selection screen of program RBDSTATE with Transaction BDM8. The selection screen is shown in Figure 19.14.

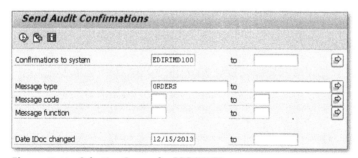

Figure 19.14 Selection Screen for RBDSTATE

CONFIRMATIONS TO SYSTEM and DATE IDOC CHANGED are mandatory parameters. The system is the receiving logical system; in this case, this is the EDI RIM. Message type identifies the IDocs to check for changes of status; in this case, this is ORDERS. If this is left blank, the system will return all IDocs changed on the selected date.

RBDSTATE selects inbound IDocs based on the message and change date entered in the selection screen. It also looks for send partner type LS for logical systems, so it will not select customer or vendor partner types.

If you were to copy RBDSTATE into a custom Z-program, you could change these parameters to retrieve status data for whatever partners you need to report on. It will still read the distribution model, read the IDoc status records, build the ALEAUD IDoc, and send it out through the outbound partner profile to your EDI or other external system.

If the program is successful, it will return a simple list of IDoc numbers for the ALEAUD IDocs returned, as in Figure 19.15.

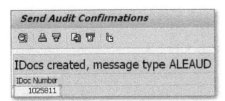

Figure 19.15 RBDSTATE Report Output

If you double-click the IDoc number, the system takes you to the IDoc tree display for the ALEAUD IDoc with all the status records it's identified based on your selection options (see Figure 19.16). This is the IDoc that will be sent to the EDI RIM through the partner profile and XML file port.

IDoc display	
▼ 🗇 IDoc 0000000001025811	
• 🗋 Control Rec.	
▼ 🗇 Data records	Total number: 000011
▼ 🗋 E1ADHDR	Segment 000001
▼ 🗋 E1STATE	Segment 000002
• 🗋 E1PRTOB	Segment 000003
▼ 🗋 E1STATE	Segment 000004
• 🗋 E1PRTOB	Segment 000005
▼ 🗋 E1STATE	Segment 000006
• 🗋 E1PRTOB	Segment 000007
▼ 🗋 E1STATE	Segment 000008
• 🗋 E1PRTOB	Segment 000009
▼ 🗋 E1STATE	Segment 000010
• 🗋 E1PRTOB	Segment 000011
▼ 🗇 Status records	
▶ 🗋 30	IDoc ready for dispatch (ALE service)
• 🗋 01	IDoc generated

Figure 19.16 IDoc Tree Display of the ALEAUD Status IDoc

It's just another IDoc. Each E1STATE segment group identifies an IDoc read based on the selection screen and provides its status record for use by the external system.

19.5 Adding Qualifiers to IDoc XML Schema

And now for something completely different. We've been looking at IDocs and ABAP and ALE configuration. But we're using XML IDocs and there is one missing link that we haven't touched yet: the XSD schema. We'll feed it to our mapping tool so we can build maps between our IDocs and our trading partners' EDI transactions.

The good news is that SAP makes it easy to get the XSD schema for all its IDocs. The bad news is that the schema are incomplete in one small but important respect for EDI and B2B: qualifiers are not included.

In this section we will get an XSD schema for an ORDERS.ORDERS05 IDoc from SAP and build an add-on schema that will provide qualifiers—*enumerators*, in the XML world—for a key segment.

19.5.1 The Issue

IDoc XSD schema are readily available from SAP. But SAP does not provide the qualifiers for qualified segments or data elements. Our EDI mapping team needs the qualifiers to build and enforce data element level rules in the translation maps.

19.5.2 The Solution

We use standard XML functionality to build an add-on schema with an enumerator data element that will be able to provide qualifiers for our IDocs.

The schema file name will be IDocQualifiers.xsd and it will be imported into the IDoc schema. The enumerator will be applied as a type to E1EDKA1 qualifier field PARVW, making the qualifiers available to the field.

19.5.3 Dependencies

IDocs are active in our SAP system, including any extended or custom IDocs we may have built.

19.5.4 Extracting an XML Schema from SAP

XSD schema for IDocs can be extracted with Transaction WE60 or through the WEDI EDI area menu path DOCUMENTATION • IDOC TYPES.

Make sure to explore the options under the DOCUMENTATION menu. Transaction WE60 supports output of IDoc documentation and metadata in a variety of formats including HTML, IDoc message type SYIDOC, ASCII, C-Header, and XML DTDs and schema.

To download the XSD schema, follow these steps:

1. Enter the name of an IDoc type into the BASIC TYPE field. We will use ORDERS05.

2. Select the menu option DOCUMENTATION • XML SCHEMA, as shown in Figure 19.17.

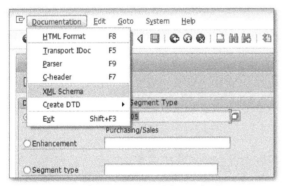

Figure 19.17 Selecting an IDoc Schema for Export

3. When the DOCUMENTATION pop-up asks "GENERATE DOCUMENTATION FOR UNI-CODE FILE?", click YES.

4. Select the menu option XML • DOWNLOAD to open a download dialog. Enter a name for the schema in the FILENAME field and navigate to a save directory on your local PC.

   A good naming convention to follow is MessageType.BasicType (for example, ORDERS.ORDERS05).

5. By default SAP offers an *.xml* file extension for the schema. Make sure you save it with an *.xsd* extension, which is the standard for XML schema.

Next find and open the schema to do a little house-cleaning before using it in any of our maps.

First change the root data element name from the IDoc basic type to the message and basic type, as detailed in Listing 19.17.

```
<?xml version="1.0" encoding="utf-8"?>
<xs:schema xmlns:xsd="http://www.w3.org/2001/XMLSchema" version="1.0">
 <xs:element name="ORDERS.ORDERS05">
  <xs:annotation>
   <xs:documentation>Purchasing/Sales</xs:documentation>
  </xs:annotation>
```

Listing 19.17 Changing the Root Data Element to Include the Message

Many basic types are used by different messages, such as the ORDERS customer PO and the ORDRSP PO acknowledgment. The EDI team wants to distinguish the schema that we use in our maps by message and basic type.

Next we will hard-code the name of the logical message to the MESTYP data element. The IDOCTYP data element is already hard-coded to ORDERS05. This is not necessary, but once again, we are creating a specific usage for this schema in our maps.

In your favorite XML schema editor, search for:

```
element name="MESTYP"
```

Add the following attribute before the closing bracket:

```
fixed="ORDERS"
```

The data element should look like this:

```
<xs:element name="MESTYP" minOccurs="0" fixed="ORDERS">
```

The last change is to search for all instances of the maxOccurs attributes that equal 999 and greater. If you find any, change the number to "unbounded". Many XML processors don't like large numbers in the maxOccurs attribute. Warning messages are returned during schema validation so it's best to change them to unbounded.

19.5.5 Creating the IDoc Enumerators

Without getting too heavily into XML terminology, an *enumerator* is a value in a list of possible values attached to the restrictions base of an XML simple type. In other words, it is the same thing as a qualifier.

SAP does not include the qualifiers when it exports the XML schema for its IDocs, such as the partner types in E1EDKA1-PARVW. These qualifiers are useful in mapping because they restrict the allowed values for a field and let the system throw an error if an incoming value is not on that list.

Without the qualifiers, we have to write our own rules or build code lists or do something else in the map to throw an error if the incoming value is not on the allowed list of qualifiers.

We can add qualifiers directly into the schema as enumeration lists attached to the qualified data elements, but that adds bulk to the schema and we would have to do it to every schema that has qualifier fields.

Because many of SAP's qualifiers are common to a large number of IDocs, the better way is to create a separate enumeration schema that includes all the SAP qualifiers you want to use across multiple schema.

You then use the XML import statement to include the enumeration schema and assign the enumerator types to the qualifier fields.

So let's create our enumeration schema. Fire up your favorite XML schema editor or load a good text editor. Enter the enumeration schema for the IDoc qualifier E1EDKA1-PARVW, illustrated in Listing 19.18.

```
<?xml version="1.0" encoding="UTF-8" standalone="yes"?>
<xs:schema xmlns:enum="urn:idocman:mapping:Qualifier"
  xmlns:xs=http://www.w3.org/2001/XMLSchema
  targetNamespace="urn:idocman:mapping:Qualifier"
  elementFormDefault="qualified" version="1.0">
<xs:simpleType name="PARVWPartnerQualifierEnum">
  <xs:restriction base="xs:string">
    <xs:maxLength value="3"/>
    <xs:minLength value="1"/>
    <xs:enumeration value="AG">
      <xs:annotation>
        <xs:documentation>Sold-to party<xs:documentation>
      </xs:annotation>
```

```
      </xs:enumeration>
      <xs:enumeration value="WE">
        <xs:annotation>
          <xs:documentation>Ship-to party<xs:documentation>
        </xs:annotation>
      </xs:enumeration>
      <xs:enumeration value="LF">
        <xs:annotation>
          <xs:documentation>Vendor party</xs:documentation>
        </xs:annotation>
      </xs:enumeration>
      <xs:enumeration value="RE">
        <xs:annotation>
          <xs:documentation>Bill-to party</xs:documentation>
        </xs:annotation>
      </xs:enumeration>
    </xs:restriction>
  </xs:simpleType>
</xs:schema>
```

Listing 19.18 E1EDKA1-PARVW Enumeration List

The design view of this schema shows how simple it actually is. In the XML world, qualifiers are created in a field with a restriction base defined by a string type with a list of enumerators. The pattern is always the same. In graphical view of our XSD editor, it looks like Figure 19.18.

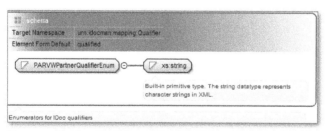

Figure 19.18 Graphical view of the IDoc Partner Enumeration List

An XSD schema is an XML file that is interpreted as a metadata dictionary. It describes the structure of an XML data file while at the same time describing its own structure. It is declared as a schema in line 2. Line 3 identifies the URL for the W3 schema standard and defines the prefix (xs:) that will be assigned to each element of the schema.

After the schema statement in line 2, it identifies the prefix (enum:) that will be used to identify its types by any other schema that uses them to define any of their data elements. The `elementFormDefault` attribute in line 5 is set to qualified, which means that the prefix is explicitly declared in any reference to the schema's type otherwise it won't be recognized.

We will see how this works when we import and apply this schema to our ORDERS. ORDERS05 schema.

The target namespace and prefix together define the namespace for the schema. The namespace defines a unique XML vocabulary in this schema. The beauty of this is that we can have multiple schema with the same data element names that are treated as unique because each has a different namespace.

In XML terminology, a namespace name is a Uniform Resource Identifier (URI) generally assigned an http: or urn: formatted name, as in our sample in Listing 19.18. It doesn't have to point to a URL address—although it could—but it does have to be unique for your development.

The other point to note is that the qualifiers are listed in a simple type that we have named for the IDoc qualifier field. The beauty of XML is that it is self-documenting, which means you can use meaningful element names to easily identify what each field means. Standard usage is to define the name in camel case—that is, upper case for each new word.

Each qualifier that we would add to this file would be defined in the same way as PARVWPartnerQualifierEnum. First declare and name the simple type, then add the restriction block. You can also add length attributes if you want to restrict the length of the data element.

The qualifiers are added as a value attribute of the data element xs:enumeration as demonstrated in Listing 19.19.

```
<xs:enumeration value="WE">
  <xs:annotation>
    <xs:documentation>Ship-to Party</xs:documentation>
  </xs:annotation>
</xs:enumeration>
```
Listing 19.19 Qualifiers Are Defined in an Enumeration Block

The structure of this block is consistent: always an enumeration element with a value attribute populated with the qualifier. You can add a description of the qualifier in a documentation element within an annotation tag. The description is optional but useful. Repeat this pattern for every qualifier you want to add to PARVWPartnerQualifierEnum.

To add qualifiers for other fields, create another simple type with a new name and a new list of enumeration blocks. It is very straightforward.

19.5.6 Using the Enumerator in an IDoc

Next we will use the qualifiers in our ORDERS.ORDERS05 schema. The first step is to import into the IDoc schema.

Open the ORDERS.ORDERS05 schema in an XML editor or text file. First we declare the enumerator prefix in the schema declaration of the IDoc schema:

```
<xsd:schema xmlns:xsd=http://www.w3.org/2001/XMLSchema
    xmlns:enum="urn:idocman:mapping:Qualifier" version="1.0">
```

We do this because the enumerator schema makes the prefix mandatory, and the IDoc schema can only recognize it if it is explicitly declared in the root schema element.

Next we add an import statement immediately after the schema element:

```
<xsd:import schemaLocation="IDocQualifiersEnum.xsd"
    namespace="urn:idocman:mapping:Qualifier"/>
```

This assumes that the two schema are in the same subdirectory. If not, the path to the imported schema must be included in schemaLocation.

The enumeration list is now ready for use in the IDoc schema. It will be assigned as a type to data element PARVW, in segment E1EDKA1. The standard listing for the data element without the enumerator type will look like Listing 19.20.

```
<xsd:element name="PARVW" minOccurs="0">
  <xsd:annotation>
    <xsd:documentation>Partner function</xsd:documentation>
  </xsd:annotation>
  <xsd:simpleType>
    <xs:restriction base="xs:string">
     <xs:maxLength value="3"/>
    </xs:restriction>
```

```
        </xs:simpleType>
</xs:element>
```

Listing 19.20 Data Element PARVW without the Enumerator Type

The type declaration with the data type and field length restrictions follows the annotation documenting the field. We will delete the simple type with its restriction base and replace it with the enumerator type PARVWPartnerQualifierEnum following the minOccurs attribute in the element tag. PARVW should now look like Listing 19.21.

```
<xs:element name="PARVW" minOccurs="0"
       type="enum:PARVWPartnerQualifierEnum">
  <xs:annotation>
    <xs:documentation>Partner function</xs:documentation>
  </xs:annotation>
</xs:element>
```

Listing 19.21 Referencing the Enumerator Type

Note the enum: prefix on the type. This is mandatory in our example. The full enumeration list in simple type PARVWPartnerQualifierEnum will now be available with all its qualifiers when we import the schema to our mapping tool to be used as a source or target structure. We can see this in the design view of our schema for E1EDKA1-PARVW shown in Figure 19.19.

Figure 19.19 Enumerator Values Linked to E1EDKA1-PARVW

19.6   Summary

"There's more than one way to skin a cat," the legendary founder of Acme Pictures, Darryl Q. Fernhausen, would say when he had trouble signing the latest wannabe starlet.

We have seen in this chapter that we have choices when it comes to custom—or even standard—solutions to issues that may crop up in the IDoc interface. We carefully went over user exit code that changes the IDoc control segment so that we could convert our partners' EDI trading partner IDs to and from our internal SAP partner numbers.

Rather than manually enter every partner profile into each SAP client that we have to work with, we wrote a simple upload program to automate it. We also looked at a program to transfer IDocs between SAP clients using ALE, and at a standard process for sending IDoc status to an external system.

Last, but not least, we got into the weeds of XML development and built an enumerator XSD schema to add the qualifiers that SAP doesn't include when it exports its IDoc schema.

We're near the end of our road now. But before we can go live, the new SAP EDI system must be tested. And so the project team turns its attention to a testing strategy for Acme Pictures.

Things don't always work out as designed. Nobody knew that better than the Great Mr. Q, who justified his many marriages by saying, "I was just testing the whole 'marriage' concept! You can't get anything right until you test it again and again." It's the same with SAP and EDI—until the system has been thoroughly tested, your design is only a paper moon. So let's look at Acme's testing strategy and see how they plan to bring their system home.

20 Testing the EDI System in SAP

The work has gone well for our Plan Q from Outer Space EDI subproject at Acme Pictures. We designed and built our interfaces in SAP and the EDI system. We've also developed some IDoc utilities and add-ons to make our lives a little bit easier.

But the proof of the pudding is in the tasting, as they say. And that means testing, and more testing, and plenty of both.

Testing is an inexact science. We try to predict the behavior of a production system that we designed based on months of research during blueprint and refined through the long and challenging development effort of realization.

We began with a vision of the completed system that was grounded in our understanding of Acme's business. Our knowledge of that business deepened as we worked with our partners to build and configure the new system.

But this was theoretical knowledge focused on the technical implementation of our piece of the puzzle. We lived and breathed EDI and IDoc interfaces throughout the development effort but were not always attuned to the big picture emerging from the efforts of every other team's contribution.

It is time to test the whole concept, as the legendary Darryl Q would say, and to prove that we got it right. And to fix it where we didn't. But before we can test we need a testing strategy, which is a substantial job in its own right.

Luckily, we have a testing specialist who's worked hard with each team to develop a test plan and a schedule. Acme is a relatively small project, so the strategy is simple and without any bells or whistles.

We will take a high-level tour of the specialist's strategy for testing our EDI interfaces in Acme's SAP system. But first we look at some of the tools SAP provides to test IDoc development.

20.1 IDoc Test Tools

EDI is a prime example of the old saying, "The more things change, the more they stay the same." These test tools largely reflect an earlier era in SAP when it was still assumed that business documents would be exchanged through file-based interfaces.

However, the vast majority of businesses continue to do EDI through file-based batch processing exchanges of standard messages. It is highly unlikely that this will change anytime soon.

SAP's IDoc test tools can be used in a number of ways:

▶ **Proof of concept**
Confirm use of a message type to post against an SAP document or data record

▶ **Posting requirements**
Confirm data required to post an IDoc to an SAP document or record

▶ **Configuration**
Confirm IDoc configuration settings such as message control, partner profiles, and ports

▶ **Development**
Debug IDoc functions and user exits

All IDoc test tools are in the TEST folder of the WEDI area menu.

20.1.1 The Main IDoc Test Tool: Transaction WE19

Transaction WE19 supports all types of unit testing. It is especially useful for inbound testing because it supports stepping through the code of an IDoc function in the ABAP debugger, invaluable for working with custom IDocs and functions and a wonderful way to learn how IDoc functions work.

Inbound IDocs can create a business document through Transaction WE19, making it the place to go to identify the message type and data requirements for posting to a particular SAP document or transaction.

The Transaction WE19 selection screen offers several options for processing IDocs; these are shown in Figure 20.1. It's generally best to begin with an existing IDoc and edit it. The other options leave you with an empty IDoc that must be populated from scratch before you can begin testing.

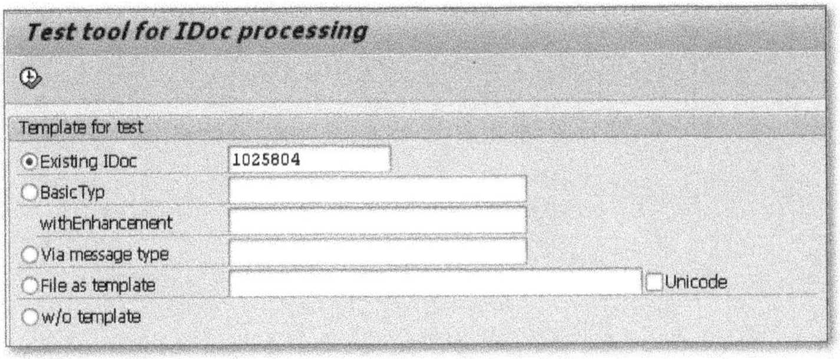

Figure 20.1 The WE19 IDoc Test Tool Selection Screen

When the IDoc loads, it appears in the edit window in Figure 20.2. From here, any existing segment can be edited by clicking on the white data line next to the segment name. This includes the control record.

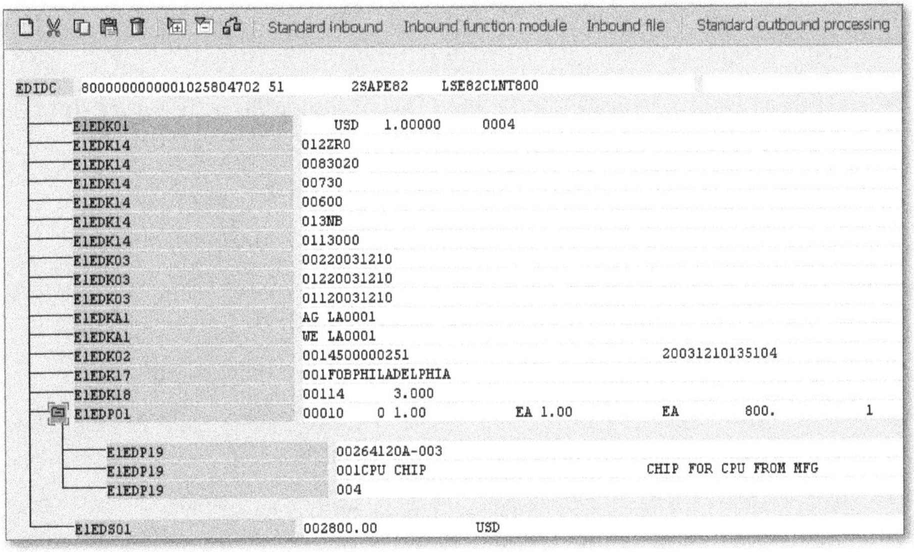

Figure 20.2 The IDoc Test Tool Edit Window

Clicking a record opens a data entry screen similar to the EDIT CONTROL RECORD FIELDS dialog box in Figure 20.3. You can change or add any values to the existing control or data segment here.

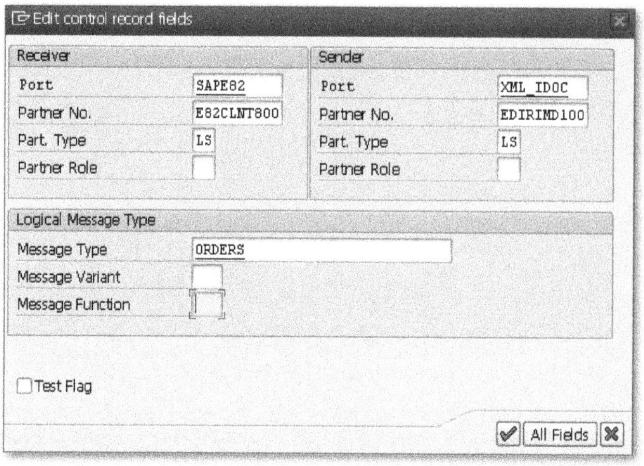

Figure 20.3 Editing Control Record Values in the IDoc Test Tool

The heavy lifting in the test tool is done through the toolbox that runs across the top of the editing window in Figure 20.2. Stepping through the features of each tool from left to the right illustrates the range of activities available in the IDoc test tool.

1. CREATING SEGMENTS icon ([F5]): Creates a new segment as a sibling or child of the selected segment.

2. CUT icon ([Shift]+[F4]): Cuts the selected segment to the clipboard.

3. COPY icon ([Shift]+[F5]): Copies the selected segment to the clipboard.

4. INSERT icon ([Shift]+[F6]): Pastes a segment from the clipboard after the selected segment.

5. DELETE icon ([Shift]+[F2]): Deletes the currently selected segment.

6. EXPAND SUBTREE icon ([Ctrl]+[Shift]+[F11]): Expands selected parent segment. If EDIDC is selected every segment below it expands.

7. COLLAPSE SUBTREE icon ([Ctrl]+[Shift]+[F12]): Collapses a selected parent segment. EDIDC collapses every segment below.

8. IDOC SYNTAX CHECK icon ([F6]): Checks IDoc syntax and returns a message reporting the results.

9. STANDARD INBOUND button ([F8]): Calls inbound processing for an IDoc through standard interface services. Confirms configuration, writes IDoc to the database, and kicks off the application function if the partner profile is set to immediate processing.

10. INBOUND FUNCTION MODULE button ([Ctrl]+[F2]): Processes the IDoc directly through its application function without calling interface services. Can be used to step through code in the ABAP debugger.

11. INBOUND FILE button ([Ctrl]+[F3]): Imports and processes an IDoc file from the app server through the file port. It first creates the file from the current IDoc, saves it to the application server, and then imports it.

    The file can be overwritten or appended with the current IDoc, creating a test file with multiple IDocs. The file can be imported into any other SAP client configured to receive the IDoc.

12. STANDARD OUTBOUND PROCESSING button ([F7]): Exports the test IDoc through the file port to an output file on the SAP application server. It can trigger outbound processing immediately even if the partner profile is set to collect IDocs for batch processing.

    Output mode is always set to 2—*Transfer IDoc immediately*, or 4—*Collect IDocs and transfer*, even if the partner profile is configured to trigger the EDI system. The EDI system can't be triggered by sending an IDoc from the test tool.

If you do a lot of IDoc interface development, Transaction WE19 is indispensable. It will help you nail down the data you need to post your IDoc against a document and confirm that your code works. It is a wonderful IDoc unit test tool but represents only the first step in the overall testing effort.

20.1.2 Outbound from Message Control: Transaction WE15

Strictly speaking, Transaction WE15 is not a test tool, although it can be used to confirm that message control is working for documents such as supplier purchase orders, deliveries, and invoices.

Transaction WE15 calls program RSNAST00, which is run after a document such as an invoice is created and IDoc output is proposed by message control but is not sent immediately after the document is saved.

`RSNAST00` is run if the date/time field in the condition record is set to 1—*Send with periodically scheduled job.*

`RSNAST00` can be used to manage the flow of IDocs and to regenerate IDoc output if there was a problem with the initial send. Figure 20.4 shows the selection screen for Transaction WE15.

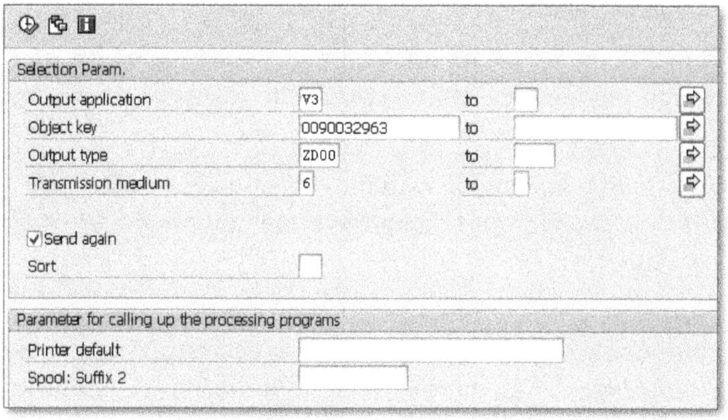

Figure 20.4 Resending an IDoc from Message Control

Transaction WE15 looks up output records for a document recorded in table NAST using the read keys entered into the selection screen. The object key is the document number with its leading zeroes. The rest you will recognize from message control.

If a NAST output record is found, `RSNAST00` identifies the processing program and form defined in message control configuration. For generation of IDocs `RSNAST00` calls form `EDI_PROCESSING` in program `RSNASTED`.

20.1.3 Outbound from IDoc: Transaction WE14

Program `RSEOUT00` is in the WEDI test folder even though it is not really a test program.

We discussed `RSEOUT00` in Chapter 7, Section 7.2.7, in the subsection Sending the IDoc to the EDI RIM.

`RSEOUT00` is used to identify and send to an external system through the outbound partner IDocs batched in the IDoc database at status 30.

20.1.4 Status File Testing: Transactions WE18 and WE17

These two transactions test an old-school status file interface. The interface updates status records in table EDIDS for an outbound IDoc with processing milestones from an external EDI system.

Transaction WE18—program `MSEIDOC1`—generates a status test file with six success and error statuses. Enter an outbound IDoc number, a directory path on the application server, and a file port, and it will create the test file and update the status table by default, if you leave the START STATUS PROCESSING IMMEDIATELY flag checked. The structure of the status file is displayed in Figure 20.5.

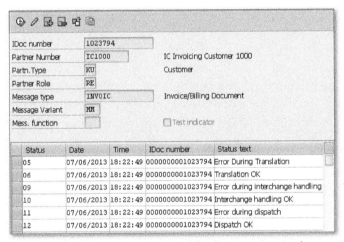

IDoc number	1023794		
Partner Number	IC1000		IC Invoicing Customer 1000
Partn. Type	KU		Customer
Partner Role	RE		
Message type	INVOIC		Invoice/Billing Document
Message Variant	MM		
Mess. function			☐ Test indicator

Status	Date	Time	IDoc number	Status text
05	07/06/2013	18:22:49	0000000001023794	Error During Translation
06	07/06/2013	18:22:49	0000000001023794	Translation OK
09	07/06/2013	18:22:49	0000000001023794	Error during interchange handling
10	07/06/2013	18:22:49	0000000001023794	Interchange handling OK
11	07/06/2013	18:22:49	0000000001023794	Error during dispatch
12	07/06/2013	18:22:49	0000000001023794	Dispatch OK

Figure 20.5 The Status File Generated by the Status Test Tool

Assuming a status file has been saved to the application server, run Transaction WE17—program `MSEIDOC0`—and enter the full directory path and file name and the file port.

The file is pulled into SAP by function `EDI_STATUS_INCOMING`. If the file is correctly populated, it will update the status record in table EDIDS for the IDoc with one record for each status reported in the file.

`EDI_STATUS_INCOMING` can be triggered by an external system through an RFC into SAP or by running an RFC script on the application server.

20.1.5 Turnaround Utility: Transaction WE12

The turnaround utility—program `MSEIDOC0`—changes any IDoc in a file on the SAP application server into an inbound IDoc and imports it for inbound testing.

The easiest way to understand the turnaround utility by breaking it down into the tasks it accomplishes:

▶ Reads the source IDoc file

▶ Copies partner number, type, and port in the SENDER tab of the selection screen into the SNDPRN, SNDPRT, and SNDPOR fields of the control segment

▶ Copies partner number, type, and port in the RECEIVER tab of the selection screen into the RCVPRN, RCVDPRT, and RCVPOR fields of the control segment

▶ Saves the edited IDoc to the target file and triggers import of the file as an inbound IDoc

There must be supporting inbound and outbound partner profiles for the values entered in the SENDER and RECEIVER tables of the selection screen, and the port must be a file port. It will not work with an XML port. The turnaround utility selection screen is shown in Figure 20.6.

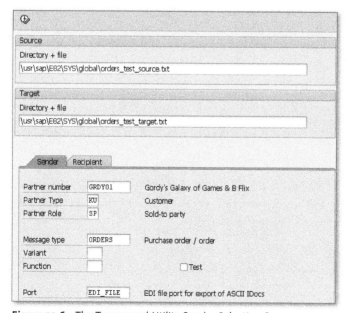

Figure 20.6 The Turnaround Utility Sender Selection Screen

An easy way to edit and export the IDoc as a file is with the Transaction WE19 test tool INBOUND FILE button. It saves the IDoc to a directory and file on the application server specified by the user. By default, the file is processed as an inbound IDoc and deleted from the application server.

To save it to the application server, uncheck the checkbox START IDOC INBOUND PROCESSING OF FILE IMMEDIATELY (see Figure 20.7). You now have a file that you can test with Transaction WE12.

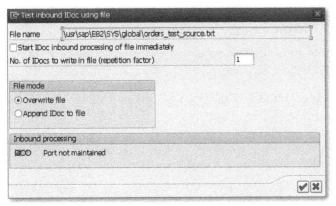

Figure 20.7 Saving an IDoc to a File from Transaction WE19

20.1.6 Inbound IDoc File Processing: Transaction WE16

Transaction WE16 is a useful way to bring IDocs into a development client for testing and debugging.

Transaction WE16 will import an IDoc even if there is no supporting partner profile and the control segments are all wrong. When we load an IDoc into a DEV client from a file for testing, we do not always care whether it passes the checks and is saved at status 64. After it's in, we can do whatever we want to it using Transaction WE19, even if it has been saved at status 56.

For quick and dirty transfer of IDocs from one client or system to another, Transaction WE16 is useful and easy to work with. Save your IDoc file in a folder on the SAP application server and enter the full path and file name in the selection screen, as in Figure 20.8. Enter a port name and execute.

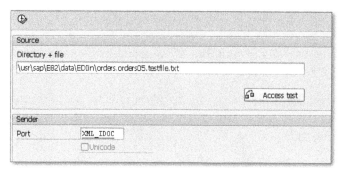

Figure 20.8 Bringing an IDoc File in with Transaction WE16

The IDoc can then be viewed and edited in any of the IDoc monitoring or test tools such as Transactions BD87, WE05, or WE19.

Transaction WE16 will support import of an IDoc through an XML file port if the IDoc file is in XML format.

20.1.7 Inbound IDocs and startRFC

`startRFC` is a trusty old SAP utility that triggers IDoc processing in SAP directly from the application server. In many companies, `startRFC` is still the only way to send IDoc files into SAP.

You may need Basis guidance to find it on your system, but `startRFC` can generally be found in a subdirectory of *\usr\sap\<SYSID>\SYS*, where SYSID is your local SAP system ID.

It can be called directly from the command line or from a script. Typically, it is by another FTP script that moves an IDoc file into the application server and the passes call parameters to a `startRFC` script, including the file name. In many older EDI environments, data are moved from system to system by FTP scripts.

Listing 20.1 is an example of a command line call to `startRFC`.

```
\\usr\sap\DEV\sys\exe\run\startrfc -3 -d DEV -u edi_user -p freddy
-c 120 -l E -h sapacdev -s 00 -g sapacdev -x sapgw00 -t -F EDI_DATA_
INCOMING -E PORT=XML_IDOC -E PATHNAME=\\datastuff\client100\EDI\INBOX\
idoc000029
```

Listing 20.1 Calling startRFC from the Command Line

The parameter switches for `startRFC` are listed in Table 20.1.

Switch	Description	Value
	Path to `startRFC` executable	*D:\usr\sap\DEV\sys\exe\run\startrfc*
-3	System control flag: log on to SAP	
-d	SAP system	dev (Acme development)
-u	User name for RFC	edi_user
-p	EDI user password	freddy
-c	SAP client for RFC	120
-I	Language	E (English)
-h	SAP application server for RFC	sapacdev (Acme dev)
-s	SAP system number	00
-g	SAP Gateway host	sapacdev
-x	SAP Gateway service	sapgw00
-t	Turns on RFC trace and saves trace file to current or specified directory; useful during testing and for troubleshooting	
-F	Message processing function to trigger by RFC	EDI_DATA_INCOMING
-E	SAP Port: XML or file port	PORT=XML_IDOC
-E	Path and file name for inbound IDOC file	PATHNAME=\\datastuff\client100\EDI\INBOX\idoc000029

Table 20.1 startRFC Call Parameters or Switches

`startRFC` uses the switches to identify a target SAP system, log in with a user name and password, and call a function module to import and process the incoming IDoc file.

Use startRFC to test inbound processing to SAP from the command line. If your EDI system does not have an IDoc adapter, startRFC may be the only way you can send IDocs into SAP. Whether for testing or production, startRFC is a useful tool to understand.

20.2   Interface Testing Strategy

Reduced to its simplest definition, testing is about reducing the risks of error before we move our system into production. The hope is that the new SAP EDI system will work as designed to support Acme's business, which is to sell its movies on DVD.

But the expectation is that stuff can go wrong. We need to eliminate this possibility as far as it is in our power to do so. The basic problem is that even if we manage to throw a lot of data at it, we will never be able to throw enough data over a long enough period of time to recreate the conditions of daily production.

But we can probably catch 95 percent of the potential system issues. Or at least the real gotchas.

We need to approach the issue in a structured and disciplined manner, which means defining and executing a testing strategy that identifies the following:

▶ Our objectives and definition of success

▶ The type of testing we need to do

▶ The number of test cycles we complete before we can declare victory and move on to cutover

▶ The components and environments of the SAP EDI system tested

▶ The level of detail we need to test

▶ Dependencies, including data requirements, for each cycle

▶ Break-fix procedures

▶ How we document our testing efforts

▶ Test team setup

▶ Roles and responsibilities for each team and each team member

After weeks of meetings with each project team during development, our testing consultant drew up a multiphase strategy that takes all of these questions into account.

For the order-to-cash interface cycle, it was determined that we will complete the following test cycles:

▶ **Unit testing**
Development objects in SAP and the EDI RIM (programs, functions, exits, maps, workflows, and so on) and interface configuration are unit tested by the developer as they are built.

▶ **String testing**
End-to-end processing flow of all interface programs in the EDI RIM and SAP, including connectivity through the IDoc adapter, are tested as development objects are built and refined in both systems. Trading partners are not included in testing.

▶ **Interface testing**
This cycle involves a more structured form of string testing that includes AS2 connectivity with the vendors and at least one customer.

▶ **Integration testing**
This cycle involves end-to-end interface runs, including connectivity with the vendors, within the context of integration testing of business processes in SAP.

▶ **Stress testing**
Here very large volumes of EDI and IDoc data run into and out of SAP and the EDI RIM, while users execute large reports and do normal daily transactional processing.

We'll address all of our testing issues as we look at each phase. But first, we need to cover some general requirements that are applicable to all of Acme's testing phases.

20.2.1 Testing Environments

We have not looked at the SAP and EDI RIM system landscapes at Acme Pictures. For our purposes, it is enough to say there are three SAP environments. Each has its own database, application, and presentation servers: DEV, QAS, and PRD.

Each system is distinguished by the client structure described in Table 20.2.

Environment	Client	Description
DEV	100	Go-forward golden client used to build QAS and PRD, with no data. Development objects are created in 100 and transported to all other clients and environments.
	120	Unit testing of development objects. Master and transactional data. Connected to EDI DEV.
	140	Data conversion test client. Client-specific configuration transported from DEV 100.
QAS	200	QAS golden go-forward client. No data. Configuration and development objects transported from DEV 100.
	240	Date conversion, interface, integration, and stress test client. Refreshed from QAS 200 before data conversion. Connected to EDI QAS.
PRD	300	Go-live production client. All configuration and development objects transported from QAS 200 during cutover. Connected to EDI PRD.
SND	120	Development sandbox for prototyping and play. Created and refreshed from DEV 120.

Table 20.2 SAP Environments and Clients at Acme Pictures

This is a simplified version of the SAP system landscape, and it's all fairly standard stuff. Development objects are created in DEV client 100 and unit tested in 120. Development objects include all IMG configuration settings, custom and extended IDocs, segments, ABAP programs, function groups, function modules, transaction codes, tables, structures, and so on.

Client-dependent objects are transported from 100 to 120 and 140. Client-independent objects are created in 100 and are immediately visible to all other DEV clients.

There's also a sandbox client for prototyping configuration and custom code before creating the objects in 100 and unit testing them in 120.

Partner profiles and file ports are special cases. They are client-dependent, only available in the client in which they were created, and cannot be transported. They must be recreated in each client where they will be used. RFC destinations are client-independent and cannot be transported to other environments such as

QAS and PRD. They are recreated each time a new system is built, although they are available to each client in that system.

Data conversion programs are developed in the Legacy System Migration Workbench (LSMW) in client 100 and tested in 120 and 140. Both ABAP programs and LSMW projects are client-independent and show up in all DEV clients after they are created and saved.

We'll test our custom partner profile load program in DEV 120 and 140, but we won't load partner profiles into client 100 because they are technically master data.

Looking at our interface test cycles, unit and string testing is done in DEV 120. Our QAS environment is reserved for the more formal and structured interface, integration, and stress test cycles.

The issue is promotion of development objects from DEV 100 to our QAS testing environment. Promotion is key to prepping QAS for testing and must be repeated each time a new testing cycle or phase begins.

All development objects are transported from DEV 100 to QAS 200. No data are loaded into 200. QAS 240 is built or refreshed from 200 after all transports have been run from DEV 100. Data conversion then proceeds into 240. All master and transactional data required for the test phase is loaded, including the partner profiles.

This is the first step in each testing cycle. It tests the data conversion projects and populates the QAS environment with the data we'll need for testing.

There will be cycles of intensive data conversion testing, but for the tests that impact our EDI interfaces, we'll load only master and transactional data that have been identified and cleansed for use in our testing.

As 240 is populated, we will add the file ports and other objects that need to be recreated each time a client is built or refreshed.

We will use a similar promotion approach for the EDI objects in the RIM, although it does not have the structured client and transport system of SAP, so it is not as tightly locked down.

EDI DEV connects to SAP DEV 120, and EDI QAS connects to SAP QAS 240. Maps, workflows, and other objects will be developed and unit tested in EDI DEV and promoted to QAS at the same time as the SAP objects.

The only other issue is EDI test data. Acme exchanges EDI transactions with Gordy's Galaxy through direct AS2 transmissions. We will copy some of those transactions to our DEV and QAS clients for testing, which is known as *carbon copying*.

For the tests where we need to mimic the flow of production data into SAP, we will create a process in the legacy system that copies EDI production data as it comes in for transfer to our new RIM EDI QAS system.

20.2.2 Break-Fix Procedures

Related to the issue of testing environments, break-fix procedures are about how we fix development objects when they fail during testing. Break-fix is relevant for the more formal testing phases in QAS.

What happens when a program fails during a test? Who fixes it? How does it get back into QAS? What happens to the test that was aborted by the failure?

Acme's break-fix procedures attempt to address these questions. They include a few guiding principles meant to minimize disruptions to testing:

▶ When a program fails during a test, testing of that program stops until the issue is fixed.

▶ The point of failure is identified, and the issue is documented in a test log with notes about the data that were being tested and relevant screenshots.

▶ The developer who coded the program fixes it. It becomes his top priority. If he is not available, the developer assigned to the test team takes care of it.

▶ The test team is available to help the developer recreate the error in DEV if necessary.

▶ The fix is coded in DEV and unit-tested by the developer, who also updates the technical specifications for the program with the change.

▶ After the developer is satisfied that the fix works, the test team does a dry run of the failed test in DEV. If it passes, the test team approves the fix, and the code is transported to QAS.

▶ When the code has been moved into QAS, the test team reruns the test from the beginning and logs the results.

Fixes that require major program changes need a round of regression testing. Everything that has been tested to the moment of failure is tested again from the beginning.

20.2.3 Test Teams and Responsibilities

Making the test team a priority is a real no-brainer. We need the right people in the right place at the right time. The same technical team will be responsible for all formal EDI interface testing in QAS.

The interface test team for the 856 includes the following roles and responsibilities:

1. SD and FI consultants:
   - Confirm document postings
   - Validate all follow-on processing and documents
   - Verify that enhancements to standard programs work according to functional and technical specifications
   - Support the business user and expert

2. Sales support or operations and accounts receivable business experts and users:
   - Run SAP portions of the test
   - Document results of each test step
   - Train in use of the transaction or business process
   - Document and log test errors with the support of the SD consultant
   - Confirm results in delivery, material, and accounting documents
   - Identify gaps in the business process

3. SAP EDI technical architect/designer:
   - Supports test and development teams in resolving system-wide issues

4. SAP development lead:
   - Monitors IDoc processing and validate syntax and configuration
   - Triggers IDoc processing
   - Verifies enhancements executed according to specifications
   - Documents and log technical issues

▸ Manages the SAP break-fix process and ensures that developers are assigned to fixes

▸ Approves program fixes and ensures they are tested in DEV

5. EDI system development lead:

▸ Triggers and monitors data flows from the EDI RIM into SAP

▸ Ensures that maps and processes execute correctly and that bugs are fixed as they are identified

▸ Manages the EDI break-fix process

▸ Assigns mapping or program fixes to the right developer

▸ Approves fixes before transporting them to EDI QAS

▸ Ensures that AS2 communications are working where connectivity with the customer is also being tested

▸ Documents and logs EDI technical issues

The test teams are supported by technical, infrastructure, and development specialists, including ABAP and EDI developers, the Basis team, and database, network, and communications support. If they are called on to fix a problem during testing, the fix becomes their first priority.

Finally, a test coordinator oversees the testing effort. At Acme, this job falls to the testing consultant. The consultant works with all teams to ensure that every test scenario and business process in every test phase is completed successfully on schedule and is signed off by project management and business owners.

The specialist defines the test strategy and schedule and works with the Basis and development teams in SAP and the EDI RIM to ensure that the test environments are ready before each test phase begins.

She helps the functional and data conversion teams identify, collect, and load clean data for each test phase into the QAS 240 test client. She also ensures that all relevant authorizations are in QAS for each tester, maintains the master list of test scenarios, keeps all teams on schedule, and helps users and support folks assess the results of each test. It's a big job indeed.

20.2.4 Documenting Tests

A number of documents will be used to support execution of test scenarios across all phases:

▶ **Business process procedures (BPPs)**
Detailed step-by-step procedures for running a transaction or business process, including screenshots and data inputs, that string together one or more transactions. BPPs are also developed as training manuals.

▶ **Test scripts**
Details of each step that will be run in a test, including data inputs, and expected and actual outputs returned, for each screen in a transaction or series of transactions. These are designed for test execution rather than training.

▶ **Issues log**
Point of failure documentation during testing. It tracks issues, fixes, data used, target and actual dates for the fix, and parties responsible.

The team will use a browser-based tool to define and record the details of testing. The BPPs and test scripts will be attached where relevant to the test step recorded in the tool.

Now we have the basic outline of Acme's test strategy and can begin working through each phase. Our main interest remains the EDI relationship with Acme's biggest customer, Gordy's Galaxy.

We begin with unit testing.

20.3   Unit Testing

Developers continue to do unit testing until the final version of their code is delivered. Believe it or not, it is one of our favorite pastimes because it lets us see the immediate results of our thinking and coding.

Unit testing is done in the DEV system. Because it involves debugging and changing data values during program runtime, it should never be done in QAS. The base process flow for unit testing is shown in Figure 20.9.

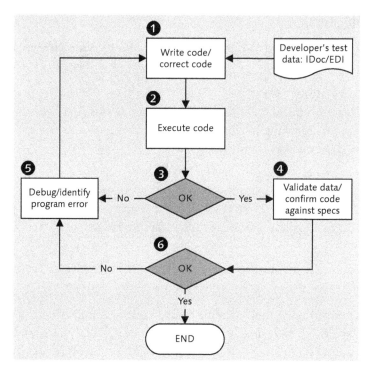

Figure 20.9 Unit Test Base Processing Flow

20.3.1 Scope

The purpose of unit testing is to confirm that the custom development object—whether a program, function, map, business process workflow, or any other object in SAP or the EDI RIM—works according to its functional and technical specifications.

It needs to work technically to fulfill the functional requirement described in the specification.

20.3.2 Criteria for Success

When do we know that unit testing is successful and we can pass our code to the next test phase? This is an informed decision that comes from several cycles of testing with different data samples that match our understanding of the requirements laid out in the specifications.

The assumption here is that we have detailed specifications and easy access to the functional consultants and business owners so that we can ask questions about the requirements when we need clarification.

20.3.3 Dependencies

Successful unit testing is dependent, first of all, on completion of functional and technical specifications.

Functional specifications are written by the functional consultant or business process owner to describe the business functionality of the program and provide data and transactional references for the programmer. They also provide test data and potential points of failure in the business functionality.

The developer works with the author of the functional specifications to understand the requirement and to provide technical background on the feasibility of the functionality.

Technical specifications are written by the developer. They provide program process flow and details of selection screen or custom transactions, tables, structures, segments, IDoc types, and so on.

Technical specifications identify tables that will be read, define formulas for calculations, and step through the program logic that will be written to meet the business requirement of the functional spec. They can get to the level of detailed pseudo code, although most old-timey programmers feel that if they are writing pseudo code, they may as well write real code. However, writing pseudo code can be a useful exercise in nailing down the basic structure and logical flow of a program before beginning to code.

The development must be created at least in an initial version. It also needs test data but these can be dummied up in the earliest phases. By the time the program is fully coded, good test data must be available.

20.3.4 Execution

Unit testing generally works on two levels:

- ▶ **Internal**
  Frequent testing of the snippet of functionality currently being coded. The aim is to ensure that syntax is correct, that the program executes, and that the tested code fragment works as expected.

▶ **Holistic**
Testing and debugging of a complete cut of the development object. The aim is to confirm syntax and execution and to step through the processing flow with test data to validate table reads, calculations, and data transformations.

This approach to developing focuses on building, testing, and debugging snippets of functionality that complete a particular task before moving on to the next. Once the logic is working, the output is validated. Ensure that all of the data expected is retrieved by spot checking documents and tables.

20.4   String Testing

String testing involves unit testing a related string of objects that comprise a program or EDI interface. Its purpose is to confirm that the end-to-end process flow of the interface works with all of its objects, whether they were developed in SAP or the EDI RIM, including connectivity between the two systems.

String testing is done in DEV by the developer with the support of the SAP EDI technical architect, members of the SAP and EDI development teams, and other resources, such as Basis, as needed.

Like unit testing, it can involve debugging and ad hoc rerunning of various pieces of an interface and should never be conducted in QAS.

Interface objects should not be transported into QAS until they have passed a string test in DEV. This is also true when an error occurs during formal testing and a fix is made to any object in the interface.

20.4.1 Scope

String testing is our first opportunity to run each interface with all its objects as an integrated process between SAP and the EDI RIM.

String testing is run for each discrete interface in the order-to-cash cycle of our SAP EDI architecture. And each interface is run as a standalone process, independently of all other interfaces.

Although the general testing process and confirmation points are essentially the same for both inbound and outbound interfaces, the objects validated and the expected results for each differ slightly.

Objects and processing points validated in string testing include the following:

- Inbound
  - Translation map
  - Connection to SAP
  - IDoc created and stored at status 64
  - Customer exit logic working, where relevant
- Outbound
  - Output control and partner profiles configuration
  - IDoc created and stored at status 30
  - IDoc successfully sent to EDI RIM
  - Translation map

We'll look at examples of both the inbound 850-ORDERS customer PO and the outbound INVOIC-810 customer invoice.

20.4.2 Criteria for Success

Success has a well-defined endpoint in string testing.

For inbound processing, the 850 purchase order must successfully translate to an IDoc and be validated against the EDI transaction set and the mapping specifications. The IDoc must also be sent into SAP and stored at status 64.

Customer exits in the IDoc function should be verified. This can also be done by processing the IDoc through the Transaction WE19 test tool debugger and ensuring that the logic works.

It is not necessary to post a sales order, although it can be a useful exercise. We have not yet set up test data in DEV to support posting a sales order.

In outbound processing, the IDoc must be generated through output control, transmitted to the EDI RIM, and translated to an X12 810 transaction set for the correct trading partner. The data in the 810 must also be validated against the IDoc and the mapping specification.

When the string test has been declared a success by the SAP EDI technical architect and the SAP and EDI development team leads, it can be submitted for approval and transport to QAS.

The test coordinator, with the support of the relevant functional team leads and project management, gives the final approval to move the interface objects into QAS.

20.4.3 Dependencies

String testing is dependent on successful completion of unit testing for each object in the tested interface: EDI RIM maps, workflows, programs, scripts, adapters; configuration in both systems; custom ABAP functions, programs, or customer exits; and so on.

The objects have been validated in unit testing against completed functional and technical specifications, including mapping specifications.

A carbon copy process is set up in legacy to copy and move EDI production transactions into a directory on the EDI RIM DEV application server for all interfaces that will be tested.

Outbound EDI transactions are also copied to compare with the mapping specifications and transactions translated in testing.

In addition, outbound string testing is dependent on the existence of business documents that generate IDocs, such as deliveries and invoices.

Master data and IDoc configuration to support outbound string testing is also required, including output control, condition records, partner profiles, file ports, and an RFC destination to call the receiving process in the EDI RIM.

20.4.4 Execution

The string test is triggered in the EDI RIM for inbound to SAP testing and in SAP for outbound to EDI interfaces. Validation along identified checkpoints in the interface flows is handled by both the SAP and EDI technical teams, depending on the system, the checkpoint object, and the expertise required for evaluation.

We begin with the inbound 850 string test.

Inbound 850 Purchase Order

The inbound X12 850 customer purchase order string test is triggered manually in EDI RIM DEV. It is not sent from the customer.

Figure 20.10 outlines the processing flow for the string test.

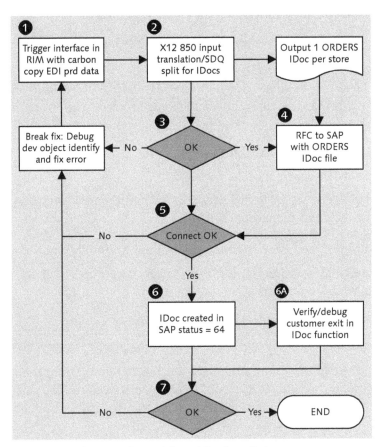

Figure 20.10 String Testing an Inbound Purchase Order

The test begins by getting an 850 interchange from Gordy's Galaxy from the carbon copy in the legacy EDI system into a directory on the EDI RIM DEV application server.

The first validation point is the translation from the X12 850 to the ORDERS IDoc. In the case of an SDQ transaction, the X12 is unwrapped at the item level and converted into one IDoc for each store level ship-to party.

The key validation is that the number of IDocs matches the number of stores ordering in the 850. We also validate that the number of materials match in both documents and we spot check quantities for store-item combinations.

Any problems in the translation are corrected and the interface is rerun from the beginning.

The next key checkpoint is the connection between SAP and the EDI RIM. If an IDoc fails to show up in SAP, we will identify and fix the problem. The error can be in any of the following:

▶ Installation and setup of JCo on the EDI RIM app server

▶ Configuration of the IDoc adapter in the EDI RIM

▶ An interruption in RFC into SAP from a network or other technical issue (may need Basis or infrastructure support to resolve)

After the error is identified, the interface is restarted from the beginning.

If the systems connect, the next validation is that the IDocs were created in SAP and are ready for application processing at status 64.

If the IDocs aren't at status 64, it is most likely due to one of two issues:

▶ IDoc syntax: Translation or data error. Fix the map or the data.

▶ Configuration: Generally related to the partner profile. Either the partner profile is missing or the control record is incorrect. The solution is to correct the partner profile or the map logic that populated the control segment and then resend the IDoc.

If any customer exits are coded in the IDoc processing function, we will run through them as well to confirm that the logic is working. The aim is not to post a sales order but to confirm that we don't hit an error when we run the IDoc processing function. If the sales order fails to post because of data issues, our test is still a success because the code ran without failing.

If there are errors and they have been fixed by the responsible developers, the interface is run again from the beginning in the EDI RIM. After the IDoc is created and stored at status 64 and any custom code in the processing function runs without failing, we can declare the test a success.

Outbound Customer Invoice

The outbound X12 810 customer invoice string test is triggered in SAP when an IDoc is generated by calling Transaction VF02 and saving the billing document.

Figure 20.11 outlines the processing flow for an outbound string test.

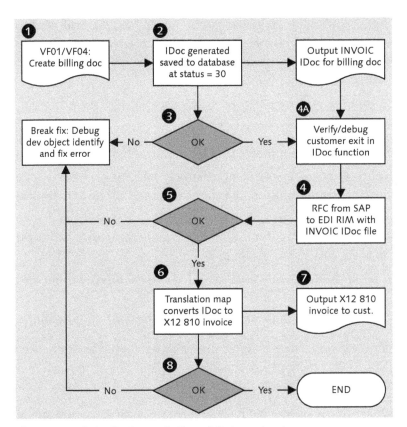

Figure 20.11 String Testing an Outbound Customer Invoice

If output control and the partner profile are configured correctly, an INVOIC IDoc is generated and stored at status 30 when a billing doc is created and saved with Transaction VF01 or with the billing due list Transaction VF31.

If there is a problem, it is most likely because the condition record has not been added for the output type and partner, or the partner profile is missing or incorrectly configured. The error needs to be identified and fixed and the IDoc generated.

If there are any customer exits in the IDoc processing function, it will be hit during IDoc generation. If it fails, we need to identify the point of failure and unit test the function until we are satisfied that it works. Then we restart the string test by generating a new IDoc out of a billing document.

If the IDoc is successfully generated, it is written to the database at status 30. The IDoc is kicked out of SAP using Transactions BD87 or WE14. We will need to confirm that SAP sends the IDoc to a file on its application server, completes the RFC to the EDI RIM, and triggers a receiving process that picks up the IDoc and sends it to the translation step.

If the transfer to the EDI RIM fails, there's a connection error, which could be prompted by one of the following circumstances:

▶ The output mode in the partner profile isn't set to start subsystem.

▶ The XML file port is not configured to automatically start the external system, is not pointing to an RFC destination, or is pointing to the wrong RFC destination.

▶ There is a problem with the RFC destination or the receiving workflow process in the EDI Rim is not correctly registered.

▶ The IDoc adapter in the EDI RIM is not configured or is incorrectly configured for receipt of RFCs from SAP.

▶ The JCo java connector on the EDI RIM application server is incorrectly installed.

In the real world, these objects are all interconnected. For example, if the IDoc adapter in the EDI RIM is incorrectly configured, the RFC destination will not register the server program and the connection will fail.

Some configuration errors may be at the Basis system level. The Basis team would then need to get involved.

Assuming no errors, or that all errors have been corrected and a new IDoc generated, the next validation point is translation.

If the map fails, the EDI team tracks down the source of the problem. It fails either because of an error in the map or because mandatory data are missing from the IDoc.

If the problem is in the IDoc, it will be fixed in SAP and resent. If it is a mapping error, the EDI team fixes the map and the SAP team regenerates the IDoc from the billing document.

If translation succeeds, we validate the data in the 810 invoice against the mapping specifications and the IDoc. We also confirm that the expected number of items translated from the IDoc to the 810 and that the ship-to partners, materials, quantities, and amounts are all correct. If there are many items, we can spot-check.

When all checks are done, we can declare the outbound string test a success.

20.5 Interface Testing

Interface testing treats each EDI interface as an integrated business process that spans development and configuration objects in SAP and the EDI RIM.

Interface testing is a more formal and structured approach run in QAS by a full test team, which includes functional and business experts in addition to the technical teams.

Connectivity with the trading partner is tested and business documents post to SAP.

The test teams are supported by the test coordinator, the SAP EDI technical architect, the development and functional teams, and other resources, such as basis and infrastructure support groups, as needed

20.5.1 Scope

Interface testing is our first opportunity to confirm results for each interface. It validates that each interface works end-to-end in a controlled QAS test environment with selected data. The aim is to identify and fix any development issues in SAP, the translation maps, or EDI processes and programs, including connectivity.

Each interface is run between SAP, the EDI RIM, and the trading partner, in the order in which it will run in production. This gives the team its first sense of where each interface fits within the overall processing cycle.

Interfaces for purchasing are run in the following order:

1. Outbound purchase order for replication: ORDERS to X12 850
2. Inbound PO acknowledgment: X12 855 to ORDRSP
3. Inbound goods receipt: X12 867 to MBGMCR
4. Inbound supplier invoice: X12 810 to INVOIC

Interfaces for the order-to-cash cycle are run in the following order:

1. Inbound customer purchase order: X12 850 to ORDERS
2. Outbound PO acknowledgment: ORDRSP to X12 855
3. Outbound ship order: SHPORD to X12 830
4. Inbound ship confirmation: X12 856 to SHPCON
5. Outbound advanced ship notification: DESADV to X12 856
6. Outbound customer invoice: INVOIC to X12 810
7. Inbound remittance advice: X12 820 to REMADV

AS2 connectivity will also be tested for the inbound 850 and outbound 810 with Gordy's Galaxy and for the outbound 830 and inbound 856 with the vendor Disc Services International (DSI).

In addition, interface testing confirms that inbound IDocs create or update relevant business documents in SAP, although posting of follow-up documents is not validated.

Acme's Project Q interface testing is scheduled to last for two weeks.

20.5.2 Criteria for Success

Interface testing builds on the success of string testing. Everything that was needed to succeed in the DEV environment for string testing must also succeed in QAS for interface testing, including:

▶ Successful translation of IDocs to X12, X12 to IDocs, and validation of all maps against mapping specifications
▶ Successful execution of all standard and custom code and configuration in SAP and the EDI RIM
▶ Inbound IDocs stored at status 64 before posting to a business document

- ▸ Outbound IDocs generated from SAP business documents and stored at status 03 after being exported to the EDI RIM
- ▸ Connectivity between SAP and the EDI RIM

In addition to these validations, connectivity with the trading partner must succeed for at least one inbound and one outbound interface.

Inbound connectivity succeeds when an X12 interchange is received into the EDI RIM by AS2 transmission and an MDN acknowledgment is returned to the partner. The RIM then sends a 997 acknowledgment to the sending partner for the inbound transaction when the functional group has been extracted from the interchange.

Outbound connectivity succeeds when an X12 interchange is sent to the trading partner and an MDN acknowledgment is immediately received. The partner follows with a 997, which is processed by the EDI RIM.

Interface testing, for the first time, validates that the inbound IDoc creates or updates an SAP document using defined test data:

- ▸ Inbound INVOIC creates an MM invoice
- ▸ Inbound ORDERS creates a sales order
- ▸ Inbound SHPCON updates pick quantity and triggers PGI
- ▸ Inbound REMADV creates a payment advice

Posting of follow-on documents is not confirmed at this point, however.

When all interfaces have been validated on the test scripts in the sequence in which they will run in the order-to-cash cycle, and all scripts are signed off, the test coordinator can declare interface testing a success.

20.5.3 Dependencies

Interface testing is dependent on the successful conclusion of unit and string testing. All development objects and configuration must be transported into the QAS environment for both systems. In SAP, QAS client 200 is built from DEV 100, and the 240 test client from 200.

Program and mapping specifications, BPPs, test scripts, issue logs, and other testing and supporting documentation are completed by the relevant teams. One test script is defined for each interface in the purchasing and order-to-cash cycles. Each testing step is described in the script. A testing schedule is defined and resources assigned to the test teams.

A complete set of master and transactional data to support all interfaces has been collected and prepped for loading. Data conversion programs were tested QAS 240. All test data are loaded, including EDPAR, EDSDC, partner profiles, and ZEDIXREF.

X12 interchanges are collected from the carbon copy in the legacy PRD EDI system to test inbound interfaces and to compare to translations generated by outbound IDocs. X12 data were selected to match the test data that we will use in SAP, particularly the ship-to locations mapped in EDPAR and the material masters.

Communications configuration is completed in the EDI RIM and on the network. AS2 profiles are set up for Gordy's Galaxy, DSI, and the firewall is open to incoming IP addresses from both partners.

Last but not least, the EDI teams at Gordy's and DSI have scheduled time for connectivity testing with Acme. They completed all their setup and configuration work in their middleware and are ready to exchange data with Acme's EDI RIM.

20.5.4 Execution

The scenarios in the scripts are the roadmaps for executing each interface test. They provide setup data for the scenario as a whole, a description of the business process, and the expected and actual results for each test step.

Many steps are common to all inbound and outbound interfaces, particularly technical processing through the EDI RIM and SAP. Differences are mainly related to the functionality of an interface.

The interface test scenario for an inbound 850 customer purchase order, for example, records the business process steps outlined in Table 20.3.

Number	Step Description	Txn	Expected Result	Result
0	Receive 850 by AS2	850	X12 decrypted	ISA number 1234
1	Send MDN to partner	850	Partner confirms MDN	OK

Table 20.3 Interface Test Scenario for the Inbound 850 PO

Number	Step Description	Txn	Expected Result	Result
2	997 generated	997	997 sent to customer	ISA number 2122. Gordy confirms
3	Translated to IDoc	850	ORDERS IDoc file	OK: File name
4	Send IDoc to SAP	BD87	IDoc at status 64	IDoc number 43456701
5	IDoc posts sales order	VA01	SO doc type ZEDI ▶ Sold-to: GRDY01. ▶ Ship-to GRDY000987. ▶ Qty: 20/Price: $11.95	SO number 20345670

Table 20.3 Interface Test Scenario for the Inbound 850 PO (Cont.)

Setup data for the scenario include Gordy's sold-to and ship-to numbers, the material being ordered by EDI, and the sales organization, distribution channel, and division used to create the sales order.

The test scenario begins with receipt of the encrypted X12 850 interchange by AS2 transmission and ends when a sales order posts to SAP. Each step touches on a key milestone in the processing cycle of the interface.

The steps are exactly the same for all inbound interfaces. The differences are in the map called and the business document posted or updated, which define the logic confirmed by the scenario.

Outbound processing is not that much different. This is illustrated by the test scenario for an outbound 810 customer invoice in Table 20.4.

Number	Step Description	Txn	Expected Results	Result
0	Create billing document	VF04	Delivery number 809899 generates billing document	Billing 907865
1	Check output	VF03	IDoc in processing log	IDoc number 245674

Table 20.4 Interface Test Scenario for the Outbound 810 Invoice

Number	Step Description	Txn	Expected Results	Result
2	Process OB IDoc	WE14	IDoc sent to EDI RIM; status = 18	OK
3	RIM picks up IDoc		IDoc number 245674 in EDI RIM	OK
4	Translated to X12 810	810	810 interchange created; IDoc status = 06	ISA number 3241
5	X12 sent to customer	810	Interchange encrypted transmitted by AS2	OK
6	MDN received	MDN	Customer sends MDN	OK; customer called
7	997 received	997	Customer returns 997 on 810	OK; ISA number 4312

Table 20.4 Interface Test Scenario for the Outbound 810 Invoice (Cont.)

The only difference between outbound scenarios involves the X12 855 PO acknowledgment interface. It adds a step to run a custom program that bundles all sales orders from one SDQ PO into a single confirmation.

Setup data to test the outbound customer invoice include Gordy's payer, bill-to, sold-to, and ship-to partners; the sales order and delivery numbers; material numbers; and output type and condition record.

The test scenario begins with generation of the billing document through the billing due list. It is dependent on the existence of a completed delivery that can be billed. It runs through all of the steps of outbound processing and ends when the translated X12 810 interchange is encrypted, sent by AS2 to Gordy's EDI team, and successfully acknowledged with an MDN.

AS2 connectivity with Gordy's is tested only once for one inbound and one outbound interface. If it succeeds once, it will always connect, unless the AS2 setup is changed by either partner. Then it needs to be retested.

The test scenario describes each processing milestone as a discrete step but the interface runs straight through once it is triggered. But the results of each step are carefully documented when the interface completes its run, including screenshots proving the expected results.

An inbound interfaces runs until it creates an IDoc at status 64, when it is processed manually by program RBDAPP01 to post the sales order.

An outbound interface runs to its end point, which is receipt of the 997 by the EDI RIM acknowledging receipt and acceptance of the X12 transaction.

Figure 20.12 outlines the process for running an interface test. This process is the same for both inbound and outbound interfaces.

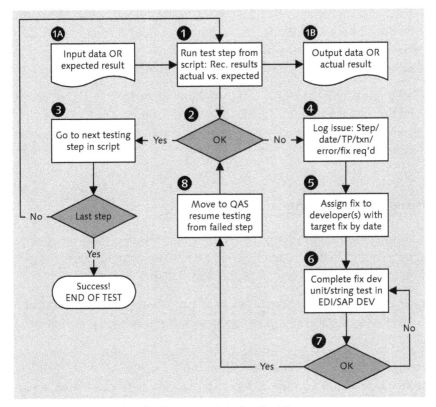

Figure 20.12 Process Flow for Running an Interface Test Step

After the interface completes its processing run, the testers go back to the beginning of the test scenario and check and document each step. If the step results match expectations, then the results are entered into the script against the step and the step is signed off.

If results *don't* match expectations, the issue is documented in the issues log and investigated by the technical team. If a programming or configuration error is identified, a developer is assigned to fix the issue.

The nature of the problem determines which developer is assigned to the fix. A translation error goes to the EDI mapper who built the map. An ABAP error goes to the SAP developer who wrote the code.

In each case, the relevant technical team lead manages the effort and ensures that the fix is tested and approved in DEV before it is transported to QAS. When the fix has been moved back to QAS, the test is run again from the beginning. Each step is validated in the order in which it appears in the scenario and success is documented. If the fix succeeds, the corrected step is signed off by the tester.

After each step has been successfully completed, the scenario is approved by the technical and functional team leads and the test coordinator. The next test scenario is then triggered and the process repeated until all interfaces have been successfully tested and signed off.

20.6   Integration Testing

Integration testing validates the design of our integrated business processes. Rather than concentrate on one end-to-end interface, we will test complete business processes that can encompass multiple interfaces and transactions.

Integration testing is about the system as a whole, particularly the points of integration between interfaces, transactions, and processes. Think of it as a dress rehearsal for production.

It is not enough to post a sales order and successfully complete all of the EDI and SAP processing behind it. That sales order must also pass all its checks and generate a confirmation to send the customer through the ORDRSP to X12 855 interface and a ship order to send to the distributor.

It must successfully post follow-up documents in inventory and accounting for each business document created or updated that requires it.

Although connectivity with trading partners is not tested, EDI documents are exchanged with the distributor DSI. The aim is to validate processing results in DSI's EDI and backend business systems.

Everybody who needs to be is either on the integration test team or called in to help if their expertise is required. Business users drive the test cycles with the support of the functional and business experts and the SAP EDI technical architect. Test teams are further supported by the test coordinator, the technical team leads, functional and development teams, and other resources and support groups as needed.

20.6.1 Scope

Integration testing emulates running Acme's business in the new system. This is done by testing real-world scenarios based on the system design and input from business process experts and users.

All systems with a stake in the new SAP environment participate in integration testing. Though our focus is Acme's new SAP EDI architecture, there are also legacy systems that support VMI processing, for example. These must also be ready for testing.

Our goal for the EDI team is to prove that the purchasing and order-to-cash cycles work end-to-end.

We look at the order-to-cash cycle here. Three business processes have been defined in integration test scenarios:

1. Drop order to distributor
   - Inbound EDI and VMI customer purchase order to SAP sales order
   - Outbound purchase order acknowledgment to the customer from the sales order to an X12 855
   - Outbound shipping order to the contract distributor from the delivery document to an X12 830
2. Shipping
   - Inbound shipping confirmation with pick quantity and post goods issue from the distributor to the delivery document

- ► Outbound advance shipping notification to the customer from the delivery to an X12 856

3. Billing and payment

- ► Outbound invoice to the customer from a billing document to an X12 810

- ► Inbound remittance advice from the customer to a payment advice note in SAP for clearing

Acme's Project Q integration testing is scheduled to last six weeks. It will run in three cycles of two weeks each. EDI-related scenarios for order-to-cash processing will be tested in the third cycle.

20.6.2 Criteria for Success

Integration testing succeeds on a micro level and a macro level. Each step of each integration test scenario, each scenario, and all three scenarios together must succeed as a whole before we can verify that we can receive orders, ship product, invoice customers, and process payments using our new SAP EDI architecture.

Everything that succeeded in previous tests must also succeed in integration testing. We will not test connectivity, but we will confirm that the vendor's EDI and business systems are updating correctly with our EDI transmissions.

All incoming IDocs post to an SAP business document. An ORDERS IDoc creates a sales order; SHPCON updates the delivery document with picking quantity and post goods issue, and REMADV creates a payment advice for clearing by accounts receivable.

In addition, all follow-up processing must succeed. Before the sales order is completed, for example, pricing must be pulled in and discrepancies between the EDI and SAP prices for an item resolved. The sold-to partner passes a credit check, and an availability check ensures that there is open inventory to fulfill the order.

All of this must be confirmed by the functional members of the test team. Only then can the test step be signed off by the tester and the ORDRSP confirmation generated by the system as the next step in test process.

This is only the beginning, of course. To confirm success for each step of the integration test scenario, all background and follow-up processing must be validated for each document or IDoc by the responsible test team members.

When all EDI test scenarios have been validated on the test scripts, all issues have been identified and resolved, and all scripts have been signed off by the integration scenario test team lead, then the test coordinator declares success and works with project management to get their final sign-off.

This is a critical step in the lifecycle of the project. Approval of integration testing means that the system is ready for prime time.

20.6.3 Dependencies

Integration testing is dependent on the successful conclusion of unit, string, and interface testing.

Development has been frozen in all systems, including SAP, the EDI RIM, and remaining legacy systems. All development objects and configuration have been completed and tested in the previous test cycles and transported into the QAS environment.

In SAP, QAS client 200 has been rebuilt from DEV 100, and the 240 test client has been refreshed and rebuilt from 200.

Integration test scenarios have been defined. One test script has been written for each EDI scenario in the order-to-cash cycle. Program and mapping specifications, BPPs, issue logs, and other supporting documentation have been updated to reflect changes from earlier test cycles. The integration test schedule has been set and the test teams have assembled.

Data conversion testing is a dry run for production cutover data loads. All master and transactional data that will be loaded into production are uploaded into QAS 240 during integration test cycle 1.

IDoc configuration and master data are set up in QAS 240, including RFC destinations, file ports, partner profiles, output types, condition records, and EDI-SAP cross-reference tables. We also pulled a large sample of X12 production data from carbon copy in the legacy EDI system.

Communications are configured between all systems, on the network, and Acme's trading partners. However, except for some EDI exchanges with DSI, AS2 communications with the partners are disabled.

20.6.4 Execution

Integration test scenarios describe end-to-end business processes that include multiple interfaces and transactions. Although the testing approach is the same for all, and the evaluation of the technical steps similar, the specifics are different for each.

We'll look at each business scenario in turn.

Drop Order to Distributor

The integration test scenario for drop order to distributor is outlined in Table 20.5. The customer order is pulled from EDI legacy carbon copy.

Number	BP Step Description	Txn	Expected Result	Result
0	Customer PO; not sent by AS2	850	PO interface triggered manually in EDI RIM; 850 is archived	ISA number 850034
1	997 generated	997	997 stops before AS2 send and is archived	ISA number 997022, archive file name
2	850 translated to IDoc	850	ORDERS XML IDoc file; IDoc is archived	OK: File name
3	IDoc sent to SAP	BD87	ORDERS = status 64	IDoc number 43456701
4	IDoc posts sales order.	VA01	SO doc type ZEDI ▶ Sold-to: GORD01 ▶ Ship-to GORD000987 ▶ Material: 39856 ▶ Qty: 20/Price: $11.95	SO number 20345670
5	Check pricing	VA01	PR00 = 11.95	OK

Table 20.5 Drop Order to Distributor Integration Test Scenario

Number	BP Step Description	Txn	Expected Result	Result
6	Credit limit	VA01	OK	OK
7	Availability check	VA01	OK	OK
8	Generate confirmation	BD87	ORDRSP = status 30	IDoc number 43456722
9	Process OB IDoc	WE14	XML IDoc sent to EDI RIM status = 18; IDoc file archived in RIM	OK
10	Translated to X12 855	855	855 interchange created IDoc status = 06	ISA number 855041
11	855 calls AS2 send	855	AS2 send fails; 855 is archived	Archive file name
12	Delivery created from sales order	VL10	▸ Shipping point: 0015 ▸ Sales order: 20345670	Del: 80345880
13	Generate ship order	BD87	SHPORD = status 30	IDoc number 43456724
14	Process OB IDoc	WE14	XML IDoc sent to EDI RIM status = 18; IDoc file is archived	OK
15	Translated to X12 830	830	830 interchange created IDoc status = 06	ISA number 830032
16	830 calls AS2 send	830	DSI receives 830; 830 file archived in RIM	MDN, DSI EDI confirms receipt
17	DSI sends back a 997	997	EDI RIM receives and archives 997	ISA number 997042
18	DSI system updated	830	DSI posts ship order	DSI EDI confirms

Table 20.5 Drop Order to Distributor Integration Test Scenario (Cont.)

The test begins when processing of an inbound 850 from the carbon copy is triggered in the EDI RIM. It ends when a shipping order posts to DSI's backend business system.

Each step represents a milestone in the processing cycle of the scenario and is described in detail by a test script.

Figure 20.13 outlines the process flow for the drop order to distribution integration test scenario.

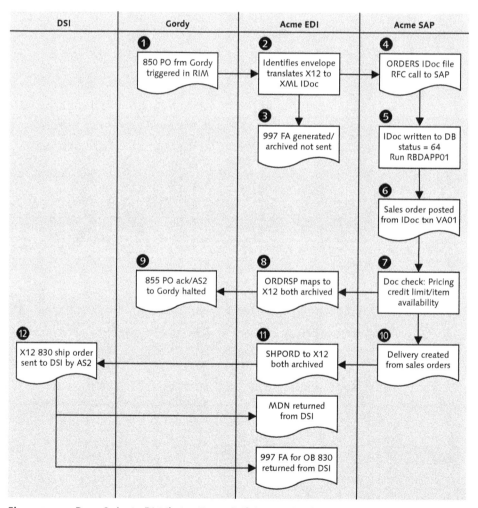

Figure 20.13 Drop Order to Distributor Happy Path Integration Scenario

Steps 0 through 3 are confirmed by the EDI team. The sales order is posted by manually running RBDAPP01 with the IDoc number. Each step is signed off by the tester as it is documented and confirmed. Errors are entered into the issues log and a developer immediately assigned to the fix.

By this point in the project lifecycle, all major development issues should have been fixed. However, integration testing introduces larger volumes of new production data and a more complete system environment that could uncover unexpected errors.

The standard break-fix process is followed for all errors. Fixes are coded and retested in DEV, transported back to QAS 240, and the integration test restarted from the beginning.

After the sales order posts, the business user validates pricing, customer credit limit, and the availability of stock. He then confirms that an ORDRSP IDoc was generated and is at status 30, ready to be sent to Gordy's Galaxy.

The IDoc is sent to the EDI system and the status updated to 18—*EDI system triggered*. The IDoc is translated to an 855 order confirmation and the IDoc status in SAP updated to 06—*Translation successful*. A failed AS2 call to Gordy is triggered and the 855 is archived.

The delivery due list is then run to create a delivery document from the sales order, and a SHPORD IDoc is generated and sent to the EDI RIM. The IDoc is translated to an 830 and sent by AS2 to DSI.

DSI responds with an MDN and a 997 functional acknowledgment. DSI's EDI team reports back to Acme that the 830 posted to a shipping order in DSI's business system. Data are compared between the two teams and, if DSI's order has everything that Acme sent in the 830, the scenario is complete.

The test coordinator confirms every step. If the results are correct, he signs off on the scenario. The team then moves on to the next test scenario.

Shipping

Table 20.6 outlines the integration test scenario for shipping.

Number	BP Step Description	Txn	Expected Result	Result
0	DSI sends ShipConf	856	Decrypted ship confirmation received; 856 archived	ISA number 856036
1	997 generated	997	997 sent to DSI MDN returned; 997 archived	ISA number 997025, DSI confirms
2	Translated to IDoc	856	SHPCON XML IDoc file; IDoc file archived	OK: File name
3	IDoc sent to SAP	BD87	SHPCON = status 64	IDoc number 43456791
4	IDoc updates delivery	VL02	Del: 80345880. Pick qty. = 20 for 39856; post goods issue	OK
5	Check picking request	VL03	Check document flow	OK; picking req: 20878752
6	Check material document	VL03 MB03	Material document for goods issue. Move type 601 relieves inventory by qty. 20 for material 39856; GL account	OK; material document number: 800365785
7	Generate customer ASN from updated delivery	BD87	DESADV = status 30	IDoc number 43456756
8	Process OB IDoc	WE14	XML IDoc sent to EDI RIM Status = 18; IDoc file is archived	OK

Table 20.6 Shipping Integration Test Scenario

Number	BP Step Description	Txn	Expected Result	Result
9	Translated to X12 856	856	856 interchange created; IDoc status = 06	ISA number 856055
10	856 calls AS2 send	856	Send fails; 856 is archived	Archive file name

Table 20.6 Shipping Integration Test Scenario (Cont.)

Setup data for the shipping scenario include DSI vendor number, Gordy's sold-to and ship-to numbers, the item shipped, sales order number, output types, and condition records.

Figure 20.14 outlines the process flow for the shipping integration test scenario.

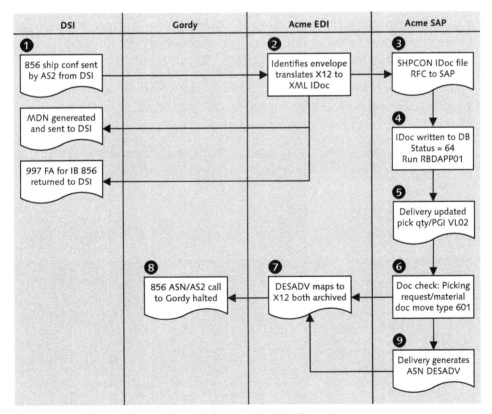

Figure 20.14 Shipping Process Happy Path Integration Test Scenario

DSI sends an 856 shipping confirmation by AS2 into the EDI RIM. An MDN and 997 are returned to Gordy, and the 856 is converted to a SHPCON IDoc. The IDoc is sent into SAP and stored at status 64. The EDI team confirms all of the previous steps before processing the inbound IDoc.

The SHPCON IDoc updates the delivery document with the pick quantity and post goods issue. The business users confirm through the document flow that a picking request and material document have been created.

The material document can also be checked with Transaction MB03. It records a 601 movement type relieving inventory for the finished goods shipped by DSI. The quantity relieved must match the quantity sent in the 856 and the GL account must be updated.

Standard break-fix processing is followed for any development or business issue that crops up at any step within the scenario.

If all follow-up processing is validated, a DESADV IDoc is generated from the delivery to be sent to Gordy as an advanced ship notification. The IDoc is stored at status 30 and outbound processing kicked off with Transaction WE14.

The IDoc is picked up by the EDI RIM, and the translation map is called. It is converted to an outbound 856 ASN, encrypted, and an AS2 call is begun but fails. The 856 is archived and the scenario is completed.

The test coordinator confirms every step and, if satisfied, signs off on the scenario. The team then moves on to the billing and payments scenario.

Billing and Payment

Table 20.7 outlines the billing and payment integration test scenario.

Number	BP Step Description	Txn	Expected Result	Result
0	Generate billing document from billing due list	VF04	Billing document created for del 80345880	Billing document: 905627712
1	Check accounting document	VF03 FB03	Accounting invoice in document flow	Accounting document: 905627712

Table 20.7 Billing and Payments Integration Test Scenario

Number	BP Step Description	Txn	Expected Result	Result
2	Confirm INVOIC IDOC generated	BD87	INVOIC = status 30	IDoc number 43456898
3	Process OB IDoc.	WE14	XML IDoc sent to EDI RIM. Status = 18; IDoc archived	OK
4	Translated to X12 810	810	810 interchange created; IDoc status = 06	ISA Number 810062
5	810 calls AS2 send	810	Send halted; 810 archived	Archive file name
6	Customer payment advice sent from EDI	820	Carbon copy 820 pulled from legacy EDI	ISA number 820055
7	997 generated	997	997 archived; AS2 to customer halted	ISA number 997045, archive file
8	Translated to IDoc	820	REMADV XML IDoc file; IDoc archived	OK: File name
9	IDoc sent to SAP	BD87	REMADV = status 64.	IDoc number 43456900
10	IDoc creates payment note	FBE1	Payment advice for invoice: 905627712	OK
11	Check payment	FBE3	Invoice, documents, and amounts match X12	OK
12	Accounts receivables runs clearing	F-28	Open items cleared, accounts updated; AR testing	OK

Table 20.7 Billing and Payments Integration Test Scenario (Cont.)

Setup data for the billing and payment scenario include Gordy's sold-to, bill-to, and ship-to numbers; item billed; delivery document number; output types; and condition records.

Figure 20.15 outlines the process flow for the billing and payment integration scenario. The test is stopped, and the standard break-fix process is used whenever any step fails to meet its expected results.

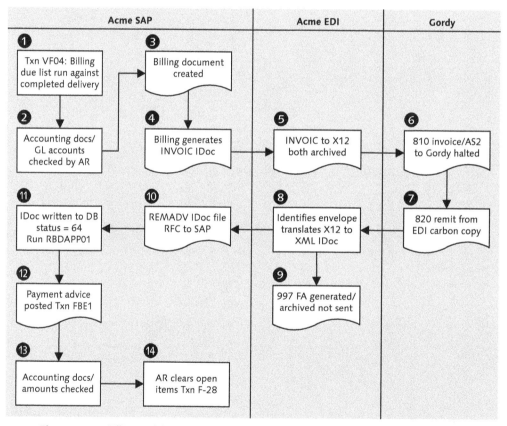

Figure 20.15 Billing and Payment Happy Path Integration Scenario

The billing due list is run with Transaction VF04 to generate a billing document against the delivery that was completed. The billing generates an accounting invoice that is validated by accounts receivable business users. We need to confirm that the correct GL accounts and profit centers were hit for the orders being billed.

If the billing document has been transferred to accounting, an INVOIC IDoc is generated from output and stored in the database at status 30.

The EDI team triggers outbound processing, the EDI RIM picks up the IDoc file, and the IDoc status in SAP is updated to 18. The translation map is called, and the IDoc is converted to an 810 customer invoice.

An AS2 call is made with the encrypted 810 invoice to Gordy's Galaxy EDI system, but it fails as expected. The 810 file is archived. Its file name and path are recorded on the test script.

An 820 interchange is then pulled from the carbon copy and used to trigger the inbound interface. It includes a line item for the invoice just translated to the 810.

The 820 generates an outbound 997, is translated to a REMADV IDoc file, is sent into SAP, and is stored at status 64. The EDI team confirms all previous steps and processes the IDoc. The IDoc creates a payment advice that the FI team validates against the invoice just sent in the 810. They also confirm that the total of all line-item payment amounts equals the total payment amount at the header level of the document.

Meanwhile, the EDI team spot-checks the payment advice and confirms that the document numbers recorded at the line-item level match those in the 820. They also validate that the line item amounts for the documents checked match those in the 820.

After all steps in the scenario have been completed, documented, and signed off, EDI testing on the order-to-cash cycle is done. The payment advice belongs to AR, which clears the payment during its own integration testing.

The test coordinator goes over every step and confirms the results. He then signs off on the scenario and presents the results for all three scenarios to the business owners and project management. If everybody is satisfied that the results meet expectations, then EDI integration testing for the new SAP system is declared a success.

20.7 Stress Testing

The goal of stress testing is to stress the system by imagining an exaggerated work-day in a production-like environment.

Both the EDI RIM and SAP are tested with massive quantities of data pulled from legacy production, inbound and outbound, while users run daily transactions and reports at an elevated pace.

Acme chose to stress test PRD after an initial build before final cutover. PRD has more resources than QAS, and Acme wants to give them a good workout in preparation for cutover.

The stress test team includes everyone who served on the integration test teams with additional technical resources from the development and Basis teams. It is managed by the test coordinator and supported by the SAP EDI technical architect.

20.7.1 Scope

Our goal is to mimic a workday on steroids. Everything that we can muster will be thrown at the EDI RIM and SAP concurrently. We will run the following jobs more or less at the same time:

▶ Regularly scheduled Basis jobs

▶ Interfaces between SAP and internal systems, particularly those that can be scheduled to send large volumes of master and transactional data through the RIM

▶ Large volumes of inbound EDI transmissions representing at least two weeks' worth of transactions

▶ Background processing of all configured inbound IDocs

▶ Background processing of delivery and billing due lists to generate large numbers of business documents and outbound IDocs

▶ Reports on large data sets run regularly by the SAP job scheduler

▶ Normal daily transactions in all functional areas by users running computer-aided testing tool (CATT, using Transaction SCAT) scripts with large data files at scheduled intervals, including end-to-end business processes such as ordering, delivery, and billing

Stress testing only lasts for one day.

20.7.2 Criteria for Success

Success is declared when the system survives the stress of the day.

Everything that was tested in previous cycles must succeed, but the goal of stress testing is not to prove functionality. It is to push the new PRD system hard and to uncover and fix performance and functionality issues in SAP and the EDI RIM.

20.7.3 Dependencies

All previous test cycles were successful and PRD is built. This includes all EDI-related configuration and master data such as file ports, partner profiles, EDPAR, and so on.

The EDI RIM PRD system has been built from QAS, JCo is installed, and the IDoc adapter is configured. Connections between the EDI RIM and SAP production systems must be working.

PRD client 300 is built by transporting all configuration and development objects from QAS 200. Data conversion programs are then run to load all master and transactional data to the client. This is not the final data load. It is a dry run for cutover conversion into PRD.

A processing schedule has been defined by the EDI coordinator. It lists all transactions, interfaces, and jobs that will run each hour throughout the day.

Batch schedules have been created in SAP and the legacy systems to trigger internal interfaces throughout the day. Jobs will be set up in the SAP job scheduler to continuously run a mix of basis programs, business reports, and IDoc batch processing for EDI.

CATT test cases have been recorded to run transactions that business users in all functional areas will normally use each day.

CATTs mimic manual data entry by recording input into the fields and screens of a transaction. The transaction can then be played back and data entered manually or from a text file.

More than one transaction can be recorded in the sequence in which each appears in a business process. This allows creation of a test case that runs an end-to-end business process manually, as a user would do in production.

For example, manual order to billing is covered by a CATT that runs Transaction VA01 to create a sales order, VL10 to generate a delivery from the order, VL02N to update pick quantities and PGI, and VF04 to generate a billing document from the completed delivery.

Each transaction in the CATT sequence is run in foreground mode. Data for each transaction are fed from a file, although data can be added or changed manually because the transaction is running in the foreground.

Input files also need to be created for each CATT. The field structure of each file corresponds to the sequence in which the fields are populated by the CATT at runtime.

A large number of inbound EDI transactions will be collected from legacy and moved to the new EDI RIM PRD system, including every transaction that will be sent to the new system.

20.7.4 Execution

The stress test follows a schedule that repeats a complete processing cycle every hour.

At the top of each hour, the EDI team releases inbound EDI transactions through the RIM. At the same time, jobs kick off in SAP to run interfaces with internal systems and output a number of resource-intensive business reports, such as currently open sales and deliveries.

The inbound IDocs hit SAP from the EDI RIM and are batched at status 64. The IDocs are processed by scheduled jobs every 15 minutes.

Meanwhile, groups of one to five users run a variety of transactions and business processes in purchasing, sales, and finance through CATT scripts. The CATTs are run in foreground processing mode and load data samples from input files that are supplemented with manual data entry.

Each group monitors and documents the results of its piece of the test. If errors occur, testing stops, and standard break-fix procedures are followed to fix the problem. After the fix has been coded and tested in DEV and QAS, it is transported back into PRD and stress testing resumes from the beginning of the current cycle.

Logging also tracks how long it takes to complete certain batch processes such as translating large EDI transactions or processing very large batches of inbound IDocs.

This documentation is used to help identify objects that can be further tuned for performance after stress testing is complete.

Any changes need to be retested and the schedule has time built in for this regression testing before cutover.

At the end of the day, the EDI test coordinator and the SAP EDI technical architect go over the results of the stress test. If everybody is still breathing and the system has not blown up like the aircraft carrier destroyed by an alien death ray in one of Acme's most famous films, the stress test is declared a success.

20.8 Summary

If Darryl Q. Fernhausen, the legendary founder of Acme Pictures, were looking down from that great studio in the sky, he would be smiling now. He would appreciate the hard work of his employees and would recognize that testing is both a significant milestone and a reward for the hard work of the whole team.

But we can't pat ourselves on the back yet. We still have to work through all test phases before we have a production system.

So we began our brief introduction to testing with a tour of some standard SAP test tools. We moved on to a discussion of Acme's strategy and looked at the differences between unit, string, interface, integration, and stress testing. Each represents an important and distinct phase in the testing cycle with its own data, resource, personnel, and acceptance requirements, and each relies on the successful completion of the previous phase before it can begin.

As important as each phases is, integration testing is the true dress rehearsal for production and must convince users that the system is ready for production. We focused on the order-to-cash cycle and outlined integration test procedures for its three key business processes: dropping an order to the distributor, shipping, and billing and payment.

Except for a little more fine-tuning of our procedures, we are almost ready for prime time. Next we consider troubleshooting and recovery options in the production system.

"Failure is opportunity in disguise," Darryl Q would tell actors who hesitated to sign with him because they believed it meant their careers were finished. "It exposes the weak points so you can fix them!" Our SAP EDI system isn't all that different, but trial and error isn't an option. We need to know in advance potential points of failure—and we need to know how to recover from them.

21   Troubleshooting and Recovery

The Great Darryl Q, legendary founder of Acme Pictures, was no programmer, but he knew more than a little about failure and recovery. The SAP EDI team can learn a lot from Mr. Q's upbeat business philosophy, even if it is sometimes a little offbeat and off-color.

We need to identify and document points of failure and recovery across the SAP EDI architecture before go-live. Months of development and testing have given us an idea of where the potential points of failure lie; now it's time to codify that knowledge for the business users and the EDI support team that will use the system every day in production.

We have two primary purposes here aimed at the business and support teams that will monitoring the EDI and IDoc data flows through the RIM and SAP:

▶ Produce a preliminary roadmap that identifies critical processing points throughout the architecture where errors can occur

▶ Document recovery processes and tools

This is about minimizing potential problems in production and keeping the business running. Acme's relationship with Gordy's Galaxy of Games & B Flix, its most important customer with more than 2,000 stores across North American, depends on it.

So in the spirit of the Great Mr. Q, let us begin by discussing the knowledge gained from failure.

21.1   Identifying Issues

This is a no-brainer. To fix a problem you have to know what the problem is. Though there may be surprises because we cannot test every possible business scenario with every possible combination of data, we do have a pretty good idea of what can go wrong where.

The good news is that technical and programming errors decrease with time. When a map or an ABAP bug is fixed, it is fixed for good, unless it is hit with unexpected data. But data and business errors are likely to continue because many of these are caused by human error.

A critical question therefore is how we define success.

21.1.1   Defining Success

Success defines a technical and business endpoint: results that are unique to the business function of a particular interface and its role within a larger process. When an interface succeeds, we do not have to do anything more (except take the next step if the interface is part of a business process that includes more than one transaction).

Technical Success

Endpoint success for an inbound interface is when an IDoc posts to a business document in SAP. For an 850 purchase order, this means creating an SAP sales order; for shipping confirmation, this means updating a delivery document with pick quantity and post goods issue.

An outbound interface succeeds when an EDI transmission translated from an IDoc is received and acknowledged by the external trading partner. The acknowledgment includes an MDN (for AS2 transmissions) and an inbound X12 997 with no error codes.

Technical success is tracked in SAP through IDoc status codes. There are two successful status codes for inbound IDocs:

▶ 64 — *IDoc ready to be transferred to application*

▶ 53 — *Application document posted*

Status 53 is the endpoint for inbound processing. Most inbound IDocs also include the document number created or updated with the success message, although not always.

Let's look at the successful status codes for outbound IDocs in the system we built for Acme Pictures:

▶ 03—*Data passed to port OK*

▶ 18—*Triggering EDI system OK*

▶ 06—*Translation OK*

Status 06 is the endpoint for outbound IDoc processing. The endpoint in the EDI system is the successful 997 functional acknowledgment, which tells us that the trading partner received the EDI transaction and found no syntax errors.

These milestones are tracked in the EDI system until we change the design and begin reporting them back to the IDoc in SAP.

Functional or Business Success

Functional success, however, is a horse of a different color. The technical interface can succeed while the business process fails.

An inbound 850 customer purchase order can translate to an ORDERS IDoc, for example, and create a sales order that is delivered, shipped, and even invoiced.

But the invoice could fail translation to an X12 810 invoice or be rejected by the customer because a key piece of data for the customer was missing or incorrect when the sales order was created. The missing data did not flag an error because it was not in a mandatory data element and could not be checked by a business rule.

This could include an incorrect customer PO number sent by mistake or a missing customer material number. These data elements are not mandatory in SAP and cannot be checked in the map. Once the sales order is created and all subsequent documents generated, these values won't appear in the outbound invoice.

From a functional and business point of view, therefore, success can only be declared when the following happens:

▶ The business document is created or updated.

▶ All data required by the document and its business process is in place, even if it's stored in a field that is not mandatory in SAP.

- All follow-up processing has been successfully triggered in SAP.

- The document flow is complete and follow-on documents are created, including all inventory and accounting documents, with all accounts correctly updated.

- The final outbound IDoc in the business process was successfully generated by message control.

- The partner successfully posts and processes the EDI transmission in his business system.

21.1.2 Defining Failure

Failure is more of a certainty than success, although it has its idiosyncrasies, too. Like success, failure is defined by results. But unlike success, failure leads to more work: we take action to correct the error.

Success in the technical system can mask failure in the business document or process. The opposite is never true; failure in the technical system is always failure across the architecture. It has to be fixed.

Technical failures tend to disappear over time as configuration and development issues are corrected. Once fixed, they stay fixed, unless something changes in the environment or unexpected data is received that exposes a real world requirement that was not foreseen.

This is true for both inbound and outbound processing.

Technical Points of Failure: Inbound

Figure 21.1 outlines potential points of failure for inbound processing.

These key processing milestones in the EDI architecture are also the potential points of failure, which isn't surprising because this is where stuff happens. Consider the following points of failure for inbound processing:

- EDI connections from the trading partner or network issues

- De-enveloping, or partner and transactional recognition

- Generation and sending of X12 997 acknowledgment

- Translation or mapping failure from logical or data error

- Workflow or adapter failures in EDI RIM (the programs that link and run the adapters and services that are the EDI system in the RIM)
- RFC through the IDoc adapter that moves the IDoc into SAP
- IDoc validation
- Incorrect or missing partner profiles or no match between control record keys and a partner profile
- Custom code in IDoc processing application fails

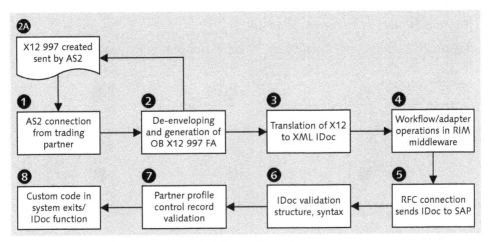

Figure 21.1 Technical Points of Failure for Inbound Processing

Status codes mark the failure of an IDoc in SAP. But if the IDoc made it into SAP and failed, every preceding step through the EDI RIM succeeded. There is always a silver lining to failure in Acme's SAP EDI architecture.

An inbound IDOC fails when the status code is one of the following:

- **56 — IDoc with errors added**
  This is usually means that no partner profile matches the partner profile keys in the IDoc control record.

- **60 — Error during syntax check of IDoc (inbound)**
  This indicates a structural problem with the IDoc, which could be caused by an IDoc build issue in the mapping or in custom code that does not raise an error.

▶ **51—Document is locked**

The IDoc function tried to access a document or table that was locked by another user or program. This can be fixed by reprocessing the IDoc when the locking process is complete. Unless an application error is raised, the IDoc will post to the business document.

In a status 60 IDoc, the segments are in the wrong order or have incorrect hierarchical relationships. The IDoc structure will be flat in the tree display, generally beginning at the segment that caused the error.

Technical Points of Failure: Outbound

Figure 21.2 outlines potential points of failure for outbound processing.

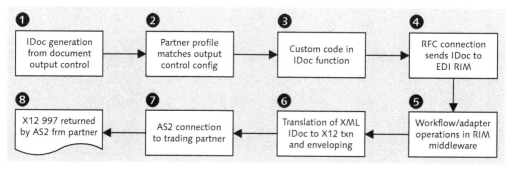

Figure 21.2 Technical Points of Failure for Outbound Processing

As with inbound interfaces, key milestones in the EDI architecture are also potential points of failure for outbound processing:

▶ IDoc generation from output control

▶ Outbound partner profile does not match message control

▶ Custom code in IDoc processing function failure

▶ RFC connection to the EDI RIM

▶ Translation errors in the map or enveloping failures

▶ Workflow or adapter failures in the EDI RIM

▶ EDI connections to the trading partner or network issues

▶ 997 with error status sent returned by the trading partner

There are more status code errors for outbound IDocs. This is driven by the design of Acme's system, particularly the status interface that we have described. It reports to SAP the status of IDoc processing in the EDI RIM.

An outbound IDoc fails when the status code is one of the following:

▸ **02—Error passing data to port**
SAP failed to write the IDoc file through the file port to the application server. Failure to write the file to the target directory could point to an authorization or other directory access issue.

▸ **03—Data passed to port OK**
The status 03 must be replaced by 18 almost immediately after outbound processing is triggered. If not this indicates a configuration error that prevents triggering the EDI system. The IDoc file has been exported to the application server but the RFC to the EDI RIM has not been begun.

▸ **05—Error during translation**
Translation failure in map reported by the status interface, most likely because of bad data. The IDoc can be corrected or a new IDoc generated from the business document and resent.

▸ **18—Triggering EDI system OK**
The status 18 must be replaced by 06 almost immediately. If it stays at 18, that indicates a failure in the status interface that could point to a translation or business process failure in the EDI RIM.

▸ **20—Error triggering EDI subsystem**
The RFC to the EDI RIM failed and the error was trapped. The IDoc was not sent to the RIM. This is most likely a communications failure. The RFC destination or XML file port are not correctly set up or there has been a system or network failure cutting the connection.

▸ **26—Error during syntax check**
The IDoc segments were not assembled in the correct order. This is most likely caused by an error in custom code building or adding segments to the IDoc.

For both inbound and outbound interfaces, the issue with technical errors in a production system is identification, break-fix, and reprocess point.

21.1.3 Functional or Business Failure

Functional or business failures are always caused by data issues, whether or not they show up as errors in the document they post to. It could be missing or incorrect data, data that does not match business rules coded in a program, or an EDI transaction sent or received out of sequence.

We have noted that it is possible for the IDoc to report success status 53 while the larger business process ultimately fails. The IDoc can create a sales order but the order could be missing business-critical data that will trigger a failure in a downstream process (for example, an invoice fails to translate or the trading partner rejects it because of missing data).

Business failures can be identified if you know the rules and the end-to-end process, and if you spot-check all documents where errors can occur.

You know, for example, that the invoice must include a customer item number or it will be rejected by the customer. You understand that in SAP data flows from the sales order through the delivery to the billing document and INVOIC IDoc. You also know that after the sales order is complete and the delivery created, data will no longer flow from the sales order to any subsequent document. So the customer item number must be in the sales order before the delivery is created or it will not make into the invoice.

The sales order is created by an ORDERS IDoc converted from an 850 customer PO. If the IDoc does not have the customer item number, the customer did not send it or it was not maintained in the customer info record. It will not get into the sales order or any subsequent document.

So we need to spot-check sales orders created by customer PO IDocs to confirm that the customer item number is there. Otherwise the downstream invoice will be rejected by the customer, unless we edit the IDoc and add the customer item number to the invoice.

Status 51 Application Errors

The easiest failures to identify are status 51 application errors that prevent the IDoc from creating or changing a business document.

Error messages always accompany IDocs at status 51. They are usually helpful in identifying the cause of the problem and are always linked to a mandatory field or business rule.

For example, if the delivery document is not configured to accept a partial delivery, or if a tolerance level has not been set, the SHPCON IDoc will fail and return status 51 if an item quantity does not exactly equal the quantity of the item in the delivery.

The errors are triggered because data in the IDoc violate business rules that are coded into the IDoc processing function or in the transaction itself.

Business Errors Reported by EDI

Errors that get past the business rules in Acme's SAP and EDI RIM systems and are rejected by the customer are reported back to Acme through two X12 transactions:

- 824, which reports on errors in the 856 advanced ship notification
- 864, which reports on errors in the 810 customer invoice.

Both transactions are text reports that reference the purchase order and document number for the transaction error—the ASN or invoice number—and include detailed text messages describing the error.

There are a few common errors for both transactions:

- Missing or incorrect GLN for the store or distribution center
- Missing or incorrect customer item number
- Missing or incorrect document numbers, particularly purchase orders

The 864 also reports an error if Gordy receives the invoice before the ASN. The invoice can only be processed by the customer after the ordered goods have been received and verified against the ASN.

Errors reported in the 864 and 824 must be resolved by Acme's EDI team and business users and then the ASN or invoice resent. Gordy will not process either document until all reported issues are fixed.

Unless there is a mapping error, in most cases data errors will be in the SAP documents. However, the SAP documents are complete, inventory has been relieved, and material movements tied to the delivery.

If the problem is with master data, the business owners fix the data. Though this will eliminate the same error in the future, this will not flow into the existing document. A good example of this is the customer material number, which can be mapped to Acme's material number in the customer material info record with

Transaction VD51. Entering the mapping will not update any existing document with the customer item number. But it will always be available for use in future documents.

The only solution is for the EDI team to edit the IDoc. This can be done in Transaction BD87 or in the archived IDoc file on the EDI RIM. But it is a trick change: the complete E1EDP19 segment to the existing IDoc would need to be added.

If we knew that this was going to happen on a regular basis, we would be safer writing an ABAP utility to update the IDoc with the missing segment or data.

Changes must be turned around quickly and the EDI transaction resent. Gordy will not process the transaction until it has received a corrected copy of the failed EDI transaction. That means no invoicing and a delay to the beginning of the payment period.

The 824 and 864 are mapped to a text report and emailed to the EDI support team as soon as they are received. Fixing the errors and resending the failed EDI transactions are top priority for the team. Business users are notified about needs to be fixed as soon as the issues are identified.

21.2   Monitoring and Recovery Tools

So where does all this magic happen? Where do we go to see whether the universe is unfolding as it should and fix it when it's not?

SAP provides powerful tools to monitor, edit, and reprocess IDocs. These monitoring and recovery tools are the starting point for our troubleshooting efforts in SAP and the EDI RIM. The tools tell us about an IDoc's current state and processing history and help us determine what went wrong and what we need to do to recover.

The SAP monitoring tools also help us identify issues in the EDI RIM thanks to the EDI data we put in the IDoc control segment during inbound and through the status interface during outbound processing. The key is understanding and cultivating your knowledge of the architecture and process, which includes the following:

▶ The end-to-end processing flow for IDocs and EDI transactions and how they get updated with status information

▶ Finding IDocs with the monitoring and recovery tools

▸ Understanding the meaning of IDoc status codes

▸ Knowing how to edit and reprocess IDocs when required

We can build custom tools to refine IDoc monitoring and troubleshooting to deal with the specific needs of our business, thanks to the standard functions that make up the IDoc interface. But the standard tools by themselves already provide a powerful platform for success.

If you are serious about the IDoc interface, know these tools well. You will spend a lot of time using them.

21.2.1 Transaction BD87: The Status Monitor

In the wrong hands, the status monitor, or Transaction BD87, is dangerous because it allows you to edit and reprocess IDocs. It is not a transaction that should be open to your business users, though it is invaluable for the EDI support team—if they know what they are doing.

No other monitoring tool has the range of functionality of Transaction BD87, although it could offer more options on its selection screen (see Figure 21.3). It would be useful, for example, to add EDI selection values included in Transaction WE05 (see Section 21.2.2, WE05: The IDoc List).

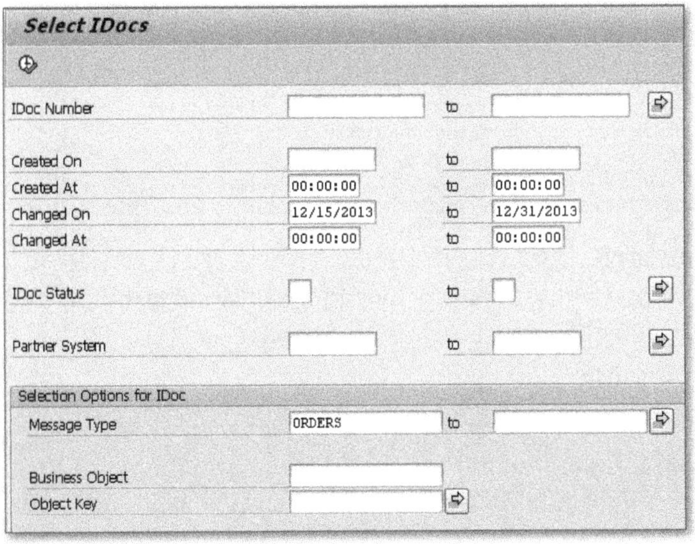

Figure 21.3 Status Monitor Selection Screen

But Transaction BD87 is just another ABAP program — RBDMON00 — that can always be copied into a custom Z program if you need to add a little more functionality. It is an ALV grid report with a lot of object-oriented programming.

It would be great fun — and you would learn a lot about the IDoc interface — to play with a custom version of Transaction BD87.

Selecting IDocs

Like all IDoc reports, Transaction BD87 pulls and formats data from IDoc tables EDIDC, EDID4, and EDIDS.

It selects IDocs with standard control record keys, including IDoc number, create and change dates and times, status, partner number, and message type. More interesting is the business object, which returns IDocs that are linked to business documents (objects) such as sales orders, deliveries, billing documents, and so on.

This can be restricted to a particular business document by entering the document number in the OBJECT KEY parameter with all leading zeroes. Multiple document numbers can be entered, but only for one business object at a time.

The business object OUTBOUNDDELIVERY (LIKP) in Figure 21.4 would return all IDocs linked to delivery 0080016955 (both the outbound ship order and the inbound ship confirmation that updated it).

| Business Object | OutboundDelivery |
| Object Key | 0080016955 |

Figure 21.4 Selecting IDocs by Business Object and Object Key

The following objects are used in the interfaces that we have built for Acme Pictures:

- **PurchaseOrder (BUS2012)**
  Links all supplier purchase orders to their outbound ORDERS and to the inbound ORDRSP PO confirmation IDocs sent back by the supplier

- **GoodsMovement (BUS2017)**
  Links all material movements, including goods receipts, to MBGMCR IDocs

- **SalesOrder (BUS2032)**
  Links sales orders to the inbound ORDERS IDocs that created them and to outbound ORDRSP they generated

▶ **OutboundDelivery (LIKP)**
Links delivery documents to the outbound SHPCON they generated and the inbound SHPCON that updated them

▶ **ItCustBillingDoc (VBRK)**
Links billing docs to the outbound INVOIC IDocs they generated

▶ **PaymentAdvice (AVIK)**
Links advice notes for payments and credits to the REMADV IDocs that created them

The IDoc Report

Transaction BD87 returns a hierarchical tree display organized by client, organized at the highest level by client and direction (see Figure 21.5).

Status Monitor for ALE Messages

IDocs	IDoc Status	Number
▶ 🔻 IDoc selection		
▼ 🗐 DO NOT CHNAGE!		558
▼ 📑 IDoc in inbound processing		67
▼ 🗐 Application document posted	53	6
▶ 🗄 MATMAS		2
▶ 🗄 STPPOD		4
▼ 🗐 Application document not posted	51	52
▶ 🗄 DELCON		1
▶ 🗄 DELINF		4
▶ 🗄 INVOIC		6
▶ 🗄 ORDERS		5
▶ 🗄 SHPCON		4
▶ 🗄 STPPOD		32
▼ 🗐 IDoc with errors added	56	9
▶ 🗄 MATMAS		7
▶ 🗄 ORDERS		2
▼ 📑 IDocs in outbound processing		491
▼ 🗐 Data passed to port OK	03	491
▶ 🗄 ALEAUD		2
▶ 🗄 DESADV		23
▶ 🗄 INVOIC		6
▶ 🗄 MATMAS		459
▶ 🗄 SYIDOC		1

Figure 21.5 Hierarchical List of IDocs Returned by Transaction BD87

Status and message type is the default grouping for each direction. There is also a count of the number of IDocs for each level.

All IDoc list processing options in Transaction BD87 are on the toolbar at the top of the screen. Functions are identified in Figure 21.6. Some of these functions are extended through menu options.

Figure 21.6 IDoc List Processing Toolbar in BD87

We will describe each tool briefly and then discuss in more detail the key IDoc display and processing functions that handle the main work of the status monitor. The toolbar functions include:

❶ REFRESH IDOC DISPLAY icon (⟨Ctrl⟩+⟨Shift⟩+⟨F3⟩): Refreshes IDoc list to reflect changes to IDoc status caused by current processing

❷ EXPAND SUBTREE icon (⟨Ctrl⟩+⟨Shift⟩+⟨F11⟩): Expands the selected node of the tree display to the next level down

❸ COLLAPSE SUBTREE icon (⟨Ctrl⟩+⟨Shift⟩+⟨F12⟩): Collapses all lower levels of a selected node

❹ DISPLAY PARTNER SYSTEMS icon (⟨F6⟩): Changes grouping of IDocs in the tree display to partner, status, and message type

❺ HIGHLIGHT MESSAGE TYPE icon (⟨F5⟩): Changes grouping of IDocs in the tree display to message type and status

❻ SELECT IDOCS button (⟨Ctrl⟩+⟨F4⟩): Opens a pop-up selection screen for filtering of IDocs in the list report, with the current select options and parameters defaulted

❼ DISPLAY IDOCS button (⟨Shift⟩+⟨F6⟩): Returns an ALV grid list with all IDocs in the selected node; double-clicking gets the same results and is quicker and more intuitive

❽ TRACE IDOCS button (⟨Shift⟩+⟨F7⟩): Traces the status of IDocs sent from the current client to an external logical system for ALE interfaces

❾ PROCESS button (⟨F8⟩): Triggers the processing program for all IDocs in a selected node

Display and process are the troubleshooting and recovery tools in the status monitor. Since we need to know what we are looking at and to understand our processing options, let's linger a little on these functions to see what they have to offer.

Display and Edit IDocs

Display is not just about looking at IDoc control, data, and status records, although this is important because it tells us what happened to the IDoc and where errors may be. Display is also about opening an IDoc for editing so that we can change and reprocess it.

We start with the list. Double-click any node to open the IDoc selection screen, an ALV grid report that lists each IDoc within that node

IDocs are listed by default by IDoc number, status, message type, status text, partner, create date and time, basic type, and number of segments.

If you click the OBJECT KEY button, however, you get a report that links the IDoc to its business document by adding the OBJECT TYPE and OBJECT KEY columns, as illustrated in Figure 21.7.

Status Monitor for ALE Messages

&ℙDisplay IDocs ▦Display relationships ▦Display status long text ⊕ Object key

IDoc Selection

IDoc number	Status	Message Type	Object Type	Object Key	Status text
993745	03	DESADV	OutboundDelivery	0080016951	IDoc sent to SAP system or external program
993746	03	DESADV	OutboundDelivery	0080016955	IDoc sent to SAP system or external program
993747	03	DESADV	OutboundDelivery	0080016955	IDoc sent to SAP system or external program

Figure 21.7 IDoc Selection Report in BD87 with Object Key Activated

The OBJECT TYPE is OutboundDelivery, and the key is the SAP delivery document number sent by the IDoc.

It is useful to know what document is linked to IDoc. A failed inbound IDoc will not create a document, for example. But we can create a document if we have incorrect or missing data that is not in a mandatory field.

It gets even better. We can go directly to the business document. Select an IDoc number and click DISPLAY RELATIONSHIPS. A dialog opens that lists the directly linked objects, demonstrating the role of the business document, the object type, and the document number, which, in the case of Figure 21.8, is outbound delivery 0080016951.

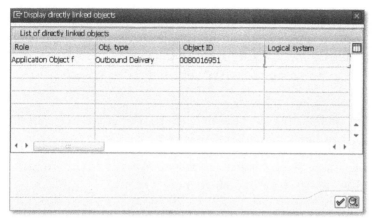

Figure 21.8 Display Directly Linked Objects from the IDoc Selection List

When you double-click the delivery number, the system calls Transaction VL03N to open the delivery document display. We can research our problem in the document itself. When done, press ⌷F3⌷ or click the green arrow to return to the linked objects dialog and, from there, back to the IDoc selection list.

Next open the tree display of a selected IDoc by double-clicking the IDoc number in the selection list.

The code behind the status monitor uses a method call to build the tree display. But you can call the same tree display in a custom program with function EDI_DOCUMENT_TREE_DISPLAY.

The tree display in Figure 21.9 illustrates the hierarchical structure of the IDoc.

We know a lot about the IDoc just from looking at it. We know that it is an outbound supplier purchase order in status 03 that has probably not been processed yet by program RSEOUT00. If it has and is still at status 03, we know there is a problem because we don't have an EDI RIM processing status yet.

We can drill deeper into the control, data, or status records, and get more information about the contents of the IDoc. We can also edit the contents of fields in the control and data records and reprocess the IDoc.

But before we look at any of this, note the Services for Object icon at the top of the screen. Click it to open a toolbar that you can also find in many business documents, including the purchase order, sales order, delivery, and billing documents.

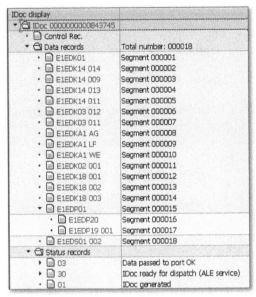

Figure 21.9 IDoc Tree Display in Transaction BD87

Click the icon to open the object services toolbar displayed in Figure 21.10. A number of features on this toolbar are well worth exploring. We'll look at each one in turn.

Figure 21.10 The Very Cool Services for Object Toolbar

❶ **Create**

This creates an attachment (uploaded from the desktop), note (typed into a text editor), or external document (referenced by a URL). These documents are then available for viewing by anyone who looks at the IDoc in SAP.

❷ **Attachment list**

This icon is only active if documents were attached with option 1; with it, you can access any attachments, notes, and external documents.

❸ **Private note**

Doesn't appear in LIST ATTACHMENTS. Only one note can be created per IDoc.

❹ Send object with note

You can sends a link to the IDoc to a wide range of individuals or groups by email, fax, X400, and more, and can also add a note or attachments from your desktop.

❺ Display relationships

This icon lists all documents and IDocs linked to the current IDoc; it supports double-click navigation to all linked objects.

❻ Workflow

Use this icon to list workflows associated with the IDoc.

❼ My Objects

This icon adds the IDoc to your objects list in the SYSTEM menu. To access the IDoc, go to the SYSTEM menu and select MY OBJECTS • EDIT OBJECTS. Double-click the IDoc number to open it in tree display.

❽ Help for the object services

Clicking this icon returns an SAP help page with detailed information about each tool on the object services toolbar, if documentation is installed.

These are all useful tools particularly if you want to pass information or observations to someone else who may need to look at the IDoc. For our troubleshooting, the most useful is DISPLAY RELATIONSHIPS. We will look at it a little more closely.

Display Relationships

Click the RELATIONSHIPS icon to open a dialog that lists all objects linked to the IDoc. This would usually include the business document and any other IDocs linked to that document and the IDoc. In our example in Figure 21.11, this is a supplier purchase order.

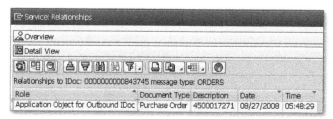

Figure 21.11 Detail View of the Objects Linked to the IDoc

When you double-click the object, SAP calls Transaction ME23N to display the purchase order. When you are done with the order, press F3 or click the green arrow to go back to the IDoc.

Click the OVERVIEW button shown at the top left of Figure 21.12 to get a tree display view of the related objects.

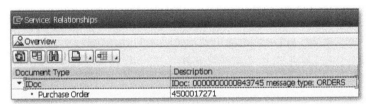

Figure 21.12 Tree Display of the IDoc's Object Relationships

This tree display begins with the IDoc as the parent and its linked document as the child. Any other IDocs associated with the document—for example, an order confirmation ORDRSP—would display as a child object of the order.

Like every other listing of linked objects and relationships, double-click to open the purchase order and return to the IDoc when you are done.

As the old saying goes, there's more than one way to skin a cat. The whole point is to give the user multiple points of view and access to a linked object or document so that we could more easily research issues we may have with either. All we need to bring to the table is an understanding of the business process, the objects, and the processing that links them.

Display and Edit the Control Record

The control and data records can be viewed and edited from the tree display in Transaction BD87 and in most other IDoc list reports that call the tree display.

There are some limits. Inbound IDocs that have been successfully processed (status 53) or copies of edited IDocs can't be edited. Most other statuses can be edited, but unless you have a really good reason, you generally only edit failed IDocs—and even then you should have a good reason.

Only fields in existing data segments can be edited through the tree display. If you need to add a segment to an IDoc (for example, an E1EDP19 segment because the customer material number is missing from an item), use the Transaction WE19 test tool. But you almost certainly will not be able to use the test tool in production.

Finally, only one IDoc at a time can be edited this way. If you know that you may have hundreds of IDocs that need to be edited at a time, you will need a custom report that supports mass update of IDocs, similar to the program we looked at in earlier in the book.

Normally, we don't edit the control record in a production environment because it defines the IDoc, although we will look at it. It is more likely that we edit a control record during development and testing. Data records are edited in the same way as the control record.

One scenario where it might be useful is if an IDoc is created in error and we want to prevent it from being processed by the next scheduled job. We can change the partner, message type, or basic type so that the control record no longer matches an existing partner profile, forcing the IDoc to fail.

To display and edit the control record, double-click the control record icon. The DISPLAY CONTROL RECORD screen opens, as in Figure 21.13. Note the SERVICES FOR OBJECT icon in the upper-left corner of screen.

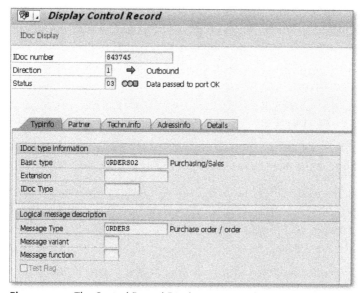

Figure 21.13 The Control Record Display Screen in the Status Monitor

The DISPLAY CONTROL RECORD screen is a formatted view of the control record in table EDIDC. All of the key fields are there.

The header area of the screen identifies the IDoc number, direction, and current status. Other control record data is displayed in five tabs organized by the type of data each holds:

- TYPINFO: IDoc message, basic type, and extended type names with message code and function

- PARTNER: Sender and receiver partners, partner types, and ports

- TECHN.INFO: SAP version, processing mode, serialization (processing sequence for a batch of IDocs), dates, and times

- ADRESSINFO: EDI sending and receiving trading partner IDs

- DETAILS: EDI control numbers, standards, and versions data

All control record data can be edited except for the header information and the TECHN.INFO tab.

To open fields for editing, select menu option CONTROL RECORD • CHANGE • DISPLAY. Make your changes and save.

Display and Edit Data Records

The data record in the tree display provides a structured view of the SDATA field in table EDID4. It also includes key control fields from the data record.

In production there may be times when we need to fix an error by changing a data record. For example, if a customer purchase order number in an invoice is incorrect, we can change it in the E1DEP02 segment.

To edit the purchase order number in the data record of an INVOIC IDoc, open the DATA RECORDS folder and double-click segment E1EDP02. The DISPLAY DATA RECORD FOR IDOC screen opens.

The header area displays control fields that cannot be edited, including IDoc number, segment name and number, parent segment number, and hierarchy level. Each populated field in the record is presented with its field name, data, and a text description.

Select menu option DATA RECORD • CHANGE • DISPLAY to open the EDIT DATA RECORD screen, as shown in Figure 21.14.

IDoc number	1023792		
Segment type	E1EDP02	IDoc: Document Item Reference Data	
Number	30		
No. higher segment	29	Hierarchy level	3

Fld name	Field contents	Short Description	
QUALF	001	IDOC qualifier reference document	▲
BELNR	4500017678	IDOC document number	▼
ZEILE	000010	Item number	
DATUM		IDOC: Date	
UZEIT		IDOC: Time	
BSARK		IDOC organization	
IHREZ		Your reference (Partner)	

Figure 21.14 Changing the UPC Number in Segment E1EDP19

Every segment field is listed and open for editing, whether populated or not. Change the purchase order number in the FIELD CONTENTS column and save.

A copy of the unedited IDoc is saved at status 33—*Original of an IDoc which was edited*, with a new IDoc number. The edited IDoc is saved at status 32—*IDoc was edited*, and can be reprocessed.

The history of both can be traced in the status record. The unedited IDoc has only one status record: 33. The edited IDoc carries forward the full status history of the original IDoc, including its most recent status 32. The edited status 32 IDoc can now be reprocessed, regardless of its previous status.

Display the Status Record

The status record in the IDoc tree display presents a formatted view of table EDIDS. Every status record stored for the IDoc is on display.

Status records are ordered from the most recent to the oldest. One look at the status folder and you know immediately if the IDoc succeeded or failed from the current status code and its accompanying message.

You also get its complete processing history from the moment it was written to the database up to its current state.

Status records can be displayed but not edited. They are the IDoc's audit trail, recording everything that happened to it throughout its lifecycle.

You can drill down in two ways to get additional information from the status record.

If there is an arrow beside the status record icon, it opens another page icon below it. Double-click the child node and a help page opens in a window. Sometimes it provides detailed information, as in Figure 21.15, but even when it is a lot thinner, this is a good starting point for research.

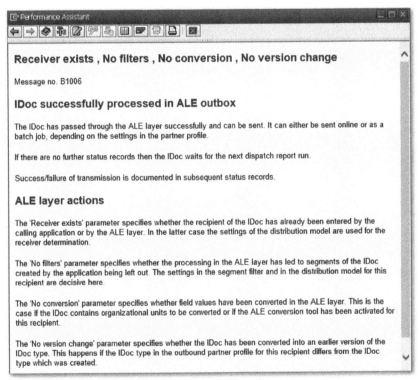

Figure 21.15 Detailed Help Screen Expands on Status Record Message

The other way to drill down is to double-click on the parent page icon itself. This opens the DISPLAY STATUS RECORD SCREEN in Figure 21.16, which shows the STS (status) DETAILS tab.

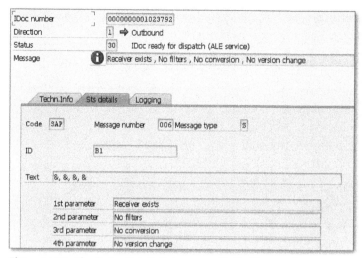

Figure 21.16 The Status Details Subscreen with its Message Data

The DISPLAY STATUS RECORD screen organizes its data in three tabs:

▶ TECHN.INFO tab: Dates and time of the log entry and database update to the current record's status code

▶ STS DETAILS tab: Data required by SAP to build the status message

▶ LOGGING tab: User, program, and subroutine that wrote the status record

You can also access the detailed message in Figure 21.15 with menu option STATUS RECORD • ERROR LONG TEXT, which is a misnomer because success messages are accessible through this menu option as well.

Processing IDocs

The status monitor in Transaction BD87 is also a frontend to all of the IDoc processing programs. It knows what program to call from the status code and direction.

Table 21.1 lists inbound IDoc processing programs called by status code.

Status	Description	Program	Txn Code
51	Application error	RBDMANI2	
56	IDoc with errors added	RBDAGAI2	BD84

Table 21.1 Inbound IDoc Processing Programs by Status Code

Status	Description	Program	Txn Code
61	Processing despite syntax error	RBDAGAI2	BD84
63	Error passing IDoc to application	RBDAGAI2	BD84
65	Error in ALE service	RBDAGAI2	BD84
60	Error during syntax check of IDoc	RBDSYNEI	
64	IDoc ready to be transferred to application	RBDAPP01	BD20
66	IDoc waiting for predecessor IDoc (serialization)	RBDAPP01	BD20
69	IDoc edited	RBDAGAIE	WPIE

Table 21.1 Inbound IDoc Processing Programs by Status Code (Cont.)

Table 21.2 lists outbound IDoc processing programs called.

Status	Description	Program	Txn Code
02	Error passing data to port	RBDAGAIN	BD83
04	Error with control information of EDI subsystem	RBDAGAIN	BD83
05	Error during translation	RBDAGAIN	BD83
25	Processing despite syntax error	RBDAGAIN	BD83
29	Error in ALE service	RBDAGAIN	BD83
26	Error during syntax check of IDoc	RBDSYNEI	
30	IDoc ready for dispatch	RSEOUT00	WE14
32	IDoc edited	RBDAGAIE	WPIE

Table 21.2 Outbound IDoc Processing Programs by Status Code

Yet Another Processing Frontend

SAP provides two other frontend programs to process IDocs. Neither has a transaction code, so if you want to use them in your system, assign a custom transaction to them. Both act as a frontend to all inbound and outbound IDoc processing programs.

▶ RBDINPUT calls all inbound IDoc processing programs. It also calls RBDCHSTA for status 62 — *IDoc passed to application* — to reset the IDoc status to 64 for reprocessing.

▶ RBDOUTPU calls all outbound processing programs.

It is too easy to process and reprocess IDocs in Transaction BD87. Select a node and click PROCESS. All IDocs in that node are processed immediately, regardless of the number of IDocs in the node.

This can be very dangerous, and it is a good reason to restrict access to Transaction BD87 in production. A thoughtless click could trigger direct processing of large numbers of IDocs that could throw balances out of whack (think inventory), process IDocs out of sequence, or cause some other business problem that forces a lot of people into unexpected recovery work.

You can also gum up performance by tying up dialog processes forced to churn through large numbers of IDocs.

At Acme Pictures, the vast majority of IDocs are processed by scheduled jobs so they use background processes. There are times, however, when we need to process IDocs in Transaction BD87.

A customer may need to resend a purchase order because of a data error in the original, and there is a rush to drop the shipping orders to the distributor. We may then process the IDocs as soon as they come in, regardless of when the next scheduled job kicks off.

At Acme we have three hard and fast rules about processing IDocs with the status monitor:

1. Never select a node and click PROCESS.

2. Only ever process the IDocs that need to be processed.

3. If we need to process more than one IDoc, always execute with a background job.

Background Processing with the Status Monitor

The good news is that Transaction BD87 supports background processing of IDoc. Select a node for processing, then go to menu option EDIT • RESTRICT AND PROCESS or press `Ctrl`+`F8`. It may be in the context-sensitive menu that pops up when you select a node and right-click for some statuses.

The restrict and process function calls the processing program for the IDoc based on current status and provides its selection screen with all of the IDoc numbers for the selected node.

To ensure that you only process the IDocs you need to do a few things:

1. Copy a list of all of the IDoc numbers that you want to process.

   You can get these by copying the IDoc number column in the IDoc selection report in Transaction BD87 or by downloading them into a text file from table EDIDC using the Data Browser (Transaction SE16).

2. Delete the numbers from the IDoc number field in the selection screen of the processing program.

3. Right-click the IDoc numbers and select DELETE SELECTION, or click the MULTIPLE SELECTION arrow and click the trash can icon when the MULTIPLE SELECTION FOR IDoc dialog opens.

4. Paste the IDoc numbers into the SELECT SINGLE VALUE tab of the MULTIPLE SELECTION FOR IDoc dialog by clicking the UPLOAD FROM CLIPBOARD icon or by pressing Shift + F12.

5. Click COPY to close the dialog and return to the selection screen.

6. In the selection screen, select menu option PROGRAM • EXECUTE IN BACKGROUND or press F9 to open the BACKGROUND PRINT PARAMETERS dialog.

7. Select an output device. LOCL is usually a good choice. Click OK and click through the formatting information dialog.

8. When the START TIME dialog opens, click IMMEDIATE and save. A background job is created and triggered to process the IDocs.

Monitor the progress of the job in the BD87 status monitor, where the IDocs change status as they post or are exported and follow the background job in the job monitor in Transaction SM37. Select all jobs under your name and the job appears is at the top of the list.

21.2.2 Transaction WE05: The IDoc List

Transaction WE05 returns an ALV grid list report of IDocs similar to the IDoc selection report in Transaction BD87. But there are key differences between the two programs.

The WE05 IDoc List, which runs ABAP program RSEIDOC2, has a more complete set of report selection criteria than BD87, including a tab with EDI-specific values that is illustrated in Figure 21.17.

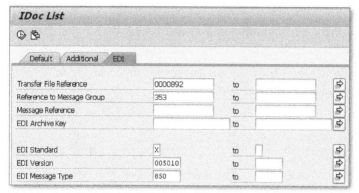

Figure 21.17 EDI Selection Values for Transaction WE05

If the EDI fields in the IDoc control record are maintained in the partner profiles, in the maps, and by the STATUS interface, IDocs can be search by the ISA, GS, or ST control numbers, the EDI standard, version, and transaction, in addition to standard search criteria as IDoc numbers, message and basic types, dates, status, partner numbers, and so on.

The report list is organized and displayed by direction, message type, and status, as shown in Figure 21.18. The full status message for a selected IDoc is displayed in two text controls at the bottom of the report list.

IDocs	Num...
▼ 🗀 Selected IDocs	000566
▼ 🗀 Outbound IDocs	000501
▶ 🗀 ALEAUD	000003
▶ 🗀 DESADV	000023
▶ 🗀 INVOIC	000005
▼ 🗀 MATMAS	000459
• 🗀 Status 3	000459
▼ 🗀 ORDCHG	000002
• 🗀 Status 3	000002
▼ 🗀 ORDERS	000007
• 🗀 Status 30	000007

Outbound IDocs ORDERS

IDoc Number	Seg...	Stat...	Stat...	Partner	Basic type	Date created	Time	Messg...
000000000102477;	28	30	◌▲◌	LI/LF/DISK01	ORDERS05	05/23/2013	19:49:43	ORDERS
000000000102477£	28	30	◌▲◌	LI/LF/DISK01	ORDERS05	05/23/2013	19:54:17	ORDERS
000000000102477§	28	30	◌▲◌	LI/LF/DISK01	ORDERS05	05/23/2013	20:29:29	ORDERS
000000000102478(	28	30	◌▲◌	LI/LF/DISK01	ORDERS05	05/24/2013	07:50:44	ORDERS
000000000102478:	28	30	◌▲◌	LI/LF/DISK01	ORDERS05	05/25/2013	15:04:04	ORDERS
000000000102478;	28	30	◌▲◌	LI/LF/DISK01	ORDERS05	05/25/2013	15:24:57	ORDERS
000000000102478;	28	30	◌▲◌	LI/LF/DISK01	ORDERS05	05/25/2013	15:54:04	ORDERS

Figure 21.18 Outbound Messages Displayed in the IDoc List.

IDocs cannot be processed with Transaction WE05. They can be edited. Double-click any IDoc in the list to open the IDoc tree display. The tree display in Transaction WE05 has all the same features as BD87, including services for objects and editing of control and data segments.

Transaction WE05 is a safer way of monitoring IDocs. In a production environment, its advantage over Transaction BD87 is its additional search options and the fact that IDocs can't be processed and reprocessed.

21.2.3 Processing Log for Output Control

You can identify outbound IDocs from within their documents by looking at the output processing log. This log does not enable follow-up processing or navigation, but it does allow quick confirmation from within a document that an outbound IDoc has been generated with message control.

The processing log for a billing document is illustrated in Figure 21.19.

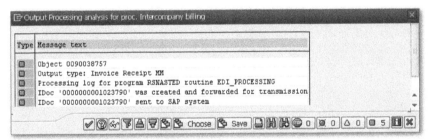

Figure 21.19 Processing Log for a Billing Document

The processing log is accessed by selecting the output type record in the output display screen in the document and clicking the PROCESSING LOG button. The following menu options in Acme's key interface documents lead to the output display window:

▸ Purchase order: Click the MESSAGES button.

▸ Sales order: Click EXTRAS • OUTPUT • HEADER • EDIT.

▸ Delivery: Click EXTRAS • DELIVERY OUTPUT • HEADER.

▸ Billing document: Click GOTO • HEADER • OUTPUT.

21.2.4 Transaction WE07: Errors History

Despite the name on its selection screen (IDoc STATISTICS), Transaction WE07 is a summary of IDoc error history. Default selection parameters are the date range (see Figure 21.20), although you can also enter minimal control segment details such as message type and basic type in the DETAIL SEL. tab.

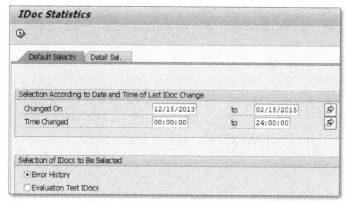

Figure 21.20 Default Selection Options for IDoc Error History

The report returns an overview of IDoc error processing during the selected date range with the total number of error IDocs (Figure 21.21).

IDocsWithErrorStatus	Number
▼ ⬜ Total IDoc Number	450
▼ ⬜ Outbound IDocs	42
• ⬜ Current in Error Status	41
• ⬜ Error Was Overcome	1
• ⬜ With Del. Indicator	0
▼ ⬜ Inbound IDocs	408
• ⬜ Current in Error Status	398
• ⬜ Error Was Overcome	1
• ⬜ With Del. Indicator	9

Figure 21.21 Overview of IDoc Error Processing History

The display is organized by direction and error disposition:

▶ CURRENT IN ERROR STATUS: Errors have not been addressed

▶ ERROR WAS OVERCOME: Errors have been fixed and the IDocs updated to a success status

▶ WITH DEL. INDICATOR: IDocs have been marked for deletion using status 68 for inbound or 31 for outbound

Double-click any of these folders to open an ALV grid list report with all IDocs in the group. The IDoc list is identical to the report in Transaction WE05. Double-click any of the IDocs to open the tree display with the same viewing and editing functionality as Transactions BD87 and WE05.

IDocs cannot be processed using Transaction WE07.

21.2.5   Transaction WE09: IDoc Search by Business Content

Transaction WE09 is one of Acme's favorite IDoc reports. We use it to find IDocs from the contents of a field in a segment.

If you have a customer PO number, for example, call up Transaction WE09 and enter in the selection screen all the keys you know into the control record section of the selection screen. At a minimum, you should know the message type, partner number, and a date range.

Then enter the segment and field names, and the purchase order number into the CRITERIA FOR SEARCH IN DATA RECORDS selection block. If we wanted to find the ORDERS IDoc with customer PO number 8888000011 from Gordy's Galaxy, we would populate the segment and field values as illustrated in Figure 21.22.

Figure 21.22 Searching for IDocs by Business Contents

You cannot use wild card characters to search, but partial entries are OK as long as the values are contiguous. In our PO number example, you can search for 88880000, but you can't search for 8888*1.

Execute the report and all ORDERS IDocs containing our purchase order number are returned in an ALV grid list that displays the expandable control record for each IDoc. If you click the IDoc number, the tree display opens with all the same functionality as Transactions BD87, WE05, and WE07.

Expand the control segment by clicking the folder icon and all segments in the IDoc open. A portion of the report is illustrated in Figure 21.23.

```
0000000000808772 11/27/2007 02:46:42 2          LS/   /APOCLNT800 53
000001 E1EDK01                            1
000002 E1EDK03                            2
000003 E1EDK03                            2
000004 E1EDKA1                            2
000005 E1EDKA1                            2
000006 E1EDKA1                            2
000007 E1EDK02                            2
```

Figure 21.23 Portion of the IDoc Display Report in Transaction WE09

Click any segment number to open the DISPLAY DATA RECORD FOR IDoc screen for that segment. The segment can be edited from here, unless the IDoc is at status 53.

It is interesting to look at the code behind this report. It is not that difficult to incorporate it into your own programs, particularly if you need to search for values in IDoc fields. Transaction WE09 runs report RSEIDOC9.

IDoc data are read by function IDOC_READ_COMPLETELY with the IDoc number in a loop on an internal table that includes control record data for all IDocs that fall within the selection parameters entered into the control record block of the selection screen. It is important to be as specific as possible to avoid pulling in large numbers of IDocs.

When the IDoc data records are retrieved for the current IDoc number, form SEARCH_DATARECORD is called. It does some funky string processing to figure out where the field that contains your value lies in the selected segment. It then calls the ABAP SEARCH command to find the value entered in the FOR VALUE field of the selection screen using the start and end position calculated for the field entered in SEARCH IN FIELD.

If the entered field value is found, the IDocs are assembled, and the report returned.

Transaction WE09 has another interesting feature. Click the DATA SOURCE button at the top of the selection screen. The report offers the option of searching for IDocs either in the database, in the archive, or both in the SELECT DATA SOURCE dialog, as illustrated in Figure 21.24.

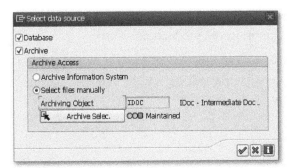

Figure 21.24 Selecting IDocs from the Database and Archive in WE09

21.2.6   Transaction WE08: IDoc Interuptus

There are a range of system logs that can also be consulted, but most of these are the purview of the Basis team. There is one that is useful for the EDI support team to know about, although the error it records rarely happens.

Transaction WE08 provides a view of table EDFI2, which logs problems in reading or deleting IDoc files by RFC function `EDI_DATA_INCOMING`.

SAP uses it to avoid processing the same IDoc record twice. The system records the name and path of the input file, records the last IDoc number generated from it, and marks the position of the last record successfully read.

Table EDFI2 also records the date and time and the ABAP program that was running when the RFC interruption occurred. Display EDFI2 using the Data Browser, Transaction SE16.

If an IDoc is partially read when an interruption occurs in the import of an IDoc file, a record will be written to EDFI2. If you attempt to reimport the IDoc file, a failure will be returned unless the EDFI2 record is deleted. This is usually handled by the Basis team, but you need to be able to recognize it so you can tell them to delete it.

This error occurs mostly during the earliest stages of development.

21.3   Recovering from Key Failure Points

Troubleshooting and recovery is about how we respond to issues as they occur in the technical or business architecture. Once we identify the issues that we are most likely to face, we can map out process flows for troubleshooting and recovery. This becomes our initial roadmap for support in the production system.

As new issues crop up in production, we identify fixes and add them to our roadmap. Continually documenting what we know as learn it is the best way to protect ourselves from what we don't know.

We will begin with the technical system.

21.3.1 Technical Troubleshooting

Technical problems are most likely to occur during development and testing.

Technical issues in production are most likely related to connectivity, changes in the network environment, or incorrectly setting up a new trading partner. How we respond depends on the direction of the interface.

Inbound

Figure 21.25 outlines an overview of our responses to potential technical issues during inbound processing.

We have already noted that errors are most likely to occur at key processing milestones in the architecture because that's where stuff happens.

Transmission failures are the most likely technical errors to occur in Acme's production system. Errors may be identified when Gordy does not receive an MDN or the business realizes that a purchase order they were expecting is overdue.

Acme's EDI team swings into action. The first step is to identify the error. A number of issues can cause transmission failures:

- ▶ Changes in the EDI partner's system that have not been communicated, such as a new IP address that is not on the safe list for Acme's firewall

- ▶ Changes in the EDI RIM that have not been communicated to the partner or that the partner has not set up, such as a target URL for AS2

- ▶ Failures in EDI or business systems, networks, communications, or other technical infrastructure at either end

- ▶ Too much traffic hitting either system at the same time

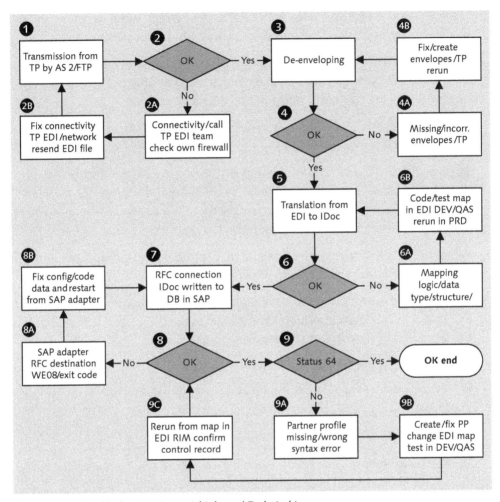

Figure 21.25 Troubleshooting Potential Inbound Technical Issues

These issues can't be fixed by Acme's EDI team alone—they need help from Gordy's EDI team or Acme's network support folk. Gordy will retransmit the interchange when the issues are addressed.

Next up is de-enveloping. These are usually one-time failures, although trading partners sometimes change their envelopes without telling us. Errors generally happen when a new partner is being set up, and envelopes have not been created or were created incorrectly.

If the envelopes exist, the issue may be that the partner and transaction are not recognized by the system and cannot be matched to their envelopes.

The EDI team fixes the issue and restarts the interchange from the point of failure. The next potential failure is translation, which could be an error in mapping logic or source file structure or a conflict between data types.

This could happen in production, particularly for a major partner who sends large volumes of EDI transmissions.

The map fix is coded and unit-tested in EDI DEV against the production data that caused the failure. When the developer is satisfied that the fix works, the map is promoted to QAS for more testing against the data that caused the failure and other production data to ensure that nothing else has gone wrong.

When the EDI lead signs off on the fix, it is promoted to production, and the transaction is rerun from the point of failure.

There may also be failures in the workflow processes that move data through the EDI RIM. These issues are technical and unique to the EDI system being used, and can be caused by a variety of factors:

- Configuration of adapters and services
- Network and technical system setup and access to file directories
- Database access or maintenance
- Memory usage, Java Virtual Machines, and so on

The EDI team monitors these processes on an ongoing basis. They are fixed immediately and tested in DEV and QAS before being brought into PRD.

Next the translated IDoc is sent into SAP through the RFC connection. The following can cause RFC failures:

- Improper installation of JCo
- Configuration errors in the SAP adapter in the EDI RIM (the adapter needs correct SAP server and login information to make the connection)
- Network or file system access issues
- RFC failure in SAP during file processing

JCo and SAP adapter configuration errors should happen only once if they occur. The EDI team fixes them, sometimes with Basis help. Network and file system access issues occur occasionally in the real world.

RFC failures in SAP occur in function `EDI_DATA_INCOMING` and can be triggered by some other problem in the system or the network.

In either case, the EDI team may need to check Transaction WE08 to ensure that no file was being processed when the failure occurred. Otherwise the team restarts the RFC connection from the EDI RIM and lets the IDocs flow into SAP.

Finally, the IDoc should be stored in the database as status 64. If not, it is most likely to be at status 56 or 60. IDocs are checked in Transaction BD87 or WE05.

Status 56 is an issue with the partner profile, which is either missing or does not match the key values in the IDoc control segment. The values that should match are the keys to inbound partner profile table EDP21:

▸ SNDPRN: Send partner number

▸ SNPRT: Send partner type

▸ SNDPFC: Send partner function

▸ MESTYP: Message type

▸ MESCOD: Message code

▸ MESFCT: Message function

▸ TEST: Test flag

Another potential failure in Acme's system occurs if table ZEDIXREF has not been updated with records for the partner and inbound transaction. This is how the SAP partner number is passed to the control segment of the IDoc.

The partner profile is created or fixed or the map is fixed to pass correct partner profile data to the control segment of the IDoc.

If the IDoc status is 60, there is a structural issue that points to an error in the map's build of the IDoc. The map is fixed and retested in DEV and QAS and promoted to PRD.

When the errors are fixed, the IDoc is resent into SAP from the IDoc adapter in the EDI RIM.

Outbound

Figure 21.26 gives an overview of our responses to technical issues that may crop up during outbound processing.

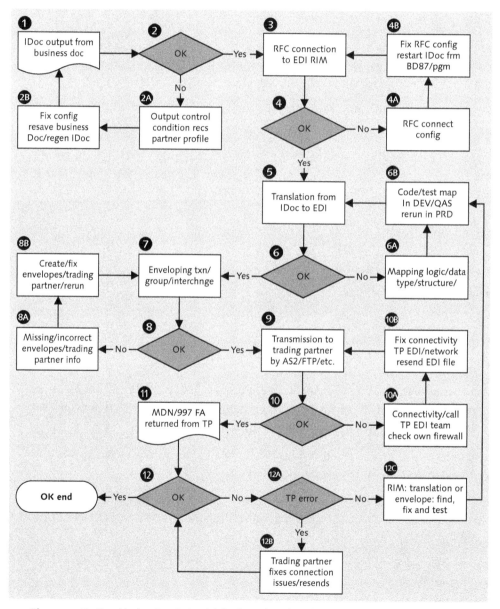

Figure 21.26 Troubleshooting Potential Outbound Technical Issues

It begins when a business document such as a sales order, outbound delivery, or invoice is created in SAP and saved. An IDoc is generated by output control. If it isn't, the error is caused by one of the following circumstances:

- Output control is incorrectly configured.
- Condition record is missing for the partner and output type.
- Partner profile is missing or incorrectly set up.
- An error in custom IDoc code in a customer exit or a custom function triggered a failure.

The output error will be identified in the output display window of the document itself. It will tell us why an IDoc was not generated if message control is set up, almost always a mismatch between output type, condition records, and outbound partner profile.

First we check the partner profile. Confirm that the message control screen has been configured. If not, add the application, output type, and process code.

If it has been entered into the partner profile, check the output type and condition records. Confirm that a condition record has been entered for the partner and output type. If a record has been entered, confirm that it is correct and that it matches the message control screen values in the partner profile.

Check also the output type and confirm that it configured for the partner type you are trying to process. If any of these values are missing or incorrect, the SAP EDI team will fix them.

If the message control and output type configuration is correct, check custom code that may be written in user exits in the IDoc processing function. We may need to debug the code to track down the error, or have our ABAP developer take care of it.

Whatever we need to fix is done in DEV, tested in DEV and QAS, and then moved back into PRD once the team leads sign off on it. We then regenerate the IDoc by going back to the document in change mode and saving it.

We should now be able to find the IDoc at status 30 with any of the IDoc list tools. The IDoc is sent out of SAP by running program RSEOUT00. If it fails to be picked up by the EDI RIM, the issue is in the RFC connection. This can be caused by several things:

- JCo is improperly installed.
- The RFC destination in SAP is not set up or is set up incorrectly.
- The EDI RIM SAP adapter is not registered as an RFC server or is incorrectly configured.
- The SAP XML file port is not configured to trigger the RFC destination for the EDI RIM.
- The partner profile is pointing to the wrong port or is not configured to start the EDI subsystem.

These issues are mostly all related. If JCo is properly installed for the inbound connection, it will work for outbound. The RFC destination can be checked in Transaction SM59. If it exists, and the connection test does not work, the SAP adapter in the EDI RIM is probably not correctly configured and the RFC destination does not recognize it as a registered server program.

If the adapter configuration is correct but the IDoc still does not trigger the EDI RIM, check the file port with Transaction WE21. Make sure that the AUTOM.START POSSIBLE flag is set in the OUTBOUND: TRIGGER tab. Confirm that the correct RFC destination for the EDI RIM is entered in the RFC DESTINATION field.

We also need to ensure that the outbound partner profile is pointing to the correct file port and that the output mode is set to START SUBSYSTEM. If it is not, the IDoc will not trigger the listening workflow in the EDI RIM.

If a network issue is preventing connection, we will need technical support from the Basis or network teams, or both.

Once RFC is working, the IDoc is picked up by the EDI RIM. The next step is translation to an EDI transaction. Mapping issues are the same as for inbound processing and are also related to enveloping.

As with inbound processing, envelopes may not have been set up or the system may not recognize the partner and transaction.

The EDI team will quickly recognize these problems because processing in the RIM will halt. The STATUS interface will report a translation failure back to SAP, but not an envelope issue. The translation failure will show as status 05 in the outbound IDoc and can be recognized in any of the standard IDoc reporting and monitoring tools.

After mapping and enveloping issues are fixed, we send the EDI transaction to Gordy's Galaxy. If the AS2—or other—transmission fails, we will work with Gordy's EDI team to identify and address the issue.

The firewall is open to all for outbound processing so new IP addresses are not an issue. However, a new IP address at Acme may indeed be an issue for the trading partner if we do not communicate with them.

Finally, Acme expects an MDN and an X12 997 acknowledgment from Gordy for all outbound interchanges.

If the MDN is not returned, Acme may not have received the transmission or they may have an issue in their system. We will need to communicate with them to make sure that they are aware of the problem.

If the 997 is not returned, or if it is returned with a syntax error, Acme's EDI team works with Gordy to resolve the issue.

There may be a glitch in Gordy's system that prevented the 997 from being sent, or the syntax error in Acme's outbound transaction may not have been critical, such as an optional text element that exceeds the length expected by Gordy's system. The acknowledgment can be handled manually.

21.3.2 Functional Troubleshooting

This is all about the data we need to create our business documents, trigger background processing in inventory management and accounting, and send an invoice to our customer so that we can get paid.

If the data are wrong, we will not get paid. It is as simple as that.

As far as direction goes, what comes in affects what goes out. Data problems in the outbound are almost always related to missing or incorrect data coming in. So it is critical to check and check again.

Inbound

We will look at an inbound 850 customer PO to illustrate the general process flow. Each interface has its own requirements but the fundamental issues—that is, identifying and fixing errors—do not differ that much. Figure 21.27 gives an overview of our responses to potential business issues during inbound processing.

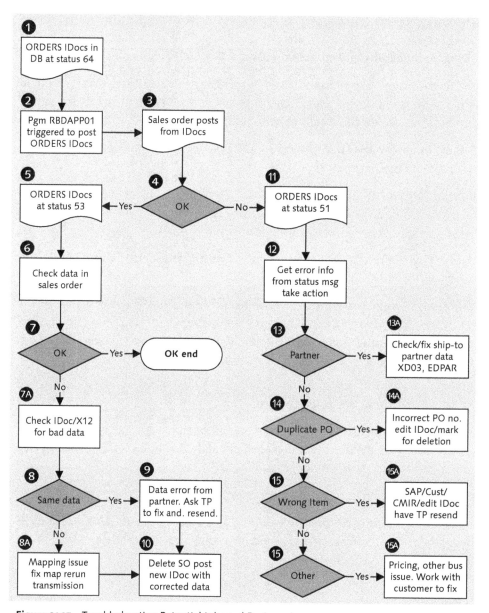

Figure 21.27 Troubleshooting Potential Inbound Business Issues

It begins with an ORDERS IDoc at status 64. Program RBDAPP01 kicks off through a scheduled job to process it and post the sales order. The IDoc status is updated to 51 if it fails to create a sales order and to 53 if it succeeds.

Status 51, as we have seen, is cleaner to deal with because we know that there is an error. First we check the status message in Transactions BD87 or WE05. That will identify any system-generated error messages.

In Acme's system, there are three key-coded checks that will return an error message to the IDoc status record if they fail:

▶ Partner does not exist at sales organization.

▶ Duplicate PO failed.

▶ Material is not defined for sales organization.

Partner Does Not Exist

The GLN is returned for the ship-to partner and does not map to the SAP partner number. Either the ship-to was not created in the customer master or a record was not entered into EDPAR mapping the SAP to the customer ship-to number.

This is fixed by creating the ship-to partner if it does not exist and then creating the EDPAR entry.

If the ship-to partner exists, make sure it is extended to the sales organization, distribution channel, and division. Then enter the record into EDPAR.

Related to this issue is a configuration error that can occur if EDSDC has not been updated with the vendor number and customer sales organization. This is a one-time setup chore with Transaction VOE2.

The IDoc can then be reprocessed with Transaction BD87.

Duplicate PO Failed

This error is returned by Acme's custom code that prevents a purchase order that has already posted and been processed from posting again.

The customer purchase order number is not mandatory in the SAP sales order. You can create a sales order without a purchase order or with an incorrect PO number.

But the customer must know what purchase order he is being invoiced against. We need to provide him with the correct PO number and ensure that we don't post the same PO twice. The problem is that the customer's order could be shipped twice if the PO posts twice, and Acme is left on the hook for the price of shipping the duplicate order.

There are, of course, other tangible and intangible costs to the relationship with the customer that should be avoided.

The only time that we do post the same PO number twice to sales orders is if we are processing customer orders with multiple ship-to partners in the SDQ segment at the line item level.

We need to determine if this is truly a second copy of the same purchase order that has already been processed, if it was an error in the EDI system, or if Gordy just sent it by mistake.

If it is a dupe, we mark the IDoc for deletion and forget about it. Chances are Gordy sent it by accident. But first we let them know about it and confirm that it was not intentional.

There could be a valid business reason for resending. Another error may have been spotted by business users at Gordy or Acme after the original IDoc posted. If that is the case, we delete the sales orders created by the original and repost the IDoc in Transaction BD87.

If it is a different order but was given the posted PO by mistake, we can edit the IDoc with Transaction BD87 in E1EDK02-BELNR where QUAL equals 001. Then we reprocess the IDoc.

Material Is Not Defined

This is a master data issue. Either the SAP item has not been created in the material master or it has not been extended to the Acme sales organization and distribution channel responsible for selling Gordy the item.

Check it. If the material exists in the right sales organization, then the issue is in the customer material info record (CMIR) in table KNMT. If CMIR does not have a record mapping the customer's item number to Acme's SAP number, this error will be returned.

The fix is to enter the missing data, wherever it may be, and reprocess the IDoc. If the IDoc got this far it will post a sales order once the material number issue is corrected.

The IDoc Posted Successfully

The IDoc successfully created a sales order and its status was updated to 53. We're done, right? Not so fast. We have already seen that a sales order can be successfully created but still be missing critical data or have wrong data.

The business owners need to spot-check the sales orders as thoroughly as possible, checking particularly for those fields that the customer needs in the invoice but that are not mandatory in SAP.

These include the purchase order number, customer item number, and whatever else the customer considers critical. We should also spot-check the item quantities against the IDoc and the X12.

These data errors can be fixed manually by the business users in the sales order. If there are a large number of errors and the fix is consistent, a mass change program can be used.

Fixing data issues in the sales order nips downstream problems in the bud. But when there are thousands of orders being created, stuff happens, and bad data get past the best guardians of the post. Some of these problems may be caught during outbound processing.

Outbound

We will illustrate the process flow by looking at an outbound 810 customer invoice. Figure 21.28 gives an overview of our responses to potential business issues during outbound processing.

We begin our outbound process with an INVOIC IDoc at status 30. Program RSE-OUT00 is triggered by a scheduled job to export our IDoc to the EDI RIM. The IDoc is updated to status 03 when it passes through the file port and to status 18 when it triggers the EDI RIM.

The RIM picks it up and hands it off to the map. Translation either succeeds or fails. Regardless, the status interface is triggered and the INVOIC IDoc in SAP is updated to 05 if translation failed or 06 if it succeeded.

If the translation fails, we analyze the data and identify where the error occurred. Unless something new has been introduced to the IDoc without telling the EDI team, it will probably be a data issue.

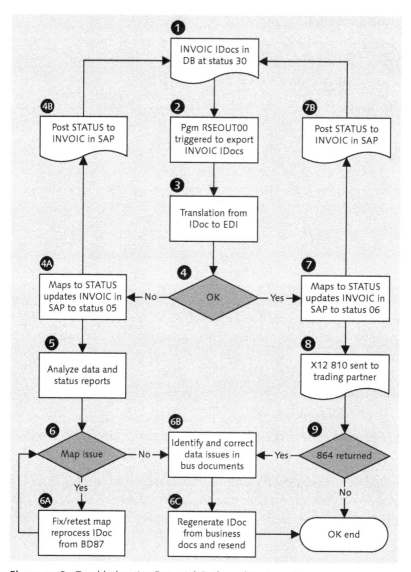

Figure 21.28 Troubleshooting Potential Outbound Business Issues

If there is a mapping issue, we will use standard break-fix procedures to correct and unit-test the map in DEV with the data that caused the failure. We will then test the corrected map with a more complete set of production data in QAS. When the fix is approved, the map is moved back to PRD and the process is rerun from the point of failure.

The vast majority of outbound translation errors in PRD are data issues. Some key value such as purchase order or customer item number is missing because it did not make it into the sales order from the original X12 850 PO.

If we set the fields that carry these values in the map to mandatory and they are not sent in the IDoc, the map will fail.

When we identify the failure, we go back to the business document in SAP and add the values and regenerate the IDoc.

If we are sending an invoice, values such as purchase order number or customer item number cannot be entered directly into the invoice. These values are pulled from other documents in the document flow that feed data into the INVOIC IDoc.

For these values, you would go to the document that holds them. To add the purchase order number or customer item number, go to the sales order overview using change Transaction VA02.

The purchase order is added to the PO NUMBER field and the customer item to the CUSTOMER MATERIAL NUMB field for the line item in the ALL ITEMS table control. Save the sales order.

You then regenerate the IDoc from the billing document with Transaction VF31 (output from billing) or Transaction WE15 (output from message control). In both, you enter the billing document number, output type, transmission medium, and a send again (WE15) or repeat processing flag (VF31).

The new values that you entered into the sales order will be pulled into the IDoc when it is regenerated. Then send the IDoc to the EDI RIM with RSEOUT00 or Transaction BD87.

If the translation succeeded, the invoice still has to get past the customer's business system. Data issues may still be caught in the customer's system, or the invoice may have arrived before the ASN.

Either way, the customer will send back an X12 864 text message with a detailed error report. If the invoice arrived before the ASN, we need to make sure that the customer receives and processes the ASN before resending the INVOIC IDoc. If we don't have to make any changes, we can resend the X12 810 invoice directly from the EDI RIM.

If there are data errors, we correct them in the business document where they occur and regenerate the INVOIC IDoc from the billing document. We then resend the IDoc to the EDI RIM and the customer.

Data errors are impossible to eliminate completely because of all the hands involved in the end-to-end process, so we have to do the best we can and continue checking.

And that's what keeps the work interesting. We build the cleanest, most efficient architecture that we can and, in the end, most of our efforts are on the data because the business depends on it. If we are successful in our build, we barely notice the system anymore—only the results.

21.4 Summary

We have come to the end of the road. Acme's new SAP EDI system is built and tested.

In this final chapter, we looked at troubleshooting and recovery. We began by considering the processing points in the technical architecture and business processes where problems are most likely to occur.

We looked at standard transactions in SAP that are useful for monitoring, troubleshooting, and recovering from IDoc issues and reviewed programs used to process or reprocess IDocs.

We then made our first stab at developing process flows for recovery in the end-to-end technical and business architecture. The idea was to develop a flexible roadmap that the support team could use in production to identify and fix issues as they come up. Unforeseen issues would be added to the process flow and other support documentation as they are recognized and addressed.

So once again, this is only the starting point. We may be ready to go live, but that doesn't mean the work ends now. It will continue for the life of the system. The bottom line is the bottom line, and nobody would appreciate this more than Darryl Q. Fernhausen, the legendary founder of Acme Picture. It's not about the shiny new SAP EDI system that we worked so hard to build, test, and implement. It's about the business it supports.

Epilogue

Twilight descends on Hollywood. The project team from Acme Pictures is gathered in the grainy duskiness of the Formosa Café. They toast each other with cocktails, laughter, and silly speeches to celebrate their successful implementation of the new SAP EDI system.

They can sense the smiling presence of the great Darryl Q. Fernhausen, the studio's legendary founder. The Formosa Café was his favorite watering spot and twilight his favorite time of day, with a Hollywood hopeful hanging on his arm, a mojito cooling his hand, and a fine Cuban Cohiba jutting from his mouth at a rakish angle.

The Formosa oozes Hollywood history, so it is the perfect spot for a post-project blowout for a movie company. The café started life in 1925 in a red trolley car on the corner of Santa Monica Boulevard and Formosa Avenue, across the street from the old United Artists Studio, now Warner Hollywood. The Formosa has lent its atmosphere to more than one movie including the gritty *film noir* crime drama *LA Confidential*.

Acme has its own history with the Formosa, which it used surreptitiously as background for a scene from its most famous crime flick, *Zombie Detectives from the Planet Ahlgor*. The scene was shot almost entirely under the table with a hand-held camera and features stunning, if somewhat jerky, close-ups of a zombie detective's shoe inching toward a pair of high heels partially veiled by the mysterious darkness. The crew also managed to catch one or two shots of the café's dark interior and red walls before being caught and unceremoniously pitched out onto Santa Monica Boulevard.

At the time, Acme Pictures was the pariah of Hollywood and couldn't get permission to film in the Formosa—or anywhere else, for that matter. The café's owner didn't want to be associated with Acme and he canceled the great Darryl Q's drinking privileges.

But *Zombie Detectives* was a huge box office hit. So there were smiles, handshakes, and cocktails all around, and the great Mr. Q was allowed to return, in light of all the publicity the movie generated. Hollywood loves a winner.

Zombie Detectives became a lucrative franchise and the Formosa never tossed out another Acme crew into the street again. The great Darryl Q was a very happy man.

Everybody on the project team was conscious of this history as they sipped their cocktails and considered the work just completed. The project had gone live without a hitch. All interfaces in the purchasing and order-to-cash cycles with Gordy's Galaxy of Games & B Flix and the supplier Disc Services International were working as expected.

The project team felt a sense of well-earned satisfaction as they toasted each other profusely in the gathering darkness of the café.

The implementation successfully replaced a hodge-podge of legacy systems and interfaces with one integrated SAP system connected to Acme's trading partners through the EDI RIM.

It is a clean environment that provides end-to-end visibility for all interfaces. The EDI portion of the RIM is modularized into processes that manage AS2 communications at one end, translation and data processing in between, and communications into or out of SAP at the other end.

The beauty of it all is that each process is linked directly to the one before it and the one after. If you jump in at any point in the chain, an interface can be easily followed in any direction to its source or destination. This gives Acme unparalleled visibility into EDI processing in SAP because key EDI system IDs are mapped to each IDoc's control segment. This makes it easy to trace the path of an IDoc through the RIM regardless of direction.

Keeping track of interfaces in legacy was one of the most time-consuming chores the EDI support team faced. Multiple systems sent and received EDI transmissions, and data were moved around by FTP scripts at the operating system level. There was no easy way to trace each step of the process from beginning to end if anything went wrong with a transmission.

And because multiple business systems exchanged documents with external trading partners, it was difficult to aggregate and analyze interfaces as a unified business process. It took all of the energy of the support team to ensure that each step of each individual interface worked as it should.

So the new SAP EDI system is a huge time saver that provides tremendous visibility into all interface processing. In fact, Acme management is still trying to figure out how much money this will save the company.

The new SAP system had already proven its worth in a major new release of a digitally remastered Blu-ray version of the famous *Zombie Detectives* series shortly after go-live, providing another good reason for the team to celebrate at the Formosa.

Gordy placed an initial order of 80,000 units for 2,000 of its stores as soon as the new release was available for ordering. The PO came in without a hitch, and the new SDQ process quickly generated 2,000 ORDERS IDocs that posted to the correct number of sales orders in SAP.

All follow-up transactions ran without any issues: the order confirmation, shipping orders, and shipping confirmations. But there was a glitch when the invoice went to Gordy: Gordy got the invoice before it had confirmed the shipment against the ASN.

Gordy sent Acme an 864 text report identifying the error. Before Acme's team could review the 864, Gordy got the ASN and confirmed the shipment. Acme's EDI team reissued the rejected invoices.

It took only one phone call to Gordy's EDI team and everybody was happy. The invoices were accepted and Gordy paid up within the 60-day payment window. Gordy sent Acme an 820 that successfully posted to a payment advice in SAP. Accounts receivable cleared it and the cycle was complete. Acme's management was pleased.

In the end, the new *Zombie Detectives* release was a great success, selling more than two million copies. Acme's new SAP EDI system handled the increased traffic to support this business without even breaking a sweat.

The EDI support team got down to the business of identifying, fixing, and recording the issues that inevitably arise in the early days of a new system. This effort led to a database of issues and solutions that proved invaluable for years to come.

As time went on and issues were fixed, there were far fewer errors, and the team was able to concentrate on defining and building audit reports in SAP and the EDI RIM.

But we're running ahead of ourselves. The new system paid for itself in a number of ways, including better visibility into EDI traffic; faster turnaround on orders and shipping with fewer errors; less paperwork, printing, and postage; better data for reporting; and more effective use of employee time. The list goes on.

The great Darryl Q. Fernhausen, lounging by that film moguls' bar in Hollywood Heaven, looked down on the scene at the Formosa Café with a satisfied smile. He could see where all this was going and felt confident that Acme would continue to grow its unique market.

He smiled, raised a toast with another heavenly mojito, took a puff of his Cohiba, and blew out a wispy halo of blue smoke.

At that moment, the group gathered in the perennial darkness of the Formosa Café toasted the great Darryl Q's memory, and recounted one of his most memorable quips.

"No matter how good it gets," he once told a tipsy director at a poolside party, "don't feel too satisfied. You can always do better. But never forget to enjoy the moment. Now...where did I put my drink?"

The Author

Emmanuel Hadzipetros has 20 years of SAP experience as a data conversion specialist and ABAP, IDoc and EDI developer in such diverse industries as pharmaceuticals, entertainment, video games, steel, utilities, and others, in four countries and three continents.

His ongoing fascination for data flows through SAP led him to B2B integration. An IDoc and XML evangelist with a practical approach to designing systems, he has built end-to-end B2B architectures from SAP through the middleware to the trading partner using such tools and standards as XI/PI, ALE, Sterling Integrator, Contivo, X12, EDIFACT, OAGIS, AS2, FTP, and others.

In his latest adventure, Emmanuel is responsible for designing the integration points in a cloud-based supply chain B2B platform for the pharmaceutical industry at a Boston area company, where he also serves as in-house SAP guru. This work includes building transactions with XSD schema and implementing GS1 standards in serialization and product tracking.

Emmanuel is a huge fan of Acme Pictures' visionary founder, Darryl Q. Fernhausen, and of his idiosyncratic approach to film-making. When he's not obsessing about XML, IDocs, and SAP data flows, Emmanuel loves to drink up the old Hollywood atmosphere of the Formosa Café while perusing the scripts of Acme's more memorable films.

Index

- ▶ Explore hundreds of the most commonly-used function modules in ABAP

- ▶ Learn about each function module's purpose and parameters, and see an example of each

- ▶ Navigate by category or use the index to easily find the function module you need

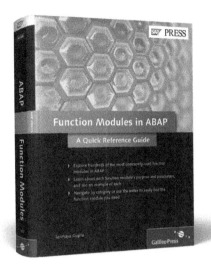

Tanmaya Gupta

Function Modules in ABAP

A Quick Reference Guide

Spending too much time on fruitless searches for the function module you need? In this compilation of the most-used function modules, you'll find essential information such as a description, parameters, prerequisites, and an example of each function module's use. Navigate this logically organized reference with the utmost ease—use different search options in the index to find the function module that will offer the most help.

977 pages, pub. 10/2013
E-Book: $59.99 | **Print:** $69.95 | **Bundle:** $79.99

www.sap-press.com/3340

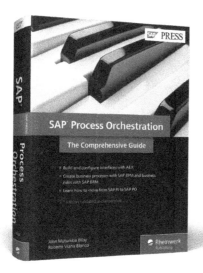

- ► Build and configure interfaces with AEX

- ► Create business processes with SAP BPM and business rules with SAP BRM

- ► Learn how to move from SAP PI to SAP PO

John Mutumba Bilay, Roberto Viana Blanco

SAP Process Orchestration

The Comprehensive Guide

Looking for smooth integration for your complex system landscape? Whether you're starting fresh or migrating from SAP PI, we've got you covered! Learn to use the AEX to configure the System Landscape Directory, work with the ES repository, and manage the integration directory in SAP PO. Build integration flows, create an SAP BPM process, and get the most out of SAP BRM. Updated with the new Push API, user-defined search, the SAP Cloud Platform Integration engine, practical exercises, and more!

908 pages, 2nd edition, pub. 09/2017
E-Book: $69.99 | **Print:** $79.95 | **Bundle:** $89.99

www.sap-press.com/4431